QUALITY AND SAFETY
IN RADIOLOGY

QUALITY AND SAFETY IN RADIOLOGY

EDITED BY

HANI H. ABUJUDEH, MD, MBA

Associate Professor of Radiology
Department of Radiology
Massachusetts General Hospital
Harvard Medical School
Boston, Massachusetts

MICHAEL A. BRUNO, MD

Professor of Radiology & Medicine
Director of Quality Services & Patient Safety
The Milton S. Hershey Medical Center
Penn State College of Medicine
Hershey, Pennsylvania

OXFORD
UNIVERSITY PRESS

OXFORD
UNIVERSITY PRESS

Oxford University Press, Inc., publishes works that further
Oxford University's objective of excellence
in research, scholarship, and education.

Oxford   New York
Auckland   Cape Town   Dar es Salaam   Hong Kong   Karachi
Kuala Lumpur   Madrid   Melbourne   Mexico City   Nairobi
New Delhi   Shanghai   Taipei Toronto

With offices in
Argentina   Austria   Brazil   Chile   Czech Republic   France   Greece
Guatemala   Hungary   Italy   Japan   Poland   Portugal   Singapore
South Korea   Switzerland   Thailand   Turkey   Ukraine   Vietnam

Copyright © 2012 by Oxford University Press, Inc.

Published by Oxford University Press, Inc.
198 Madison Avenue, New York, New York 10016

www.oup.com

Library of Congress Cataloging-in-Publication Data
Quality and safety in radiology / edited by Michael A. Bruno, Hani H. Abujudeh.
p. ; cm.
Includes bibliographical references and index.
ISBN 978-0-19-973575-4 (pbk. : alk. paper)
I. Bruno, Michael A.   II. Abujudeh, Hani H. [DNLM: 1. Radiology—organization & administration.
2. Quality Assurance, Health Care—methods.   3. Quality Control.
4. Safety Management—methods.   WN 100]
616.07'570289   dc23 2011043409

This material is not intended to be, and should not be considered, a substitute for medical or other professional advice. Treatment for the conditions described in this material is highly dependent on the individual circumstances. And, while this material is designed to offer accurate information with respect to the subject matter covered and to be current as of the time it was written, research and knowledge about medical and health issues is constantly evolving and dose sched-ules for medications are being revised continually, with new side effects recognized and accounted for regularly. Readers must therefore always check the product information and clinical procedures with the most up-to-date published product information and data sheets provided by the manufacturers and the most recent codes of conduct and safety regulation. The publisher and the authors make no representations or warranties to readers, express or implied, as to the accuracy or completeness of this material. Without limiting the foregoing, the publisher and the authors make no representations or warranties as to the accuracy or efficacy of the drug dosages mentioned in the material. The authors and the publisher do not accept, and expressly disclaim, any responsibility for any liability, loss or risk that may be claimed or incurred as a consequence of the use and/or application of any of the contents of this material.

1 3 5 7 9 8 6 4 2
Printed in United States of America
on acid-free paper

This book is dedicated to the first and best quality and safety professionals we ever knew: Feryal Fakhry Arnout (now deceased) and Sarah Jean Bruno, our mothers. They kept us safe and taught us the value of quality while we were still young and impressionable.

—HHA

—MAB

FOREWORD

New advances in radiology are helping to transform the way medicine is practiced in the 21st century. Gone are the days of exploratory laparotomies or exploratory brain surgery for diagnostic purposes. Gone also are many invasive procedures for the diagnosis or treatment of many diseases and conditions affecting every organ system in the body. Simply stated, the ability to visualize and diagnose disease through contemporary noninvasive imaging methods and gain access to disease for treatment purposes through minimally invasive image-guided interventions is a better, safer way to deliver care to patients.

Among the important implications of the enhanced standing of radiology in medical practice comes the responsibility for imaging specialists to ensure that what they do meets the highest possible quality and safety standards, first because it is the right thing to do and second to address the quality and safety expectations of a broad stakeholder community comprised of patients, other providers, regulators, and the public, among others.

It is precisely for the purpose of helping radiologists, technologists, nurses, and other people who work in the field achieve the goal of high quality and safety that Drs. Hani Abujudeh and Michael Bruno have produced their book *Quality and Safety in Radiology*. They are to be congratulated on creating a book that brings together the myriad threads that comprise the quality and safety agenda for the specialty of radiology, first as an efficient reference book but also as a guide at a very practical level for imaging providers.

Drs. Abujudeh and Bruno have invited experts who are recognized nationally and internationally for their special knowledge about quality and safety issues in radiology to contribute to the volume.

Chapters cover not only regulatory considerations and details such as checklists for interventional procedures, but also address quality and safety from the viewpoint of patients and other stakeholders and provide information on how to teach key elements of the quality and safety agenda to others. Taken together, this new book represents the most comprehensive contemporary source for this information.

Current events at the time of publication of *Quality and Safety in Radiology* include an unprecedented number of news articles reporting errors in diagnostic imaging leading to overdoses of radiation. On top of these stories, a tsunami in Japan resulted in damage to several nuclear reactors, resulting in the release of radioactive material that found its way literally around the world. These events have caused concerns on the part of the public about the safety of radiation, including that associated with medical imaging, and whether the people responsible for applying it have been as diligent as they should have been in their efforts.

To address the concerns coming from the public, referring physicians, and regulators, imaging providers must redouble their efforts to improve quality and safety. These concepts and this commitment must be daily companions to all of us who practice radiology. Abujudeh and Bruno's outstanding new book, *Quality and Safety in Radiology*, is a welcome addition to our armamentarium in pursuing our quality and safety goals and should become part of every radiologist's personal library.

James H. Thrall, MD
Chairman, Department of Radiology
Massachusetts General Hospital
Juan M. Taveras Professor of Radiology
Harvard Medical School

PREFACE

Excellence is an art won by training and habituation. We do not act rightly because we have virtue or excellence, but rather we have those because we have acted rightly. We are what we repeatedly do. Excellence, then, is not an act, but a habit.

—ARISTOTLE[1]

This book is designed to assemble, succinctly and in one volume, the essential working knowledge and current practice of a very young and rapidly evolving field: Quality & Safety (Q&S), as uniquely applied to the specialty of diagnostic radiology. Although most of the basic concepts, methods, and jargon are derived from the more general Q&S movement in American (and increasingly, international) health care, much is unique to radiology. Thus, in recent years, a distinct subspecies of *radiology* Q&S has arisen out of the efforts of many radiologists and other professionals from leading institutions worldwide to selectively adapt the core quality concepts and best-practices used in other disciplines to address the unique needs of our specialty.

The field now known as diagnostic radiology can be said to have a definite beginning, as radiology, even in its most simple form, was not possible before Roentgen's 1895 discovery. Likewise, the Q&S movement in American medicine had a definite beginning—namely, the 1999 publication of *To Err Is Human*,[2] the landmark monograph from the Institute of Medicine, which is cited or mentioned by nearly all of the contributors to this book. Although 1999 will seem like very recent history to most of us, it is worth noting that this landmark publication occurred well prior to the widespread adoption of picture archiving and communication system (PACS) systems in radiology, and in fact was more than 2 years before the 2001 introduction of the now-ubiquitous iPod. It was also less than

1 year after the relatively inauspicious founding of a tiny Internet start-up company named Google, Inc. Actually, by the time *To Err Is Human* was published, Google, Inc. had grown from its original two founders to a total of eight employees.[3] Clearly, there has been sufficient time since then for the development of the ideas, methodologies, and infrastructures that have fundamentally changed the lives of millions of people—whether by making a large, seemingly infinite store of knowledge on the Internet instantaneously searchable on the one hand, thereby fueling human productivity and creativity in previously unimagined ways, or by fundamentally changing the core culture and practices of American medicine, thereby resulting in greatly enhanced patient safety and greater consistency in the quality of health care delivery on the other.

Within departments of radiology, distinct and customized Q&S programs had been established at most major institutions by 2005, and since then, a substantial body of knowledge, experience, and perspective has accumulated in radiology Q&S—sufficient to warrant publication of the first-ever textbook entirely devoted to this topic. But because the field is "embryonic" in the sense of it still being very much in a state of rapid development, it is quite possible that a future second edition of this textbook will be very different from the volume you now hold. Yet, a great deal of what is contained here is not likely to change very much—including the basic foundation concepts upon which current

Q&S practices are constructed. Fashions are fleeting, specific goals may shift, priorities always evolve, and methods become more refined with time, but the basic tenets remain unchanged—such as the ideal of placing the needs of the sick and suffering above all else, and first and foremost for physicians to do no (preventable) harm.

In a very real sense, the Q&S movement in radiology is a direct consequence of an underlying commitment to the core agenda of physicians since the time of Hiippocrates, and is a direct extension of that which we commonly refer to as "professionalism." Although the term has been used to describe a wide range of specific behaviors and even the clothing and personal grooming of physicians, the essence of professionalism for a physician is altruistically serving their patient's needs in all situations, including advocating on behalf of individual patients when the health care delivery system is flawed in some way or fails to put the patient's needs first. Of course, to do this effectively, the physician must also be well-trained and competent, and his or her methods and judgments must be guided and informed by the best available medical science. Whenever possible, mistakes must be avoided, and when impossible to avoid, mistakes must become opportunities for learning and improvement—indeed, we must learn from *all* mistakes, our own and those of our colleagues, and thus continuously improve our performance so that we can truly put the needs of our patients first. Thus, at its core, the Q&S movement is the very definition of professionalism in medicine.

As noted by Lesser, Lucey, et al. in their recent (and excellent) practical review of what sorts of behavior constitutes professionalism in medicine,[4] health care is a fundamentally human activity requiring a large number of human actions and interactions, each of which must be guided by an overarching set of values that leads to consistently desirable behaviors on the part of physicians and others who provide health care. Since it is based on the *intrinsic* values held by the individual people involved, true professionalism results from each individual's own *intrinsic* motivation and each person's own intrinsic sense of the meaningfulness and purpose of his or her work, and thus results in consistently patient-centered (professional) behaviors.

For radiologists, this includes such diverse behavioral goals as reliably good attention to handwashing during patient encounters, generating clear and decisive written reports, keeping up with the field's demands for lifelong learning, being mindful of patients' fears and concerns during procedures (even those which we may consider "minor"), aggressively pursuing accurate clinical information from our clinical colleagues to inform our interpretations, and working forthrightly—and often against our own financial interests—to limit imaging to that which is clinically appropriate.

Our main goal for this textbook is to supply enough knowledge, background, and perspective to enable the novice reader to function competently in the radiology Q&S arena, and also to provide valuable resources and guidance to the experienced person as well. We hope to provide all readers with a solid basis from which to grow their own personal knowledge and expertise as the field continues to evolve. The "state-of-the-art" is a rapidly moving target, but we have attempted to provide just that for the present time, as well as a volume that can serve as a reference and a guide to further learning.

We have been extremely fortunate to have received the help of a truly outstanding group of volunteer contributors, most of whom are recognized leaders in their subject matter areas, and all of whom have given generously of their time, effort, expertise, and depth of knowledge to bring this project to completion. Because of their extraordinary effort, a great deal of material has been condensed into this small volume, in the hope of making a complex and sometimes bewildering field into something understandable, accessible, and manageable. We shall be forever in their debt.

We will close our preface, and begin the text, with one final thought. When we first discussed writing a book on Q&S in radiology, we had initially contemplated a text for people who, like us, had taken on the role of Q&S Officer for their radiology departments or institutions, a diverse (and growing) population. Later, we reasoned that we should also try to serve the needs of administrators and managers, mostly nonphysician professionals who also need to understand Q&S concepts in order to lead effectively and assure the best use of resources in this task. But ultimately, in thinking about the "target audience" for a book such as this, we came to realize that Q&S is not just the job of the Quality Officer, nor for that matter only for the department administrator, operational manager, or chairperson. Indeed, quality is truly *everyone's* calling, and *everyone's* responsibility. So, accordingly, we have tried to make this a book that would be useful for everyone in radiology who has an interest in the topic.

Michael A. Bruno
Hani H. Abujudeh

REFERENCES

1. Durant W. *The story of philosophy: The lives and opinions of the world's greatest philosophers.* New York: Pocket Books, 1991 (as quoted in reference 4).

2. Kohn LT, Corrigan JM, Donaldson MS, eds. *To err is human: Building a safer health system.* Washington DC: National Academy Press, 2000. Published by the Institute of Medicine and available online at http://www.nap.edu/readingroom

3. Google. Google Company History. Accessed at Google's own "Corporate History" website: http://www.google.com/corporate/history.html

4. Lesser CS, Lucey CR, Egener B, et al. A behavioral and systems view of professionalism. *JAMA.* 2010;304(24):2732–7.

CONTENTS

Contributors   *xv*

PART ONE: *Core Concepts in
Radiology Quality & Safety*   *1*

1. Basic Definitions   3
   Aine Marie Kelly

2. Components of a Comprehensive
   Radiology Quality, Safety, and
   Performance Improvement Program   *12*
   *Olga R. Brook, Ronald L. Eisenberg,
   Chun-Shan Yam, Phillip M. Boiselle, and
   Jonathan B. Kruskal*

3. *Primum Non Nocere*: A Few Words on the
   Primacy of Patient Safety   *26*
   Michael A. Bruno

4. Practical Quality Assurance   *29*
   David M. Paushter and Richard L. Baron

5. Root Cause Analysis (RCA) and
   Health Care Failure Mode and
   Effect Analysis (HFMEA)   *39*
   Rathachai Kaewlai and Hani H. Abujudeh

6. Patient Perspectives on Service and
   Quality in Clinical Imaging   *47*
   Frank J. Lexa

7. Just Culture: A Shared Commitment   *52*
   K. Scott Griffith and David Marx

8. Communication of Radiology Results   *59*
   Sarwat Hussain

9. Teamwork and Communication
   in Radiology   *68*
   Karen Miguel

10. The Joint Commission, National Patient
    Safety Goals, and Radiology: Making
    the Grade   *80*
    *Laura P. Rossi, Mildred M. LeBlanc,
    Karen Miguel, and Kathleen A. Tobin*

11. Errors in Radiology: Why We Have to
    Classify Radiology Errors and
    How We Do It   *93*
    Jonathan B. Kruskal and Olga R. Brook

12. The Role of the Apology in Radiology   *104*
    Stephen R. Baker

13. Universal Protocols and the Checklist   *111*
    Rathachai Kaewlai and Hani H. Abujudeh

14. Peer Review in Radiology   *117*
    *Rathachai Kaewlai, Valerie P. Jackson,
    and Hani H. Abujudeh*

15. Radiation Dose in Medical Imaging:
    Clinical and Technological Strategies
    for Dose Reduction   *126*
    *Mi Sung Kim, Sarabjeet Singh, and
    Mannudeep K. Kalra*

PART TWO: *Management Concepts
in Radiology Quality & Safety*   *145*

16. Key Performance Indicators
    in Radiology   *147*
    Rathachai Kaewlai and Hani H. Abujudeh

17. Six Sigma and Lean: Opportunities
    for Health Care to Do More and
    Better with Less   *161*
    Jamlik-Omari Johnson

18. Stakeholder Management and
    Best Practices   166

    Giles W.L. Boland

19. Assessing Physician Performance   175

    James R. Duncan and Stephen Currie

20. Predicting System Performance   184

    James R. Duncan and Elio Beta

21. Control Charts and Dashboards   196

    *Joseph R. Steele, John A. Terrell, David M.
    Hovsepian, and Victoria S. Jordan*

22. Governmental and Outside Agencies'
    Influence on Radiology Quality   210

    *Dipti Nevrekar, James P. Borgstede,
    and Judy Burleson*

23. Pay-for-Performance and Quality in
    Radiology   223

    David A. Rosman and Sanjay Saini

24. ACR Appropriateness Criteria   231

    Michael A. Bettmann

PART THREE: *Educational and
Special Concepts in Radiology
Quality & Safety*   239

25. Teaching Quality and Safety to
    Radiology Residents and Fellows   241

    Michael A. Bruno and Donald J. Flemming

26. Simulation   245

    Sharjeel H. Sabir and Jeffrey B. Cooper

27. Evidence-based Radiology and Its
    Relationship with Quality   255

    Francesco Sardanelli

28. Quality in Pediatric Imaging   291

    Sjirk J. Westra

29. Quality in Interventional Radiology   302

    Gloria M. Salazar and Hani H. Abujudeh

30. Pregnancy in Radiology   314

    *Mannudeep K. Kalra, Michael F. Greene,
    and Robert L. Brent*

31. Afterword: Quality and Ethics   332

    Richard Gunderman and Jordan Swensson

Index   339

CONTRIBUTORS

Stephen R. Baker, MD
Professor and Chair of Radiology
Associate Dean-Graduate Medical Education
New Jersey Medical School
Newark, New Jersey

Richard L. Baron, MD
Professor of Radiology
Dean for Clinical Practice
University of Chicago Medical Center
Chicago, Illinois

Elio Beta, BS
Medical Student
University of Illinois College of Medicine
    at Urbana-Champaign
Urbana, Illinois

Michael A. Bettmann, MD
Professor and Vice Chair for Interventional
    Services
Department of Radiology
Wake Forest University Baptist Medical Center
Winston-Salem, North Carolina

Phillip M. Boiselle, MD
Professor of Radiology, Harvard Medical School
Vice Chair of Quality, Safety, & Performance
    Improvement
Department of Radiology
Beth Israel Deaconess Medical Center
Boston, Massachusetts

Giles W.L. Boland, MD
Vice Chair Business Development
Department of Radiology
Massachusetts General Hospital
Associate Professor Radiology
Harvard Medical School
Boston, Massachusetts

James P. Borgstede, MD, FACR
Professor and Vice Chair
Department of Radiology
University of Colorado
Denver, Colorado

Robert L. Brent, MD, PhD
Thomas Jefferson University
Alfred I. duPont Hospital for Children
Laboratory of Clinical and Environmental
    Teratology
Wilmington, Delaware

Olga R. Brook, MD
Beth Israel Deaconess Medical Center
Department of Radiology,
Boston, Massachusetts

Judy Burleson, MHSA
Director, Metrics
Quality and Safety
American College of Radiology
Reston, Virginia

Jeffrey B. Cooper, PhD
Professor of Anaesthesia
Harvard Medical School
Department of Anesthesia, Critical Care
    & Pain Medicine
Massachusetts General Hospital
Boston, Massachusetts
and
Executive Director
Center for Medical Simulation
Cambridge, Massachusetts

Stephen Currie, BS
Medical Student
Washington University School of Medicine
St. Louis, Missouri

James R. Duncan, MD, PhD
Associate Professor of Radiology and Surgery
Mallinckrodt Institute of Radiology,
    Interventional Radiology Section
Washington University School of Medicine
Medical Director of Vascular Access
St. Louis Children's Hospital
St. Louis, Missouri

Ronald L. Eisenberg, MD, JD
Associate Professor of Radiology
Harvard Medical School
Radiologist
Beth Israel Deaconess Medical Center
Boston, Massachusetts

Donald J. Flemming, MD
G. Victor Rorher Professor of Radiology
Vice Chair for Education
The Milton S. Hershey Medical Center
Penn State College of Medicine
Hershey, Pennsylvania

Michael F. Greene, MD
Department of Obstetrics and Gynecology Service
Massachusetts General Hospital
Harvard Medical School
Boston, Massachusetts

K. Scott Griffith, MS
Chief Operating Officer
Outcome Engenuity, LLC
Curators of the Just Culture Community
Plano, Texas

Richard Gunderman, MD, PhD
Professor
Radiology, Pediatrics, and Medical Education
Indiana University
Indianapolis, Indiana

David M. Hovsepian, MD
Professor
Stanford University Medical Center
Palo Alto, California

Sarwat Hussain, MD
Professor and Vice-Chairman of Radiology
University of Massachusetts School of
    Medicine
UMass Memorial Healthcare
Worcester, Massachusetts

Valerie P. Jackson, MD
Eugene C. Klatte Professor and Chair
Department of Radiology
Indian University School of Medicine
Indianapolis, Indiana

Victoria S. Jordan, PhD, MBA
Director, Quality Measurement and
    Engineering
University of Texas MD Anderson Cancer
    Center
Houston, Texas

Jamlik-Omari Johnson, MD
Assistant Professor of Radiology and Imaging
    Sciences
Chief, Division of Emergency Radiology
Emory University
Atlanta, Georgia

Rathachai Kaewlai, MD
Radiologist
Massachusetts General Hospital and Harvard
  Medical School
Boston, Massachusetts
Current: Ramathibodi Hospital
Mahidol University
Bangkok, Thailand

Mannudeep K. Kalra, MD
Assistant Professor of Radiology
Massachusetts General Hospital
Harvard Medical School
Boston, Massachusetts

Aine Marie Kelly, MD, MS
Associate Professor of Radiology
Division of Cardiothoracic Radiology
Department of Radiology
University of Michigan Hospitals
Ann Arbor, Michigan

Mi Sung Kim, MD
Department of Radiology
Myongji Hospital, Kwandong University
  College of Medicine
Dukyang-ku, Koyang, Kyunggi, Korea
and
Massachusetts General Hospital Imaging
Massachusetts General Hospital
Boston, Massachusetts

Jonathan B. Kruskal, MD, PhD
Professor of Radiology
Harvard Medical School
Chairman, Department of Radiology
Beth Israel Deaconess Medical Center
Boston, Massachusetts

Mildred M. LeBlanc, BSN, MPA
Patient Safety Staff Specialist
Edward P. Lawrence Center for Quality and Safety
Massachusetts General Hospital
Boston, Massachusetts

Frank J. Lexa, MD
Vice Chairman and Professor of Radiology
Drexel University College of Medicine
and
Project Faculty
Spain, United Arab Emirates, and East Asia
  Regional Manager
Wharton Global Consulting Practicum
and
Adjunct Professor of Marketing
The Wharton School
Philadelphia, Pennsylvania
and
Professor of Business Development in the
  Life Sciences
Instituto de Empresa
Madrid, Spain

David Marx, JD
Cheif Executive Officer
Outcome Engenuity, LLC
Curators of the Just Culture
  Community
Plano, Texas

Karen Miguel, RN, MM-H
Patient Safety Officer
Massachusetts General Hospital Imaging
  Department
Massachusetts General Hospital
Boston, Massachusetts

Dipti Nevrekar, MD
Department of Radiology
University of Colorado
Denver, Colorado

David M. Paushter, MD, FACR
Professor and Interim Chair
Department of Radiology
The University of Chicago School of
  Medicine
Chicago, Illinois

David A. Rosman, MD, MBA
Instructor in Radiology
Department of Radiology
Harvard Medical School
Massachusetts General Hospital
Boston, Massachusetts

Laura P. Rossi, RN, MSN
Staff Specialist
Office of Quality and Safety
Massachusetts General Hospital
Boston, Massachusetts

Sharjeel H. Sabir, MD
Clinical Fellow in Radiology
Massachusetts General Hospital
Boston, Massachusetts

Sanjay Saini, MD, MBA
Professor of Radiology
Harvard Medical School
Vice Chairman for Health System Affairs
Massachusetts General Hospital
Boston, Massachusetts

Gloria M. Salazar, MD
Assistant Radiologist
Division of Vascular Imaging and
   Intervention
Director of Quality Assurance
Department of Radiology
Harvard Medical School
Massachusetts General Hospital
Boston, Massachusetts

Francesco Sardanelli, MD
Associate Professor of Radiology
Università degli Studi di Milano
Dipartimento di Scienze
Medico-Chirurgiche Radiology Unit,
IRCCS Policlinico San Donato
Milan, Italy
and

Director of the European Network for Assessment
   of Imaging in Medicine (EuroAIM)
Vicepresident of the European Society of
   Breast Imaging (EUSOBI)

Sarabjeet Singh, MBBS, MMST
Massachusetts General Hospital Imaging
Massachusetts General Hospital
Boston, Massachusetts

Joseph R. Steele, MD
Associate Professor
Division of Diagnostic Imaging
University of Texas MD Anderson Cancer Center
Houston, Texas

Jordan Swensson, MD
Transitional Resident, Methodist Hospital
Indiana University School of Medicine
Indianapolis, Indiana

John A. Terrell, MS
Senior Industrial Engineer
University of Texas MD Anderson Cancer Center
Houston, Texas

Kathleen A. Tobin, RN, BSN
Quality and Safety Specialist
Massachusetts General Hospital Imaging
   Safety Office
Boston, Massachusetts

Sjirk J. Westra, MD
Associate Professor of Radiology
Harvard Medical School
Pediatric Radiologist
Department of Radiology
Massachusetts General Hospital
Boston, Massachusetts

Chun-Shan Yam, PhD
Assistant Professor of Radiology
Beth Israel Deaconess Medical Center
Harvard Medical School
Boston, Massachusetts

I

Core Concepts in Radiology
Quality & Safety

1

Basic Definitions

AINE MARIE KELLY

Quality of care is the degree to which health services to individuals and populations increase the likelihood of desired health outcomes and are consistent with current professional knowledge.[1] The Institute of Medicine (IOM) report *Crossing the Quality Chasm* alluded to quality and safety concerns with poor system design and a provider-centric (rather than patient-centric) system.[2] The IOM has outlined six aims for redesigning health care systems in the 21st century to make them safe, patient-centered, effective, efficient, timely, and equitable.[2] The IOM report, *To Err Is Human: Building a Safer Health System,* highlighted the potential benefits to health care in the United States from improvements in the quality of care.[3]

TOTAL QUALITY MANAGEMENT

Total quality management (TQM) is associated with the development, deployment, and maintenance of organizational systems that are required for various business processes. It is based on a strategic approach that focuses on maintaining existing quality standards, as well as on making incremental quality improvements. It can also be described as a cultural initiative, as the focus is on establishing a culture of collaboration among various functional departments within an organization for improving overall quality.

Quality management (or TQM) has its origins in the 1950s, when W. Edward Deming, an industrial engineer of the post World War II era, brought his expertise to the Japanese manufacturing industries.[4] Deming's concepts included a systematic way to guarantee that organized activities would happen as planned, without any errors that could increase the overall cost of production. Deming described the *plan-do-study-act* (PDSA) or *Deming cycle* to continuously augment the performance of complex systems.[5]

In today's extremely competitive economic environment, quality management processes used by industrial companies and businesses have become commonplace in hospitals. These quality processes have proved successful in improving quality and controlling costs and are therefore being increasingly and rapidly applied to radiology departments and practices. An understanding of quality initiatives as they apply to radiology requires an overview of the many (often overlapping) terms used to describe and define these. In essence, a variety of processes can be introduced to monitor quality (quality control, quality assurance, quality improvement) and safety (risk management) under a departmental aegis that serves as a cog in the larger institutional culture of safety (or TQM).[6]

SYSTEMS FAILURES AND APPROACHES

Breaches in quality and safety can be viewed as either human or system issues or a combination of both.[7] In complex systems, including health care, several components or steps are involved in the process of health care delivery. Defenses, barriers, and safeguards are often put in place at key positions. These can rely on engineered technologies (e.g., alarms, physical barriers, and automatic shutdowns), humans (e.g., control room operators, pilots, nurses, pharmacists, clerks, surgeons, anesthetists), or procedures and administrative controls (e.g., a 14-step procedure to putting in a central line).[7,8] In theory, these defenses and barriers are intact, but in practice, they usually have many "holes." These have been likened to the holes in Swiss cheese, but unlike in the cheese, the holes in these systems are opening, closing, and moving constantly. According to this "Swiss cheese theory," when the holes or deficiencies line up, it allows for potential hazards and accidents to occur.[7]

Similarly, the approaches taken to ensure quality and safety can be focused primarily on people, or systems, or both. A comprehensive management program can be directed to or concentrated on several targets, including the person, the team, the task, the workplace, and the institution as a whole.

The basic framework used to evaluate health care quality improvement efforts is the structure, process, and outcome triad described by Donabedian in the late 1970s.[9] To date, a lot of the quality and safety literature has focused on processes and outcomes, with less emphasis placed on structure. Structural elements include physical facilities, management personnel, culture, organizational design, information management, and incentives.

QUALITY INDICATORS OR METRICS

The terms *quality indicators* or *metrics* are used to describe data that can be used by hospitals or organizations to measure quality and safety, monitor trends, or make a comparison to another institution or agency.[10] These indicators can relate to any aspect of patient care, including prevention, inpatient care, and patient safety. Quality indicators can be used to assess the effects of health care program and policy choices, and quality management initiatives. Many quality indicators were developed in the 1990s as part of the health care utilization project (HCUP), a federal-state-private collaboration designed to build uniform databases from administrative hospital-based data.[11] These quality indicators concerned three main areas: preventable and avoidable hospital admissions, adverse outcomes, and procedures (inappropriate utilization). The Agency for Health-care Quality and Research (AHRQ) has expanded

and refined the original HCUP quality indicators and divided these into similar domains of prevention, in-hospital events, and patient safety, as well as developing pediatric quality indicators.[12]

In 2006, the Intersociety Conference (comprising 53 professional radiology societies) held a conference on quality in radiology and developed 49 metrics to assess and improve the quality of practice.[13] These were grouped into categories of access and appropriateness, patient safety, interpretation, and the use of satisfaction surveys.[13] Examples of quality metrics that can be used in radiology include the percentage of phone calls answered within 2 minutes, the percentage of patients scheduled within 5 minutes, the percentage of patients in whom the examination is initiated within x minutes of registration, the positive rate for high-cost or high-risk examinations, the frequency with which expensive equipment is inoperative, the frequency with which information technology is inoperative, whether the modality is accredited by a recognized accrediting body, the waiting time from the initiation of a request to the actual procedure, comfort of the waiting area, radiology staff helpfulness, level of information and education given to patients in the radiology department, standardized protocol use, standardized report use, report finalization time, and critical incident reporting, to name but a few.

FLOWCHARTS AND GRAPHICAL TOOLS

Flowcharts and graphical tools are used to provide graphical representations of troubleshooting issues and processes related to quality. Some of these tools are described in more detail in Chapter 21.

The *Ishikawa diagram* (also known as a *fish bone diagram* or *cause-and-effect diagram*) depicts the causes of a certain event or events. The purpose of these diagrams is to break down into successive layers of detail the root causes that might contribute to a particular effect. The categories typically include people, methods, materials, machines, measurements, and environment (Figure 1.1). A *check sheet* is a document used to collect data in real time, at the location where the data are generated. Blank spaces are left for information to be filled in, as either qualitative or quantitative data. Data are recorded by making marks or "checks" in the spaces. Check sheets are usually divided into regions, with different regions having different significance. *Control charts* are also known as *Shewhart charts* or *process-behavior*

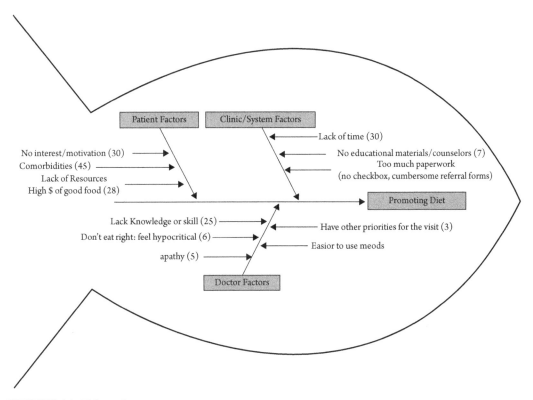

FIGURE 1.1 Ishikawa chart.

Reprinted from Fluker SA, Whalen U, Schneider J, et al. Incorporating performance improvement methods into a needs assessment: experience with a nutrition and exercise curriculum. *J Gen Intern Med*. 2010 Sep;25 Suppl 4:S627–33. With permission of the publisher, Springer Science + Business Media.

charts. Shewhart was the first to study quality as an industrial process in 1931.[14] Using samples of success as the numerator, and total opportunities as the denominator, events can be graphed to evaluate performance over time. An average line can be used to illustrate deviations of the data from the average, and upper and lower control limits can be used to depict the acceptable range (Figure 1.2). A *histogram* can be plotted to show the frequencies of events occurring within ranges of values;

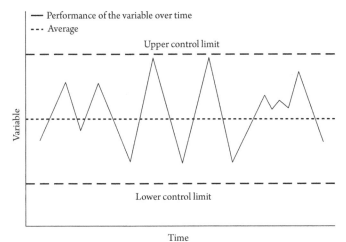

FIGURE 1.2 Control chart.

for example, the numbers of calls answered within 2 minutes. The *Pareto chart* contains both bars and a line graph, with the bars representing individual variables or values, and the line representing the cumulative total (Figure 1.3). The purpose of the Pareto chart is to highlight the most important quality issues, which are usually depicted from left to right in decreasing order of frequency or importance. A *scatter plot* or *scatter graph* displays data as a collection of points (dots), with each point having the value of one variable on the *x* axis and of another variable on the *y* axis. If one variable is independent and under the control of the user or experimenter, it is usually displayed on the horizontal or *x* axis. A *flowchart* (or *runchart*) depicts an algorithm or a process by showing the steps as boxes connected in order with arrows. Flowcharts are useful in analyzing, designing, documenting, or managing a process or program (Figure 1.4).

range, it is deemed acceptable. Quality control sets the baseline or minimal level of quality and has been likened to an apple grower rejecting rotten apples at the time of packing, thus ensuring that apples for sale meet minimal market expectations.[15]

Within radiology, QC involves the regular, intermittent technical testing of medical equipment and the evaluation of image quality to ensure conformity to regulations. Quality control typically deals with issues such as acceptance testing and the preventive maintenance of imaging equipment, the evaluation of shielding around x-ray facilities, the measurement of processing parameters (such as developer temperature, developer pH, base and fog, speed and contrast), the measurement of radiation dose (such as kVp, mAs, scanner output, and effective dose), and image parameters (such as image contrast, resolution, artifacts, appropriate labeling, and consistency).

QUALITY CONTROL

In the industrial or health care setting, the purpose of quality control (QC) is to establish ranges of acceptability for specific measures or data points.[4] Action is taken only when a measurement falls outside the range. If the measurement falls within the

QUALITY ASSURANCE

Quality assurance (QA) is a more comprehensive quality management program used to ensure excellence in health care through the systematic collection and evaluation of data.[4] Although QA involves QC, it focuses on specific indicators believed to

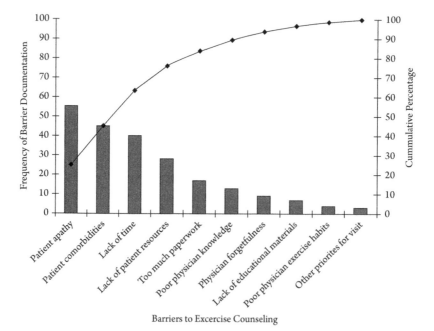

FIGURE 1.3 Pareto chart.

Reprinted from Fluker SA, Whalen U, Schneider J, et al. Incorporating performance improvement methods into a needs assessment: experience with a nutrition and exercise curriculum. *J Gen Intern Med.* 2010 Sep;25 Suppl 4:S627–33. With permission of the publisher, Springer Science + Business Media.

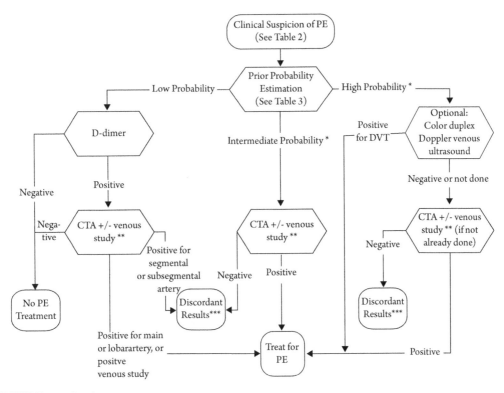

FIGURE 1.4 Flowchart.

Reprinted from Green LA, Frey KA, Froehlich JB, et al. *Venous thromboembolism* (VTE). Ann Arbor, Michigan: University of Michigan Health System, 2009. (Accessed on July 28, 2001 at www.med.umich.edu/umhs/health-providers/clinical_care_guidelines.html.) With permission.

affect the quality of services. With regard to the apple grower example, QA would involve more effort—such as pruning, fertilizing, and infection control during growth—to reduce the number of rotten apples at the time of packing.[15]

These indicators can be related to the main areas of structure, processes, outcomes, or patient-centeredness. In diagnostic imaging, these might include access to services, appropriateness of utilization, patient selection parameters, timeliness of scheduling, scheduling process, patient prescreening, imaging modality and protocol selection, waiting times, waiting room amenities, technical effectiveness and efficiency, patient safety, imaging interpretation, prior imaging availability, repeat rate, pathology correlation, missed diagnosis rate, reporting timeliness, report finalization, critical findings reporting, and in-service education. The ultimate aim of any QA program is to enhance patient care, and QA programs guide decisions made in imaging practices with respect to clinical practice and operational functioning.

QUALITY IMPROVEMENT AND CONTINUOUS QUALITY IMPROVEMENT

Quality improvement (QI) or continuous quality improvement (CQI) refers to proactive processes that aim to improve and enhance the quality of care and services.[16] These methods combine professional knowledge with knowledge about making improvements.[17] The philosophy is based on the continuous improvement of processes associated with providing services that meet or exceed the patient's or referring clinician's expectations. Continuous QI determines that every activity in an imaging facility be identified and that clear standards (indicators) be set and measured to allow processes to be continually improved. The outcome is a more efficient operation, which should save money and increase the quality of the health care delivered. Returning to the apple grower example, QI (or CQI) would include analyzing the growth, production, and handling of the apples, and developing and implementing measures to improve the number, size, and taste of the apples.[15]

Continuous QI promotes two basic organizational changes: first, to highlight and correct mistakes after the fact, and to analyze, understand, and improve the work process; and second, to accept QM as a dynamic and never-ending process. Continuous QI focuses on four main issues: determining and meeting needs of patients and consumers, taking a holistic approach to QI based on identifying causes of poor performance, using fact-based management and scientific methodology, and empowering practitioners to improve quality on a daily basis. The most common QI methodologies used in health care include PDSA, Six Sigma, and lean management.

As an example, QI and CQI could be applied to radiology in the case of adverse events, such as an anaphylactic reaction to intravenous iodinated contrast or nephrogenic systemic fibrosis (NSF) following gadolinium. As a *reactive* process, the QA system would track and report the adverse event. The QA process, however, lacks the methodologies to use these data to realize systematic improvements. On the other hand, QI (or CQI) is a *proactive* approach that attempts to anticipate problems before they occur and improve the way a system functions. For example, the occurrence of adverse reactions to iodinated contrast or gadolinium could be prevented through prescreening patient questionnaires or by using more detailed request forms. After determining the problem, CQI looks for possible structural changes within the system and tries to determine proactively other weak points in the process.

RADIOLOGY QUALITY MAP
A radiology quality map is a graphical representation of the patient's path through the diagnostic (and interventional) radiology department (Figure 1.5). It outlines those steps where opportunities exist for process and outcome improvement in the radiology profession.[18] This map can act as a framework upon which to build a TQM program for radiology practice and radiology departments.

For example, the first step in the radiology encounter is the ordering of the examination by the referring physician. The physician may order the wrong examination because she is not up to date with the current literature or be is unaware of the appropriateness criteria for that particular diagnostic imaging test and clinical indication. The physician may ask for a "high-resolution" study because she wants thinner "slices" or collimation, or she may ask for intravenous contrast when it is not needed. The scheduler may misinterpret what the physician said over the phone or her writing on the request form. Finally, the diagnostic imaging examination may not be necessary at all, but the physician requests it anyway for other reasons (overutilization).

The second step in the process is appointment scheduling, whether this be routine, urgent or emergent, outpatient or inpatient. Timeliness of scheduling is important and measurable, and this has ramifications for outcomes in patient care. Other factors to consider at this stage might include screening for renal impairment, diabetic drug (metformin) use, and allergy to intravenous contrast.

The third step is the initial radiology encounter, which occurs when the patient arrives at the radiology department. Aspects include the wait time, which is measurable and a determinant of patient satisfaction, waiting room appearances and comfort, and staff (reception, nursing, and paramedical) interpersonal skills. Patient education takes place,

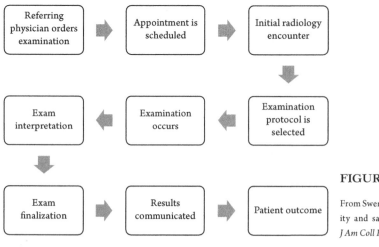

FIGURE 1.5 Radiology quality map.

From Swensen SJ, Johnson CD. Radiologic quality and safety: mapping value into radiology. *J Am Coll Radiol.* 2005;2(12):992–1000.

including appropriate preparation for the examination and advice about what to expect. In some radiology centers, screening for renal impairment, diabetic drug (metformin) use, and contrast allergies might take place at this point.

The fourth step is selection of the appropriate examination protocol by the radiologist. This will include the imaging modality to be used, the "slice" thickness or collimation, the extent of anatomical coverage, the field of view, the use of oral and/or intravenous contrast, pulse sequences, expiratory and prone images, or the number of phases or "runs" to be used. Standardization of protocols is generally recommended, since findings are more accurately compared if the previous and follow-up study protocol parameters are the same.

The fifth step is the performance of the diagnostic imaging examination. This includes patient comfort (appropriate discretion and privacy), and safety issues such as prevention of falls and nosocomial infections. Process effectiveness and efficiency include wait time for intravenous injections and the scan, scan performance time, and time to complete the examination in full. Safety issues that can occur during this time include wrong patient selection, examination mislabeling, incorrect examination or procedure, incorrect radiation dose, wrong procedure side or site, and contrast-induced nephropathy or nephrogenic systemic fibrosis.

The sixth step is the interpretation of the examination. The accuracy of interpretation has a critical impact on outcome and is directly related to overall quality. Inaccuracies may occur due poor study quality, missing or inaccurate clinical information, unavailability of prior reports or images, detection or perception errors, interpretation errors (misjudgment), lack of knowledge on the part of the reporting radiologist, and communication errors.

The seventh step is report finalization, which makes the information available to the referring physician. Time to final report signing can be measured and should be actively monitored.

The eighth step is communication. Report quality measures include timeliness, accuracy, reliability, brevity, clarity, and clinical relevance. Standardized lexicons or terminology, such as the mammography BIRADS system, provide a uniform method by which to communicate and access information.[19] Structured reports increase the efficiency of the reporting process and reduce transcription errors.[20] Currently, it is the radiologist's responsibility to communicate findings to the referring physician,

particularly for urgent, unexpected, or significant findings.[21]

PLAN-DO-STUDY-ACT CYCLE

The PDSA cycle involves a trial-and-learning approach in which a hypothesis or solution is generated and then tested on a small scale before making any changes to the whole system.[14] The entire process is dependent on data collected through observation and statistical analysis. First, a functional system is identified, such as patient scheduling, equipment performance, image interpretation, or report distribution. Work teams comprise all parties that interact with the system being studied. A system flowchart (such as a fishbone diagram, Pareto chart, or scatter plot) is created and, following this, observations are made of problems that exist or areas that can be improved. Next, testing is initiated and a course of action to improve the process is planned. Finally, the effects of changes to the system are monitored and feedback is given.

The sequence of four repetitive steps of quality planning (plan), quality steering (do), quality assurance (study), and quality improvement (act) is carried out over the course of short cycles. Small changes can be incorporated quickly at the end of each cycle, with additional new changes added for subsequent cycles. An example that would be applicable to radiology is of enhancing patient safety through feeding tube insertion.[5] This process might include assessing current complication rates, identifying vulnerable populations, selecting the appropriate feeding tube, providing adequate supervision, utilizing technology-guided insertion, reassessing complication rates, and finally, implementing explicit policies and procedures.[5]

SIX SIGMA

The Six Sigma model was developed by Motorola in 1987 as a company-wide quality improvement concept.[22] Six Sigma is a quality system model based on reducing variability within a process and moving the mean to a gold standard. Six Sigma stands for six standard deviations from the arithmetic mean. This allows only 3.4 defects per million opportunities. By measuring the number of defects in a process, one can systematically determine how to avoid them and reach a zero defects level. The phases of the Six Sigma process are to identify the process and key customers, define customers' needs, measure performance, analyze data, set priorities, and launch improvements to integrate and disseminate Six Sigma throughout the organization.[4] The elements of Six Sigma (define, measure, analyze, improve, and control) align themselves nicely with good medical practice. A perceived weakness of Six Sigma is its complexity, with its rigorous adherence to the problem-solving process resulting in overkill for simple problems with obvious solutions.[9]

LEAN MANAGEMENT TECHNIQUES/PROCESSES

Lean principles came from the Japanese manufacturing industries' (Toyota Production System) lean management and lean manufacturing policies.[23] In the 1990s, the term "lean" was coined to describe the set of tools designed to eliminate or reduce waste.[9] The expenditure for resources, other than to create value for the customer or consumer, was regarded as wasteful and a target for elimination. As waste is eliminated, production times and costs are reduced. Lean principles focus on getting the right things to the right place, at the right time and in the right quantity to achieve perfect workflow. Wastes include overproduction, unnecessary transportation, inventory (not producing an income), motion, defects, overprocessing, and waiting (not producing an income). Leans tools include value stream mapping (drawing a map of the process from concept to product), the five S's (sorting, setting in order, systematic cleaning, standardizing, and sustaining), production leveling (making small batches rather than bulk), pull systems (ordering only the number of new parts needed), and mistake proofing. The lean technique's strengths lie in its customer focus and the use of standardized solutions to common problems. Lean is weak, however, on organizational infrastructure, deployment plans, analytical tools, and quality control mechanisms.[9]

ROOT CAUSE ANALYSIS

Root cause analysis (RCA) is a methodology aimed at identifying and solving the root causes of problems or incidents. The practice of RCA is based on the principle that problems are best solved by attempting to correct or eliminate root causes, rather than by merely addressing the current or downstream symptoms. By focusing corrective measures at root causes, it is hoped that the likelihood of problem recurrence will be minimized. However, it is recognized that complete prevention of recurrence by a single intervention is not always possible. Thus, RCA is often considered to be an iterative process, and is frequently viewed as a tool within the CQI process.

QUALITY AND SAFETY

Safety is the foundation of any quality management program. Patients assume that they will be safe while in the radiology department. Like quality metrics, safety metrics are available that relate to radiology, including image labeling, hand hygiene, wrong patient studies, medication errors, wrong side studies or interventions, falls in the radiology department, infection rates after radiological procedures, complication rates after radiologic procedures, contrast-induced nephropathy, specimen labeling errors, and critical test reporting.[16]

THE AMERICAN COLLEGE OF RADIOLOGY AND QUALITY

The American College of Radiology (ACR) defines quality of care as "the degree to which health services for individuals and populations increase the likelihood of desired health outcomes and are consistent with current professional knowledge."[24] Specifically with regard to diagnostic imaging, "Quality is the extent to which the right procedure is done in the right way, at the right time, and the correct interpretation is accurately and quickly communicated to the patient and referring physician."[24] The goals are to maximize the likelihood of desired health outcome and satisfy the patient.

The ACR has for a long time been concerned with quality in radiology and has undertaken many activities to enhance the quality of radiologic care.[25] These include several accreditation programs, which currently cover the areas of mammography, breast magnetic resonance imaging (MRI), stereotactic breast biopsy, breast ultrasound, computed tomography (CT), MRI, nuclear medicine and positron emission tomography (PET), radiation oncology, and ultrasound.[26] The ACR practice guidelines and technical standards also provide guidance for the performance of imaging in all areas, including patient selection and considerations, performing personnel qualifications, required technical parameters, minimum technical requirements, equipment specifications, and report documentation.[27]

REFERENCES

1. Becher EC, Chassin MR. Improving quality, minimizing error: Making it happen. *Health Aff (Millwood).* 2001;20(3):68–81.
2. Battles JB. Quality and safety by design. *Qual Saf Health Care.* 2006;15 Suppl 1:i1–3.

3. Blackmore CC. Defining quality in radiology. *J Am Coll Radiol*. 2007;4(4):217–23.

4. Erturk SM, Ondategui-Parra S, Ros PR. Quality management in radiology: Historical aspects and basic definitions. *J Am Coll Radiol*. 2005;2(12):985–91.

5. Sorokin R, Gottlieb JE. Enhancing patient safety during feeding-tube insertion: A review of more than 2,000 insertions. *JPEN J Parenter Enteral Nutr*. 2006;30(5):440–5.

6. Kruskal JB, Anderson S, Yam CS, Sosna J. Strategies for establishing a comprehensive quality and performance improvement program in a radiology department. *Radiographics*. 2009;29(2):315–29.

7. Reason J. Human error: Models and management. *BMJ*. 2000;320(7237):768–70.

8. Velmahos GC, Toutouzas KG, Sillin LF, Chan L, Clarck RE, Theodorou D. et al. Cognitive task analysis for teaching technical skills in an inanimate surgical skills laboratory. *Am J Surg*. 2004;187(1):114–9.

9. Vallejo B. Tools of the trade: Lean and Six Sigma. *J Healthc Qual*. 2009;31(3):3–4.

10. de Vos M, Graafmans W, Kooistra M, Meijboom B, Van Der Voort P, Westert G. Using quality indicators to improve hospital care: A review of the literature. *Int J Qual Health Care*. 2009;21(2):119–29.

11. Health Care Utilization Project (HCUP) quality indicators. Accessed April 15, 2010 at: http://www.qualityindicators.ahrq.gov/hcup_archive.htm

12. Agency for Healthcare Research and Quality (AHRQ) quality indicators. Accessed April 15, 2010 at: http://www.qualityindicators.ahrq.gov/general_faq.htm#1

13. Dunnick NR, Applegate KE, Arenson RL. Quality—radiology imperative: Report of the 2006 Intersociety Conference. *J Am Coll Radiol*. 2007;4(3):156–61.

14. Varkey P, Reller MK, Resar RK. Basics of quality improvement in health care. *Mayo Clin Proc*. 2007;82(6):735–9.

15. Lau LS. A continuum of quality in radiology. *J Am Coll Radiol*. 2006;3(4):233–9.

16. Johnson CD, Krecke KN, Miranda R, Roberts CC, Denham C. Quality initiatives: Developing a radiology quality and safety program: A primer. *Radiographics*. 2009;29(4):951–9.

17. Applegate KE. Continuous quality improvement for radiologists. *Acad Radiol*. 2004;11(2):155–61.

18. Swensen SJ, Johnson CD. Radiologic quality and safety: Mapping value into radiology. *J Am Coll Radiol*. 2005;2(12):992–1000.

19. Liberman L, Menell JH. Breast imaging reporting and data system (BI-RADS). *Radiol Clin North Am*. 2002;40(3):409–30, v.

20. Reiner BI. The challenges, opportunities, and imperative of structured reporting in medical imaging. *J Digit Imaging*. 2009;22(6):562–8.

21. Lucey LL, Kushner DC. The ACR guideline on communication: To be or not to be, that is the question. *J Am Coll Radiol*. 2010;7(2):109–14.

22. Motorola University Six Sigma in action. Accessed August, 17, 2010 at: http://www.motorola.com/Business/US-EN/Motorola±University

23. Toyota Production System. Accessed August, 17, 2010 at: http://www2.toyota.co.jp/en/vision/production_system/

24. Hillman BJ, Amis ES, Jr., Neiman HL. The future quality and safety of medical imaging: Proceedings of the third annual ACR FORUM. *J Am Coll Radiol*. 2004;1(1):33–9.

25. Deitch CH, Sunshine JH. The relationship of managed care to business, professional, and organizational aspects of radiology practices. *AJR Am J Roentgenol*. 2004;182(1):29–38.

26. ACR Website. Accreditation Programs. Accessed April 15, 2010 at: http://www.acr.org/accreditation.aspx

27. ACR Website. Practice Guidelines and Technical Standards. Accessed April 15, 2010 at: http://acr.org/SecondaryMainMenuCategories/quality_safety/guidelines.aspx

2

Components of a Comprehensive Radiology Quality, Safety, and Performance Improvement Program

OLGA R. BROOK, RONALD L. EISENBERG, CHUN-SHAN YAM,
PHILLIP M. BOISELLE, AND JONATHAN B. KRUSKAL

To ensure safety, provide high-quality care, and optimize clinical performance by physicians, the introduction of processes of comprehensive continuous quality management is essential. Many of these processes are now mandated by organizations and stakeholders that regulate our profession; whether it is the Joint Commission, the American College of Radiology (ACR), the Accreditation Council for Graduate Medical Education (ACGME), the American Board of Radiology (ABR), or insurance payers, more and more quality- and performance-related demands are being made on our daily practice.

Performance improvement programs are more likely to be effective when they subscribe and adhere to recognized principles. Appropriately selected and collected data should be actively, continuously, effectively, and visibly managed by a team that consists of qualified and enthusiastic personnel. The monitored metrics should be mission driven and benchmarked against appropriate standards. Suitable tools should be used for data analysis and trends identification. Furthermore, proactive systems should be employed to minimize risk. There also should be a mechanism for managing severe adverse and sentinel events. Such events have to be managed promptly and effectively, ensuring that action items identified from a root cause analysis and any implemented changes are continuously monitored to determine their efficacy.

Monitoring of all implemented changes should be performed to determine progress toward relevant evidence-based benchmarks. Ultimately, all the members of a department are responsible for improving quality and safety. However, the chairman and the quality director are responsible for the practical implementation of the performance improvement program. For all participants, participation must be easy rather than burdensome. The staff involvement in the quality assurance process should be rewarded, and timely feedback should be provided for all reported events. Performance improvement is a process that differs from analyses made in commercial companies, where increased revenue is the major goal. In medicine, the benefit to the individual patient is the primary aim, with less emphasis placed on economic implications. The following are what we consider the essential components for establishing a quality, safety, and performance improvement program in a large academic radiology department.

LEADERSHIP

Institutional Leadership and Culture

To achieve meaningful and sustained improvement in an organization, it is essential that hospital leadership actively participates in all processes and values, and rewards quality-related initiatives. Visible leadership and implementation of a culture that emphasizes, supports, and values continuous quality improvement, patient and staff safety, and performance improvement is essential if such processes are to be successful at the departmental level.

Quality Team

Convening a team of quality champions is essential to facilitate productive and meaningful change and improvement. For most radiology departments, such a team may include a physician Director of Quality, a Director of Departmental Operations, a nurse assigned to quality initiatives and auditing, physician and technologist champions, enthusiastic trainees, and representation from hospital leadership, including members from the Departments of Risk Management and Healthcare Quality.

Just Culture

David Marx[1] introduced the phrase *"just culture"* when he outlined the principles for achieving an environment in which staff members feel comfortable disclosing errors, including their own. Whereas many traditional health care cultures hold individuals accountable for all errors, a just culture recognizes that individual practitioners are not accountable for system failings over which they have no control. A just culture recognizes that competent professionals make mistakes, but does not tolerate disregard for risks to patients or misconduct. Such a culture should minimize fear among participants and should identify and introduce proactive rather than reactive monitoring processes.

Engaging Staff

Attention should be paid to engaging physicians in the processes of quality and performance improvement. Such buy-in is challenging, but ultimately can be very rewarding by following processes such as those described by Reinertsen et al.[2,3,4] Lessons we have learned from this effort include making physicians partners in the improvement processes and having their involvement visible and prominent. The champion physicians should be identified, trained, and supported as they acquire the skill to manage projects and develop engaging methods for quality improvement.[5] Examples of valuable physician involvement in the quality improvement process include standardizing what can be standardized, using data positively rather than punitively, and making the right thing easy to try and do.

In addition, it is important to build trust with each initiative, communicate candidly and often, choose messages and messengers thoughtfully, and value the time of everyone involved as much as your own.

Patient and Staff Safety

There is an increasing awareness of safety issues that impact both patients and hospital staff, as well as the implementation of strategies to minimize or prevent such events from occurring. In the imaging environment, patients and staff are subjected to a series of specific risks that must be monitored and prevented. The most common examples include patient falls, medication misadministration, radiation exposure errors, needle sticks, and ergonomic injuries. The following are essential components of a patient and staff safety program.

Adverse Event Reporting Systems

Adverse event reporting systems should permit anonymous, nonpunitive reporting of adverse events, including near-misses.[6] In a radiology department, such events may be related to patient safety, technical quality problems, procedural complications, and diagnostic or interpretive errors. To improve participation, it is helpful to define specific criteria for reporting cases, provide feedback to the submitting staff member, and publicize the advantages and benefits of such a system. The system may reside within a department of radiology or be hospital-wide, and it must be actively and regularly managed. This management should include fair and effective review of all adverse events, monitoring to identify trends, and appropriate follow-up of all action items resulting from the submitted cases. In our experience, an additional useful component is the facilitation of interdepartmental reporting and exchange of cases. This process should preserve confidentiality, and all data should be afforded protection similar to that given to other peer review material.

Systems for Communicating Results

According to the Joint Commission, a system should exist whereby (a) critical results are communicated in a timely manner to the appropriate person (Figure 2.1A), and (b) this communication is documented (Figure 2.1B). Many radiologists remain frustrated by difficulties in identifying the responsible physician to whom results should be communicated. National Patient Safety Goal (NPSG) number 2 requires that, once results are communicated,

(A)

Record of Notifications of Critical Radiology Findings
Case Submission

Please Provide the Following Information

[1] Result to Communicate:
Question of left lower lobe opacity. Suggest dedicated chest
PA and Lat X-ray to evaluate.

[2] Note to Coordinator:

Submit   Cancel

(B) **Critical Communication (clip=▓▓▓▓▓) --> Results Communicated..**

▓▓▓▓▓▓▓▓▓ (BIDMC - Radiology)
Sent: Wednesday, August 18, 2010 11:13 AM
To: ▓▓▓▓▓ (BIDMC - Radiology)
Cc: ▓▓▓▓▓ (BIDMC - Radiology)

```
Critical Communication (clip=▓▓▓▓) --> Results Communicated..
MRN=▓▓▓▓   Clip=▓▓▓▓.
Study Date=20100816
Study Type=MR UROGRAM(MR ABDANDPEL WANDW/OC)
Commmunications=1. 1-cm lesion in the left ureter approximately 9
cm proximal to the
ureterobladder junction consistent with urothelial carcinoma.

2. There is no evidence of other lesions within the kidneys,
right ureter or
urinary bladder.

Note=Results communicated with Dr. ▓▓▓▓ via email. Email
response was received on 08/17/10-6:03 PM confirming he has
viewed patient's results. -▓▓▓▓▓
```

FIGURE 2.1 (A) The electronic system for communication of critical results to the clinician. In Box 1, the radiologist is submitting the findings, which must be reported to the referring physician, with special instructions to the coordinator (in Box 2) if needed. The coordinator identifies the responsible physician, communicates the results (via fax, e-mail, phone), and documents the communication in the feedback e-mail to the radiologist (B) with additional documentation in the Critical Results Communication database.

they are to be written down and read back to ensure accuracy. Because of the volume of abnormal results and the challenge of defining and distinguishing urgent and critical results, efforts have been directed toward developing automated communication systems[7] that can help manage and follow-up such cases. We have developed an electronic messaging system that permits radiologists to submit online requests to communicate significant, but not emergent, abnormal findings and recommended follow-up to two communications facilitators, who contact referring health care providers by e-mail or telephone. All of our 10,000 cases during a 3-year period were successfully communicated, with more than 80% within 48 hours, and satisfaction among referring physicians with the system was high.[8]

Audits
Audits may be performed through direct observation of clinical activities, or through the random review of patient charts for assessment hospital- and patient-level quality-of-care metrics. The most common audit

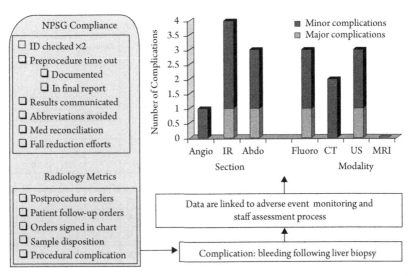

FIGURE 2.2 The monitoring of compliance with the Joint Commission's National Patient Safety Goals (NPSGs) and several radiology-specific metrics. When note is made that an adverse event (e.g., bleeding requiring hospital admission) occurred following an imaging-guided procedure (e.g., ultrasonography-guided liver biopsy), the review process is used to link this information to an adverse event reporting system, to ensure that the event has been or is now being recorded. The data are then further linked to the departmental procedural complication key performance indicator. Abdo, abdominal imaging; Angio, angiography; IR, interventional radiology

is performed to monitor compliance with the Joint Commission's NPSGs (Figure 2.2). It is important to define specific measures before evaluating charts and to be sensitive to the fact that hospital-level qualities of care differ among institutions.[9]

Environmental and Safety Walkabouts

A formal but unannounced walkabout is a very effective way of evaluating safety processes and staff awareness of them in a clinical department. Not only can useful data be collected (Figure 2.3A and 2.3B) and procedures put in place to improve safety mechanisms, but the presence of an evaluating team with representation from senior hospital executives sends a message to all staff that safety is taken seriously. This message can be further reinforced if visible steps are taken to improve staff and patient safety in the workplace. From a regulatory perspective, the Joint Commission expects health care organizations to conduct such patient safety walkabouts. These walkabouts can focus on the environment of care or on patient care and safety. They also can serve as safety and security inspections to ensure that Occupational Safety and Health Administration (OSHA) standards are upheld, material safety data sheets are readily available, all guests are registered and identified by a clearly visible badge, staff are

aware of the locations and function of surveillance systems and alarms, and staff are familiar with emergency codes.

Safety and Risk Reporting Mechanisms

With the increasing deployment and utilization of electronic health care records, electronic systems are being developed for the reporting and management of safety events (Figure 2.4). The many existing systems give staff the opportunity to report not only adverse events, but also near-misses, so that steps can be introduced to prevent errors from occurring.

Compliance with National Patient Safety Goals

In keeping with Joint Commission requirements, institutions are expected to develop systems for monitoring and ensuring compliance with the NPSGs, most of which is applicable to radiology department. Specifically, all staff working in a radiology department are expected to adhere and be compliant with the Universal Protocol, verify and document patient identity; perform a preprocedure pause or "time-out" prior to every interventional procedure to verify the side, site, and nature of the procedure; and document this time-out in the record. In addition to adoption

(A)

Breast Imaging Observation Audit Tool

Date: _____ Time: _____

Site: _____

Observer: _____

Instructions:

Indicate YES if compliant

Indicate NO if you observe defects

Observation #	1	2	3	4	5	6	7	8	9	10	Total Yes
Hand Hygiene											
Before Patient Contact?	Y/N	Y/N	Y/N	Y/N	Y/N	Y/N	Y/N	Y/N	Y/N	Y/N	
After Patient Contact?	Y/N	Y/N	Y/N	Y/N	Y/N	Y/N	Y/N	Y/N	Y/N	Y/N	
Wristband checked?	Y/N	Y/N	Y/N	Y/N	Y/N	Y/N	Y/N	Y/N	Y/N	Y/N	
Pt. verified w/2 Identifiers	Y/N	Y/N	Y/N	Y/N	Y/N	Y/N	Y/N	Y/N	Y/N	Y/N	

Patient confidentiality maintained?	Y/N
Supplies expiration checked ?	Y/N
Sharps containers needing to be replaced?	Y/N
Medications expiration checked & secure ?	Y/N
Exam Gloves stocked & available in all sizes?	Y/N
Refrigerated reagents expiration and clarity verified ?	Y/N
Fluid Shield Masks with visors available?	Y/N
ID badges worn by all staff?	Y/N
No food or beverages in the clinical area	Y/N

Timeout Audit	Obs 1	Obs 2	Obs 3	Obs 4	Obs 5
Date					
MRN					
Consent Available					
Patient actively identified					
Procedure verified					
Side/Site verified					
Allergies reviewed					
Patient off anticoagulants appropriately					
Relevant lab tests acknowledged					
All team members participated in time out					

FIGURE 2.3 Various charts and questionnaires used in departmental walkabouts for collecting safety data.

of the Universal Protocol, the new National Safety Goals for 2010 require use of two patient identifiers, timely reporting of critical tests and critical results, labeling medications to improve their safety, and meeting hand hygiene guidelines and preventing surgical site infections in order to reduce the risk of health care–associated infections.[10]

Professional Assessment/Performance Evaluation

Regulatory and credentialing organizations now require that hospitals establish systems for assessing and managing staff performance. The radiology community has responded to these requirements by developing peer review processes (Figure 2.5)

(B)

Ultrasound Observation Audit Tool

DMonth/Yr: _____

Site: _____

Observer: _____

Instructions:
Indicate YES if compliant
Indicate NO if you observe defects

Observation #	1	2	3	4	5	6	7	8	9	10	Total Yes
Hand Hygiene											
Before Patient Contact?	Y / N	Y / N	Y / N	Y / N	Y / N	Y / N	Y / N	Y / N	Y / N	Y / N	
After Patient Contact?	Y / N	Y / N	Y / N	Y / N	Y / N	Y / N	Y / N	Y / N	Y / N	Y / N	
Wristband checked?	Y / N	Y / N	Y / N	Y / N	Y / N	Y / N	Y / N	Y / N	Y / N	Y / N	
Pt. verified w/2 Identifiers	Y / N	Y / N	Y / N	Y / N	Y / N	Y / N	Y / N	Y / N	Y / N	Y / N	

Patient confidentiality maintained?	Y / N
Supplies or Meds not expired and secure?	Y / N
Supplies 18″ from ceiling?	Y / N
GUS system is clean?	Y / N
Sharps containers needing to be replaced?	Y / N
Exam Gloves available in all sizes?	Y / N
N95 Respirator available in 2 brands & 2 sizes?	Y / N
Fluid Shield Masks with visors available?	Y / N
ID badges worn by all staff?	Y / N
Compressed gas cylinders secured?	Y / N
Sink area counters clear 10″ each side?	Y / N

Timeout Audit	Obs 1	Obs 2	Obs 3	Obs 4	Obs 5
Date					
MRN					
Consent Available					
Patient actively identified					
Procedure verified					
Side/Site verified					
Allergies reviewed					
Patient off anticoagulants appropriately					
Relevant lab tests acknowledged					
All team members participated in time out					

FIGURE 2.3 (*Continued*).

and by mandating that all radiologists participate in a practice quality improvement project to maintain certification.[11]

Peer Review Process

Participation in peer review processes is no longer an option for many radiologists. Peer review is one means of evaluating radiologists' performance and offers an opportunity to reduce errors and improve patient care.[12] Peers who are being reviewed need not be radiologists, but may also be technologists or other members of a department. For example, random radiographs can be evaluated (hard copy or on a picture archiving and communication system [PACS]) for defined quality indicators as a metric of technologists' performance. Recordings of telephone conversations can be reviewed to evaluate customer service and staff performance in a scheduling office. Patient satisfaction surveys can be amended to include feedback about all staff,

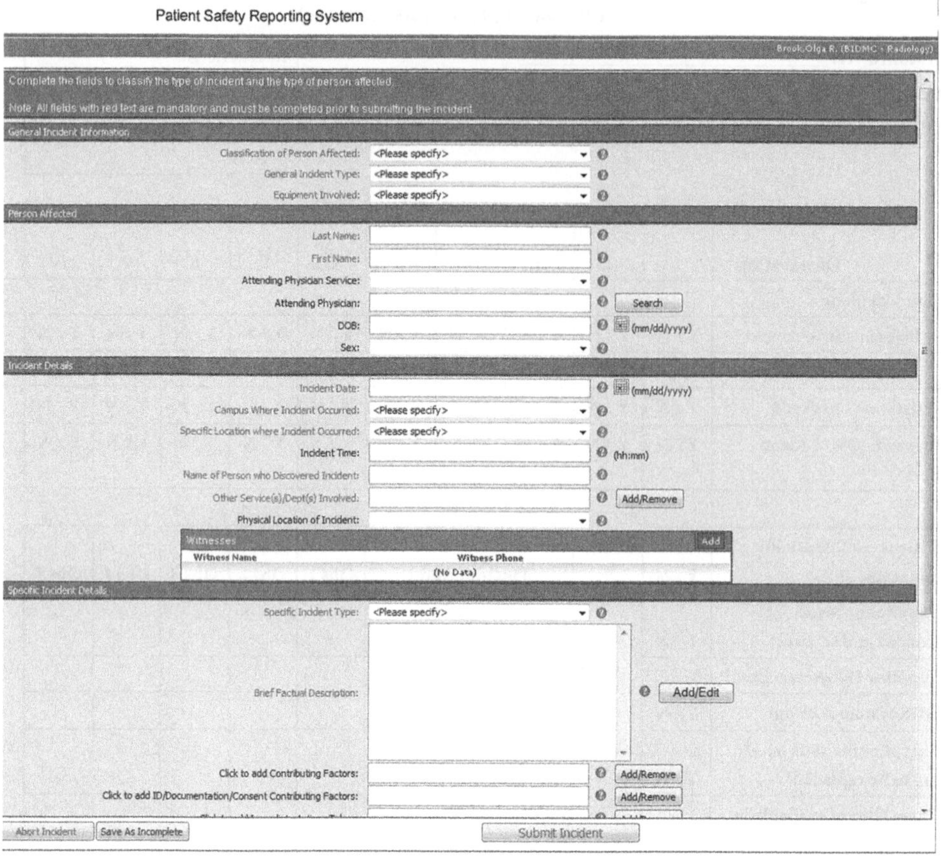

FIGURE 2.4 The electronic system for submission of an incident report. The report can be submitted by any staff involved. Its structure facilitates full description of the incident. Immediate e-mails are sent to the designated staff to ensure prompt response.

including nurses, front office personnel, transport facilitators, physician extenders, technologists, and all clinical staff.

For peer review of physician performance, the challenge is to convince radiologists that the task of double reading or reinterpreting studies is beneficial rather than a bureaucratic requirement. The process of peer review is mandated by many regulatory groups, including the ABR and the ACR. As a component of Part IV of the ABR maintenance of certification program, there is a requirement to evaluate performance, which can be accomplished using a peer review system.[11] Many hospitals and regulatory organizations now require that all active staff physicians participate in peer review of clinical performance. Some departments have linked participation in peer review with incentive systems.

Peer review of radiologists exists in many forms, ranging from national programs managed by the ACR to simpler systems developed within departments or institutions. Most radiologists are aware of the ACR *RadPeer* program,[13] whereby agreement with interpretation of prior studies is ranked on a scale of 1 to 4 (Figure 2.6). Many departments have established peer review systems that are either similar to the ACR system or that have radiologists blindly interpret a certain number of pre- or randomly selected cases. What all systems have in common are anonymous reporting and fair analysis, minimal effect on work flow, ease of participation, no punitive aspect, and integration into the department quality assurance program.[13] Ideally, such systems can be integrated at the national level, allowing benchmarking of a radiologist's performance. Although radiologists may still be reluctant to participate, the increasing regulatory requirements will ultimately make this mandatory.

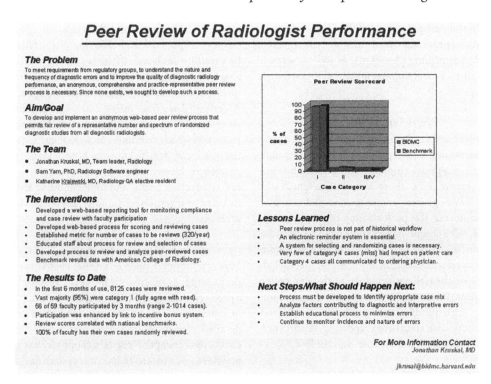

FIGURE 2.5 Screen shot illustrates how data from a selected performance indicator ("Peer Review of Radiologist Performance") are collected and depicted as a dashboard.

Diagnostic and Procedural Competencies
Although peer review systems tend to focus more on diagnostic and interpretive reviews, systems for measuring procedural competencies must be developed. Such systems do exist for trainees but have not yet been fully developed at the staff level. Recently, a radiologist-specific system has been proposed that incorporates multisource evaluation of competency, including professional standing, physician clinical performance assessment, and direct evaluation

FIGURE 2.6 Screen shot from Radiology RAD Review quality assurance program. For each study, a peer radiologist grades the agreement with the original interpretation on a 1–4 scale. The submission is within one screen; the data about the study are automatically pulled in from a radiology information system (RIS) by submitting the clip of the exam, which minimizes interference with workflow.

of technical and procedural skills. To be effective, evaluation processes must include management of underperforming physicians, as well as steps to stimulate technical improvement and maintenance of competency.[14]

Physician Scorecard

Regulatory and credentialing organizations, as well as an increasing number of hospitals, are introducing the concept of comprehensive physician scorecards (Figure 2.7). These are often aligned with the ACGME general competencies that are used for monitoring the performance of residents and fellows.[15] The comprehensive physician scorecard of an attending radiologist should include customizable key performance indicators (KPIs) that include metrics of clinical performance with peer review agreement rate, rate of complications; research metrics with funding and publications achieved; compliance with structured reporting, report turnaround time, and hand hygiene, and the like.[16]

Customer/Stakeholder Affairs

It is important to know precisely who your customers are, determine their needs and expectations, continually try to exceed them, and frequently assess their opinions of your services. There may well be multiple simultaneous customers, both external (patients) and internal (referring physicians, payers, radiology department staff). Hospital or medical school leaders and trustees, members of the court of public opinion, organizations that regulate health care finances, and even politicians should all be included in the enlarging group of stakeholders impacted by imaging services.[17]

Customer Surveys

Surveys of patients and referring physicians must be carefully analyzed. Patients can provide invaluable feedback and should be involved in peer review, quality review, and 360-degree evaluation processes. Alderson[18] lists four major categories to consider when evaluating customer satisfaction: knowing the factors on which customers base their evaluations of the quality of service, knowing how to identify your customers, knowing how to measure your customers' satisfaction levels, and understanding the need to balance interpersonal and technologic skills in practice.

Mystery Shoppers

Mystery shoppers pose as normal customers while performing a specific task—such as purchasing a product, asking questions, registering complaints, or behaving in a certain way—and then provide detailed reports or feedback about their experiences. The concept of "mystery shoppers" has gained popularity as a means to monitor system access and to directly evaluate scheduling, access to next available appointment, and human interactions.[19] Furthermore, these mystery shoppers are valuable for providing feedback regarding cleanliness, waiting room chatter, and comments from real patients.[20]

Process Improvement and Performance Indicators

Several recent articles in the imaging literature describe the use of KPIs by radiology departments to manage their clinical operations.[15,21,22] Although these tools are increasingly popular and their number and variety continue to expand, KPIs alone

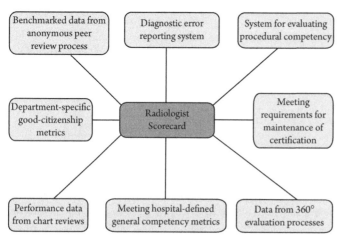

FIGURE 2.7 Options that can be used to assess the performance of a radiologist (scorecard), including an anonymous process for comparing performance with that of peers; means of evaluating diagnostic or procedural performance (chart, morbidity and mortality reviews); and a variety of metrics defined by departments (good citizenship criteria), the hospital administration (general competencies and peer evaluations), and the American Board of Radiology (maintenance of certification).

cannot help a department reach its goals. These indicators should be coordinated and aligned with a strategic operating plan. Templates are available to guide radiology departments in creating comprehensive strategic plans and communicating them to other entities within the health care organization.

In some radiology departments, KPIs resemble a random collection of metrics. Patient access to radiology services, turnaround time in diagnostic reporting, and peer-review audit rates each may seem important in its own right. However, as the quantity and range of indicators increase, so do the resources required to measure them and the focus needed to select those that should actually be monitored. Establishing a properly targeted and organized set of KPIs, ideally derived from the strategic planning process, will help the leadership team identify the most important problems or opportunities that should be addressed.

The strategic planning continuum can be divided into two realms: the definition of guiding principles (values, mission, and vision), and the development of a time-sensitive operating plan (goals, objectives, and actions) that is aligned with those principles. Overriding all activities are the *values* of a department, the core beliefs or ethical principles that guide every function and activity. These values may be linked to those of the institution or correspond to the culture of a department and its leadership, and they should guide departmental decision-making processes, behaviors, and interactions. The *mission statement* is the most basic embodiment of a business strategy[23] and sets forth the purpose of the organization. Based on core values, the mission statement is a road map that guides the organization in a particular direction. The *vision* is the destination that will be reached by adhering to the mission. By communicating a shared vision and road map, the well-crafted mission statement can help align and inspire members of the group. By providing a moral compass, the statement can allow ethical decisions to be made while avoiding prolonged debate and indecision. The vision and mission statements should be developed by senior management, but deployed only after carefully obtaining buy-in from department members.

The development of an operating plan starts with the careful selection of *goals*, each of which is designed to be achieved in 1 year or more. Goals can be considered as a short-term vision for the organization. A series of *objectives*, similar to the mission statement, provides the road map for reaching these goals. At a more detailed level, tasks, action items, or tactics tied to responsible individuals or groups are set as milestones by which progress toward an objective can be measured. How are strategic opportunities best identified and translated into goals? One useful tool that provides a framework is SWOT (strengths, weaknesses, opportunities, and threats) analysis, in which internal strengths and weaknesses and external opportunities and threats to a process are identified during brainstorming and environmental analysis.

Finally, in one of the last steps in the development of the operating plan, the leadership chooses a set of KPIs that will provide crucial insight into how well the objectives of the plan are being met. Key performance indicators are most useful when formulated as an integral part of the operating plan, because they are better aligned with the specific tasks that must be accomplished to reach the current goals of the organization.

How does a department optimize its use of KPIs? For departments that are commencing their strategic planning journey, objectives must be in place for achieving defined goals before selecting KPIs. Then, KPIs can be selected on the basis of the objectives and tactics that are to be used to achieve these goals.

Managing KPIs appropriately, actively, and continuously is an important component of clinical operations. Data may be displayed on electronic dashboards, which may be equipped with alarm indicators when specified thresholds are exceeded or not met. Data are most useful when they automatically populate the fields in a database[24] and are continuously depicted and updated instead of being manually transcribed and evaluated later. We have found that the assignment of responsibility to the right person for each KPI, and the linking of KPIs to specific metrics, benchmarks (when available), targets, objectives, and a timeline, are vital for ensuring the active and continuous collection and appropriate management of information.

In departments with sophisticated data engineering capabilities, the concepts of "bubble up" and "drill down" can be introduced: When measures drop below or rise above the defined target, a red flag (bubbling up) notifies the responsible administrator, who then can take appropriate action. Such action might involve delving deeper (drilling down) into the data to perform a root cause analysis. Practicality must guide decisions about who has access to and manages the data, since the amount of information collected is vast and the burden of continuous data analysis is heavy. Much of the necessary data analysis can be performed by designated staff at intervals of their choosing.

The prioritization of goals also varies according to the departmental vision and mission. However, many departments will probably assign high priority to improving productivity, maximizing revenues, improving customer service, and enhancing quality of care and patient safety. To adeptly navigate through the current environment, successfully manage change, and make sound decisions about complex issues, radiologists should develop some familiarity with the process and terminology of strategic planning.[25]

Educational Components

Although not typically included in a list of essential components, an educational program is an especially useful adjunct in academic departments of radiology, where ACGME and ABR requirements must be taught and monitored. This program should encompass staff training and self-improvement. An array of educational products can be used to stimulate staff engagement and participation, improve management of collected data, and meet regulatory requirements. Examples include the ACGME Outcome Project for residents and the ABR-mandated practice quality improvement project required to receive maintenance of certification.

The two major goals of the ACGME Outcome Project are to ensure that residency program educational content is aligned with the changing needs of the health care system, and that residency programs have outcome assessment systems that provide sound measures of the programs' educational effectiveness. To accomplish these goals, the ACGME has identified six general competencies, which are grounded in a national consensus on what residents in all specialties should know and be able to do.

The six general competencies include: (1) *patient care* that is compassionate, appropriate, and effective for the treatment of health problems and the promotion of health; (2) *medical knowledge* about established and evolving biomedical, clinical, and cognate (e.g., epidemiological and social-behavioral) sciences and the application of this knowledge to patient care; (3) *practice-based learning and improvement* that involves investigation and evaluation of one's own patient care, appraisal and assimilation of scientific evidence, and improvements in patient care; (4) *interpersonal and communication skills* that result in effective

information exchange and teaming with patients, their families, and other health professionals; (5) *professionalism*, as manifested through a commitment to carrying out professional responsibilities, adherence to ethical principles, and sensitivity to a diverse patient population; and (6) *systems-based practice*, as indicated by actions that demonstrate an awareness of and responsiveness to the larger context and system of health care and the ability to effectively call on system resources to provide care that is of optimal value.[26] The evaluation of residents must use dependable measures to assess their competences, including mechanisms for providing regular and timely performance feedback and the use of assessment results to achieve progressive improvements in resident competence and performance.

Morbidity and Mortality or Peer Review Conference

The morbidity and mortality or peer review conference has long served as a means of reviewing errors and adverse events in an environment that facilitates learning, encourages accountability, and promotes leadership and academic development.[27] To facilitate reporting of errors, an electronic submission system is developed (Figure 2.8A). After the case is submitted, it is reviewed by authorized staff members and then evaluated at the quality assurance conference. The results of these evaluations are submitted on the feedback form (Figure 2.8B). Mandated by the ACGME, these conferences must occur in all training institutions and can even be structured to meet the ACGME's general competencies.[25] Talner and D'Agostino[28] found that, far from being an "unnecessary evil thrust on us by the meddlesome medical bureaucracy," the meeting can be a useful teaching exercise and a successful recruiting tool for prospective residents.

Radiology Resident Quality Assurance Elective Programs

Quality assurance elective programs or rotations are now being offered.[29] These can be designed to meet the ACGME outcomes project requirements, to train residents to undertake their practice quality improvement projects, and to support the ACGME practice-based learning competency training.

Grand Rounds

Some radiology departments hold quality assurance grand rounds as an educational means of engaging staff in the principles and processes of quality and

(A)

Department of Radiology - Confidential Peer Review
Online Quality Assurance and Performance Improvement Reporting System

Chest ⊙	Abdominal (MRI) ⊙	Emergency ⊙	IR ⊙
Abdominal (CT) ⊙	Mammo ⊙	OB (US) ⊙	Nuc Med (NM) ⊙
Abdominal (US) ⊙	MSK ⊙	Neuro (CT, MRI) ⊙	Not sure(?) ⊙

Clinical issue: ⊙   Technical issue: ⊙

Patient Information: _____   ☑ Not related to a patient case

Medical record number: _____   Clip#(BID or BIDN)

Please provide a brief summary of pertinent issues:

_____

.> 2048   (characters left)

How was this matter brought to our attention?

☐ Radiology Colleague   ☐ non-Radiologist physician
☐ I made or detected the error   ☐ Patient or patient relations
☐ Other department at BIDMC   ☐ Other hospital
☐ HCQ/risk management

Thank you for your input.
When you press SUBMIT this confidential information will be submitted to the Radiology QA Group for review.

[Submit]

(B)

Department of Radiology - Confidential Peer Review
Online Quality Assurance and Performance Improvement Reporting System

Case Information

Section: Abd Modality: CT Patient MRN: 2445819 CLIP No: 5373560
Patient Case Related: NO Category:

Summary of pertinent issues:
rt adrenal lesion, with extension into IVC through rt superior adrenal vein is not mentioned in the report
lt 10th posterior rib pathological fracture, lt inferior pubic ramus lytic lesion is not in the report (" evidence of lytic lesions)
kidney is not excreting contrast on the delayed imaging - not in the report
study reviewed at the conference

Reason of submitting: [- I made or detected the error]
Case Review:
Issues identified from review:
Risk reduction strategy:
Action plans:
Responsible person:
Timeline for completion:
Measures of effectiveness:
Supervison:
Was supervison a contributing factor? ⊙ Yes ⊙ No
If yes, please explain
Disclosure:
Was error disclose? ⊙ Yes ⊙ No
If yes, by and to whom?
and what was disclosed?

Classification:
⊙ procedure complication - minor
⊙ procedure complication - major
⊙ equipment-related
⊙ technical error
⊙ interpretive error
⊙ miss or near-miss
⊙ communication error
⊙ delay in diagnosis

Notifications:
Has or will case be presented at section M & M?   ⊙ Yes ⊙ No
Should this case be presented at QA Ground Rounds? ⊙ Yes ⊙ No
Should another department be notified of this case?   ⊙ Yes ⊙ No
If yes, which department?

Context:
For serious adverse events, please provide context of case

FIGURE 2.8 (A) Screen shot of the Quality Assurance Database submission form. The form requires choosing the modality and classification of the issue under clinical or technical realms. This automatically directs the form to the designated staff member. (B) Screen shot of electronic form for error evaluation. Issues identified from the review are submitted. Risk reduction strategies, along with action plan, a responsible person, and timeline for completion, are required next steps for the quality assurance process. Error disclosure is an integral process of any error evaluation.

safety. We have held monthly quality assurance grand rounds for the past 3 years, with participation from all sections of the department. Indeed, elevating these sessions to the level of grand rounds sends a powerful message of how highly the departmental leadership values quality assurance.[25] Quality assurance grand rounds can also be designed to meet requirements for earning category 1 risk management credits, serve to provide an annual overview of the departmental quality management structure, and help orient new residents and faculty to the processes for case reporting and peer review.

Tools for Improving Departmental or Organizational Performance

A variety of problem-solving quality management methods are used for improving organizational or departmental performance. These can be integrated into an organization's total quality management program and range from the basic model for improvement, developed by Associates in Process Improvement,[30] to more complex models such as Six Sigma and the balanced scorecard. Six Sigma is a management philosophy that sets ambitious objectives to force accountability by minimizing mistakes and maximizing value.[31] This method is being increasingly used in radiology departments that constantly strive for zero technical defects.[32]

The balanced scorecard, first developed by Robert Kaplan and David Norton[33] at Harvard Business School in 1990, is a key management tool that provides a framework for translating organizational vision into strategies that incorporate all quantitative and abstract measures that are of true importance to that organization. By focusing not only on financial outcomes but also on human issues, the balanced scorecard helps provide a more comprehensive view of a business, which in turn helps organizations act in their own best long-term interests. This is particularly relevant to the health care field. The strategic management system helps managers focus on the performance metrics while balancing financial objectives with customer and employee perspectives, as well as with internal processes. Implementing balanced scorecards typically includes four processes: translating the vision into operational goals, communicating the vision and linking it to individual performance, business planning, and providing feedback and learning and adjusting the strategy accordingly.

In summary, a comprehensive quality and performance improvement program possesses many components. Starting with strong leadership support and identification of a dedicated team, this effort should be focused on patient and staff safety and include professional assessment and performance evaluation, education, and involvement of patients and other stakeholders at all levels, while being compliant with National Patient Safety Goals and the guidelines and requirements of the ACGME, ABR, ACR, and Joint Commission.

REFERENCES

1. Marx D. Patient safety and the "just culture": A primer for health care executives. New York: Columbia University, 2001. Accessed November 24, 2008 at: http://www.mers-tm.net/support/marx_primer.pdf.
2. Reinertsen JL. Engaging physicians. How the team can incorporate quality and safety. *Healthc Exec.* 2008 May-Jun;23(3):78, 80–1.
3. Palmersheim TM. The 1999 ICSI/IHI colloquium on clinical quality improvement: "Quality—settling the frontier." *Jt Comm J Qual Improv.* 1999 Dec;25(12):654–68.
4. Palmersheim TM. The 2000 ICSI/IHI Colloquium on Clinical Quality Improvement: "Cultivating quality—growing and nurturing clinical quality improvement in health care." *Jt Comm J Qual Improv.* 2000 Sep;26(9):554–8.
5. Yackanicz L, Kerr R, Levick D. Physician buy-in for EMRs. *J Healthc Inf Manag.* 2010 Spring;24(2):41–4.
6. Kruskal JB, Yam CS, Sosna J, Hallett DT, Milliman YJ, Kressel HY. Implementation of online radiology quality assurance reporting system for performance improvement: Initial evaluation. *Radiology.* 2006;241:518–27.
7. Choksi VR, Marn CS, Bell Y, Carlos R. Efficiency of a semiautomated review process for notification of critical findings in diagnostic imaging. *AJR Am J Roentgenol.* 2006;186:933–6.
8. Eisenberg RL, Yamada K, Yam CS, Spirn PW, Kruskal JB. Electronic messaging system for communicating significant, but not emergent, abnormal imaging results. *Radiology.* 2010;257:724–731.
9. Gibbs J, Clark K, Khuri S, Henderson W, Hur K, Daley J. Validating risk-adjusted surgical outcomes: Chart review of process of care. *Int J Qual Health Care.* 2001;13:187–96.
10. The Joint Commission. 2010 Hospital National Patient Safety Goals, July 2010. Accessed August 3, 2010 at: http://www.jointcommission.org/PatientSafety/NationalPatientSafetyGoals/
11. Strife JL, Kun LE, Becker GJ, Dunnick NR, Bosma J, Hattery RR. American Board of Radiology perspective on Maintenance of Certification: Part IV—practice quality improvement for diagnostic radiology. *RadioGraphics.* 2007;27:769–74.

12. Halsted MJ. Radiology peer review as an opportunity to reduce errors and improve patient care. *J Am Coll Radiol.* 2004;1:984–7.

13. Borgstede JP, Lewis RS, Bhargavan M, Sunshine JH. RADPEER quality assurance program: A multifacility study of interpretive disagreement rates. *J Am Coll Radiol.* 2004;1:59–65.

14. Mendiratta-Lala M, Boiselle P, Kruskal JB. Measuring and managing procedural competency of staff radiologists. *Radiographics.* 2011;31:1477–1488.

15. Donnelly LF, Strife J. Performance-based assessment of radiology faculty: A practical plan to promote improvement and meet JCAHO standards. *AJR Am J Roentgenol.* 2005;184:1398–1401.

16. Abujudeh HH, Kaewlai R, Asfaw BA, Thrall JH. Quality initiatives: Key performance indicators for measuring and improving radiology department performance. *Radiographics.* 2010 May-Jun;30(3):571–80.

17. Adams HG, Arora S. *Total quality in radiology: A guide to implementation.* Boca Raton, FL: St. Lucie, 1994.

18. Alderson PO. Noninterpretive skills for radiology residents: Customer service and satisfaction in radiology. *AJR Am J Roentgenol.* 2000;175:319–23.

19. Steiner K. The mystery shopper: An anonymous review of your services. *Health Care Strateg Manage.* 1986 Jun;4(6):9–11.

20. 'Mystery shoppers' can uncover ED weaknesses. *ED Manag.* 2006 Dec;18(12):140–1.

21. Nagy PG, Warnock MJ, Daly M, Toland C, Meenan CD, Mezrich RS. Informatics in radiology: Automated Web-based graphical dashboard for radiology operational business intelligence. *RadioGraphics.* 2009; 29(7):1897–1906.

22. Ondategui-Parra S, Bhagwat JG, Gill IE, Nathanson E, Seltzer S, Ros PR. Essential practice performance measurement. *J Am Coll Radiol.* 2004;1(8):559–66.

23. Camponovo EJ, Forman HP. The business of radiology and the mission statement. *J Am Coll Radiol.* 2004;1(2):108–12.

24. Kruskal JB, Reedy A. Invited commentary. *Radiographics.* 2010;30 (3): 580–2.

25. Gill IE, Ondategui-Parra S, Nathanson E, Seiferth J, Ros PR. Strategic planning in radiology. *J Am Coll Radiol.* 2005;2(4):348–57.

26. Common Program Requirements: General Competencies Approved by the ACGME Board February 13, 2007. Accessed August 3, 2010 at: http://www.acgme.org/outcome/comp/GeneralCompetenciesStandards21307.pdf

27. Kravet SJ, Howell E, Wright SM. Morbidity and mortality conference, grand rounds, and the ACGME's core competencies. *J Gen Intern Med.* 2006;21:1192–4.

28. Talner LB, D'Agostino H. The department of radiology quality assessment meeting: An unexpected teaching bonus. *Invest Radiol.* 1994;29:378–80.

29. Krajewski K, Siewert B, Yam S, Kressel HY, Kruskal JB. A quality assurance elective for radiology residents. *Acad Radiol.* 2007;14:239–45.

30. Langley GL, Nolan KM, Nolan TW, Norman CL, Provost LP. *The improvement guide: A practical approach to enhancing organizational performance.* San Francisco: Jossey-Bass, 1996.

31. Sander W. Six Sigma: The breakthrough management strategy revolutionizing the world's top corporations. *Qual Prog.* 2000;33:106–107.

32. Kang JO, Kim MH, Hong SE, Jung JH, Song MJ. The application of the Six Sigma program for the quality management of the PACS. *AJR Am J Roentgenol.* 2005;185:1361–5.

33. Kaplan RS, Norton DP. *The balanced scorecard: Translating strategy into action.* Boston: Harvard Business School Press, 1996.

3

Primum Non Nocere

A Few Words on the Primacy of Patient Safety

In medical circles, the word "quality" is rarely used unpaired with the word "safety." Indeed, the genesis of the medical profession's current laser-like focus on quality concepts and practices began as a response to a very immediate concern about patient safety in the hospital setting. Although there were a few articles published in the medical (including radiological) literature prior to the turn of the current century, most sources cite the publication of the Institute of Medicine's call to arms *To Err Is Human* in 1999 as the beginning of medicine's "quality era."[1] That book presented evidence of a surprisingly large number of preventable deaths that had occurred among hospitalized patients. Suddenly, it seemed that hospitals were really not very safe places to be, in stark contrast to the much more favorable public impression of hospital safety that prevailed prior to the book's publication. It was even suggested by some statistically inclined observers that it might be safer for patients to leap from their hospital's rooftops than for them to lie in a hospital bed! The distress caused by this revelation spread through the public imagination, and pervaded establishments and organizations of medical care and medical professionals in the United States. The response was quick, comprehensive, and far-reaching. Much productive change in the area of quality and safety in health care has occurred in the intervening decade. But it is worth remembering that, in the beginning, the focus of professional and organizational effort was toward improving patient safety first and foremost—including the development of novel strategies for error prevention, the establishment of safety goals and safeguards, and the fostering of the "culture of safety" concept into the machinations of health care delivery.

In the beginning, the focus of these safety efforts was justifiably directed to areas outside of diagnostic radiology, especially in the prevention of medication errors, iatrogenic infections, falls, and common preventable surgical errors and complications. Practical strategies for such things as promoting widespread hand hygiene compliance, medication reconciliation, surgical site marking, and procedural "time-outs" were soon developed. It did not take very long, however, for the safety imperative to spread down from the medical and surgical units to the hospital's lower levels, where the radiology departments are housed. According to an article by Erturk et al. in 2005, most radiology departments had active safety programs in place or under development by the time of their 2005 survey.[2]

By 2005, the leaders of the "safety movement" in medicine had long since made the connection between patient safety, system performance, and the extensive prior industrial experience with continuous quality improvement (CQI), quality control, and quality assurance, and had began to adapt concepts that had been useful in diverse industries, such as aviation and automobile manufacturing, toward improving the quality—and by extension the safety—of medical practice. Such terms as "lean," "Six Sigma," "flowcharting," and "dashboarding," which are discussed in detail in other chapters of this book, became familiar to physicians and hospital administrators, who has-tened to identify the "key performance indicators" (KPIs) for their radiology departments and then set out to measure them, improve them incrementally, and then measure them again, which is the essence of the "plan-do-study-act" cycle.

In reflecting on the past 10 years of work in the patient safety arena, it is clear that the most vital, central feature of a successful safety program, whether in radiology or in other medical specialties, has been in fostering a "culture of safety." Although there is no clear roadmap for accomplishing this, a few guiding principles can be named. These include, at a minimum:

- *Making the safety of patients the universal first priority* for the entire organization—starting with top leadership. Safety must trump all other concerns, efficiencies, and expediencies.
- *Creating a habitual mindfulness of safety issues* at all times by everyone in the organization; this is a learned behavior requiring practice and encouragement.
- *Making it clear that everyone in the organization is empowered to act* in the interests of patient safety as needed, without fear of undue recrimination should other management concerns be neglected.
- *Ensuring that all errors and "near-misses" are brought to light* and systematically evaluated in an organized way. In general, this requires fostering an atmosphere conducive of the self-reporting of errors, one that is free of recrimination and without undue fear of con-sequences, the so-called "blameless culture," which has recently been rearticulated as the "just culture," as discussed in Chapter 7. This is the most difficult cultural change to bring about within the medical community, which historically has been a very blame-oriented and punitive culture when errors (inevitably) occur, and this particular cultural change requires constant effort and maintenance by departmental leaders in order to keep the ten-dency toward "blamefulness" at bay. Clearly, there is a risk of causing complacency toward mistakes if the presumption of blamelessness is taken to an extreme; however, there is a recognized even greater risk of the unwanted suppression of vital information on errors and patterns of error needed for optimal risk reduction when individual errors cannot safely

be acknowledged by the individuals involved, and the underlying issues fully analyzed.

In radiology, our KPIs are diverse and wide-ranging, including such seemingly unrelated items as rapid report turnaround times, good patient access to imaging, the optimal use of information technology by radiology providers, report format-ting and clarity/legibility, good hand hygiene, responding to issues raised in patient satisfaction surveys, preventing adverse events with intrave-nous contrast administration, and keeping radia-tion exposures for common examination types as low as is reasonably achievable. Some of these (e.g., radiation safety, hand hygiene, and contrast safety) would be considered part of a patient safety program, whereas others (e.g., report formatting and report turnaround times, patient wait times, etc.) would be considered to be part of good radiol-ogy operations management. In the final analysis, however, and especially for radiologists, the pri-macy of patient safety in this milieu remains undi-minished. Within the departments of radiology, by the very nature of the type of service provided, issues that affect patient safety must always receive top priority.

Maximizing operational quality by optimizing efficiency and cost-effectiveness is indeed impor-tant, and can consume much of our time and effort. There is a risk, however, that quality efforts could become inappropriately blended with superficially similar, but not exactly corresponding CQI goals of sound business management. Overlap of business quality improvement and clinical quality and safety functions can result in "mission creep" by the quality management group, and are best avoided. If the gen-esis of the quality movement in medicine (including radiology) was in an almost obsessive-compulsive fixation on enhancing patient safety, perhaps there might be a future undesirable exodus from the movement, a shift in focus that finds us less con-cerned with safety issues and instead intent on chas-ing progressively more abstract ideas and derivative measures of "quality." There is a danger inherent in this as we may indeed find ourselves expending our limited attention, energy, time, and other resources for process improvement on goals that are ultimately less important than patient safety.

In the current health care payment climate, novel "pay for performance" plans (see Chapter 23), created by third-party payers—however well-intentioned—have often focused on narrowly defined quality metrics. Such incentive-payment schemes may have myriad unintended consequences, such as putting subtle (or not-so-subtle) pressure on departmental leaders, quality committees, and quality workgroups to prioritize initiatives that may enhance reimbursement and marketplace competitiveness (such as improving patient satisfaction and optimizing staff courteousness, for example) over patient safety-related initiatives. It would be naïve to presume that health care organizations will be able to commit unlimited resources to quality improvement work. This means that, inevitably, not everything worth doing in the quality arena can and will ultimately be done. There will always be pressure on organizational managers to show a return on investment dollars in the form of near-term financial returns or at least cost-avoidance. While the financial health of our practices and institutions matters a great deal—and while the practice of medicine is undeniably at its core a business venture—to physicians and to our patients, the practice of medicine is also a sacred trust, one not subject to the many large and small compromises inherent to running a successful business.

Radiologists, as the physicians in the imaging enterprise, have a unique duty to patients that goes beyond the duty of a business to its customers. First, and to the extent humanly possible, that duty is to put the patient's needs first, and *do no harm*. Thus, the radiologists on the quality team/working group must serve as the primary advocates for the continued primacy of patient safety in the hierarchy of competing organizational priorities within the quality agenda.

Our hospitals, clinics, and outpatient imaging centers currently are much safer today than they were a mere decade ago. Our patients have benefited from safety gains that are the direct and tangible result of sustained individual effort and organizational investments in the area of quality and safety that began with the publication of *To Err Is Human*. But systems as complex as these cannot yet be made error-free; in fact, perfection will likely remain beyond our human reach forever. Although much progress has been made—including measurable and statistically significant progress in many, many KPIs—nothing has eclipsed the central importance of our safety mission, and nothing has changed the rank-ordering of our priorities in that regard. When we say "Quality and Safety," therefore, it is understood that we always mean "safety first."

REFERENCES

1. Kohn LT, Corrigan JM, Donaldson MS, eds. *To Err Is Human: Building a safer health system.* Washington DC: National Academy Press, 2000. Available online at: http://www.nap.edu/readingroom
2. Erturk SM, Ondategui-Parra S, Ros PR. Quality management in Radiology: Historical aspects and basic definitions. *J Am Coll Radiol.* 2005;2:985–91.

4

Practical Quality Assurance

DAVID M. PAUSHTER AND RICHARD L. BARON

If you don't know where you are going, any road will take you there.

—AFTER LEWIS CARROLL[1]

The need to improve quality in medicine has been well documented,[2] and pressures abound from government agencies, third-party payers, medical certification boards,[3] and others[4] to require physicians to participate in organized quality improvement processes in their practices. Educational materials in print forms and symposia are widespread on the basics of "how to do" quality improvement processes. The focus of this chapter is to learn how to integrate the continuous quality improvement (CQI) process into the routine of a radiology practice. An emphasis is placed on understanding how the realities of a radiology practice can put roadblocks in place that may undermine the successful implementation of a quality program, and how these can be overcome by avoiding common pitfalls in the process of project design.

The quality improvement process in radiology is often thought of as a method of improving patient outcome quality or patient safety through an approach of methodological consistency.[5–7] Nonmedical businesses have used the CQI process for many years, not just as a quality measure for safety in industrial operations, but as a well-documented method to improve operational efficiencies. This not only can enhance productivity (financial benefit) but can dramatically improve employee functioning, making it easier to achieve goals and create better job satisfaction.[8,9] At the University of Chicago, the Department of Radiology first implemented the CQI process as part of a strategic business plan to improve radiology operations, with its emphasis arising from the operations and function viewpoint, rather than directed primarily at patient quality. The conceptual framework empowered functioning units/teams within the department with a skill set to solve locally identified problems in their daily operations, obviating the need to merely pass along the problem to a more central, remote, and distracted manager or team to solve. The process of identifying problems and solving them locally has the potential to produce more rapid, focused change, and therefore a better result.[10] Why wouldn't practicing radiologists want to embrace such a process, which could rapidly solve the irritants in their daily work operations (improving operational quality), and, at the same time, put in place a system to improve patient care (patient and outcomes safety/quality)?

THE PROCESS OF CQI

The process of CQI relies on the ability to either define a specific parameter best state (using either published benchmarks or an internally derived goal) or identify a specific problem in operations/procedures that needs to be overcome. In either case, the importance of determining the proper measurement technique and ultimate goal cannot be overemphasized.[11] It is often stated that if "you can't measure it, you can't manage it." Whether setting a goal for best practice or solving an identified operational problem, the process of CQI begins with measuring the baseline state, rather than relying on anecdotal information as the key driver. This is done by gathering the appropriate data, which can then be sorted and analyzed. Following a thoughtful analysis, potential barriers to improved performance can be identified through a root cause analysis. Focusing on basic elements of the data and the process, one can then construct an improvement plan to address identified deficiencies or problems. Following implementation, one then recycles through the process of remeasuring and analyzing the outcome data and implementing additional interventions as required.[6,7] This is continued indefinitely until reaching the prescribed goal, after which time continued measurements and review assure that the operational improvements are sustained.

The steps of the CQI process are:

- Identify the problem and determine benchmark.
- Measure baseline performance.
- Analyze data to determine quality solutions.
- Implement process change.
- Remeasure performance and compare with benchmark.
- Implement process change as needed.
- Remeasure on an ongoing basis.

POTENTIAL ROADBLOCKS TO CQI SUCCESS

The realities of implementing the described CQI process have shown that it is not as easy as it may appear to successfully tackle one specific project, let alone develop a widespread culture of embracing the process throughout all areas of a radiology department. Without understanding the many underlying roadblocks that exist within the typical radiology department practice and culture, it has proven difficult for radiologists to successfully implement sustainable quality improvement processes. In addition, failing to properly set up a structured and sustainable CQI methodology within a department, or to manage a specific project, can result not only in failure to achieve specific project goals but may undermine the future of the department's entire CQI process. Some potential roadblocks are described here.

Lack of Training

Gaining sustained attention from physicians and radiologists to analyze their practice details and develop a robust CQI program is a difficult task. Physicians often consider analyzing and "proving"

quality an affront to their expertise, rather than a necessary and integrated part of clinical practice. Although training in medical school and residency is geared toward maximizing the quality of individual patient care, historically, there has been little formal education in evaluating and improving the process of care. Independent thinking and action has been fostered and even cherished in traditional medical training programs, with little emphasis on collaboration among peers, let alone with departmental and institutional administration. Coupled with these training, mentorship, and attitudinal limitations, most physicians have not been exposed to those existing models of business analytics and change management that have proven valuable in guiding the CQI process.[8,9] In short, the work cannot be accomplished without adequate motivation, skills, and tools.

Compounding this lack of knowledge about CQI is the misconception in academic environments that CQI projects and their associated processes are analogous to research initiatives. Although significant similarities exist between the quality process and research approaches, the CQI imperative of improving quality through measurement and intervention on a continuous basis has a different thrust than a time-limited research project. A number of radiology specific CQI training resources are now available in print,[6,10–12] online (the Radiological Society of North America, the Society for Cardiovascular and Interventional Radiology), and in meeting format, and these can assist in the formation and expansion of a quality program. Taking advantage of these resources may help avoid potential pitfalls and provide needed structure to developing programs.

Ever-present Distractions

Numerous distractions to a practicing radiologist make it difficult for CQI to truly become part of a radiologist's culture. The highest priority in any practice is to complete ever-increasing (hopefully) volumes of clinical work. With decreasing reimbursements per unit of effort, there is a natural inclination for radiologists to spend more time performing the clinical work through either prolonged working hours or a reduction in time spent on nonclinical activities during the workday. Many radiology groups regularly monitor the relative value unit (RVU) production of each member or utilize other productivity indicators and place an emphasis on these for salary impact.[13–15] Radiologists practicing in academic centers may have additional competing and time-consuming priorities, such as research and education that they may perceive as key drivers for determining their career success. The current economic recession exacerbates these distractions, with departments' annual budgets facing cutbacks and therefore limiting support staff to aid in CQI functions. Without adequate resource allocation to build a robust, integrated CQI platform, inordinate time and attention may be spent solving individual problems as they occur, rather than appropriately triaging available resources for process improvement.

For CQI to successfully compete with professional pressures, whether clinical, teaching, or research, integration of the process into daily work is needed. Processes that allow this to occur in seamless fashion, particularly picture archiving and communication system (PACS)-based or other electronic solutions, permit ongoing data accrual without requiring offline tasks of busy radiologists.[12] As requirements for ongoing databases for maintenance of certification become routine, this will spur development of generic data accrual and manipulation programs integrated with PACS. If not available, shared desktop folders with electronic data entry or transfer into spreadsheet format for database mining still allows reasonable workflow to occur.

Culture

The culture of the work environment and practice traditions may create roadblocks. An individual radiologist may feel that, as only one member of a large group, and working relatively independently throughout the day to complete individualized tasks, he or she is just one "cog in the wheel" and can't have much of an impact in improving operations and quality. In addition, the culture of a radiology practice often inherently allows one to adopt the "I'm on staff" mentality. In this scenario, individuals do not have an adequate impetus to strive to enhance their performance as a key component of the larger group, at times feeling that a salaried position in a large institution guarantees them ongoing employment, regardless of their individual performance. This may result in an incongruous feeling of entitlement for salary, time, and resources despite mounting financial pressures on the parent organization. Finally, payers historically have financially rewarded radiologists for the mere process of generating a report regardless of the effort, quality, or accuracy of that report. Successful radiology groups

will develop a culture that recognizes that the long-term sustainability of a practice will require a definition of quality reporting that goes beyond the minimum required for reimbursement. All of these cultural issues and potential roadblocks must be overcome in order for CQI to be embraced and successful throughout a radiology organization

Insufficient Resources

With declining reimbursement, often all available resources, including personnel, are focused toward direct patient care. This has become particularly acute as the financial crisis has impacted patient volumes for many facilities, resulting in layoffs of "ancillary personnel." Success of a CQI program in this environment rests on the belief that improving the quality of care is not only in the best interest of the patient, but a driver of the business model as well. In the direct sense, payers are clearly moving toward a "pay for performance" mindset that will result in proof of quality, providing a larger service population and higher payments. Indirectly, improving quality is typically associated with increased operational efficiency and decreased expense related to duplication of efforts and patient complications. Therefore, providing adequate resources for CQI is supported by business logic as well as patient concerns.

To summarize, the success of a CQI process depends not just on the participation of all radiologists in a department, but on their embracing quality as a constant of and essential of their professional lives, thereby making the program a high priority, a requirement to successfully change culture. The business model has long ago demonstrated that those individuals working directly on the activity production line are the best sources for identifying operational inadequacies. If the associated departmental technical staff and ancillary personnel do not sense that the radiologists are involved and actively promoting process improvement, they too will not become engaged.

Other roadblocks to successful CQI implementation include:

- Lack of education and exposure
- Culture of independence
- Distraction of daily work
- Lack of obvious rewards
- Head in the sand
- Lack of empowerment
- Inadequate resources

KEYS TO GAINING THE ATTENTION AND MOTIVATION OF RADIOLOGISTS

Leadership

First and foremost, the leadership of the department and parent organization must visibly and palpably embrace the importance of a CQI program on an ongoing basis. Hospital administration, department chairs, section chiefs, and technology leaders must demonstrate their participation frequently and consistently. At the University of Chicago, this is done in a variety of ways. The institutional physician and administrative leadership participate in all quality committee activities and make it a priority to attend and actively contribute to standing meetings. Every department is required to participate in monthly hospital meetings, which include reporting on the status of quality initiatives. Each department has a designated "quality chair" with administrative power, typically the director of clinical operations (vice chair), who actively attends bimonthly quality chair meetings, as well as monthly combined physician and administration quality assurance meetings. Each section chief, the imaging modality managers, and key administrators in radiology are required to attend monthly departmental quality meetings supported by leadership. These meetings all represent oversight and review assemblies that discuss the continual ongoing work done on projects throughout the department on a regular basis. At the end of each year, the institution has a "Quality Fair," where numerous exhibits reporting on quality initiatives from all departments are highlighted and awards are given to promote recognition for excellence. Within each department, leadership must provide acknowledgment to those individuals and teams putting efforts into CQI programs.

Continuous Process Philosophy

The "C" (representing continuous) in CQI is a key concept required to successfully integrate a quality program into daily practice. Several aspects of the process must be continuous and regular. First, quality must be consistently seen as important to leadership and continually reinforced by their actions.

Second, leadership must see that frequent updates are made concerning not just the overall program, but that also key communications are made to those involved on the status of all projects. The regularly scheduled committee and operational meetings discussed above must occur in an ongoing fashion. Infrequent meetings without interval updates allow last-minute flurries to disrupt the CQI process and perpetuate the image of an intermittent process. Team members must have accountability, which requires assigned responsibilities with recognized and published time frames to achieve them. All too often, CQI meetings are postponed or prove fruitless due to lack of forward motion on assignments. Distributing "dashboards" demonstrating critical data measures over time for multiple department initiatives can be very helpful in allowing all department members to see the progress of all CQI projects at a glance and allowing participants to feel as if it is almost "real-time" in effect.[9] Color coding indicator results, often depicted as green (meeting target), yellow (approaching target), and red (not gaining traction) can be an effective means of keeping issues in front of targeted teams with easily grasped status reports.

Communications to all involved personnel should not be limited to data presentation or to formal CQI meetings, but verbal discussion of CQI initiatives can and should occur in a wide range of operational meetings that take place within the department and between departments. These informal communications are essential for widespread awareness and for maintaining vitality in specific projects.

Third, keeping the actual work of a project flowing continually will keep the initiative and associated issues in the foreground.

Finally, whenever possible, try to keep data accumulation continual and part of routine operations rather than intermittent and/or retrospective. These combined efforts allow quality assurance to permeate all areas within a department with a singular focus.

Building an Awareness of Impact and Rewards

If developing a CQI program is to truly be a priority for a radiology department, there must be a clear perception of the potential impact of the needed improvements, and conversely, of the impact of noncompliance to all working in the department. Building an awareness of requirements to comply with American Board of Radiologists (ABR), Center for Medicare and Medicaid Services, external quality organizations, and third-party payers' quality programs and initiatives, and their regulatory and financial impact, is essential for radiologists. Many third-party payers have developed payment contingencies for reimbursement depending on meeting specified quality goals, and these will only escalate in the future as health care organizations move increasingly to "pay for performance." Development of a strong CQI process will provide the framework for meeting or exceeding present and future expectations placed on health care providers. In aligning incentives in the department of radiology at the University of Chicago, a significant portion of the annual bonus reimbursement to radiologists has depended on sectional goals weighted toward participating in the department CQI process, rather than focusing on individual goals or metrics, such as individual productivity. When sectional participation in the CQI process is made a basic requirement, successful distribution of bonus funds is not based on meeting any predetermined target, but on active participation in the ongoing practice of improving care. This can positively impact the individual radiologist's engagement in departmental CQI processes and foster attainment of sectional and departmental goals. Rewards are key to driving behavior, and the end result of a CQI project producing increased operational efficiency or patient outcome/safety will be a sufficient driver for most physicians. Public laudations and honors, however, are effective tools to reward exemplary process participation. The use of money in the bonus pool acts as a positive tool to direct radiologists toward key areas requiring group focus and concentration that the department wants to emphasize, beyond the accepted standard operations.

Appropriate Project Selection for Group Participation

To overcome the roadblocks discussed, the projects chosen must reflect clinical or operational concerns that allow vesting among all parties involved. If the issues to be evaluated are not perceived as relevant or problematic, motivating participants will prove difficult. Projects will be best supported if they are in line with the focus and direction of the department and institution. Further, a "stand alone" project with an idiosyncratic focus is unlikely to garner the adequate institutional or departmental resources required for success. In addition, local culture may dictate the chances for success based upon prevailing practice and political climate. The contemplated intervention or measured parameter must be within the sphere of departmental control, since altering behavior is a daunting task under the best of circumstances.

From a practical viewpoint, projects must be broad enough to effect recognizable and pertinent

change, but not so all-encompassing as to become mired in the CQI process. The ability to dissect a large-scale problem into identifiable simpler units that can be individually altered is essential. Solutions aimed at altering one or two factors are significantly more likely to come to fruition than are those involving changing multiple parameters simultaneously. Although multiple-parameter interventions may prove successful, unnecessary changes in process may be made at the expense of the patient or department. The quality parameters to be reviewed must be clear and easily measurable, with data accrual and analysis not exceeding the time and resource commitment available to the team. Benchmarks of success should be culled from the available literature, professional society resources, or local norms[6,7,11] and must be tempered by practice circumstances that may not allow achieving a "perfect" score.

Data Accrual and Interpretation

Continuous QI data must be readily available from existing sources, such as radiology information systems (RIS), PACS, or billing systems, and simply transferred or exported to an easily manipulated electronic database. The ability to enter and cull data during day-to-day work improves the constancy of information and participation in the CQI process.[12] Data should be accurate, representative, and reproducible; thus, methods of data accrual or the data source should not be changed in midstream. Information accrued should be of sufficient granularity to understand the factors that may limit quality and permit recognition of improvements after intervention. Finally, data analysis should be straightforward, not relying upon complex statistical manipulation to gauge success.

Some further keys to the success of CQI include:

- Make it relevant.
- Align incentives.
- Keep it simple (focus).
- Minimize resources required.
- Define responsibilities and timelines.
- Keep the "C" in CQI.

ILLUSTRATIVE PROJECTS

Case Project 1: Decreasing Nondiagnostic Pulmonary Emboli CTA Examinations

Tables 4.1 and 4.2 summarize key aspects from a CQI project undertaken at the University of Chicago by the chest section several years ago to

TABLE 4.1 ADEQUACY OF PULMONARY EMBOLUS COMPUTED TOMOGRAPHY (CT): PROJECT OUTLINE

- Identify all PE CT scans on a daily basis.
- Review reports for nondiagnostic/suboptimal studies.
- Review exams for vessel opacification >200 HU, motion and noise artifacts.
- Classify and quantify causes of poor quality.
- Intervene with appropriate modifications.
- Remeasure.

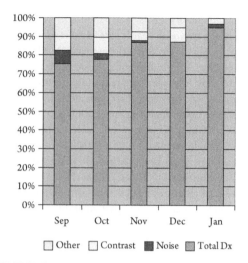

FIGURE 4.1 Adequacy of pulmonary embolus computed tomography (CT): Results.

address nondiagnostic computed tomography (CT) scans in evaluating patients for suspected pulmonary embolic disease. An initial assessment confirmed the section's anecdotal experience that a significant proportion (25%) of CT examinations were nondiagnostic due to technical factors. Through a 6-month process, using the principles of CQI (initial assessment, measurement, analysis, intervention, followed by repeating these cycles), the nondiagnostic examination rate rapidly decreased to 5% (Figure 4.1). This process involved all chest radiologists in assessing exams on an ongoing basis, thus allowing data collection to become an accepted part of the daily practice. In addition, the process required collaboration between the professional and technical staff, including leadership. This process fostered collaborative review of interventions and impact, allowing the expertise of physicians and technologists in the department to optimize the patient outcome in a way that would not have been possible working in a more isolated fashion.

TABLE 4.2 ADEQUACY OF PULMONARY EMBOLUS COMPUTED TOMOGRAPHY (CT): INTERVENTIONS

- Interventions based on reviewers' input and initial results
- Bolus tracker location: Change from aorta to PA
- Tracker image: Slightly higher mA to improve quality
- IV process: Specify above wrist and a least 20 g
- Arm position: Raised with hands on scanner
- Contrast bolus: Increase from 4 to 5 cc/sec
- Breath-hold instructions: Avoid deep breath
- Protocols: Standardize across multiple CT units

- Training: In-service education for technologists, sharing data and process

Case Project 2: Adequacy of History Provided on Radiology Requisitions

Several years ago, the pediatric radiologists at the University of Chicago attempted to solve a nationally recognized and long-standing problem impacting radiology care, that of inadequate history provided on requisitions. The pediatric section focused on improving the adequacy of critical history provided by referring caregivers on requisitions for neonatal intensive care unit (ICU) chest radiograph examinations. The methodology for this project is summarized in Table 4.3. After implementing the initial baseline measurement and preliminary analysis, the intervention steps outlined in the table were undertaken. After 5 months, the first reanalysis was performed; the data from the baseline and post intervention are displayed in Figure 4.2. The data demonstrated a slight decline in the quality of history provided after intervention. The project was abandoned by the participants for a variety of factors, unfortunately accompanied by a feeling of hopelessness to achieve change.

TABLE 4.3 IMPROVING HISTORY PROVIDED ON REQUISITIONS: METHOD

- Review of imaging requisitions from pediatric neonatal and cardiac intensive care units
- Review panel composed of a pediatric radiologist, a radiology resident, a pediatric intensivist, and two pediatric residents to assess adequacy of history, without detail of specific provider, time of order, or type of exam
- Individual educational outreach to pediatric intensivists individually, rotating pediatric residents on the radiology service, and two lectures at clinical morning report on this topic by a pediatric radiologist
- Resample adequacy of requisition history at 5 months

Despite the best intentions, this project demonstrates the problems that can occur when the principles detailed earlier in this chapter are not taken into consideration in planning a CQI project. Most importantly, no engagement was made of all the parties necessary to achieve change. Although the radiology faculty and staff were truly invested in all ways (accuracy of imaging interpretation, billing compliance, and operations required this information, and a sectional bonus relied on the process instituted), the department of pediatrics was not. Without broad-based involvement of the pediatricians (faculty, residents, and practicing support staff), achieving change was unlikely. Success would have required their leadership to embrace accurate and complete patient histories as a high priority and to adhere to all of the leadership requirements for success (visible presence, frequent communications, department rewards for participation, etc.). Gaining the attention of physicians from the distracters described earlier is extremely difficult, and without prioritization from the external department leadership, their true engagement was significantly limited. This design flaw was not recognized or addressed during planning and implementation, resulting in a disconnect between the project planners, who desired change, and the disinterested providers. Those issues that went wrong included:

- Lack of engagement of all required participants
- Inadequate support of leadership
- Data insufficiently granular
- Data accrued infrequently and not communicated to key personnel
- Interventions not derived from data analysis

This project had preplanned interventions developed prior to data collection, similar to a scientific project, rather than using data analysis to detect issues and trends that would direct the development of potential interventions. Although the CQI process is in some ways similar to a scientific project approach, there are two key structural differences. First, the CQI process should determine potential interventions only after data collection and analysis, whereas scientific experimental methodology

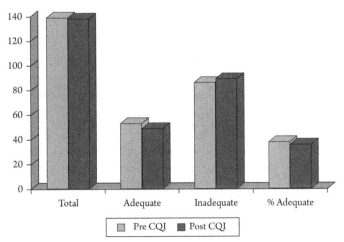

FIGURE 4.2 Improving history on imaging requisitions: Results.

classically employs a prestudy hypothesis and single intervention prior to initiating the formal experiment. Second, the scientific method typically involves one predetermined set of experiments with a single endpoint analysis to determine whether change occurred, whereas CQI is an iterative process with multiple repeated measurements, often following sequential interventions directed by the data.

The selection of appropriate measures to be used in data collection and subsequent postintervention monitoring is essential for a successful CQI project. Proper measures can quickly identify problems, guide analysis toward suitable interventions, and allow postintervention analysis. In this specific case, only the number of requisitions that were adequate versus inadequate was obtained, thus limiting detailed analysis and potentially more successful interventions. The stratification of data by subcategories (perhaps particular shifts of clinical service, or specific ordering physician) might have identified specific problem areas that could have benefitted from tailored interventions with a higher likelihood of change. By analyzing the data in smaller but more frequent intervals, success or lack thereof could have been assessed and more specific interventions planned during the project period. More frequent and more detailed analysis could have been accomplished without stressing resources, since shorter bursts of frequent activity incorporated into the daily routine are less burdensome than completing a larger task at a later date.

The use of more frequent, detailed data gathering would have allowed for several of the key requirements for successful CQI to have been in place. First, measurable data on a linear scale relating to specific providers could have been accrued, with the potential for changing individual behavior, and reinforced through serial communications of data. Merely publicly providing associated data with specific names will frequently engage individuals to alter behavior to avoid being perceived as not performing to standards. Second, frequent communications to all project participants, including those ordering and performing the examinations, would have kept the project's goals and rationale in the foreground.

The project addressed an important issue, involved substantial time and effort from multiple individuals and, when it failed to develop the hoped-for changes over time, affected morale among those involved and certainly endangered their enthusiasm

over participating in the departmental CQI program. Learning from these experiences, the pediatric radiology section subsequently chose a more internally focused project to standardize radiologist reporting systems for renal hydronephrosis on ultrasound examinations; this program was extremely successful, requiring only a short time to collect data and implement significant changes. All participants were engaged with the process, communication occurred continually at multiple levels (including leadership), patient care improved, and participants were financially rewarded through the bonus system.

Case Project 3: Improving Quality of Plain Film Radiographs of Joints/Extremities

When the musculoskeletal imaging section at the University of Chicago first participated in CQI, they chose to tackle improving the quality of plain film radiographs of joints and extremities. Typical of many large institutions, these examinations are performed at multiple sites throughout the hospital, including portable services, and are often performed on sick and poorly mobile patients. Without prior CQI education or participation, the section's first attempt was structured in a manner that paralleled a physician's practice, with characteristics focusing on anecdotal experiences and without organized documentation and analysis. The methodology for this project is shown in Table 4.4.

This example tackled a project that was limited to radiology personnel; therefore, in contrast to

---

TABLE 4.4 IMPROVING THE QUALITY OF MUSCULOSKELETAL PLAIN FILMS

- Data acquisition: 2 days/month
- All plain films evaluated by one attending and one resident
- Type of exam, location of facility recorded
- Exams rated as poor quality flagged for review
- Data analysis: Certain exams and facility location correlated with lower exam quality
- Intervention: Flagged exams anecdotally presented at quarterly technologists' meetings
- Resampling: 3-month intervals with no significant improvement in exam quality

---

the preceding case illustration, it should have been easier to engage the physicians and staff to develop needed change. However, intermittent data gathering with infrequent accrual dates spread over a 3-month period resulted in limited engagement of the radiologists and lack of project visibility as a priority process. This project would have had greater initial traction had there been substantially more frequent data gathering for analysis, acquiring more data points over short periods of time. The data collection could have been accomplished by having a supervising technologist with appropriate expertise perform the assessments, with ongoing collaborative exam review with the radiologists (reducing radiologist time on the project). This would also have kept the project visible to those technologists who were the targeted change agents.

Lack of focus in this project and limited ability to measure and manage the data/process were evident. Rather than using sporadic exam assessments to motivate technologic staff for improvement, data should have been organized and reviewed to provide a measurable scale of quality (perhaps percent of cases determined to be of poor quality) that could be tied to specific exam performance techniques and locations. Further categorizing the data as to the etiology of the quality issue should have been included, so that (1) interventions could be planned to eliminate or reduce the problem, and (2) data could be tracked for serial analysis and uncovering of trends. In this fashion, the most approachable or obvious problems could have been addressed, with subtler or more complex issues tackled as the project advanced. "Keep it simple" does not suggest limiting CQI projects to minor but achievable arenas, but refers to developing a focus that is clear and well-defined at each step, to allow for targeted data accrual, assessments that will be meaningful, and specific, focused interventions that will have a high likelihood of initiating change. Among the issues that went wrong:

- Infrequent data accrual
- Low project visibility
- Lack of objective, quantifiable quality parameters
- Poorly focused data and interventions

The development of capabilities to participate more efficiently in CQI improves with practical experiences. Learning from this project, the following year, the musculoskeletal section embarked on a more focused process to reduce magnetic resonance imaging (MRI) scan time for specific procedures. Using the CQI process optimally over a 6-month period, they substantially reduced scan time, improving both patient satisfaction and departmental efficiency. At the annual University of Chicago Medical Center Quality Fair, this exhibit received the award for the best quality improvement project within the hospital. The musculoskeletal section project for this year is to tackle the quality of MRI images, in some ways similar to the plain film project of several years ago. The differences in their current planning emphasize how they have learned to plan CQI projects and remove roadblocks before they occur. In this new project, each MRI examination will be graded for quality on a 1–5 scale at time of original interpretation. Those deemed 3–5 (lesser quality) will be noted in an electronic folder embedded within the PACS system, detailing the basis of problem and location of the MRI unit. After 200 examinations, the database will be reviewed and analysis of average score grouped by location, type of examination, and performing technologist. Depending on the data, the team will determine whether a focused plan for intervention should be based on which examinations are most problematic, which locations (or technologists) are most problematic, or which artifact/quality issue is most prevalent. Key to this more advanced project is simplified and systematic data collection that is incorporated in the radiologist's work routine. This integration also optimizes project visibility to radiologists to ensure that data collection is complete and inclusive. Projects that require reopening patient files at a later date to retrospectively review images or gather information are too time-consuming for radiologists and staff and can be a serious roadblock. Gathering the pertinent information at the time of patient care delivery and incorporating it into the operational routine is a key component to maximizing the potential for project success.

A central theme early in the department of radiology's approach to CQI was to assume that academic radiologists were trained in scientific methodology, and with minimal introduction to CQI processes, they could develop and institute well-designed CQI projects. The problems we encountered in these early projects revealed that specific education and training focusing on methodology is essential for a successful program. Many medical centers today have embraced institutional programs in quality management and have put in place institutional resources and experienced personnel to lead local programs. Departments should take advantage of this expertise and seek experienced advice in CQI planning and implementation.

CONCLUSION

We have demonstrated the keys to successful implementation of a CQI process and reviewed potential roadblocks that can be overcome. Regardless of how well an organization or business performs, ongoing monitoring of performance and searching for improvement solutions will provide a basis for future programmatic success. By engaging all individuals in the process throughout an organization using the principles of simplification and clarity, measuring to manage achievable goals, and high-priority communications and rewards, departments can reap the benefits of improved operations, patient safety, and a professionally stimulated staff.

REFERENCES

1. Carroll, L. *The Complete, Fully Illustrated Works.* New York: Gramercy Books, 1995.
2. Kohn L, Corrigan J, Donaldson M, eds. Committee on Quality of Health Care in America, Institute of Medicine. *To err is human: Building a safer health system.* Washington, DC: National Academies Press, 2000.
3. Strife J, Kun L, Becker G, Dunnick NR, Bosma J, Hattery RR.. The American Board of Radiology perspective on maintenance of certification: Part IV—Practice quality improvement in diagnostic radiology. *AJR.* 2007;188:1183–6.
4. Donnelly L, Strife J. Performance-based assessment of radiology faculty: A practical plan to promote improvement and meet JCAHO standards. *AJR.* 2005;184:1398–1401.
5. Boland GW. Herding cats toward best practices: Standardizing the radiologic work process. *AJR.* 2009;193:1593–5.
6. Johnson C, Miranda R. Aakre K, et al. Process improvement: What is it, why is it important, and how is it done? *AJR.* 2010;194:461–8.
7. Steele J, Schomer D. Continuous quality improvement programs provide new opportunities to drive value innovation initiatives in hospital-based radiology practices. *J Am Coll Radiol.* 2009;6:491–9.
8. Lexa F, Berlin W, Boland G, et al. ACR white paper: Task force to evaluate the value add impact of business models. *J Am Coll Radiol.* 2009;6:681–93.
9. Reiner B. Quantifying radiation safety and quality in medical imaging 3: The quality scorecard. *J Am Coll Radiol.* 2009;6: 694–700.
10. Donnelly L, Dickerson J, Lehjkamp T, et al. Operational rounds: A practical administrative process to improve safety and clinical services in radiology. *J Am Coll Radiol.* 2008:5;1142–9.
11. Liu P, Johnson D, Miranda R, et al. A reference standard-based quality assurance program for radiology. *J Am Coll Radiol.* 2010;7: 61–6.
12. Khorasani R. You should harmonize your quality, safety and IT programs. *J Am Coll Radiol.* 2009;6:399–400.
13. Ding A, Saini S, Berndt E. Radiologist productivity: What, why and how. *J Am Coll Radiol.* 2009;3:824–7.
14. Duszak R, Muroff L. Measuring and managing radiologist productivity, part 1: Clinical metrics and benchmarks. *J Am Coll Radiol.* 2010;7: 452–8.
15. Duszak R, Muroff L. Measuring and managing radiologist productivity, part 2: Beyond the clinical numbers. *J Am Coll Radiol.* 2010;7: 482–9.

5

Root Cause Analysis (RCA) and Health Care Failure Mode and Effect Analysis (HFMEA)

RATHACHAI KAEWLAI AND HANI H. ABUJUDEH

Having a problem is, by nature, a state of disaffection, undesirability, and difficulty in any person's life. However, problems also represent challenges that encourage people to overcome them by finding ways to identify causes, eliminate them, establish more pleasant circumstances, and prevent them from recurring. Problems occur every day in every section of any hospital. The reactive identification of causes is the most important step to solving problems. However, the proactive identification of potential problems, which prevents them from occurring in the first place, is even more effective. In this chapter, we discuss two different, but related, processes: root cause analysis (RCA) and health care failure mode and effect analysis (FMEA), which are commonly used to tackle any already existing problems, and to proactively prevent them from occurring, respectively.

ROOT CAUSE ANALYSIS

After problems have occurred and initial damage control has been put in place, an in-depth investigation into the cause (or causes) of the problem is a usual first step within the corrective action process. Causes identified in an initial action may represent simply symptoms (signs of a problem), first-level causes (direct cause leading to a problem), or higher-level causes. *Root causes* are the highest-level, specific, underlying causes of a problem that can reasonably be identified and managed, and for which effective recommendations for preventing recurrences can be generated (1). Tackling and removing causes other than root causes may only temporarily relieve the problem. Given the significance of finding the root causes in problem-solving, RCA has become paramount in driving quality management systems in health care.

Root cause analysis is a structured process that focuses on events that have already surfaced, caused an actual defect, or contributed to a problem. It aims to determine what happened, how it happened, and why it happened, thus initiating the actions necessary to eliminate future occurrences of similar problems (2). It helps in the recognition of deep, less-than-visible factors that have contributed to the identified event and is a prerequisite to any corrective action plan. Root cause analysis is most effective when it is well defined, equipped with adequate resources, and carried out by trained personnel. Complete assessment of root causes by RCA allows one to plan specific elements of corrective action connected to the identified causes and to prevent the recurrence or prolongation of the event. Root cause analysis has been popularized in the U.S. health care system by the Joint Commission (JC) and the U.S. Veterans Hospital Administration as a systematic analytic approach to health care improvement since the 1990s (3,4). The Joint Commission requires organizations to perform an RCA for every sentinel event, which it defines as "an unexpected occurrence involving death or serious physical or psychological injury, or the risk thereof"(5). Currently, 27 U.S. states have mandatory adverse event reporting systems in place for documenting such occurrences (6). Although certain sentinel events are not subject to review by the Joint Commission under the sentinel event policy, RCA should be performed for every sentinel event, to probe reasons for those problems that have already occurred as well as for that have almost occurred (near-misses) (7). To produce viable results, RCA must be a part of the whole organization's continuous improvement process. Typically, RCA is performed by a small team, with members selected from all levels associated with the event. Analysis includes defining the event, identifying the causes, and devising solutions. The team typically meets at least weekly, with each meeting lasting less than 2 hours. Once solutions have been designed, usually within approximately 2 months, the decision to implement the recommended changes can take days to months to complete.

The 11 steps in performing RCA (8) are outlined in Table 5.1 and each step is described in details. A framework for RCA and an action plan in response to a sentinel event can help start an RCA process; a sample framework is accessible at the Joint Commission's website (9).

Step 1: Organizing a Team

Root cause analysis is best applied by a group of people working together in an open, honest, and trustful

---

TABLE 5.1   ELEVEN STEPS OF ROOT CAUSE ANALYSIS AS SUGGESTED BY THE JOINT COMMISSION

1. Organize a team
2. Define what happened (the event)
3. Identify and define the process(es) related to the event
4. Identify proximate causes
5. Design and implement any necessary "quick fix" interim changes
6. Identify root causes
7. Identify potential risk reduction strategies
8. Formulate and evaluate proposed improvement actions; identify measures of success
9. Develop and implement an improvement action plan
10. Evaluate and fine-tune improvement efforts
11. Communicate the results

Reprinted with permission from Joint Commission. Root cause analysis tools to help with root cause analysis. *Jt Comm Perspect Patient Saf.* 2002;2.

atmosphere that stimulates the sharing of important information to reach the root cause, to devise solutions that will terminate the root cause and eventually eliminate the problem. The RCA should be performed by staff at all levels who have fundamental knowledge of the specific process involved. It is also important to include staff who will likely ultimately be responsible for removing the identified root case (10). The typical design of an RCA team includes 4–10 members selected from those areas that experienced the problem, area manager or supervisor with decision-making authority, physicians, respected and credible leaders with broad knowledge, and quality improvement experts. In essence, the team should include representatives from three categories of organizational staff: leaders, caregivers with hands-on experience in the process being examined, and a facilitator (10). A team of less than 10 members tends to be most efficient, whereas a team with less than four members will likely provide less creativity, a limited knowledge base, and inadequate experience to solve the problem and devise solutions.

Because most RCAs investigate errors that have occurred during clinical care, physician involvement in the RCA process is crucial. A physician's first-hand experience and critical knowledge of the process is a vital input into possible root causes. In fact, the Joint Commission's Accreditation Committee will not accept an RCA of a medical care process if no physician has participated in the analysis (11). The RCA process may benefit from the inclusion of caregivers directly involved in the event, who can offer an insight into understanding what occurred and how its recurrence can be prevented. However, the downside may be intimidation of involved caregivers, thus leading to limited information being disclosed and feelings of discomfort among the RCA team when questioning the involved caregivers. Hospitals should consider caregiver involvement on an individual basis (12).

Step 2: Define What Happened (the Event)

Understanding the nature of the event (problem) is vital before starting the analysis. This step involves asking the "who, what, when, where, and why" of the event (2) to get complete information and understanding. Gathering data and analyzing the event is the major task in this step (1). Once the problem is adequately defined, the framework for identifying those issues that lie beneath the problem (i.e. practices, documents, excuses, speculations, confusion, etc.) can be created.

Step 3: Identify and Define the Process(es) Related to the Event

Several approaches, tools, and techniques can be used to uncover the causes of a problem using RCA. The flowchart is one of many useful tools that can be used to paint a picture of process(es) involved in the event. Preparation of the chart should begin as soon as the team starts to collect information about the event. A quick and easy way to get a complete flow of the process(es) related to the event is to perform brainstorming. As data input increases, the flowchart will begin to look like a skeleton chart of causes and effects. Each process related to the event should be identified and defined. The chart is modified as more relevant facts are uncovered, and until the team is satisfied with its thoroughness (1).

Step 4: Identify Proximate Causes

Proximate causes are superficial, obvious, or immediate causes pertaining to the event, usually found during early stages of RCA process (8). By asking why the problem occurred during brainstorming, ideas are generated about possible causes. When several proximate causes are identified, the RCA team can explore the most critical process in the event by determining its importance and relevance. The major contributors to the event, or causal factors, are those that, if eliminated, would have either prevented the event or reduced its severity (1).

It is critical that the RCA team not point fingers at an individual as a cause of the problem (event). In fact, RCA should banish anxiety about assigning of blame to those involved. The RCA should probe instead those obstacles that prevented the individual from performing optimally and appropriately in a task. In modern medicine, medical errors are considered symptoms of system-wide disease, and the disease (not its symptoms) must be treated (13). Therefore, RCA must be dedicated to investigating and improving systems-related problems. If the team believes that individual unacceptable behavior had, at least in part, caused the problem, it should refer relevant information to peer review or to another appropriate body in the hospital for further assessment (13).

Step 5: Design and Implement Any Necessary "Quick Fix" Interim Changes

Some potentially serious outcomes related to the problem can compromise patient care. Therefore, it is necessary that the organization respond promptly and appropriately to alleviate the problem and prevent a similar problem from recurring during the period of RCA process. These "quick fix" interim changes can be designed based on the proximate causes. Structure, the culture of the health care organization, and the pressures of potential serious outcomes related to the event may require this "quick fix." (14) The RCA team, however, should not rely on this quick fix to solve the problem in the long run. Instead, the team should continue working to determine the root cause and possible long-term solutions.

Step 6: Identify Root Causes

To identify the root cause, the team relies heavily on internal logic and reasoning skill. The events are usually the result of several combined contributors, but the most obviously visible factor may be given all the attention. However, if only one obvious factor is addressed, the RCA team will be unlikely to accomplish its real task (1). To reach conclusions, other presumptive and contributing causes need to be eliminated. *Presumptive causes* are those apparent at the beginning or during data collection that, after verification, have no data to support them as the real cause of the problem. *Contributing causes* are those that contribute to an event but, on their own, would not cause or prevent the occurrence. The *root cause* is the most basic reason for a problem and it requires corrective action.

Several rounds of drilling down into the problem and its causes can lead to the true root cause. Therefore, it is important not to stop the analysis too soon. A good facilitator on the RCA team plays an essential role in insisting on continuing the RCA until the root cause is reached. The Five Rules of Causation (15) is a tool developed to help create minimum standards for searching out root causes in the RCA process. It helps minimizing biases occurring during the RCA process (Table 5.2).

Step 7: Identify Potential Risk-reduction Strategies

After identifying the root causes of the event, attempts are made to provide potential fixes or risk reduction strategies. This is a critical process that defines the usefulness of the RCA process. Without generation of recommendations following identification of the root causes, the RCA is wasted (1). Tools that can be utilized by the team to search for potential fixes may include Six Thinking Hats, a team process that forces members to think based on roles that differ from their usual ones. Breaking root causes down into smaller recognizable causes

---

TABLE 5.2   FIVE RULES OF CAUSATION

---

1. Rule 1: Causal statements must clearly show the "cause-and-effect" relationship. This is the simplest of the rules. When describing why an event has occurred, you should show the link between your root cause and the bad outcome, and each link should be clear to the RCA team and others. Focus on showing the link from your root cause to the undesirable patient outcome you are investigating. Even a statement like "resident was fatigued" is deficient without your description of how and why this led to a slip or mistake. The bottom line: The reader needs to understand your logic in linking your causes to the outcome.

2. Rule 2: Negative descriptors (e.g., poorly, inadequate) are not used in causal statement. As humans, we try to make each job we have as easy as possible. Unfortunately, this human tendency works its way into the documentation process. We may shorten our findings by saying "maintenance manual was poorly written" when we really have a much more detailed explanation in our mind. To force clear cause-and-effect descriptions (and avoid inflammatory statements), we recommend against the use of any negative descriptor that is merely the placeholder for a more accurate, clear description. Even words like "carelessness" and "complacency" are bad choices because they are broad, negative judgments that do little to describe the actual conditions or behaviors that led to the mishap.

3. Rule 3: Each human error must have a preceding cause. Most of our mishaps involve at least one human error. Unfortunately, the discovery that a human has erred does little to aid the prevention process. You must investigate to determine WHY the human error occurred. It can be a system-induced error (e.g., step not included in medical procedure) or an at-risk behavior (doing task by memory, instead of using a checklist). For every human error in your causal chain, you must have a corresponding cause. It is the cause of the error, not the error itself, which leads us to productive prevention strategies.

4. Rule 4: Each procedural deviation must have a preceding cause. Procedural violations are like errors in that they are not directly manageable. Instead, it is the cause of the procedural violation that we can manage. If a clinician is violating a procedure because it is the local norm, we will have to address the incentives that created the norm. If a technician is missing steps in a procedure because he is not aware of the formal checklist, work on education.

5. Rule 5: Failure to act is only causal when there was a preexisting duty to act. We can all find ways in which our investigated mishap would not have occurred, but this is not the purpose of causal investigation. Instead, we need to find out why this mishap occurred in our system as it is designed today. A doctor's failure to prescribe a medication can only be causal if he was required to prescribe the medication in the first place. The duty to perform may arise from standards and guidelines for practice; or other duties to provide patient care.

Source: U.S. Department of Veterans Affairs. Using the five rules of causation. Accessed May 31, 2010, at: http://www4.va.gov/ncps/cogaids/Triage/index.html#page=page-9

---

with known solutions will help generate potential fixes for complex root causes.

Step 8: Formulate and Evaluate Proposed Improvement Actions

Identify Measures of Success
Once the RCA team devises risk reduction strategies or potential fixes, a pilot test of the solutions on a small scale is highly recommended.[16,17] By performing the pilot test, the team is able to monitor the results for unintended consequences and refine the improvement actions accordingly. If good results are achieved, the team can be confident about the fixes before committing significant organizational resources. In addition, identifying measures of success will help facilitate leadership buy-in for the improvement actions (17).

To formulate and evaluate proposed improvement actions, a scientific method such as the plan-do-study-act (PDSA) cycle can be used (17). The PDSA cycle helps the team to decide what needs to be changed or improved, determine how the change can be accomplished, test the change, assess the effects of the change, implement successful improvements, or rehypothesize and conduct another experiment for change. In this step, the team should identify measures of success that are related to improvement actions as well (17).

Step 9: Develop and Implement an Improvement Action Plan
Effective action plans do not rely on memory or vigilance, but rather aim at redesigning processes, software, and workspaces (2). Development and implementation of an improvement action plan

should reach a consensus among relevant personnel, departments, hospitals, and stakeholders at all levels. In this way, the appropriate level of the health care system is remediated (16).

Step 10: Evaluate and Fine Tune Improvement Efforts

To best evaluate and fine tune these efforts requires the development of high-quality measures of effectiveness and performance for the improvement actions (2). Measures must be related to improvement and validate the success of the improvement actions. They must be clear, quantifiable, and include numerators, denominators, and thresholds. They must show the impact of actions on the root causes, and if relevant, demonstrate change over time (17).

Evaluating the results of the improvement action plan requires data collection and a comparison of data against internal references, external standards, practice guidelines, targets, or thresholds. If data indicate that goals have been achieved, the team will focus on communicating, standardizing, and rolling out successful improvement initiatives (17).

Step 11: Communicate the Results

To build trust, motivate participation, and encourage performance of personnel toward improvement, it is important to communicate the results of the RCA process to everyone involved, including management (18). This may be done using a root cause summary table listing the causal factors, root cause identification, and recommendations. Communicating the conclusions and recommendations with organization leadership buy-in is critical to the success of improvement initiatives (17). It may, however, take days or months before the change is complete.

Limitations and Difficulties

The usefulness of RCA lies relies on its quality. The quality of RCA is a reflection of input data, and the conversations, thoughts, and relationships of members of the RCA team. It is true that people share what they know only when an atmosphere of openness, trust, and honesty is present (18). Inherent biases—we all are human—will arise during the analysis process. People tend to select and interpret data to support their prior opinions and to please a powerful audience. To avoid such deviations, adequate resources and assurances of psychological safety should be sufficiently provided to the RCA team, so that they can pursue facts and dig out the causes of problems (18).

Root cause analysis is time-consuming and labor-intensive. Therefore, organizations should approach RCA systematically rather than independently, which can be done by drawing lessons across investigations. Organization should focus on preventing issues that could arise while conducting RCAs as well. These include a lack of time, resources, feedback, and fear of retribution experienced by RCA team members (19).

HEALTHCARE FAILURE MODE AND EFFECT ANALYSIS

Despite the great potential for RCA to mitigate health care hazards, it has methodological limitations. By itself, RCA is an uncontrolled case study with hindsight bias (20). The depth of the root causes identified can be influenced by current concerns of the day. The frequency and manifestation of certain problems are unpredictable, making it is difficult in these cases to discern if the root causes established by the RCA are the actual causes of the problem. To proactively identify risks to patient safety and reduce medical/health care errors, a new approach, *health care failure mode and effect analysis* (HFMEA), was developed by the U.S. Veterans Administration National Center for Patient Safety (NCPS) (21).

Healthcare FMEA focuses on the system and uses a multidisciplinary team to evaluate processes within it. Failure mode and effect analysis aims to correct system errors before they lead to adverse events. *Failure modes* are different ways in which a certain process fails to achieve its intended purpose. During the HFMEA process, the team identifies the topic and its potential failure modes, determines their severity and probability, prioritizes those failure modes, develops appropriate actions, and defines outcome measures (21). The technique has been promoted for use in U.S. hospitals and is recognized in a White Paper published by the American Society for Healthcare Risk Management (ASHRM) (22).

The five steps to performing HFMEA are outlined in Table 5.3 and explained in the following text.

Step 1: Define the Topic

This is one of the most important steps in performing HFMEA. The topic selected should be in a high-risk or high-vulnerability area. Because the process requires significant time and effort to complete, only one or two topics may be performed annually within

TABLE 5.3   FIVE STEPS OF
RADIOLOGY FAILURE MODE AND
EFFECT ANALYSIS (RFMEA)

1. Define the topic.
2. Assemble the team.
3. Graphically describe the process.
4. Conduct a hazard analysis.
5. Define actions and outcome measures.

a division or department. The HFMEA should have a clear definition for analysis, and the potential sources of topics may include (but are not limited to) sentinel events and incident reports (21).

Step 2: Assemble the Team

Similar to performing an RCA, the HFMEA team should include all levels of personnel related to the topic, in order to gain insight into how the process is actually conducted. It should also include leaders and quality improvement experts to help initiate the project and provide support when the team's final recommendation is made. In addition, having a person without knowledge of the process may be useful, to ensure that various viewpoints are presented within the team as well. Having someone who is unfamiliar with the topic of interest can help encourage a critical review of practices and standards, and the detection of potential weaknesses that others may miss (21).

Step 3: Graphically Describe the Process

The HFMEA team starts by identifying processes and subprocesses within the defined topic. Then, these processes and subprocesses are numbered consecutively. All processes and subprocesses should be identified before proceeding to the next step (21). If the team believes that the topic is too large or complicated, it should identify a portion of it on which to focus and analyze. In this way, the team will have an adequate amount of time to spend on the important portion of the topic; will be able to limit attempts to overanalyze a large, complex topic; and will be able to reach a timely conclusion to the analysis (21).

Step 4: Conduct a Hazard Analysis

After identifying all processes and subprocesses, the team lists all possible potential failure modes for each and numbers them consecutively. Failure

modes can be ascertained from various sources, such as brainstorming or by asking simple questions: "Why did it happen?" "What might happen?" "What could happen to the patient?" (23) Cause-and-effect diagramming, Joint Commission Sentinel Event Alerts, Institute for Safe Medication Practices (ISMP) information, and Food and Drug Administration databases also can be used to obtain failure modes (21).

The next step involves determining the severity and probability of each failure mode (21). The team assigns a severity score (What would be the impact if this happened to a patient?) and probability score (How likely is this to happen?) for each failure mode. A hazard scoring matrix is then utilized to determine whether the specific failure mode warrants further action. Table 5.4 represents a guide to performing hazard scoring for each failure mode. Areas that the team might want to mitigate are those with high criticality (a single-point weakness which, if it fails, would result in adverse event), high detectability (a hazard that is very obvious and which, if it fails, could result in adverse event), or a lack of effective control measures.

Step 5: Actions and Outcome Measures

At this step, solutions to overcome failure modes are suggested by the team. After selecting specific failure modes to tackle, the team suggests solution

TABLE 5.4   GUIDE TO PERFORMING
HAZARD SCORING FOR ALL FAILURE
MODES

Severity
  1 = No harm to patient or process
  2 = Mildly harmful to patient or process
  3 = Moderately harmful to patient or process
  4 = Severely harmful to patient or process
Probability
  1 = Rare (1 time/month)
  2 = Uncommon (1 time/week)
  3 = Occasional (less than 2 times/day but more than 1 time/week)
  4 = Frequent (more than 2 times/day)
Criticality
  Ask the question "Is there redundancy?"
Detectability
  Ask the question "Is this totally obvious?"

and develops actions for each. Outcome measures should be identified. Then, the team appoints a person to be responsible for completing or ensuring the completion of each action (21). In this step, it is critical to success that management/administration concurs with each recommendation or suggestion for action made by the HFMEA team.

In the radiology department, HFMEA can be a useful approach for a number of common sources of error, including patient identification, preparation, and consent; administration of pharmaceuticals; radiation exposure; monitoring during an examination; and maintenance of a safe working environment (24, 25). Published examples of radiology FMEA (RFMEA) topics include screening of diabetic patients before interventional procedures (24), ordering of radiologic studies, and misadministration of intravenous contrast medium in outpatient radiology (26). In these articles, the authors have demonstrated a successful approach to reducing errors in their departments. The success of RFMEA relies greatly on strong clinical and administrative support (24).

Although HFMEA seems to be very useful in proactively identifying and preventing the problems we face in many health care processes, it is very time-consuming and costly. Therefore, it is appropriate to select only one or two priority HFMEA topics per year. Since the system itself can be large and complicated, it is difficult to completely analyze and derive meaningful solutions for failure modes. The scope of HFMEA can be initially determined by departmental leaders on the basis of the resources available to support such projects and later adjusted by team members (24). The results of HFMEA may be difficult to measure if outcome measures are not well defined. A culture of reporting errors within an institution can potentially hinder the measurement of outcome recommendations provided by this analysis (27).

REFERENCES

1. Rooney JJ, Vanden Heuvel LN. Root cause analysis for beginners. *Quality Progr.* 2004:45–53.
2. Bagian JP, Gosbee J, Lee CZ, Williams L, McKnight SD, Mannos DM. The Veterans Affairs root cause analysis system in action. *Jt Comm J Qual Improv.* 2002;28:531–45.
3. Spath P. *Error reduction in health care: A systems approach to improving patient safety.* Washington: AHA Press, 1999.
4. Stalhandske E, Bagian JP, Gosbee J. Department of Veterans Affairs patient safety program. *Am J Infect Control.* 2002;30:296–302.
5. Joint Commission. Sentinel event. Accessed May 31, 2010, at: http://www.jointcommission.org/sentinelevents/
6. Rosenthal J, Takach M. 2007 guide to state adverse event reporting systems. State Health Policy Survey Report 2007.
7. Joint Commission. Root cause analysis learning from your near misses. *Jt Comm Perspect Patient Saf.* 2001;1.
8. Joint Commission. Root cause analysis tools to help with root cause analysis. *Jt Comm Perspect Patient Saf.* 2002;2.
9. Joint Commission. Root cause analysis matrix. Accessed May 31, 2010, at: http://www.jointcommission.org/NR/rdonlyres/3CB064AC-2CEB-4CBF-85B8-CFC9E7837323/0/se_root_cause_analysis_matrix.pdf
10. Joint Commission. Root cause analysis pulling together the right team for an effective root cause analysis. *Jt Comm Perspect Patient Saf.* 2001;1.
11. Joint Commission. Integrating physicians into the root cause analysis process. *Jt Comm Perspect Patient Saf.* 2002;22.
12. Joint Commission. Risk management including caregivers involved in a sentinel event in the root cause analysis process: pros and cons. *Jt Comm Perspect Patient Saf.* 2003;3.
13. Joint Commission. Root cause analysis questions and answers. *Jt Comm Perspect Patient Saf.* 2001;1.
14. Edmondson AC. Learning from failure in health care: Frequent opportunities, pervasive barriers. *Qual Saf Health Care.* 2004;13(Suppl 2):ii, 3–9.
15. U.S. Department of Veterans Affairs. Using the five rules of causation. Accessed May 31, 2010, at: http://www4.va.gov/ncps/cogaids/Triage/index.html#page=page-9
16. Wu AW, Lipshutz AK, Pronovost PJ. Effectiveness and efficiency of root cause analysis in medicine. *JAMA.* 2008;299:685–7.
17. Joint Commission. Root cause analysis practical tips for implementing the results of an RCA. *Jt Comm Perspect Patient Saf.* 2003;3.
18. Carroll JS, Rudolph JW, Hatakenaka S. Lessons learned from non-medical industries: Root cause analysis as culture change at a chemical plant. *Qual Saf Health Care.* 2002;11:266–9.
19. Braithwaite J, Westbrook MT, Mallock NA, Travaglia JF, Iedema RA. Experiences of health professionals who conducted root cause analyses after undergoing a safety improvement programme. *Qual Saf Health Care.* 2006;15:393–9.
20. Reason JT. *Human error.* New York: Cambridge University Press, 1990.
21. DeRosier J, Stalhandske E, Bagian JP, Nudell T. Using health care Failure Mode and Effect Analysis: The VA National Center for Patient Safety's prospective risk analysis system. *Jt Comm J Qual Improv.* 2002;28:209, 248–267.

22. Gilchrist M, Franklin BD, Patel JP. An outpatient parenteral antibiotic therapy (OPAT) map to identify risks associated with an OPAT service. *J Antimicrob Chemother.* 2008;62:177–83.

23. Kimchi-Woods J, Schultz JP. Using HFMEA to assess potential for patient harm from tubing misconnections. *Jt Comm J Qual Patient Saf.* 2006;32:373–81.

24. Abujudeh HH, Kaewlai R. Radiology failure mode and effect analysis: What is it? *Radiology.* 2009;252:544–50.

25. Thornton E, Brook OR, Mendiratta-Lala M, Hallett DT, Kruskal JB. Application of failure mode and effect analysis in a radiology department. *Radiographics.* 2010 Oct 27. [Epub ahead of print]

26. Ouellette-Piazzo K, Asfaw B, Cowen J. CT health-care failure mode effect analysis (HFMEA): The misadministration of IV contrast in outpatients. *Radiol Manage.* 2007;29:36–44;quiz 45–37.

27. Esmail R, Cummings C, Dersch D, et al. Using Healthcare Failure Mode and Effect Analysis tool to review the process of ordering and administrating potassium chloride and potassium phosphate. *Healthc Q.* 2005;8(Spec No.):73–80.

6

Patient Perspectives on Service and Quality in Clinical Imaging

FRANK J. LEXA

Diagnostic imaging represents one of the great triumphs of medicine in the last 100 years. Many of the most important modern medical inventions are now in the armamentarium of radiology, from x-rays through computed tomography (CT), magnetic resonance (MR) imagery, ultrasound, and positron emission tomography (PET). These technologies, their applications, and the interpretation of their diagnostic information has been minutely examined from the perspective of the radiologist. This chapter focuses on the patient—how she or he experiences an imaging procedure, and how that molds his or her perspectives on the quality of service provided.

THE CONSUMER REVOLUTION

We begin by providing a broader perspective on the consumer revolution occurring in the United States and other nations as this chapter goes to press in late 2011. Within a single generation, a profound change has occurred in how U.S. citizens view their relationship with medical practitioners. Previously, this relationship was likely to be fairly patriarchal (or matriarchal), with the patient often taking a passive role in the medical system. Doctors and hospitals had reputations that often determined patient choice, but hard data was difficult or impossible for patients to find, and the system was often opaque to the lay public. Now, patients can (and do) run their doctor's names through search engines that provide both professional and amateur evaluations and ratings. These latter ratings are not only analogous to but are sometimes run by the same corporations that provide user ratings for everything from restaurants to plumbers and dog walkers. In the course of this revolution, patients have come to place a much higher emphasis on the service aspects of their experiences in the medical systems. They expect more courtesy and more respect for their feelings and needs than those of a generation ago. Patients are also far less tolerant of waiting for appointments and/or of being delayed during their visits to medical facilities. Two generations ago, long waits in a physician's reception area to see a doctor were so common that they had become a cliché, as well as standard comedic fare on television and other media. Today, long wait times are an almost sure way to get a failing grade from a busy patient. Time pressures on patients have increased, and their expectations have changed. In some regions of the United States and in other countries where the government takes direct responsibility for medical services, long waiting times may also have strong negative political repercussions.

The consumer revolution includes both technical and nontechnical components. The former is driven by the increasing availability of information from sophisticated web sites and a generation that is both savvy and comfortable with using web tools. These are the patients who call your facility and ask how many Tesla your MR system generates, if you are going to use a specific gadolinium-based contrast agent, and/or if you have an MOC neuroradiologist who will read their study. On the nontechnical side, patients are focusing on elements of the process that are more readily apparent to consumers—availability of appointments, timeliness, friendliness, waiting room amenities, etc. Although high technology consumer gadgetry is the more interesting and innovative component of the consumer revolution, we will focus on the latter in this chapter—the nontechnical aspects of patient care—since they are more universal and have significant impact on patient perceptions of quality of care.

The first step toward superior service is for medical practitioners to understand the significant perceptual gap that exists between our customers and us (1). As this chapter is being written, there are approximately 30,000 practicing radiologists in the United States, and the U.S. population has recently surpassed 300 million. That gives a ratio of about 10,000 customers per radiologist. Given the disparity in size and the gap in technical expertise, it is no surprise that there are significant differences in how the two groups view an imaging encounter.

What follows is based upon work that began in the middle of the first decade of the 21st century and was first published by Lexa in 2006 (1). This is an ongoing project, involving surveys and interviews with imaging patients in major U.S. metropolitan areas. Since that first report, this effort has continued to grow and expand in size and scope.

WHAT PATIENTS WANT

One of the stronger messages of this chapter is that you should be surveying your patients yourself. Although many national organizations may collect information about you, there is no substitute for knowing your patients and understanding their perspectives. That said, however, certain issues are sure to arise almost universally within large metropolitan practices, so it's possible for you to learn from the experiences of those practices that are comparable to your own. Remember, however, that a large nation like the United States has remarkable diversity by region, setting, culture, demographics, and a host of other factors. This diversity will contribute to variances from nationally averaged data in your practice setting, or may even uncover elements that are unique to your practice or locale. By surveying your patients yourself, you can discover those factors and then track how well you are doing.

A FRAMEWORK FOR ANALYSIS

There are many ways to obtain and analyze information about how patients evaluate their experience with you. A good framework that I have used for understanding the patient's perspective of an imaging encounter is to break the process down into temporal steps and then analyze what matters to the patient at each of those time points. Here is a sample framework that covers common issues that patients identify as important at each step:

Prearrival

Patients begin their assessment of your facility before they ever meet you. This includes brochures, word of mouth, web presence, and pretty much any other public branding or marketing that you do, often including a drive-by look at your facility. Many patients are already forming an assessment at this stage. This perception intensifies with their first contact: How easy are you to reach? How many rings does it take for someone to answer the phone? Does your elderly patient have to navigate past a voice robot to get to a human? Do you put people on hold or route them to voice mail? Is your website useful to them, or is it frustrating to use or even useless?

Next comes scheduling. If you cannot accommodate their work and family commitments and if you inconvenience them, then, not surprisingly, patients will see your staff as insensitive and/or inflexible. The person who answers your phone can either mitigate or amplify their frustration. A pleasant person who explains things well and is understanding can help greatly with how the patient perceives the experience. The same scheduling outcome can be perceived differently—for example: The patient may feel lucky to get an appointment at such an important and busy place, or the patient may feel that your rude and inflexible staff makes him wonder if it is worth coming there at all. It is worth reminding you at this point that most of your customers are not happy about having to come to your facility. They are worried and/or frightened by the prospect of the test and its outcome. Someone who is friendly and understanding on the phone will go a long way toward helping them to calm down, regardless of the scheduling issues per se. Obviously, not everyone can get their first choice in an appointment.

A tip from other successful service businesses (such as restaurants) is to make sure that you ask for their first, second, and third choices (and try to understand the preferences that are driving them), put these in the record, and then work to try to accommodate them. If this isn't possible up front, then make sure that the patient will be alerted if something better for them does open up.

Arrival

The perception of your service and quality is next affected by the patient's first physical contact. Is your location easy to find? Could your directions be understood by someone with a 10th-grade education or by the patient being evaluated for early Alzheimer's disease? Is it easy to park? Are you in a part of the country where people want a valet to park their car, or are you located where they would resent or mistrust that service? If they haven't seen your facility before, now they are looking at it carefully. Even if they haven't a clue about what things like digital mammography or FLAIR imaging means, they can and do look for cues that they can understand. If your facility is clean and well maintained, they will be more comfortable and more likely to be forgiving of minor service problems than if the facility is dirty, with a cracked window, burned-out light bulbs, and out-of-date magazines. The analogy that we hear repeatedly is that of the restaurant with dirty bathrooms. You may not have access to the kitchen, and you may not understand any of the elements of the art of great cooking even if you did look in the kitchen, but everyone can recognize a poorly maintained bathroom and most people start to get concerned about the rest of the facility when they see one.

First Connection

All of us want to be acknowledged by friendly, helpful personnel. This is particularly true when one is sick or worried about his health. When a patient arrives at your facility, he wants to be greeted in a caring, cheerful manner. Failure to do this, either because the front desk person is rude, overworked, or distracted by a phone call, or for any other reason, sends a strong negative message to your patients. Making people line up like they would at the Department of Motor Vehicles adds to their level of anxiety and alienation. One of the greatest worries patients have at this point is that they will be delayed, and then arrive late for whatever they have to do next. Reassurance at this point and helping them get started with whatever paperwork or preparation for the scan that needs to be done helps them feel that things are moving forward on time.

The Keystone

Most patients rank their experience with the physician or technologist as the most important step in the process. Unfortunately, outside of mammography and interventional suites, most radiologists remain unseen by patients during their diagnostic testing. That is a story for another chapter, but until this paradigm changes, the technologist will be the person with the most influence on how your service and quality are perceived by patients. For most of your customers, the chance to speak to a medical professional about their test and how they are cared for during the test are the most memorable parts of the entire experience. A positive interaction here can make up for cold, stale coffee and other minor missteps in their experience with you. On the other hand, a bad experience with the technologist usually can't be fixed easily, if at all.

The next question is more profound: What do they want from their time with your technologists or (occasionally) physicians? The first answer may surprise you: They want to be reassured. Many are worried or fearful about the safety of the test. This is layered on top of the anxiety they have over their health. Because many patients are trying hard to be brave, they may not share this with you. Yet, my patient surveys and focus group work consistently show that patients do harbor a great deal of anxiety and fear about the hazards of imaging. Some of this may be irrational, and patients are always relieved to hear that their dental work won't be pulled out or their childhood memories erased by the MRI. Some fears may be out of proportion, and a caring technologist or radiologist can explain that the radiation risks of a single CT scan are negligible or nonexistent and, in any case, are well worth the knowledge that they are not harboring a lethal aneurysm or malignant tumor. Sometimes, they may even know at some level that the fear is irrational, but they need the TLC anyway. The latter point is one of context and timing: If someone has an irrational fear of flying, what they need from you in the next seat on the plane is a friendly face and a kind word. Perhaps when you are back on the ground you can give them the statistics lecture and "reassure" them that their cab ride to the airport was orders of magnitude more dangerous than their flight. A technologist who can talk people through procedures and allay their fears is one of your practice's most important assets.

To provide great service, other important tasks at this point include creating a clear picture of the examination and setting clear expectations for the patient. More than one patient has told me that the referring physician's office told them the MRI would last a half an hour. When the technologist didn't explain the actual likely length, let alone the variability of the examination, the predictable result was that, by 40 minutes, the patient assumed that we had found a malignant brain tumor. Patients usually have lots of questions, and you have to remember that not all of them are always asked. Preparation is the key here: If the technologist can provide a clear picture of the noise, the need to hold still, and other details, then the patient will be calmer and less likely to be worried in the course of a standard examination. Again, an empathetic technologist can sense this and make the experience much better for your patients.

The Main Event

The imaging experience depends upon the modality employed and the specifics of the test. Nevertheless, there are common elements that patients react to during their tests. The first is having a private, safe place where they can get changed in a dignified fashion. The Health Insurance Portability and Accountability Act (HIPAA) rules have codified some elements of this, but if you don't see the issue here, then you probably haven't been a patient yourself yet, and you should try to hear their side. During the test, patients appreciate the knowledge that they can talk to the technologist if something doesn't feel right or if they are frightened. Responsiveness is everything at this point. Amenities also help, but again, a friendly technologist outweighs audiovisual systems, nicer robes, and the like. Some patients may be trying to be stoic, but asking them periodically to make sure that they are comfortable is the right thing to do.

Disembarking

For many patients, the end of the exam is a particularly important moment. Continuing with our airline analogy, they have landed safely. Their fears are allayed for now, and they can get out the door and get on with their lives. One of the consistent complaints that I hear from patients is about delays at this point. If they have to wait around while films are compared or disks are burned, then the analogy is that of arriving at an airport only to be told that there is no gate agent to let you off the plane. You can expect to get very low marks if you make people wait 20–30 minutes at this point. If you need to, offer them options, so that they feel that they have

some control over the situation rather than that they are at your mercy. Perhaps they can go get a cup of coffee, or return tomorrow to pick up a disk, or have it mailed. Giving them choices is much better than holding them captive.

A related issue works the other way. You may be finished with them, but they may not be finished with you. They may be looking to you for guidance: How do they get to their next appointment, when will their doctor get the results, should they move up their appointment with their doctor? Again, having a pleasant, helpful person who can smoothly guide them makes a large difference.

It is worth remembering and emphasizing that in most complex encounters, there is disproportionate impact at the beginning and the end. With the former, it is a "first impression" or "blink" effect. If they missed your exit on the expressway due to poor directions and were caught in a subsequent traffic jam, they are going to need a very good experience on site with you to make up for that. With the latter, just think about which strikeout you remember from a Little League game: the one buried in the middle of the third inning or the last one, when the game is lost and everyone goes home? Sometimes the player who gets the game-ending strikeout is remembered decades later by his former team mates and coaches as the kid who lost the game. In the physical imaging encounter, this is your penultimate chance to make a positive difference, so make the most of it.

Last Chance or Beginning of the Next Time

The end of the physical encounter on site is not quite your last chance in the patient's experience. When I began this work, I found that one area in which most imaging centers were deficient was in following up after a patient left. It always strikes me as a peculiarly passive way of treating people in what is supposed to be a service-oriented field. First off, you need to do some follow-up interviewing to find out how you are doing. It is beyond the scope of this chapter to discuss survey techniques, but asking how you are doing is the right first step in trying to take care of patients and respond to their concerns (2).

Another reason is to create a relationship with your patients that extends beyond the single encounter. As an example, many groups never let people know what other services they provide. More than once, I have been sitting in a radiology waiting room as part of my consulting work and overheard a patient talking with a friend or family member. While they are waiting for their CT scan, you can hear them wondering aloud if there is a good place nearby where they can get their next mammogram—this while the mammogram room is less than 20 feet away!

CONCLUSION

This chapter has provided an introduction into why and how patients usually view imaging services differently than you do as a professional. I have provided a framework for radiologists to start to think about the imaging experience from the patient perspective, and I've supplied examples from my survey and focus group work of the common concerns that determine how patients evaluate our services. Finally, I would

encourage your to embark on this work yourself. This is part and parcel of creating and building relationships with your patients, and that is what physicians and other professionals should be doing—not merely providing a business service, but having a physician–patient relationship, and this depends upon good communication and action on your part.

REFERENCES

1. Lexa, FJ. 300,000,000 customers: Patient perspectives on service and quality. *J Am Coll Radiol.* 2006;3:346–50.
2. Lexa FJ, JW Berlin. The architecture of smart surveys: Core issues in why and how to collect patient and referring physician satisfaction data. *J Am Coll Radiol.* 2009; 6(2):106–111.

7

Just Culture

A Shared Commitment

K. SCOTT GRIFFITH AND DAVID MARX

THE NEED FOR A FAIR AND JUST CULTURE

Creating a Learning System

Event reporting and investigation remains a central task in the management of patient safety risk. The Joint Commission requires investigation of "sentinel events." Every state board requires investigation of at least some level of event—if only to determine if an unsafe provider is present. The Agency for Healthcare Research and Quality (AHRQ) dedicated the majority of its initial patient safety research to improvement in event reporting and investigation systems. Simply put, the lessons we can learn through event reporting and investigation are an essential element of patient safety and risk management.

Central to event investigation is the need to uncover meaningful information to mitigate future risk. It is a common perception today that current organizational and regulatory safety cultures within health care do not support open and honest reporting or participation in event investigations. In the watershed *To Err Is Human* report, the Institute of Medicine (IOM) recommended that Congress "pass legislation to extend peer review protections to data related to patient safety and quality improvement that are collected and analyzed by health care organizations for internal use or shared with others solely for the purpose of improving safety and quality."

Whether it is the threat of punitive action within an organization, from a state board, or merely exposure to a lawsuit, there are ample reasons why a single provider who makes an error would not come forward or honestly report his or her participation in an event. What type of disciplinary policy an organization has in place (in the spectrum from "blame-free" to "highly punitive") will be key in determining an organization's ability to identify and mitigate risk. Health care practitioners often believe that nothing happens to the data they generate—so why bother reporting?

The "highly punitive" culture refers to organizations that may, as perceived by the workforce, take some form of punitive action against those individuals who admit to making a mistake. This is a culture that deters reporting of events and instead relies more on professional expectations of perfection as the principle driver of safety.

The "blame-free" culture has been promoted as an antidote to the highly punitive culture. The theory here is that, since health care professionals do not intend to make mistakes, there is little value in reprimanding or disciplining the erring professional. It is a culture intended to facilitate the reporting of events—giving the workforce assurances that disciplinary action will not be taken against those who report their errors. The blame-free philosophy promotes the "system," rather than the people as the cause of all undesirable outcomes. Unfortunately, the blame-free system is both theoretically flawed and of little practical value to health care.

A Balanced Accountability

At the heart of this controversy lies a fundamental *just culture* issue: What system of accountability best supports system (and patient) safety? In a just culture, neither a blame-free nor a punitive perspective is deemed optimal. The answer lies in the balance of accountability, in which both systems and individuals are held appropriately accountable (Figure 7.1).

The just culture is a higher level of development in our learning of how to be effective health care leaders; it's a major evolution in learning from our mistakes in the complicated work of health care. The United Kingdom National Patient Safety Agency calls it an "open and fair" culture (see www.npsa.nhs. uk). Whatever the word used to describe it, the just culture sits squarely in the space between a highly punitive and a blame-free culture. The just culture maintains the balance between open reporting and individual accountability to help facilitate a maximum level of safety. The just culture focuses on the system, yet does not lose sight of the physician, pharmacist, or nurse as components within the system. It is both good system design and good component reliability that produces good patient safety outcomes.

At the heart of just culture is a process for allocating responsibility for events—that is, determining what problem is caused by the system, and what problem is caused by the component. In today's health care environment, both requirements and accountability for system success are largely placed on the component (e.g., physician, nurse). Although this approach may seem expedient, the larger question of system performance can only be assessed through analysis of the whole. To move away from a very component-focused system, it is necessary to devise a system to determine where accountability for events will rest. The just culture answers the

question of when disciplinary action taken against individuals (whether they are front-line providers, leaders, executives, or regulators) will best serve system safety. Ultimately, the just culture leads us to better management of the critical elements within our control: designing safe systems and helping staff make safe behavioral choices.

System Design

We must design systems that anticipate human error, capture errors before they become critical, and permit recovery when the consequences of our errors do reach our patients. We must design systems that will facilitate people in making good decisions—decisions that best support them in getting the job done safely and correctly the first time.

Human Behavior

Although we must anticipate that humans will make mistakes, our management of behavioral choices will improve our chances of achieving the outcomes we desire. We must learn how to productively coach around reliable behaviors, and recognize when remedial and disciplinary actions will best serve system safety.

Everything we do in the just culture, and through developing an open learning culture, is directed at these two management tasks: better system design and helping staff make better behavioral choices.

A SET OF BELIEFS

To implement a just culture, an organization should begin with a core set of beliefs. These are simple

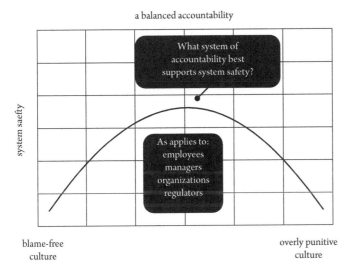

a balanced accountability

What system of accountability best supports system safety?

As applies to:
employees
managers
organizations
regulators

system saefty

blame-free culture

overly punitive culture

FIGURE 7.1 Balanced accountability chart.

truths about the predictable fallibility of humans within social systems and the management of risk. What follows are six beliefs that are essential to the success of the just culture journey.

To Err Is Human

We have all heard this phrase. In critical, high-risk jobs, however, we often expect that humans will be immune from human error. We expect that professionals, with the proper training and tools, should be perfect. After all, these tasks are so critical that we cannot afford for them to be foiled by human error. Under these critical circumstances, we demand that humans will simply be perfect.

It is this notion of perfect performance that we must abandon for a more realistic view that humans will make mistakes. It has been said that human error is the downside of having a brain. Clearly, this is the case. To be effective leaders, we must look beyond the human error to the systems in which people function, and to their behavioral choices within those systems.

To Drift Is Human

To many, this phrase is likely not as familiar, but it is a phrase that applies to all of us. Unlike human error, which is unintentional by definition, drifting refers to intentional behaviors that unknowingly create risk. In every human endeavor, we will drift away from what we have been taught. There are many reasons for drifting; the two most prevalent are our desire to accomplish more (causing us to drop perceptibly less important tasks), and our fading perceptions of risk as we become increasingly comfortable and competent with the task at hand.

Consider driving an automobile. Remember being told that our hands were to be at the 10 and 2 o'clock positions so that we were alert and in control of our car? Where are your hands today? One hand lying on the window, one at 6 o'clock on the wheel? Perhaps one hand is on a cup of coffee or holding a cell phone?

We must believe that to drift is human. We must believe that even the most dedicated and professional people will drift—even when working with the most well-designed system or procedure. It is our tendency as humans to drift, and it is our job as leaders to predict, identify, and minimize the chances of drift.

Risk Is Everywhere

Health care is a complex system that is risk-prone by definition. Although this concept might go without saying, it is important to reinforce its importance. Risk, technically speaking, is the product of the likelihood of occurrence and the severity of outcome. Something that is perceived as high risk has a combination of likelihood and severity that is perceived as being toward the higher end of the risk spectrum. Helicopter skiing and mountain climbing are generally considered high risk; there is a high likelihood that things can go awry and, when they do, the outcomes are generally severe. We don't usually perceive poker and bridge, on the other hand, to be high-risk endeavors. It's important to recognize that not all risks are bad; it's about identifying the risks we take that do not provide any benefit or utility, and then working to manage those risks.

In the just culture context, it is important always to be looking for the risk around us. A just culture is an environment in which people can raise their hands not only when they have made a mistake, but when they simply see a risk that should be remedied.

We Must Manage in Support of Our Values

Unfortunately, we will see behaviors among people that are inconsistent with organizational values. In a just culture, it is our job to proactively seek out and manage those behaviors that are inconsistent with these values. When assessing human behavior, ask whether the behavior is consistent or inconsistent with the values of your organization. In this model, the procedures we create are subordinate to the values we hold. Why is this? It is because, as fallible system designers and procedure authors, we will sometimes create rules that will not match the circumstances at hand. What we know through experience within the justice system is that we humans will ultimately judge each other based not upon compliance, per se, but on whether we believed the individual did the right thing under the circumstance at hand.

In the hospital setting, safety is but one value. Privacy, dignity, compassion, fiscal responsibility, and even basic access to care will rightfully compete with safety. In a just culture, we assess how individuals, whether staff, managers, contractors, or executives, are making decisions in alignment with the shared values of the organization.

We Are All Accountable

Accountability is a fundamental component of a just culture. The question is really how we should respond when someone has acted inconsistently with our shared institutional values. Accountability in this context is not about who pays for the harm to a patient (the remedy); rather, it is about the accountability of the human system components within the larger objectives of the system. What can be expected of people, and what are they accountable for as a critical component of the health care system?

Progress Can Be Measured

Within a just culture, the inputs (i.e., system design and human behavior) are managed to improve the outputs (organizational performance). Measuring how well the organization responds to events and behaviors leads to predictable rates of errors and precursor events. This approach to managing risk through the just culture foundation will demonstrate improved system performance.

THE THREE BEHAVIORS IMPORTANT TO RISK MANAGEMENT

In a just culture, three behaviors can be managed (human error, at-risk behavior, and reckless conduct), and each has its own safety-supportive management response.

Human Error

So, what is human error? It is, simply put, doing something other than what was intended. Consider a world-class, professional golfer such as Phil Mickelson at the golf course. We are watching the tournament on our television. Phil is 150 yards from the 18th and final hole, down by one stroke, and he needs to put it into the hole to tie the match. He hits the ball, and it comes to a rest just 6 inches from the hole.

The crowd goes wild. Now, given that Phil Michelson needed to sink the shot into the hole, has he made a mistake? Would the crowd be jumping up and down in frustration because he has made a mistake? No! Even though the shot did not achieve its intended outcome, we would not call it a mistake. Rather, given the expected reliability of hitting the hole from 150 yards away, we would say that he did a great job.

Now, if he had made the shot, tied the round, but then incorrectly signed his scorecard (resulting in a one-stroke penalty), we would then say that he had made a human error. Our belief that Phil Mickelson did other than he should have done leads us to apply the label of human error.

Consider the human reliability curve shown in Figure 7.2. The curve is a conceptual model for managing human error. First, the curve shows a

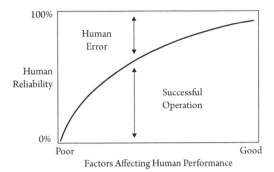

FIGURE 7.2 Factors affecting human performance chart.

relationship between system design and the rate of human error. As the factors affecting human performance improve, our reliability (probability of a successful outcome) improves. As the factors affecting human performance degrade, our reliability decreases. It is important to recognize that no task will ever have 100% reliability.

In working within a just culture, part of our job is to consider job performance reliability. It may be that people generally do a particular task at 99.9% reliability. The same group of people may perform other tasks at only 95% reliability. Only organizations can decide what reliability is appropriate for particular tasks.

Consider the simple task of waking up and getting to work on time. For this task, most of us are likely to be in the 95%–99% reliability range. Factors in our system that impact our reliability include our choice to use an alarm, the time we get to sleep the night before, the activities we plan to do before we get to work, or the reliability of our transportation choice, to name only a few. If you live a considerable distance from work, travel routes with highly variable traffic loads, and leave yourself only a small margin for deviation, you may have a less-than-desired reliability. However, if you have an important meeting the following morning, you may wisely decide that the risks of being late are great—thus providing the impetus to use a second alarm and leave even earlier than usual.

Increasingly, we are learning more about how humans perform within the work place. We know that either too little work stress or too much stress will cause performance to degrade. On the too-little stress side, we have a tendency to be mentally off task, allowing our minds to be cluttered with non-task thoughts and prone to making errors. On the high-stress side, if we have too much activity for our minds to organize and remember, our risk of human error again increases. Factors such as information, equipment characteristics, unique job and task considerations, qualification and skills, individual performance factors such as fatigue or life changes, environmental conditions (both physical and organizational), communication, and supervision all shape the natural error rate for the task performed. Any of these factors can lead to human error.

Looking back at our human reliability curve, what then is our task within a just culture? From a safety perspective, it is to provide people with the best opportunity to get the job done safely. And, from an economic perspective, it is providing people the best opportunity to get the job done right the first time.

We can never design an error-free system. If a task is very safety sensitive, great effort may be expended to control the risk of undesirable outcomes. Perhaps two people will perform the task, each checking the other. Or, some part of the task may be automated (e.g., allowing a computer to check certain math calculations). Conversely, if the task is rarely performed and does not have a critical safety impact, we may be willing to accept a lower level of proficiency because the cost of additional training or system changes far outweighs the cost of the error and its accompanying rework.

At-risk Behavior

At-risk behaviors are behavioral choices that increase the risk of error, but of which people are not aware of the increased risk. These are not intentional risk-taking behaviors, but the subtle drifting away that we see in every human endeavor. Of the three behaviors discussed here, at-risk behaviors are the most difficult to manage.

Most people make decisions in life based upon the outcome they expect or desire from their conduct. Consider your decision to speed. (If you do not speed, then consider those around you who do.) How do you react when you see a speed limit sign on the side of the road? Do you slow down? Does mere recognition that you are speeding cause you to reduce your speed? The answer is generally no! Yet, when most of us see a police car on the side of the road ahead, we do slow down. The police car represents an immediate, potential undesired outcome—that of a fine for violating the speed limit. As humans, the outcomes we seek drive our conduct even more than do rules.

When facing two possible choices of conduct (e.g., to speed or not to speed), humans make decisions by weighing the incentives and/or consequences of each choice. The chart in Figure 7.3, with columns for desired and undesired behaviors, illustrates that process.

Under each of the behaviors is a list of incentives for choosing one behavior over another. Saving time is the general reason for speeding, while following the law and reducing the risk of an accident are the general reasons for obeying the speed limit. Each incentive to engage in a behavior can be ranked by the strength of its influence.

To rank the incentives, we can classify them as strong or weak based upon the criteria shown in Table 7.1. Strong incentives involve immediate and certain consequences, whereas weak incentives involve delayed or uncertain consequences, and/or just the rules themselves.

There is one strong incentive to speed—the immediate and certain savings of time. There are two weak incentives to follow the speed limit—the limit (rule) itself, and the uncertain and delayed risk of an accident or ticket (sanction). Given this balancing of incentives, you would expect to see speeding on the road (and, in fact, in most places you do). The police car parked on the side of the road, however, represents an immediate and relatively certain consequence of a ticket, adding a strong incentive to follow the speed limit—at least when the police car is in sight. In fact, the police car parked on the side of the road is such a powerful visual incentive that you may find yourself slowing down even when you're not speeding!

The value of the incentives chart, however, is not that it predicts the rate of specific behaviors, but that it provides a mapping of what factors should be addressed to reduce the occurrence of any

Desired Behavior	Undesired Behavior
Following the Speed Limit	Exceeding the Speed Limit
Follow Law (weak)	Save Time (strong)
Reduce Risk of Accident (weak)	

FIGURE 7.3 Desired versus undesired behavior chart.

TABLE 7.1 STRENGTH OF
INCENTIVES CHART

Strength of Incentives

Certain consequences are stronger than uncertain
consequences.

Immediate consequences are stronger than delayed
consequences.

Consequences are stronger than rules or other
preconditions.

particular behavior. The choices are either to eliminate incentives for the undesirable behavior, or
increase the incentives for the desirable behavior.

There are no absolutes in the evaluation of
at-risk behavior. What one person perceives as a
strong incentive to engage in a particular behavior,
another person may perceive as weak. What remains
constant, however, is that humans will drift away
from rules or policies as they gain comfort with the
tasks they are performing.

Additionally, groups as a whole will exhibit
similar at-risk behaviors that will become opportunities for management. As one person has apparent
success with an at-risk behavior, he or she is likely to
influence other people, until the behavior becomes
the group norm.

Reckless Behavior

Consider two examples of at-risk behavior on the
road: speeding, and driving with only one hand on
the steering wheel. In these cases, the driver does not
recognize or appreciate the increased risk of harm.
We engage in these behaviors believing we are driving
safely (particularly because we drive like this so often
without mishap). In contrast, there are behaviors
on the road in which the driver does recognize and
appreciate the increased risk of harm that may result,
and knows that the risk is both significant and unjus-
tified. Driving while intoxicated, drag racing, and
intentionally driving on the wrong side of the road are
examples of reckless conduct. These behaviors carry
with them the recognition that the risk is great, and
that the risk is unjustifiable; these behaviors are reckless toward the safety of others on the road.

A person engaging in reckless conduct recognizes the risks associated with the chosen behavior.
Specifically, reckless conduct involves a conscious
disregard of a substantial and unjustifiable risk of
causing harm. It is the one behavior we can expect
each other to absolutely avoid. It is also a behavior

where disciplinary action is effective in correcting
the conduct.

The Use of Punishment in Response to Behaviors

It is important to identify where corrective action
has historically not worked well. What we have traditionally done is to discipline based upon the event's
outcome, or sometimes for just the mere presence
of human error. This strategy is not supportive of a
learning culture, and it is not productive of overall
efforts to reduce risk.

Making corrective action contingent upon an
error alone will not serve to effectively deter error, but
will serve instead to hinder the fostering of a learning
culture. In a just culture, we can and should expect
people to come forward when they make an error, so
that together we can learn how to best reduce the risk
of future error. Disciplining someone for a human
error will not serve system safety. In any organization, how likely are people to come forward when they
know they face corrective action for human error?

Should disciplinary action be used to deter
at-risk behavior? After all, doesn't the potential for
corrective action act as an incentive to choose the
proper behavior and a deterrent to the undesirable
behavior? There are two factors that weigh toward
not using corrective action in response to at-risk
behavior. The first is that organizations, somewhere
along the way, have most likely tacitly approved certain at-risk behaviors and overlooked others. Most
organizations have allowed at-risk behaviors to grow
because they have resulted in savings of time and/or
resources. Disciplinary action also tends to be coun-
terproductive because people are not likely going to
be honest about at-risk behaviors the next time an
error or event is investigated when discipline is the
potential response.

In many cases, at-risk behaviors will remain
hidden until a specific event reveals their presence.
In balancing learning and deterrence, the interests
of safety are best served by learning about the at-risk
behaviors, so that we are able to design incentives to
facilitate safer behaviors.

So, how does one manage reckless conduct? It is
here, in a just culture, that disciplinary action becomes
a viable and productive option. Humans cannot control when they will make an error—they can, however,
control their behavioral choices. In some cases, such
as with at-risk behavior, the individual does not perceive the risk. In other cases, an individual recognizes

TABLE 7.2   THREE BEHAVIOURS

The Three Manageable Behaviors		
Human Error	At-risk Behavior	Reckless Behavior
A product of our current system design and our behavioral choices	A choice where the risk is believed to be insignificant or justified	A conscious disregard for a substantial and unjustifiable risk
Manage through changes in: • Choices • Processes • Procedures • Training • Design • Environment	Manage through: • Removing incentives for the behavior • Creating incentives for better choices • Increasing situational awareness	Manage through: • Remedial action • Punitive action
Console	Coach	Punish

the risk, but chooses to act in conscious disregard of a substantial and unjustifiable risk. The reasons for engaging in reckless conduct are as varied as the conduct itself, but none of the reasons can excuse recklessness toward the safety or lives of fellow employees, clients or patients, or the general public. It is here that discipline serves as a deterrent against future choices to engage in the reckless conduct. The individual's conduct will determine the level of corrective action that should be taken, but by adding the threat of corrective action, an immediate and certain disincentive has been added to engaging in the reckless conduct. Generally, as we discover more about the precursors to human error, many of today's at-risk behaviors will move into the zone of reckless conduct as organizations identify a substantial and unjustifiable risk(s) associated with the behavior (see Table 7.2).

CONCLUSION

In summary, the just culture model assists organizations to place less focus on events, errors, and outcomes, and more focus on understanding risk, system design, and the management of behavioral choices. In this model, errors and outcomes are the outputs to be monitored; system design and the behavioral choices are the inputs to be managed. This philosophy leads to a set of attributes and behaviors for the organization. These include:

- Creating an environment of internal transparency around risk

- Striving to understand why human errors occur within the organization
- Striving to understand why at-risk behaviors occur within the organization
- Learning to see common threads—to prioritize risk and interventions
- Working to design systems that reduce the rate of human error and at-risk behavior, or mitigate their effects
- Learning when to console and when to coach
- Limiting the use of warnings and punitive actions to the narrow circumstances in which they benefit system safety
- Using data to build both unit and organizational models of risk
- Learning to measure patient safety risk, at both the unit and organizational level

Finally, a just culture foundation is built upon shared commitment. Executives, managers, and employees alike must mutually agree to demonstrate the values held dear by the organization. Working together, the just culture becomes the visible bond between individuals who believe in the principles of fairness, consistency, and continuous improvement. A just culture can transform an organization from reactive to proactive in the management of risk while simultaneously maximizing both system and human reliability.

8

Communication of Radiology Results

SARWAT HUSSAIN

The single biggest problem in communication is the illusion that it has taken place.

—GEORGE BERNARD SHAW

COMMUNICATION: THE PROBLEM

Excellence in communication is the single most important determinant of the perception of quality in any department of radiology, probably exceeding other factors related to technical skills, quality of images, or accuracy of interpretation. Proper communication must be assured at various levels and in different forms. Professional and courteous verbal interaction with referring physicians, patients' families, radiology staff, and faculty assures the delivery of high-level, clinically competent patient care, and it results in superior reputation. Effective communication between patients and caregivers has been shown to have positive effects on health management outcomes, medical costs, and patient satisfaction, while patient satisfaction studies have indicated that as many as 30% of unsatisfactory patient responses are related to problems with perceived abrasive or incomplete communication.

There are many aspects of communication in radiology. The mode, contents, and the speed of communicating is generally determined by the clinical need to respond to the level of urgency, regulatory compliance, quality mandates, departmental policy, or clinical etiquettes, and in response to clinicians' practice pattern. All of these issues can cover predictable scenarios but cannot fully substitute for the on-the-spot judgment and experience of a seasoned radiologist. To support high-quality clinical care, accurate imaging results must be conveyed to those responsible for treatment decisions in a timely manner.

In radiology, communication with referring providers most commonly occurs in an asynchronous manner via written report, e-mail or voice mail, or text messaging. More recently, electronic text messaging has become commonly used to send radiology reports, request call-backs, or even transmit images. Synchronous or real-time communication occurs via telephone conversations to convey critical results, or via face-to-face interactions during consultation and clinico-radiological conferences.

LEGAL ASPECTS OF COMMUNICATION IN RADIOLOGY

A radiology report is the final product of the department of radiology. The contents of the imaging report must reach the referring physician in a timely fashion, so that he or she may take the appropriate patient management actions.

In the past, the notification responsibility of the radiologists was considered completed with the sending out of the radiology report to the referring physician or service. Not as a matter of routine, but as a matter of courtesy or excellence of service, a radiologist may have telephoned the referring physician if, in the judgment of the radiologist, the patient required immediate medical attention. No serious consideration was given to the possibility of radiology results not reaching the referring physician and, consequently, not being acted upon. The same was true of other clinical disciplines, in which a written report was considered sufficient.

In today's climate of increasing litigation, and as the health care system strives for excellence in patient care, a prolonged turnaround time or a missing or overlooked radiology result that contains important diagnostic indicators may have potentially devastating clinical consequences. One study has shown that, in 1 week, a primary care physician (PCP) reviews about 800 clinical chemistry, 40 radiology, and 12 pathology reports, and must communicate with 200 physicians in more than 100 practices. This burden on the PCP further increases because, in 14% of practices, laboratory (6.1%) and radiology (3.8%) results are missing at the time of patient visits. Only through the joint efforts of radiologists and referring providers can the communication gap can be filled.

In more recent years, radiologists have been given an irrefutable legal responsibility to ensure that the benefits of an important radiological diagnosis accrue to the patient in a timely fashion. Communication of a diagnosis has become as important as the diagnosis itself. Courts have repeatedly stressed that the interpreting radiologist is liable if a radiology report is not conveyed within a timeframe that does not adversely affect patient care. For example, in a case decision, the Arkansas Supreme Court opined that "with the patient in the peril of his life, it does him little good if the examining doctor has discovered his condition, unless the physician takes measures and informs the patient or other responsible for his care, of that fact."

The liability for inadequate communication arises independently of any professional guidelines. The following three examples of reported case law confirm that a radiologist has a duty to directly communicate positive findings to the attending physician or to the physician who ordered the study. These cases represent the views of courts from three different jurisdictions, Washington State, Ohio, and New Jersey.

In the first case, a Washington State Appellate Court case from 1973, a radiologist reported x-ray findings of a young boy to the referring emergency room (ER) physician. After the patient left the ER, the ER physician mailed the radiology report to the boy's attending physician, who claimed never to have seen the report. The ER physician was held accountable. His defense's argument was that the ER physician had the right to assume that the attending physician had received and acted upon the report. The Court disagreed and stated that "because of the

medical significance of the x-ray report...a personal contact was required to ensure prompt action."

In a 1979 Ohio case, the Court of Appeals stated, "In certain situations, direct contact with the treating physician is necessary beyond communication through administrative channels." In 1987, the New Jersey Court of Appeals reiterated the language from the 1979 Ohio decision and added that, "communication of an unusual finding in an x-ray, so that it may be beneficially utilized, is as important as the finding itself."

In each of these cases, a physician was found responsible for patient harm caused by the delay in proper treatment because the radiology report with positive results was not directly communicated to the referring provider. Courts have consistently opined that the burden of delivery of critical results rests upon the interpreting radiologist.

According to a 10-year study of 184 lung cancer claims ending in 2005, the Physician Insurers Association of America (PIAA) reported the total indemnity payout for all the claims was $75,530,437, or an average of $410,491 per claim, with an average defense cost of $46,870 per claim. Of the 184 claims, 100 (56.2%) were the result of a communication error that ended in death or harm to the patients.

Typically, a medico-legal case takes 4 to 6 years to come to trial. This can place a severe financial and psychological burden on the defendant. Clearly, no practitioner wants to face the prospect of protracted litigation, and in the event of a lost case, increased insurance premiums and inclusion in the National Practitioner Data Bank. Similarly, no patient wants to lose an opportunity for life-saving treatment because of a lost or misplaced radiology report or because an incidental finding went untreated.

COMMUNICATION: AMERICAN COLLEGE OF RADIOLOGY STANDARDS

Many lawsuits against radiologists, some successful, led to the development of American College of Radiology (ACR) Standards and Guidelines. One purpose of the guidelines was to define the communication responsibility of radiologists and assure that a record is kept of reports containing important radiological findings.

As many as 25% of all ACR members are involved in at least one malpractice claim involving allegations of communication failure, and the average payout was $1.9 million. Studies have revealed that

70%–80% of legal actions against radiologists involve some form of communication breakdown, with 60% of these involving the failure to communicate urgent or unexpected findings directly to the referring physician. In one survey, physician's practice communication problems in diagnostic testing accounted for 50% of all errors.

In 1991, the ACR issued the first set of Standards on Communication in Radiology. These standards proposed the contents and structure of a radiology report. The standard also elaborated on those circumstances requiring direct communication with the referring provider prior to sending a formal written report. The standard stated that "direct communication of unusual, unexpected, or urgent findings to the referring physician" was required "in advance of the formal written report."

The standard alerted radiologists to three scenarios requiring direct communication: detection of conditions carrying the risk of acute morbidity or mortality and requiring immediate treatment or intervention; detection of a condition of nonacute morbidity or mortality, but sufficiently serious to require notification and evaluation or initiation of treatment; and any discrepancy between an emergency or preliminary report and a final written report. Additionally, the ACR clarified that the referring and treating physicians also shared responsibility for obtaining the results of imaging studies. In reality, this statement did not alter the radiologist's burden of responsibility for appropriate communication. It is important to note that using common sense and following the guidelines is sound risk management practice that can save lives and reduce the likelihood of expensive and stressful litigation. However, adherence to the guidelines does not guarantee a good outcome in the case of litigation, nor will ignoring the recommendations always invite a lawsuit.

Several revisions have been made to the ACR standards. One purpose of these revisions was to change the name from "ACR Standards" to "ACR Guidelines" on communication, which would clarify these mandates of communication without placing member radiologists at undue risk for litigation. The ACR mandates on communication have in fact been invoked by both plaintiff and defendant attorneys in cases where communication was an issue.

In 2003, after revisions by an ACR-appointed task force, the Communication Standards became the ACR Communication Guidelines. Added to the section on "direct communication" was the provision that, when a care provider cannot be reached, the patient himself should be informed of a diagnosis requiring immediate attention. With this revision, the mandate to directly communicate the "unusual" findings was eliminated.

In 2003, the ACR task force also examined how the Standards were being used by the public, ACR members, lawyers, hospitals, and insurance companies. As a result of this research, the standards were divided into two groups and renamed. Those standards that focused on recommended conduct in specific areas of radiological practice became "practice guidelines," and those standards that described technical parameters and contained equipment specifications became "technical standards." The communication standard fell into the first category and became the ACR Practice Guideline for Communication of Diagnostic Radiology.

The communication guideline emphasized not only the mode of direct communication of imaging results, by telephone or in person, but also stressed timely delivery to the treating physician. The guideline is a reflection of the current state of legislation regarding a radiologist's duty to communicate findings and how that communication should take place, depending upon the urgency of treatment and the unexpected nature of the findings. The new guidelines further illuminated those situations that may require nonroutine communication, or communication that goes beyond the usual administrative channels, for reporting on certain types of imaging results. These were derived from the ACR task force's review of legal counsel from many cases brought against radiologists. A summary of these cases illustrated three primary situations in which a communication failure resulted in serious harm to the patient and loss to the radiologist: urgent findings not communicated in a timely manner, inconsistent findings between preliminary and final reports not appropriately addressed, and unexpected or incidental findings not appropriately addressed.

COMMUNICATING MAMMOGRAPHY REPORTS

The communication of mammography reports is governed by the U.S. Food and Drug Administration (FDA) Mammography Quality Standard Act (MSQA) of 1994. The report of each examination must be conveyed to both the referring provider and the patient. Referring providers receive formal mammography reports through the usual channels. A written notification of a normal mammography report, in lay terms, must be provided to the patient within 30 days of mammography. This is generally done via first-class mail. In the case of Birads categories 4 or 5 ("Suspicious" or "Highly suggestive of malignancy"), results are treated as critical results and mandate immediate communication to the health care provider and that a record of that communication be kept on file. For referring providers, direct telephone communication is preferred over certified mail or e-mail. The patient will receive a summary of the abnormal report, in lay terms, via certified mail.

Patients who do not have a health care provider must receive a normal mammography report as above. The breast imaging facility accepting such patients must maintain a system to refer patients to a health care provider when a mammogram is abnormal.

CRITICAL RESULTS COMMUNICATION AND NATIONAL PATIENTS SAFETY GOALS

Critical Results

In 1997, the Board of Commissioners of the Joint Commission established a national database of sentinel events at accredited institutions. Analysis of these events led to the emergence of a pattern of prevalence of patient harm. A broadly based representative group worked with the Joint Commission to develop Patient Safety Goals, as well as a system of implementation and audit. In 2002, this effort culminated in the issuance of the first set of National Patient Safety Goals (NPSGs). The objective of the Joint Commission's NPSGs is to focus on specific improvements in patient safety. The Joint Commission recognized that systematic improvement in the design of health care delivery is pivotal to system-wide improvement in all aspects of patient safety.

Compliance with these goals became a requirement for maintaining accreditation. Based on continued analysis of sentinel events, the NPSGs are renewed yearly. Although many of the NPSGs deal with communication, NPSG 2 and its requirements define the mode and content of communication as a matter of Joint Commission regulatory compliance, subject to audit during the accreditation process. The NPSG 2 and its requirements are described here.

NPSG 2: Improve the Effectiveness of Critical Communication Among Caregivers

Requirement 2A. For verbal or telephone orders, or for telephonic reporting of critical test results, verify the complete order or test result by having the person receiving the order or test result read-back the complete order or test result.

Requirement 2B. Standardize a list of abbreviations, acronyms, and symbols that are to be used throughout the organization.

Requirement 2C. Measure, assess, and, if appropriate, take action to improve the timeliness of reporting, and the timeliness of receipt by the responsible licensed caregiver, of critical test results and values.

Requirements 2A and 2C are discussed further in the following sections.

Implementation

To implement NPSG 2—Improve the Effectiveness of Communication Among Caregivers—the salient requirements are (1) timely and direct communication with referring providers, (2) maintenance of a verifiable record of communication, and (3) timely escalation of fail-safe processes when referring providers are not immediately available.

Effective implementation of critical communication requires both a change in the work habits of radiologists and a commitment by hospital leadership and referring physicians. Clinical, administrative, and information technology (IT) resources must continuously work together until compliance is achieved and maintained. Developing and implementing a system for critical result communication can be onerous. In a 2008 report on critical results by the Imaging Performance Partnership on Critical Result Communication, only 42% of the 51 department surveyed had developed Joint Commission-compliant policies for critical communication, and only 31% (or 92 departments) had achieved 90% compliance with the critical result communication requirements.

Methods of Critical Communication, Automated or Manual

Currently, two methods are used to communicate critical results: the first is labor-intensive manual communication using a telephone and physically recording elements of communication within the radiology report; the second method uses commercially available or in-house developed automated computer systems that are expensive and difficult to implement due to poor acceptance by referring providers.

Developing a Critical Result Communication Policy

A first step toward compliance is to develop, in conjunction with and approved by hospital leadership, a departmental policy on critical result communication that incorporates the spirit and requirements of the NPSG 2. The policy document should contain clear definitions of terms, the delineation of a time line, and clarification of its objectives and expectations.

The appendices to the policy are populated with specific details. The contents of appendices may be developed in-house or adopted from the literature.

For instance, the Massachusetts Coalition for the Prevention of Medical Errors (MCPME) has suggested categories designated by urgency and timelines. These are emergent (Red alert), which indicates that communication must occur within 1 hour or less (in practice, such communication is immediate and interruptive); urgent (Orange alert), which indicates that communication can occur within 8 hours; and nonurgent (Yellow alert), which indicates that communication can wait up to 24–96 hours. Table 8.1 depicts the diagnoses under each category. The Yellow category is included in the list in order to assure that follow-up of potentially important incidental findings, such as thyroid, lung, or adrenal nodules, is not overlooked.

TABLE 8.1 CRITICAL RESULTS CALLING POLICY

Critical Values, Department of Radiology

Red Alert: Level I EMERGENT - Call Result Within 1 Hour	Orange Alert: Level II URGENT- Call Result Within 8 Hours	Yellow Alert: Level III Important Incidental Communicate Within 3 Days
Airway compromise, any cause	Suspected child abuse	Suspicious lung nodule
Brain herniation	Hydrocephalus Gr III (neonate) unsuspected	Adrenal nodule
New significant or tension pneumothorax	Shunt malposition, extraventricular	Thyroid nodule
Unexpected free air in the abdomen	Possible/probable active tuberculosis	Suspected malignancy (for example solid renal mass)
Leaking/ruptured/dissected aortic aneurysm		
Ectopic pregnancy		
Acute spinal cord compression		
Acute epi- or subdural hematoma		
New pulmonary embolism on CT pulmonary angiogram		
Significantly misplaced tubes or catheters		
Bowel obstruction (volvulus, etc.)		
Unstable fracture		
Acute vascular compromise, limb, organ		
Myocardial ischemia; large territory at risk		
Retained surgical foreign body		

Communication Process

1. ED 6–3511(U)/4–6481(M) responsible MD; IP/OP; page/text page ordering MD call xxx–xxxx "Critical Result."
2. Fail-safe: Division Chief; Department Chair; Chief Quality Officer (Klugman); Chief Medical Officer (Tosi).

It is noteworthy that there is neither a specific Joint Commission mandate nor any national consensus on the list of critical diagnoses or the timeline of communication. Populating the list of critical diagnoses and incidental findings is entirely a local decision. Examples of common diagnoses deemed critical are aortic dissection or rupture, pulmonary embolism, pneumothorax, unstable spine fractures, stroke, limb or gut ischemia, and pneumoperitoneum.

Definitions

In its latest revision, the Joint Commission no longer differentiates between critical results and critical tests. *Critical result* is the only term to be used and is defined as a "potentially life-threatening or significant unexpected diagnosis." Critical results must be communicated only when positive diagnoses are made; for example, pulmonary emboli on a computed tomography (CT) angiogram. As stated above, the Joint Commission allows accredited institutions to define their own lists of critical diagnoses. Differentiation is also made between the critical categories and "stat" designations for emergency department (ED) studies or requests from referring providers. Stat studies are generally read in real time, but unlike critical tests, they do not require keeping a verifiable record of result communication.

In many hospitals, the department of radiology or emergency radiology services is located adjacent to the main ED for easy access. Patient care teams from the ED frequently walk over to review studies with radiologists. Notwithstanding the informality of these visits, a verifiable record of critical communication must be kept in all cases.

Critical results communication may not be necessary when a patient with a known critical diagnosis is referred from an outside institution.

Having completed the critical result policy, implementation requires consensus among the radiology implementation team, referring providers, and administrative leadership, under the general directions of a hospital-wide quality improvement body.

Elements of Critical Result Communication

There are four elements of documentation in critical result communication. These are *name, time, date,* and *write-down read-back* (WDRB). Consistent use of these elements assures that a verifiable record of the interaction is available to demonstrate compliance, perform audits, and provide feedback to the individual radiologist on their performance. Recording both the first and last name of the result's recipient is recommended; however, stating the last name with identifying suffix (e.g., Dr. Smith of primary care or Nurse Jones of ICU night shift) is also acceptable. The use of first names only ("Nurse Susan") is not acceptable.

Write-down and read-back assures that the receiver has understood the results and that the results were accurately conveyed to the right person. The process of WDRB is as follows: The sender concisely states information to the receiver. The receiver then writes down the statement and reads it back or repeats what he or she has heard. The sender then provides an acknowledgment that the read-back was correct, or makes a correction. There is no consensus as to whether WDRB is necessary when a critical result is received by an attending physician, as the chance for misunderstanding is minimal. Proponents argue that if the attending is on the road or at home, the results may be forgotten; therefore, WDRB must be assured, even if the receiver has to pull over to the road side and write down the result.

Unacceptable forms of critical communications include answering machines, pages, and e-mail. Only physicians, registered nurses, nurse practitioners, and physician assistants are authorized to receive critical results. Unit secretaries, nursing assistants, and medical students are not.

Compliance

It is necessary to set a goal for compliance within a given timeframe. A 90% compliance rate is a reasonable target to strive for. Once this goal is consistently achieved, the target may then be increased. Reminders to radiologists summarizing the policy, defining expectations, and clarifying legal and regulatory imperatives, in the form of handouts, Power Point presentations, in-service training, and orientation sessions for new staff help to improve compliance.

Performing a periodic audit for compliance is more important than is the method of audit or statistical analysis. For statistical analysis, it is difficult to establish a numerator. In some departments, 1,000 randomly picked radiology reports are analyzed. In others, a dual approach is made to determine a numerator: for example, critical result reports are tagged with unique identifier, and a radiology information system (RIS) word search is performed for critical results that were not communicated as such.

Auditing the compliance of individual radiologists and the department as a whole is important. Data mining for audits, in a manual system, can be facilitated by flagging reports containing records of critical result communication with unique identifier symbols, such as "*+*." To search the RIS for reports for which critical communication should have occurred but did not, the system is queried for keywords in critical communication lists, such as "aortic dissection," "pulmonary embolism," "pneumothorax," "spine fracture," "cerebral hemorrhage," "intestinal obstruction," "perforation," and the like. From the accrual of this search, a certain number of reports, perhaps 100 per month, can be manually audited for compliance. All reports should be reviewed by a radiologist to separate compliant from noncompliant reports. A noncompliant report would be one in which at least three elements of communication—name, time, and date—are not recorded.

To enhance compliance, it is important that violators of the critical result policy are given regular feedback in writing, detailing the missing element in the record of communication. Records of noncompliance are not only shared with individual staff members, but also reported collectively at department meetings and to the relevant hospital committee. Another source of noncompliance data may be the referring physician, who may complain when a critical result is not conveyed in a timely manner.

Because of inaccuracies in hospital information system (HIS) listed contact information for physicians caring for inpatients, reporting radiologists may spend 30 minutes or more tracking down referring providers. A fail-safe process should be detailed in the critical communication policy. If a reasonable effort to contact a referring physician fails, a fail-safe or escalation process should be invoked. The steps of escalation in the contact effort may be to relevant departmental division head, then to the department vice chair or chair, followed by the hospital's chief quality or safety officer and chief medical officer. Invocation of the escalation policy can help to alert the referring providers.

Emergency department physicians can view images in real time, but teams of ED physicians and trauma surgeons frequently visit to discuss cases with the on-duty radiologist. In this scenario, the necessary step of recording the name of a specific physician is sometimes skipped. Such a pitfall should be avoided through in-service training.

THE ROLE AND PROMISE OF INFORMATION SYSTEMS AND TECHNOLOGY IN COMMUNICATING RADIOLOGY RESULTS

In the current health care environment, there is growing expectation for not only rapid and accurate transmission of information, but also its timely delivery to the responsible clinician. Technology has the potential for improving this and many other aspects of patient care. With this in view, the federal government has recently approved the American Recovery and Reinvestment Act of 2009, which seeks to "preserve and improve affordable health care and modernize the nation's infrastructure" through implementation of electronic medical records (EMRs) and electronic health records (EHR).

Many new systems are in use or are being introduced to facilitate the communication and documentation processes. One such system is the audit trail and node authentication (ATNA) integration profile, which contributes to access control by limiting network access between nodes and limiting access to each node to authorized users. Network communications between secure nodes in a secure domain are restricted to only other secure nodes in that domain. Secure nodes limit access to authorized users as specified by the local authentication and access control policy.

Implementation of a critical communication policy, whether by manual or automated methods, requires commitment from leadership and the involvement of a radiologist interested in performance improvement, as well as an administrator to lead the implementation and manage the policy audit.

The communication of results may be synchronous or asynchronous. A synchronous communication is interruptive, real-time, face-to-face or telephonic, and requires an immediate response. Asynchronous communication is noninterruptive and occurs via a RIS, an HIS, mail, e-mail, or text messaging.

With some exceptions, the majority of radiology reports are communicated asynchronously. For communication of routine outpatient and inpatient reports, sufficient redundancy is usually built into the system so that reports are available in a timely fashion or can be accessed online as needed. In the rare event that a report is untraceable, the study may have to be repeated. Acknowledgment of the receipt of routine radiology reports is legally not necessary at this time.

Built into the RIS is the ability to run reports on many aspects of turnaround time, such as by source of origin, whether inpatient or outpatient, and against the target turnaround time. However, reports containing important or unexpected high-risk diagnoses must be conveyed synchronously, within minutes of interpretation. The record of the audit of this verifiable communication is necessary for departmental quality performance under Joint Commission compliance and accreditation requirements.

THE COMMUNICATION RESULTS MANAGEMENT TOOL

The NPSG 2 requirement for critical communication has led to a search for an automated solution that can ensure critical result delivery, acknowledgment, and documentation; provide a list of failed deliveries and escalate them for further intervention; provide a means of auditing and evaluating compliance; and decrease the burden of critical results delivery on the radiologist's workflow productivity.

Currently, several commercially produced systems are available, featuring different solutions. One generic type of system is a *communication result management tool* (CRMT). Veriphy (Nuance, Burlington, Massachusetts) is one such commercially available CRMT product. Typically, CRMT systems promise the timely delivery of critical results, and they record the detail of steps and the contents of the critical communication in the institution's picture archiving and communication system (PACS), order entry system, HIS, or RIS. An early version of this solution was initially adopted by numerous large academic medical centers. Typically, these CRMT systems had features that allowed the radiologist to select the provider to be contacted and the degree of urgency, recorded the message contents, and produced a receipt confirming message delivery. These system had the further ability to generate an audit report on these components of communication for quality improvement and Joint Commission compliance. The early version of CRMT was fraught with problems and did not fulfill its expected role. Therefore, most centers discontinued their use in less than 2 years. The major pitfalls of CRMT included:

- A failure to estimate the value and role of human intervention; unlike laboratory findings, discussion between referring

physicians and radiologists can contribute to improvement in diagnosis and patient management.
- Messages that were either never delivered or were sent to the wrong receiver
- Inaccurate referring physician contact information, ever-changing physician schedules, and changes in ordering and receiving physicians with shifts
- Referring physician complaints regarding repeated or after-hours reminders not appropriate for the level of urgency
- The need to escalate contact efforts for undelivered results
- The difficulty of acknowledging the receipt in an automated system, which created further obstacles to the acceptance of CRMT

To solve these problems, commercial vendors are developing different approaches and workflows for critical result management. Some use speech recognition; others do not. One vendor has a web-based program, whereas another integrates seamlessly with an existing HL7 data stream. (HL7 is a standard in common use in many HIS for data transmission.)

For a department of radiology, the ability to maintain a record of communication, acknowledgment, and subsequent audit fulfills the promise of automation to facilitate workflow. Automated systems can eliminate the need for manual labor at every stage of implementation and audit for compliance.

Finding solutions to some of the drawbacks of automated critical communication and audit systems poses challenges for IT, because provider directories and contact information are often held in different computer systems within an institution. This information drifts out of date very rapidly, and technologies are being developed that allow for the easy creation and real-time updating of provider directories at reasonable cost. Integrated health care enterprises (IHE) are beginning to use lightweight directory access protocols and domain name system queries to update the contents of personnel directory information on a real-time basis.

Future CRMT solutions may develop technologies that enable systems to know, in real time, which providers are present in the institution or on duty and are available to receive communication from the department of radiology. This may include the use of radio frequency identity tags on pagers or phones to identify provider locations within the perimeter of the institution. Using this technology with built-in escalation protocols, the system would only try to reach those who are immediately within the vicinity of the workplace, rather than those who are unavailable. A further refinement of the system, using an acknowledgment tool, could include the ability to order the next appropriate test or begin treatment based on the imaging examination. Such interactive programs would improve message receipt and acknowledgment, thus enabling easier and more timely follow-up and, most importantly, improved provider acceptance.

SELECTING A COMMUNICATION RESULT MANAGEMENT TOOL

Before selecting a system for communication and acknowledgment, it is of paramount importance to assure collaboration among the administration, IT team, radiologists, and the referring providers. Guidelines must be developed with input from all stakeholders. These guidelines must define critical diagnoses, the methods of communication, escalation policies, and fail-safe mechanisms. The escalation algorithm is especially challenging in teaching hospitals, where the resident or hospitalist caring for a patient may change several times a day. In such institutions, unless process is in place to escalate the communication to the responsible physician on duty, the result may not be received and urgently needed action may never take place. It should be noted that a list of critical diagnoses may be service- or physician-dependent. The participation of referring providers in the decision-making process serves to enhance compliance, whereas their exclusion is a potential roadblock.

For successful implementation, the radiologists and the referring providers must fully realize that the communication tool or system is not used simply for the convenience of radiologists or to pester referring physicians. Demonstrating successful implementation of critical results communication is, in fact, a requirement for maintaining the accreditation of the institution. Although many technical challenges remain, referring provider buy-in remains the most critical element for the success of automated systems.

Many in-house developed e-mail alert systems with return receipt capability are currently in use. The process begins with radiologists tagging a report with a searchable unique identifier, statement, or sign. A language text query technology is set to periodically search for the unique identifier in finalized radiology reports. When the statement is found, the system automatically sends an alert message to the physician's e-mail addresses, after automatically retrieving the physician e-mail address from the contact repository. The system then captures and displays the log information of all alerts. The log is used for audits and problem solving.

9

Teamwork and Communication in Radiology

KAREN MIGUEL

ealth care is changing. After a decade of warning calls from watchdog groups and regulatory bodies for the need to improve teamwork and communication, these efforts are finally being integrated into medical and nursing schools' curricula, hospital formal standards, and regulatory requirements. Institutions are beginning to recognize the positive impact team training has on patient outcomes. Patient safety depends on strong teamwork and communication amongst caregivers.

Organizations such as the Institute of Medicine (IOM), The Leapfrog Group, the Institute for Health Improvement (IHI), and the Joint Commission have advocated for systems improvements, as well as for evaluation and impact measurement procedures. Efforts to support and reward have been developed to shift the paradigm from mandates and reprimands to positive changes in behaviors and culture. The primary focus has become to identify the necessary improvements to the delivery system, with the goal of reducing the likelihood of reoccurrence.

Accepting that errors are inevitable is the first step in increasing safety in any environment. Management of these inevitable errors has become the focus for many high-reliability industries, such as aviation, the nuclear energy industry, and more recently, health care. Each of these organization's safety platforms shares two key elements: the adoption of specific teamwork and communication behaviors, and the implementation of safety tools, such as

checklists and standardization of processes and procedures that complement these behaviors. For health care, the risk of human error requires us to put systems in place and provide new skills and tools—all with the goal of changing the culture and ultimately improving patient outcomes. To that end, teams make fewer mistakes than do individuals when they are performing their responsibilities.[1] Alternatively, poor team performance has contributed to 40% of delays in operating room (OR) cases and contributed to 30% of adverse events for a specific series of OR cases reviewed.[2] The effectiveness of team training on team performance across all industries has been cited numerous times in the literature.[3,4]

Those organizations showing success in team training and improved communication have leadership at all levels willing to abandon cultural precedents that link performance with autonomy. Instead, in these organizations, we see a primary commitment to a culture of safety at the core of the institution's or department's goals and mission. Team training optimizes patient outcomes by improving communication through key teamwork skills. It requires a committed leadership to build a culture that sustains continued growth and positive momentum, as well as a fundamental foundation supported by ongoing education and continuous data transparency. These conditions must all be in place for the value of the program to be realized, and for the measurable benefits of improved safety to prevail.

HEALTH CARE AND CREW RESOURCE MANAGEMENT

The most highly used team training strategy in health care is *crew resource management* (CRM), modeled after a similar program in the aviation industry, which places an emphasis on the role of human factors.[5] Crew resource management is an active process, first used by airline flight teams, that draws from all its available resources to achieve safe and efficient flight operations. Its aim is to provide individual, team, and system processes to prevent, discover, and mitigate errors before the errors become an accident or adverse outcome. In health care, team training success is evaluated by drawing comparisons between staff perception of their safety environment through the use of safety attitudinal questionnaires (SAQ), as well as through active observations of those behaviors. General teamwork training in health care emphasizes team concepts such as communication, awareness, and continuous learning.

Elements of CRM have been adopted by many areas of health care, specifically the OR, anesthesia, and labor and delivery. Other specialty areas, such as radiology, are beginning to appreciate its benefits as well. Image-guided interventional suites have become the ORs of the future, and are prone to the same type of errors—including communication errors—traditionally associated with ORs. With the projected growth of image-guided interventions performed by radiologists, the need for team training has never been more imperative.

Communication failures remain the root cause of over two-thirds of all unintended patient harm. Clearly, more focus needs to be directed to learning ways to communicate effectively. Key behavioral markers of CRM include the use of briefings; inquiry and rebriefings; structured communication, such as SBAR (see below); closed-loop communication; appropriate assertion and the use of critical language; and debriefing.[6]

Briefings are useful for "getting everyone on the same page," or for establishing a common method for communicating key elements of a situation in a timely and concise manner. Briefings are usually informal, set the tone for the procedure or the day, and are owned by the entire team. Briefings should not be confused with the time-out procedure of the Universal Protocol; there are similarities, but the distinction is clear. Both are initiated by the leader—in the case of radiology, this is the proceduralist—but briefings offer a chance for everyone to speak up, and they send a clear message of collective ownership by encouraging team members to raise concerns as they are realized.

In settings such as the procedural suite, OR, or the labor and delivery area, it is imperative for everyone on the team to have an understanding of the overall "big picture." This form of situational awareness is a process by which the key operator "rebriefs" by informing the team of any changes to the intended plan, so that they have an opportunity to ask questions to assure they will be able to react accordingly and predict alternate needs moving forward.

A common method of structured communication is *SBAR*. By stating what is going on with a patient (*the Situation*), the salient points of the patient history (*the Background*), the caregiver's thoughts on what the patient's issue are (*the Assessment*), and what the caregiver believes may be necessary as a next step (*the Recommendation*), a clinical communication exchange between team members can happen effectively and efficiently. Although the recommendation offered may not become the ultimate decision, the laying out of the issue in a clear, concise manner is of great benefit to patient outcome.

Fundamental to the Read Back/Feed Back National Patient Safety Goal, *closed-loop communication* describes the practice of repeating back information when one member the team makes a request of another. Closed-loop communication is used when a medication or a specific device is requested, and the team member carrying it out repeats back what was heard.

Appropriate assertion teaches people how to speak up and share their concerns, as well as how to use *critical language*, common phrases that all staff members understand. Appropriate assertion strikes a balance between persistence and politeness, and is centered on not backing down when an issue requires attention and a clear resolution. By using common critical language for such urgent situations through phrases like "I'm concerned, something is not right, I need you to come and evaluate the patient now," the staff drives home the urgency of the situation and the clear request for action. This key element of critical language (also used in commercial airlines) is essential to safe care, as it creates a clearly agreed-upon model for clear and direct communication to get the person to stop and listen to the need.[7]

The final key element of CRM is debriefing. *Debriefing* is a process for constructive discussion of the team's performance during a procedure or as a wrap-up at the end of day. It is intended to discuss what went well, what did not go well, and what was learned, as well as what steps can be taken to improve the process the next time. It allows for all domain experts to voice ideas positively, starting with the least senior staff, so the collective wisdom of the team is captured and continuous learning occurs.[6]

MASSACHUSETTS GENERAL HOSPITAL PILOT PROGRAM

In 2007, the leaders of a radiology department at a large academic medical center in Boston, Massachusetts General Hospital (MGH), tested the potential benefits of CRM training. A pilot study was developed for two interventional radiology (IR) areas, vascular and neurology, and ran for more than 24 months, with specific aims of improving staff perception of safety and improving communication skills and team practices to ultimately lead to mitigating errors and decreasing threats for errors.

Using an SAQ—the Agency for Healthcare Research and Quality (AHRQ)'s *Hospital Survey on Patient Safety Culture*—researchers were able to evaluate staff's perception of a safety culture in their work environment before and after team training. This survey was chosen from several available surveys as it had been designed, tested, and revised by AHRQ and was currently being utilized by nearly 300 hospitals across the country. With a focus on 12 areas of patient safety culture, it was designed to capture staff opinions about patient safety issues, event reporting, and medical errors (Figure 9.1).

The clinical arena lacked a procedure or method to measure the success of team practice through behaviors. Directly correlating mitigation or prevention of errors to CRM in health care was not possible at that time. However, high-risk, high-hazard industries like aviation had begun to successfully show the causal effect between the cultural integration of team behaviors and an increase in the identification, communication, and mitigation of existing or potential threats before they became errors. When staff perceptions of safety are favorable, staff are less prone to act unsafely, which has been shown to be an indication of fewer errors and injuries. These measurements are difficult to validate due to the subjective nature of the process, but do possess "face validity." These standardized methods for measuring behavior were validated using trained observers in the procedural setting.

Building upon the limited research in measuring observational behavior in clinical areas and the current functional methodologies, a simple observation tool was designed for use by the trained observers during procedural observations[8] (Figure 9.2). The behavioral markers observed were briefing and rebriefing, SBAR, closed-loop communication, verbal knowledge sharing, appropriate conflict resolution and assertion, and debriefing.

The overarching aim of the observation tool was to be as diverse as possible, so that it could be used to measure team behaviors over a wider range of health care settings.

Recognizing that leadership commitment was the critical component to the team training success, it was acknowledged that staff perception of the training program, as well as the behaviors observed, was a direct evaluation of leadership's influence on the program. The main goals were first to reduce threats and mitigate errors by improving communication skills and team practices, and second, to improve staff perception of safety. The team training program consisted of three components: framing, training, and sustaining.

Framing

Framing included informing the staff about the program and obtaining pretraining observational data. Executive sponsors, individuals selected from high-level leadership, were asked to provide program oversight to ensure the availability of adequate resources, and they met biannually to review the data and advise on areas of necessary focus. A steering committee, comprised of leadership from nursing, physician, technologist, and education, identified process and outcome measures that were of interest for their area, in addition to the previously identified measurements of the study. The committee reviewed the progress and determined needs as necessary. A subgroup of the steering committee, the working group, participated in a 4-hour training session to learn the process for collecting observational data, as well as for obtaining a minimum number of weekly observations.

Training

There were two components to the training: group team training to perform the procedures, and observer training. The group team training took place off the main campus, and all staff was required

This survey asks for your opinions about patient safety issues, medical error, and event reporting in your hospital and will take about 10 to 15 minutes to complete.

*An "event" is defined as any type of error, mistake, incident, accident, or deviation, regardless of whether or not it results in patient harm.

**"Patient safety" is defined as the avoidance and prevention of patient injuries or adverse events resulting from the processes of health care delivery.

SECTION A: Your Work Area/Unit

In this survey, think of your "unit" as the work area, department, or clinical area of the hospital where you spend most of your work time or provide most of your clinical services.

What is your primary work area or unit in this hospital? Mark ONE answer by filling in the circle.

a. Many different hospital units/No specific unit	h. Psychiatry/mental health
b. Medicine (non-surgical)	i. Rehabilitation
c. Surgery	j. Pharmacy
d. Obstetrics	k. Laboratory
e. Pediatrics	l. Radiology
f. Emergency department	m. Anesthesiology
g. Intensive care unit (any type)	n. Other, please specify:

Please indicate your agreement or disagreement with the following statements about your work area/unit. Mark your answer by circling the appropriate number.

Think about your hospital work area/unit...	Strongly Disagree	Disagree	Neither	Agree	Strongly Agree
1. People support one another in this unit	1	2	3	4	5
2. We have enough staff to handle the workload	1	2	3	4	5
3. When a lot of work needs to be done quickly, we work together as a team to get the work done	1	2	3	4	5
4. In this unit, people treat each other with respect	1	2	3	4	5
5. Staff in this unit work longer hours than is best for patient care	1	2	3	4	5
6. We are actively doing things to improve patient safety	1	2	3	4	5
7. We use more agency/temporary staff than is best for patient care	1	2	3	4	5
8. Staff feel like their mistakes are held against them	1	2	3	4	5
9. Mistakes have led to positive changes here	1	2	3	4	5
10. It is just by chance that more serious mistakes don't happen around here	1	2	3	4	5
11. When one area in this unit gets really busy, others help out	1	2	3	4	5
12. When an event is reported, it feels like the person is being written up, not the problem	1	2	3	4	5
13. After we make changes to improve patient safety, we evaluate their effectiveness	1	2	3	4	5
14. We work in "crisis mode" trying to do too much, too quickly	1	2	3	4	5
15. Patient safety is never sacrificed to get more work done	1	2	3	4	5
16. Staff worry that mistakes they make are kept in their personnel file	1	2	3	4	5
17. We have patient safety problems in this unit	1	2	3	4	5
18. Our procedures and systems are good at preventing errors from happening	1	2	3	4	5

SECTION B: Your Supervisor/Manager - Please indicate your agreement or disagreement with the following statements about your immediate supervisor/manager or person to whom you directly report. Mark your answer by circling the appropriate number.

	Strongly Disagree	Disagree	Neither	Agree	Strongly Agree
1. My supervisor/manager says a good word when he/she sees a job done according to established patient safety procedures	1	2	3	4	5
2. My supervisor/manager seriously considers staff suggestions for improving patient safety	1	2	3	4	5
3. Whenever pressure builds up, my supervisor/manager wants us to work faster, even if it means taking shortcuts	1	2	3	4	5
4. My supervisor/manager overlooks patient safety problems that happen over and over	1	2	3	4	5

SECTION C: Communications How often do the following things happen in your work area/unit? Mark your answer by circling the appropriate number.

Think about your hospital work area/unit...	Never	Rarely	Sometime	Most of the time	Always
1. We are given feedback about changes put into place based on event reports	1	2	3	4	5
2. Staff will freely speak up if they see something that may negatively affect patient care	1	2	3	4	5
3. We are informed about errors that happen in this unit	1	2	3	4	5
4. Staff feel free to question the decisions or actions of those with more authority	1	2	3	4	5
5. In this unit, we discuss ways to prevent errors from happening again	1	2	3	4	5
6. Staff are afraid to ask questions when something does not seem right	1	2	3	4	5

Content taken from the AHRQ Safety Climate Survey

FIGURE 9.1 Safety attitudinal questionnaire (SAQ).

Reproduced from the Agency for Healthcare Research and Quality (AHRQ) Hospital Survey on Patient Safety Culture, 2004.

to attend. The team was taught the key concepts of team training, which included interactive practice sessions focused on those concepts. Observer training was aimed at calibrating each observer and included a subsequent training session in which each participant observed communication interactions, rated them, then compared scores with other observers. The framework for teaching was preceded by the explanation of leadership expectations at all levels, as well as the department's commitment to fostering an environment of openness and mindfulness of errors.

Sustaining

Training was recognized as successful and valuable when results showed a persistent improvement in and sustainment of the adoption of the key components of team training. Clearly, the participants were implementing these concepts in their daily work. Measurement would be made through frequent and

SECTION D: Frequency of Events Reported In your hospital work area/unit, when the following mistakes happen, how often are they reported? Mark your answer by circling the appropriate number.

	Never	Rarely	Sometime	Most of the time	Always
1. When a mistake is made, but is caught and corrected before affecting the patient, how often is this reported?	1	2	3	4	5
2. When a mistake is made, but has no potential to harm the patient, how often is this reported?	1	2	3	4	5
3. When a mistake is made that could harm the patient, but does not, how often is this reported?	1	2	3	4	5

SECTION E: Patient Safety Grade
Please give your work area/unit in this hospital an overall grade on patient safety. Mark ONE answer.

(A) Excellent   (B) Very Good   (C) Acceptable   (D) Poor   (E) Failing

SECTION F: Your Hospital - Please indicate your agreement or disagreement with the following statements about your hospital. Mark your answer by circling the appropriate number.

Think about your hospital...	Strongly Disagree	Disagree	Neither	Agree	Strongly Agree
1. Hospital management provides a work climate that promotes patient safety	1	2	3	4	5
2. Hospital units do not coordinate well with each other	1	2	3	4	5
3. Things "fall between the cracks" when transferring patients from one unit to another	1	2	3	4	5
4. There is good cooperation among hospital units that need to work together	1	2	3	4	5
5. Important patient care information is often lost during shift changes	1	2	3	4	5
6. It is often unpleasant to work with staff from other hospital units.	1	2	3	4	5
7. Problems often occur in the exchange of information across hospital units	1	2	3	4	5
8. The actions of hospital management show that patient safety is a top priority	1	2	3	4	5
9. Hospital management seems interested in patient safety only after an adverse event happens	1	2	3	4	5
10. Hospital units work well together to provide the best care for patients	1	2	3	4	5
11. Shift changes are problematic for patients in this hospital	1	2	3	4	5

SECTION G: Number of Events Reported
In the past 12 months, how many event reports have you filled out and submitted? Mark ONE answer.

(a.) No event reports   (b.) 1 to 2 event reports   (c.) 3 to 5 event reports
(d.) 6 to 10 event reports   (e.) 11 to 20 event reports   (f.) 21 event reports or more

SECTION H: Background Information

This information will help in the analysis of the survey results. Mark ONE answer by circling the corresponding letter.

1. How long have you worked in this hospital?

a. Less than 1 year	b. 1 to 5 years	c. 6 to 10 years
d. 11 to 15 years	e. 16 to 20 years	f. 21 years or more

2. How long have you worked in your current hospital work area/unit?

a. Less than 1 year	b. 1 to 5 years	c. 6 to 10 years
d. 11 to 15 years	e. 16 to 20 years	f. 21 years or more

3. Typically, how many hours per week do you work in this hospital?

a. Less than 20 hours per week	b. 20 to 39 hours per week	c. 40 to 59 hours per week
d. 60 to 79 hours per week	e. 80 to 99 hours per week	f. 100 hours per week or more

4. What is your staff position in this hospital? Mark ONE answer that best describes your staff position.

a. Registered Nurse	h. Dietician
b. Physician Assistant/Nurse Practitioner	i. Unit Assistant/Clerk/Secretary
c. LVN/LPN	j. Respiratory Therapist
d. Patient Care Assistant/Hospital Aide/Care Partner	k. Physical, Occupational, or Speech Therapist
e. Attending/Staff Physician	l. Technician (e.g., EKG, Lab, Radiology)
f. Resident Physician/Physician in Training	m. Administration/Management
g. Pharmacist	n. Other, please specify:

5. In your staff position, do you typically have direct interaction or contact with patients?

a. YES, I typically have direct interaction or contact with patients.   b. NO, I typically do NOT have direct interaction or contact with patients.

6. How long have you worked in your current specialty or profession?

a. Less than 1 year	b. 1 to 5 years	c. 6 to 10 years
d. 11 to 15 years	e. 16 to 20 years	f. 21 years or more

Comments: Please feel free to write any comments about patient safety, error, or event reporting in your hospital.

Content taken from the AHRQ Safety Climate Survey

FIGURE 9.1 (*Continued*).

consistent observations of team behaviors through a set number of required observations from each of the observers, and through the delivery of the AHRQ's safety attitudinal survey, administered at pretraining and at 1-year intervals, to measure staff attitudes about their behavior.

The steering committee and the work group were responsible for tracking and generating any results for the specific process and outcome measures that were identified at inception.

THE PILOT RESULTS

Agency for Healthcare Research and Quality Safety Survey

The comparison between the 2007 and the 2008 surveys showed a statistically significant improvement in overall staff perception (Figure 9.3). Teamwork within the IR area was scored based on whether staff supported each other, treated each other with respect, and worked together as a team. These scores increased

Communication and Teamwork Skills Assessment – Team

Observer ID: ______ Case ID :________ Date:____________ Observation Start/End Time_____/_____

Team Members (by role, not name): ______________________________

Procedure:______________ Institution/Hospital: ____________ Specialty/Department ______________________________

Segment of Procedure (circle one): Pre procedure Intra Procedure Post Procedure

Standard CATS Behaviors				
Behavior	Observed, Adequate	Observed, Mediocre	Expected/Not Observed	Comments
Briefing / Re-briefing (formal)				
Verbal Knowledge Sharing - Ideas, Plans, Concerns				
SBAR				
Closed Loop				
Appropriate Conflict Resolution				
Debriefing				

Climate Assessment

After you complete your observation please answer the following questions based on your assesment of the environment you observed.

Professional	5	4	3	2	1	Unprofessional
Collaborative/Collegial	5	4	3	2	1	Uncooperative/Divided
Respectful	5	4	3	2	1	Disrespectful
Attentive/Interested	5	4	3	2	1	Detached/Uninterested

Additional Comments:

Frankel©2007 Not for Distribution Partners HealthCare - Patient Safety

FIGURE 9.2 Communication and Teamwork Skills (CATS) observation tool.

Adapted from Frankel A, Gardner R, Maynard L, Kelly A. Using the Communication and Teamwork Skills (CATS) assessment to measure health care team performance. *Joint Comm J Quality Patient Safety*. 2007;33(9):549–58. Reprinted with permission from Allan Frankel, MD.

by 9 percentage points post training (56%–65%) and reflected a stronger team dynamic shared across staff demographics. The patient safety composite showing the highest average percent increase was management expectations and actions for promoting the patient safety (71%–82%), indicating that there was strong leadership presence throughout the program. The highest overall improvement post-training for a single composite (39%–57%) was staff perception that there was a nonpunitive response to errors, thereby making staff feel more comfortable in reporting errors without fear of repercussions or long-term personnel issues. This indicates that staff feel safer sharing adverse events, rather than being preoccupied with potential punitive measures. In fact, two-thirds of respondents reported one or more adverse events, and this increase reflected confidence that they were able to report these occurrences without fear of retribution.

Observational Scores

There were three observation data collection points: pretraining, immediate post-training (0–6 months), and sustaining (6–12 months), with a focus on the six behavioral markers discussed earlier (Figure 9.4). The marker that showed a steady increase over time was closed-loop communication (pretraining, 51%; post-training, 64%; sustaining, 74%). This exemplified the team's ability to embrace a shared mental model and the importance of clear communication. Briefing (pretraining, 0%; post-training, 75%; sustaining, 65%) showed significant improvement post-training but had slightly fallen during the sustaining period. SBAR (pretraining, 0%; post-training, 38%; sustaining, 58%) showed significant improvement post-training and had continued to improve during the sustaining period. These were newly acquired skills for staff, taught for the first time during training. Half of the observations showed that debriefing was performed after training, but fell off during the sustaining period (pretraining, 0%; post-training, 50%; sustaining, 38%). The highest marker for gain and sustain was in the area of appropriate conflict resolution and assertion (pretraining, 0%; post-training, 100%; sustaining, 98%).

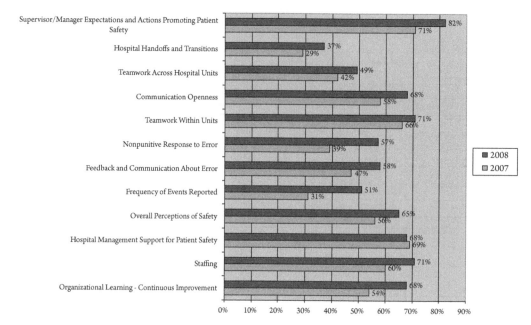

FIGURE 9.3 Staff survey results: AHRQ safety attitudinal questionnaire.

The pilot program had achieved its intended goals of improving staff perception of safety and of improving communication skills and team practices to ultimately lead to mitigating errors and decreasing threats for errors. This was represented in the overall scores of the safety culture survey and the comparative scores of the observational data. One additional positive outcome was an increase in the reporting of near-misses and adverse events into a "glitch book," which was a book in which staff anonymously catalogued concerns they had about particular case events. The glitch book entries were used at multidisciplinary staff meetings to address concerns in a nonthreatening and objective manner.

One admitted limitation of the pilot was a lack of set outcomes for specific behavioral markers and

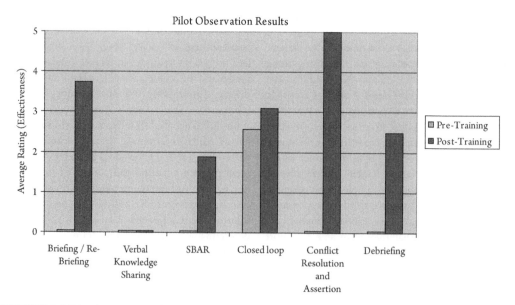

FIGURE 9.4 Pilot observation results.

attitudes, which would have made it easier to focus re-education and learning sessions on specific areas of concern. A second limitation was the inability to directly correlate, through a causal effect, the number of adverse events with serious patient outcomes to the adoption of high-performance team skills after training. As this data point was not established from the onset, the ability to accurately measure and compare serious patient outcome rates was not possible. A third limitation was the lack of an infrastructure to support a well thought out plan for sustaining the program. The pilot was intended to provide support from the Corporate Safety Office of this academic medical center over a 2-year timeframe, and there were no site-specific resources or plan to continue the pilot for the long term.

HARDWIRING FOR SUCCESS OR PUTTING IT ALL TOGETHER

One year after the team training program and pilot study, the newly formed Radiology Safety Office reviewed the current platform and provided the necessary support and redirection needed to expand the team program throughout all six IR areas. When interviewed post-pilot, leadership determined their departmental priorities and the biggest concerns for each area involved improving communication. Based on this feedback, there was a need for attention to providing clarity, as well as managing concerns about the program and its intended goals. Also cited was the lack of team dynamics training refreshers. There was a need for an educational platform that provided staff access to online resources, such as learning modules, and to active learning strategies, such as mock codes in vitro or simulation lab environments utilizing team algorithms. Building on the success, as well as learning from the shortcomings of the pilot, the platform for the team program was directed at the development of three critical success factors: engaging leadership; creating an educational curriculum that focused on new staff, as well as on refresher training for all staff; and establishing a mechanism to present meaningful and useful data in order to guide improvements at the divisional level.

Engaging Leadership

Both structural and philosophical changes must take place for a paradigm shift in human behavior to occur. Team training demands sponsorship and commitment from all levels of employees, especially leadership. Strong leadership is required to build a culture that sustains continued growth and positive momentum. An effective leader needs to create an "agenda for change" with two major elements in mind: a *vision*, with the long-range organizational interests in mind, and a *strategy* for achieving that vision, balancing the competing internal and external forces. The agenda must provide direction while managing the concerns of major stakeholders. Radiology leaders must have a vision and serve as a model for teamwork while providing motivation through open acknowledgment of new ideas and innovations. Leaders must also be willing to commit adequate resources to assure sustainability.

Program leaders should consider several factors before initiating a team training program. Aligning team training expectations and safety aims with organizational goals and communicating the importance of this issue to the department are paramount to the success of any new program. MGH Imaging made this a strategic priority for the department with its initial focus on the interventional suites. The program was communicated at the annual strategic retreat to all levels of medical and operational leadership. All frontline staff was informed of the program goals, their role, and the role of their leadership, as well as of how these goals aligned with departmental and hospital missions. Divisional leaders spoke of the program in regular staff meetings and wherever there was an opportunity to communicate.

We started by asking executive leadership to appoint a single leader who believed in the program and was vested in providing the sponsorship required to engage/re-engage peers. This physician leader had also played a vital role in the pilot project's success and was committed to leading the effort. Next, we defined leadership expectations and resource requirements to ensure commitment to sustaining the program (see Table 9.1). Carried over from the pilot, leadership acknowledged that staff perception of the training program, as well as the behaviors observed, was a direct evaluation of leadership's influence on the program.

Continuous Learning and Reinforcement

Depending on the size of the group and the resources available, many options are available for continued staff education. Live classroom training may be held in 4-hour sessions, while online training can be divided into modules lasting 20–40 minutes each. Depending on a facility's resources and access, active learning strategies, such as simulation or in vitro

TABLE 9.1 LEADERSHIP
EXPECTATIONS AND RESOURCE
REQUIREMENTS NEEDED TO SUSTAIN
THE TEAM TRAINING PROGRAM

The Steering Committee and Work Group will:

  a. Meet regularly

  b. Ensure that data collection is performed (observations, etc.)

  c. Review data as it is returned and evaluate course of program

  d. Review that feedback of information is effective.

  e. Define areas for follow-up training

  f. Administer follow-up Safety Climate Survey (every yearly)

  g. Redesign program to continually focus on improving outcomes as desired by department, such as (but not limited to):

    i. Efficiency, i.e. procedure turnover time

    ii. Patient Centeredness, i.e. patient satisfaction

    iii. Complications, i.e. adverse event rates

    iv. Threats: (recurrent events that predispose to errors)

    v. Close Calls: incident report data

    vi. "Good Catch" books where hopefully # of reports will increase and the severity of harm will decrease

drills that use mock codes, can be used after initial exposure to the curriculum and will greatly enhance the adoption of behaviors. As basic concepts, the "how" may fade after time, so it is important to reassert "why" it is important for teams to work well together.[9] A plan for regularly required refresher training should also be taken into consideration.

For best results, identifying trained professionals to deliver the training material, providing appropriate and frequent notifications of the upcoming training programs, and allocating time for staff to participate must all be coordinated by leadership.

For training to be a success, trainees must be ready and motivated to learn. By setting the right expectations, clarifying what team training is and what it is not, and framing the program in a positive context, leaders set the program up for success. Providing staff with resources and information before the training makes it more likely that they will be engaged and willing to learn. Consider providing information not only about the training sessions and the day itself, but also information on human factors and the science of errors, to help frame the message that patient safety and improving outcomes is critical to good practice.

Work with leadership to assure that staff will be given time off from daily obligations to attend and participate without distraction. Teams that are intended to work together should also train together.

Determining who will provide the training and where it will be held is important. Seek out professionals who understand adult learning methods and who are content experts.

At MGH, prior to initiating training, several weeks were dedicated to obtaining a baseline sense of the staff's perception of their work environment and how they interacted with each other while performing procedures. An industry-recognized SAQ was administered, and 20–40 observations for each IR division were collected. Six interventional specialties required team training. Based on the size of each, two live 4-hour training sessions were administered. All role groups, including new residents and fellows, participated in the training. The live team training was provided by an outside consultant contracted to support the program infrastructure. The sessions were run 6 months apart, thus allowing for the opportunity to learn and make improvements from the earlier session. These took place in an off-site facility adjacent to the hospital, allowing staff to be removed from their daily obligations while providing convenient access. Each interventional division closed routine scheduling for the afternoon(s) and provided only necessary emergent coverage as determined by the division. Staff was informed that this training was mandatory.

In addition to live training, the consultant provided training for site-based observers and a data management platform to manage the data from both the annual SAQ and the observational data. Each division selected two to three staff representing physician, nurse, and technologist role groups to become site-based observers. The 4-hour observer training focused on training the observers to recognize the key behaviors of good teamwork and communication. To ensure interrater reliability, short videos of clinical scenarios were reviewed, rated, and discussed to "calibrate" the observer pool. The schedule for collecting observations was set at quarterly, and would run for a period of 1 month, in which time each division was expected to collect a minimum of 20 observations. Quarterly recalibration sessions for trained observers were also instituted in the weeks prior to the collection period. This 1.5-hour session was a web-based interactive format run by the outside consultant.

The long-term plan for an educational curriculum at MGH is comprised of both a didactic and an active learning model. Annually, all new residents and fellows are required to attend a 4-hour live training session. New staff is also encouraged to join. Biannually, staff is required to complete a series of online learning modules focused on human factors and systems engineering, as well as on the basic behavioral components of teamwork and communication. Simulation provides the learner an opportunity to practice teamwork skills under similar conditions they face daily and will increase the likelihood that these behaviors are brought back into the care areas.[10] Active learning, such as simulation or mock drills, can also begin to address issues that may likely arise among team members in the form of competing priorities and goals, such as communication breakdowns, failures to reach agreement, and poorly coordinated activities.[10]

Two forms of teams work within the interventional areas: those that always work together as "fixed" teams and those who may never have met or at minimum do not always work together, such as anesthesia-supported cases or computed tomography- and magnetic resonance imaging-guided interventional procedure teams. These types of teams were positioned to address a variety of scenarios.

Measurement

Measuring the effectiveness of team training is a critical success factor for sustained change and continuous improvement. Training effectiveness must be assessed at multiple levels. It is imperative to measure staff's perception of their safety environment, and—even more importantly, albeit more costly—to measure the degree to which the transferred skills are observed. At the highest and most efficient level is the ability to measure the transferred teamwork skills against organizational improvements and patient outcomes.

At MGH, the annual SAQ draws both staff's perception of safety in the workplace and staff's feelings of how their divisional and executive leadership communicate overall and manage issues around safety (Figure 9.5). The observational data by the IR division is shared with the local leadership team, as well as with the steering committee made up of all divisional leaders and key departmental members (Figure 9.6). The successes are shared and the areas of concern elicit discussion for improvement. The ultimate goal is to include teamwork behavior into risk assessment of adverse events and to celebrate every opportunity of success.

CONCLUSION

Talk is cheap, as we are often reminded. The message before, during, and after a program's inception must be clear: namely, that teamwork matters. Before embarking on adopting a program of this magnitude, an organization must be invested both culturally and financially. Positioning a teamwork training initiative as an organizational priority

MGH Interventional Radiology

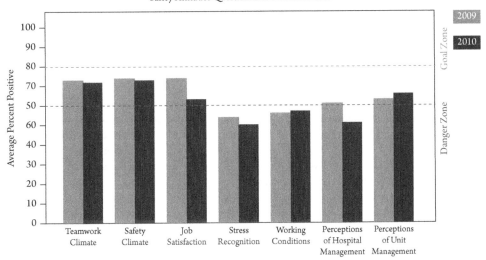

FIGURE 9.5 Safety attitudinal questionnaire results 2009–2010.

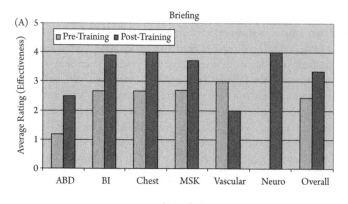

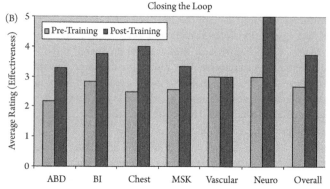

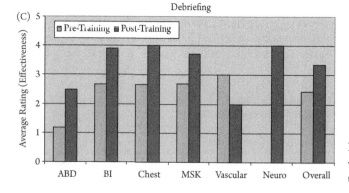

FIGURE 9.6 Domain scores (pretraining vs. post-training). (A) Briefing. (B) Closing the Loop. (C) Debriefing.

should be included into departmental mission statements and reflected in departmental policies.

The adoption of CRM concepts by high-risk industries is shown to have made remarkable differences in safety outcomes by effecting cultural change. It has been shown that team practices have limited the impact of adverse events in the OR by as much as 20%.[2] By applying CRM to health care, we take the first step in moving the paradigm toward a culture of safety. Cultural change is a slow process, and for high-reliability organizations that embrace collaboration, the ability to enhance patient safety

is clearly within reach. A second positive outcome possible through the adoption of CRM is the improvement in staff perception of safety in their work environment, demonstrated through safety culture survey results. In addition, direct observational data reflects the positive effects of team training behaviors, as well as illuminating those areas needing further attention. Adherence to both will support the cultural adoption of high-performing team behaviors in a team setting.

Communication and teamwork engagement is designed to bring threat and error management principles and high-reliability theories to the sharp end of patient care. The work requires executive sponsorship and engaged unit-based leadership, allowing cycles of engagement to repeat over time. The process also requires a strong organizational commitment to manage errors and a just culture that supports a nonpunitive approach to those errors that will inevitably occur. The participants of team training are exposed to concepts that will widen the lens through which they see the environment of care. Accepting the fact that humans are not error-proof and never will be, we will begin to become keenly focused on ways to mitigate the risk of harm to our patients. Hospitals and health care systems are best served by building on cultural assessments that measure the culture of patient safety and enable radiology leadership to answer the fundamental question: "Are we safer?"

REFERENCES

1. Amalberti R, Auroy Y, Berwick D, Barach, P. Five system barriers to achieving ultrasafe health care. *Ann Int Med.* 2005;142(9):756–65.
2. Christian CK, Gustafson ML, Roth DM, Sheridan TB, Gandhi DK. A prospective study of patient safety in the operating room. *Surgery.* 2006;139:159–73.
3. Baker DP, Day R, Salas, E. Teamwork as an essential component of high-reliability organizations. *Health Serv Res.* 2006;41(4):1576–98.
4. Salas E, Weaver S, DiazGranados D, Lyons R, King H. Sounding the call for team training in healthcare; some insights and warnings. *Acad Med.* 2009;84(10):s128–31.
5. Salas E, Almeida SA, Salisbury M, King H, Lazzara, EH. Teamwork and communication. what are the critical success factors for team training in health care? *Jt Comm J Qual Patient Saf.* 2009;35(8):398–405.
6. Leonard M, Frankel A, Simmonds T. *Achieving safe and reliable healthcare; strategies and solutions.* Chicago, IL: Health Administration Press, 2004.
7. Leonard M, Graham S, Bonacum D. The human factor: The critical importance of effective teamwork and communication in providing safe care. *Quality Safety Health Care.* 2004;13(1):85–90.
8. Frankel A, Gardner R, Maynard, L, Kelly A. Using the communication and teamwork skills (CATS) assessment to measure healthcare teamwork performance. The joint commission journal on quality and patient safety. *Jt Comm J Qual Patient Saf.* 2007;33(9):549–58.
9. Helmreich RL, Merritt AC, Wilhelm JA. The evolution of crew resource management training in commercial aviation. *Int J Aviation Psychol.* 1999;9(1): 16–32.
10. Salas E, Wilson K, Lazzara E, King H, Augenstein J. Simulation-based training for patient safety: 10 principles that matter. *Patient Safety.* 2008;4(1):3–8.

10

The Joint Commission, National Patient Safety Goals, and Radiology

Making the Grade: A Guide to Achieving Joint Commission Standards

LAURA P. ROSSI, MILDRED M. LEBLANC, KAREN MIGUEL, AND
KATHLEEN A. TOBIN

Regulatory forces are increasingly having an impact on the health care systems in response to public demands for safe, quality care that can be delivered at a reasonable cost. Although standards for quality have always been important to health care organizations, accreditation and certification processes have had a more significant influence on market forces and health care financing in recent years. Various organizations promulgate practice and care standards for health care professionals in different specialties; however, the Joint Commission for the Accreditation of Hospitals remains the preeminent authority for the accreditation of organizations providing inpatient and ambulatory services. The purpose of this chapter is to review those Joint Commission standards that apply to radiology settings and discuss the strategies for addressing these standards in practice.

THE JOINT COMMISSION AND ITS RELATIONSHIP TO RADIOLOGY PRACTICE

The mission of the Joint Commission is "to continuously improve health care for the public, in collaboration with other stakeholders, by evaluating health care organizations and inspiring them to excel in providing safe and effective care of the highest quality and value."[1] Established in 1951, as a result of the collaboration of the American College of Surgeons (ACS) with other professional and hospital associations, the Joint Commission has promulgated standards and conducted accrediting surveys since 1953. The Joint Commission carries out this mission primarily through the development and dissemination of standards, as well as through a survey process that provides a score based on the extent to which standards are found to have been implemented appropriately. Less well known are the Joint Commission processes to address and respond to patient complaints.

The Joint Commission routinely monitors each state's legislative and regulatory activities in order to identify new opportunities for state reliance on the Joint Commission accreditation and certification. Each state varies in terms of its recognition and reliance on the Joint Commission for quality oversight and regulatory authority.

The Joint Commission also has a significant influence on the federal agenda related to health care issues. Because the Joint Commission is considered to have and enforce standards that meet or exceed Medicare requirements, it is recognized by the federal government as having deeming authority to enforce the standards mandated by the Conditions of Participation (CoP) required by the Center for Medicare and Medicaid Services (CMS).[2] The CoP define the eligibility requirements for institutions participating in and receiving payment from CMS programs and include a range of quality standards related to governance, patient rights, infection control, quality assessment, and medical records. Full compliance with these conditions is required for an organization to receive reimbursement for services from Medicare and Medicaid.

Health care organizations seeking to demonstrate their compliance with these requirements may choose to be surveyed either by an accrediting body, such as the Joint Commission, or by a state agency on behalf of CMS. The deemed status relationship involves open and ongoing communications between the Joint Commission and CMS related to the accreditation process for hospitals, home health agencies, hospices, laboratories, nursing homes, ambulatory care centers, and managed care plans. The CMS periodically validates the Joint Commission's survey process, the coordination of receipt and follow-up related to complaints about a health care organization, and the reporting of major changes in an organization's accreditation status under these programs.

When the Social Security Amendments of 1965 were initially passed, hospitals with Joint Commission accreditation were considered to have met the Medicare CoP. In 2008, the Medicare law was changed, requiring the Joint Commission apply to CMS for a continuation of its deeming authority, similar to the application process required of other accrediting bodies. In November 2009, the Joint Commission's deemed status was extended through July 15, 2014.

The CMS now conducts random validation surveys and complaint investigations of organizations accredited by the Joint Commission. The CMS undertakes such unannounced surveys to validate the Joint Commission survey findings, as well as to assess the hospital's compliance with the CoP. Each year, a selected group of hospitals who have undergone a Joint Commission survey will also undergo a CMS validation survey. The Joint Commission must provide CMS with their accreditation decision reports for hospitals selected for validation surveys and any other data as requested. In addition, the Joint Commission must provide CMS with a list of, and any related documentation for, organizations that are denied accreditation or receive a conditional or preliminary denial of accreditation.

Accreditation Requirements Specific to Radiology

The recent Medicare Improvements for Patients and Providers Act (MIPPA) now requires imaging centers be accredited by the Joint Commission, the American College of Radiology, or the Intersocietal Accreditation Commission (IAC) in order to receive Medicare reimbursement for magnetic resonance imaging (MRI), computed tomography (CT), and nuclear medicine by January 1, 2012. Among the new requirements for radiology are the maintenance of a proper level of training and education for physicians and staff, the use of imaging equipment that adheres to strict standards of performance and operates under proper safety guidelines, and the establishment of a quality assurance program that upholds the defined standards.[3,4]

Radiology departments are also obliged to address various specialty-specific regulations and standards, as set by the U.S. Food and Drug Administration (FDA) for mammography and nuclear medicine. Although not directly related to the Joint Commission, we mention them here for completeness in addressing radiology quality and safety standards.

Mammography

In 1992, Congress enacted the Mammography Quality Standards Act of 1992 (MQSA) to ensure that all women have access to quality mammography for early detection of breast cancer. Congress charged the FDA with the task of developing and implementing MQSA regulations. The FDA began the enforcement process for these standards in 1995. Subsequent amendments to the standards were introduced in 1998 and 2004, eventually extending the program until the current time. The FDA's website for the Mammography Program within the Center for Devices and Radiological Health serves as an excellent resource for mammography facility personnel, inspectors, and other interested individuals about the implementation of these standards.

Nuclear Medicine

The U.S. and Nuclear Regulatory Commission's (NRC) has a series of licensing requirements and regulations to guide the operation of diagnostic nuclear medicine facilities. These regulations are focused on the proper use of radioactive materials in medical diagnosis, treatment, and research to assure patient, employee, and general public safety, as well as environmental protection. The NRC provides a means for reporting emergency and nonemergency safety issues 24 hours a day. Serious safety events involving a nuclear facility or radioactive materials should be reported, including accidents involving a nuclear reactor, nuclear fuel facility, or radioactive materials; lost or damaged radioactive materials; or any threat, theft, smuggling, vandalism, or terrorist activity involving a nuclear facility or radioactive materials. (NRC website) The NRC's most recent revision includes regulations related to the medical use of byproduct material. The Society for Nuclear Medicine[5] has published a comprehensive reference that integrates all of the requirements and provides specific guidance related to the approaches for meeting them.

JOINT COMMISSION STANDARDS AND PERFORMANCE CRITERIA

The Joint Commission standards are revised and put forth annually and are organized into several chapters (see Table 10.1). Each chapter has a different level of relevance for various areas of the hospital; however, familiarity with the content of each chapter is warranted to assure that radiology department policies, procedures, and standards are consistent with the Joint Commission standards, as well as with what is happening across the health care system seeking accreditation. For example, the Joint Commission's expectations related to the management of sentinel events are addressed in chapters related to leadership and performance improvement. These chapters include specific standards related to developing a safety culture, and to reporting and investigating adverse events. The performance improvement chapter provides guidance

---

TABLE 10.1 JOINT COMMISSION HOSPITAL ACCREDITATION STANDARDS

Environment of Care (EC)

Emergency Management

Human Resources (HR)

Infection Prevention and Control (IC)

Information Management (IM)

Leadership (LD)

Life Safety (LS)

Medication Management (MM)

Medical Staff (MS)

National Patient Safety Goals (NPSG)

Nursing (NR)

Provision of Care, Treatment, and Services (PC)

Record of Care, Treatment, and Services (RC)

Rights and Responsibilities of the Individual (RI)

Transplant Safety (TS)

Waived Testing (WT)

---

about data collection, priority setting, and evaluation of improvement initiatives.

In addition, the Joint Commission has specific policies related to the types of sentinel events that may require their review. A sentinel event is defined as "an unexpected occurrence involving death or serious physical or psychological injury, or the risk thereof. Serious injury specifically includes loss of limb or function. The phrase 'or the risk thereof' includes any process variation for which a recurrence would carry a significant chance of a serious adverse outcome."[6] Generally, sentinel event reporting to the Joint Commission is considered to be voluntary, although the Joint Commission may request specific reports as they become aware of them. The National Quality Forum has developed a series of definitions for serious reportable events (SREs) that are well accepted across the country. Familiarity with these definitions is advisable for all staff with responsibilities related to quality and safety (see Table 10.2).

In 2002, the National Patient Safety Goals (NPSGs) were established and now undergo a regular review with the established chapters in an effort to assist organizations in establishing a focus on specific areas related to patient safety. The NPSGs are developed by the Patient Safety Advisory Group, a multidisciplinary panel of recognized professionals with expertise in patient safety. This group systematically reviews the literature and feedback from patient care areas to advise the Joint Commission on the available evidence and face validity of specific goals and the ways in which the goals should be prioritized, as well as on the feasibility of implementation. The most current NPSGs and a related plan for implementation at the department level is displayed in Table 10.3.

The Patient Safety Advisory Group also recommends specific issues and actions that are highlighted in the Joint Commission Sentinel Event Alerts. The first alert was published in February 28, 1998, and intended to disseminate information about trends in the occurrence of sentinel events and suggested strategies for their prevention. Since that time, 46 sentinel alert newsletters have been published (see Table 10.4). Although sentinel alerts are not considered to be mandatory standards, they provide important insights into specific safety issues and how they can be addressed. In our institution, sentinel alerts are reviewed by hospital administration and referred to the quality staff in clinical departments with related subject matter expertise

---

TABLE 10.2　NATIONAL QUALITY FORUM SERIOUS REPORTABLE EVENTS (SRE)

---

1. Surgical Events

   Surgery performed on the wrong body part

   Surgery performed on the wrong patient

   Wrong surgical procedure performed on a patient

   Unintended retention of a foreign object in a patient after surgery or other procedure

   Intraoperative or immediately postoperative death in an ASA Class I patient

2. Product or Device Events

   Patient death or serious disability associated with the use of contaminated drugs, devices, or biologics provided by the health care facility

   Patient death or serious disability associated with the use or function of a device in patient care, in which the device is used or functions other than as intended

   Patient death or serious disability associated with intravascular air embolism that occurs while being cared for in a health care facility

3. Patient Protection Events

   Infant discharged to the wrong person

   Patient death or serious disability associated with patient elopement (disappearance)

   Patient suicide, or attempted suicide resulting in serious disability, while being cared for in a health care facility

4. Care Management Events

   Patient death or serious disability associated with a medication error (e.g., errors involving the wrong drug, dose, patient, time, rate, preparation, or route of administration)

   Patient death or serious disability associated with a hemolytic reaction due to the administration of ABO/HLA-incompatible blood or blood products

   Maternal death or serious disability associated with labor or delivery in a low-risk pregnancy while being cared for in a health care facility

   Patient death or serious disability associated with hypoglycemia, the onset of which occurs while the patient is being cared for in a health care facility

   Death or serious disability (kernicterus) associated with failure to identify and treat hyperbilirubinemia in neonates

   Stage 3 or 4 pressure ulcers acquired after admission to a health care facility

   Patient death or serious disability due to spinal manipulative therapy

   Artificial insemination with the wrong donor sperm or donor egg

5. Environmental Events

   Patient death or serious disability associated with an electric shock while being cared for in a health care facility

   Any incident in which a line designated for oxygen or other gas to be delivered to a patient contains the wrong gas or is contaminated by toxic substances

   Patient death or serious disability associated with a burn incurred from any source while being cared for in a health care facility

   Patient death or serious disability associated with a fall while being cared for in a health care facility

   Patient death or serious disability associated with the use of restraints or bed rails while being cared for in a health care facility

6. Criminal Events

   Any instance of care ordered by or provided by someone impersonating a physician, nurse, pharmacist, or other licensed health care provider

   Abduction of a patient of any age

   Sexual assault on a patient within or on the grounds of the health care facility

   Death or significant injury of a patient or staff member resulting from a physical assault (i.e., battery) that occurs within or on the grounds of the health care facility

---

Reprinted with permission from National Quality Forum (NQF).

TABLE 10.3   PROPOSED PLAN FOR ADDRESSING 2011 NATIONAL PATIENT SAFETY GOALS

Patient Safety Goal	Process/Metrics

Goal 1:
Improve the accuracy of patient identification.
A. NPSG.01.01.01: Use at least two patient identifiers when providing care, treatmen;, and services.
B. NPSG.01.03.01: Eliminate transfusion errors related to patient misidentification.
  • Use two identifiers
    Specimen labeling
  • Two persons hanging blood. Use a two-person verification process, or a one-person verification process accompanied by automated identification technology, such as bar coding.
    (See also NPSG.01.01.01, EPs 1 and 2)
	Process
	  • Staff members are educated in the radiology procedure for patient identification using two identifiers as part of their competency based orientation process.
	Metric
	  • Work Instruction sheet (WIS) used for monthly audits by managers (100%)
	Process
	  • Specimen Labeling: Departmental policy has been developed and education provided to staff with specifics on specimen staff labeling.
	Metric
	  • Surveillance rounds observations quarterly

Goal 2:
Improve the effectiveness of communication among caregivers.
• NPSG.02.03.01: Report critical results of tests and diagnostic procedures on a timely basis.
	Process
	  • New process requiring critical test results be communicated in a live person-to-person call within 40 minutes of the study's final reading.
	  • Task force to define reporting criteria for other clinically significant results that are not considered critical test results.
	Metric
	  • A quarterly audit is performed to assure that the reporting of the critical result is documented in the radiologist's report

Goal 3:
Improve the safety of using medications.
• NPSG.03.04.01: Label all medications, medication containers, and other solutions on and off the sterile field in perioperative and other procedural settings.
• NPSG.03.05.01: Reduce the likelihood of patient harm associated with the use of anticoagulant therapy.
	Process
	  • Custom labels are included in the IR procedural trays
	Metric
	  • Quarterly surveillance rounds to capture compliance
	  • Activated clotting time processes are defined by the laboratory point-of-care testing regulations.

- NPSG.03.06.01: Maintain and communicate accurate patient medication information. *N.B. The types of medication information to be collected in non–24-hour settings and different patient circumstances such as radiology should be defined.*

Process
- Modified medication reconciliation is used in: Nuclear Medicine, CT, MRI, and for nonsedation IR cases. Modality-specific forms capture pertinent patient information on current medications.
- Full medication reconciliation is required for invasive procedures being performed under sedation or anesthesia. Radiology follows hospital procedure

Goal 7:

Reduce the risk of health care-associated infections.
- NPSG.07.01.01: Comply with either the current Centers for Disease Control and Prevention (CDC) hand hygiene guidelines or the current World Health Organization (WHO) hand hygiene guidelines.
- NPSG.07.03.01: Implement evidence-based practices to prevent health care-associated infections due to multidrug-resistant organisms in acute care care organizations.
- NPSG.07.04.01: Implement evidence-based practices to prevent central line-associated bloodstream infections.
- NPSG.07.05.01: Implement evidence-based practices for preventing surgical site infections.

Process
- As defined by the Infection Control department, Radiology complies with the regulations surrounding hand hygiene, line placement, precautions and prevention of surgical site infections

Metric
- Departmental monthly hand hygiene audit results are included in the hospital's hand hygiene database.

Goal 15:

The organization identifies safety risks inherent in its patient population.
- NPSG.15.01.01: Identify patients at risk for suicide.

Process
- Screening of inpatients at the point of hospital admission according to the hospital policy. This standard does not apply to outpatients.

Goal - Universal Protocol

The organization meets the expectations of the Universal Protocol.
- UP.01.01.01: Conduct a preprocedure verification process.
- UP.01.02.01: Mark the procedure site.
- UP.01.03.01: A time-out is performed before the procedure.

Process
- Implement hospital-wide policy using form customized to radiology-specific practices including use of imaging for site verification
- Live 4-hour training for all IR staff in Teamwork and Communication

Metric
- Perform monthly audits re: UP performance
- Quarterly recalibration of and observations of team functioning
- Annual safety survey

From National Patient Safety Goals. © The Joint Commission, 2011. Reprinted with permission.

for further analysis and interpretation. Over the course of time, several alerts have referenced safety issues in radiology. Although the relationship of the Joint Commission is generally with the institution within which a radiology department operates, the standards and NPSGs apply to all clinical services and departments within the hospital. For example, many standards related to infection control will apply hospital-wide, whereas specific standards guiding the performance of diagnostic tests and procedures may be more of a priority and concern for radiology staff.

It is beyond the scope of this chapter to discuss all the Joint Commission standards and their application to radiology. The most clinically relevant issues for radiology and common strategies for addressing these areas are discussed here. The intent is to model how each Joint Commission standard should be interpreted, prioritized, and operationalized in practice. This process can be applied to each of the chapters and may be prioritized and acted upon differently depending on the institutions and their specific needs.

IMPLEMENTATION OF STANDARDS AND ONGOING REGULATORY READINESS

Efforts to maintain regulatory readiness requires attention at many levels to assure consistency between institution-wide efforts and department operations. The spirit of the standards set forth by the Joint Commission is intended to assist organizations in demonstrating their capacity for quality and safety, as well as for discovering opportunities for improvement. The accreditation survey process frequently creates a sense of challenge among staff preparing for a visit. Systematic review and purposeful preparation for this process cannot be underestimated and is critical to a positive and successful experience.

The Massachusetts General Hospital (MGH) Imaging Department has a robust infrastructure that is aligned with the hospital leadership to promote the Joint Commission standards (see Figure 10.1). The hospital's Center for Quality and Safety oversees the preparation and implementation of Joint Commission standards for the hospital. At the radiology department level, the quality and safety structure is led by a radiologist in collaboration with two registered nurses, who oversee the review and evaluation of radiology practice across the inpatient and ambulatory sites. Once the standards are

understood, and the department's status in relation to the achievement of these standards has been assessed, radiology leadership has the opportunity to work with members of the hospital leadership to share best practices and identify department challenges that may require support. Frequently, issues such as Universal Protocol have an impact across department lines and require an institution-wide consensus to set standards and policy. In other situations, a centralized hospital-wide leadership group can foster collaborative problem-solving among specific departments that must work together to assure proper patient identification and correct ordering procedures. Institution-wide forums can promote the identification of common themes and sharing of best practices that can benefit more than one department in planning for improvements, as well as create an overall sense of team spirit in maintaining regulatory readiness.

CONTINUOUS JOINT COMMISSION READINESS: THE MASSACHUSETTS GENERAL HOSPITAL EXPERIENCE

A catchy and readily identifiable theme can be helpful in promoting a guide to regulatory readiness among all hospital employees. At MGH, "Excellence Everyday" (EED) is the theme that serves as the foundation for Joint Commission preparation. It defines the central structure responsible for overseeing the process and a decentralized group of "champions" identified from each hospital department and patient care unit to which feedback can be directed. This strategy provides a vehicle for communicating updates and feedback to frontline staff, as well as a means of recognition for successful efforts. In a similar way, department- and unit-based champions serve as a designated group who can assist with the evaluation of improvement initiatives, as well as serve as resources from whom information about area-specific safety concerns can be drawn. This group is also instrumental in providing feedback to the leadership group about the common learning needs that might exist among the staff. Group forums for EED Champions are held on a regular basis and with increasing frequency during the preparation for a Joint Commission survey; these forums provide the opportunity to share challenges and best practices in addressing the standards.

Meeting the standards requires an infrastructure to support monitoring, data analysis, feedback

TABLE 10.4   SENTINEL EVENT ALERTS

Issue 46: A follow-up report on preventing suicide: Focus on medical/surgical units and the emergency department 11/17/2010

Issue 45: Preventing violence in the health care setting 06/03/2010

Issue 44: Preventing maternal death 01/26/2010

Issue 43: Leadership committed to safety 08/27/2009

Issue 42: Safely implementing health information and converging technologies 12/11/2008

Issue 41: Preventing errors relating to commonly used anticoagulants 09/24/2008

Issue 40: Behaviors that undermine a culture of safety 07/09/2008

Issue 39: Preventing pediatric medication errors 04/11/2008

Issue 38: Preventing accidents and injuries in the MRI suite 02/14/2008

Issue 37: Preventing adverse events caused by emergency electrical power system failures 09/06/2006

Issue 36: Tubing misconnections—a persistent and potentially deadly occurrence 04/03/2006

Issue 35: Using medication reconciliation to prevent errors 01/25/2006

Issue 34: Preventing vincristine administration errors 07/14/2005

Issue 33: Patient controlled analgesia by proxy 12/20/2004

Issue 32: Preventing, and managing the impact of, anesthesia awareness 10/06/2004

Issue 31: Revised guidance to help prevent kernicterus 08/31/2004

Issue 30: Preventing infant death and injury during delivery 07/21/2004

Issue 29: Preventing surgical fires 06/24/2003

Issue 28: Infection control-related sentinel events 01/22/2003

Issue 27: Bed rail-related entrapment deaths 09/06/2002

Issue 26: Delays in treatment 06/17/2002

Issue 25: Preventing ventilator-related deaths and injuries 02/26/2002

Issue 24: A follow-up review of wrong site surgery 12/05/2001

Issue 23: Medication errors related to potentially dangerous abbreviations 09/01/2001

Issue 22: Preventing needlestick and sharps injuries 01/08/2001

Issue 21: Medical gas mix-ups 07/01/2001

Issue 20: Exposure to Creutzfeldt-Jakob disease 06/01/2001

Issue 19: Look-alike, sound-alike drug names 05/01/2001

Issue 18: Kernicterus threatens healthy newborns 04/01/2001

Issue 17: Lessons learned: Fires in the home care setting 03/01/2001

Issue 16: Mix-up leads to a medication error 02/27/2001

Issue 15: Infusion pumps: Preventing future adverse events 11/30/2000

Issue 14: Fatal falls: Lessons for the future 07/12/2000

Issue 13: Making an impact on health care 04/21/2000

Issue 12: Operative and post-operative complications: Lessons for the future 02/04/2000

Issue 11: High-alert medications and patient safety 11/19/1999

Issue 10: Blood transfusion errors: Preventing future occurrences 08/30/1999

Issue 9: Infant abductions: Preventing future occurrences 04/09/1999

Issue 8: Preventing restraint deaths 11/18/1998

Issue 7: Inpatient suicides: Recommendations for prevention 11/06/1998

Issue 6: Lessons learned: Wrong site surgery 08/28/1998

Issue 5: Board votes to increase time frame for submitting root cause analysis 07/24/1998

Issue 4: Examples of voluntarily reportable sentinel events 05/11/1998

Issue 3: Board of commissioners affirms support for sentinel event policy 05/01/1998

Issue 2: Board to review modifications to sentinel event procedures 03/20/1998

Issue 1: New publication announcement 02/28/1998

to staff, and ongoing improvement. In our organization, safety report trending and routine auditing provide the major source of data to identify priorities requiring improvement. Aggregated reports for selected issues that cross hospital departments are generated and distributed centrally from the hospital's Center for Quality and Safety. The radiology department leadership must be prepared to demonstrate the evolution of their quality plan, including the rationale for selected project and priority setting. Access to meaningful data that supports the focus and scope of the plan is critically important. Although it is important to demonstrate outcome achievement, it is equally important to demonstrate how ongoing efforts have been tested and evaluated. In general, staff leading quality efforts should initiate a cycle of timely data analysis and feedback to staff that produces an ongoing stream of ideas for improvement that can be tested.

Reason[7] suggested that safety reporting data can provide key information about the types of issues that affect the smooth flow of patients through the system on a daily basis. For such data to be useful in guiding organizational learning, there must be a sense of shared value for reporting among staff and a level of trust that such reports will be handled in a just manner. Members of the organization should have a common understanding of where the lines between acceptable and unacceptable behavior are drawn, with the latter suggesting a possible need for disciplinary action. Creating a culture of safety requires a process for blame-free reporting and trust that safety events will be addressed in a just manner. This calls for the hospital and department leadership to uphold performance standards and policies that define acceptable behavior, while carefully differentiating between human errors and an individual's conscious decisions to violate standard operating procedures.

When staff members report an unexpected event, the leadership's response and management of the event is critical to building a foundation that supports a safety culture and encourages staff to report their concerns regularly without fear of retaliation or unjust disciplinary action. Not only is leadership focus on the event at the time of its occurrence critical, but the degree to which staff at large are involved in an open discussion of safety events is key to establishing a safety culture, assuring continued reporting, and maximizing the organizational learning from the event.

Staff meetings and departmental newsletters can provide effective vehicles for communication and for stimulating dialogue about what is observed at the point of care delivery and how safety issues can be prevented. As staff members become more aware of quality and safety concerns, the conversations about practices, routines, and safety events become more sophisticated. Ongoing leadership development and training for managers requires a concerted effort to encourage an open discussion of challenging issues and facilitate consensus about the direction for improving systems.

All MGH employees are trained to report deviations from what is "ordinarily expected," as well as "near-misses," in the hospital-wide electronic safety reporting system. Reports involving radiology patients and staff are reviewed on a daily basis. Serious injury is rare but carefully investigated, according to criteria established by local and national regulations. More common are routine occurrences that suggest systems or processes that

FIGURE 10.1 Massachusetts General Hospital (MGH) imaging quality and safety structure.

influence a staff member's ability to carry out standard operating procedures. A selected number are de-identified and shared widely with all staff during staff meetings or through a monthly publication called "Safety Moments."

Feedback to staff is considered an essential strategy to facilitate insight and changes in behavior and to impact practice. Mugford, Banfield, and O'Hanlon[8] conducted a comprehensive review of the literature related to this topic and concluded that the greatest influence is likely to result if it is part of an overall strategy targeting decision makers committed to a review of their practice. Furthermore, feedback is more likely to have a direct impact on practice when it is presented close to the time of decision making. Some investigators have suggested that the layout and quantity of information displayed has an impact, although there is no consensus related to this.

At MGH, a mixed approach is used, combining the use of audit and direct feedback. Managers at each radiology site routinely audit the extent to which the standards are being met in their area through routine supervision and auditing of daily operations and practices. Although area managers follow-up on specific audit findings and safety events in their area, the department's quality staff examines these aggregate data for trends and establishes priorities for a focused quality improvement effort across all radiology sites. The radiology quality staff conducts routine surveillance rounds of each modality and off-site facility on a quarterly basis. Surveillance includes a review of the medical record, and interviews and observations of both the clinical and non-clinical staff, as well as of the environment of care. Such rounds provide an opportunity for reinforcing standards and providing real-time feedback to the staff. Follow-up reports with written and mutually agreed upon recommendations are provided to guide managers. Implementation of improvement plans can be derailed by unanticipated hurdles and delays, therefore subsequent rounds are used to track progress and closure on an initiative when possible.

Setting Priorities at the Department Level

From October 1, 2009 through September 30, 2010, a total of 1,871 safety events related to patient care and system issues affecting the radiology department were reported. Of these, 826 (44%) required that radiology quality staff to assume a primary responsibility for follow-up inquiries and to develop a plan of action due to the scope and focus of the reported event. Of these 17, approximately 2%, were considered to be serious events requiring in-depth follow-up and/or intervention. Reports not requiring specific intervention at the time of the event are analyzed in the aggregate to identify evidence suggestive of new signals/trends, as well as of the achievement of improvement goals.

The 826 events occurred in various radiology locations across our system and were classified in the following categories (see Table 10.5). The highest volume of events is in the diagnostic test category, in which the most common specific event is "test not ordered correctly." This represents an important safety risk for patients, as well as a productivity concern. Staff members at all levels in a radiology department provide an important safety net through their conscientious attention to details in identifying and interviewing patients about the test they expect or need to have done. When discrepancies are noted, staff members take steps to contact providers and clarify orders; however, this takes substantial time and impacts the flow of patients over the course of a day. To address this in a systematic fashion, the quality staff identified key information to facilitate identification of areas and providers who are prone to incorrect orders. This information is expected to reveal trends and common errors that could be resolved through a system improvement, such as computerized prompts and decision support aids when orders are entered. Examining the process flow from ordering to completion of tests can also reveal potential learning needs of the staff involved. Collaboration with services in which trends are identified can also be useful in developing meaningful improvements.

The category of Medication/IV Safety largely captures the number of infiltrations and extravasations. Adverse drug reactions (ADRs) are known complications of many radiology procedures; however, these events are routinely reported and monitored by the pharmacy, along with other ADRs reported from other clinical areas. On the other hand, Care Coordination includes "failure in system of patient care," which includes a myriad of factors that are tracked to detect trends related to scheduling and communication among patients and providers.

Analysis of safety reporting data can also provide key information related to the achievement of NPSGs. Monthly reports suggest that the major goals of concern for the radiology department are related to communication among caregivers, patient identification, Universal Protocol, and patient falls.

TABLE 10.5   SAFETY REPORTING BY CATEGORY AND VOLUME (OCTOBER 2009
THROUGH SEPTEMBER 30, 2010)

	Volume of Safety Events Responsible for Follow-up/Investigation, by General Event Type				
	Q1FY10	Q2FY10	Q3FY10	Q4FY10	Total
Total	202	285	218	121	826
Adverse drug reaction	23	37	19	9	88
Airway management	4	3	3	3	13
Blood/blood product	0	2	0	0	2
Care/service coordination	30	38	31	11	110
Diagnosis/treatment	5	6	11	5	27
Diagnostic test	54	113	58	28	253
Employee general incident	0	0	0	1	1
Environment	1	3	3	5	12
Fall	10	14	8	6	38
ID/documentation/consent	11	16	13	4	44
Infection control	1	2	0	1	4
Lab specimen/test	0	1	1	4	6
Line/tube	13	8	5	2	28
Medication/IV safety	33	28	36	20	117
Risk register entry	1	0	1	1	3
Safety/security/conduct	5	9	15	9	38
Skin/tissue	8	2	5	4	19
Surgery/procedure	3	3	9	8	23

The respective opportunities for improvement inform the development of a quality and safety plan for the department (see Table 10.3). For example, events identified as issues involving communication among caregivers have resulted in a new process and standard for defining and reporting critical test results. The plan related to patient identification and Universal Protocol is largely attached to the implementation of hospital-wide policies. The increasing numbers of interventional radiology procedures makes these goals an essential priority for which hospital administration provides support to assure consistency with other procedural areas, such as the operating room and cardiac catheterization lab. Routine audits provide essential surveillance data related to the implementation of these important policies.

Patient falls represent a special challenge in the radiology environment. An increasing numbers of outpatients who are elderly and have some chronic illness or physical incapacity experience a high risk of falling when they arrive for a radiology procedure. The literature suggests a variety of risk assessment and surveillance strategies to address the issue of falls.[9] Although these do not exclusively pertain to the radiology practice, this is considered a concern for radiology departments and requires purposeful evaluation and planning. Following a series of falls, our department implemented a falls risk assessment that led to a reduction in the number of injuries resulting from falls and an increased proportion of falls involving preventative assistance to the floor over the last 2 years. The risk assessment involves a brief three-question survey that is completed by each outpatient upon arrival to the department. Patients are asked if they feel weak or dizzy, if they have a history of falls, and if they use an assistive device to ambulate. A "yes" response to any of those factors is identified as a fall risk, and the patient's ID band and exam requisition are marked with a yellow sticker.

This alert was intended to facilitate closer monitoring and more timely assistance by the staff. Initially, this improvement effort did not produce a significant reduction in the number of falls reported, although a decrease in the number of severe injuries from falls was observed. An ongoing review of falls suggested some new factors be considered in a revised and updated risk assessment. A task force was formed to consider a plan for the next iteration of improvements. This group incorporated the expertise of both geriatric and child life specialists, in addition to the EED Champions' feedback from modality-specific environmental surveillance rounds. As a result, the task force recommended a plan that included attention to staff education needs, new patient assessment factors, specific preventive interventions, and documentation in the medical record.

Frequently, a department has other priorities for quality and safety that are not specifically called for in the standards but that provide useful examples of how the department views and addresses patient and staff concerns. For example, team training was a departmental priority in the context of improving communication, particularly during interventional procedures when the Universal Protocol was required. Strategies for conducting briefings and debriefings, including closed-loop communication and appropriate assertion (see Chapter 9), can be useful in encouraging staff members to raise questions without fear of reproach or retaliation. This requires a substantial commitment on the part of leadership in various areas of the department to provide resources for training, as well as for ongoing monitoring of behavior and attitudinal change. For further guidance in this area, refer to Chapter 9.

Another example is related to our department's concern about ergonomics and its impact on the access of disabled patients, as well as the ability of staff to safely move patients; this issue led to a focused effort by the Quality and Safety Council. This involved a formal evaluation to assure compliance with the Americans with Disability Act (ADA), following which transfer devices such as ceiling lifts and handrails were obtained and placed in areas with identified needs. Consultation with occupational health experts prompted a survey of the staff and an evaluation of the environment in each modality to determine necessary improvements to prevent staff and/or patient injury. In particular, a review of the repetitive arm motion required in ultrasound and related staff injuries revealed a need for new tables that were more appropriately positioned.

Maintaining Readiness for the Survey Process

Assuring regulatory readiness is definitely a team sport. One might say that the outcome of the survey process is similar to that of an athletic team's playing season, for which the off-season training effort is so critically important. The challenge is to create a process that assures the sustainability of standards that are currently met, as well as movement forward with ongoing improvements. In recent years, the Joint Commission has established a more rigorous process involving an unannounced visit, a tracer methodology, and public reporting of survey findings. In this new process, specific types of patients are selected and their hospital stay is traced. In tracing the patient's stay, Joint Commission surveyors examine the extent to which any standards applicable to the patient's care are met. For example, a patient with an acute stroke might be selected, and the care of this patient is then "traced" from the emergency department, through radiology, and into an inpatient unit or intensive care unit. The tracer methodology involves face-to-face interviews with staff caring for patients, as well as with the patients and family members themselves. Mock surveys are conducted on a regular basis and have been particularly helpful in preparing and guiding staff. Anecdotal experience suggests that the more attention paid to the implementation of the standards within day-to-day operations, the more likely staff are to be aware of the issues, and thus, prepared for the questions that can be posed by surveyors.

There is some variation in the length and duration of the survey process across institutions and settings depending on the size, type, and complexity of the institution. An institution's prior survey findings and corrective actions may also influence the process. Since the visit is unannounced, an institutional and department plan for greeting surveyors and engaging them in a positive dialogue about quality efforts is critical. Qualified tour guides should be identified in advance and available to assist surveyors in getting around the institution and accessing the necessary information. These guides, while frequently knowledgeable members of the institution's leadership staff, must also be prepared to refrain from providing surveyors with information unless asked. The focus is generally on allowing the staff to provide the answers and more accurately demonstrate the application of the standards at the point of contact with patients. A plan should be available for how and where the surveyors will be met, so that department managers are prepared in a timely manner to make necessary staff available during operating hours.

When the survey is completed, an exit interview with the institution's leadership staff is held to review preliminary findings. The survey team prepares a formal, consensus report that specifically describes areas that require correction and further action before accreditation status can be granted. The Joint Commission process for accreditation is thought to have an important impact on efforts to reduce error and improve safety, although the specific impact on measures of patient safety is unclear. [10,11] Public reporting of Joint Commission survey results has only recently been instituted, and its full impact on an institution's performance improvement efforts remains to be seen.

CHALLENGES AHEAD

In the acute setting, radiologists find themselves engaged in an increasing number of acute and emergency interventions requiring timely imaging prior to treatment and prompt intervention, such as in the area of acute stroke management. The demands for quick readings as a prerequisite for treatment and other production pressures have the potential to affect the accuracy and timeliness of reporting results. Ultimately, this has the potential to impact the flow and clinical course of patients as they move through the system.

The role of the radiologist is expanding beyond that of the diagnostician to that of interventionalist in some situations that require clarity about the responsibilities for preprocedure evaluations, consultation, and follow-up. The standard operating routines for radiology will need to keep pace with regulatory requirements as more invasive procedures, previously done only in the operating room, are now extended into the radiology setting.

Additional challenges present with an increasing volume of sicker patients undergoing radiology procedures on an outpatient basis.[12] The demands for some triage and assessment of patients at the time of scheduling and upon entry into the department are likely to be necessary to prevent untoward events. For example, knowledge of assistive devices, the need for interpreters, and prior comorbid conditions will be needed to prevent falls, miscommunication, and adverse reactions.

CONCLUSION

Meaningful integration of quality and safety efforts within the departments' day-to-day operations is critical to develop and reinforce processes that support a culture of quality and safety. This requires a framework that supports reporting concerns and must include regularly scheduled and ongoing opportunities for education and feedback about standards and performance measures.

Preparing for a Joint Commission survey requires a focused effort to interpret and implement standards within each department. Department efforts should be well coordinated with other institutional efforts to address standards, to assure consistency and avoid duplication. Staff at all levels, including physicians and particularly those in leadership positions, should routinely be involved in a review of the department's regulatory readiness and plans for improvement.

REFERENCES

1. The Joint Commission, 2011. Accessed at: www.jointcommission.org
2. Menendez JB. The impetus for legislation revoking the Joint Commission's deemed status as a Medicare accrediting agency. *JONA'S Healthcare Law, Ethics, and Regulation.* 2010;12(3):69–76.
3. HCPro. 2009 MPFS offers imaging implications. *Radiology Administrator's Compliance & Reimbursement Insider.* October 2008;5(10):1–7.
4. Wiley G. MIPPA accreditation countdown: ACR, IAC, or Joint Commission? *Radiology Business Journal.* September 2010. Accessed at: http://www.intersocietal.org/iac/news/pressmedia.htm
5. Siegel JA. *Guide for diagnostic nuclear medicine.* Reston: Society of Nuclear Medicine, 2001.
6. The Joint Commission. *Hospital Accreditation Standards.* Oakbrook Terrace: The Joint Commission, 2009.
7. Reason J. *Managing the risks of organizational accidents.* Aldershot: Ashgate Publishing, 1997.
8. Mugford M, Banfield P, O'Hanlon M. Effects of feedback of information on clinical practice: A review. *BMJ.* 1991;303(17):398–402.
9. Fox NM, Vanderford V. Preventing falls in radiology. *Radiol Tech.* 2000;72(1): 63–66.
10. Devers KJ, Pham HH, Liu G. What is driving hospitals' patient safety efforts. *Health Affairs.* 2004;23(2):103–115.
11. Miller MR, Pronovost P, Donithan M, Zeger S, Zhan C, Morlock L, Meyer GS. Relationship between performance measurement and accreditation: Implications for quality of care and patient safety. *Am J Med Care Qual.* 2005;20(5):239–52.
12. Hammons TF, Piland NF, Small S, Hatlie MJ, Burstin HR. Ambulatory patient safety: What we know and need to know. *J Ambulat Care Manage.* 2003;26(1): 63–82.

11

Errors in Radiology

Why We Have to Classify Radiology Errors and How We Do It

JONATHAN B. KRUSKAL AND OLGA R. BROOK

The road to wisdom? Well, it's plain And simple to express: Err And err And err again But less And less And less.

—PIET HEIN

In this chapter, we describe latent and active failures in diagnostic radiology and illustrate an error classification system based on the expertise of psychologists and the Joint Commission.

To err is human, yet society demands that medical professionals be errorless, perfect. For radiologists, being held to such standards is particularly challenging due to the rapidly advancing science of image acquisition, the art of digital image interpretation in an era of multiplanar availability, and our reliance on referring physicians to provide us with appropriate clinical information. Furthermore, the Joint Commission now requires performance evaluation processes for all physicians, as well as the development of comprehensive error detection systems that incorporate root cause analyses for all sentinel events[1] and will hopefully permit identification of opportunities for minimizing the incidence and impact of our errors. In addition, the classification of medical errors is absolutely essential for their management. The classification identifies the weak link in the radiological process and then highlights the underlying processes that have predisposed to the error occurrence. The error classification system also provides a framework for an adequate allocation of resources when planning a change in the radiology process. We should not fail to seize an opportunity for improvement when an error occurs.[2]

Diagnostic errors are often unrecognized or unreported and may be associated with high morbidity.[3,4] The science of measuring such errors

is underdeveloped,[5,6] and the implementation of a peer review process in diagnostic radiology is one method to respond to this need. The wide spectrum of interrelated contributing factors makes the classification of medical errors difficult. This has led to the development of many systems, few of which are widely accepted or simple to use. Nevertheless, it is important for radiologists to have a user-friendly classification of errors that provides a conceptual framework within which contributing factors can be identified and strategies implemented to reduce or eliminate them.

In this chapter, we describe factors that contribute to radiology errors, and we illustrate a classification system, based on the expertise of psychologists as well as the Joint Commission,[1] which has been valuable for managing errors in our practice.

DEFINITIONS OF ERRORS AND ADVERSE EVENTS

An *error* is a deviation from the expected norm, regardless of whether it results in any harm. It is frequently merely a symptom of a flawed underlying process that can be remedied. An *adverse event* is an occurrence with harmful consequences to a person receiving care. Thus, driving through a red light is an error regardless of whether an accident ensues. In the case of an accident, the vehicle may be adversely affected or even destroyed, but the driver may experience no injury at all. In medical terms, this would be considered a *near-miss event*, a subset of the adverse event, in which the patient fortunately sustained no harm (which could have resulted from the error) or one in which timely steps were taken to prevent harm from occurring. Adverse events thus can be categorized along a spectrum ranging from a near-miss experience to loss of life.[7]

COMMON MYTHS CONCERNING HUMAN ERRORS AND THEIR MANAGEMENT

James Reason has highlighted a number of myths pertaining to errors.[8] A common misconception is that errors are intrinsically "bad." Yet, there may be a positive aspect to an error or seemingly poor outcome, such as Alexander Fleming's discovery of penicillin in a discarded Petri dish contaminated with a mold that turned out to be *Penicillium*. Moreover, detection and analysis of errors will guide interventions that improve future performance, minimize the incidence or impact of subsequent errors, and prevent more serious errors from occurring.

Individuals who make errors are not inherently less experienced, more careless, or less well-trained than those who do not. Indeed, the Institute of Medicine (IOM) reported that 90% of medical errors result from systemic problems rather than individual factors.[9] Errors will continue to occur unless the initial error is properly addressed and potential contributing factors from the individuals involved are resolved. Returning to the motor vehicle analogy, the driver either may have intended to speed through the red light or there was a fault in one of the vehicle's operating systems. The contributing factor—reckless driving or faulty equipment—must be addressed to prevent further, perhaps even graver, errors. Consequently, error detection systems must not only be able to detect such behavior, but must provide structures for managing and providing appropriate remediation for such acts.

Another common belief is that errors are random occurrences. Although this may initially appear to be true, errors frequently reflect longstanding substandard practices (often recognized in retrospect, but not acted upon or detected at the time of occurrence), coupled with latent system failures that caused the errors to occur. For example, failure to perform a time-out prior to a procedure may lead to anaphylaxis in a patient with an allergy to latex. The error is clear—use of latex gloves—however, the important contributing factor and substandard practice—failure to perform the time-out—may be missed and not addressed. Similarly, another myth is that it is easier to change the behavior of an individual than the process itself; instead, substandard practices are more amenable to change than are habits and human behavior. By performing timeout script a standard practice before any procedure, involving all staff, providing a time out structured list will make greater impact than trying to make one physician errorless.

Although many physicians believe that errors are rare in medical practice, this has been dispelled by data in the IOM report, *To Err Is Human*.[9] This misconception about the rarity of errors may be due to the lack of error detection or reporting systems, or to the paucity of published and scientifically rigorous data. Many physicians are reluctant to expose their errors due to the fear of litigation, even though studies have shown that open discussion of errors does not increase the likelihood of a lawsuit[10] and may even significantly decrease the number of claims and overall annual litigation expenses.[11] Therefore, when a medical error occurs, the best way to decrease the risk of litigation is to provide full disclosure to the patient.[12] The culture of full disclosure ideally should be taught as a part of medical school curriculum, and appropriate facilities should be available throughout medical training and hospital practice. Independent services are also emerging that facilitate the difficult process of disclosure.[13]

More than 50 years ago, Garland[14] observed that experienced radiologists miss about 10% of abnormalities on chest radiographs. Two decades later, a similar error rate was confirmed in the interpretation of chest radiographs,[15] bone studies, gastrointestinal series,[16] and special procedures.[17] Retrospective reviews have indicated that a large number of breast[18] and lung[19,20] carcinomas could be seen on reevaluation of prior examinations that had been incorrectly interpreted as normal. Among the numerous ways suggested to reduce the occurrence of radiologic errors are appropriate clinical history, comparison with previous imaging studies, double interpretation, and a lower volume of cases per unit time.[21] The most recent data from the RADPEER Quality Assurance Program of the American College of Radiology reports a disagreement rate between initial interpretations and overreads of about 3%, which varied substantially among specific imaging facilities.[22]

System- or process-related failures are very frequent,[23] but in most cases, fortunately, do not

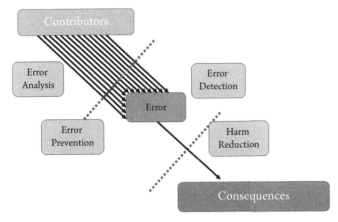

FIGURE 11.1 Complex analysis of an error. When analyzing an error, multiple facets should be addressed: error detection systems, contributors to the error with prevention systems, consequences of an error, and harm reduction measures.

cause harm. Although there may be numerous predisposing factors and near-miss events, only an accidental alignment of a series of latent errors may result in a real adverse event. Consequently, it is essential to establish error detection systems to detect those seemingly minor or near-miss occurrences before they inevitably lead to an adverse event (Figure 11.1).

GENERAL APPROACHES FOR CLASSIFYING ERRORS

Why Classify Errors?

Classifying errors permits the development and implementation of detection and analysis systems to minimize the occurrence of errors or the degree of their resulting harm. Furthermore, the Joint Commission requires all accredited institutions to have error detection systems, to establish proactive rather than reactive processes for managing errors, and to perform a root cause analysis for all sentinel events. Here, we describe a practical radiology-specific classification system that takes into account our varied modes of practices and imaging technologies.

Classification Systems

Although several error classification systems have been developed for use in medicine,[7,24,25,26] none was customized for diagnostic radiology. Most concentrate more on human error than on system processes. Renfrew et al.[27] proposed a scheme that focuses on perceptual errors, classifying them as related to complacency, faulty reasoning, lack of knowledge, underreading, poor communication, false-negative causes, and complications. Even though human error in radiology is highly important, this classification does not take into account many predisposing

factors, such as management issues, understaffing, ergonomics, and work volume.

Reason's Swiss Cheese Model of Medical Error

In 1990, British psychologist James Reason introduced risk analysis and management systems to human error[23] and described two basic approaches.[28] The *person approach* assigns blame for an error to an individual. The *system approach* acknowledges that humans make mistakes and errors are to be expected. However, it views these as a consequence and instead focuses on identification of an underlying systems failure. Therefore, numerous safeguards, defenses, and barriers must be implemented to prevent an error from occurring and to reduce its impact, with stress placed on seeking possible or latent failures within the system.

Highly technical, complicated systems have multiple levels of defenses (physical, electronic, personal, procedural, and administrative) against errors (Figure 11.2). Unfortunately, none of these defenses functions perfectly. Holes in the defenses are considered *latent failures*, but no single one will result in an adverse event. A human error will usually not cause an adverse event if all safeguards are in place. Examples of such safeguards in interventional radiology include the preprocedure time-out, checking the consent form and ensuring that this matches the request, verifying the patient identification, checking for allergies, and being aware of the patient's coagulation status. National Patient Safety Goals have been developed in part to plug latent failure holes (Figure 11.3). The existence of multiple holes in a system, coupled with the high likelihood of some active failure, makes a medical error virtually inevitable.

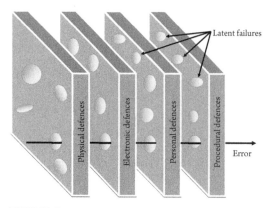

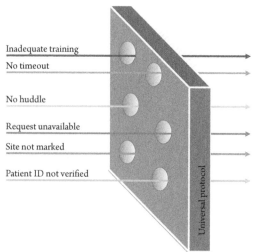

FIGURE 11.2 Reason's Swiss cheese model of latent and active contributors. A series of safeguards (slices of Swiss cheese) exist in the system or should be introduced to minimize the chance of an error occurring. Within each layer of defense, there are latent factors (holes in the cheese) that predispose to errors. A single latent failure is unlikely to result in an error. However, when properly aligned and in the presence of an active failure, the error is likely to be manifest. Therefore, when introducing steps to prevent errors, attention should not focus only on human failures, but also on introducing safeguards to prevent latent failures from aligning.

Figure 11.4 illustrates an example of successful implementation of defenses (Figure 11.4) and an active failure (Figure 11.5)—a junior resident missing a subtle finding on a computed tomography (CT) scan. In a properly functioning system with all barriers intact, an attending radiologist will discover the problem during a formal readout. Thus, the resident's "failure" will not result in a manifest error. System factors that may have been in place to prevent such an error include a policy requiring that an attending reviews all cases, a culture in which residents preview all cases prior to readout, a protocol that optimizes depiction of subtle findings, a distraction-free and ergonomic reading environment, and a requirement that ordering physicians provide relevant clinical information to facilitate interpretation. Nevertheless, even if both the resident and attending miss the finding, there may be no adverse consequence to the patient.

FIGURE 11.3 Introduction of a specific safeguard: the Universal Protocol. The Joint Commission introduced the Universal Protocol to improve compliance with National Patient Safety Goals. This requires preprocedure verification (including confirmation of patient identity [ID]), marking the site and side of a proposed procedure, and performing a preprocedure time-out to verify the nature of the procedure— steps that ensure that many latent contributors can be prevented from resulting in overt errors. In this example, when adherence to the Universal Protocol is present, all but one factor on the left are prevented. The only exception is inadequate training, which is considered a latent organizational failure. For this reason, more than a single safeguard is usually required to ensure adequate prevention of an error.

surrounded by active and latent contributors (Figure 11.6), all of which interact with each other directly or indirectly, like pieces of a puzzle. This approach considers issues specific to contemporary diagnostic radiology, such as communication of abnormal results, technical contributors, and patient factors. It facilitates root cause analysis of adverse events by emphasizing the detection and management of all underlying latent errors. The focus on potential systems errors, rather than on human issues, makes it more likely that involved radiologists will participate in the investigation and implementation of change.

CLASSIFYING RADIOLOGICAL ERRORS

We approach errors using a system in which the patient is at the center of all errors, closely

Contributors and Causes

For a medical error to be manifest at the clinical level, there must be a convergence of active (human) factors, facilitated by a combination of predisposing

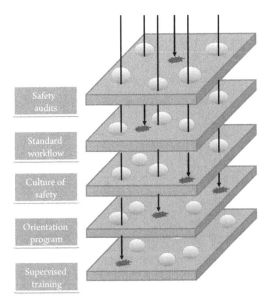

FIGURE 11.4 Safeguards and defenses. A series of five safeguards and defenses have been introduced (listed to the left of the figure) to minimize the chances of latent errors aligning to produce an error. By undertaking regular safety audits, introducing standardized workflow in procedure areas, instilling a culture of safety throughout a department, training and orienting all new hires, and ensuring that all procedures are properly supervised, the effects or complications relating to latent contributors residing within a system can be minimized and even prevented.

(latent) failures. Therefore, the goal of error analysis and proactive safety systems is to identify dormant latent failures before they enable an active error to occur. Rather than blaming individuals, it is very important to analyze near-misses or adverse events to highlight predisposing systems factors. Unlike active failures, which may be difficult to foresee, latent conditions can be identified and treated before an adverse event occurs—a proactive approach, rather than reactive risk management.[23,28]

Latent Failures

Latent failures represent predisposing conditions that enable an error to occur (Table 11.1). These errors may lie dormant for a prolonged period, remaining undetected due to an absence of surveillance, absent root cause analysis processes, or lack of a culture that stresses patient safety. Staff may be aware of such conditions but be unwilling to report them; if latent failures are not properly reported, they may not be adequately addressed by those in management positions.

Latent factors can be considered technical or systems-related (Figure 11.7). *Technical* latent factors include those relating to equipment and engineering (construction and design flaws, ease of use, safety issues); departmental design; workflow design; hardware, software, and equipment failures; picture archiving and communication system (PACS) and the integrity of the digital environment; materials and material management (contrast agents, devices); protocols, policies, rules, and regulations; and routine maintenance of all systems involved. Technical issues are particularly relevant in a radiology department, where they can be minimized by routine equipment maintenance and adherence to safety guidelines, which should be clear and easy to implement lest they cause potentially dangerous ambiguity.

System latent factors include staffing, duty hours, ergonomics, the departmental culture of safety and leadership training, supervision, and departmental governance. System errors occur due to failures of higher-level decision makers, managers, and maintenance personnel. Although remote from the error itself, both in space and time, system failures generally have substantial influence.

Communication Failures

Poor communication lies at the heart of many medical errors.[24] Although most commonly considered as failure to transmit critical or urgent, important, incidental or unexpected results, communication errors encompass a far broader scope in daily practice. They include incomplete or inaccurate information, questionable consent and disclosure processes, inadequate documentation, and failure to perform or ineffective performance of the preprocedure time-out. Communication failures need not be limited to verbal interchange. They may be in written or electronic format, with incorrect or inaccurate radiology reports representing a large source of communication errors. Absent communication, or failure to communicate correctly, can be an equally egregious error. A poorly performed study due to failure to communicate instructions to a deaf or non-English speaking patient may result in acquisition of diagnostically inadequate images. Rather than representing any fault of the patient, this should be considered a failure of appropriate communication and the image acquisition processes.

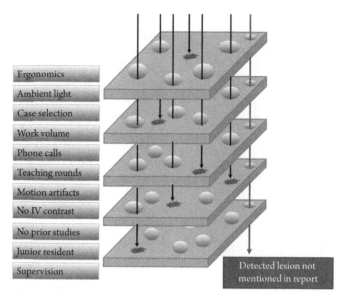

FIGURE 11.5 Insufficient safeguards. If insufficient safeguards or defenses exist, an error is likely to ultimately occur. In this example, despite the demonstration that some defenses effectively minimize or prevent errors from occurring, a dangerous situation will arise when a series of latent contributors align. Here, a combination of poor ergonomics and ambient light, frequent telephone disturbances, working with an inexperienced resident, and other factors listed to the left of the figure align to enable an error to occur. A lesion detected during a readout session was not mentioned in the report, possibly with important consequences for the patient's care. Such contributing factors should be identified through the root cause analysis process and steps put in place to prevent this from occurring again.

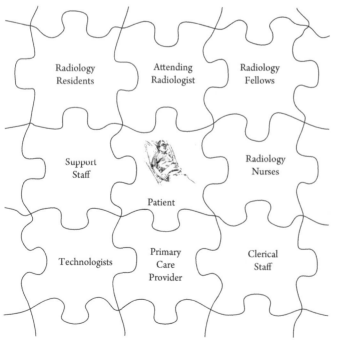

FIGURE 11.6 The patient and practitioners. The patient experience in a radiology department is impacted by a number of practitioners, all of whom are linked directly and indirectly, like pieces of a puzzle. Any break in this puzzle will impact the experience and outcome. Such breaks can occur due to latent factors or from active human errors (knowledge-based, skill-based, violations of rules and guidelines, or any combinations of these). Root cause analysis of human contributors should therefore consider all practitioners involved in patient care, not just the individual most closely associated with error occurrence.

TABLE 11.1   COMPARATIVE
DEFINITION OF LATENT VERSUS
ACTIVE FAILURE

Latent Failure	Active Failure
Preconditions for unsafe acts	Unsafe acts that are directly linked to an accident
Less apparent	Readily apparent
System related	Person related
Dormant for a long time	Felt immediately
Predispose to error	"Sharp end"

Communication errors can be categorized into three classes: errors of documentation, communication of inaccurate or incomplete information, and failures in the communication loop.

Documentation

With the increasing complexity and frequency of imaging studies, it is essential that each step in the process be clearly documented and verified. Many errors occur through inaccurate, inadequate, or insufficient documentation. The widespread deployment of electronic medical records may provide systemic checks to minimize errors from occurring. Nevertheless, the electronic systems have to be made user-friendly and convenient to use. An appropriate orientation to the electronic systems also aids in preventing new trainees from making errors due to lack of experience.

Inaccurate or incomplete information most frequently involves failure of the ordering physician (or scheduling office) to provide essential clinical data, such as a history of previous allergy to contrast material. However, this term also can reflect failure of radiologists to adequately explain their thoughts and opinions in the official radiology report. For example, describing a distended, edematous gallbladder in the report, without concluding that these findings may represent acute cholecystitis in the appropriate clinical setting, represents an error of inaccurate/incomplete information.

Communication Loop Failures

The interaction among referring physicians, scheduling services, technologists, and radiologists forms a radiology communication loop (Figure 11.8) that is highly susceptible to error and must be subjected to continuous scrutiny and

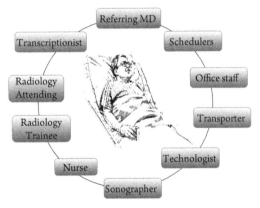

FIGURE 11.8 The radiology communication loop. A series of practitioners participate in the care of a patient visiting a radiology department. Each interlinked person plays an essential role in ensuring a satisfying and successful outcome. From the referring physicians' interaction with schedulers, to the patients' interaction with office and welcoming staff, including extenders such as valet parking attendants, transport technologists, imaging technologists, nurses, and physicians, each link in this chain communicates with others, and each is equally important to maintain integrity of the chain. Any break may have serious consequences. As an example, should a breakdown occur during the transcription phase, results may not be received or incorrect results may be transferred. Such breaks can be prevented by the insertion of appropriate safeguards (see Figure 11.9).

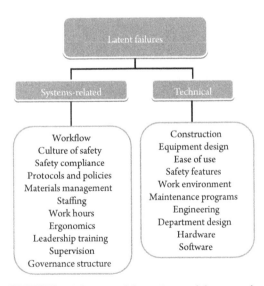

FIGURE 11.7 Latent failures. Latent failures can be categorized as systems-related or technical. This figure illustrates examples of such latent failures that may occur in an imaging environment.

documentation. The infrastructure for convenient and Health Insurance Portability and Accountability Act (HIPAA)-compliant communications channels among all parties involved should be developed, including phone, beeper, or electronic communications.

Our department has developed various strategies to safeguard the radiology communication loop (Figure 11.9). An electronic protocol and schedule ensures timely and exact protocol details; additionally, a time-out consisting of double verification of patient identity and the type of procedure is made prior to performing every examination. Technologists change the status of each study on PACS after verifying its arrival and completion. An automatic update of the study list ensures that each case is promptly read by a radiologist. In addition, we have developed a convenient electronic notification system to convey significant but not emergent findings to the referring physician.[29] Finally, follow-up multidisciplinary conferences provide important feedback to radiologists, including quality improvement.

Active Failures or Human Errors

Active failures or human errors include procedural complications or mistakes and diagnostic misses and misinterpretations. However, they may occur due to patient factors or involve one or more practitioners involved in the study, as illustrated in Figure 11.5, as well as be secondary to latent contributors, such as scheduling the incorrect examination. An active failure is usually person-related, and its consequences are immediately felt by the system (Table 11.1). Active failures may be ascribed to human failures (more specifically, failure of execution of a task, inadequate planning, or behavior-related failures), patient-based failures, and external failures.

Failures of execution,[30] which refer to procedures that are adequately planned but incorrectly performed, may be divided into slips and lapses. A *slip* is a problem of attention, such as omission of safety procedures, misordering, mistiming, and intrusion. Similarly, an abnormality may "slip" out of our attention when we are distracted during the readout. Safeguards against such distractions include an ergonomically designed workplace, properly positioned ambient light, prohibitions on phone calls, and a quiet environment. *Lapses* are related to memory and include the omission of planned items. For example, a radiologist may properly identify an abnormality but simply forget to include it in the report. One technique for eliminating such lapses is structured reporting.

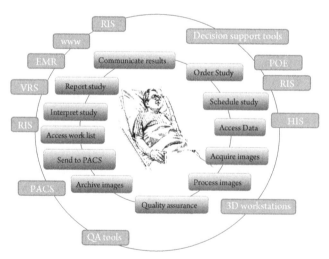

FIGURE 11.9 The radiology imaging chain. Encircling the patient is an interlinked series of events that occur from the time a study is ordered until the results are communicated to the ordering provider. At each stage of this process, latent or active failures may result in breakage of a link, which in turn can be prevented by inserting appropriate safeguards. In this example, the recent introduction of a series of digital safeguards illustrates how conventional steps of the imaging chain can be "protected." Such digital safeguards range from provider order entry (POE) systems, radiology information systems (RIS) and hospital information systems (HIS), standard tools of quality assurance (QA), picture archive and communication systems (PACS), voice recognition systems (VRS), the electronic medical record (EMR), and the internet via the world wide web (www).

Mistakes or *failure of intention* can be rule-based or knowledge-based. *Rule-based mistakes* occur in familiar surroundings, when the radiologist misapplies a good rule due to failure to notice contraindications. For example, it is a good rule that a young female patient with right lower quadrant abdominal pain, nausea, leukocytosis, and a dilated appendix with surrounding fat stranding most likely has acute appendicitis. However, failure to notice an enlarged ovary with a large cyst and deviation of the uterus in this patient would cause the radiologists to miss an ovarian torsion with secondary changes in the appendix. Another source of error is to apply a poor rule. An example is reviewing only axial and reconstructed CT images, but not the scout view, which might be the only image on which an abnormality can be detected. *Knowledge-based mistakes*, which reflect a failure to know what one is doing or to not realize that what one is doing is incorrect, occur in unusual and novel situations, when one "fixates" on a particular hunch or hypothesis. To prevent this error, it is important to leave options open and avoid the "satisfaction of search," as well as not neglect contradictory evidence or suggestions, even when they come from support personnel or subordinates.

Human errors may be deliberate and intentional, usually associated with motivational problems (low morale, poor supervision, or perceived lack of concern). They may be categorized as negligent behavior, recklessness, and intentional rule violations, all of which we have previously addressed.[31] Methods for determining accountability and culpability have been previously illustrated.[32] The most important question is whether the physician passes the so-called "substitution test"—whether peers or the "reasonable radiologist" would have acted in a similar manner. If not, it is necessary to assess the contributions from training, supervision, and experience. Any perceived deficiencies that are identified require remedial training with ongoing monitoring and supervision. It may even be appropriate to refer the physician to a disciplinary body or to adjust his or her duties.

External Causes

Some mistakes and failures are inevitable and beyond radiologist or organizational control and responsibility. Examples include electrical failures, magnet quenches, CT malfunctions, and a flood or earthquake. Defensive strategies and safeguards can diminish the impact of errors arising from external causes. For example, there should be an alternative, readily available source of electricity (such as a power generator) in case of an electrical failure. Manual air bags should be available in the radiology department to care for ventilated patients. Policies defining contingency plans must be established in case essential pieces of equipment do not function properly.

Most errors have more than one contributing failure. With medical mistakes, an active human error is readily apparent, whereas latent system and technical failures may not be readily identified. The most important part of any investigation is to unearth all predisposing latent failures, for without them an active failure alone will usually not result in a medical error.

The patient and nonradiology personnel can also contribute to medical errors. Patient factors that may contribute or predispose to an error include physical attributes (weight, body habitus, presence of hardware, language barriers), comorbidities, allergies, age, lack of prior experience with similar procedure or study, and an inability to comprehend or follow instructions.

CONSEQUENCES OF AN ERROR

Consequences of radiological errors can impact the patient and his or her immediate circle, as well as other imaging staff who were directly involved and members of the medical team. There also are more global consequences of error that may affect the practice, the institution, the profession, the procedure, or even the imaging study.

The Patient

The impact of an error on a patient includes physical, psychological, and financial components. The initial response must be to make every effort to treat the patient and to minimize the degree of physical harm. Once the patient is stable, the severity and permanence of the physical harm should be assessed. Similarly, there should be measurement of the psychological effect of an error on the patient, which often is greater than physical impact. In most situations, the patient should be offered appropriate care free of charge, including a follow-up plan to manage any resulting harm and referrals to appropriate specialists.

Staff and Other Customers

The impact on the radiologist involved in an error, especially the psychological impact, may be devastating. It also can affect all personnel involved in patient care (technologists, nurses, physicians, and the institution). The "second victim" of the medical error refers to the physician and other members of the medical team involved in the adverse event.[33] At times, the psychological impact may be so grave as to disable all future professional activity. When necessary, counseling should be provided to all personnel impacted emotionally by a serious event.

Global Considerations

Nonmedical impacts of the error include legal, social, and economic effects on both the patient and the system. These issues frequently contribute to the reluctance of the medical profession to disclose medical errors. However, full disclosure about an adverse event and measures taken to diminish the likelihood of its recurrence may significantly aid in the patient–radiologist relationship, improve the patient's well-being, and decrease the likelihood of litigation.[10,11,12]

STRATEGIES FOR MANAGING AND MINIMIZING DIAGNOSTIC ERRORS

An important goal of error analysis is to create processes aimed at reducing or preventing the occurrence of errors and minimizing the degree of harm. The development of an effective system for detecting and appropriately managing errors is essential to substantially ameliorate their consequences. At this stage, the error analysis process identifies contributing factors to enable the implementation of concrete steps to prevent such errors from occurring in the future. Active and comprehensive management of errors and adverse events requires ongoing surveillance processes.[32]

Minimizing the incidence and extent of active errors requires reliable reporting mechanisms coupled with policies that define mechanisms of case review and management. Educational programs, morbidity and mortality meetings, and a comprehensive and respected root cause analysis process are also essential components of this comprehensive approach.

CONCLUSION

In summary, we propose an error classification system for diagnostic radiology that includes personnel, communication, cause, and impact characteristics. Rather than focusing the investigation on blaming individuals for active failures, the primary effort should be to discover latent system failures that can be remedied at a departmental level. This will result in decreasing the likelihood of future errors and diminishing their adverse impact.

REFERENCES

1. Joint Commission. Accepted: New and revised hospital elements of performance related to CMS application process. *Jt Comm Perspect.* 2009;29(10):16–19.
2. Gunderman RB, Burdick EJ. Error and opportunity. *AJR Am J Roentgenol.* 2007;188:901–3.
3. Croskerry P. Clinical cognition and diagnostic error: Applications of a dual process model of reasoning. *Adv Health Sci Educ Theory Pract.* 2009;14 (Suppl 1): 27–35.
4. Croskerry P. A universal model of diagnostic reasoning. *Acad Med.* 2009;84(8):1022–28.
5. Newman-Toker DE, Pronovost PJ. Diagnostic errors: The next frontier for patient safety. *JAMA.* 2009;301(10):1060–62.
6. Newman-Toker DE, Camargo CA Jr, Hsieh YH, Pelletier AJ, Edlow JA. Disconnect between charted vestibular diagnoses and emergency department management decisions: A cross-sectional analysis from a nationally representative sample. *Acad Emerg Med.* 2009;16(10):970–97.
7. Chang A, Schyve PM, Croteau RJ, O'Leary DS, Loeb JM. The JCAHO patient safety event taxonomy: A standardized terminology and classification schema for near misses and adverse events. *Int J Qual Health Care.* 2005;17:95–105.
8. Reason J. Beyond the organisational accident: The need for "error wisdom" on the frontline. *Qual Saf Health Care.* 2004;13(Suppl 2):ii28–33.
9. Kohn LT, Corrigan JM, Donaldson MS, eds. *To err is human: Building a safer health system.* Washington, D.C.: National Academy Press, 2000.
10. Stewart RM, Corneille MG, Johnston J, Geoghegan K, Myers JG, Dent DL, et al. Transparent and open discussion of errors does not increase malpractice risk in trauma patients. *Ann Surg.* 2006;243:645–9.
11. Clinton HR, Obama B. Making patient safety the centerpiece of medical liability reform. *N Engl J Med.* 2006;354:2205–2208.
12. Feinmann J. You can say sorry. *BMJ.* 2009;339:b3057. doi:10.1136/bmj.40018.430972.4D.
13. Medically Induced Trauma Support Services. Accessed at: www.mitss.com
14. Garland LH. Studies on the accuracy of diagnostic procedures. *AJR.* 1959; 82:25–38.
15. Herman PG, Gerson DE, Hessel SJ, et al. Disagreement in chest roentgen interpretation. *Chest.* 1975;68:278–82.
16. Brady AP, Stevenson GW, Stevenson I. Colorectal cancer overlooked at barium enema examination and colonoscopy: A continuing perceptual problem. *Radiology.* 1994;192: 373–8.

17. Lehr JL, Lodwick GS, Farrell C, et al. Direct measurement of the effect of film miniaturization on diagnostic accuracy. *Radiology.* 1976;1881:257–63.

18. Warren RM, Duffy SW. Comparison of single reading with double reading of mammograms, and change in effectiveness with experience. *Br J Radiol.* 1995 Sep;68(813):958–62.

19. Austin JHM, Romney BM, Goldsmith LS. Missed bronchogenic carcinoma: Radiographic findings in 27 patients with a potentially resectable lesion evident in retrospect. *Radiology.* 1992;182: 115–23.

20. Forrest JV, Friedman PJ. Radiologic errors in patients with lung cancer. *West J Med.* 1981;134:485–90.

21. Berlin L. Accuracy of diagnostic procedures: Has it improved over the past five decades? *AJR Am J Roentgenol.* 2007 May;188(5):1173–8.

22. Borgstede JP, Lewis RS, Bhargavan M, Sunshine JH. RADPEER Quality Assurance Program: A multifacility study of interpretive disagreement rates. *J Am Coll Radiol.* 2004;1:59–65.

23. Reason J. The contribution of latent human failures to the breakdown of complex systems. *Philos Trans R Soc Lond B Biol Sci.* 1990;327:475–84.

24. Woolf SH, Kuzel AJ, Dovey SM, Phillips RL Jr. A string of mistakes: The importance of cascade analysis in describing, counting, and preventing medical errors. *Ann Fam Med.* 2004;2:317–26.

25. Vincent C, Taylor-Adams S, Stanhope N. Framework for analysing risk and safety in clinical medicine. *BMJ.* 1998;316:1154–7.

26. Vincent C. Understanding and responding to adverse events. *N Engl J Med.* 2003;348:1051–6.

27. Renfrew DL, Franken EA Jr, Berbaum KS, Weigelt FH, Abu-Yousef MM. Error in radiology: Classification and lessons in 182 cases presented at a problem case conference. *Radiology.* 1992;183:145–50.

28. Reason J. Human error: Models and management. *BMJ.* 2000;320:768–70.

29. Eisenberg RL, Yamada K, Yam CS, Spirn PW, Kruskal JB. Electronic messaging system for communicating significant, but not emergent, abnormal imaging results. *Radiology* (in press).

30. Reason J. Safety in the operating theatre – Part 2: Human error and organisational failure. *Qual Saf Health Care.* 2005;14(1):56–60.

31. Kruskal JB, Anderson S, Yam CS, Sosna J. Strategies for establishing a comprehensive quality and performance improvement program in a radiology department. *Radiographics.* 2009;29(2):315–29.

32. Kruskal JB, Siewert B, Anderson SW, Eisenberg RL, Sosna J. Managing an acute adverse event in a radiology department. *Radiographics.* 2008;28(5):1237–50.

33. Wu AW. Medical error: The second victim. The doctor who makes the mistake needs help too. *BMJ.* 2000;320(7237):726–7.

12

The Role of the Apology in Radiology

STEPHEN R. BAKER

The resolution of disputes, misunderstandings, and offenses, whether they be emotional, physical, legal, or medical, is a continual project in social relations. A mark of any civilization is the way in which wrongs done to an individual or group, either actual or only perceived, are dealt with so that violence is excluded and some measure of closure is reached to the satisfaction of all parties.

One means by which harmony can be restored after an error is committed or a harm is endured is through the use of apology. Offered correctly and with acceptance by the offended, an apology can sometimes have an almost magical effect on relations between the two parties, allowing the air to clear once again. No wonder it is a desired expectation in many instances, functioning as a fitting resolution to an event caused by the hurtful action of one person against another.

In this era of omnipresent public scrutiny, with information and judgments instantaneously rendered and then disseminated and often manipulated by the media, any well-known individual who, by utterance, gesture, or deed, appears to violate tacitly accepted codes of conduct or morality and thereby inflicts pain and suffering against another, is seemingly obliged to apologize, often in a public forum. Nearly always, such so-called admissions of guilt are self-serving accounts that fail to set things right. Yet, in each instance, they reaffirm the societal notion that apology is a fitting emotional restorative that, when employed, can obviate the persistence of

the antagonism even though the physical disruption cannot be undone.

The noun "apology" also has a distinct diplomatic definition. The relations between nations, once strained and sometimes persistently so, often provide opportunities for political leaders to issue statements of apology as representative of their regret for some violation of human rights, even if it occurred long ago. Here, too, for some festering international disagreements, an apology is seen as a necessary expedient to be pronounced before relations can improve. Yet this definition, pertinent enough for current events and historical deliminations, is irrelevant for the application of apology to the relationship between caregiver and patient. Instead, we should focus only on the private use of this rhetorical expedient where its effectiveness can be assessed.

Therefore, an analysis of the value of its inclusion in the verbal repertoire of a physician is germane to the enhancement of quality. The reasons for its formal incorporation are manifold, reflecting the differing and sometimes divergent sensibilities of the various stakeholders in health care delivery. For patient advocates, apology can be considered a humane impulse crucial to the maintenance of dignity of the ill and injured and the preservation of empathy by doctors for sufferers. For some physicians, apology is seen as another means of avoiding tort actions against them, given the presumption that its rendering will be viewed by the harmed patient as a compelling gesture provided by a compassionate professional who inadvertently erred. Therefore, they hold to the notion that by apologizing they need not be punished, even though they may have damaged a patient or his or her family member. And, risk management officers may consider apology to be a money-saving maneuver because the accepters of an apology are perceived to be less apt to become litigants in a suit against one of the health care workers they represent.

Hence, it is important to acknowledge the increasing implementation of apology in hospital procedures and policies, as well to highlight both its benefits and the illusions about its benefits, each of which has promoted its administrative acceptance. Apology has also been interwoven into recent legislation, passed by a majority of states in an effort to manage malpractice costs. The implication of these initiatives for medicine in general and radiology in particular deserve discussion as well.

Yet, before one uncritically embraces apology as a panacea for what might ail the doctor–patient relationship, it is helpful to understand what apology is and what it is not, how it is presented artfully and how it is botched, and when it is likely to be successful and when it is apt to fail. To delve into these questions, one must define the term clearly and consider its constituent elements.

THE ELEMENTS OF APOLOGY

The earliest recorded definition of apology in the Western literature was published in 1544, when it was characterized as a frank acknowledgment of the commission of an offense with an expression of regret for it, by way of reparation. Yet, about the same time, another term, similar in spelling and directed to the same concern, was also defined. That term is *apologia*.[1] It refers to an oral or written defense with no accompanying repentance or effort of restitution. It is crucial to distinguish the two. Apologia entails an account, often qualified by contingencies, whereas apology requires at the very least an acknowledgment of wrongdoing without qualification by the particularities of circumstance.

By contemporary definition (New Universal Unabridged Dictionary), an apology is defined as a frank, regretful admission that one has done wrong.[2] On the other hand, an apologia is an explanation for a course of action or belief, without suggestion of guilt or error.[3] The word "but" often is part of an apologia, but could never be included in an apology.

For example the assertion, "I caused harm by my action, but I was not myself today" is an attempt to explain an untoward action, yet it avoids the placement of guilt by the offender on himself. Hence, it is perfectly in accord with the meaning of an apologia. In fact, most so-called public apologies are really just apologias, as they are accounts of how external imperatives have made someone do or say the wrong thing.

A true apology, in contrast, avoids the deflection of responsibility away from the offender. It must include a congeries of elements that conform to the rubric "It was not justified even if justifiable." Hence, an apology places responsibility squarely upon the perpetrator and not on external influences that compelled him or her to perform the offense.

Two contemporary commentators have parsed the elements of apology, each providing a checklist, if you will, of the constituent components of an apologetic utterance. In 1971, Erving Goffman, a sociologist, described nine components of an apology, all of which are essential for its empathetic legitimacy.

- An expression of embarrassment or disgrace
- Clarification that one knows the error
- Articulated sympathy for the imposition of the sanction
- A verbal rejection of the wrong
- A vilification of the self
- An espousal of the right way
- Avowal to pursue that right way
- The performance of penance
- A resolution to make restitution[4]

The last element, may not necessarily involve the exchange of some material good but a declaration to never do it again could suffice. Yet, Goffman's lengthy roster does not reference the confession of sorrow or regret. A slightly different characterization of apology has been offered by contemporary Canadian philosopher Tavuchis, who maintained that sorrow and regret are essential to an apology. He reduced an apology to four essentials:

- Acknowledgment of the offense through speech
- Admission of fault for the violation inducing harm
- Expression of genuine sorrow or remorse
- Provision of an explicit offer of restitution or a promise to reform[5]

Like many precepts seemingly newly discovered and announced, these two "dissections" of apology are not entirely novel in the history of thought. Much the same notions were described by Maimonides in the 12th century, as he focused on the necessity of articulating expressions of regret and restitution after an injury was committed.

What, then, is the utility of a true apology? Is it merely a form of oral recapitulation of the record of harm—in essence, no more than an ineffectual announcement with little substantive import for conciliation? Or, can it be something more transformative, a statement purposive and compelling in intent and exculpatory in expectation? If so, does it then have tactical implications for the doctor–patient dialog and, consequently, for the potential remedies that the patient and/or his family will pursue in response to the damages that have been experienced by them?

According to Disraeli, "Apologies only account for that which they do not alter." If we accept that insight in factual terms and also in affective terms, at least at the time of the commission of the injury or neglect, then Disraeli is absolutely correct. But if we consider that the task of an apology is to resolve conflict even in the face of an admitted offense, then Disraeli's view is incorrect. Because, as Tavuchis informs us, there is a peculiar and perhaps ineffable power in an accepted apology for both the offender and the affected.[5] While it reiterates the reality of the event, it supersedes it as well. This paradoxical effect is bound up with the uncertainty of its acceptance, even when the apology is brought forth with earnestness and passion and when it encompasses all the aforementioned elements that distinguish it.

THE PSYCHOLOGY OF APOLOGY

For the offender, an apology often requires substantial psychological and emotional effort. It is painful in anticipation, and haunted by the fear that it may fail to be embraced by the offended. Furthermore, despite the rhetorical skills that the harmer could possess, he or she knows that any such presentation, no matter how eloquently rendered, will not necessarily pass muster. Even though it may be expertly narrated, the genuineness of the confession will be discerned to be distinct from the smoothness of its delivery. It is just as possible to be effective for those halt of speech as it is for the most accomplished orator, if all the elements of apology are communicated forthrightly and are perceived in that light by the victim.

Therefore, true apologies cannot be transmitted by e-mail or any other form of communication having only a unidirectional flow of information. An apology only becomes authentic and transformative in the context of a conversation. Moreover, an apology is not likely to be successful when there are many witnesses to it. In that setting, the offender can impress the audience with his or her thespian qualities, which may at the same time place the offended party in the position of having to measure his response in accord with his opinion about how a bystander might view it. An apology is a performance, but it is for the harmed to hear and consider, not for a crowd to accept or reject. What is more, an apology will not be meaningful if the cultural differences between the two parties are so wide that the value system of each has limited points in common. And, rendered in person, the heartfeltness of a true apology can be supported by appropriate gestures or gesticulations of contrition by the offender that further affirm the intent and sincerity of the verbal confession and pledge that are crucial to its acknowledgment by the offended.

After an apology is tendered, the initiative then shifts to the injured party to grant a measure of forgiveness to complete the moral transaction that forms the essence of the apology ritual. The word "ritual" is apt here because an apology is more than a procedural exercise. Rather, it is actually an encounter that could be assigned within the broader scope of a "religious" experience because a true apology, genuinely accepted, is in essence a "transfiguration" of regard. It immediately renders social concord, to the immense relief of both, often leading to the forging of a closer and enduring bond between the two as together they have participated in a shared experience in which each has gained insight into the deeply felt sensibilities of the other.

Once an apology is accepted, the negotiation for restitution is generally a genial one, because both the offender and the offended have accepted the principle of exchange of something, either goods themselves or promises of better behavior. Now the focus is on the specifics of the transaction, rather than on the establishment and articulation of its appropriateness.

APOLOGIES AND DISCLOSURE

In the past few years, there has been increasing interest and activity in full disclosure and the use of the apology in medicine, manifested by the implementation of a wide range of initiatives that integrate apology into medical care, making it a component of the acknowledgment of error for a range of clinical encounters, including emergency diagnosis and treatment. The reasons for such attention are several and complementary.

Modern, technologically intensive, and depersonalized health delivery has engendered the unintended consequence of deflecting concern from the notion of the whole patient, one who is a sapient and sensitized participant in his care. As a result, this neglect has widened opportunities for error. But, in the past decade, there has been a renewed interest in the documentation and reporting of medical mistakes. The collective consciousness was stimulated, perhaps, by the Institute of Medicine's "manifesto," *To Err Is Human*, in 1999.[6] Adverse event reporting has now become a required metric. As a result, the recording of error has become a nationwide expectation, and the rules of disclosure have been codified by state laws, federal mandates, and regulatory demands.

An increasingly accurate and comprehensive delineation of error is sought by patient advocates as a desideratum of good medicine. Nonetheless, with respect to a lay opinion, a consensus has not emerged about the extent of the recognition and the repercussions of adverse occurrences. Although all will attest generally to the ill effects of error with regard to the assignment of responsibility and punishment, for many, their specific opinions about it are seemingly contradictory, depending upon how questions are posed to them. For example, one survey substantiated the presumed notion that patients want information to prevent another error from occurring and, most importantly, have a right to know about what has happened to them. Yet, that did not translate into confirming perceptions about the terms of physicians' accountability. In this investigation, nearly all the former patients queried would want to be told of an untoward outcome and how it happened, and nearly everyone would like the doctor to say he was sincerely sorry. Yet, 63% of the same respondents would want the doctor to be reprimanded, 38% want the responsible physician to be placed on probation or have his license rescinded, and 65% claimed that they have the right to expect that doctors will not make errors.[7]

Moreover, most would want an apology, but the timing and terms of it could influence their desire to seek redress through legal action. Nearly 50% maintained that, if an apology was given promptly and with appropriate sentiment, they would have avoided initiating a malpractice suit.[8] Hence, as patients are now becoming more engaged in their care, and the justification for disclosure is more explicit and transparent, then apology, at least as a defensive maneuver, is being touted as a protective device for physicians, either to avoid a tort action entirely or to change the terms of engagement between doctor and patient to include on-demand accountings of damage and response. It is claimed that such a transaction, post apology, could eventuate in a lower payout. This would replace the usual situation today of an apology-absent scenario in which the characters are lawyers, the setting is a courtroom, the discussion is testimony, and, if fault is decided through verdict or settlement, payment is made and malpractice premiums for the defendant are ultimately increased.

An explicit, clearly delineated "true" apology, at least as a defensive maneuver, could be reckoned as a protective device for physicians. It could function as an intention to avoid a lawsuit because, by providing a measure of relief through a verbally expressed empathy, it could transform a confrontation into a congenial arrangement between doctor and patient. And, by offering apology as an initiative even before harm is felt or even if it does not occur at all, some maintain that mutual respect could be strengthened even more. This aggressive approach—an up-front apology—has been deployed for many years and with success at the Lexington VA hospital complex, where errors are admitted to the patient even if no untoward result has or will occur. And, offers of restitution are made that can vary from cash awards to help in seeking satisfaction through administrative assistance.[1]

According to a Lexington VA spokesman, rancor is reduced and cooperativeness and the restoration of satisfaction are enhanced. Yet, although such a program has merit and serves the particular needs of the patient population at that institution, its widespread application is doubtful. For one thing, other groups of patients elsewhere may be more sophisticated and litigious. The dialog with patients at the Lexington VA is conducted by specifically trained administrators. The physicians who committed the error are not permitted to speak with patients because of the apprehension by the director of the hospital that such doctors are too emotionally affected to be appropriate apologizers. Yet, this protocol will probably not gain general acceptance as it may not be enthusiastically appreciated by patients elsewhere, who are perhaps more suspicious of the motives behind administrative apologies. What is more, apology by proxy is patronizing to caregivers as well. In fact, it should be considered only as an expedient because it violates the canons of apology. As both Tavuchis and Goffman maintain, an apology can only be meaningful when those who caused the harm plead for forgiveness for it.

A true apology uttered by the physician who committed the error can be allied to risk management stratagems to reduce malpractice payments. It is not necessary to have a substitute stand in for the doctors. Rewards can be lessened for malpractice actions if admission of guilt is readily made, transferring the impetus to the assessment of damages rather than strenuously resisting the ascertainment and acknowledgment of blame in cases where the offense is obvious. Such an initiative has reduced aggregate legal costs at the University of Michigan and at other institutions.[1] There, malpractice cases in which there is no error are vigorously defended, whereas in those instances in which clear error has occurred, prompt admission is given and reparation is made without the delay occasioned by protracted legal wrangling.

And yet, overall, the linkage between apologies and the avoidance of malpractice suits is problematic in practice even if they are seen to be causally related phenomena in prospect. The tendency to sue by the plaintiff or plaintiff's relative depends on the severity of the injury or its treatment complications initially, upon the residual effects of either, upon the cost of treatment immediately and long term, and upon the extent and perception of disability. It also depends on the age of the patient. For example, permanent harm to a child may be less likely to result in acceptance of forgiveness by the parents than would temporary discomfort or illness experienced by an adult. Furthermore, after death or paralysis, a loved one may not be persuaded from seeking legal redress even if the apology is sincere, the remorse genuine, and the restitution substantial.

Nonetheless, in the last 10 years, mindful that errors will occur whenever physicians in an attempt to heal instead do harm, lawmakers have increasingly inserted themselves into medical practice by formulating and enacting legislation that provides some relief to physicians. These statutes have sought to protect physicians from the seemingly unbridled claims of patients. Their foundation has been the widespread perception that numerous settlements and judgments, some of them supposedly enormously generous, have expanded to an immoderate degree the costs of health care in general and the burden to doctors, particularly. That such risks to individual

caregivers do exist is true, but across the country, the extent of malpractice awards as a percentage of medical care is small and is probably dwarfed by the accumulating costs of superfluous care, which is rife in diagnostic imaging, manifested by the widespread overutilization of radiologic procedures.

The anguish of physicians and the economic concern of the electorate have stimulated the passage of these laws, which have been designed to "immunize," in varying degrees of comprehensiveness, defendants who have taken the occasion to apologize to their patients. These statutes can be assigned to one of two groups.[9]

The "I am sorry you were harmed" laws, which by 2008 had been passed in 26 states, assert that expressions of commiseration regret, condolence, sorrow, and the like are not admissible in court (Table 12.1).[9-33] The Texas statute passed in 1999 has been the model for legislation of similar ilk approved in many other states.[29] In essence, these laws mandate that empathetic gestures in speech

TABLE 12.1   "I AM SORRY YOU WERE HARMED" LAWS*

State	Year Passed
California	2000
Delaware	2006
Florida	2002
Georgia	2005
Hawaii	2007
Illinois	2005
Louisiana	2005
Maine	2005
Maryland	2004
Massachusetts	1986
Missouri	2005
Montana	2005
North Carolina	2004
Ohio	2004
Oklahoma	2008
Oregon	2003
South Dakota	2005
Tennessee	2003
Texas	1999
Vermont	2005
Virginia	2005
Washington	2002
West Virginia	2005
Wyoming	2004

*Apology in which fault or liability is admissible in a civil action.

are protected. But, on the other hand, admissions of wrongdoing are not protected and these, then, are admissible. The language of the Virginia statute summarizes this distinction:

> In any civil action brought by an alleged victim of an unanticipated outcome of health care, or in any arbitration or medical malpractice review panel proceeding related to such civil action the portion of statements, writings, affirmations, benevolent conduct, or benevolent gestures expressing sympathy, or general sense of benevolence, which are made by a health care provider or an agent of a health care provider to the patient, a relative of the patient, or a representative of the patient shall be inadmissible as evidence of an admission of liability or as evidence of an admission against interest. A statement of fault that in part of or in addition to any of the above shall not be made inadmissible by this section.

In contrast, the "I am sorry I harmed you" laws go one step further.[31] With them, admissions of fault of liability, of responsibility for harm are also not admissible in court. The Colorado statute, one of five such laws (the others were passed in Arizona, Connecticut, New Hampshire, and South Carolina), is typical[34–38] (Table 12.2):

> In any civil action brought by an alleged victim of an unanticipated outcome of medical care, or in any arbitration proceeding related to such civil action, any and all statements, affirmations, gestures, or conduct expressing apology, fault, sympathy, commiseration, condolence, compassion, or a general sense of benevolence which are made by a health care provider or an employee of a health care provider to the alleged victim, a relative of the alleged victim,

or a representative of the alleged victim and which relates to the discomfort, pain, suffering, injury, or death of the alleged victim as the result of the unanticipated outcome of medical care shall be inadmissible as evidence of an admission of liability or as evidence of an admission against interest.[35]

Yet, by these legal codifications, are physicians sheltered? And if they are, then will patients be less able to seek and receive compensation for the damages they have been subjected to as a consequence? And what about the restorative effect of an apology when the legal, if not also the moral cost of such an admission is obviated by protection from penalty. Can there really be a true apology when, within the context of an "I am sorry I harmed you" law, a "shield" is provided? Moreover, what is the point of an apology anyway, if some of the risks attended on its rejection are trivialized by safety from mandated payment transfer? Does the apology lose its empathic power when one of its adverse consequences is minimized or removed?

These questions are provocative, but even today the data are limited and conclusions for the maintenance of the doctor–patient relationship in general and its influence on the likelihood and extent of settlements and verdict research are unknown.

Perhaps it is likely that answers to these questions will emerge over time, at least with respect to primary caregivers. But, for radiologists, what about the implications for apology in general and the effect of laws related to it? The text of the apology statutes focuses directly on the content of the dialog between the physician who is apt to be the primary caregiver and the patient. Certainly not in most instances is the radiologist in on the conversation. Accordingly, the referring physician can apologize, but the radiologist has little opportunity to do so unless he or she has performed an interventional procedure. It is more likely for the radiologist, often distant in space and frequently separated in time from the patient, to be the odd man or woman out in any prospective apology colloquy. Having little occasion to profess before the patient either "I am sorry your were harmed," or "I am sorry I harmed you," the radiologist is more apt not to be forgiven but rather to be made a scapegoat. Therefore, I sense that both types of laws are a trap for radiologists, be they in the emergency reading room, in a clinic, in a hospital, or with even more susceptibility providing teleradiology interpretations from afar.

TABLE 12.2   "I AM SORRY THAT I HARMED YOU" LAWS*

State	Year Passed
Arizona	2005
Colorado	2003
Connecticut	2005
New Hampshire	2005
South Carolina	2006

*Apology in which fault or liability is inadmissible in a civil suit action.

CONCLUSION

Apologies can be miraculous in their resolution of discord. They are an essential component of compassionate medical care. Yet, what is not emphasized is that they are nonetheless risky even when some measure of protection is provided by either type of malpractice statute. And referring physicians, while they are our colleagues, are also not necessarily our allies when an affective apology can reduce their liability.

The only way we can ameliorate the enlargement of risk is to develop a closer connection with our referrers and patients, as we have done for breast imaging and interventional radiology. As our practices are currently constituted, we cannot really enjoy a close relationship with our patients. Hence, we must collaborate more closely with the clinicians we serve. To do this requires enhancement of opportunities to establish interactive dialogs in real time with them, rather than to just continue the unidirectional transmission of information, often with articulation by us and clinician reception separated in time. The only way to make us more intimate collaborators in effect and in spirit is to replace communication with consultation, to interact face to face, not just by computer to computer. Only by becoming real consultants in time and place will we gain a measure of comfort that our referrers will include us in the apology when we err in interpretation or when we both err in transmitting imaging test results.

REFERENCES

1. Taft L. Apology and medical mistake: Opportunity or foil? *Ann Health Law.* 2005;14:55–94.
2. *Webster's New Universal Unabridged Dictionary.* New York: Barnes & Noble, 1996.
3. Berlin L. Will saying "I'm sorry" prevent a malpractice lawsuit? *AJR Am Roentgenol.* 2006;187:10–5.
4. Goffman E. *Relations in public.* New York: Harper&Row; 1971:95–187.
5. Tavuchis N. *Mea culpa: a sociology of apology and reconciliation.* Stanford, CA: Stanford University Press; 1991:15–44.
6. Kohn LT, Corrigan JM, Donaldson MS, eds. *To err is human: Building safer health system.* Washington DC: National Academy Press, 2000.
7. Witman AB, Park DM, Hardin SB. How do patients want physicians to handle mistakes? A surgery of internal medicine patients in an academic setting. *Arch Intern Med.* 1996;156:2565–9.
8. Mazor KM, Simon SR, Yood RA, et al. Health plan members' views about disclosure of medical errors. *Am Intern Med.* 2004;140:409–18.
9. Sack K. Doctors say "I'm sorry" before "see you in court." *The New York Times.* May 18, 2008A1.
10. Tex Civ Prac & Rem Code Ann § 18.061.
11. Cal Evid Code §1160.
12. Del Code §4318.
13. Fla Stat Ann §90.4026.
14. Ga Code Ann §24-3-37.1.
15. Hawaii Stat Ann §626-1.
16. 110 Ill Comp Stat Ann 5/8-1901.
17. La Rev Stat Ann §13:3715.5.
18. Me Rev Stat Ann Title 24, §2907.
19. Md Code Ann, Cts & Jud Proc §10-920.
20. Mass Gen Laws ch 233, §23D.
21. Mo Ann Stat §538.229.
22. Mont Code Ann §26-1-814.
23. NC Gen Stat Ann §8C-1, Rule 413.
24. Ohio Rev Code Ann §2317.43.
25. Okla Stat Title 63, §1-1708.1H.
26. Ore Rev Stat Ann §677.082.
27. SD Code Ann §19-12-14.
28. Tenn R Evid Rule 409.1.
29. Tex Civ Prac & Rem Code Ann §18061.
30. Vt Stat Ann §1912.
31. Va Code Ann §8.01-52.1.
32. Wash Rev Code Ann §5.66.010.
33. W Va Code Ann §55-7-11a.
34. Ariz Rev Stat Ann §12-2605.
35. Colo Rev Stat Ann §13-25-135.
36. Conn Gen Stat Ann §52-184D.
37. NH Rev Stat Ann §507-E:4.
38. SC Code Ann §19-1-190.

13

Universal Protocols and the Checklist

RATHACHAI KAEWLAI AND HANI H. ABUJUDEH

A wrong-site surgery or procedure generally defines those surgical procedures performed either on the wrong body side, wrong body part, or wrong patient, or a wrong surgical procedure performed on a patient.[1] Policy-makers have coined the term "never events" to describe these shocking medical errors.[2,3] Media coverage of wrong-site surgical events has been steadily increasing in the past 15 years, indicating increasing public interest in and concern for this particular area of safety in surgical care delivery.[4] In January 2003, the Joint Commission made elimination of wrong-site surgery/procedure one of its National Patient Safety Goals (NPSGs). In 2004, the Universal Protocol (UP) was implemented for all accredited facilities as a means of preventing wrong-site surgery.[5] Wrong-site surgeries or procedures occur across surgical specialties, including radiology. Therefore, it is critical for radiologists to understand the concepts and methods used in the proactive prevention of wrong-site surgeries/procedures. In this chapter, we discuss the magnitude of error in a wrong-site surgery/procedure, the implications of a wrong-site surgery/procedure, and how to prevent its occurrence through the use of the Joint Commission's UP.

MAGNITUDE AND CAUSES OF WRONG-SITE SURGERY/PROCEDURE

Wrong-site surgery/procedure is, overall, a rare event. However, it is the most common sentinel event reported to the Joint Commission, accounting for 13.5% of 6,428 total reports as of September 30, 2009.[3] In 2008, the Joint Commission received approximately 115 reported cases of wrong-site surgeries, which has markedly increased compared with data gathered before 1999, when reported cases were less than 30 per year.[5] It is believed that wrong-site surgery is underreported, and may occur 1,300–2,700 times per year[6] or in approximately 1 in 50,000–100,000 procedures performed in the United States.[7] This type of error is more common in certain fields associated with bilaterality, such as orthopedic surgery.[7] Wrong-side errors occur more frequently than wrong patient or wrong procedure errors.[1] Although its incidence is very low, wrong-site surgery can significantly impact patients' lives and quality of life, attract media attention, and undermine public confidence in the health care system and care providers.

Since these are rare events, most personnel in the operating room environment—including physicians—have never experienced one or may not believe it could happen to them.[8]

It is believed that wrong-site surgery usually stems from a lack or breakdown of systematic verification of the site of surgery, patient identification,[2] and communication.[1] Underlying factors contributing to wrong-site surgery are numerous and may include high workload, multiple team members, diffusion of authority, poor teamwork, poor leadership, lack of accountability, problem in team communication, poor handoff of operating room personnel, wrong processes performed, inappropriate workflow, unawareness of operating policies, and other issues.[1,6,8,9] These factors may be categorized as related to organizational culture, interpersonal dynamics, or hierarchical structures in the operating room. In addition to these factors as contributors to wrong-site surgery, compliance with safety protocols by persons who perform procedures is another important element. Recent research by the Pennsylvania Patient Safety Authority found that the most common source of errors leading to wrong-site surgery was a lack of surgeon compliance and adherence to the safety protocol.[8] A lack of empathy within the health care organization was also noted as a factor contributing to wrong-site surgery. Many of these factors are amenable to organizational cultural and policy changes.

EFFORTS TO PREVENT WRONG-SITE SURGERY/ PROCEDURE

To effectively prevent a wrong-site surgery/ procedure, it is important to view the problem as stemming from errors in process, not as errors caused by individuals. In many cases, the physicians involved in wrong-site surgeries or procedures are held culpable and punished. For example, in 1994, an orthopedic surgeon practicing in Florida was charged with performing an extremity amputation on the wrong side and was blamed as the cause of the error.[10] But because several processes occur before the actual performance of a surgery or procedure, the causes of mishap can be numerous, and attempts to fix those causes can potentially help to reduce wrong-site surgery/procedure errors.

In 1994, the Canadian Orthopaedic Association made a recommendation for marking the incision site with a permanent marker prior to the patient entering the operating room.[11] Following this recommendation, in 1998, the American Academy of Orthopaedic Surgeons' instituted a campaign called "Sign Your Site." In 2002, the National Quality Forum identified 27 serious, reportable events in health care that are largely preventable and of concern to both the public and health care providers. The Forum coined the term "never events" to describe these medical errors.[12] Three of these "never events" are wrong-site surgery/procedure involving a wrong body part, wrong patient, or wrong procedure performed on a patient. In the following years, the Joint Commission made wrong-site surgery/procedure prevention one of their NPSGs and approved the UP for Preventing Wrong Site, Wrong Procedure, and Wrong Person Surgery. The UP became effective July 1, 2004, for all Joint Commission-accredited hospitals, ambulatory care, and office-based surgery

facilities. Since then, the UP has been continuously updated, with the latest version issued on September 2009 as "2010 Universal Protocol."

Several other efforts have been recommended in the international community, most prominently the 2008 World Health Organization (WHO) surgical safety checklist.[7] The WHO checklist aims to promote safe surgery and address other aspects of surgery as well (i.e., postprocedure sign-out); this differs from the UP, which targets prevention of wrong-site, wrong-procedure, and wrong-person surgeries. Both endorse preprocedure verification, site marking, and a time-out before the procedure.[13] It should be noted that, according to the Joint Commission publication,[13] compliance with the WHO surgical safety checklist does not ensure compliance with the UP. Other efforts to prevent wrong-site surgery/ procedure include the Australian Ensuring Correct Patient, Correct Site, Correct Procedure Protocol in 2004,[14] and the U.K.'s National Patient Safety Agency guidelines in 2005.[15]

In this chapter, we focus only on the UP.

WHAT IS THE UNIVERSAL PROTOCOL?

The UP is a three-step process that includes strategies to prevent wrong-site surgery/procedure. These steps are performed preoperatively to confirm the patient's identity, mark the operative site, and take a final time-out before the surgery/procedure starts. The three steps are complementary to each other and intentionally add redundancy to the practice to ensure safety. The UP consists of (1) preprocedure verification, (2) procedure site marking, and (3) hard-stop time-out. These require active communication among all members of the surgical/procedural team. The UP is consistently initiated by a designated team member and conducted in a fail-safe mode (i.e., the procedure is not started if a team member has concerns).[16]

WHEN TO PERFORM THE UNIVERSAL PROTOCOL

The UP is mandated and required by the Joint Commission in all patients before undergoing all surgical and nonsurgical invasive procedures.[17]

The Joint Commission defines invasive procedures as "operative procedures in which skin or mucus membranes and connective tissues are incised, or an instrument is introduced through a natural body orifice." These encompass several services, including all procedures listed in the surgery section of the current procedural terminology (CPT) list, percutaneous transluminal angioplasty, and cardiac catheterization, as well as minimally invasive procedures involving biopsies or placements of probes or catheters requiring entry into a body cavity through a needle or tracer.[18] When applying this definition of the UP, several procedures are exempted from procedure site marking (step 2 of UP). In radiology practice, these exempted procedures include those in which there is a lack of right/left distinction based on external landmarks, history or prior studies, and situations in which right/left distinction is determined or confirmed through intraprocedural imaging before intervention.[19] Peripheral intravenous line insertion, nasogastric tube insertion, urinary bladder catheterization, single-organ cases, interventional cases for which the catheter/instrument insertion site is not predetermined, and procedures performed in premature infants (in whom the mark may cause a permanent tattoo)

and in the patient who is profoundly medically unstable or in arrest are exempted from site marking.[20] In addition, the Society of Interventional Radiology (SIR) has opined that, in procedures in which vascular access is simply a means of providing a route of access to perform a procedure or to provide central venous access, skin marking at the vascular access site is not needed.[19] In cases in which both right- and left-sided structures are known to be abnormal (e.g., bilateral hydronephrosis), the SIR recommends that skin marking be performed even if intraprocedural imaging is employed.[19] However, even if the procedure is not subject to skin marking, the preprocedural verification and hard-stop time-out must still be performed.[19]

THREE COMPONENTS OF UNIVERSAL PROTOCOL

The three components of the UP are shown in Table 13.1.

TABLE 13.1   DEFINITION AND ELEMENTS OF THE UNIVERSAL PROTOCOL (UP)

	Definition	Elements*
UP.01.01.01	Conduct a preprocedural verification process	1. Implement a preprocedure process to verify the correct procedure, for the correct patient, at the correct site. 2. Identify items that must be available for the procedure and use a standardized list to verify their availability. 3. Match the items that are to be available in the procedure area to the patient.
UP.01.02.01	Mark the procedure site	1. Identify procedures requiring marking of incision or insertion site. 2. Mark the procedure site before the procedure is performed. 3. Procedure site marking is performed by a licensed independent practitioner who is ultimately accountable for the procedure and will be present when the procedure is performed**. 4. Use unambiguous method and type of mark for site marking. 5. A written, alternative process is in place for patients who refuse site marking or when it is technically or anatomically impossible or impractical to mark the site.
UP.01.03.01	A time-out is performed before the procedure	1. Conduct a time-out immediately before starting the invasive procedure or making the incision. 2. The time-out is standardized, initiated by a designated team member, and involves the immediate members of the team, including the individual performing the procedures, the anesthesia providers, the circulating nurse, the operating room technician, and other active participants. 3. Perform a time-out before each procedure if two or more procedures are being performed on the same patient and the person performing the procedure changes. 4. During the time-out, the team members agree, at a minimum, on correct patient identity, correct site and procedure to be done. 5. Document the completion of the time-out.

*These are similar for ambulatory health care, critical access hospital, hospital, and office-based surgery.
**Exemptions apply.

Preprocedural Verification

The three elements of preprocedural verification are:

- Implement a preprocedure process to verify the correct procedure, for the correct patient, at the correct site. It is important to verify patient, procedure, site, and side at every stage, from the time a decision is made to perform a procedure to the time the patient undergoes the procedure. These stages include the time of procedure scheduling, preadmission testing and assessment, admission or entry to the facility for the procedure, and at any time the responsibility of care is transferred to another health care team member. Verification should be performed with patient involvement as much as possible. A standardized list (or checklist) is typically used to induce physicians to adhere to safety measures and help avoid human failures of omission.[21] The checklist should contain simple, clearly defined items that encompass verification of correct patient identification (with two identifiers); correct procedure, site, and side; and completion of a consent form.
- Identify items that must be available for the procedure and use a standardized list to verify their availability.
- Match the items that are to be available in the procedure area to the patient. Documentation of the use of a standardized list on a per-patient basis is not required, although it is expected that the list be used for every patient.[17]

Procedure Site Marking

There are five elements of procedure site marking:

- Identify procedures requiring marking of incision or insertion site. If the procedure to be performed is not exempted from site marking, the site (or sites) to be operated must be marked.
- Mark the procedure site before the procedure is performed.
- Procedure site marking is performed by a licensed independent practitioner who is ultimately accountable for the procedure and will be present when the procedure is performed. In limited circumstances, the licensed independent practitioner may delegate site marking to a qualified individual who is permitted by the organization to participate in the procedure, is familiar with the patient, and will be present when the procedure is performed, including residents qualified through a medical residency program, licensed advanced practice registered nurses, and physician assistants who perform duties requiring collaboration or supervisory agreements with a licensed independent practitioner. This option is available when it is not feasible for the person responsible for the procedure to mark the site.[17]
- Use unambiguous methods and types of mark for site marking. The site to be marked must be at or next to the procedure site. Nonprocedure sites should not be marked to avoid confusion. The mark must be on the skin (use of adhesive site markers is not recommended), unambiguous, clearly visible, and made with a permanent marker so that it is not removed during site preparation. Each organization may use different methods of marking, but the protocol should be consistent in order to prevent any ambiguity. The National Patient Safety Agency of the United Kingdom recommends the use of an arrow drawn on the skin and pointing to the site and discourages the use of a cross because of its double meaning. The American Association of Orthopaedic Surgeon recommends that surgeons write their initials or name on the operative site. At the authors' institution, the site is marked with the word "YES." When two or more procedures will be performed on a patient, two sites are marked using different words or symbols.
- A written, alternative process is in place for patients who refuse site marking or when it is technically or anatomically impossible or impractical to mark the site.

In the 2010 revision of the UP, the Joint Commission provided more flexibility to site marking by allowing organizations to develop alternative processes for site marking.[17]

Hard-Stop Time-Out

A time-out is a brief pause before the incision/puncture to confirm the correct patient, correct site, and correct procedure. These three items are considered most essential to the time-out process in the 2010 UP. Other items that an institution may consider including in the time-out (but not required by the Joint Commission) are complete and accurate consent form, agreement on procedure to be done, correct patient positioning, relevant images properly labeled and displayed, need for preprocedural antibiotics administration, and safety precautions based upon patient history or medications used. During the time-out, all other activities must be suspended (hard stop). Any team member can ask for clarification or verification. All members must be in agreement before proceeding with the incision or puncture. Active communication among team members is crucial to a proper time-out. Each member is required to explicitly state his or her name and role in the procedure, and the patient's name, procedure, and procedure site. This step is critical because its omission was identified as a major contributor to wrong-site surgery/procedure in a study of 427 cases.[22] In many sentinel events, someone on the team recognized an error but did not speak up or was ignored.[2] Patients, to the extent possible, are encouraged to participate in the time-out with active responses. There are five elements in the hard-stop time-out:

- Conduct a time-out immediately before starting the invasive procedure or making the incision.
- The time-out is standardized, initiated by a designated team member, and involves the immediate members of the team, including the individual performing the procedures, the anesthesia providers, the circulating nurse, the operating room technician, and other active participants.
- Perform a time-out before each procedure if two or more procedures are being performed on the same patient and the person performing the procedure changes.
- During the time-out, the team members agree, at a minimum, on correct patient identity, and the correct site and procedure to be done.
- Document the completion of the time-out.

CONCLUSION

Benefits and Demonstrated Outcomes of Using the Universal Protocol

The UP utilizes a group effort to prevent the error of wrong-site surgery/procedure. On the basis of openly shared information and opinions among team members, it has been shown that groups faced with complex problem-solving situations often identify better solutions than do any individual in that group can by acting alone. Similarly, in an operating/interventional suite, team-based decision-making can yield a better outcome than would a single physician.[16] In a prospective investigation of physician self-reported wrong-site and wrong-patient procedures, nonsurgical specialties contributed equally with surgical disciplines to adverse outcome. This emphasizes the need to expand the UP into nonsurgical specialties to produce visible effects in decreasing wrong-site and wrong-patient procedures.[23] A few studies have shown the good results of utilizing the UP in various practices. In a large study of 37,133 briefings and debriefings in a tertiary-care medical center in Michigan, it took 2.9 and 2.5 minutes, on average, to perform a briefing and debriefing, respectively. These centers achieved a 76%–95% compliance rate and showed that it was feasible to implement these processes in the operating room across a diverse cohort of surgical specialties and surgeons.[8] Another study, in a combat zone hospital in Iraq, showed no cases of wrong-site surgery in a total of more than 900 procedures performed under a well-implemented UP policy.[24]

REFERENCES

1. Senders JW, Kanzki R. The egocentric surgeon or the roots of wrong side surgery. *Qual Saf Health Care.* 2008;17:396–400.
2. Lum F, Schachat AP. The quest to eliminate "never events." *Ophthalmology.* 2009;116:1021–1022.
3. Agency for Healthcare Research and Quality. Never events. Accessed May 31, 2010, at: http://www.psnet.ahrq.gov/primer.aspx?primerID=3
4. Google. 1980–2010 trends in search of "wrong site surgery." Accessed May 31, 2010, at: http://news.google.com/archivesearch?um=1&cf=all&ned=us&hl=en&q=wrong+site+surgery&cf=all
5. Joint Commission. Total sentinel events reported by year. Accessed May 31, 2010, at: http://www.jointcommission.org/NR/rdonlyres/67297896-4E16-4BB7-BF0F-5DA4A87B02F2/0/se_stats_trends_year.pdf
6. Seiden SC, Barach P. Wrong-side/wrong-site, wrong-procedure, and wrong-patient adverse events: Are they preventable? *Arch Surg.* 2006;141:931–9.
7. World Health Organization. WHO surgical safety checklist and implementation manual. Accessed May 31, 2010, at: http://www.who.int/patientsafety/safesurgery/ss_checklist/en/index.html
8. Joint Commission. Time out! Conducting a final verification before surgery. *Jt Comm Perspect Patient Saf.* 2009;9:1–11.

9. Berenholtz SM, Schumacher K, Hayanga AJ, et al. Implementing standardized operating room briefings and debriefings at a large regional medical center. *Jt Comm J Qual Patient Saf.* 2009;35:391–7.

10. Associated Press. Stiff penalty recommended for surgeon. *Sarasota Herald-Tribune.* October 1995, p. 48.

11. Furey A, Stone C, Martin R. Preoperative signing of the incision site in orthopaedic surgery in Canada. *J Bone Joint Surg Am.* 2002;84-A:1066–68.

12. Kizer KW, Stegun MB. Serious reportable adverse events in health care. In Henriksen K, Battles JB, Marks ES, Lewin DI, eds. *Advances in Patient Safety: From Research to Implementation*, vol. 4. Rockville, MD: Agency for Healthcare Research and Quality, 2005.

13. Joint Commission. Clarification: Compliance with the Universal Protocol. *Jt Comm Perspect Patient Saf.* 2009;29:9.

14. Australian Commission for Safety and Quality in Health Care. Ensuring correct patient, correct site and correct procedure in radiology, nuclear medicine, radiation therapy and oral surgery. Accessed May 31, 2010, at: www.safetyandquality.gov.au

15. Rhodes P, Giles SJ, Cook GA, et al. Assessment of the implementation of a national patient safety alert to reduce wrong site surgery. *Qual Saf Health Care.* 2008;17:409–15.

16. Barbieri RL. Is this tool the cure for wrong-site surgery and other OR errors? *OBG Management.* 2009;21(3).

17. Joint Commission. Approved: Revised Universal Protocol for 2010. *Jt Comm Perspect Patient Saf.* 2009;29(10):3.

18. HCPro. Q&A: What is an invasive procedure? Accessed May 31, 2010, at: http://www.hcpro.com/CCP-232176-862/QA-What-is-an-invasive-procedure.html

19. Angle JF, Nemcek AA, Jr., Cohen AM, et al. Quality improvement guidelines for preventing wrong site, wrong procedure, and wrong person errors: Application of the Joint Commission "Universal Protocol for Preventing Wrong Site, Wrong Procedure, Wrong Person Surgery" to the practice of interventional radiology. *J Vasc Interv Radiol.* 2008;19:1145–51.

20. Association of periOperative Registered Nurses. Best practices for preventing wrong site, wrong person, and wrong procedure errors in perioperative settings. *AORN J.* 2006;84(Suppl 1).

21. Pronovost P, Needham D, Berenholtz S, et al. An intervention to decrease catheter-related bloodstream infections in the ICU. *N Engl J Med.* 2006;355:2725–32.

22. Clarke JR, Johnston J, Finley ED. Getting surgery right. *Ann Surg.* 2007;246:395–403, discussion 403–395.

23. Stahel PF, Sabel AL, Victoroff MS, et al. Wrong-site and wrong-patient procedures in the Universal Protocol era. *Arch Surg.* 2010;145:978–84.

24. Harrington JW. Surgical time outs in a combat zone. *AORN J.* 2009;89:535–7.

14

Peer Review in Radiology

*RATHACHAI KAEWLAI, VALERIE P. JACKSON,
AND HANI H. ABUJUDEH*

Physicians' performance is one of the most difficult yet critical aspects to assess when undertaking to improve medical care quality.[1,2] As the medical profession heads into the new era of a quality-minded health care system, it needs to ensure itself, the public, payers, and governing authorities of its assessability and accountability. In the past decade, several groups have expressed significant interest in holding physicians accountable for their actions, for example, through reports such as the Institute of Medicine's *To Err Is Human* and its follow-up report *Crossing the Quality Chasm*.[3] Issues of medical errors have caught the attention of the lay public and have driven several attempts by all parties involved to tackle quality problems in health care. The medical profession has the choice of either monitoring itself or being monitored by others.[1]

Performance measurement is not new in medicine. Medicine has long relied on a process called "peer review" to protect its professionalism and quality of care.[4] Since the start of its quality assurance program in 1979, the Joint Commission has shaped the quality of medical practice in the United States. Peer review is now viewed as a clinical performance measurement and improvement process.[4] The Joint Commission has two programs aimed at the systematic measurement of physicians' professional performance: ongoing professional practice evaluation (OPPE) and focused professional practice evaluation (FPPE). The OPPE encompasses the routine monitoring of competency of current medical staff members, whereas the FPPE is focused on concerns derived from the OPPE or used in new medical

staff credentialing and privileging.[5] Peer review is considered an essential component for these evaluations and for working toward optimal physician performance. Quality gaps, specifically in terms of performance, occur in all specialties, including radiology. Radiologic error rates are no different than for other fields.[6] Peer review is a method that most radiology departments utilize in the measurement of performance in the area of radiologist medical and clinical knowledge.[7] In this chapter, we discuss methods of performance evaluation, radiological errors and diagnostic accuracy, the what and why of peer review, how to perform peer review, limitations of peer review, and measurement of outcome.

WHY IT IS IMPORTANT TO MEASURE PERFORMANCE

Even with technological progress in medicine, there is always room for improvement in the development and advancement of medical professional standards.[6] The systematic monitoring, analysis, and improvement of a physician's performance are important to ensure a high quality of care. Peer review plays an important part in this assessment.[8,9] The reasons for performing peer review are broad but may be categorized as the following:

- *Maintenance of professional standards*. The results of peer review can be an incentive to improve the accuracy and consistency of individual physician performance.[6] An individual's desire for self-improvement, based on ethical insight, is essential to improving performance.[10]

- *Requirement of governing authorities.* On a local or regional level, physician performance and competency evaluations may be tied to institutional accreditation and payments from third parties (e.g., Medicare). Failure to evaluate physicians' performance and competency, therefore, may lead to loss of accreditation and profit. At a national level, performance evaluation is one of the four components of the American Board of Medical Specialties (ABMS) and the American Board of Radiology (ABR) maintenance of certification (MOC) programs. The Joint Commission also provides guidelines to develop peer review programs, in which considerable flexibility in implementing strategies is allowed.[3]
- *Institutional medical staff obligation.* It is the responsibility of the institutional medical staff to undertake mutual accountability for quality. The medical staff is obligated to ensure that their physicians are competent; otherwise, everyone is at greater risk (community, organization, referring physicians, practicing physicians).[5]

HOW TO MEASURE PERFORMANCE

There are several ways to measure the performance of radiologists and other physicians. These include peer review (retrospective case review); professional auditing of reports with standard references; surveys of colleagues, referring physicians, and patients; and examinations or tests. If data are systematically aggregated and analyzed, the use of any of these methods can be very useful for ongoing, continuous quality improvement. Thus, in addition to peer review, the potential list of performance measurement methods for radiologists includes:

- *Professional auditing of reports with standard references.* When a gold standard is available for comparison with the imaging report, it can be used for professional audits. For example, the results of histopathology or follow-up can be correlated with imaging interpretation. This method, although very definitive and useful, is limited because only a minority of patients will have biopsy, surgery, or adequate clinical follow-up data available.[6]

- *Surveys.* Surveys of referring physicians and patients are usually done to assess the nontechnical components of a radiologist's performance and competency. Surveys can also be useful if the referring physician knows the patient's outcome and can assess the accuracy of the radiologist's interpretation. A disadvantage of surveys is that they are subjective.
- *Examinations and tests representative of the work.*[9]
- *Analysis of aggregate data.*

PEER REVIEW PROCESS

The literal meaning of "peer review" is simply an evaluation by a colleague.[10] However, in contemporary medicine, the meaning of peer review is the "evaluation of a physician's professional performance for all defined competency areas using multiple data sources."[5] A broader and more comprehensive framework for physician's performance assessment was introduced when the Joint Commission and the ABMS adopted the Accreditation Council on Graduate Medical Education (ACGME)'s six general competencies of physicians. The ACGME's six general competencies include patient care, medical/clinical knowledge, interpersonal and communication skills, professionalism, systems-based practice, practice-based learning and improvement. Thus, the new meaning of "peer review" has surpassed a mere case review, which is just one tool with which to evaluate physician's competency. Current concepts of peer review are not limited to technical competency or retrospective record review.[4] Currently, peer review is conducted by committees and important decisions are made by consensus, thus making the process fairer and more efficient.[4,5] Multiple data sources are included in the review, such as case reviews of significant events, measures of policy compliance, and clinical data or perception data. The review aims to provide an accurate, continuous, systematic reflection of the performance of physicians and systems, to achieve continuous improvement in the quality of care.[5,10]

RADIOLOGY PEER REVIEW

Radiology is no more immune to medical errors than other specialties.[6] Diagnostic errors are relatively common and may result in delayed diagnosis and treatment.[11] Errors can occur in multiple phases of the care provided in radiology departments; for example, mistakes can be made in patient identification, positioning, examination protocol, radiation dosage, image interpretation, or the communication of findings. Of these, the most important aspect is, perhaps, image interpretation because it holds a strong connection with patient health outcomes.[6] There is a wide variability in the diagnostic accuracy of image interpretation,[12] which may be a result of different study designs and different samples of images and radiologists.[6] These variations may be case-specific or due to radiologist inconsistency. To measure and monitor the diagnostic accuracy of image interpretation, one needs to understand the subjective and variable nature of image interpretation. Variability or error of image interpretation is due in part to the high degree of natural variation in both normal anatomy and pathology.[6] Three sources of variability or error in image interpretation are (1) differences in visual observation (detection), (2) differences in interpretation of a perceived finding (interpretation), and (3) different thresholds of concern about perceived abnormalities (level of confidence).[6] *Errors* differ from *variability* in that they imply an incorrect interpretation when a correct one is possible. Therefore, error can only arise in cases in which the correct interpretation is not in dispute.[13]

In radiology, peer review is probably the most commonly used performance evaluation method. Peer review can be uniquely feasible in radiology because the average case volume per radiologist exceeds that of many other specialties. Diagnostic accuracy can be gauged by examining agreement in interpretation among radiologists,[2] and it is likely less time-consuming compared with case review in other specialties. Peer review can be performed reactively or proactively.[14] The reactive method is used when discrepant reports are found during routine clinical work. The proactive method involves an assigned double interpretation of imaging studies by separate radiologists. The latter has the advantage of being a less-biased system because a predetermined fraction of routine work is sampled for double interpretation, and selection bias can be avoided. However, it is time-consuming and costly. The former system, on the other hand, provides a quick, timely audit of discrepant imaging reports, but it may be easily biased and very subjective.[2] It should be noted, however, that both systems are limited by the use of gold standards or "expert opinion," without histopathologic proof or clinical follow-up. Whatever method is used, the department should make sure that the process is consistent and systematic, and that the performance measures are evidence-based, reproducible, accepted, and agreed-upon by the majority of radiologists. The measures should occur

in adequate numbers, so that meaningful statistical assessment can be achieved as well.[7]

Before setting up a peer review system, it is critical to create a positive peer review culture within an institution or a group to avoid reluctance to perform this task. An ideal peer review system should be nonpunitive, consistent, and fair to those individuals being evaluated and to those who perform the evaluation. This should result in a real improvement of performance.[5,15] The review process should use effective and efficient committee structures and defined processes. To exercise fairness in the peer review system, physician performance measures must be valid and accurate, and potential biases must be minimized. The feedback should be timely and useful.[5] The peer review should gauge reliable data for the ongoing evaluation of physician's performance,[2] as well as provide improvement strategies. With the use of poor methods, one cannot expect the acceptance of results or improvement.[5]

Setting Up a Peer Review System

Good preparation and management is required to set up of an effective peer review system. Beyond promoting a positive attitude toward peer review in a department or institution, the recruitment of a peer review committee, selection of peer review methodology, process organization, and stimulation of change in performance are keys to achieving good outcomes from peer review.[10]

Physicians are often motivated to participate in peer review, but they can be hesitant to offer criticism to their colleagues. A well-designed program using a team approach can alleviate the concern of an individual peer reviewer and avoid putting the department chair or any other single individual in the position having to discuss subjective and often emotional issues when errors are observed. A typical professional peer review committee is comprised of 5–10 physicians who regularly meet to discuss concerns, including clinical issues, documentation issues, or complaints involving patient care.[10,16] The committee members may be selected by department chair and administration, and should include all subspecialties, representing the whole group of radiologists. Each member may serve staggered terms to ensure that there are always experienced members on the committee to provide expertise and to mentor new members.[16,17]

Steps in Peer Review

Several methods of peer review can be used in radiology. As noted previously, the two main categories are reactive and proactive systems. Each system has its own benefits and disadvantages. One should keep in mind that both systems rely upon an expert opinion or consensus to reach a conclusion. However, any peer review system that is well designed, structured, and created to capture ongoing information is helpful in performance evaluation and can offer a balanced platform for constructive feedback. The review process can be either paper-and-pencil or computerized, depending on the resources of each institution. Computer-based systems, especially those with online web-based mechanisms, are more convenient and generally easier to use.[18] All peer review systems require similar components, including case identification, case screening and assignment of reviewer, radiologist review, committee review, input from the involved radiologist, committee decision, communication of findings, and improvement plan assignment with follow-up.[5]

- *Case identification.* The reactive and proactive peer review systems are categorized based on this step. Studies may be randomly selected a radiological information system (RIS) query (i.e., proactive method) or identified from the occurrence reporting system, in which radiologists or referring physicians submit discrepant reports to the peer review committee (i.e., reactive method). Cases may also be identified from other departments, conferences, patient complaints, or the risk management office. In any method, the department should develop clear peer review criteria and ensure that all parties are aware of the criteria, in order to increase the number of case referrals for peer review. Less strict criteria can provide a broader scope of review, increase the number of problems identified, and magnify the number of quality improvement projects related to them.[4] If the process is done reactively, the system should be able to move through the identified cases for review in a timely fashion.[5] The framework/criteria for cases included in the peer review system can be dynamic, depending on the results of monitoring and outcome measures.[4]
- *Case screening and assignment of radiologist reviewer.* The peer review committee screens the identified cases to ensure that the issues are radiologist-related. Then, appropriate radiologist reviewers are assigned to review

each case. At this point, the committee should identify potential conflicts of interest that may result in bias during the review. There should be clearly defined inclusion and exclusion criteria during this screening. If the process is done reactively, the screener should provide the reviewer with specific quality concerns, so that the reviewer can provide specific responses.

- *Radiologist review.* Case assignment can be done automatically on a rotating basis, by subspecialty, or by the committee chair after his or her initial assessment. Ideally, assignment should be done quickly, and a clear timeframe should be set for the reviewer to review his or her cases, so that committee can receive the results before the next meeting. The reviewer's job is to make an initial judgment of the accuracy of the initial imaging interpretation and categorize the degree of agreement based on the rating system used within the department or institution. In cases of major disagreement, the reviewer's documentation of rationale and questions should be requested. To minimize personal bias when matching the reviewer with the radiologist under review, a predetermined assignment order can be used.
- *Committee review.* If the initial review shows appropriate interpretation, the cases should be reported to the peer review committee for approval. However, if there is major discrepancy, the case(s) should be placed on the agenda for discussion by the peer review committee. The committee, as a group, then will decide either to confirm or dismiss the reviewer's concerns. If the committee dismisses the reviewer's concerns, it should determine how that decision might apply to future cases. In this step, the committee should have a predefined mechanism to nullify under- or overscoring by initial radiologist reviewers, which could be done by using another member of the committee or a committee chair as a secondary reviewer.[5] By providing redundancy (e.g., having more reviewers), the system defends against accusations of intentional and sham peer review from others.[19] Another means of strengthening peer review is to use reviewers from different specialties or subspecialties in a peer review committee. This multispecialty

or multi-subspecialty review committee may provide different viewpoints on the cases and may potentially result in a fairer scoring. The committee should identify and manage potential conflicts of interest between the reviewer and radiologists under review.

- *Input from the involved radiologist (radiologist under review).* If the peer review process is performed reactively, the committee may choose to obtain input from the radiologist under review, either before or after the initial review. The former has an advantage of avoiding discussing those cases that have a clear explanation. If the peer review process is done proactively, contacting the involved radiologist after the initial review is appropriate since it can avoid unnecessary interruptions if the committee thinks the interpretation was correct. It is critical that the committee protects the radiologist reviewer's anonymity at all steps and minimizes personal appearance of the involved radiologist. Communications to the involved radiologist should come from the committee, not the reviewer.
- *Committee decision.* After receiving the initial review and input from the involved radiologist, the committee discusses the cases and finalizes the case rating by voting. All information should be available to all members before voting, through the use of forms or other methods of correspondence. The committee should define the threshold for focused review of cases (i.e., major discrepancy resulting in morbidity or mortality) and set a predetermined number of cases that require focused review for each level in the rating system .
- *Communication of findings.* The committee should communicate all outcomes (either exemplary, appropriate, or needing improvement) to the involved radiologist and, when suitable, identify opportunities for improvement from a systems perspective.
- *Improvement plan assignment with follow-up.* If the peer review committee finds major discrepancies in the cases of the involved radiologist, it must determine the next step needed to improve that radiologist's performance. In this step, the peer review committee may report the results of the evaluation and its suggestions to the

department chair. Follow-up on these actions should be implemented based on departmental policy. The peer review committee should avoid any action beyond providing suggestions to the administration and should leave the decision to implement an improvement plan to a separate party. In this way, the peer review committee remains neutral and avoids conflicts.

Adaptations of Peer Review Methods

Adaptation of the aforementioned peer review system may include a group review of cases (reactive review of submitted cases) in a conference setting,[7] integration of peer review into daily clinical workflow by providing prior interpretations with every new imaging study for discrepancy (proactive review),[3] and random selection of cases from prior months for reinterpretation and discrepancy scoring by randomly assigned peers (proactive review).[3] Many of these steps can be done electronically, as with case selection, case routing for peer review, scoring, and communication of findings.[18] Regardless of the adaptations chosen, the peer review committee must explore those discrepancies found and believed to be important to their institutions and suggest an improvement plan to the administration.

Minimization of Bias During Peer Review

It is important for peer review to be fair to all parties, including those under review and those who review others. *Bias* is a tendency or preference toward a particular perspective or result that, if not minimized, can erode the peer review culture and potentially result in nonacceptance, diminished reliability or accuracy of the results, and poor compliance with performance improvement strategies. Minimization of bias is a critical aspect to consider when setting up and performing peer review. One should attempt to minimize bias at every step of peer review, although it can never be completely eliminated. There are three major types of bias: human nature, systematic, and statistical bias. *Human nature bias* is related to psychological shortcuts produced by human beings to reduce complexity and ambiguity during evaluation. It is the view of the world created by an individual's or a group's experiences. *Systematic bias* reflects flaws in the evaluation system itself that can influence decision-making by an individual and lead to incorrect results. *Statistical bias* represents errors in sampling, which can result in incorrect conclusions in statistical analysis. In general, to minimize bias in peer review, one needs to look for it in the structures, procedures, and results of the review, and then manage it through policies and systems. Table 14.1 describes various potential methods to minimize bias in peer review system.

Case Rating/Scoring

Case rating/scoring is important for ensuring fairness for all parties, defining thresholds for further evaluation (focused review), allowing medical staff and the peer review committee to set targets and address different levels of discrepancy found during peer review, and simplifying the results of review for departmental or institutional staff. Multiple case rating/scoring systems exist for peer review, as shown in Table 14.2. To select the right system for use, one must consider several aspects that may contribute to rating, including ease of use and understanding, practicality, and validity. A good rating/scoring system should allow users to rate each case using categories that focus on only one aspect of evaluation, which makes the rating/scoring easier and more reliable. For example, the rating/scoring system should have separate categories for accuracy of interpretation, documentation, and potential clinical outcome. Each category should have at least three levels for case rating, allowing for uncertainty or gray areas (i.e., correct, questionable, incorrect). If one would like to include reasons for discrepancy (e.g., knowledge, judgment, communication) in the scoring system, this should be a separate category

that will allow further analysis of the root cause of discrepancy and potential improvement. Another potentially important category that can be included in peer review is the radiologist's contribution to patient harm. Actual and potential harm should be scored separately, and their sum can be used as an overall harm score.

RADPEER AND ERADPEER

RADPEER (and its electronic version, eRADPEER) is a peer review system designed by the American College of Radiology (ACR) for use by any radiology group. RADPEER was piloted as a paper-based system in 2002 and offered to all participants in 2003, while eRADPEER was made available online in August 2005.[20] The RADPEER or eRADPEER process is conducted during routine interpretation of current images. If previous images of the same area are available when a new study is being interpreted, the reviewer reviews the images and report of the prior study and scores the accuracy using a standardized 4-point rating scale (Table 14.2). This is considered a proactive method of peer review that is simple and easy to use, although its limitation lies in the use of the gold standard of another radiologist's opinion.

There is an annual fee for the use of RADPEER and eRADPEER, and at least two radiologists (the reviewer group) are required as reviewers. Once the reviewer group applies to the program, a group identification number is assigned. The group then assigns each radiologist a number known only to

TABLE 14.1 METHODS TO REDUCE OR MINIMIZE BIAS IN PEER REVIEW SYSTEM

Methods to Reduce or Minimize Bias (5)	
Human nature bias	Use a committee, rather than an individual, to make a final determination and resolve peer review problems.[5,16]
	Protect reviewer's anonymity.
	Decrease variance in rating/scoring of discrepancy.
	Create and follow a strong conflict-of-interest policy.
	Use multispecialty, multi-subspecialty peer review committee to bring all perspectives to the peer review.
Systematic bias	Ensure the system is consistent and respects the radiologist's rights.
	Use a case rating/scoring system in which each category rates only one concept (i.e., separate clinical outcomes, appropriateness, and documentation scoring).
	Use external peer review.
Statistical bias	Measure the issues relevant to radiologists' performance.
	Choose the right type of measures for the questions.
	Examine the reliability and accuracy of the measures used.

TABLE 14.2 CASE RATING/SCORING SYSTEM USED IN RADIOLOGY

RADPEER[9]

Score	Meaning	Optional
1	Concur with interpretation	
2	Discrepancy in interpretation/not ordinarily expected to be made (understandable miss)	a. Unlikely to be clinically significant b. Likely to be clinically significant
3	Discrepancy in interpretation/should be made most of the time	a. Unlikely to be clinically significant b. Likely to be clinically significant
4	Discrepancy in interpretation/should be made almost every time – misinterpretation of finding	a. Unlikely to be clinically significant b. Likely to be clinically significant

Melvin et al.[25]

Grade	Significance
0	None
1	Minor (incidental to treatment/management)
2	Significant (affects treatment/management, not outcome)
3	Major (affects outcome)

Soffa et al.[26]

Grade	Meaning
1	Interpretation expected and acceptable; reviewer comfortable with interpretation
2	Interpretation varies slightly, but not totally unexpected; reviewer still comfortable with interpretation
3	Interpretation varies moderately; reviewer uncomfortable with interpretation, which might adversely affect patient condition
4	Interpretation varies significantly; reviewer very uncomfortable with interpretation, which probably would adversely affect patient condition

the group. Reports are generated based on each group practice. Aggregate data from RADPEER and eRADPEER include summary statistics and comparisons for each radiologist by modality, summary data for each facility by modality, and data summed across all participating facilities.[9] Individual radiologist information and protected patient health information are not transmitted to the ACR, so confidentiality is not an issue.[20] The program has grown substantially since 2007, after the ACR mandated that all sites applying for voluntary accreditation programs show evidence of a physician peer review program.[9] Eventually, RADPEER and eRADPEER should allow benchmarking of individual and group performance against a national norm.[21]

EXTERNAL PEER REVIEW

External peer review is another type of peer review system that utilizes different resources (outside of a home institution) to acquire fair, efficient, and useful information to evaluate and improve physician performance.[5] The Joint Commission requires a solid internal peer review system, as well as clear policies for obtaining external peer review evaluations.[19] Typically, an external peer review is sought when there is doubt of the unbiased and objective review of the quality of care delivered. In this regard, external peer review can provide recommendations for actions based on objective and unbiased review and reassurance that the standard of care has been delivered.[19] Other potential circumstances that may require external peer review include lack of internal expertise, lack of internal resources, ambiguity, credibility, and legal concerns, and for benchmarking purposes. A good external peer review policy should not only address the circumstances that require external peer review, but also the decision maker (one who determines when external review is required), case selection technique, reviewer selection technique, and potential use of results from the review.[5]

POTENTIAL OBSTACLES, LIMITATIONS, AND FUTURE OF PEER REVIEW

Peer review processes may not be easy to perform. Physician reviewers may feel reluctant to perform peer review because it can have negative influences on their relationships with colleagues,[5] and some radiologists fear having their work evaluated by their peer group.[10] Other detracting factors include the effect on time, the increased workload, and financial and practical objections,[10] as well as the potential of information becoming available to the public and/or legal system.[5] Even with the RADPEER and eRADPEER programs, which are viewed as minimally intrusive and less time-consuming than other peer review methods, poor radiologist compliance was considered a substantial problem. Radiologist shortage, increased workloads, and decreased payments per service have been cited as potential obstacles in this national program.[8] Staff commitment to peer review and financial compensation are also issues. Based on a recent survey of 339 institutions (including 61 teaching hospitals) in the United States, only a small fraction of time was devoted to peer review (1.1 full-time employee per 100 beds or 0.2% of average hospital staffing). Approximately 80% of peer reviewers were not compensated.[4]

Lack of peer review's demonstrable impact on patient care may also be a reason for poor radiologist compliance. This may be overcome by optimally selecting for review only those cases that have a high frequency of interpretive error or the potential for high morbidity or high financial cost in the event of an error.[22]

Peer review systems using double interpretation of imaging studies possess some inherent limitations because the gold standard for "correct interpretation" is expert consensus, not pathology or clinical follow-up. Such opinion-based standards could vary substantially.[23] Therefore, radiology groups should consider measuring their radiologists' performance by other means as well. In addition, some measures of expectations for radiologist performance will not be found in radiology reports. By obtaining the views of others (i.e., colleagues, patients, referring physicians), physicians' performance evaluations can potentially be positioned to meet the measures of all six core competencies of ACGME.[24]

Since higher demands from the public and controlling bodies can be expected in the future, it is important for radiology to improve its current peer review by looking beyond simple methods of double reading and determination of disagreements on retrospective review of cases. Although these methods can provide useful information, it is unclear whether they accurately reflect the capabilities of a typical general radiologist.[1] The development of indicators and systematic, preferably electronic, methods that will continuously determine when an incorrect diagnosis has been made and provide electronic feedback to the radiologist; a national-level peer review program; and research in the field of outcome improvement are required. Dr. Philip Cascade pointed out more than a decade ago that, "by achieving these goals it will be possible not only to make the statement but to provide objective proof to the public, payers, the government, and accrediting agencies such as the Joint Commission that radiology is best practiced by radiologists."[1]

REFERENCES

1. Cascade PN. Quality improvement in diagnostic radiology. *AJR Am J Roentgenol.* 1990;154:1117–20.
2. Mahgerefteh S, Kruskal JB, Yam CS, Blachar A, Sosna J. Peer review in diagnostic radiology: Current state and a vision for the future. *Radiographics.* 2009;29:1221–31.
3. Halsted MJ. Radiology peer review as an opportunity to reduce errors and improve patient care. *J Am Coll Radiol.* 2004;1:984–987.
4. Edwards MT. Peer review: A new tool for quality improvement. *Physician Exec.* 2009;35:54–59.
5. Marder RJ, Burroughs JH. *Peer review best practices case studies and lessons learned.* Marblehead, MA: HCPro, Inc., 2008.
6. Alpert HR, Hillman BJ. Quality and variability in diagnostic radiology. *J Am Coll Radiol.* 2004;1:127–32.
7. Donnelly LF. Performance-based assessment of radiology practitioners: Promoting improvement in accordance with the 2007 joint commission standards. *J Am Coll Radiol.* 2007;4:699–703.
8. Borgstede JP, Lewis RS, Bhargavan M, Sunshine JH. RADPEER quality assurance program: A multi-facility study of interpretive disagreement rates. *J Am Coll Radiol.* 2004;1:59–65.
9. Jackson VP, Cushing T, Abujudeh HH, et al. RADPEER scoring white paper. *J Am Coll Radiol.* 2009;6:21–25.
10. Grol R. Quality improvement by peer review in primary care: A practical guide. *Qual Health Care.* 1994;3:147–52.
11. Brenner RJ, Lucey LL, Smith JJ, Saunders R. Radiology and medical malpractice claims: A report on the practice standards claims survey of the Physician Insurers Association of America and the American College of Radiology. *AJR Am J Roentgenol.* 1998;171:19–22.
12. Potchen EJ, Cooper TG, Sierra AE, et al. Measuring performance in chest radiography. *Radiology.* 2000; 217:456–9.

13. Robinson PJ. Radiology's Achilles' heel: Error and variation in the interpretation of the Rontgen image. *Br J Radiol.* 1997;70:1085–98.

14. Lee JK. Quality—a radiology imperative: Interpretation accuracy and pertinence. *J Am Coll Radiol.* 2007;4:162–5.

15. Guthrie M. Guidelines for disciplinary action from peer review. *Physician Exec.* 2009;35:78–79.

16. Agee C. Professional review committee improves the peer review process. *Physician Exec.* 2007;33: 52–55.

17. Agee C. Improving the peer review process: Develop a professional review committee for better and quicker results. *Healthc Exec.* 2007;22: 72–73.

18. Kruskal JB, Yam CS, Sosna J, Hallett DT, Milliman YJ, Kressel HY. Implementation of online radiology quality assurance reporting system for performance improvement: Initial evaluation. *Radiology.* 2006;241:518–27.

19. Lauve R. Peer review and privileging. One pill cures all—but it's tough to swallow. *Physician Exec.* 2006;32:40–45.

20. American College of Radiology. RADPEER™. Accessed February 21, 2010, at: http://www.acr.org/ SecondaryMainMenuCategories/quality_safety/ radpeer.aspx 21. Amis ES, Jr. What is a good radiologist? *J Am Coll Radiol.* 2004;1:155.

22. Sheu YR, Feder E, Balsim I, et al. Optimizing radiology peer review: A mathematical model for selecting future cases based on prior errors. *J Am Coll Radiol.* 2010;7:431–8.

23. Abujudeh HH, Boland GW, Kaewlai R, et al. Abdominal and pelvic computed tomography (CT) interpretation: Discrepancy rates among experienced radiologists. *Eur Radiol.* 2010;20:1952–7.

24. Lockyer JM, Violato C, Fidler HM. Assessment of radiology physicians by a regulatory authority. *Radiology.* 2008;247:771–8.

25. Melvin C, Bodley R, Booth A, Meagher T, Record C, Savage P. Managing errors in radiology: A working model. *Clin Radiol.* 2004;59:841–5.

26. Soffa DJ, Lewis RS, Sunshine JH, Bhargavan M. Disagreement in interpretation: A method for the development of benchmarks for quality assurance in imaging. *J Am Coll Radiol.* 2004;1:212–7.

15

Radiation Dose in Medical Imaging

Clinical and Technological Strategies for Dose Reduction

MI SUNG KIM, SARABJEET SINGH, AND MANNUDEEP K. KALRA

CLINICAL AND TECHNOLOGICAL STRATEGIES FOR COMPUTED TOMOGRAPHY RADIATION DOSE REDUCTION

Since ionizing radiation has been discovered, it has been a double-edged sword. Radiation has benefited mankind in several areas, most notably in medicine, but when used inappropriately, it can also result in harm in the form of tissue damage and carcinogenesis. According to the National Council on Radiation Protection and Measurements (NCRP), in 2006, in the United States, medical exposure constituted nearly half of the total radiation exposure from all sources, including natural background radiation.[1] Much of the increase in medical radiation exposure has come from increased use of computed tomography (CT) scanning in modern medical practice.[1] Therefore, appropriate use of CT scanning and a reduction of radiation dose associated with CT scanning is of paramount importance. In this chapter, we discuss various clinical and technological strategies for CT radiation dose reduction.

MAGNITUDE OF USE OF COMPUTED TOMOGRAPHY

Worldwide, use of radiation has increased remarkably in the last quarter century, most noticeably from increased use of radiation-based medical imaging. According to the NCRP's report, the per capita dose from medical exposure of the U.S. population

in 2006 was about 3.0 milli-Sievert (mSv; a unit of effective dose), and the collective dose was about 900,000 person-Sievert, in comparison with 0.54 mSv per capita effective dose and 124,000 person-Sv collective dose in 1982.[1]

The largest contribution and increase have come primarily from increased use of CT scanning, which is a relatively high-dose procedure compared to diagnostic radiography (Table 15.1). The Nations Scientific Committee on the Effects of Atomic Radiation 2000 report on medical radiation exposure stated that, worldwide, CT constitutes 5% of radiologic examinations and contributes 34% of the collective dose.[2]

RISKS WITH LOW RADIATION DOSE IMAGING TECHNIQUES

The harmful effects of radiation have been categorized into two main types: deterministic risks and stochastic risks. *Deterministic risks* result from cell death and occur when radiation dose exceeds a certain threshold level. The severity of deterministic effects depends directly on the amount of radiation dose. These effects are generally not seen when a single exposure time is less than 150 mSv, a threshold rarely seen with single or even multiple CT examinations. Thus, deterministic risks are rarely seen with diagnostic x-ray-based examinations, including CT scanning, because radiation doses typically do not reach the threshold level. Examples of deterministic effects include cataracts, skin damage, depression

TABLE 15.1   COMPUTED TOMOGRAPHY (CT) CONTRIBUTIONS TO MEDICAL RADIATION EXPOSURE IN THE WORLD

Country (Data Year)	Number of CT Examinations (%)*	% Collective Dose
[2]United Nations Scientific Committee on the Effects of Atomic Radiation (UNSCEAR 2000)	(5%)	34%
[3]U.S.A (2006)	67,000,000 (17%)	49%
[4]U.K (1999)	–	40%
[5]Poland (1999)	460,000	–
[6]France (2002)	4,200,000 ~ 6,000,000 (8%)	39%

Superscripts on countries represent the number of references.
*Numbers in parentheses are percentage of number of CT examinations to the total number of medical radiation-based imaging procedures.

of red blood cell formation, and decrease in fertility. Recently, some of the deterministic effects, such as skin erythema and hair loss, have been reported with CT examinations performed at radiation doses of several times greater than that needed for a routine CT (see http://www.medicaldeviceguru.com/showthread.php?p=10331).

The main concern with radiation dose associated with medical imaging, including CT scanning, is therefore that of the stochastic effects of radiation. Examples of stochastic effects are radiation-induced carcinogenesis and mutagenesis. These stochastic effects do not require a threshold radiation dose and can occur at any dose. Although the severity of stochastic effects is not related to the amount of radiation dose, the frequency or the chances of their occurrence increases with increasing radiation dose. Therefore, to minimize the frequency of occurrence of stochastic effects, radiation dose must be reduced.[7] In humans, radiation-induced mutagenesis has never been reported, so that the risk of radiation-induced carcinogenesis is of main concern with CT scanning.

Recently, x-rays at low radiation dose have been officially classified as a carcinogen by the World Health Organization's International Agency for Research on Cancer,[8] the Agency for Toxic Substances and Disease Registry of the Centers for Disease Control and Prevention,[9] and the National Institute of Environmental Health Sciences.[10] Until now, the most comprehensive epidemiologic data supporting the harmful carcinogenic effect of radiation dose have been obtained from atomic bomb survivors in Japan. These data show a statistically significant increase in the incidence of solid cancer from 1958 to 1994 at effective dose estimates in excess of 50 mSv.[11] Prior studies have showed that

CT examinations can have effective dose estimates in the range of 10–25 mSv per exam.[11-14] Therefore, it would not be uncommon for a patient's estimated exposure to exceed 50 mSv with one or more CT examination. Sodickson et al.[15] have recently reported cumulative radiation exposure and lifetime attributable risk (LAR) of radiation-induced cancer from CT scanning in adult patients from a single hospital in the United States. The authors projected that, in their institution, as many as 15% of patients undergoing CT scanning received an estimated cumulative effective dose of more than 100 mSv, and 4% of patients received between 250 and 1,375 mSv. At these levels of radiation doses, the authors estimated mean and maximum LAR of radiation-induced cancer at 0.3% and 12%, and 0.2% and 6.8% for radiation-induced cancer mortality, respectively.

Although data exist on use of CT scanning, associated radiation dose, and projected risk of cancer incidence and mortality, to our best knowledge, most studies do not take into account that many patients undergoing CT scanning may be extremely sick or may have terminal illnesses or ailments. In such circumstances, where beneficial informati~ may be obtained from CT, there is an un⸍ resentation of risk estimates in the ⸍' oversight or data about the a⸍⸍ management or decisio⸍ tion obtained fro⸍

AP}
COMP

In order to mai⸍
outlook with CT

strategy for CT radiation dose reduction or optimization is to ensure that CT is indeed indicated for the clinical information desired. Once it is agreed that CT scanning will add substantial information to patient care, radiologists, physicists, and technologists should make all efforts to ensure that CT scanning is performed at as low as reasonably achievable (ALARA principle) radiation dose while maintaining the diagnostic confidence of the interpreting radiologist.

To address the issue of appropriateness of CT scanning, a few institutions have developed or have obtained access to sophisticated decision support and radiology order entry systems. At Massachusetts General Hospital (MGH), an online radiology order entry system coupled with a decision support program enables physicians to not just order and schedule CT examinations from their personal computers but also to obtain information about the probability or the improbability of acquiring desired information from CT scanning for a particular patient age, gender, and clinical concern or indication. These systems use guidelines recommended in the Appropriateness Criteria developed by the American College of Radiology, as well as by the task forces of subspecialty referring physicians and radiologists in the hospital. The system also informs the physician about prior imaging tests and their reports in order to avoid inadvertent duplicate ordering of CT examinations and reduce the probability of exposing patients to unnecessary radiation.

Once the appropriateness of CT scanning is established, efforts should be made to reduce radiation dose based on patient age, size (weight or body mass index), clinical indication, body region being scanned, and presence of prior imaging test. Several strategies can help to reduce the population-based radiation dose from CT. These include limiting the use of CT according to clinical indications, avoiding multiphase scans, tailoring CT protocols to specific clinical issues, making judicious choices for repeat or follow-up CT, and adjusting technical scanning parameters appropriately.[16]

SCANNING PARAMETERS AFFECTING COMPUTED TOMOGRAPHY RADIATION DOSE

...d tomography scanning parameters that
...ct or indirect influence on radiation dose
...ized in Table 15.2. Radiation dose is

linearly related to tube current, scan time, and scan volume. Tube current is the most commonly manipulated scanning parameter for adjusting CT radiation dose. A recent survey found that reduced tube current is the most common modification reported by 93% of CT users, followed by increased pitch (43%) and reduced peak kilovoltage (39%).[17] To optimize radiation dose, the most important thing a radiologist or a technologist can do is to adjust or modify tube current according to patient body size, always using less radiation dose for smaller and younger patients. Alternatively, users can employ automatic exposure control techniques to adapt tube current to patient size.

Previous studies in the head, neck, chest, abdomen (for several specific clinical indications), and pediatric pelvis have suggested that it is possible to reduce tube currents used without jeopardizing image quality.[18–21] Cohnen et al.[18] reported that in cadavers, with reduction of tube current and voltage in the conventional and helical modes, acceptable image quality head CT scans can be obtained with

---

TABLE 15.2   PARAMETERS AFFECTING IMAGE QUALITY OR RADIATION DOSE WITH COMPUTED TOMOGRAPHY (CT) SCANNING

CT Parameters That Have a Direct Influence on Radiation Dose

Tube current (mA)
Tube voltage (kVp)
Scan length
Detector collimation
Table speed
Pitch
Gantry rotation time
Dose reduction technique such as automatic exposure control
Use of shielding:
Out-of-plane (lead aprons or eye shields)
In-plane (bismuth eye, thyroid, and breast shields)

CT Parameters That Do Not Have a Direct Influence on Radiation Dose

---

Reconstructed slice thickness
Reconstruction kernel: Smooth, sharp
Image processing technique: SoftMip, Ray Sum projection
Reconstruction technique: Filtered back projection
Iterative reconstruction
Noise reduction filters

---

a radiation dose reduction of up to 40%. Naidich et al.[19] assessed the utility of low radiation dose chest CT using reduction of mA in a preliminary study of 12 patients. Diederich et al.[20] assessed the use of low tube current for detection of pulmonary nodules with 50 mA at a pitch of 2:1 or with 25 mA at a pitch of 1:1, as compared with standard-dose CT (250 or 100 mA at a pitch of 1:1; 200 mA at a pitch of 2:1).

Pitch is defined as the ratio of the table feed in millimeter per gantry rotation and the total collimated width of the x-ray beam or the used detector width. In single detector row helical CT, as pitch increases, radiation dose decreases if all other parameters are held constant. Vade et al.[21] showed that, for single detector row helical CT, increasing the pitch from 1.0:1 to 1.5:1 resulted in a 33% dose reduction without any loss of diagnostic information.

On the other hand, most modern multidetector row CT scanners automatically adjust tube current to neutralize the effects of pitch change on CT radiation dose. For example, with increases in pitch, these scanners automatically increase the tube current to maintain constant image noise and therefore a relatively constant radiation dose. Conversely, when the pitch is decreased, tube current is automatically decreased too. Most vendors also set their automatic tube current modulation techniques to increase or decrease the tube current automatically with any change in the pitch, in order to maintain constant image noise and radiation dose. Thus, for most modern multidetector scanners, pitch changes should be made for other overriding issues, such as desired speed of scanning and image quality. For example, when performing CT angiography or CT imaging in patients who cannot hold still or who can hold their breath for only a very short time, a higher pitch may help decrease scan duration. For most body imaging work except for cardiac imaging and CT angiography, a pitch of close to or slightly higher than 1:1 is generally sufficient. When performing coronary CT angiography on a single source multidetector CT, an overlapping pitch of 0.2 to 0.35:1 is used to enable multisegment image reconstruction in different segments of cardiac cycles.

On dual-source multidetector CT, a higher pitch of up to 0.6:1 is used to reduce radiation dose for gated cardiac CT while acquiring data from two simultaneously operating x-ray tubes and detector assemblies. For noncardiac CT angiography, in order to reduce scan duration and enable the use of a compact high injection rate contrast medium

bolus, generally, a pitch of greater than 1:1 should be used. For subjects with higher body weight, who tend to have noisier images, it is again important to use a lower pitch of less than 1:1 in order to improve image quality, as compared to smaller patients.

Tube potential determines the x-ray beam energy, and radiation dose is proportional to the square of the tube voltage. Wintermark et al.[22] showed that 80 kVp acquisitions of perfusion CT studies of regional cerebral blood flow were associated with increased contrast enhancement with a reduced radiation dose, as compared with 120 kVp acquisition. It is imperative that most CT perfusion studies of the head be performed at lower kVp and lower tube currents in order to decrease radiation exposure from this otherwise higher radiation dose CT procedure.

In a recent study, it was shown that chest CT acquired at 80kVp can also provide acceptable image quality in adults weighing less than 75 kg.[23] Wintersperger et al.[24] evaluated an abdominal CT angiography protocol using 100 kVp and concluded that tube voltage reduction from 120 to 100 kVp allows for substantial reduction of patient radiation dose in abdominal CT angiography without change in image quality.

Gantry rotation time is also directly related to the radiation dose, and a slower gantry rotation implies higher radiation dose and vice versa. Generally, in order to minimize the scan duration and reduce possibility of motion artifacts, faster gantry rotation speeds are used (0.4–0.5 second), except for larger patients, in whom a higher radiation dose is achieved using slower gantry rotation (0.8–1 second).

Protecting radiosensitive organs, such as the breast, eye lenses, and gonads, is an easy way to reduce the radiation dose to these organs. Lead shields, such as lead body aprons and eye shields, have been used routinely in conventional radiography to reduce scattered radiation to body parts outside the primary region being imaged. Due to the tight x-ray beam collimation used in modern multidetector row CT scanners, there is little external scattered radiation dose to patients undergoing CT scanning. In fact, most scattered radiation exposure from CT results from internal scattering, which occurs due to interaction and deflection of x-ray photons from the imaged body region. This explains why out-of-plane shielding is unlikely to be an effective way of reducing scattered radiation dose with CT scanning. An exception to this general principle is the use of barium sulphate suspension as an oral contrast agent in pregnant patients undergoing chest CT. A recent study has shown that if pregnant patients are administered up to 40% barium sulphate oral contrast agent prior to their chest CT, the fetal radiation dose can be reduced by as much as 90%.[25]

In-plane shielding for CT scanning has been introduced to protect radiosensitive organs within the scanning range. These in-plane shielding devices partially block the x-ray beam to the underlying radiosensitive surface tissues, such as eyes, thyroid, and breasts, and thus reduce radiation dose while allowing enough x-ray beam to pass to generate a diagnostic CT image. The in-plane shields operate on the premise that most of the radiation dose to these radiosensitive superficial structures is contributed by rays directly incident upon them; hence, partial blockage of these x-rays with use of in-plane shields will reduce radiation dose to these structures. Bismuth is being currently used for in-plane shielding as it provides greater attenuation and is more elastic and moldable to the body surface than lead. Hohl et al.[26] demonstrated a radiation dose reduction of 30%–50% to thyroid and breasts with use of bismuth-based shields in an anthropomorphic phantom study. In this study, image noise in the thyroid, breast, and superficial anterior aspect of the phantom was increased with use of shields, but placement of a spacer between shield and surface resulted in a decrease in the image noise.

SIZE-BASED STRATEGIES FOR DOSE REDUCTION

Computed tomography radiation dose should be adjusted depending on the patient's size. Prior research from several distinguished authors has suggested adjusting tube current based on patient size in both adults and, more importantly, in children (smaller patients require a lesser dose and larger patients need a greater dose).[18–20,27–28] Donnelly et al.[27] have reported a 30%–50% dose reduction for pediatric CT performed with mAs adjustment and reductions based on weight of the children. In adult patients, Kalra et al.[28] have reported substantial reduction in radiation dose from abdominal CT with decrease in tube current on the basis of patient weight and cross-sectional dimensions. They showed that image quality at

50% reduced tube current (120–150 mA) was acceptable when compared with images obtained at standard tube current (240–300 mA) with a four-detector row multidetector CT scanner, although standard dose images were less noisy and more visually pleasing in patients weighing less than 81.6 kg, a cross-sectional area of less than 800 cm^2, a circumference of less than 105 cm, an anteroposterior diameter of less than 28 cm, and a transverse diameter of less than 34.5 cm. Conversely, imaging quality with reduced tube current CT was unacceptable in patients weighing more than 81.6 kg and having larger abdominal circumferences. In fact, for every 4 cm decrease in patient diameter in the region being scanned, the tube current time product can be reduced by 50% without substantially affecting the image quality.[29] Therefore, children or lighter patients must be scanned at lower radiation doses.

In a landmark study published in the *American Journal of Roentgenology*, Frush and colleagues[30] introduced the concept of color-coded CT protocols to adapt scanning parameters to children's weight or length based on the Broselow Luten pediatric color-coded system, in order to reduce radiation dose in a seamless and stratified manner. In 2009, Singh et al.[31] reported substantial radiation dose reduction with another color-coded pediatric CT protocol system based on patient weight, body region, clinical indication, and the number of prior CT examinations while using a combined tube current modulation technique (Table 15.3). These authors achieved 16%–89% radiation dose reduction for chest and abdominal CT performed using an automatic exposure control technique within a controlled minimum and maximum tube current range. For children weighing less than 20 lbs, 80 kVp was used, and for those between 21–60 lbs, 100 kVp was used for radiation dose reduction.

In summary, size-based adjustment of CT radiation dose can be performed using both fixed tube current or automatic exposure control techniques and lower kVp in children and with automatic exposure control for adults.

CLINICAL INDICATION STRATEGIES FOR DOSE REDUCTION

Following size-based adjustment of CT parameters, the next step toward dose reduction involves

TABLE 15.3   COLOR-CODED COMPUTED TOMOGRAPHY (CT) PROTOCOL SYSTEM

PINK ZONE
Most ROUTINE OR RULE OUT abdominal indications

	Weight	Noise Index	Minimum mA	Maximum mA	kVp
BABIES	<20 lb	5	65	130	80
CUTIES	21–60	7	80	160	100
KIDDIES	61–100	10	95	190	120
TEENIES	100–200	12	110	220	120
BIGGIES	>200	15	130	300	120

GREEN ZONE
First chest CT, first stone CT, follow-up abdominal CT

	Weight	Noise Index	Minimum mA	Maximum mA	kVp
BABIES	<20 lb	7	50	100	80
CUTIES	21–60	9	60	120	100
KIDDIES	61–100	11	70	140	120
TEENIES	100–200	13	80	160	120
BIGGIES	>200	16	90	240	120

RED ZONE
Follow-up chest CT, multiple prior abdominal CT, bone, or MSK indications

	Weight	Noise Index	Minimum mA	Maximum mA	kVp
BABIES	<20 lb	8	50	100	80
CUTIES	21–60	10	50	100	100
KIDDIES	61–100	12	50	100	100
TEENIES	101–200	14	50	100	120
BIGGIES	>201	18	75	150	120

GRAY ZONE
CT Angiography

	Weight	Noise Index	Minimum mA	Maximum mA	kVp
BABIES	<20 lb	5	100	200	80
CUTIES	21–60	7	120	240	100
KIDDIES	61–100	10	95	190	100
TEENIES	101–200	12	110	220	120
BIGGIES	>201	15	130	300	120

Upon receipt of CT examination in children (≤18 years of age) in the online radiology order entry system, pediatric radiologists prescribe a "color" in the radiology protocoling system based on specific clinical indication and number of prior examinations for the same indication. Technologists weigh the patient to determine the weight subzone within the prescribed color zone. For example, for an index CT examination for ruling out appendicitis in a 4-year-old child, the radiologist enters "pink" in the protocoling system and if the child weighs 40 lbs, the technologist selects "pink cutie" protocol, which is preprogrammed into the scanner user interface. Technologists have to type the protocol (such as pink cutie) used for scanning in radiology information system for assessing compliance.

the creation of specific protocols or the use of modified scan parameters to further reduce radiation for specific clinical indications. Prior studies have shown that reduced-dose CT scanning can be performed for certain clinical indications, such as for the evaluation of urinary stones, appendicitis, CT colonography (CTC), most bone indications, pulmonary nodules, CT-guided biopsy, shunt patency in hydrocephalus, cystic fibrosis, and bronchiectasis.[32-56]

Hydrocephalus, Craniosynostosis, and Computed Tomography Perfusion

Computed tomography is the modality of choice when it comes to the assessment of shunt system integrity, size change in the ventricular system, and identification of any shunt-related complications in patients with hydrocephalus. Udayasankar et al.[32] reported that low-dose nonenhanced head CT performed at 80 mA provides relevant diagnostic information in children with ventricular shunt, resulting in a 63% mean dose reduction on a four-row multidetector CT scanner.

Head CT is routinely used in the preoperative assessment and the evaluation of postoperative neurologic complications in patients with craniosynostosis. Craven et al.[33] found that low-dose CT technique at 85 mA results in retained image quality for 3D reconstructions and reduced the dose to the eye lenses, which are at risk for radiation-induced cataract. At our institution, we use a fixed mA of 50 and 100 kVp to reduce radiation dose while maintaining image quality in patients undergoing CT for craniosynostosis.

Another important indication for adjusting scanning parameters for dose reduction is in CT perfusion for evaluation of acute strokes. In contradiction to routine head CT examinations, which are generally performed at 120 or 140 kVp, a perfusion head CT must be performed at 80 kVp and up to 200 mAs to reduce radiation dose. Reduction of tube potential for perfusion CT will cut the dose by 2.5- to 3-fold, compared to the higher kVp scanning indicated for routine head CT.

Paranasal Sinuses Abnormalities

In CT of the paranasal sinuses and the neck, the most radiation-sensitive organs are the thyroid gland and the eye lens.[34] Limiting and reducing the radiation dose to the eye is important, especially in young patients and in patients who require repeat or follow-up CT scanning. Marmolya et al.[35] have suggested a low-dose paranasal CT protocol at 16 mAs for axial scanning and at 23 mAs for coronal scanning, for reduction of radiation dose in head phantom and patient studies. Given the improved z-axis resolution with modern multidetector row CT scanner, radiation dose has been further decreased by completely eliminating the use of direct coronal plane scanning in most patients. Hagtvedt et al.[36] demonstrated that the diagnostic yield of 40 mA sinus CT scans are adequate for the evaluation of patients with acute sinusitis, in comparison with standard-dose CT performed at 200–240 mA.

Cervical Spine Trauma

Computed tomography is the preferred initial imaging technique to assess acute blunt cervical spine trauma because of its accuracy, speed, and reduced patient manipulation. Mulkens et al.[37] reported the application of low-dose CT in acute blunt cervical trauma using combined or xyz-axis automatic tube current modulation technique with a 61%–71% dose reduction, compared with standard-dose CT. In another study, a 37% reduction in the CT dose index (CTDI) volume and DLP was noted for cervical spine CT performed with z-axis or xyz-axis automatic tube current modulation, compared to fixed tube current technique.

Benign and Indeterminate Chest Diseases

Dose requirements of the chest CT are much smaller than those of abdomen CT because of low x-ray absorption in the lungs.[16] In addition, as chest structures have higher inherent contrast between blood vessels and mediastinal fat, and between lung lesions or vessels and surrounding air-filled lung parenchyma, increased noise associated with low-dose chest CT is not as damaging to the diagnostic confidence as increased noise in relatively low-contrast abdominal structures. Therefore, chest CT should be performed at a lower radiation dose as compared to an abdominal CT. As mentioned earlier, several studies have reported no significant difference in detection of lung nodules on chest CT obtained at 10%–30% of the standard tube currents.[19,20] Karabulut et al.[38] showed that low-dose CT scanning at 50 mA showed no significant difference in the detection of pulmonary nodules, compared with standard-dose CT using 200 mA. Rusinek et al.[39] reported that 20 and 200 mAs chest CT had equal sensitivity for detection of 3 mm lung nodules. Gartenschlager and colleagues[40] also noted that, compared to 200 mA standard-dose CT, 30 mA low-dose CT had 85% sensitivity and 93% specificity in the detection of pulmonary nodules.

In evaluation of asbestos-related pleural-based plaques and thickening, the reliability of low-dose CT has been shown. Michel et al.[41] reported that low-dose high-resolution chest CT (120 kVp, 60 mAs) is adequate for evaluation of asbestos-related pleural disease compared to conventional-dose HRCT (140 kVp, 220 mAs), with up to 75% reduction in radiation dose.

In patients with cystic fibrosis, chest CT is used to monitor the onset and progression of lung manifestations from an early stage (bronchiectasis, peribronchial thickening, consolidation, and air trapping). Loeve et al.[42] suggested an ultra-low-dose CT protocol for assessment of all cystic fibrosis-related structural lung abnormalities in children, with an end-expiratory CT performed at fixed a 25 mA (effective tube current–time product of 10 mAs) and with a reduction of radiation dose by up to 75%.

For subjects being assessed for diffuse lung disease with high-resolution chest CT, imaging is performed generally in the supine position in inspiration and expiration, followed by acquisition of CT images in the prone position. In such instances, the initial volumetric acquisition of inspiration-phase images should be followed by a step-and-shoot or nonhelical mode of image acquisition with spacing (0.6–1 mm images at 20 mm interval) to reduce radiation dose.

Computed Tomography-guided Biopsy or Procedures

Computed tomography fluoroscopy provides real-time reconstruction and display of CT images during interventional procedures, and thus results in increased target accuracy and reduced intervention times. However, radiation dose is crucial because prolonged CT fluoroscopy exposure times can increase radiation dose to both the patient and the radiologist. The options available for dose reduction during CT-guided interventional procedures include reduction in tube voltage, tube current, slice thickness, patient coverage, number of acquisitions, and length of procedure. Heyer et al.[43] reported CT-guided transbronchial bronchoscopic biopsy using a low-dose protocol (80 kV, 20 mAs, 5-mm collimation, 10-mm slices) for the diagnostic pathway of solitary pulmonary nodules in patients who had undergone unsuccessful conventional bronchoscopic biopsy. For nonfluoroscopic CT-guided procedures, radiologists must decrease the scan length and adjust other scanning parameters to reduce radiation dose. In our institution, the initial lesion-localizing image series is followed by very limited scan length acquisition only through the lesion being targeted for the procedures. All subsequent scan series are then acquired with tight collimation and modified scan parameters (80–100 kVp, 100 mAs in step-and-shoot scanning mode) to reduce radiation dose.

Gastrointestinal and Urinary Abnormalities

Low-dose CT protocols have been used to detect urinary calculi, with sensitivity and specificity similar to those of conventional-dose CT protocols. Prior studies have reported a 31% reduction in effective tube currents and a 66% reduction in radiation dose for kidney stone protocol CT, compared to standard-dose CT with similar diagnostic performance.[44,45] Kluner et al.[46] documented 97% sensitivity and 95% specificity for detection of urinary calculi using an ultra-low-dose protocol performed at a mere 6.9 mAs. Recently, Jellison et al.[47] have reported the use of very-low-dose kidney stone protocol CT performed at 7.5 mA for detection of distal ureteral calculi in a cadaveric model, with up to a 95% decrease in radiation dose to a level equivalent to the dose of a single KUB radiograph.

High inherent contrast at the air–soft tissue interface in a distended colon allows for marked reduction in radiation exposure. Studies have shown that polyp detection remains unimpaired despite substantial increase in image noise in CTC performed at extremely low radiation doses.[48–50] Fisichella et al.[50] showed that low-dose CTC at 10–50 mA using automatic tube current modulation was equivalent to standard-dose CTC performed at 40–160 mA for detection of 6 mm or larger polyps.

Although there is controversy about which appendiceal CT technique is optimal, studies have shown that low-dose CT protocols using decreased tube currents provide similar diagnostic performance as standard-dose CT protocols. A recent study has reported that low-dose unenhanced four-detector row CT at 30 mAs has similar diagnostic performance as standard-dose unenhanced CT at 100 mAs for the diagnosis of acute appendicitis.[51]

Use of CT in the evaluation of acute abdominal pain has increased to a large extent because of the high accuracy of CT in the diagnosis of specific diseases and condition such as appendicitis, diverticulitis, urinary tract calculi, and free air, as well as rapid patient throughput with CT. Udayasankar et al.[52] reported that an ultra-low-dose technique with z-axis automatic tube current modulation (noise indexes 25 or 35 and minimum and maximum tube currents of 25 and 200 mA, respectively) provides rapid and accurate diagnostic information in patients with acute abdominal pain for detection of free air, stones, and intestinal obstruction, with a 78% mean dose reduction compared to standard-dose CT.

Multidetector row CT urography has become the most robust imaging tool for evaluation of the urinary tract because of the superior contrast resolution of CT urography compared to the excretory urography. Computed tomography urography, however, involves higher radiation exposure than routine abdominal CT or the conventional excretory urography.[53] This increase in radiation dose with CT urography is primarily due to multiphase imaging, in which images are acquired without contrast, and then in nephrographic and excretory phases following contrast administration. Compared to the three-phase CT urography protocol, in MGH, a two-phase CT urography protocol is used to reduce radiation dose without compromising the diagnostic yield of the procedure. This is accomplished by acquiring a single-phase postcontrast image following a biphasic administration of contrast bolus (40 cc of intravenous contrast at 1–2 cc/sec followed 10 minutes later with an 80 cc bolus of intravenous contrast at 3–4 cc/sec, with scanning performed 100 sec after administration of the second bolus). This split-bolus technique allows the initial contrast bolus to opacify the collecting system; in time, the contrast from the second bolus results in nephrographic phase of contrast excretion. Yanaga et al.[54] have reported a low-voltage technique (80 kVp) combined with a adaptive noise reduction filter for CT urography with 50% dose reduction compared to standard-dose CT generally performed at 120 kVp.

It is common practice to use the same CT protocols when abdominal and pelvic CT scans are performed simultaneously. Kamel et al.[55] have suggested the use of lower mAs (80 mAs) for evaluation of the pediatric pelvis, with acceptable anatomic detail and diagnostic image quality compared to standard-dose CT of 240 mAs.

Orthopedic Trauma

A low-dose CT protocol using lower fixed tube current or automatic tube current modulation may be acceptable in the evaluation of the skeletal system because skeleton is a relatively high-contrast anatomic structure. For example, Chapman et al.[56] have suggested that 16-MDCT using z-axis automatic tube current modulation was optimal at 100 kVp, with a noise index of 20 and minimum amperage of 25 mA, for the evaluation of posttraumatic pediatric elbow.

STRATEGIES TO REDUCE DOSE FOR FOLLOW-UP COMPUTED TOMOGRAPHY EXAM

In patients undergoing follow-up CT scanning specifically for a nonmalignant disease, low-dose CT may be acceptable because noisier images may be adequate for evaluation of specific lesions or abnormalities seen on prior imaging examination. This helps reduce cumulative radiation doses to those patients undergoing serial follow-up studies for benign disease processes. Singh et al.[31] have reported a 50%–65% dose reduction for follow-up chest CT and a 25%–80% dose reduction for follow-up abdominal CT in children using a color-coded protocoling system that employs an automatic exposure control technique and decreases both the kVp and mAs for children with prior imaging tests for the same clinical indication (Figure 15.1).

In adults, use of low-dose CT protocols for detection and follow-up of pulmonary nodules has been

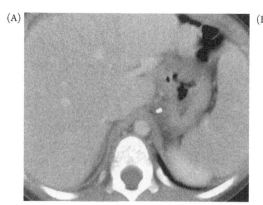
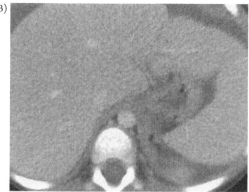

(A)   (B)

FIGURE 15.1 Two-year-old boy (14 lbs, transverse diameter 17.8 cm) was evaluated with abdominal computed tomography (CT) to assess recurrence of left adrenal neuroblastoma. The initial abdominal CT (A) was performed with scan parameters of 120 kVp and 93–119 mA, resulting in CT dose index (CTDI) volume of 3.8 mGy. Follow-up CT (B) with reduced radiation dose using scan parameters of 120 kVp and 45–62 mA resulted in radiation dose of 1.8 mGy. (A) Initial abdominal CT. (B) Lower-dose follow-up abdominal CT.

described in the literature.[57] Gergely and colleagues[57] have reported the use of an ultra-low-dose CT protocol (120 kV, 5 mAs, effective dose of 0.12 mSv) for detecting lung nodules in follow-up of cancer patients compared with standard-dose CT (120 kV, 150 mAs, effective dose of 4.8 mSv). Jiménez et al.[58] have suggested that chest CT scanning limited to just six preselected CT levels instead of the entire chest provides the same radiologic information at the follow-up study for the monitoring of respiratory disease progression in children with cystic fibrosis.

Kalra et al.[45] found that use of a z-axis modulation technique (noise indexes of 14 and 20) resulted in a 43%–66% reduction in radiation dose without compromising stone depiction in patient undergoing follow-up CT for kidney stones when compared with a previous fixed tube current (200–300 mA) technique. In our institution, initial stone protocol CT is performed at a 25 noise index, and follow-up stone protocol CT is performed at a noise index of 30 for a prospective slice thickness of 5 mm and 120 kVp.

TECHNOLOGICAL STRATEGIES FOR COMPUTED TOMOGRAPHY DOSE REDUCTION

Technical innovations to enable radiation dose optimization for CT scanning include improvement in detector efficiency with better pre-patient x-ray beam collimation, reduction in soft x-rays with bow-tie and beam-shaping filters, reduction in overbeaming with section collimation, and development of adaptive dose shielding, automatic exposure control (AEC), automatic centering technique, improved image postprocessing, and image reconstruction techniques.

To reduce the radiation dose to patients who are not directly incident on the detector assembly, online pre-patient collimation cams have been added to most modern multidetector row CT scanners. These cams help improve scanner efficiency by removing unnecessary x-rays that do not help in image formation but add to radiation dose to the patients.

Since the cross-section of most patients is oval or noncircular in shape, the attenuation of the x-ray beam in the peripheral regions is less than in the central region. Bow-tie or beam-shaping filters are designed to reduce the incident x-rays in the peripheral region. They attenuate and harden the beam spectra to efficiently penetrate the patient, as well as to selectively remove the soft x-rays, which are unlikely to reach the detectors, and thus decrease absorbed radiation. These filters help reduce surface radiation dose by 30%–50% compared with the dose from flat filters.

At the x-ray source, recently some vendors have introduced adaptive section collimation to reduce radiation dose at the margins of the scanning range, which extends beyond the edge of the detector assembly (referred to as overranging) in multidetector-row CT scanners at the beginning and the end of the scan range. The overranging x-rays do not take part in image formation and therefore decrease scanner dose efficiency and increase patient radiation exposure. Adaptive collimation dynamically cuts off the overranging x-rays and thus improves scanner efficiency and reduces radiation dose to patients.

Recently, a new feature on dual-source 64-channel multidetector row CT scanners (Siemens Definition Flash, Siemens Medical Solutions, Forchheim, Germany) has been introduced that turns off the x-rays for part of the x-ray tube rotation when it is producing x-rays that will be incident upon radiosensitive organs such as the breast and thyroid gland. This helps avoid direct exposure to the radiosensitive organs when they lie in the region being scanned.

From an image processing perspective, Meyer et al.[59] have reported on the use of softMip for low-dose CT image datasets, which decreases image noise while increasing image contrast. This technique allows review of low-dose CT with less image noise and has been assessed for low-dose kidney stone protocol CT and CT angiography studies. Recently, Seo et al.[60] investigated the use of the sliding slab ray-sum technique for low radiation dose unenhanced CT of acute appendicitis. With this technique, in a relatively thick slab, the pixel values are averaged along the viewing direction and the image quality is usually better than source thin sections due to canceling out of image noise in the thick slab images.

Along with the iterative reconstruction technique, AEC techniques represent important technologic breakthroughs for dose optimization in CT. Automatic exposure control techniques modulate tube current on the basis of the size, shape, and geometry of the body region being scanned.[61] Although most modern multidetector row CT scanners utilize AEC techniques, there is considerable difference in the definition of targeted image quality between different scanner vendors. With AEC, tube current may be modulated as a function of projection angle (angular or xy-axis modulation), in the longitudinal direction or along patient length (z-axis or longitudinal modulation), or in both angular positions and longitudinal direction (combined or xyz-axis modulation). In electrocardiographically gated cardiac CT, tube current can be modified based on the electrocardiograph (ECG) pulsing window specified by the user.

Angular (xy-axis) modulation adapts the tube current to minimize x-rays in certain projection angles as the x-ray tube rotates around the patient (for example, in the anteroposterior direction compared to the lateral direction). Reduction in tube current with this type of modulation technique is based on the asymmetry of the cross-section of the body region being imaged, as well as the fact that image noise is predominantly determined by x-rays projecting through the part of the cross-section that most attenuates the x-rays. The latter provides an opportunity, therefore, to reduce tube current at other projection angles without increasing the overall radiation dose. The greater the asymmetry of the cross-section (elliptical compared to circular cross-section), the greater will be dose reduction with angular modulation. Greess et al.[62] have reported a 10%–60% reduction in radiation dose (neck, 22% dose reduction; thorax, 23% dose reduction; abdomen, 23% dose reduction; thorax and abdomen, 22% dose reduction) with use of angular modulation for pediatric patients undergoing body CT.

Longitudinal (z-axis) modulation uses localizer radiograph data to estimate patient size and regional attenuations and then adjusts the tube current to maintain noise level or image quality reference values specified by the user within a user-specified range of tube current. This technique reduces or increases the tube current along patient length based on the increase or decrease in overall regional attenuation at different section positions in an attempt to maintain a constant desired or specified image quality. Kalra et al.[63] reported that z-axis tube current modulation using a noise index of 10.5–12 and an mA range of 10–380 resulted in reduced tube current time product and similar image noise and diagnostic acceptability for abdominal CT compared with a fixed tube current technique (200–300 mA). Similarly, Namasivayam et al.[64] demonstrated a radiation dose reduction of 21% for a noise index of 8 (150–440 mA) and 33% for a noise index of 10 (75–440 mA) for neck CT compared with a fixed current technique of 300 mA.

Combined (xyz-axis) modulation combines the advantages of angular and longitudinal modulation

techniques for adjusting tube currents to obtain a user-specified image quality, such as noise index (AutomA3D, GE Healthcare, Waukesha, Wisconsin) or reference mAs (Care Dose 4D, Siemens Medical Solutions). Mulkens et al.[44] reported a 25%–31% reduction in effective tube current with the use of a combined modulation technique for scanning subjects with kidney stones compared with application of a fixed tube current technique. Rizzo et al.[65] showed that a combined modulation technique with a reference mAs of 160 resulted in a substantial reduction of radiation dose of 42%–44% with uncompromised diagnostic acceptability, compared with a constant tube current technique of 160–200 effective mAs for abdominal and pelvic CT.

A fourth type of automatic tube current modulation is relevant for the ECG gated or tagged CT angiography of the thorax and the heart. This ECG-based tube current modulation technique enables the user to reduce tube current in those phases of cardiac cycles in which full-resolution images are not required or not as critical. Users can control the amount of tube current reduction (80%–96% of the maximum mA) for such phases or pulsing windows of the cardiac cycle by specifying the phases in which full tube current is required. These phases are generally specified by the user or by the scanner itself based on clinical area of interest and heart rate as portion or percentage of R-to-R wave peaks on ECG tracing tagged to the scan acquisition. Some scanners also allow the user to control the minimum mA for the tube current modulation. Dose reduction with this technique depends on the width of the selected pulsing window, as well as on the heart rate. With a higher heart rate, due to shortening of diastolic phase compared to the systolic phase, there is less dose savings with this technique. Conversely, at slower heart rates, this technique saves more radiation dose. Likewise, dose savings with this technique is also directly related to the width of the selected pulsing window. This technique can help reduce the radiation dose by 20%–50% compared to nonmodulated ECG gated studies.[66] The ECG tube current modulation technique should not be confused with prospective ECG-triggered CT scanning, which involves a sequential or step-and-shoot mode of scanning and turning off of the x-ray tube during certain phases of the cardiac cycle to reduce radiation dose. Most coronary artery calcium scoring CT studies are performed with ECG-triggered image acquisition. When the heart rate is below 60–65 beats per minute, coronary CT angiography can also be performed using prospective ECG triggering technique to reduce radiation dose. In contradiction to the ECG-mediated tube current modulation, prospectively triggered CT image acquisition does not allow evaluation of cardiac function. Shuman et al.[67] have reported that 64-detector-row multidetector CT angiography performed with prospective ECG triggering technique had similar subjective image quality scores, but a 77% lower radiation dose when compared with a retrospective ECG-gating technique.

Optimal centering of patients in the CT gantry is important for radiation dose optimization, as well as for the efficacy of AEC techniques. Prior studies have reported that off-centering of patients is extremely common and causes errors in tube current modulation that can outweigh the dose reduction gained by use of AEC.[68,69] Recently, automatic patient centering software has been assessed to help radiologic technologists accurately center patients in the gantry isocenter, based on the information obtained from the lateral localizer radiograph. Li et al.[70] have reported radiation dose savings of up to 30% in surface radiation dose with an automatic centering technique in patients undergoing chest or abdominal CT using the z-axis AEC technique.

Noise reduction filters help improve acceptability of low-dose CT by decreasing noise in low-dose CT images while maintaining other features of the image, such as image sharpness and contrast. These filters operate on *digital imaging and communications in medicine* (DICOM) images and can be either linear or nonlinear. Linear filters may blend smaller structures in the background and thus reduce lesion conspicuity and low-contrast resolution. Alvarez et al.[71] reported a 17% reduction in image noise with use of two-dimensional linear filters. The nonlinear filters are region specific, which implies that noise

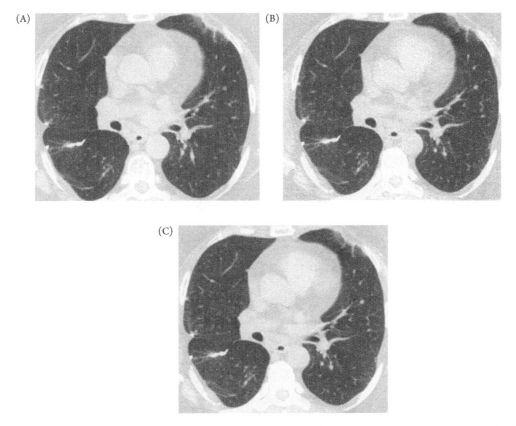

FIGURE 15.2 A 67-year-old woman (170 lbs, transverse diameter 41 cm) underwent chest computed tomography (CT) for follow-up of lung cancer. Transverse chest CT images showed multiple pulmonary nodules. Use of two-dimensional (2D) adaptive filters lowers image noise in 40 mAs image (C) and enhances the visibility of small structures compared to 40 mAs (B) and 150 mAs (A) unprocessed images. (A) 150 mAs, unprocessed image. (B) 40 mAs, unprocessed image. (C) 40 mAs, processed image.

and radiation dose reduction has to be determined specifically for different body regions. Prior studies with nonlinear filters revealed the potential for decreased noise in low-dose CT images but image contrast and sharpness was affected adversely as well, raising concerns over loss of lesion conspicuity with application of these filters.[72,73] Kalra[72,73] documented that noise reduction filters reduced image noise on low-dose chest CT (110–140 mA) and low-dose abdominal CT (120–150 mA), but they compromised lesion conspicuity and image contrast in comparison to unfiltered standard-dose CT images (chest CT, 220–280 mA; abdominal CT, 240–300 mA). Some of these limitations have not been reported with more recent nonlinear filters. For example, Funama et al.[74] have recently reported a 50% radiation dose reduction without loss of liver lesion detectability with application of adaptive nonlinear filters. Singh et al.[75] reported a dose

reduction of 35% for pediatric chest and abdominal CT examinations, a 75% dose reduction (down to 40 mAs) for chest CT (Figure 15.2) in adult patients, and a 50% dose reduction (down to 100 mAs) for adult abdominal-pelvic CT (Figure 15.3) with adaptive nonlinear two-dimensional filters.

The extent of radiation dose reduction for CT scanning may also be restricted or harmful to the diagnostic confidence of interpreting radiologists because the current CT reconstruction technique using filtered back projection (FBP) does not produce consistent diagnostic-quality images with reduction in radiation dose. Recent developments in iterative reconstruction techniques for CT scanning allow for improvements in image quality at both standard and low radiation dose CT acquisitions. The most noticeable benefit of iterative reconstruction is that it is able to incorporate into the reconstruction process a physical model of the

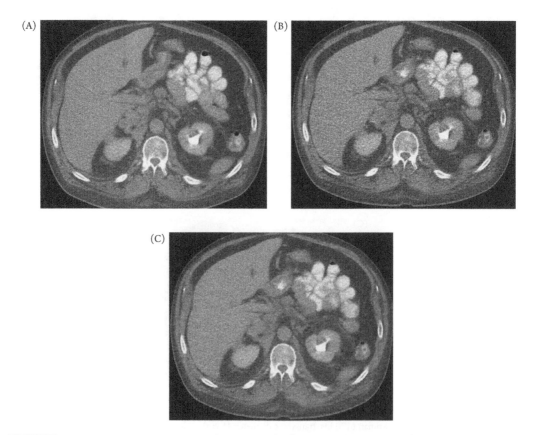

FIGURE 15.3 Transverse abdominal computed tomography (CT) images in 53-year-old man (230 lbs, transverse diameter 44 cm) showed enlarged and nodular right adrenal gland and paracaval lymphadenopathy. Low tube current (100 mAs) image (C) post processed with 2D adaptive filter resulted in lower image noise compared to 100 (B) and 200 mAs (A) unprocessed images. (A) 200 mAs, unprocessed image. (B) 100 mAs, unprocessed image. (C)100 mAs, processed image.

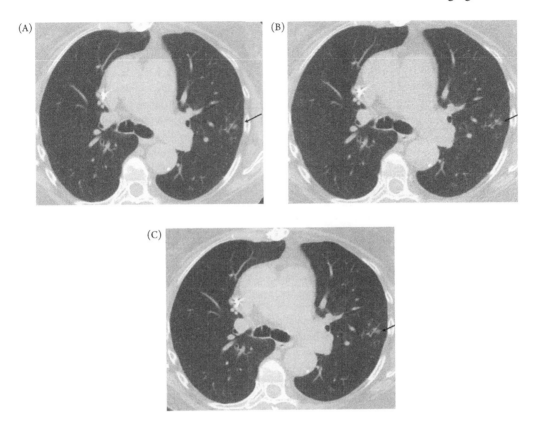

FIGURE 15.4 Transverse chest computed tomography (CT) images of a 74-year-old woman (193 lbs, transverse diameter 43 cm) with clustered nodular opacity in left upper lobe. These images were reconstructed with filtered back projection (FBP) (150 mAs-FBP [A] and 40 mAs FBP [B]) and adaptive statistical iterative reconstruction (ASIR) 70% technique (C). ASIR technique lowers image noise and makes 40 mAs CT images diagnostically acceptable, hence allowing reduction of tube current to 40 mAs. (A)150 mAs FBP. (B) 40 mAs FBP. (C) 40 mAs ASIR.

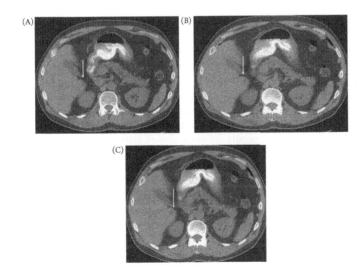

FIGURE 15.5 Transverse abdominal computed tomography (CT) images of a 62-year-old man (203 lbs, transverse diameter 43 cm) with a subcentimeter sized hepatic cyst in segment 5. These images were reconstructed using filtered back projection (FBP) (200 mAs FBP [A] and 100 mAs FBP [B]) and adaptive statistical iterative reconstruction (ASIR)50% technique (C). ASIR technique lowers image noise and renders 100 mAs CT images diagnostically acceptable, hence allowing a 50% dose reduction. (A) 200 mAs FBP. (B) 100 mAs FBP. (C) 100 mAs ASIR.

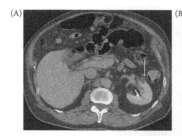
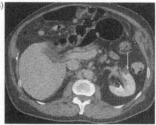
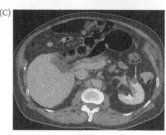

FIGURE 15.6 A 73-year-old man (153 lbs, transverse diameter 29 cm) with known history of renal neoplasm underwent abdominal computed tomography (CT). Images were reconstructed using filtered back projection (FBP) (200 mAs FBP [A] and 100 mAs FBP [B]) and adaptive statistical iterative reconstruction (ASIR) 50% technique (C). ASIR images have lower image noise as opposed to FBP, and 100 mAs tube current-time product level was diagnostically acceptable with ASIR. (A) 200 mAs FBP. (B) 100 mAs FBP. (C) 100 mAs ASIR.

CT system that can accurately characterize the data acquisition process, including noise, beam hardening, scatter, and so forth, which helps in improving image quality at lower radiation dose CT acquisitions. Although these positive attributes of iterative reconstruction techniques have been known for decades, iterative reconstruction for CT images has been approved for clinical CT scanning very recently. As iterative reconstructions are computationally much more intensive compared to the FBP technique of image reconstruction, their implementation has only become possible with the availability of much faster computer processing capabilities and a refinement of the iterative reconstruction process itself. Currently approved iterative reconstruction technique for CT is based on a purely statistical model of iterative reconstruction, as other versions of the technique are still slower for image reconstruction and therefore remain experimental at the time of writing. A discussion of the basic physical foundation of the iterative reconstruction process is beyond the scope of this chapter.

Hara et al.[76] have recently reported a 32%–65% dose reduction with the use of a statistical iterative reconstruction technique for body CT without any compromise in image quality. In a single-institution retrospective study, Prakash et al.[77,78] documented that this technique can allow an average of 28% and 25% dose reductions for chest and abdominal CT examinations, respectively, compared to the FBP technique. In prospective blinded randomized studies, Singh et al.[79,80] have recently reported

that statistical iterative reconstruction technique can permit the reduction of tube currents down to 40 mAs for chest CT (Figure 15.4) and 100 mAs for abdominal CT (Figures 15.5 and 15.6) examinations without affecting diagnostic confidence or lesion detectability.

CONCLUSION

In summary, exponential growth in the use of CT has spurred justified concerns over the potential effects of associated radiation dose and has contributed to the development of clinical and technologic strategies for reducing radiation dose. Appropriate and systematic radiation dose optimization exercises require close collaboration among radiologists, technologists, physicists, and the regulatory authorities. Efforts to reduce CT radiation dose must begin with a clear understanding of the risk versus benefits of performing CT examination in the first place, and then applying the "as low as reasonably achievable" principle for radiation dose reduction.

REFERENCES

1. National Council on Radiation Protection and Measurements. Ionizing radiation exposure of the population of the United States: Recommendations of the National Council on Radiation Protection and Measurements. Report no. 160. Bethesda, MD: NCRP, March 2009.
2. United Nations Scientific Committee on the Effects of Atomic Radiation. 2000 report to the General Assembly, Annex D: Medical radiation exposures. New York: United Nations, 2000

3. Mettler FA, Thomadsen BR, Bhargavan M, Gilley DB, Gray JE, Lipoti JA, et al. Medical radiation exposure in the U.S. in 2006: Preliminary results. *Health Phys.* 2008 95:502–507.

4. Crawley MT, Booth A, Wainwright A. A practical approach to the first iteration in the optimization of radiation dose and image quality in CT: Estimates of the collective dose savings achieved. *Br J Radiol.* 2001;74:607–14.

5. Staniszewska MA. Evaluation of patient exposure in computerised tomogram in Poland. *Radiat Prot Dosimetry.* 2002;98:437–40.

6. Scanff P, Donadieu J, Pirard P, Aubert B. Population exposure to ionizing radiation from medical examinations in France. *Br J Radiol.* 2008;81:204–13.

7. International Commission on Radiological Protection. ICRP publication 73: Radiological protection and safety in medicine. A report of the International Commission on Radiological Protection. *Ann ICRP.* 1996;26.

8. World Health Organization, International Agency for Research on Cancer. Overall evaluations of carcinogenicity to humans, list of all agents evaluated to date. Accessed February 4, 2007, at: http://monographs.iarc.fr/ENG/Classification/Listagentsalphorder.pdf

9. Agency for Toxic Substances and Disease Registry. Toxicological profile for ionizing radiation. Accessed at: http://www.atsdr.cdc.gov/toxprofiles/tp149.html

10. U.S. Department of Health and Human Services, Public Health Service, National Toxicology Program. Report on carcinogens. 11th ed. Accessed February 15, 2007 at: http://ntp.niehs.nih.gov/index.cfm?objectid_32BA9724-F1F6-975E-7FCE50709CB4C932

11. Pierce DA, Preston DL. Radiation-related cancer risks at low doses among atomic bomb survivors. *Radiat Res.* 2000;154:178–86.

12. Conference of Radiation Control Program Directors. Thirty years of NEXT. Accessed at: http://www.crcpd.org/Pubs/NextTrifolds/ThirtyYearsOfNEXT.pdf

13. Regulla DF, Eder H. Patient exposure in medical x-ray imaging in Europe. *Radiat Prot Dosimetry.* 2005;114:11–25

14. Stabin MG. Doses from medical radiation sources. Accessed at: http://hps.org/hpspublications/articles/dosesfrommedicalradiation.html

15. Sodickson A, Baeyens PF, Andriole KP, Prevedello LM, Nawfel RD, Hanson R, et al. Recurrent CT, cumulative radiation exposure, and associated radiation-induced cancer risks from CT of adults. *Radiology.* 2009;251:175–84.

16. Rehani MM, Berry M. Radiation doses in computed tomography: The increasing doses of radiation need to be controlled. *BMJ.* 2000;320:593–4.

17. Karabulut N, Ariyürek M. Low dose CT: Practices and strategies of radiologists in university hospitals. *Diagn Interv Radiol.* 2006;12:3–8.

18. Cohnen M, Fischer H, Hamacher J, Lins E, Kotter R, Modder U. CT of the head by use of reduced current and kilovoltage: Relationship between image quality and dose reduction. *AJNR Am J Neuroradiol.* 2000;21:1654–60.

19. Naidich DP, Marshall CH, Gribbin C, Arams RS, McCauley DI. Low-dose CT of the lungs: Preliminary observations. *Radiology.* 1990;175:729–31.

20. Diederich S, Lenzen H, Windmann R, Puska Z, Yelbuz TM, Henneken S, et al. Pulmonary nodules: Experimental and clinical studies at low-dose CT. *Radiology.* 1999;213:289–98.

21. Vade A, Demos TC, Olson MC, Subbaiah P, Turbin RC, Vickery K, et al. Evaluation of image quality using 1:1 pitch and 1.5:1 pitch helical CT in children: A comparative study. *Pediatr Radiol.* 1996;26:891–3.

22. Wintermark M, Maeder P, Verdun FR, Thira JP, Valley JF, Schnyder P, et al. Using 80 kVp versus 120 kVp in perfusion CT measurement of regional cerebral blood flow. *AJNR Am J Neuroradiol.* 2000;21:1881–4.

23. Sigal-Cinqualbre AB, Hennequin R, Abada HT, Chen X, Paul JF. Low-kilovoltage multi-detector row chest CT in adults: Feasibility and effect on image quality and iodine dose. *Radiology.* 2004;231:169–74.

24. Wintersperger B, Jakobs T, Herzog P, Schaller S, Nikolaou K, Suess C, et al. Aorto-iliac multidetector-row CT angiography with low kVp settings: Improved vessel enhancement and simultaneous reduction of radiation dose. *Eur Radiol.* 2005;15:335–41.

25. Yousefzadeh DK, Ward MB, Reft C. Internal barium shielding to minimize fetal irradiation in spiral chest CT: A phantom simulation experiment. *Radiology.* 2006; 238: 751–8.

26. Hohl C, Wildberger JE, Suss C, Thomas C, Muhlenbruch G, Schmidt T, et al. Radiation dose reduction to breast and thyroid during MDCT: Effectiveness of an in-plane bismuth shield. *Acta Radiol.* 2006;47:562–7.

27. Donnelly LF, Emery KH, Brody AS, Laor T, Gylys-Morin VM, Anton CG, et al. Minimizing radiation dose for pediatric body applications of single-detector helical CT: Strategies at a large children's hospital. *AJR Am J Roentgenol.* 2001;176:303–306.

28. Kalra MK, Prasad S, Saini S, Blake MA, Varghese J, Halpern EF, et al. Clinical comparison of standard-dose and 50% reduced-dose abdominal CT: Effect on image quality. *AJR Am J Roentgenol.* 2002;179:1101–6.

29. Maher MM, Kalra MK, Toth TL, Wittram C, Saini S, Shepard J. Application of rational practice and technical advances for optimizing radiation dose for chest CT. *J Thorac Imaging.* 2004;19:16–23.

30. Frush DP, Donnelly LF. Helical CT in children: Technical considerations and body applications. *Radiology.* 1998;209:37–48.

31. Singh S, Kalra MK, Moore MA, Shailam R, Liu B, Toth TL, et al. Dose reduction and compliance with pediatric CT protocols adapted to patient size, clinical indication, and number of prior studies. *Radiology.* 2009;252:200–208.

32. Udayasankar UK, Braithwaite K, Arvaniti M, Tudorascu D, Small WC, Little S, et al. Low-dose nonenhanced head CT protocol for follow-up evaluation of children with ventriculoperitoneal shunt: Reduction of radiation and effect on image quality. *AJNR Am J Neuroradiol.* 2008;29:802–806.

33. Craven CM, Naik KS, Blanshard KS, Batchelor AG, Splencer JA. Multispiral three-dimensional computed tomography in the investigation of craniosynostosis: Technique optimization. *Br J Radiol.* 1995;68:724–30.

34. Hein E, Rogalla P, Klingebiel R, Hamm B. Low-dose CT of the paranasal sinuses with eye lens protection: Effect on image quality and radiation dose. *Eur Radiol.* 2002;12:1693–6.

35. Marmolya G, Wiesen EJ, Yagan R, Haria CD, Shah AC. Paranasal sinuses: Low-dose CT. *Radiology.* 1991;181:689–91.

36. Hagtvedt T, Aaløkken TM, Nøtthellen J, Kolbenstvedt A. A new low-dose CT examination compared with standard-dose CT in the diagnosis of acute sinusitis. *Eur Radiol.* 2003;13:976–80.

37. Mulkens TH, Marchal P, Daineffe S, Salgado R, Bellinck P, te Rijdt B, et al. Comparison of low-dose with standard-dose multidetector CT in cervical spine trauma. *AJNR Am J Neuroradiol.* 2007;28:1444–50.

38. Karabulut N, Törü M, Gelebek V, Gülsün M, Ariyürek MO. Comparison of low-dose and standard-dose helical CT in the evaluation of pulmonary nodules. *Eur Radiol.* 2002;12:2764–9.

39. Rusinek H, Naidich DP, McGuinness G, Leitman BS, McCauley DI, Krinsky GA, et al. Pulmonary nodule detection: Low-dose versus conventional CT. *Radiology.* 1998;209:243–9.

40. Gartenschlager M, Schweden F, Gast K, Westermeier T, Kauczor H, von Zitzewitz H, et al. Pulmonary nodules: Detection with low-dose vs conventional-dose spiral CT. *Eur Radiol.* 1998;8:609–14.

41. Michel JL, Reynier C, Avy G, Bard JJ, Gabrillargues D, Catilina P. An assessment of low-dose high resolution CT in the detection of benign asbestos-related pleural abnormalities. *J Radiol.* 2001; 82:922–3.

42. Loeve M, Lequin MH, de Bruijne M, Hartmann IJ, Gerbrands K, van Straten M, et al. Cystic fibrosis: Are volumetric ultra-low-dose expiratory CT scans sufficient for monitoring related lung disease? *Radiology.* 2009;253: 223–9.

43. Heyer CM, Kagel T, Lemburg SP, Walter JW, de Zeeuw J, Junker K, et al. Transbronchial biopsy guided by low-dose MDCT: A new approach for assessment of solitary pulmonary nodules. *AJR Am J Roentgenol.* 2006;187:933–9.

44. Mulkens TH, Daineffe S, De Wijngaert R, Bellinck P, Leonard A, Smet G, et al. Urinary stone disease: Comparison of standard-dose and low-dose with 4D MDCT tube current modulation. *AJR Am J Roentgenol.* 2007;188:553–62.

45. Kalra MK, Maher MM, D'Souza RV, Rizzo S, Halpern EF, Blake MA, et al. Detection of urinary tract stones at low-radiation-dose CT with z-axis automatic tube current modulation: Phantom and clinical studies. *Radiology.* 2005;235:523–9.

46. Kluner C, Hein PA, Gralla O, Hein E, Hamm B, Romano V et a. Does ultra-low-dose CT with a radiation dose equivalent to that of KUB suffice to detect renal and ureteral calculi? *J Comput Assist Tomogr.* 2006;30:44–50.

47. Jellison FC, Smith JC, Heldt JP, Spengler NM, Nicolay LI, Ruckle HC, et al. Effect of low dose radiation computerized tomography protocols on distal ureteral calculus detection. *J Urolo.* 2009;182:2762–7.

48. van Gelder RE, Venema HW, Serlie IW, Nio CY, Determann RM, Tipker CA, et al. CT colonography at different radiation dose levels: Feasibility of dose reduction. *Radiology.* 2002; 224:25–33.

49. Hara AK, Johnson CD, Reed JE, Ahlquist DA, Nelson H, Ehman RL, et al. Reducing data size and radiation dose for CT colonography. *AJR Am J Roentgenol.* 1997;168:1181–4.

50. Fisichella VA, Båth M, Allansdotter Johnsson A, Jäderling F, Bergsten T, Persson U, et al. Evaluation of image quality and lesion perception by human readers on 3D CT colonography: Comparison of standard and low radiation dose *Eur Radiol.* 2010; 20(3):630–9.

51. Keyzer C, Tack D, de Maertelaer V, Bohy P, Gevenois PA, Van Gansbeke D. Acute appendicitis: Comparison of low-dose and standard-dose unenhanced multidetector row CT. *Radiology.* 2004;232:164–72.

52. Udayasankar UK, Li J, Baumgarten DA, Small WC, Kalra MK. Acute abdominal pain: Value of noncontrast enhanced ultra-low-dose multi-detector row CT as a substitute for abdominal radiographs. *Emerg Radiol.* 2009;16:61–70.

53. Eikefjord EN, Thorsen F, Rorvik J. Comparison of effective radiation doses in patients undergoing unenhanced MDCT and excretory urography for acute flank pain. *AJR Am J Roentgenol.* 2007;188: 934–9.

54. Yanaga Y, Awai K, Funama Y, Nakaura T, Hirai T, Roux S, et al. Low-dose MDCT urography: Feasibility study of low-tube-voltage technique and adaptive noise reduction filter. *AJR Am J Roentgenol.* 2009; 193:W220–W229.

55. Kamel IR, Hernandez RJ, Martin JE, Schlesinger AE, Niklason LT, Guire KE. Radiation dose reduction in CT of the pediatric pelvis. *Radiology.* 1994;190:683–7.

56. Chapman VM, Kalra MK, Halpern E, Grottkau B, Albright M, Jaramillo D. 16-MDCT of the posttraumatic pediatric elbow: Optimum parameters

and associated radiation dose. *AJR Am J Roentgenol.* 2005;185:516–21.

57. Gergely I, Neumann C, Reiger F, Dorffner R. Lung nodule detection with ultra-low-dose CT in routine follow-up of cancer patients. *Rofo.* 2005;177:1077–83.

58. Jimenez S, Jimenez JR, Crespo M, Santamarta E, Bousono C, Rodriguez J. Computed tomography in children with cystic fibrosis: A new way to reduce radiation dose. *Arch Dis Child.* 2006;91:388–90.

59. Meyer H, Juran R, Rogalla P. SoftMip: A novel projection algorithm for ultra-low-dose computed tomography. *J Comput Assist Tomogr.* 2008;32:480–4.

60. Seo H, Lee KH, Kim HJ, Kim K, Kang SB, Kim SY, et al. Diagnosis of acute appendicitis with sliding slab ray-sum interpretation of low-dose unenhanced CT and standard-dose IV contrast-enhanced CT scans. *AJR Am J Roentgenol.* 2009;193:96–105.

61. McCollough CH. Automatic exposure control in CT: Are we done yet? *Radiology.* 2005;237:755–6.

62. Greess H, Nomayr A, Wolf H, Baum U, Lell M, Bowing B, et al. Dose reduction in CT examination of children by an attenuation-based on-line modulation of tube current (CARE dose). *Eur Radiol.* 2002;12:1571–6.

63. Kalra MK, Maher MM, Toth TL, Kamath RS, Halpern EF, Saini S. Comparison of z-axis automatic tube current modulation technique with fixed tube current CT scanning of abdomen and pelvis. *Radiology.* 2004;237:347–53.

64. Namasivayam S, Kalra MK, Pottala KM, Waldrop SM, Hudgins PA. Optimization of z-axis automatic exposure control for multidetector row CT evaluation of neck and comparison with fixed tube current technique for image quality and radiation dose. *AJNR Am J Neuroradiol.* 27;2221–5.

65. Rizzo S, Kalra MK, Schmidt B, Dalal T, Suess C, Flohr T, et al. Comparison of angular and combined automatic tube current modulation techniques with constant tube current CT of the abdomen and pelvis. *AJR Am J Roentgenol.* 186;673–9.

66. Hausleiter J, Meyer T, Hadamitzky M, Huber E, Zankl M, Martinoff S, et al. Radiation dose estimates from cardiac multislice computed tomography in daily practice: Impact of different scanning protocols on effective dose estimates. *Circulation.* 2006;113:1305–10.

67. Shuman WP, Branch KR, May JM, Mitsumori LM, Lockhart DW, Dubinsky TJ, et al. Prospective versus retrospective ECG gating for 64-detector CT of the coronary arteries: Comparison of image quality and patient radiation dose. *Radiology.* 2008;248:431–7.

68. Matsubara K, Koshida K, Ichikawa K, Suzuki M, Takata T, Yamamoto T, et al. Misoperation of CT automatic current modulation systems with inappropriate patient centering: Phantom studies. *AJR Am J Roentgenol.* 2009;192:862–5.

69. Gudjonsdottir J, Svensson JR, Campling S, Brennan PC, Jonsdottir B. Efficient use of automatic exposure control systems in computed tomography requires correct patient positioning. *Acta Radiol.* 2009;50:1035–41.

70. Li J, Udayasankar UK, Toth TL, Seamans J, Small WC, Kalra MK. Automatic patient centering for MDCT: Effect on radiation dose. *AJR Am J Roentgenol.* 2007;188:547–52.

71. Alvarez RE, Stonestrom JP. Optimal processing of computed tomography images using experimentally measured noise properties. *J Comput Assist Tomogr.* 1979;3:77–84.

72. Kalra MK, Wittram C, Maher MM, Sharma A, Avinash GB, Karau K, et al. Can noise reduction filters improved low radiation-dose chest CT images? Pilot study. *Radiology.* 2003;228:257–64.

73. Kalra MK, Maher MM, Sahani DV, Blake MA, Hahn PF, Avinash GB, et al. Low-dose CT of the abdomen: Evaluation of image improvement with use of noise reduction filters pilot study. *Radiology.* 2003;228:251–6.

74. Funama Y, Awai K, Miyazaki O, Nakayama Y, Goto T, Omi Y, et al. Improvement of low-contrast detectability in low-dose hepatic multidetector computed tomography using a novel adaptive filter: Evaluation with a computer-simulated liver including tumors. *Invest Radiol.* 2006;41:1–7.

75. Singh S, Sharma A, Digumarthy S, Sjoberg J, Shepard J, Kalra MK. Two-dimensional image filters for reducing radiation dose for multidetector chest CT: A double blinded study. *RSNA.* 2008; doi:10.1148/radiol.1101450.

76. Hara AK, Paden RG, Silva AC, Kujak JL, Lawder HJ, Pavlicek W. Iterative reconstruction technique for reducing body radiation dose at CT: Feasibility study *AJR Am J Roentgenol.* 2009;193:764–71.

77. Prakash P, Kalra MK, Digumarthy SR, Hsieh J, Pien H, Singh S. Radiation dose reduction with chest CT using adaptive statistical iterative reconstruction technique: Initial experience. *J Comput Assist Tomogr.* 2010;45:202–210.

78. Prakash P, Kalra MK, Kambadakone AK, Pien H, Hsieh J, Blake MA, et al. Reducing abdominal CT radiation dose with adaptive statistical iterative reconstruction technique. *Invest Radiol.* 2010;34:285–289.

79. Singh S, Kalra M, Hsieh J, Pien H, Shepard J, Digumarth S. Adaptive statistical iterative reconstruction for dose reduction in chest CT. *RSNA.* 2009.

80. Singh S, Kalra MK, Hsieh J, Doyle MM, Prakash P, Blake MA Comparison of iterative and filtered back projection techniques for abdominal CT: A prospective double blinded clinical study. *RSNA.* 2009.

II

Management Concepts in Radiology Quality & Safety

16

Key Performance Indicators in Radiology

RATHACHAI KAEWLAI AND HANI H. ABUJUDEH

The improvement of health care quality has become an important national and international policy today.[1,2] Conceptual frameworks for monitoring, measuring, and managing the performance of health systems have been developed in many countries to ensure effectiveness, equity, efficiency, and quality.[3,4] Health professionals and policy-makers constantly seek to improve the quality of individual provider, facility, and overall health systems.[5] With growing demand from health care purchasers, providers, governing authorities, and the public, the need to assess and monitor the quality of health care is increasingly important.[1] However, as the old management adage says, you cannot manage what you cannot measure. Elements of health care quality must be measurable, so that they can be managed, evaluated, monitored, and improved. Some elements in the quality of care are easy to define and measure, while others are not.[6] Radiology practices are faced with pressures, both internal and external, to measure their quality. Mandatory radiology quality reporting criteria developed by the Centers for Medicare and Medicaid Services (CMS) and third-party payers are in place. Part IV of the American Board of Radiology (ABR)'s maintenance of certification (MOC) program requires practice quality improvement projects of all diagnostic radiology board recertification and certificates of added qualification.[7] The Joint Commission and employer-sponsored health care purchasing groups are requesting hospitals, where many radiology practices are based, to provide and track information about effectiveness and quality

of care.[7,8] Radiology practices are also encountering increased competition and reduced reimbursement rates that demand the development of tools to assess and increase the efficiency of their activities.[8,9]

It is time for radiology practices to develop a standard set of measures for the evaluation of their operations and patient care.[10] In this chapter, we discuss performance measurement, performance indicators (PIs), key performance indicators (KPIs), methods to develop and maintain such indicators, and their limitations.

ASSESSMENT OF HEALTH CARE QUALITY

In general, the assessment of quality of care can be viewed in three different layers.[6] The core or deepest layer is the care provided by practitioners and other providers, and here assessment can be performed in regards to technical (knowledge, judgment, skill) and interpersonal issues. The middle layer is care implemented by patients; this care is contributed to by patients themselves, their families, and providers. Amenities lie between the core and the middle layer. The outer layer is care received by the community as a whole, which is judged by accessibility to care, and the performance of provider, patient and family. As suggested by Donabedian,[11] the steps for assuring quality of care may include determining what to monitor, prioritization of monitored factors, selecting an approach to assess performance, formulating criteria and standards, obtaining necessary information, choosing how to monitor,

TABLE 16.1   A SEQUENCE OF STEPS FOR ASSURING QUALITY OF CARE

Determining what to monitor

Determining priorities in monitoring

Selecting an approach (or approaches) to assessing
  performance

Formulating criteria and standards

Obtaining the necessary information

Choosing how to monitor

Constructing a monitoring system

Bringing about behavior change

constructing a monitoring system, and bringing about behavior change (Table 16.1).

PERFORMANCE INDICATORS

Performance indicators are those elements of practice performance that can be measured and that carry consensus or evidence that they can be used to assess quality.[8] They are an important component of and supplement to quality management, and can be applied to clinical, financial, organizational, and health system performance.[8] They require an operational definition of quality to be developed; hence, they are considered to be a quantitative measure of quality.[12] Ideal PIs should be attributable to health care, linked to health outcome, scientifically sound, sensitive to change, well defined, easily measurable, reflective of a variety of care dimensions, relevant to policy and practice, feasible to collect and report, and compliant with national processes of data definitions. In addition, ideal PIs should not be vulnerable to the random variation associated with rare events. It should be noted that no PIs have all of these ideal characteristics. Perhaps the most important criterion is that the PI is attributable to health care (i.e., the PI contains a link between the provider and an action that the provider has some control over).[8] A good set of PIs should reflect the needs of and be agreed to among all stakeholders in health care (health funders, providers, and consumers). It should also be applicable across a range of organizational settings.

Since quality may mean different things to different people, the perspectives of performance for key stakeholders may vary. Each stakeholder brings to the table a unique view of health care quality and a distinct political agenda on health care issues.[12]

To develop and implement meaningful, scientifically sound, generalizable, and interpretable PIs, one needs to consider the purpose of performance measurements as viewed by different parties. The design of PIs is intimately related to their intended purposes.[8] Different stakeholders may use PIs for health care purchasing, utilization, or performance improvement.[2]

THREE TYPES OF PERFORMANCE INDICATORS

Generally, a quality indicator system is designed in line with Donabedian's structure, process, and outcome definitions.[13] These three approaches are influenced by probability. They are not precisely separated, but rather represent a series of causes and effects. Structure influences process, and process influences outcome.[11] Knowledge of structure–process and process–outcome linkage should be established before any particular component can be used as a measure of quality.[6] The higher the degree/firmness of linkage, the more credible the judgment of quality can be.[11] Outcome and process measurements are more commonly seen in the current development of PIs rather than in structural measurements.[13] However, good performance management systems should include an appropriate combination of all types of PIs.[14]

Outcome

The outcome of medical care is the effect of care on a patient's health and well-being; this could be survival, recovery and restoration of function, or death. Outcome has been frequently used as an indicator of quality of medical care[15] and is considered by practitioners to be "what matters most."[11] Examples of quality outcome measure are surgical fatality rate, perinatal mortality, and contrast extravasation rate.[10] The benefits of using outcomes for the assessment of performance and quality of care are that their validity and stability is seldom questioned,[15,16] they are fairly concrete and amenable to more precise measurement,[15] and they reflect and embody the overall care (quality, quantity of life added by clinical intervention) done for a patient.[11,14,16] Focusing on outcome measurements may help direct clinical attention toward a single goal (the patient's health status), rather than toward specific interventions, and may nurture innovations and technologies for long-term health benefits.[14] Although outcome measures have several advantages, they should be used with discrimination[15] because several limitations exist. Endpoints, such as fatality, may not be relevant to care in some disease conditions that are end-staged or that produce crippling conditions. Several processes and factors influencing outcome may render it invalid. Many outcomes are evident only after a long period of time.[17] Either good or bad outcomes usually do not provide insight into the nature and location of a defect or strength to which the outcome might be attributed.[15] When interpreting outcome measures, risk adjustment for specific clinical conditions may be required, thus making data collection lengthy and costly.[2]

However, despite many limitations, outcomes remain the ultimate proof of the effectiveness and quality of medical care.[15] To develop and use outcomes as a PI, one must be aware that the outcome selected is relevant to the objective of care and achievable by good care. Outcome must be the first-hand result of health care contributed by the provider, not of other nonmedical factors that may have intervened. Trade-offs between one outcome and the alternative may have to be weighed; for example, having a shorter life at a higher functioning level versus a longer life with greater disability. To monitor outcome, one must track the consequences of not taking action to obtain a complete picture of performance. Last, measures of other factors used to achieve the outcome have to be taken into account.

Process

Process indicates actions of giving and receiving care, covering both patient's and practitioner's activities from seeking care to implementation of treatment.[6] Assessment of the process can be based on variable considerations, such as appropriateness, completeness, justification of diagnosis and treatment, technical competence, and the like.[15] The advantages of using process over outcome measures[11] are that process measures are able to identify smaller variation in quality of care; are quickly measurable and updated in real time with appropriate use of information technology;[14] are valuable in themselves, regardless of clinical outcome (i.e., speed of access to care); readily attributable to providers; and are easy to understand and interpret.[2] Process indicators can give a clear indication of the remedial action required for poor performance. These indicators also require less risk adjustment for patient illness, compared with outcome measures.[2] Measurement is desirable particularly when the process is unambiguously associated with improved patient health outcomes; this strong relationship between process and outcome measures needs to be emphasized.[14]

Structure

Structure is the setting in which the care takes place.[15] Material resources (facilities, equipment, money), human resources (number, qualifications of personnel), and organizational structures (medical staff organization, methods of peer review, and methods of reimbursement) are attributes of structure.[6] Administrative and related processes that support and direct the provision of care may be included in this category.[15] Given the extent of structure, it could be the major determinant of quality of care since it reflects how the health care system is organized.[11] Examples of structure indicators are adequacy of facilities and equipment, staff qualifications, administrative structure and operations, etc. The major obstacles for use of structure indicators are that their relationships with process and outcome are usually not well established.[15]

The use of a combination of the three types of indicators is likely the best course in the development of performance measurement indicators. The team intending to develop indicators should have a thorough understanding of the strengths and limitations of these three types of quality measures, which will assist them in selecting an appropriate mix of indicators to be used in a particular institution.[18] The precise mix should be determined by the nature of the organization, stakeholders' needs, what is considered important to each setting, and the availability of the needed information.[11]

SEVEN STEPS TO DEVELOP PERFORMANCE INDICATORS

Step 1: Define Stakeholders and Use for Measurement

The stakeholders who will use performance indicators strongly influence the development of such indicators. In general, care providers use indicators to evaluate and enhance their performance through quality improvement initiatives. Health care purchasers and patients use indicators to help in health care decision-making—for example, to select a hospital or a care provider. Government authorities and third-party payers monitor organizations through these indicators.[2] Because each stakeholder brings its own perspective of how indicators will be used (i.e., different domains of process, different units of analysis), the indicators must be valid to stakeholders' needs and also represent an important domain of quality.[18] To develop such indicators that can be fully functional and valid to each stakeholder, one should clarify the goals and purposes of quality indicators for each stakeholder.

For care providers, the goal of indicators is the improvement of health care processes as a part of their internal organizational quality improvement initiatives. Indicators often require significant technical details, and the link between process and outcome should be clearly established. The unit of analysis here tends to be small, such as individual unit, practice, or practitioner. For these stakeholders, the practical interpretation or visual impact of differences in graphic presentation (i.e., acceptable, unacceptable) is often more important than statistically significant results.[2]

For health care purchasers and patients, the goal of indicators is to aid in making health care decisions (purchasing care). Indicators should be easily understandable and have clearly established links to outcomes that can be perceived by patients, benefits managers, and enrollees. Statistical significance becomes more important for these stakeholders because patients and enrollees need to make decisions for better care. Here, summary or aggregated data are typically used.[2]

For government authorities and third-party payers, the goals of indicators are the monitoring and regulation of health care organizations. Indicators must be strongly linked to outcomes and be accepted by the clinical community, even though they may not be used for direct clinical feedback. Indicators for this group of stakeholders are usually summary measures for relevant unit of analysis.[2]

Each team (Table 16.2) will need to develop multiple indicators—each providing insights into a different domain of quality as viewed by all major stakeholders—that can be used to completely evaluate quality of care.[18]

Step 2: Choose Clinical Area to Evaluate
Performance indicators are designed as a means to improve the clinical, service, and financial performance of an institution. To choose an area to evaluate through the use of indicators, one should consider the impact of morbidity, mortality, or cost as related to that specific area. In some cases, care providers may want to focus on areas with a particular problem of care. Another rationale that can

help in choosing the area to evaluate is the cost of data collection and the potential cost savings from improving the aspect of care being evaluated. Care providers may be reluctant to pursue the measurement of a certain aspect of care if it will result in higher costs after improvement. In addition, the volume measured should also be high enough to produce meaningful statistical results. Once the goals and use of indicators have been defined, and clinical areas have been selected for evaluation, one can move on to organizing an assessment team.

Step 3: Organize Assessment Team
Members of the assessment team should include representatives of care areas, quality personnel with knowledge of measurement, and appropriate advisors. Advisors should come from each stakeholder group and from the administration whose resources will be used. Since the development of indicators requires intensive resources and is costly, joint efforts to share indicators among different parts of an institution, or across institutions or professional societies may lead to the most efficient use of resources. In addition, use of measures that have been published,[19] or developed by national organizations, such as the National Committee on Quality Assurance (www.ncqa.org), the CMS (www.cms.gov), or the Institute for Healthcare Improvement (www.ihi.org) can save time and money.

Step 4: Select Aspect of Care or Process Criteria To Be Measured
The team creates a framework of care by examining all aspects of the care process and defining the links between them. The framework is used in selecting the aspect of care to be measured. By simply asking if the process could go wrong at each step, the team derives many potential measures.[18] In the radiologic framework,[20] the process of care usually starts when a referring physician orders an imaging test. The radiology department then schedules the procedure, and the protocol is selected for each patient. The examination is performed. The radiologist interprets, then finalizes the report and communicates its results to the referring physician. The patient's outcome depends upon the final diagnosis and the treatment given by the referring physician.

Potential indicators that can arise in the first step of ordering the imaging test are, for example, correctness, completeness and appropriateness of orders, safety, or utilization. Then, the team needs to evaluate each potential indicator to see whether it is

TABLE 16.2   STRATEGIC AREAS OF RADIOLOGY DEPARTMENT
PERFORMANCE AND CORRESPONDING KEY PERFORMANCE
INDICATOR (KPI) COMMITTEE DUTIES

Strategic Area and KPI Committee	Committee Duties
Patient safety and quality of care	Review existing and potential measures that directly or indirectly pertain to patient safety and quality of care within the department (e.g., number of falls, rate of hand hygiene compliance).
Customer service	Review existing and potential measures that directly or indirectly pertain to patient, employee, and system-wide satisfaction with service provided by the department (e.g., patient satisfaction survey results).
Operations management	
Utilization	Review existing and potential measures that directly or indirectly pertain to all facets of operations within the department (e.g., number of patients imaged, resource utilization, examination duration).
Information technology	Review existing and potential measures that directly or indirectly pertain to the state of information technology within the department (e.g., duration of picture archiving and communication system downtime).
Innovation	Review existing and potential measures that directly or indirectly pertain to the development of new and innovative programs and initiatives within the department (e.g., number of new patent applications).
Education	Review existing and potential measures that directly or indirectly pertain to department-provided training and credentialing of both clinical and nonclinical staff (e.g., number of continuing education units awarded).
Research	Review existing and potential measures that directly or indirectly pertain to research activities within the department (e.g., number of papers published).
Financial management	Review existing and potential measures that directly or indirectly pertain to financial management within the department (e.g., gross revenue, technical relative value units).

For each main strategic area or each subcategory, a KPI committee may be formed to identify relevant KPIs and metrics.
Reprinted with permission from Abujudeh HH, Kaewlai R, Asfaw BA, Thrall JH. Quality initiatives: Key performance indicators for measuring and improving radiology department performance. *RadioGraphics*. 2010;30:571–80.

feasible to measure, reliable, and valid. Useful indicators are those that, if improved, will translate into improved outcome. This emphasizes the importance of a linkage between structure and process, and process and outcome. Additionally, the team should make sure that providers and managers are able to influence the process component of that indicator to make it valid. The team should also evaluate existing indicators for their measurability, reliability, and validity.[18]

Step 5: Write Indicator Specifications

Once the team agrees upon valid, reliable, and measurable indicators, they must state the specifications of each indicator. These specifications help identify target populations and the data to be actually collected. Specifications should identify a unit of analysis (patient, provider, provider group, hospital unit, hospital, health system, or insurer), a definition (yes-no result, proportion, ratio, average), inclusion and exclusion criteria, prevalence versus incidence, a definition of the risk-adjustment strategy (if required, particularly with outcome indicators), the data source and collection procedures (where and how data will be obtained), and data collection specifications.

Step 6: Perform Preliminary Tests

Preliminary tests of indicators and data collection methods should be performed on a small sample to identify areas needing modification, and to test the scientific strength of the indicators. Indicator reliability may be tested by repeated measurement of the same area; reliable indicators should yield comparable results. Indicator validity is tested by confirming that the scores obtained from using the indicators are in line with outcome measures.

Step 7: Write Scoring and Analytical Specifications

The team should define acceptable performance and scoring with all stakeholders involved in particular indicators. All stakeholders should agree on what constitutes acceptable performance.[18] This process of benchmarking reflects the goal that each stakeholder wants to achieve. Typically, benchmarks are performance levels achieved by top-performing groups in society at large,[21] either nationally or internationally—but not perfection. It is not always possible to find widely available benchmarks for every process; therefore, the choice of benchmarks for specific indicators needs to be made based upon the availability of data.[21]

The team also needs to develop an analytical plan, which is a detailed plan for how indicators will be analyzed and by what type of statistical tools and degree of significance.

KEY PERFORMANCE INDICATORS

The performance indicators created by the assessment team will be assigned various levels of importance. Those that are most critical for the current and future success of the organization/institution are called *key performance indicators* (KPIs). Characteristics of KPIs may include the following[22]:

1. *Nonfinancial.* PIs those are expressed with currency terms are results of action. Although financial measures can provide a clear picture of where the organization/institution is heading, they do not clarify what exactly needs to be done to improve the results. Key PIs influence management aspect of the organization, whereas governance is impacted by financial metrics.

2. *Frequently measured.* Since KPIs are considered "key" to the organization, they are monitored frequently in terms of hours or days. They are current- or future-oriented measures, as opposed to past measures, meaning that they are monitored daily, 24/7 (current measures) or focused on the next day/week/month/quarter (future-oriented measures).

3. *Acted on by chairman and senior management team.* Again, since KPIs are the key to success,

they receive constant attention from the head of the organization and the senior management team.

4. *Understood by all staff and teams.* Individuals in the organization know the KPIs for their organization, so that they can work accordingly toward the same goals that the organization is pursuing.

5. *Linked to a team.* The KPI ties responsibility to a team or an individual, so that, when needed, the chairman or senior management team can act directly and swiftly through the team.

6. *Have significant impact and influence on the success of the organization.*

7. *Have positive impact on other performance indicators.*

Fewer than 20 KPIs are likely adequate for an organization, as recommended by Kaplan and Norton. Too few KPIs can be too restrictive and may not be sufficient to represent all critical aspects of the organization's performance. Too many KPIs, however, may reflect an incomplete analysis of the organization's existing PIs. Careful selection of PIs likely yields a reduced number of KPIs that truly reflect the critical aspects of organizational performance and that can provide useful information for improvement. In addition to the KPIs, teams in different units use PIs to continuously monitor their performance. The suggested ratio of PIs to KPIs for institutional use is 8:1.[22] The total number of PIs may appear small, but very often various teams will find that many PIs are simply variations of others. These PIs can be standardized and combined to minimize the use of resources in monitoring performance.

IMPLEMENTATION OF PERFORMANCE INDICATORS

The most critical step for success in performance measurement is in how the PIs and KPIs are introduced and implemented in the organization. Their creation, by itself, is only a starting point. Four foundation stones for the successful development and utilization of KPIs in any organizations are a strong partnership with all organization's members and customers, a transfer of power to the front line, the integration of measurements, the reporting and improvement performance, and the linkage of performance measures to the organization's strategy.[22] Since the changes brought about via PIs and

KPIs can be great, a significant, mutual understanding and acceptance of the need for change among management, employees, unions, and customers is very important. The organization's management needs to provide effective top-down and bottom-up communication pathways and to empower their front-line employees to take actions in situations negatively affecting KPIs. Performance is measured and reported in a way that results in action. Management must ensure that employees perceive performance measurements as a positive way to ensure the success of the organization. KPIs and PIs must be linked to the organization's strategy for success (its vision, mission, and values).[22]

To implement PIs and KPIs in the organization, one may appoint a project facilitator who has experience in performance measures and implementation, and who possesses a motivating character to assist the process of implementation. The facilitator will help the assessment team (PI development team) to present the PIs and KPIs to the senior management for their approval and commitment, select appropriately small PI/KPI teams from different units of the organization, provide insights to the teams, and help the teams in troubleshooting. A database of all PIs and KPIs should be made that includes details about the PIs and KPIs (description, how to measure, type, person/team responsible, frequency of measurement, data sources of measures, linkage to core success of organization, etc.). The database will create a comprehensive, accessible resource for everyone in the teams and in the organization, thus making KPI use widespread in the organization and helping their use become a part of organizational culture.[22]

POTENTIAL PERFORMANCE INDICATORS AND KEY PERFORMANCE INDICATORS IN RADIOLOGY

By utilizing a quality map provided by Swensen (Figure 16.1), the assessment team has a visual framework of how a radiology department operates and which processes have the potential to develop performance measures. Several potential PIs and KPIs in radiology practice have been published in the literature,[10,18] and some of them are summarized in Tables 16.3–16.8. Outcome measures are a result of care provided by radiology practices, and these may include contrast extravasation rates and diagnostic accuracy of imaging interpretation. These indicators are most meaningful to patient care. However, these also are difficult to measure and infrequently developed in radiology. Based on research by Maher,[10] only 21% of their 257 radiology PIs were considered outcome measures, whereas process and structure measures accounted for 45% and 34% of all measures, respectively. To provide an accurate reflection of radiology's contribution to patient care, outcome and process measures are the two most important indicators to develop. Once the indicators are identified by the organization, not all of them need to be monitored. Those measures that must be included in every organization are those required by regulatory agencies, payers, or CMS (Table 16.9). Otherwise, the organization should have an ongoing process to assess for proper indicators that are most meaningful to and aligned with the organization's mission and vision.

As of 2009, the American Board of Radiology's Maintenance of Certification program requires all radiologists to participate in the Physician Quality

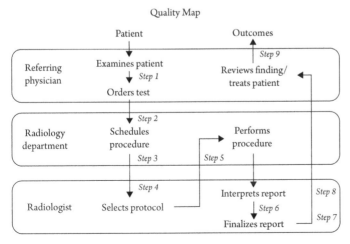

Quality Map

FIGURE 16.1 Radiology quality map. Reprinted from Swensen SJ, Johnson CD. Radiologic quality and safety: Mapping value into radiology. *JACR.* 2005;2:992–1000, with permission from Elsevier.

TABLE 16.3   RADIOLOGY-SPECIFIC KEY PERFORMANCE INDICATORS (KPIS) THAT RELATE TO CORE FUNCTIONS OF OPERATIONS MANAGEMENT

Key Factor and Related KPIs	Metrics
Clinical performance	
Intradepartmental division success rates*	Peer review of image interpretation by staff, correlation of radiologic findings, complications rate
Department-wide success rates	False-positive and false-negative rates, peer review agreement rate, percentage of examinations with unnecessary recommendations
Communication with referring physicians	Audits of e-mail alerts sent to physicians, rate of compliance with standardized protocols, and rate of compliance with report quality standards
Research	
Funding	Amount of funding received, source of funding, contribution of radiology department resources to research
Publications	Numbers of publications in peer-reviewed and non-peer-reviewed journals, rank of authors, number of patents
Patient experience (service level)	
Outpatient service	Survey of patients receiving preappoinment examination information and education, measurement of waiting time from patient arrival to beginning of examination, measurement of appointment delay from scheduled examination time to beginning of examination, outpatient report turnaround time
Outpatient access	Appointment availability (overall score, percentage of open slots for the next 30 days)
Inpatient service	Inpatient report turnaround time, inpatient imaging turnaround time
Resource utilization and productivity	
Equipment idle time	Percentage of time when equipment is unavailable because of unscheduled downtime
Equipment utilization	Ratio of number of hours available to number of hours in use
Equipment staffing level	Ratio of numbers of imaging staff (technologists, technologist assistants) to number of machines
Professional staffing level	Ratio of reports generated (relative value units) per professional full-time employee (radiologist)
Technical staff productivity	Number of examinations performed (relative value units) per staff full-time employee (technologist, technologist assistant)

*Refers to the success rate within each of 11 subspecialty-based divisions (e.g., international radiology, breast imaging) in the radiology department.

Reprinted with permission from Abujudeh HH, Kaewlai R, Asfaw BA, Thrall JH. Quality initiatives: Key performance indicators for measuring and improving radiology department performance. *RadioGraphics.* 2010;30:571–80.

Reporting Initiatives (PQRI). The program defines five categories needed for reporting, including patient safety, accuracy of interpretation, report turnaround time, practice guidelines, and technical standards and referring physician surveys.[7] Many of these requirements fit into the indicators that any departments would be able to gather data on, as a group or an individual radiologist. The programs will also help increase quality awareness within the radiology group and improve relations between radiology practices and their hospitals.

VARIATIONS IN INTERPRETING PERFORMANCE INDICATORS

The development of indicators to measure health care performance is one of many steps in performance measurement. To be confident that the measured performance accurately reflects actual performance, one needs to consider variations that may influence a PI.[14,22] Many sources of variation exist, therefore PIs need to be adjusted before a

TABLE 16.4 RADIOLOGY-SPECIFIC KEY PERFORMANCE INDICATORS (KPIS) THAT RELATE TO ENABLING FUNCTIONS OF OPERATIONS MANAGEMENT

Key Factor and Related KPIs	Metrics
Employee development	
Licensing and certification	Percentage of jobs with competency-based assessment, percentage of staff who have completed competency assessment, percentage of staff who meet or exceed continuing education requirements, percentage of staff licensed (e.g., by the American Registry of Radiologic Technologists), percentage of staff with a master's degree, percentage of divisions with a Technologist III, percentage of clinicians with a doctorate of philosophy (Ph.D.)
Education access and use	Number of courses or training sessions requested and delivered, number of training seats available, percentage of training seats filled, percentage of staff attending training courses
Application and transfer of knowledge	Percentage of courses with measured outcomes, percentage of course evaluations completed, number of academic papers written and published, number of presentations delivered internally and externally, percentage of full-time staff who are preceptors, percentage of full-time staff who are student mentors
Employee empowerment	Number of staff who have moved to new positions or roles within the institution, ratio of average number of active council members to total number of staff, number and percentage of nonmanagerial staff in leadership positions on strategic councils, number of suggestions from staff, number of process improvement initiatives undertaken and number of those completed
Informatics support	
Downtime	Hours of scheduled downtime for maintenance, hours (minutes) of unscheduled downtime
Data integrity	Number of instances and volume of lost data or images
Service provision	Number of different systems supported, number of users supported, volume of data managed, number of appropriate service calls filed, number of inappropriate service calls filed, average delay in response to service call
Resources used	Number of informatics support staff
Technology replacement and project management	Numbers of hardware and software installations, upgrades, and replacements completed; number of informatics projects initiated and number of those completed; person-hours spent on informatics improvements and upgrades; success rate of informatics projects initiated; spending on technology as a proportion (percentage) of departmental budgeted expenses
Demand generation	
No. of new referrers	Numbers of new referring physicians recruited inside and outside an institution
Total no. of referrers	Total number of current referring physicians inside and outside an institution
Demand generated	Total number of referrals from all physicians
Effort expended	Total number of initiatives undertaken to increase demand and awareness
Analyses and forecasts	
Effort expended	Number of analyses and forecasts provided
Quality	Deviation of actual results from forecasts, number of analyses used by management

Reprinted with permission from Abujudeh HH, Kaewlai R, Asfaw BA, Thrall JH. Quality initiatives: Key performance indicators for measuring and improving radiology department performance. *RadioGraphics*. 2010;30:571–80.

TABLE 16.5   RADIOLOGY-SPECIFIC KEY PERFORMANCE INDICATORS (KPIS) THAT
RELATE TO FINANCIAL MANAGEMENT

Key Factor and Related KPIs	Metrics
Net income	
Revenue	Measure of total amount billed, measure or estimate of total amount reimbursed
Expense	Measure of fixed (overhead) costs, measure of variable costs (correlated with the number of examinations performed), and measure of costs due to errors (as a result of lawsuits, unnecessary examinations, and repeat examinations)
Variance from budget	
Revenue	Variance between actual revenue and revenue line in budget
Expense	Variance between actual expense and expense line in budget
Fiscal efficiency	
Efficient use of labor	Ratio of total labor costs (salary, benefits, and contract labor) to total revenue
Efficient use of assets	Net return on total assets
Billing effectiveness	
Total rejections	Total amount of bills rejected by insurers
Effectiveness of precertification process	Difference between cost of precertification and revenue collected for precertified examinations

Reprinted with permission from Abujudeh HH, Kaewlai R, Asfaw BA, Thrall JH. Quality initiatives: Key performance indicators for measuring and improving radiology department perform ance. *RadioGraphics.* 2010;30:571–80.

conclusion can be drawn about stakeholder performance.[14] Performance indicators can be categorized by sources into:

1. *Clinical team.* Patient care is often delivered by more than one clinical team; therefore, outcome of care is likely a result of collaboration between several teams and may also be influ-enced by factors outside the institution of care (i.e., referral practice). Outcomes of radiologic care, both diagnostic and interventional, often are the results of collaboration among radio-logical, surgical and medical teams.[14]

2. *Patients.* Different combinations of patient types being treated may account for differ-ent outcomes, either in diagnosis, severity

TABLE 16.6   RADIOLOGY-SPECIFIC KEY PERFORMANCE INDICATORS (KPIS)
THAT RELATE TO PATIENT SAFETY AND QUALITY OF CARE

Key Factor and Related KPIs	Metrics
Patient safety	
Compliance with directives	Number of new quality and safety projects completed, rates of compliance with JCAHO and Health Insurance Portability and Accounting Act requirements and institutional policies
Policy formulation	Number of new or updated quality and safety policies, average age of policies, age of oldest active policy
Incident reporting	Total number of incident reports (number of preventative reports plus number of adverse outcome reports)
Patient experience	Patient satisfaction with quality and safety of care (numeric rating on a scale of 0–10)

Reprinted with permission from Abujudeh HH, Kaewlai R, Asfaw BA, Thrall JH. Quality initiatives: Key performance indicators for measuring and improving radiology department performance. *RadioGraphics.* 2010;30:571–80.

TABLE 16.7   RADIOLOGY-SPECIFIC KEY PERFORMANCE INDICATORS (KPIS)
THAT RELATE TO MANAGEMENT OF EXTERNAL STAKEHOLDERS

Key Factor and Related KPIs	Metrics
Referring physicians and their staff	
Satisfaction	Survey of referring physicians, survey of their staff (numeric rating on a scale of 0–10)
Report turnaround time	Outpatient report turnaround time, inpatient report turnaround time
Comments	Numbers of complaints, requests, and compliments received by telephone or e-mail
Patients	
Satisfaction	Numeric rating on a scale of 0–10
Outpatient access	Appointment availability as a score and as a percentage of openings in the schedule for the next 30 days
Comments	Numbers of complaints, requests, and compliments received by telephone or e-mail

---

Reprinted with permission from Abujudeh HH, Kaewlai R, Asfaw BA, Thrall JH. Quality initiatives: Key performance indicators for measuring and improving radiology department performance. *RadioGraphics*. 2010;30:571–80.

of disease, or complications.[14] To interpret the indicators accurately, particularly outcome measures, one needs to consider risk adjustment procedures. The risk adjustment procedure can be performed using statistical methods that allow interpretation of outcomes for specific clinical conditions. It requires definition and measurement of several patient characteristics, including anatomical, physiological and health status.[2]

3. *Institution*. Certain institutional arrangements, the level and nature of resources available to the assessment team, and the seniority of support staff can potentially limit the development and utilization of PIs.[14]

4. *External environment*. Performance outcomes are affected not only by factors in the hospital, but also by access to care (geographic location, transport infrastructure), care arrangement (social care, insurance), employment status, and society at large.[14]

5. *Random fluctuation*. Randomness of differences in measured performance can occur even in well-controlled systems. In the health care business, random fluctuation should be taken into account when interpreting the results of PIs.[14]

POTENTIAL PITFALLS IN UTILIZATION AND IMPLEMENTATION OF INDICATORS

Several barriers and pitfalls in the use and implementation of indicators can be related to users and systems. The perceptions of users/stakeholders are among the most important pitfalls and barriers to the use and implementation of PIs. If the indicators are perceived as irrelevant to the context of care (lack of face validity), they will likely be unsuccessful. Caregiver perception that indicators may be used in a punitive way will likely result in poor acceptance and use as well.[8] Caregivers may influence the results of indicators by adjusting/altering variables other than clinical quality (so-called *gaming*). For example, caregivers may select only easy cases for review, so that favorable outcome figures are achieved.

When indicators have a narrow target in one or a few areas of a department, staff may pursue that target to the expense of the system objectives as a whole (so-called *suboptimization*).[17] For example, if the only target is to reduce the turnaround time of radiology reports, it may decrease the quality of interpretation. In addition, other important areas may be inadvertently neglected and excluded from the performance evaluation (so-called *tunnel vision*).[17] Since there may be many different priorities for performance measurement and improvement in an institution, the assessment team should be clear about which indicators are considered most important to them, always being aware that priorities can differ among physicians, managers, patients, and administrators. The assessment team may tend to focus on short-term issues of performance evaluation at the expense of long-term considerations (so-called *myopia*). Since the results of long-term PIs emerge much more slowly, a lack of their use may erode preventive services.[17]

TABLE 16.8   RADIOLOGY-SPECIFIC KEY PERFORMANCE INDICATORS (KPIS) THAT RELATE TO MANAGEMENT OF INTERNAL STAKEHOLDERS

Key Factor and Related KPIs	Metrics
Diversity	
Function	Number of teams or projects including representatives of three or more areas of function
Age	Measured in years as the mean and standard deviation across the department
Ethnicity	Demographic variance from the population served
Level of education	Percentages of radiology department staff with each academic degree, compared with percentages of staff with the same degree in other departments of the hospital
Harassment-free work environment	Comparison of annual number of reported incidents or complaints of harassment with national statistics
Compensation and recognition	
Recognition of performance excellence	Number of awards distributed, total dollar amount of pay incentives disbursed for excellent performance
Actual and relative pay scales	Comparison of pay at each level with that at the same level in other radiology departments, overall rank among radiology departments (percentile)
Resources	
Equipment quality	Average age (in months) of major imaging and information technology systems, number of late-generation imaging devices variance in number of hours of scheduled maintenance from manufacturer recommendations
Equipment availability	Machine downtime not due to scheduled maintenance (in hours per week or month)
Equipment diversity	Number of machine manufacturers represented
Equipment staffing levels	Ratio of imaging staff (technologists and technologist assistants) to imaging machines
Continuing education	
Access	Annual numbers of courses and training programs offered
Utilization	Percentages of staff participating (department-wide and per role within the department)
Work-life balance	
Vacation utilization	Number of vacation days available, ratio of vacation days used to days available
Workload	Average overtime hours worked (per employee)
Commute	Average hours spent commuting to work (per employee)
Variety of work	Average number of different examination types performed by technologist
Participation	
Staff influence on departmental governance	Unique count of council members
Attrition and retention	
Staffing level	Percentage of full-time positions not filled by full-time employees
Continuity of staffing	Number of temporary employees divided by total number of positions, average years of service (obtained by dividing total years of employment for all staff by the number of staff)
Staff turnover	Attrition rate (number of staff who retired, resigned, or died in the previous year)
Employee satisfaction	Numeric rating on a scale of 0–10

Reprinted with permission from Abujudeh HH, Kaewlai R, Asfaw BA, Thrall JH. Quality initiatives: Key performance indicators for measuring and improving radiology department performance. *RadioGraphics*. 2010;30:571–80.

TABLE 16.9 EXAMPLES OF RADIOLOGY PERFORMANCE INDICATORS

Structure indicators
- Presence of policy for critical test result communication
- Percentage of radiologists with board certification

Process indicators
- Appropriateness of exam ordering
- Time from order to completion of computed tomography (CT) examination
- Patient waiting time
- Critical test reporting rates
- Error rates of imaging labelling

Outcome indicators
- Contrast extravasation rates
- Contrast-induced nephropathy rates
- Diagnostic accuracy of imaging interpretation

Performance indicators that can be considered as high value in radiology[10]
- Critical-test result communication timeliness
- Time to diagnostic mammography
- Contrast extravasation rate
- Mammography call-back rate
- Peer-review rate of agreement
- Emergency and inpatient report turnaround time
- Structured reporting frequency
- Medication list documentation rate
- Radiation dose exposure documentation rate
- Interventional radiology complication rate

Radiology-related performance indicators that are tracked by the Centers for Medicare and Medicaid Services (CMS) through 2010 Physician Quality Reporting Initiative (PQRI) Program[24]
- Indicator #112: Screening mammography (percentage of women aged 40 through 69 years who had a mammogram to screen for breast cancer within 24 months)
- Indicator #145: Exposure time reported for procedures using fluoroscopy (percentage of final reports for procedures using fluoroscopy that include documentation of radiation exposure or exposure time)
- Indicator #146: Inappropriate use of "probably benign" assessment category in mammography screening (percentage of final reports for screening mammograms that are classified as "probably benign")
- Indicator #147: Correlation with existing imaging studies for all patients undergoing bone scintigraphy (percentage of final reports for all patients, regardless of age, undergoing bone scintigraphy that include physician documentation of correlation with existing relevant imaging studies that were performed)
- Indicator #195: Stenosis measurement in carotid imaging studies (percentage of final reports for all patients, regardless of age, for carotid imaging studies performed that include direct or indirect reference to measurements of distal internal carotid diameter as the denominator for stenosis measurement)

To prevent potential pitfalls in the use and implementation of indicators, PIs must be reviewed regularly to assess their methodology, unit of analysis, and financial impact.

CONCLUSION

The health care system is complex, difficult to understand, and hard to manage. Given the current concern for health care accountability and quality, a robust policy approach to performance monitoring must be devised to support the growing demands of the public for high-quality care. As Donabedian once stated "the most important single condition for success in quality assurance is the determination to make it work. If we are truly committed to quality, almost any reasonable method will work. If we are not, the most elegantly constructed of mechanisms will fail."[23]

REFERENCES

1. Groene O, Skau JK, Frolich A. An international review of projects on hospital performance assessment. *Int J Qual Health Care.* 2008;20:162–71.

2. Rubin HR, Pronovost P, Diette GB. The advantages and disadvantages of process-based measures of health care quality. *Int J Qual Health Care.* 2001;13:469–74.

3. Arah OA, Klazinga NS, Delnoij DM, ten Asbroek AH, Custers T. Conceptual frameworks for health systems performance: A quest for effectiveness, quality, and improvement. *Int J Qual Health Care.* 2003;15:377–98.

4. Gibberd R, Hancock S, Howley P, Richards K. Using indicators to quantify the potential to improve the quality of health care. *Int J Qual Health Care.* 2004;16 Suppl 1:i37–43.

5. Evans DB, Edejer TT, Lauer J, Frenk J, Murray CJ. Measuring quality: From the system to the provider. *Int J Qual Health Care.* 2001;13:439–46.

6. Donabedian A. The quality of care. How can it be assessed? *JAMA.* 1988;260:1743–8.

7. Steele JR, Schomer DF. Continuous quality improvement programs provide new opportunities to drive value innovation initiatives in hospital-based radiology practices. *J Am Coll Radiol.* 2009;6:491–9.

8. Crampton P, Perera R, Crengle S, et al. What makes a good performance indicator? Devising primary care performance indicators for New Zealand. *N Z Med J.* 2004;117:U820.

9. Schaedig C. Using metrics and dashboards to forecast business. *Radiol Business J.* 2008. Accessed May 30, 2010, at: http://www.imagingbiz.com/articles/view/using-metrics-and-dashboards-to-forecast-business/Update: June 15, 2008.

10. Maher B, Pratt S. What is Quality Radiology? *Radiol Business J.* 2008. Accessed May 30, 2010, at: http://www.imagingbiz.com/articles/view/what-is-quality-radiology/. Updated: September 1, 2008.

11. Donabedian A, Bashshur R. *An introduction to quality assurance in health care.* New York: Oxford University Press, 2003.

12. Ibrahim JE. Performance indicators from all perspectives. *Int J Qual Health Care.* 2001;13:431–2.

13. Chiu WT, Yang CM, Lin HW, Chu TB. Development and implementation of a nationwide health care quality indicator system in Taiwan. *Int J Qual Health Care.* 2007;19:21–28.

14. Goddard M, Davies HT, Dawson D, Mannion R, McInnes F. Clinical performance measurement: Part 1—getting the best out of it. *J R Soc Med.* 2002;95:508–10.

15. Donabedian A. Evaluating the quality of medical care. *Milbank Mem Fund Q.* 1966;44(Suppl):166–206.

16. Mant J. Process versus outcome indicators in the assessment of quality of health care. *Int J Qual Health Care.* 2001;13:475–80.

17. Rubin HR, Pronovost P, Diette GB. From a process of care to a measure: The development and testing of a quality indicator. *Int J Qual Health Care.* 2001;13:489–96.

18. Abujudeh HH, Kaewlai R, Asfaw BA, Thrall JH. Quality initiatives: Key performance indicators for measuring and improving radiology department performance. *Radiographics.* 2010;30:571–80.

19. Swensen SJ, Johnson CD. Radiologic quality and safety: Mapping value into radiology. *J Am Coll Radiol.* 2005;2:992–1000.

20. Schoen C, Davis K, How SK, Schoenbaum SC. U.S. health system performance: A national scorecard. *Health Aff (Millwood).* 2006;25:w457–75.

21. Parmenter D. *Key performance indicators: Developing, implementing, and using winning KPIs.* Hoboken, NJ: John Wiley & Sons, Inc., 2007.

22. Goddard M, Davies HT, Dawson D, Mannion R, McInnes F. Clinical performance measurement: Part 2—avoiding the pitfalls. *J R Soc Med.* 2002;95:549–51.

23. Donabedian A. The effectiveness of quality assurance. *Int J Qual Health Care.* 1996;8:401–407.

24. Centers for Medicare & Medicaid Services. Physician Quality Reporting Initiative (PQRI) 2010. Accessed May 30, 2010, at: http://www.cms.gov/PQRI/. Updated: April 21, 2010.

17

Six Sigma and Lean

Opportunities for Health Care to Do More and Better with Less

JAMLIK-OMARI JOHNSON

LEAN: A BRIEF OVERVIEW

Lean manufacturing, lean production, lean enterprise, and lean thinking or often simply, "lean," is a production practice borrowed from the Japanese manufacturing industry. Although the term *lean manufacturing* was first coined in 1988 by John Krafcik, the concept is a generic process management philosophy derived mostly from Taiichi Ohno's influence on the Toyota Production System.[1] Lean considers the expenditure of resources for any goal other than the creation of value for the end customer to be wasteful and thus a target for elimination. Working from the perspective of the customer who consumes a product or service, value is defined as any action or process for which a customer would be willing to pay. Lean is centered on preserving value with less work.[2,3]

The common goals of lean manufacturing systems include:[4,5]

- *Improve quality.* To stay competitive in today's marketplace, a company must understand its customers' wants and needs and design processes to meet their expectations and requirements.
- *Eliminate waste.* Waste is any activity that consumes time, resources, or space but does not add any value to the product or service.
- *Reduce time.* Reducing the time it takes to finish an activity from start to finish is one of the most effective ways to eliminate waste and lower costs.
- *Reduce total costs.* To minimize cost, a company must produce only to customer demand. Overproduction increases a company's inventory costs because of storage needs.

The elimination of waste is the goal of lean. The acronym, TIMWOOD identifies the seven types of waste[6]:

- Transport (moving products that is not actually required to perform the processing)
- Inventory (all components, work in process and finished product not being processed)
- Motion (people or equipment moving or walking more than is required to perform the processing)
- Waiting (waiting for the next production step)
- Overproduction (production ahead of demand)
- Overprocessing (resulting from poor tool or product design creating activity)
- Defects (the effort involved in inspecting and fixing defects)

In summary, lean is a set of principles and techniques that drive organizations to continually add value to the product they deliver by enhancing process steps that are necessary, relevant, and valuable while eliminating those steps that fail to add value. Moreover, lean thinking is an integrated approach to designing, doing, and improving the work of people who have come together to produce and deliver goods, services, and information. Used in manufacturing for decades, lean thinking is associated with enhanced product quality and overall corporate success.[7]

SIX SIGMA: A BRIEF OVERVIEW

Although credit for coining the term "Six Sigma" is generally given to a Motorola and one of its employees, Bill Smith (1929–1993),[8] the concepts of Six Sigma actually evolved over centuries. The roots of Six Sigma as a measurement standard can be traced back to German mathematician and physicist Carl Friedrich Gauss (1777–1855), who introduced the concept of the normal curve.[9] Six Sigma as a measurement standard in product variation can be traced back to the early 20th century when American statistician, engineer, and former Bell Telephone employee Walter Shewhart (1891–1967) showed that three sigma from the mean is the point at which a process requires correction.[10] The popularity of Six Sigma was evident in it widespread adaptation among key players across the manufacturing industry, such as General Electric and Sony.

The maturity of a manufacturing process can be described by a sigma rating indicating its yield, or the percentage of defect-free products it creates. A six-sigma process is one in which 99.99966% of the products manufactured are statistically expected to be free of defects or 3.4 defects per million. In the case of Motorola, it set a goal of six sigmas for all of its manufacturing operations. This goal became the catch phrase for the management and engineering practices used to achieve it.

Six Sigma is a process improvement strategy that strives to improve the quality of an end product by identifying and removing the causes of error (defects) and minimizing variability in manufacturing and business processes. This methodology uses a set of quality management methods, employs statistical methods, and creates a special infrastructure of people within an organization. Each Six Sigma project carried out within an organization follows a defined sequence of steps and has quantified financial targets geared toward cost reduction and profit increase.

At the core of any Six Sigma project is a group of individuals who are familiar with the organization and the particular problem being addressed. They are in turn guided by a group of specialists savvy in implementing Six Sigma processes. Six Sigma is an organized process of data analysis based on a five-step problem-solving methodology: Define, Measure, Analyze, Improve, and Control (or DMAIC).

- *Define.* Clearly define the goals of the team. Identify the process that needs to be improved and the factors that are essential to performing the process. Map the most significant steps of the process.
- *Measure.* The team identifies the key factors that influence the final outcome and collects the relevant baseline data.
- *Analyze.* The team analyzes the data to determine and verify cause-and-effect relationships. The team determines the nature of the relationships and attempts to ensure that all factors are considered. They identify which relationships have the maximal significance on variation in the process and output. They seek out the root cause of the defect under investigation.
- *Improve.* The team creates strategies to improve the high-impact factors based upon the data analysis. Once improvement strategies are implemented, the outcomes are measured again.
- *Control.* The team checks the post implementation data against the baseline data to determine if the anticipated performance measures have been met. If the process is successful and there has been process improvement, plans are made to sustain improvement or to further improve output. The team must control the future state process to ensure that any deviations from the target are corrected before they result in defects.[11]

LEAN AND SIX SIGMA IN HEALTH CARE

Lean and Six Sigma are business management strategies commonly used in production industries to improve process efficiency and quality. Manufacturing has employed these technologies for decades in the pursuit of continuous improvement to maximize profits and maintain a competitive edge. The application of these principles in the health care setting, although relatively novel, is easily applied and highly applicable. These methodologies provide a mechanism to identify opportunities for improvement in patient care delivery systems.[12]

Health care costs in the United States have continued to rise steadily since the 1980s. Medical errors are one of the major causes of deaths and injuries in thousands of patients every year, contributing to soaring health care costs.[13] In the 1980s, many health care systems adopted industrial quality management methods including total quality management (TQM) and continuous quality improvement (CQI). These methodologies required a uniform commitment to quality in all areas of an organization to meet a consumer's perceptions of quality and acted on opportunities to improve the efficiency, effectiveness, and value of services provided to customers. TQM consists of five major tenets:

- Produce quality work the first time.
- Focus on the customer.
- Have a strategic approach to improvement.
- Improve continuously.
- Encourage mutual respect and teamwork.

CQI consists of four components:

- Achievement objectives and goal identification
- System process analysis
- Action planning and implementation
- Performance measurement and follow-up.

Although these approaches gained popularity during the 1990s, many critics voiced skepticism about the effectiveness of these programs and their impact on health care delivery, patient outcomes, and, ultimately, costs.[14–17]

Adaptation of lean and Six Sigma principles stem from a tradition of quality and process improvements. Six Sigma seeks a nonexistent error rate. It is ripe for health care because many health care processes require a near-zero tolerance for mistakes. In health care, management can superimpose Six Sigma onto existing TQM efforts, so that minimal disruption occurs in the organization. Integrating Six Sigma into the existing TQM program facilitates process improvement through detailed data analysis. Using the Six Sigma metrics, internal project comparisons facilitate resource allocation while external project comparisons allow for benchmarking. Thus, the application of Six Sigma makes TQM efforts more successful.[18]

However, implementing a Six Sigma project is not a minor undertaking. Six Sigma projects not only require significant financial resources and employee time, the projects necessitate making difficult decisions about relationships among stakeholders,

employee retention, and jobs. The institutional milieu must be considered prior to instituting Six Sigma principles. If the institution has a history of making data-driven decisions, or at least has displayed openness to operating in that manner, there exists a good chance of success. The departmental leadership should approve a comprehensive scope for the project. The project scope should also have the support of the institutional leadership. The project scope should address the desired outcomes, the resources available to undertake the project, a reasonable timeline for completion, and any foreseeable political hurdles. The scope should be comprehensive enough to form a major component in the bid package to hire a consulting firm or a job description for an in-house expert. A senior-level, full-time project manager is necessary. The project manager must have sufficient authority to independently enable cooperation among the stakeholders. An information technology liaison with intimate knowledge of the hospital information systems is important. A multidisciplinary steering committee should include physicians and other caregivers, and modality, ancillary, and administrative representatives. Having representation outside the department undergoing the change is highly desirable. The size of the group should be small enough to be nimble and effective, but large enough to provide a variety of viewpoints. The team should keep in mind the five phases of Six Sigma, which are summarized by the acronym DMAIC: Define, Measure, Analyze, Improve, and Control.[19]

The principles of lean management have permeated many sectors of the business world, secondary to the success of the Toyota Production System. These management and engineering methodologies enable workers to eliminate mistakes, reduce delays, lower costs, and improve the overall quality of the delivered product or service. Lean management principles can be applied to health care. Their implementation within the ambulatory care setting is predicated on the continuous identification and elimination of waste within any process. The key concepts of flow time, inventory, and throughput are utilized to improve the flow of patients throughout the health care enterprise and to identify points that slow this process. Nonessential activities are shifted away from bottlenecks, and extra work capacity is generated from existing resources. The additional work capacity facilitates a more efficient response to variability, which in turn results in cost savings and a more efficient use of limited resources.[20]

Early successful examples of juxtaposing lean and Six Sigma strategies on existing quality principles include improving report turnaround times, reducing emergency department wait times, reducing surgical site infections, and decreasing operating room turnaround times.[21-23]

CONCLUSION

Health care systems, providers, and support personnel have experienced continued surges in the demand for services over a number of decades.[24] At the same time, the health care system is challenged to deliver improved quality of care at lower cost. The health care system can benefit from the application of lean and Six Sigma methodologies used by other industries to meet similar challenges. Lean Six Sigma process improvement methodologies have been used in manufacturing for decades. These principles are applicable in the health care setting as a way to identify opportunities for improvement in patient care delivery. Lean Six Sigma methodologies can been used in a variety of clinical applications. Optimizing patient services requires a combination of well-trained and dedicated personnel, cutting-edge technology, and a thoughtful examination of workflow, processes, and productivity.

Sharply increased competition, governmental regulation, and decreased funding sources threaten the status quo in most health care organizations, which must now decrease costs while improving service. These organizations must reevaluate their business practices and ensure that they are performing at peak efficiency. Meaningful cost savings come from changing the way services are delivered, not just from simple belt-tightening.[25] In recent years, most hospitals have gone through several rounds of cost-cutting initiatives. Although it is necessary and prudent to closely monitor operating costs and staff utilization, the focus needs to shift from simply cutting cost to improving systems in an effort to boost revenue.[26] It is a tall order: Health care organizations are asked to show better outcomes, more efficiency, improved patient and provider satisfaction, and cost reduction in the system.

Lean Six Sigma, a process-focused strategy and methodology for business improvement, can be used to improve care processes, eliminate waste, reduce costs, and enhance patient satisfaction. Health care, as with any other service operation, requires systematic innovation efforts to remain competitive, cost efficient, and up-to-date. Lean thinking and Six Sigma can be combined to provide an effective framework for producing systematic innovation efforts in health care. Controlling health care cost increases, improving quality, and providing better health care are some of the benefits of this approach. It is no surprise that many health care organizations are turning to the lean Six Sigma methodologies to hardwire process excellence into their organizations as means for survival. If the health care system and its team of players is not actively involved in data collection and measurements to improve the delivery, quality, and value of its product and services, another entity will indeed assume this role.

REFERENCES

1. Krafcik JF. Triumph of the lean production system. *Sloan Management Review.* 1988;30(1):41–52.
2. Womack JP, Jones DT, Roos D. *The machine that changed the world: The story of lean production.* New York. Harper-Collins, 1990.
3. Holweg M. The genealogy of lean production. *J Operations Management.* 2007;25(2):420–37.
4. Liker JK. *The Toyota Way: 14 management principles from the world's greatest manufacturer.* New York: McGraw-Hill, 2004.
5. Feld WM. *Lean manufacturing: Tools, techniques, and how to use them.* Boca Raton, FL: St. Lucie Press, 2001.
6. Womack JP, Jones DT. *Lean thinking.* New York: Free Press, 2003:352.
7. Dickson EW, Singh S, Cheung DS, Wyatt CC, Nugent AS. Application of lean manufacturing techniques in the Emergency Department. *J Emerg Med.* 2009;37(2):177–82.
8. Tennant G. *Six Sigma: SPC and TQM in manufacturing and services.* Farnham, U.K.: Gower Publishing, Ltd., 2001:6.
9. Dunnington GW. *Carl Friedrich Gauss: Titan of science.* Winchester, VA: The Mathematical Association of America, 2003.
10. Bayart D. Walter Andrew Shewhart. In CC Heyde, E Seneta, eds., *Statisticians of the centuries.* New York: Springer, 2001:398–401.
11. Snee RD. Six Sigma: The evolution of 100 yeas of business improvement methodology. *Int J Sigma Competitive Advantage.* 2004;1:4–20.
12. Loree A, Maihack M, Powell M. The path of least resistance: Is there a better route? *Radiol Manage.* 2003;25(5):48–51.
13. Kumar S, Steinebach M. Eliminating US hospital medical errors. *Int J Health Care Qual Assur.* 2008;21(5):444–71.
14. Shortell SM, Jones RH, Rademaker AW, et al. Assessing the impact of total quality management and organizational culture on multiple outcomes of care for coronary artery bypass graft surgery patients. *Med Care.* 2000;38(2):207–17.

15. Zbaracki MJ. The rhetoric and reality of total quality management. *Admin Sci Quarterly*. 1998;43(3): 602–36.

16. Blumenthal D, Kilo CM. A report card on continuous quality improvement. *Milbank Q*. 1998;76(4):625–48.

17. Bigelow B, Arndt M. Total quality management: Field of dreams? *Health Care Manage Rev*. 1995;20(4): 15–25.

18. Revere L, Black K. Integrating Six Sigma with total quality management: A case example for measuring medication errors. *J Healthc Manag*. 2003 Nov-Dec;48(6):377–91; discussion 392.

19. Benedetto AR. Six Sigma; not for the faint of heart. *Radiol Manage*. 2003;25(5):40–53.

20. Casey JT, Brinton TS, Gonzalez CM. Utilization of lean management principles in the ambulatory clinic setting. *Nat Clin Pract Urol*. 2009 Mar;6(3): 146–53.

21. Jimmerson C, Weber D, Sobek DK II. Reducing waste and errors: Piloting lean principles at Intermountain Healthcare. *J Qual Patient Care*. 2005;31(5): 249–57.

22. San DC. Six Sigma method application in reducing ED wait times. *Acad Emerg Med*. 2002;9:395.

23. Pexton C, Young D. Reducing surgical site infections through Six Sigma and change management. *Patient Safety Qual Healthcare*. Accessed at: http://www.psqh.com/julsep04/pextonyoung.html

24. MacKenzie R, Capuano T, Durishin LD, Stern G, Burke JB. Growing organizational capacity through a systems approach: One health network's experience. *Jt Comm J Qual Patient Saf*. 2008 Feb;34(2): 63–73.

25. Hanwell LL. Strategic repositioning: A practical approach to reducing costs and enhancing quality. *Radiol Manage*. 1996 Mar-Apr;18(2):54–58.

26. Aloisio JJ. Proposed: Improve efficiency, reimbursement and LOS through better utilization of inpatient imaging procedures. *Radiol Manage*. 2002 Mar-Apr; 24(2):36–39.

18

Stakeholder Management and Best Practices

GILES W.L. BOLAND

No corner of medicine is immune from the massive gauntlet thrown down by the Institute of Medicine's (IOM) estimation that at least 98,000 patients die each year from medical error.[1] Although many, if not most, radiological procedures are relatively non–life- threatening, there remains the potential to do harm, both in the short and longer term. Interventional radiological procedures carry significant risk of immediate harm to the patient, whereas excessive radiation dose from the inappropriate use of computed tomography (CT) may harbor an as yet unproven risk of many cancer deaths.[2-3] Besides, considerable variation exists within radiology, with no two departments likely following similar protocols and practices. This variation can sometimes lead to idiosyncratic behavior in workflow and image interpretation, potentially creating an unnecessary risk in relation to patient outcomes.[4] Further undermining the pursuit of excellence has been the massive increase in demand for imaging services over the last decade, without the necessary bandwidth or expertise to adapt uniformly across the profession; not every practice has been able to adopt best practices.[4-10] Indeed, not all imaging departments have fully embraced the IOM's heed to, at all times, reduce the risk of morbidity and mortality to each and every patient. Fundamentally, this requires vision and leadership to affect culture change among all staff within an imaging department. This chapter first outlines the challenges facing imaging departments, particularly relating to safety and quality, and then discusses how leadership and vision are key to addressing these challenges.

RAISED EXPECTATIONS

Over the last 15 years, there has been a massive increase in demand for imaging services spawned by the introduction of faster and better machines combined with innovative imaging protocols that have transformed the practice of radiology, such that imaging is now on the critical pathway to most disease diagnosis and management.[5] This, however, has come at a cost, as it has raised stakeholder (referring physicians and patients) expectations.[5] Stakeholders now demand and expect fast access to high-end, costly imaging services, and rapid report turnaround in order to expedite the diagnostic dilemmas and evaluate optimal treatment pathways.[5] Further compounding this dynamic has been a relative shortage of equipment and radiologists to meet the demand. In short, there has been a supply-and-demand problem. Although this dynamic now demonstrates some sign of easing,[11] for much of the last decade, imaging departments and radiologists have struggled to keep up with imaging demand. This has, at least at times, led to lack of attention on quality initiatives designed to reduce morbidity and mortality, primarily as radiologists have been too focused on delivering basic clinical services.[6] Furthermore, considering that the practice of radiology is dynamically evolving with the delivery of new equipment and protocols, it is no wonder that many departments and radiologists struggle to keep pace with these innovations. This inability to embrace the full value from these developments is unfortunate, as often they are designed to improve safety and quality.

QUALITY AND SAFETY FACTORS IN CONTEMPORARY IMAGING PRACTICES

Although Hippocrates' general charge is to do no harm to the patient, there are a variety of specific quality and safety agenda that contemporary radiologists must address before they can at least be confident they are delivering appropriate value, given current limitations in knowledge, skill, and technology. Imaging departments should develop strategies to address each one of these, simply to keep pace with the rate of change, let alone attempt to forge new and innovative workflows and procedures designed to enhance quality and safety. This will usually require a vision within the department to understand that quality and safety are paramount to delivering value to patients, which ultimately will be set by departmental leaders, who are charged with setting departmental direction and key agenda. Without strong leadership, many initiatives will either fall short, confuse employees, or ultimately fail. Specific initiatives that departmental leaders must address include (not in order of importance):

- Utilization management and procedure appropriateness
- Imaging protocols
- Radiation dose
- Patient access
- Procedure and modality safety
- Image interpretation
- Peer review
- Report format and delivery
- Culture of quality and safety

Each will be discussed in turn.

UTILIZATION MANAGEMENT

Radiologists are often criticized for recommending too many additional imaging studies. This at times is unfair, given pressures of patient or referring physician demand and expectation, medico-legal issues, or lack of specificity of the imaging modality. Many of these pressures place the radiologist in a position where he or she feels compelled to pursue the definitive diagnosis, if possible, at all costs. Patients and referring physicians, too, are caught up in the belief that imaging can readily diagnose many diseases—sometimes, not surprisingly, given the advances in image quality, protocol development,

and radiologist subspecialist expertise. However, this belief often leads to overuse of resources, which, when used inappropriately, leads to unnecessary costs, wasted time, unfounded hope, and sometimes compromised safety, which at its worst can have fatal consequences. Suppose a referring physician believes a contrast-enhanced CT scan of the abdomen is indicated for relatively minor abdominal pain. This is not a case in which the test is absolutely contraindicated, but perhaps in this case, patient pressure has forced the physician's hand and a CT is requested to rule out a significant underlying pathology. Let us assume that the yield from this test will very likely be negative (sometimes useful to the referring physician in itself), and the test was not indicated. This leads to unnecessary anxiety for the patient as he waits for the procedure to be performed (sometimes days or weeks), the use of an expensive resource that could be used for someone else, and unnecessary costs to the patient and insurance company. However, and perhaps more sinister, is the fact that the patient, particularly if young, will be unnecessarily exposed to the risk from excessive radiation (to be discussed later) and to the potentially harmful effects of intravenous contrast media usage, rarely a fatal event.

In other words, patients should only receive an imaging test when absolutely necessary, and both radiologist and referring physician need to weigh the risk versus the benefits of performing the test. Hitherto, however, too many departments and hospitals have been relatively lax in achieving this goal, rather making the assumption that both radiologist and referring physician would naturally only perform the test under these premises.[4] But referrers and radiologists are sometimes too busy, underinformed, or intimidated, or they lack the will to change this dynamic. In addition, there is an inherent conflict of interest for the radiologist and health care provider, as imaging can be lucrative to both parties, potentially reducing the urgency to enforce best practices, albeit subconsciously.

On the other hand, many, perhaps most, radiologists and referring physicians strive to maintain high standards but fail due to the complexity of indications, which, as mentioned, are often changing due to the arrival of new equipment and protocols.

Given these dynamics, it is critical that individual radiologists and radiology leaders strive to maintain current best practices by mandating a culture and policy whereby radiologists and referring physicians work together to understand when an imaging test is indicated and when it is unlikely to yield value. Unfortunately, however, given the challenges outlined above, even with the best will in the world, it will not be possible for individuals to achieve this goal, despite their best efforts.

Fortunately, however, information systems are now available that can remove much of the variation in image referrals and direct referring physicians toward the appropriate imaging test (if it is indicated in the first place). Electronic decision support (DS) physician tools can be highly effective at reducing inappropriate utilization. These DS tools are designed to ensure that the referring physician only orders a test when it is indicated, usually using a scheduling algorithm that often employs nationally based standards, including those of the American College of Radiology (ACR).[12-16] The physician will only be allowed to proceed if the imaging request meets these guidelines. These electronic algorithms are highly complex and sophisticated, and with appropriate referring physician education and support, they have proven to be widely acceptable and effective within institutions.[13-16] Furthermore, as the process is electronic, physicians can be monitored to determine their performance, and further supported and informed as needed. These DS tools have also been demonstrated to have a significant impact on reducing image utilization, with one study demonstrating a 19% decrease in certain cross-sectional imaging requests within one institution.[14] This serves to reduce cost, eliminated the delivery of unnecessary radiation, and permit the referring physician to be directed by accepted institutional guidelines, rather than by his own, at times idiosyncratic, behavior. This can have a reassuring effect on the referring physician, who can now be relatively secure in the knowledge that the test is not indicated, rather than practicing defensive medicine in the fear that he might be punished for getting it wrong.

Decision support tools are becoming widely available in medicine as a whole, and are likely to be the only effective and sustainable method of standardizing the referral process and realistically reducing inappropriate utilization.

IMAGING PROTOCOLS

As discussed, the rapid introduction of newer and better machines, combined with imaging protocols designed to take maximal advantage of newer software and hardware, can frequently result in many radiologists and radiology departments (let alone referring physicians) failing to take full advantage of the value that these new developments offer.[4]. This is not surprising, given the myriad number of imaging protocols sometimes unique to a specific manufacturer. Many of these protocols are designed to reduce patient dose (to be discussed in the next section) or to enhance imaging quality and the diagnostic capability of the modality in question. Occasionally, this may mean that imaging can replace a more invasive, more costly, and potentially harmful test. Many smaller departments and radiology groups simply do not have the bandwidth and expertise that readily allows them to stay abreast of these developments.

However, given that these newer protocols are usually designed to improve the quality and safety of imaging procedures, it is vital that even small radiology departments assign an individual or team to introduce the latest accepted standard within the industry, particularly if their imaging equipment permits it. This, naturally, takes the radiologist away from his or her busy clinical schedule, but without a dynamic response to this agenda, radiologists are potentially denying their patients the opportunity for a safer, less costly environment. Radiology leaders need to delegate this responsibility to the appropriate individuals and insist that frequent review of best practices is maintained. It will have the added benefit of demonstrating to referring physicians that radiologists have the best interests of the patient at heart.

RADIATION DOSE

It has been known ever since Marie Curie died in 1934 of aplastic anemia that excessive radiation is harmful to health.[17] Radiologists are taught in their training to follow the ALARA principle (the acronym for "as low as reasonably achievable"), to deliver the minimal radiation dose necessary to achieve diagnostic images. Recently, reports have highlighted this issue, with one paper predicting that there will be an excess of 15,000 U.S. deaths a year due to the increase in CT usage over the last decade.[2,3] Although the science and predictions are questioned by some, the fact remains that radiation can be harmful. It is perhaps surprising therefore that there has not been a more consistent effort by all radiology departments to mandate major dose reduction programs and protocols, particularly given the existing wealth of research material on dose reduction programs,[12, 18-21] including those from the ACR.[22] Dose reduction might include minimizing anatomical coverage, the number of slices obtained, and the mAs and kVp output delivered by CT scanners. This assumes, of course, that the test was clinically indicated in the first place and, as mentioned, many radiologists and referring practitioners believe that an unacceptable level of unnecessary imaging and overutilization occurs. One report estimated that up to a third of CT scans performed in the United States might be inappropriate.[23] As discussed, DS information systems likely offer the only sustainable way of reducing inappropriate utilization.

Radiologists must seriously address the radiation dose problem, mainly to ensure that each patient receives the minimal dose necessary to generate diagnostic images. Until radiology departments consistently deliver significant dose reduction programs on their CT scanners, they will continue to be criticized for a lack of due diligence and safety by both the scientific community and the press.

Many departments have mandated and introduced dose reduction programs, but have failed to sufficiently educate and inform their referring physicians of these major benefits to patients, such that referrers are left thinking that their departments are delivering harmful doses to their patients. On the contrary, the dose from some of these protocols is ten times less than the standard dosage regimes used in earlier years.[24] It is unfortunate that provocative and attention-grabbing scientific manuscripts have often used dosage calculations from earlier and less sophisticated equipment and protocols; part of the problem, however, lies within the radiology community, which has not sufficiently published, educated, and advertised these recent substantive improvements in radiation dose protocols. Radiology departments and individual radiologists need to not only embrace dose reduction programs, but to understand its implications so that they can educate both patients and referrers to their benefits once instituted. This will demonstrate to both parties that radiologists are serious about patient safety and quality and remove some of the fear and misunderstanding concerning radiation. After all, many CT examinations are indeed indicated, so radiologists need to encourage referrers and patients alike towards it proper use, with the appropriate dose. All radiologists should be familiar with their department's dose reduction programs and the risks these entail.

PATIENT ACCESS

Although expeditious patient access to imaging tests once requested may not seem, at first glance, a quality initiative, it does provide the referring physician the opportunity to either rapidly diagnose a potential disease or rule out a disease of concern—a major quality initiative. Rapid patient access to imaging modalities is now expected by both referrers and patients alike. Anything that slows down patient access will likely not only lead to patient and referring physician frustration but to a potential delay in diagnosis. It is therefore imperative that radiology departments first understand this critical dynamic; it's not so much that it pleases the referrers—it is because it helps referrers meet their obligations toward higher-quality patient care.

Radiology managers should critically evaluate their whole imaging algorithm, from scheduling to wait-times, to modality throughput and report turnaround. (The latter will be discussed later.) Ultimately, it will be modality capacity that will determine the ability for schedulers to provide convenient and expedited access for patients. Maintaining and increasing modality capacity, although a crucial quality initiative, is often seen as a cost burden to departments rather than an opportunity and a key quality metric. For instance, if the patient backlog for magnetic resonance imaging (MRI) examinations exceeds the modality's ability to handle these patients, then patient access and wait times for examinations will never improve, and in fact, will lengthen further. Too often, managers may believe that the only effective way of handling this situation is to purchase more equipment, an expensive and usually unnecessary maneuver. However, by understanding how many days or weeks it takes to reduce, or ideally remove, this backlog, managers can then manipulate the modality schedule to adapt to patient demand. For instance, managers can either increase the hours of operation or reduce the examination length, and ideally both. Increasing the hours of operation may seem expensive (the addition of variable costs), but can usually be readily offset by additional revenue, with the primary advantage of meeting patient and referring physicians demand for greater patient access.[5]

Reducing the examination length is more challenging, but departments should critically evaluate their workflow and look for opportunities to reduce redundant or inefficient practices. For instance, it has been demonstrated that CT examination throughput times can be reduced to approximately 10 minutes through the use of additional technologists and parallel process work practices.[25] Weekend scheduling, particularly for MRI procedures, may be more convenient for patients, and Sunday can sometimes be the busiest day for these modalities.[25] Finally, the creation of additional capacity is essential to permit urgent patient add-on procedures, an inevitable daily event, which is often challenging as it frequently means displacing less urgent patients. By freeing up additional time, these add-on patients are more easily accommodated within a busy day's schedule.

Aside from workflow management at the modality level, managers should reevaluate their scheduling process to take advantage of any opportunities they have created. This may entail hiring more scheduling staff, or, perhaps preferably, moving to an electronic online order entry system as previously described.[15,16] This facilitates a uniform scheduling process, with the added convenience of permitting the real-time evaluation of potential openings. An electronic order entry system, particularly when a DS system is embedded into the process, leads to a standardized scheduling process that adheres to best practice guidelines.

PROCEDURE AND MODALITY SAFETY

Although this vital aspect of overall patient safety will be addressed in more detail in other chapters, departments and all personnel must, at all costs, strictly adhere to best practices concerning modality and procedure safety. It clearly is of little or no value to the patient have access to the most modern and sophisticated equipment and highly skilled subspecialty radiologists, only to succumb to a major accident in the MRI or suffer from a poorly managed reaction to injected intravenous contrast material. First, the correct patient should be imaged in the first place (or undergo his or her interventional radiology procedure). Recently, methodologies such as the time-out procedure have minimized (but probably not eliminated) this risk. Policies and procedures should be rigorously adhered to throughout the imaging process, as many steps in the process are potential areas for error. Fortunately, electronic systems can help reduce error, making it is less likely that images will be lost or the examination assigned to the wrong patient, although no area is immune from error. A culture of quality and safety (to be discussed later) will help all personnel to strive toward developing, maintaining, and improving best practices.

Basic safety and quality principles must be adhered to, with a zero-tolerance policy. For instance, all relevant personnel must be familiar with procedures to manage adverse reactions to intravenous contrast. For instance, the emergency cart must be regularly checked for the appropriate equipment and drugs, technologists and radiologists should be familiar with their location, and radiologists must be familiar with the latest resuscitation guidelines. One day, somewhere within the organization, a patient will have a potentially life-threatening contrast reaction, possibly at an outpatient imaging center, where there will be little or no help from hospital-based personnel.

As discussed under the radiation section, all radiologists must insist on low-dose radiation protocols. Recently, the press has reported on patients who received many times the accepted best practice doses for certain imaging procedures, either due to lack of knowledge, insufficient training, or simple error.[26]

IMAGE INTERPRETATION

Although a few computer-aided diagnostic algorithms exist for image interpretation, the vast majority of images are still interpreted by individuals. Referring physicians and patients therefore have to rely on and trust that radiologists are sufficiently trained, proficient, and adherent to best-practice guidelines. Unfortunately, but understandably, there are few uniform and standardized guidelines on image reporting. For instance, it is highly likely that one department will report differently on an imaging study compared to another. This may exist even within the same division within a department. For instance, while one radiologist may recommend a follow-up imaging examination for a possible abnormality identified on a different modality (i.e., a contrast-enhanced CT examination following an ultrasound examination), another radiologist may recommend yet a different modality from the first radiologist, possibly at a different time interval, and some radiologists may recommend no follow-up imaging at all. It has further been demonstrated that more senior radiologists (those who have been longer in clinical practice) have a lower recommendation rate for subsequent imaging than do newer qualified fellows.[4]

Although there are no easy answers to help standardize these discrepancies, it behooves all radiologists to regularly educate themselves as to the best imaging practices, either through journals, educational conferences either at their institution, or formal radiological courses. Radiologists should be encouraged to subspecialize where possible, which in all likelihood increases the specificity and accuracy of their reports (although there is a relative paucity of data to support this widely held assumption).

More fundamental practices must be adhered to, such as reviewing any necessary prior imaging. This is facilitated with the almost universal contemporary use of picture archiving and communication systems (PACS), in which prior imaging is readily available. Not so straightforward, however, is what to do when the prior imaging has been performed at an outside institution. Not only may the reporting radiologist not know about any relevant prior imaging, but the images usually are never available in real time. The onus, however, is on the reporting radiologist to inform the referring physician of the necessity to obtain any relevant prior imaging from outside institutions and to amend the report, if necessary, once this becomes available. A further problem arises when referring physicians enter radiology reading rooms asking for outside images to be reviewed. Paradoxically, it is currently far quicker and easier to review hard copy film rather than images on CD ROMs. Often the CD formats are not recognized by the host PACS or even personal computers (PC), the images are small, the software to manipulate the images is unfamiliar, and it is difficult to compare an image on a PC to one on a PACS. Programs are becoming available that facilitate the incorporation of outside images into host PACS, but issues of patient identity (unique medical record number) remain challenging as these unique identifiers often differ from one institution to the next, thus risking that a patient's images may be incorrectly assigned to another. Sometimes, for data integrity issues, organizations refuse to import outside images, making the role of the diligent radiologist even harder. Despite these hurdles, the reporting radiologist should make his or her best attempt to incorporate outside images or offer to evaluate outside images should a referring physician wish it.

Finally, it is becoming commonplace for all patient data to reside in an electronic medical record (EMR). Progressive departments have been able to link the EMR to the PACS, such that all patient clinical data is available to the radiologist once a patient is selected from the PACS worklist. This has the potential to redefine the accuracy, succinctness, and relevance of the radiologist's report. The radiologist can now evaluate clinical data in real time, offering greater opportunity to incorporate relevant clinical data into his or her report. In a patient with fever, for instance, the radiologist can seamlessly evaluate any relevant clinical, surgical, and biochemical findings that might explain the patient's fever and use this to dictate a report with the likelihood of greater specificity toward the appropriate diagnosis. This methodology will undoubtedly be standard within

a few years, and radiology leaders should encourage their hospital administrators to expedite the development and implementation of such systems into their workflow.

PEER REVIEW

It is perhaps surprising that many radiology departments still do not have systematic and transparent peer review programs. The ability and necessity to regularly review reporting errors and/or variations in practice styles, meaning, or format is critical for patient care and education. Part of the problem lies in the fact that few comprehensive and usable programs facilitate peer review, although the ACR is promoting RADPEER.[28] Although there is no obligation to embrace this peer review program, it is certainly preferable to use this if no other peer review program is in place. However, peer review programs are not complicated; they simply take additional time and resources—perhaps the main impediment to departments who have considered introducing them. But workload or cost should not trump the importance of maintaining a program for all reporting radiologists on a regular basis. This might involve re-review of a small percentage of films either by a peer (hence, peer review) within the organization, or the process may be outsourced to another organization. Furthermore, regular meetings at which "missed cases" or aberrant reports are evaluated are crucial. In many institutions, the offending radiologist may never know he or she made a potentially harmful mistake, and therefore it is the obligation of radiology departmental leadership to insist upon programs that can inform radiologists (within a supportive environment) in a timely fashion when they cause harm to patients. Too often, peers feel intimated or too distracted to point out to their colleagues when errors are made. This culture needs to change to one in which all radiologists take the responsibility to inform their colleagues when errors are noted. It is the responsibility of radiology leadership to set a tone of quality and safety (to be discussed at the end of this chapter) within the department, such that radiologists can learn from each other, with the goal of minimizing future errors to the benefit of patient care.

REPORT FORMAT AND DELIVERY

The accuracy of reporting has already been discussed, and it can be improved with access to prior imaging and electronic medical records to enhance the specificity and quality of the report. However, reports are often delivered in a variety of styles and format, and this is known to frustrate referring physicians as the trawl through different report styles to find the relevant findings and recommendations. It is not unusual for one radiologist reporting on a particular patient to dictate a long, verbose report, while another, perhaps on a follow-up examination, delivers a medium-length report, and yet another a short report, sometimes with lack of pertinent negatives. It is highly likely that this scenario will persist unless guidelines from managers and leaders indicate the necessity for radiologists to dictate their reports according to a departmental standard. This goal is made far easier with the use of macros, ideally tailored to the type of investigation in question.[29] This process is further enhanced with the use of voice recognition (VR) technology, whereby radiologists can simply input their findings (positive or negative) directly into a template that they can see on-screen. In fact, VR offers further advantages in that, once dictated, the record is available for immediate final signature and dissemination across the health care network. No redundant loop of off-site transcription by a third party delays the delivery of the report, particularly as third-party output requires further analysis and editing by the reporting radiologist before it can be finally signed. Therefore, VR not only offers to the opportunity to standardize reports, but to expedite delivery. Both of these quality measures can impact patient care. Referring physicians prefer to have a final, not preliminary, report and ideally prefer standardized reports in which they can readily navigate to the clinical findings. Some radiologists complain that VR is less productive than standard digital dictation, but newer programs are highly accurate and fast. Even if there is a slight reduction in productivity, the ability to deliver expeditious finalized, standardized reports should trump the radiologist's desire to be slightly more productive. Therefore, the final output and product of the whole radiology process—namely, the radiology report—is enhanced to the benefit of radiology customers—the referring physicians and patients.

CULTURE OF QUALITY AND SAFETY

All radiology departments should always strive to maintain the highest levels of quality and safety. Ultimately, this is likely only achieved with strong, sometimes decisive, but meaningful and transparent

leadership. There will likely be little buy-in from radiology departments if leaders simply dictate quality and safety measures, without explaining why they are needed and the costs to individuals (managers, referring physicians, radiologists, and patients alike) should these not be developed, introduced, and maintained. Leaders and managers need to create an environment in which quality and safety are paramount within a department and insist on zero tolerance toward individuals, practices, and workflows that are not in the best interests of the patient. This may sometimes require a change in the emphasis of the department away from radiology value unit (RVU) productivity toward quality and safety. This can be a challenge, considering that the worth of many radiologists is measured in terms of RVU productivity, which says little of their quality and safety. Furthermore, measures to enhance quality and safety often take reporting radiologists away from their inclination to generate more financially rewarding RVUs.

Given that quality and safety measures generally do not contribute to the financial bottom-line of either the department or the individual radiologist (at least in the short term), there are inherent conflicts of interests in diverting precious time toward nonremunerative quality and safety measures. This is a particular challenge to radiology leaders and managers, but it is a pathway they must insist upon. To change the culture to one of safety and quality, rather than outright productivity at all costs, will require regular communication, educational briefings, the development of teams to devise and implement best practices, and ultimately the reevaluation of results after evaluating and monitoring performance.

Performance monitoring and measurement offers managers and leaders the best opportunity to transform their departments once and for all into ones that insist on best practices. The ability to measure performance across a range of quality parameters is becoming relatively seamless through the use of electronic information systems. Key performance indicators (KPIs) can be developed that indicate how quality and safety measures are performing, and the data can be used to iterate workflows and procedures accordingly. These indicators may include patient satisfaction, patient access time, hand hygiene, adherence to standardized reports, compliance with directives, and incident reporting, among many others.[29] Furthermore, departmental data can be shared privately across the organization, a key tool to help personnel understand how their performance compares to departmental goals and other individuals. It can be difficult, particularly for physicians, to embrace changes that optimize quality and safety without access to meaningful, timely, and accurate data. Some departments have used these data to develop pay-for-performance measures on key quality indicators that reward radiologists when they meet these quality initiatives.[30] A recent study demonstrated a dramatic reduction in report turnaround times after the introduction of pay-for-performance measures.[30]

Departmental leaders and mangers must therefore embrace the quality and safety initiative, which often requires departmental and sometimes organization culture change. Teams must be delegated to devise and implement policies designed to enhance the patient experience and safety. Information systems offer the opportunity to effectively monitor a wide range of meaningful data that can be used to reduce inefficiencies, correct mistakes, and ultimately effect cultural change. Once radiology personnel recognize that the monitoring of quality and safety performance is integral to regular practice, and that there is commitment to continually improve and if necessary correct aberrant practices or behaviors, then any resistance to the quality and safety agenda should dissolve.

REFERENCES

1. Kohn LT, Corrigan JM, Donaldson MS, eds. *To err is human: Building a safer health system*. Washington, DC: National Academy Press, 1999.
2. Brenner DJ, Eric J. Hall EJ. Computed tomography—An increasing source of radiation exposure. *NEJM.* 2007;357:2277–84.
3. Smith-Bindman R, Lipson J, Marcus R, Kim KP, Mahesh M, Gould R, et al. Radiation dose associated with common computed tomography examinations and the associated lifetime attributable risk of cancer. *Arch Intern Med*. 2009;169: 2078–86.
4. Boland GWL. From herding cats towards best practices: Standardizing the radiologic work process. *AJR.* 2009;193:1593–5.
5. Boland G. Stakeholder expectations for radiologists: Obstacles or opportunities. *JACR.* 2006;3:156–63.
6. Muroff LR. Taking your practice to the next level. *JACR.* 2009; 5(9):986–92.
7. Muroff LR, Rao V. Radiology's image problem: Ponder the words of some thought leaders in the field. *JACR.* 2008;5:616–8.
8. Collins J. Evidenced-based medicine. *JACR.* 2007;8: 551–4.
9. Erturk SM, Ondategui-Parra S, Otero H, Ros PR. Evidenced-based radiology. *JACR.* 2006;3:513–9.
10. Swensen SJ, Johnson CD. Radiologic quality and safety: Mapping value into radiology. *JACR*. 2005;2: 992–1000.
11. Sunshine JH, Maynard CD. Update on the diagnostic radiology employment market: Findings through 2007–2008. *JACR.* 2008;5:827–33.
12. ACR Appropriateness Criteria® October 2008. Access June 2010 at: http://www.acr.org/SecondaryMain MenuCategories/quality_safety/app_criteria.aspx
13. Rosenthal DI, Weilburg JB, Schultz T, , Miller, JC,, Nixon V., Dreyer, KJ and Thrall, HF. . Radiology order entry with decision support: Initial clinical experience. *J Am Coll Radiol*. 2006;3:799–806.
14. Sistrom CL, Dang PA, Weilburg JB, MD, Dreyer KJ, Rosenthal DI, Thrall JH. Effect of computerized order entry with integrated decision support on the growth of outpatient procedure volumes: Seven-year time series analysis. *Radiology*. 2009;251:147–55.
15. Morin RL, Rosenthal DI, Stout MB. Radiology order entry: Features and performance requirements. *JACR.* 2006: 3:554–7.
16. Lehnert BE, Bree RL. Analysis of appropriateness of outpatient CT and MRI referred from primary care clinics at an academic medical center: How critical is the need for improved decision support? *JACR.* 2010;3:192–97.
17. Marie Curie. Accessed October 2010, at: http://nobelprize.org/nobel_prizes/physics/laureates/1903/marie-curie-bio.html
18. Kalra MK, Maher MM, Toth TL, Hamberg LM, Michael A. Blake MA, et al. Strategies for CT radiation dose optimization. *Radiology*. 2004;230:619–28.
19. Huda W, Vance A. Patient radiation doses from adult and pediatric CT. *Am J Roentgenol*. 2007;188:540–6.
20. Kalra, MK, Rizzo SM, Novelline RA. Reducing radiation dose in emergency computed tomography with automatic exposure control techniques. *Emerg Radiol*. 2005;11:267–74.
21. Boland GWL. The CT dose and utilization controversy: The radiologist's response. *JACR.* 2008;5: 696–8.
22. ACR practice guideline for diagnostic reference levels in medical x-ray. Accessed June 2010, at: http://www.acr.org/SecondaryMainMenuCategories/quality_safety/guidelines/med_phys/reference_levels.aspx
23. Slovis TL, Bedon WE. Panel discussion. *Pediatr Radiol*. 2002;32:2442–4.
24. Lee CH, Goo JM, Ye HJ, Ye SJ, Park CM, Chun EJ, Im JG. Radiation dose modulation techniques in the multidetector CT era: From basics to practice. *Radiographics*. 2008;28:1451–9.
25. Boland GWL. Maximizing outpatient CT productivity: Use of multiple technologists to increase patient throughput and CT capacity. *J Am Coll Radiol. JACR.* 2008;5:119–25.
26. Boland GWL. Hospital owned and operated outpatient imaging centers: Strategies for success. *J Am Coll Radiol*. 2008;5(8):900–6.

27. Radiation overdoses point up dangers of CT scans. Accessed November 2010, at: http://www.nytimes.com/2009/10/16/us/16radiation.html

28. RADPEER™. Accessed November 2010, at: http://www.acr.org/secondarymainmenucategories/quality_safety/radpeer.aspx

29. Boland GWL. Voice recognition technology for radiology reporting: Transforming the radiologist's value proposition. J Am Coll Radiol. 2007;4(12):865–867.

30. Abujudeh HH, Kaewlai R, Asfaw BA, Thrall JH. Quality initiatives: Key performance indicators for measuring and improving radiology department performance. Radiographics. 2010;30(3):571–80.

31. Boland GWL, Gazelle GS, Halpern E. Radiologist report turnaround times: Impact of pay for performance measures. AJR Am J Roentgenol. 2010;195(3):707–11.

19

Assessing Physician Performance

JAMES R. DUNCAN AND STEPHEN CURRIE

You cannot improve things that you cannot measure.

—LORD KELVIN, CIRCA 1890

Mention assessment to most health care professionals and you evoke angst along with memories of standardized tests and No. 2 pencils. As a result, most radiologists are reluctant to participate in voluntary testing. Still, the same individuals recognize the value of collecting and analyzing information prior to making decisions, such as hiring new staff, recommending a treatment strategy, attending an educational course, or purchasing equipment. In each case, gathering data, analyzing it, and making a decision are attempts to predict the future and maximize the likelihood of the desired outcome.[1] Patients wish to follow the same process when choosing their health care provider, whether it is an individual radiologist, hospital-based radiology group, or freestanding imaging center. As a result, patients, referring physicians, regulatory agencies, and third-party payers all wish to collect data on physician performance, analyze it, and use it to guide their choices. Radiologists should recognize that the same data can also be used to guide process improvement efforts.[2] In both cases, measurements are the starting point for any data-driven decision-making process.

ASSESSMENT AS AN ATTEMPT TO UNDERSTAND A SYSTEM'S INNER WORKINGS

Despite advances in noninvasive neuroimaging, we cannot truly monitor a person's thought process. Instead, we attempt to infer that process by observing stimulus–response pairs. Human information

processing can be considered a system that captures sensory data, uses it to drive decision-making, and generates observable actions (Figure 19.1).[3-7]

This model resembles the system that computers use to process information and act on it. Our sensory organs are analogous to input devices, such as mice and keyboards. Our working and long-term memory are represented by the computer's random access memory and hard drive, respectively. Our motor units are analogous to printers, video monitors, and computer-controlled robotic arms. Cognitive psychologists and computer scientists also recognize that parallels exist between the algorithms that drive decision-making in both systems.[8] In computers, the algorithms are explicitly described in the software. When provided with identical inputs, these algorithms produce consistent results. In humans, the algorithms are referred to as *mental models* and tend to be biased by recent events and other factors that are often difficult to quantify.[9] As a result, although mental models are more nuanced, they tend to produce more variable results.[10]

When designing physician assessments, we typically treat the capabilities of sensory organs, working memory, long-term memory, and motor unit as constants. We are most interested in the candidate's decision-making algorithms. As above, we cannot directly observe those mental models, but rather we attempt to infer them from our observations of how the candidate responds to various stimuli. Although we might begin formulating a decision

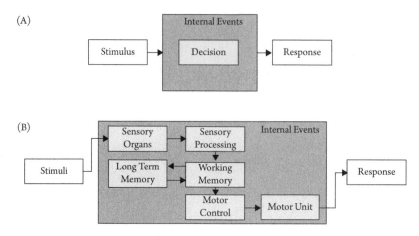

FIGURE 19.1 Models of human information processing. Human behavior is often depicted using stimulus–response pairs (A). Research in neurosciences and cognitive psychology provides a more detailed understanding (B) of how sensory information is captured, processed, and the results forwarded to working memory. Once a decision is made, the planned action is formulated and appropriate signals are conveyed to motor units.[4–7]

about a candidate's competence after observing the first stimulus–response cycle, it is usually best to delay the final decision until enough information is available to make a valid decision.

COLLECTING ENOUGH INFORMATION TO MAKE A VALID DECISION

Validity is a commonly abused term. Although it is common to find phrases such as "valid data" or "a validated test," such terminology suggests that validity is an open-or-shut case, in which, once the data collection vehicle is declared valid, the results can be trusted no matter what circumstances surrounded data collection. Validity is better characterized as a property of the decision made following data collection.[1,2] It is crucial to recognize that validity is conditional and that new information can challenge the validity of a prior decision.[11] Kane and other assessment experts suggest the validity argument should be viewed as a debate.[12,13] For physician assessment, the examiner should be prepared to stand in front of a review board and declare "based on my observations of the candidate's performance and my belief that these observations reflect an accurate sample of the tasks required during patient care, I believe the candidate is competent and recommend that the board certify the candidate." In this process, the examiner reviews the data and makes a claim. Members of the review board might refute the claim by arguing the analysis was flawed or the observations excluded key aspects of patient

care. The examiner might revise the claim, collect additional data, or argue against those criticisms. In its purest form, the debate is an attempt to uncover the truth before making an informed decision. It resembles a courtroom scene, complete with opposing counselors, rules of evidence, judges, and juries.

The conditional nature of validity means that, before making a claim, one should attempt to collect sufficient evidence to support that decision against any reasonable challenge. Still, one has to balance the costs required to collect information against the diagnostic yield of each piece. Information science uses bandwidth to describe information gathering.[14] Limited bandwidth means that the amount of information we can collect from any single stimulus–response cycle is limited, and the number of stimulus–response cycles is constrained by the observation time. Assessments use three strategies to address bandwidth limitations.[15–17] The first is to increase the information yield of any stimulus–response cycle. For multiple choice items, the information yield can be calculated using the number of alternatives the candidate must reasonably consider before making a decision. The second strategy is to increase the number of cycles per unit time. This can be accelerated by having informative stimuli stacked up and ready to present to the candidate. The third approach is to expand the observation period. A single exam might use 4–8 hours to present hundreds of items, or the certification board might use a series of exams to collect the information it needs to make its decision.

TEST ITEMS AS STIMULI

Test items should be viewed as stimuli that are presented to the candidate in an attempt to learn about the candidate's mental models. Stimuli come from two potential sources. *Real stimuli* are those that occur during the course of actual work. If you plan to use your observations to predict the candidate's decision making abilities during patient care, you will want to observe performance during actual clinical work. *Simulated stimuli* are recreations of stimuli encountered in work environments.[18] Sports provide an excellent analogy.[19] Analysis of responses to game day stimuli is usually the best predictor of future game day performance. However, performance during practice scenarios is often also used to predict game day performance. Further, practice scenarios are often used to improve game day performance.

DESIGNING ASSESSMENTS USING SIMULATED STIMULI

Simulation-based assessments provide the test designer with numerous choices about which stimuli to present, how to grade responses, and how those scored items will be combined to make decisions. The ability to retrieve and reuse stimuli means that examinations can be prepared ahead of time and delivered in focused testing sessions. Further, the results from different candidates can be compared because they experienced the same stimulus. As a result, standardized exams have been the predominant data source for high-stakes decisions throughout medical training. The design of these standardized exams consists of four stages: domain, task, evidence, and decision modeling.[20]

SIMULATION-BASED ASSESSMENT DEVELOPMENT: MODELING THE DOMAIN

The wide gamut of possible stimuli means that choices must be made as to which stimuli should appear on the exam. The domain model uses data from the work environment to drive decisions about what types of stimuli will be needed to support the claim that performance on the exam is a useful predictor of clinical performance. The domain model typically uses surveys, workplace observations, and other datasets to determine what topics should appear on the examination and how many questions should be allotted to each topic.[21] Test designers use the domain model to create the test blueprint.

We recently suggested using billing data to construct the domain model.[22] The advantage of this approach is that billing records are detailed, accurate, stored in reliable databases, and continually updated. These billing records include operator, date of service, service site, and current procedural terminology (CPT) codes. The large number of CPT codes used in radiology facilitates construction of detailed domain models at the national (Figure 19.2) and individual levels (Figure 19.3). Test designers can use these results to help create individualized test blueprints. Such individualized but data-driven domain modeling techniques will increase in importance as physician assessment becomes a more frequent occurrence. The Joint Commission's ongoing professional practice evaluation (OPPE) and the American Board of Medical Specialties' maintenance of certification (MOC) programs are clear examples of this trend.

SIMULATION-BASED ASSESSMENT DEVELOPMENT: SELECTING THE TASK MODEL

The next step in assessment design is deciding how evidence of the candidate's decision-making skill will be elicited for each particular topic found on the test blueprint. The task model defines how a stimulus will be presented and the response recorded. Multiple choice questions are typical stimuli, and responses are recorded by having the candidate use a pencil to fill an oval or click with a mouse to indicate the chosen answer. Since multiple choice items are relatively easy to create and score, they provide test designers with an efficient and effective method of assessing decision-making skills in different segments of the domain. However, multiple choice items provide limited information because correct responses can result from guessing. In addition, many stimulus and response pairs contain cues that artificially increase the probability that the candidate will select the correct answer even though he or she does not possess the desired mental model. For example, any veteran of multiple choice questions knows to eliminate choices that include key words such as "always" or "never."

Although text-based multiple choice items have long been used to assess a radiologist's skills, the introduction of computer-based testing and its ability to reproduce radiographic images, as well as record details of the candidate's response, allows

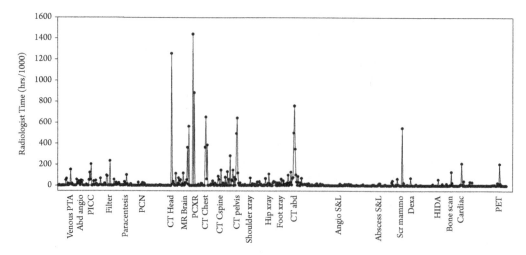

FIGURE 19.2 Nationwide domain model for radiologists. Data from the American Medical Association's Resource Based Relative Value Scale Data Manager 2009 was used to estimate how radiologists spend their time when caring for Medicare patients. For each current procedural terminology (CPT) code, the data on Medicare Utilization and Physician Time was used to calculate how radiologists across the nation spent their time in 2007. The resulting time in thousands of hours (y axis) was plotted against CPT code (x axis). Short descriptions for high-frequency codes are indicated. As expected, the combination of frequency and time/code led to clearly identifiable peaks for chest radiography, head computed tomography (CT), abdominal/pelvic CT, head magnetic resonance imaging (MRI), screening mammography, peripherally inserted central catheters, and other exams/procedures.

test designers to begin using new task models (Figure 19.4). Such task models will likely be more informative since they avoid the hidden cues found in multiple choice questions and also better recreate the stimuli encountered during a radiologist's workday.

WORKPLACE ASSESSMENTS

There are several compelling reasons to collect data from workplace activities and use these datasets to assess physician performance.[21] First, patients are most interested in how well physicians will perform during their procedure. Physician

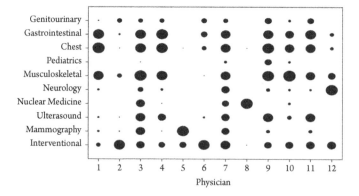

FIGURE 19.3 Individual domain model for radiologists. Departmental billing data was collected and each current procedural terminology (CPT) code was assigned to a modality/section. The logarithm of code frequency in each category was used to determine symbol diameter, and the results displayed for 12 different radiologists. Physicians 3 and 7 practiced in a community hospital and thus interpret or perform a wide array of exams. Physicians 2 and 6 are from the interventional radiology section. Physicians 8 and 6 are from the nuclear medicine and mammography sections. The mammographers, as well as members of the abdominal and cardiothoracic sections (Physicians 10–12) perform biopsies, and this accounts for codes that mapped to the interventional segment of the domain model. Unpublished data from Sridhar and Duncan.

Central Venous Catheter
Tip Position

A. Examine the image
B. Determine optimal
position for the
tip of the specified
catheter
C. Move the arrow so
that its tip matches
that location
D. Save your answer

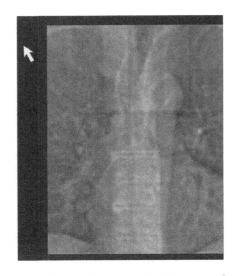

FIGURE 19.4 Task model for central venous catheter placement. One key aspect of placement is catheter tip position, and this task model provides a simple means of determining the candidate's target position for the catheter tip. By repeating this item with different catheter types (e.g., Port-A-Cath and tunneled dialysis catheter), the test designer can also determine if the candidate's mental model takes catheter types into account.

performance on standardized tests is useful only if the relevant knowledge, skills, and abilities transfer to clinical work. Second is the fact that simulation-based assessments provide only brief snapshots of performance. It makes little sense to base decisions on a dataset that captures the candidate's performance from a few hours every several years. A far larger dataset could be obtained by continually monitoring performance throughout the year. Third is the Hawthorne Effect, in which people tend to improve their performance when they believe they are being watched.[23] If assessment is intermittent, we can expect candidates will adjust their performance during the observation period. Fourth, workplace assessment minimizes the problems that occur from flawed domain and task models. The assessment is based on what the individual actually does in the workplace, rather than on what the test designer believes this individual does.

The problem with workplace assessments has been lack of standardized test items. Objectively measuring responses to the numerous stimuli found in the workplace is exceedingly difficult. This complicates efforts to generate scorable items and use the results to make valid decisions about the candidate's competence. However, Deming, Box, and others provide ideas about how to use workplace observations to guide improvement efforts.[24–27]

CONVERTING OBSERVED EVENTS INTO ITEM-LEVEL SCORES

In both simulation- and workplace-based assessments, the examiner must convert observable events into item-level scores. Test designers use evidence models to develop the algorithms for converting raw test data into item-level scores.[28] For the multiple choice items found in simulation-based assessments, the algorithms simply compare the candidate's response to the "correct" response found in the answer key. Scoring algorithms for other task models are more complicated (Figure 19.5).

CONVERTING SCORES INTO A FINAL DECISION

It is rare that the final decision depends on the results of a single item. Instead, the results of multiple items are collected and combined to yield a final decision.[16] The process used to aggregate the results of multiple test items and use that data to render final judgment about the candidate's overall skills, knowledge, and abilities is governed by the decision model.[20] Since some items might be considered more important than others, the aggregation algorithm lends more weight to those items. Finally, whereas *criteria-referenced decision models* have a defined set point needed to pass the assessment, *normative decision models* allow only a certain fraction of the candidates to pass the exam and vary the passing score to achieve this.[16]

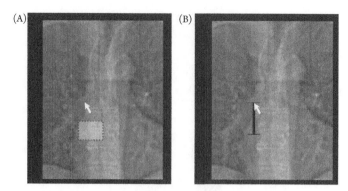

FIGURE 19.5 Evidence models for central venous catheter placement. The candidate's response is indicated by the arrow. For this example, the optimal catheter tip location is the cavoatrial junction, which is located two vertebral bodies below the carina (reference). Panel A illustrates an all-or-nothing scoring key, in which the candidate only receives credit if the arrow tip is within the box. Panel B illustrates a graduated scoring key, in which the distance between the candidate's choice and the optimal point is measured and the amount of partial credit awarded depends on that distance.

ASSESSING RADIOLOGIST PERFORMANCE IN THE WORKPLACE

Routine assessment of radiologist performance in the workplace requires a reliable, continuous, and unbiased flow of data. Although some might suggest using diagnostic miss and/or complication rates to assess performance, these untoward events are typically detected by having subject matter experts review medical records. The costs of such chart review necessitates limiting either the sample size or sampling frequency.[29] The large number of subject matter experts needed to routinely assess radiologist performance on a large scale makes this method impractical. Further, there are concerns about how each examiner's personal definition of diagnostic misses and/or procedural errors might bias the dataset.

Another approach is to capture and analyze data that results from normal work processes.[24–26] Since radiologists use ionizing radiation in their work, we and others recognized that radiation metrics could be used to assess physician performance.[3,30] This is particularly true in fluoroscopy, since the radiologist is directly involved imaging decisions.[1] During procedures such as balloon angioplasty, the radiologist extracts information from the fluoroscopic image and uses that information to guide the procedure. The result is a tight linkage between information gathering, data analysis, and decision-making. In contrast, during purely diagnostic fluoroscopic procedures, the radiologist uses ionizing radiation to collect information that is later condensed into a written report. The referring physician uses that report or his or her own analysis of the images to guide treatment. This workflow has prompted a generation of radiologists to capture key findings on film. In both cases, the radiologist controls the information-gathering process. The dynamic information provided by the fluoroscopic image creates a feedback loop, in which the radiologist monitors the procedure and adjusts technique to answer the clinical question or administer treatment. This ability to dynamically control the process means that the radiologist is uniquely positioned to balance the benefits and risks of ionizing radiation during fluoroscopic procedures (Figure 19.6).

MULTIPLE FACTORS INFLUENCE RADIATION USE DURING FLUOROSCOPIC PROCEDURES

When compared to standardized tests, workplace assessment introduces additional variables (Figure 19.7). Variations in problem difficulty, available tools, and workplace environment confound efforts to link the observed results to radiologist skill. Although the overall system is more complex, it is still possible to deconvolute the dataset by capturing data on these other factors. Workplace assessment requires a reliable and robust system for capturing and storing data. Although many elect to build ad hoc data capture systems and specialized databases, we and others have elected to extract data from administrative datastreams. Since these systems are commonly part of the billing process, they are designed to be highly reliable, and the

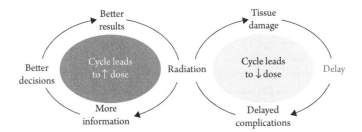

FIGURE 19.6 Competing processes driving radiation use. In most cases, the left-hand loop tends to drive radiation dose because the radiologist gets rapid feedback about how more radiation leads to more diagnostic information, better decisions, and better clinical results. The right-hand loop, with its long delay between tissue damage and observable complications, is much more difficult to integrate into the radiologist's decision-making.

data is continually reviewed to ensure its accuracy. Further, since multiple providers submit billing information to national third-party payers, the data fields and data elements are standardized. This standardized format also allows one to leverage the large amount of information stored in datasets that are linked to the billing process. Finally, billing data is stored, and this allows retrospective review.

CAPTURING DATA ON RADIATION USE FROM DAILY WORK

We recently leveraged the radiology information system (RIS) to reliably capture data on radiation use while maintaining the links to the other variables

shown in Figure 19.7. The RIS provided the necessary linkages to physicians, technologists, date of service, supplies, imaging equipment, CPT codes, and patient attributes. While we hope to someday electronically transfer dose metrics directly from imaging equipment to the RIS, this project started with manual entry of fluoroscopy time. Fluoroscopy time was chosen because the RIS had a field configured for this data, and detailed examination of radiation use in selected procedures suggested that fluoroscopy time would be a useful performance measure.[3] In addition, Medicare's Physician Quality Reporting Initiative provided an incentive for capturing this data in the billing stream. Efforts are under way to routinely capture kerma area product (KAP),

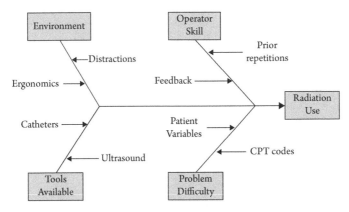

FIGURE 19.7 Factors influencing radiation use during fluoroscopic procedures. Ishikawa or "fishbone" diagram illustrating the cause-and-effect relationship between multiple variables and radiation use. The variables are grouped into four broad categories that reflect ideas drawn from the human factors and assessment literature.[31] That research indicates that system performance is influenced by the combination of operator skill, problem difficulty, available tools, and environmental factors. In this model, current procedural terminology (CPT) coding patterns can be used to estimate the operator's prior experience and procedure difficulty. Although experience tends to promote expertise, that benefit can be destroyed by poor equipment or an environment filled with distractions. Conversely, improved tools tend to simplify difficult procedures.

reference point air kerma, and number of images. Ideally, the interfaces needed to electronically transfer these and other data elements directly from the imaging equipment into the RIS will become available but, in the meantime, we only collect KAP and the other metrics in cases where the fluoroscopy time exceeds 30 minutes and/or reference point air kerma is greater than 2 Gray.

USING THIS DATA FOR ONGOING PROFESSIONAL PRACTICE EVALUATION

The Joint Commission requires hospitals to continually evaluate the professional practice quality of each medical staff member. The resulting Ongoing Professional Practice Evaluation (OPPE) program can be viewed as a high-stakes assessment because the results are meant to guide decisions about whether to renew, revise, or revoke that physician's medical staff privileges. The Joint Commission recognizes that hospital administrators lack the expertise to make these assessments and therefore requires hospitals to establish peer review processes in which medical staff collect and analyze the

necessary data. Ideally, these decisions start with datasets that are objective, accurate, and reflect key attributes of actual clinical practice. This part of the process mirrors how domain and task models are used to design assessments. Evidence models are then used to transform the raw data into performance means.

Our current evidence model borrows ideas from item response theory (IRT), particularly the idea that the probability of completing any fluoroscopic procedure within a particular time will depend on problem difficulty and operator skill.[32] This prompted an attempt to begin estimating problems with different degrees of difficulty and linking the results to the granular procedure nomenclature provided by CPT coding. The results shown in Figure 19.8 indicate that the performance curves shift appropriately (Figure 19.8). These curves do not consider the influence of other factors, such as patient attributes, operator experience, or variable working conditions (e.g., emergent vs. routine procedures). Still, the evidence suggests that OPPE-mandated peer review could use fluoroscopy data to begin identifying trends associated with performance issues. The decision model, which dictates exactly how this data will be combined with other

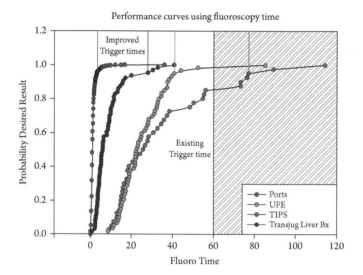

FIGURE 19.8 Performance curves for common interventional procedures. current procedural terminology (CPT) codes were used to identify common procedures within the dataset. The fraction of cases completed versus fluoroscopy time was plotted to create performance curves. These graphs illustrate the dataset's central tendency and variation. Ports are a simple procedure since 95% of the cases are completed with less than 4 minutes of fluoroscopy. The central tendency is best evaluated by assessing the 50th percentile (0.5 probability of the desired result), whereas variation is assessed by the curve's slope. This analysis illustrates that performance during transjugular intrahepatic portosystemic shunting (TIPS) is highly variable, and this variability makes it difficult to predict how much fluoroscopy the next TIPS will require. The gray area indicates a standardized trigger value of 60 minutes will fail to identify problems that occur with Port-A-Cath placement and transjugular liver biopsies.

measures of performance to decide whether to renew, revise, or revoke clinical privileges, is in the very earliest stages of development.

CONCLUSION

When assessing physician performance, one should recognize that the quality of the results will depend on the thought and care that went into designing the assessment process. Although simulation-based assessments that utilize multiple choice questions have long been the norm for medical education, there are substantial advantages to expanding to new task models and workplace-based assessments.

REFERENCES

1. Duncan JR, Evens RG. Using information to optimize medical outcomes. *JAMA*. 2009;301: 2383–5.
2. Bucholz EI, Duncan JR. Assessing system performance. *J Vasc Interv Radiol*. 2008;19: 987–94.
3. Beta E, Parikh AS, Street M, Duncan JR. Capture and analysis of data from image-guided procedures. *J Vasc Interv Radiol*. 2009;20: 769–81.
4. Schmidt R, Lee T. *Motor control and learning: A behavioral emphasis*, 4th edition. Champaign, IL: Human Kinetics, 2005.
5. Fitts P. The information capacity of the human motor system in controlling the amplitude of movement. *J Exp Psych*. 1954;47:381–91.
6. Reason JT. *Human error*. New York: Cambridge University Press, 1990.
7. Reason J. Human error: Models and management. *BMJ*. 2000;320:768–70.
8. Minsky M. Society of the mind. New York: Simon & Schuster, 1986.
9. Gagne R, Wager W, Golas K, Keller J. *Principles of instructional design*, 5th edition. Belmont, CA: Wadsworth/Thomson Learning, 2005.
10. Dawes RM, Faust D, Meehl PE. Clinical versus actuarial judgment. *Science*. 1989;243:1668–74.
11. Messick S. Validity. In: Linn RL, ed. *Educational measurement*, 3rd ed. New York: American Council on Education, Macmillan Publishing; 1989:13–103.
12. Kane M. Certification testing as an illustration of argument-based validation. *Measurement*. 2004;2:135–70.
13. Kane M. Validation. In: Brennan R, ed. *Educational measurement*, 4th ed. Westport, CT: Praeger Publishers; 2006:17–64.
14. Pierce JR. *An introduction to information theory: Symbols, signals & noise*, 2nd, rev. ed. New York: Dover Publications, 1980.
15. Brennan R. *Educational measurement*, 4th ed. Westport, CT: Praeger Publishers, 2006.
16. Kubiszyn T, Borich G. *Educational testing and measurement*, 8th ed. Hoboken, NJ: John Wiley & Sons, Inc., 2007.
17. Clauser BE, Margolis MJ, Swanson DB. An examination of the contribution of computer-based case simulations to the USMLE step 3 examination. *Acad Med*. 2002;77:S80–2.
18. Dillon GF, Boulet JR, Hawkins RE, Swanson DB. Simulations in the United States Medical Licensing Examination (USMLE). *Qual Saf Health Care*. 2004;13(Suppl 1): i41–5.
19. Williams AM, Hodges NJ. *Skill acquisition in sport: Research, theory and practice*. London/New York: Routledge, 2004: xxii.
20. Mislevy RJ, Steinberg LS, Almond RG. On the structure of educational assessments. *Measurement: Interdisciplinary Research and Perspectives*. 2003;1: 3–62.
21. Raymond M. Job analysis and the specification of content for licensure and certification examinations. *Appl Measure Educ*. 2001;14(4):369–415..
22. Sridhar S, Duncan JR. Strategies for choosing process improvement projects. *J Vasc Interv Radiol*. 2008;19:471–7.
23. Parsons HM. What happened at Hawthorne?: New evidence suggests the Hawthorne effect resulted from operant reinforcement contingencies. *Science*. 1974;183:922–32.
24. Deming W. *The new economics for industry, government, education*, 2nd ed. Cambridge, MA: The MIT Press, 2000.
25. Deming W. *Out of the crisis*. Cambridge, MA: The MIT Press, 2000.
26. Box G. *Improving almost anything: Ideas and essays*. Hoboken, NJ: Wiley-Interscience, 2006.
27. Liker JK. *The Toyota way: 14 management principles from the world's greatest manufacturer*. New York: McGraw-Hill, 2004.
28. Williamson DM, Mislevy RJ, Bejar II. *Automated scoring of complex tasks in computer-based testing*. Mahwah, NJ: Lawrence Erlbaum Associates, 2006.
29. Swanson DB, Norman GR, Linn RL. Performance-based assessment: Lessons from the health professions. *Educat Res*. 1995;24:5–11.
30. Miller DL, Kwon D, Bonavia GH. Reference levels for patient radiation doses in interventional radiology: Proposed initial values for U.S. practice. *Radiology*. 2009;253:753–64.
31. Sanders M, McCormick E. *Human factors in engineering and design*. New York: McGraw-Hill, 1993.
32. Embretson SE, Reise SP. *Item response theory for psychologists*. Mahwah, NJ: Lawrence Erlbaum Associates, 2000.

20

Predicting System Performance

JAMES R. DUNCAN AND ELIO BETA

We strive to predict the future because every planned action is an attempt to influence future events. Even though our predictions can never be completely accurate, every plan includes a mental model of how the planned action might lead to the desired outcome. These plans are based on our analysis of prior events because we recognize that past performance is the best method of predicting future events. We look for recurring patterns in the circumstances leading up to key events and build an understanding of the linkages between actions and outcomes. We then adjust our actions to maximize the probability of the desired outcome.

USING PRIOR EXPERIENCE TO CREATE AND REVISE OUR MENTAL MODELS

We study the past because that experience leads us to create, and then refine, mental models that describe the linkage between cause and effect, input and output, stimulus and response.[1-5] The utility of our mental models is judged by their ability to accurately predict future events when provided with data regarding prior events. Having created reliable and robust mental models, we attempt to pass them along to our colleagues and students.[6,7] We verbally describe our thought process, put our ideas on paper, or provide step-by-step guidance through procedures. Each is an attempt to communicate these models. However, many of these attempts fail because we cannot directly transfer this knowledge (Example 1). To learn from our experience, our colleagues and students must pay attention to the stimuli we provide, link those events to their own preexisting mental models, revise their mental models, and test the results.[8] These recipients might test their new mental models using a series of internal mental simulations in which prior stimulus–response pairs are run through the model.[1] The recipients might also test their mental models while performing procedures to see if these new models accurately predict observable events.[9] In each case, the recipient only accepts the new model if it satisfactorily explains the linkages between past and future events.[1] Further, the recipient's model will almost certainly differ from our model. As a result, we cannot expect the results of our training to perfectly transfer to our students.

Example 1: Communicating Mental Models

Radiologists commonly instruct patients to hold still and stop breathing during image acquisition. We provide these instructions because we know that movement can degrade the images. Most adult patients understand that we have valid reasons for these instructions and will make every effort to comply, even though they don't fully understand our rationale. In some cases, we might provide a more detailed expectation by stating that they will need to hold still without breathing for 10–15 seconds. We might also tell them that they will likely experience a warm feeling during contrast injection and that the x-ray machine will make a whirling sound. We provide these additional instructions because we recognize that, when patients have a reasonable expectation of the upcoming events, they will be better prepared to comply with our instructions. These explanations foster "shared mental models." The problem is that patients might not comply with our instructions for a variety of reasons. Some patients might fully understand our instructions but will not be able to comply because they have a decreased respiratory reserve or an involuntary tremor. Others might not know exactly when they should hold still or stop breathing. Others might not comprehend the instructions because room noise interferes with verbal communication and leads to communication failures. Finally, young children and non-English speaking patients will not understand our verbal instructions even when the room is quiet and the instructions are clear. All of these examples illustrate the difficulty of communicating a simple mental model and observing the desired result.

TRANSFER OF TRAINING OCCURS WITHIN INDIVIDUALS

The mental models used in our daily work as radiologists were developed through an extensive series of experiences that began before grade school and continued throughout college, medical school, residency training, and fellowship. The simple hand movements we learned and practiced as children impacted the manual dexterity available to us when we were first asked to start intravenous lines or perform image-guided biopsies. The algorithms used to plan these tasks and the motor control programs used to execute them are continually refined, even in the absence of instructors.[5,9] When faced with a task, we first search our memory for an example that is comparable to the current task. If the prior plan and execution were successful, we typically adopt that approach.[1] If the prior repetition was unsuccessful or suboptimal, we are faced with decisions about using the plan anyway, revising the plan, searching for another comparable set of circumstances, or solving the problem de novo.[1,10,11] This illustrates how we are constantly transferring and adapting knowledge gained from prior experience to the current task.

PROBLEMS WITH TRANSFER

Although we strive to do everything possible to improve the probability that the future follows the desired course, there is no guarantee that some unpredicted event will subvert the chain of events.

All predictions are imperfect because, as illustrated in Example 2, it is impossible to completely recreate any set of circumstances.

Example 2: Repeating a Simple Task

Consider the simple task of measuring a pulmonary nodule on a computed tomography (CT) scan. The results from repeated measurements will almost certainly vary, even though the computer displays an exact copy of the original image. The number and spatial distribution of photons reaching our retina will vary from moment to moment due to slight fluctuations in ambient light, viewing angle, and other factors. This will influence our ability to discern the edge of the nodule. Further, as we position the electronic calipers, our movements reflect the firing of numerous motor neurons and how individual muscle cells respond to those commands. As a result, even if your measurement plan remains constant, your execution will vary since the start and end points cannot be exactly reproduced. The results can be further biased by factors such as fatigue or perhaps an unconscious tendency to report that the nodules decrease in size whenever we learn that a patient is undergoing chemotherapy.

This illustrates the problems associated with applying mental models learned from prior experience to the current problem. Transfer of training should be considered a four-dimensional problem, in which data from one time and place are applied to a problem that occurs at another time and place. If all other factors are equal, predictions will improve as differences in time and space decrease. Repeating an identical task in the exact same location means that we only have to consider how performance might change over time (Equation 1). In such circumstances, the predicted future performance will approximate the prior performance if the interval between the two performances is suitably small.

$$\text{Predicted Performance (t)} = \text{Prior Performance} \ (t - x) + \Delta \qquad \text{(Equation 1)}$$

where $\Delta \downarrow$ to 0 as $x \to 0$.

MEASURING PERFORMANCE

Measurement theory contends that each observation will vary around the true value.[12–15] Although any individual measurement can differ from the true value, if an infinite number of measurements were summed, the sum of these differences would be zero (Equation 2). As a result, efforts to ascertain the true value will improve, if one makes a number of repeated measurements (Example 3).

$$\text{Observed Performance} = \text{Actual Performance} + \delta$$
(Equation 2)

where, for repeated measurements, $\Sigma\delta \to 0$ as the number of measurements increases.

Example 3: How Repeated Measurements Allow Greater Confidence in Results

A series of histograms illustrate how averages of repeated measurements allow greater confidence in the result (Figure 20.1). In this example, a 2.0 cm nodule was measured 10,000 times, and errors in measurement caused a standard deviation of 0.2 cm. Panel A illustrates the results when single measurements were used to estimate the true nodule diameter. In panels B and C, 3 and 20 measurements, respectively, were averaged and the average used to estimate the nodule diameter.

PERFORMANCE WILL VARY ACCORDING TO SKILL AND TASK DIFFICULTY

Test theory[15,16] suggests that the probability of any performance meeting predetermined criteria will depend on two factors: the individual's skill and problem difficulty (Equation 3). We use the term "skill" to describe the relevant knowledge, proficiencies, and abilities needed to achieve the desired result in the task at hand and abbreviate skill as "S" in the resulting equations. Highly skilled individuals are termed experts, and their expertise is valued because they tend to reliably produce the desired result. Although we might assign a simple task to a novice instead of an expert, doing so increases the risk of an undesirable result.

$$\text{Predicted Performance (t)} = F(S_t, D)$$
(Equation 3)

where S_t is skill available at time (t) and D is the problem difficulty.

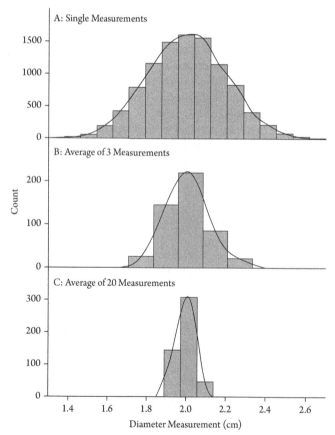

FIGURE 20.1 Distribution of single or multiple measurements with mean of 2.0 cm and standard deviation of 0.2.

This equation indicates that the linkage between skill and the observed performance is not absolute (Example 4). Great skill does not guarantee superior performance. The expert might still fail due to fatigue, performance anxiety, and chance events. Such failures will be rare if the expert is given a simple problem. Conversely, the lack of skill does not guarantee failure, since a novice can occasionally achieve the desired result, especially if there are a limited number of possible results (e.g., multiple choice or true–false tests).

Example 4: How the Probability of Success Varies with Task Difficulty and Skill

The probability of success during an image-guided biopsy depends on the operator's skill, as well as the depth and size of the lesion. Task difficulty is therefore determined by the size and depth of the target. This dependency on target size and distance is easily illustrated using a sporting analogy. In football, the difficulty of a field goal attempt is largely determined by yardage (Figure 20.2). Skilled kickers are often successful at 40 yards or more (upper panel). However, as skill decreases, the performance curve shifts to the left (lower panel). Conversely, a rightward shift is evidence of additional skill. In this example, task difficulty only depends on yardage, but we acknowledge that task difficulty will also depend

on other factors, such as crosswinds and field conditions. By analogy, an uncooperative patient will tend to decrease the probability of a successful biopsy.

Tests are used to help estimate a person's skill. This proposed linkage among the observed result, skill, and task difficulty suggests that several factors should be considered when designing tests (Example 5). First, differences in skill can best be observed by creating tests that include tasks of the appropriate difficulty. Second, multiple task repetitions should be used to refine the skill estimate (Example 3). Third, a well-designed test can help us predict future results if there is no change in skill or task difficulty over time.

Example 5: Estimating Skill from Observed Results with Different Test Items

Consider how a test with three different items might be used to estimate the skill levels of three individuals. If each individual is given one chance at each item, it is likely that the expert (*dashed line*) will succeed at two of the three items, and the novice will fail at two of the three items (Figure 20.3). Since the intermediate (*solid line*) might succeed at one or two of the three items, there is a 50/50 chance of the intermediate being classified as an expert or a novice. Repeating the test improves the ability to accurately classify the three individuals. However, it

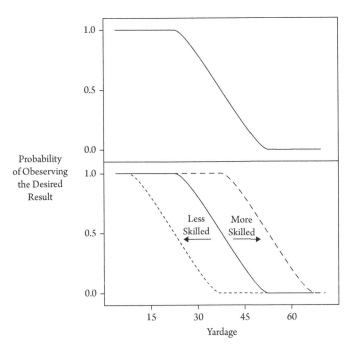

FIGURE 20.2 Probability of observing the desired result depends on the combination of task difficulty and operator skill.

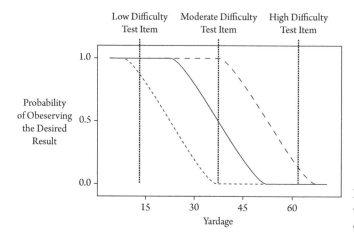

FIGURE 20.3 Using different items with different levels of difficulty to assess operator skill.

seems wasteful for the expert to repeat the low- and medium-difficulty tasks. It is also inefficient to have the novice repeat the two more difficult tasks. If testing time is limited, one should use the results of each testing round to predict each individual's skill, and use that information to choose items for the next testing round. This strategy is known as *adaptive testing*, and it can markedly improve one's ability to accurately predict future performance.[16]

SKILL CAN CHANGE OVER TIME

The discussion thus far does not address how skill might change over time. Since skill can clearly increase or decrease over time, the skill available at any point in time, S_t, represents a balance between skill acquisition and skill loss (Equation 4). Equation 4 also includes a factor, $S_{t=0}$, to account for pre-existing skill or inborn aptitude.

$$S_t = S_{t=0} + S \text{ (gained through training or experience)}$$
$$- S \text{ (lost over time)} \qquad \text{(Equation 4)}$$

Skill Acquisition

Human performance tends to improve with practice,[17,18] and this phenomena is expressed as the *power law of practice*. This relationship is widely used to predict how training or experience will influence future performance.[18] Practice leads to increased skill, which in turn improves the chance of the desired performance. Equation 5 explicitly describes how skill might increase with practice.

$$S \text{ (gain)} = k * \ln \text{ (task repetitions)} \qquad \text{(Equation 5)}$$

Although our model predicts that skill will increase according to the logarithm of task repetitions, we readily acknowledge that the amount learned from any single task repetition and applied to the next repetition will also depend on feedback and transfer of training. Equation 6 therefore acknowledges that the slope of the learning curve (k) includes factors for transfer of training ($\beta_{P \to A}$) and feedback (α).

$$k = \alpha\beta_{P \to A} \qquad \text{(Equation 6)}$$

where $\beta_{P \to A}$ indicates how well experience with the practice task (P) prepared the candidate to perform the assessment task (A).

The transfer of Training Factor: $\beta_{P \to A}$

Although multiple repetitions of the same or similar tasks are commonly treated as identical, time and other factors mean that the circumstances surrounding the first, second, third, fourth, or nth task repetition will never be completely identical to the task of interest. The nth+1 repetition can be considered a test, and the prior repetitions constitute pretest practice. Even though the practice repetitions (P) will never exactly recreate every aspect of the assessment task (A), we suggest that skills gained during practice will transfer to the assessment task (P→A). Thus, we contend that the transfer factor ($\beta_{P \to A}$) approaches 1.0 as the differences between the practice and assessment tasks become infinitesimally small. We expect that any well-designed practice activity will minimize the probability of negative transfer and suggest that $\beta_{P \to A}$ will almost always vary between zero and 1.0.

Example 6: Transfer of Training

There is considerable debate regarding the transfer of training, especially how transfer decreases as task attributes vary.[10] Consider four related tasks, A, B, C, and D, where the tasks vary in a single dimension (Figure 20.4).

It is relatively easy to prove that practicing Task A leads to improved performance on Task A. It is also possible to measure how practicing Task A tends to improve performance on Task B. Such results reflect what has been termed "near transfer." It has proved much more difficult to measure how much practicing task A leads to improved performance on tasks C and D. We contend that attempts to measure such "far transfer" are hampered by two problems. First is the difficulty of measuring small signals in the midst of noise.[19] The noise can quickly make it nearly impossible to recognize the pattern. Second is the need to consider multiple dimensions when considering transfer coefficients.

The simplest dimension to consider is time. Our model predicts that performance on some future task will depend on the amount of prior practice and how well the skills learned through practice transfer to that future task. The accuracy of these predictions will tend to decrease as one looks further and further into the future (Equation 1). Stated another way, it is much easier to make specific and accurate predictions about tomorrow's performance than next year's. This stems from the realization that every factor influencing task performance will tend to drift over time. Some might suggest they would counter such drift by recording every task variable and use that data to recreate the future task. Given the problems with exactly measuring anything (Example 2), communicating those results (Example 1), and the inability to observe/measure every possible variable, it is simply impossible to counter such drift. As a result, one obtains the following diagram (Figure 20.5), which illustrates how an apparently identical task changes over time.

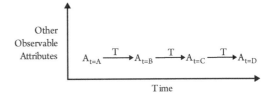

FIGURE 20.5 How the progression of time means that tasks can never be reproduced.

In this model, the transfer factor can be determined from the length of the connecting arrow, which reflects the interval between task repetitions (T). However, differences in nonobservable or previously unknown variables can distort the transfer factor (Figure 20.6).

The Feedback Factor: α

Feedback or knowledge of results clearly promotes learning since a pattern of failed predictions will prompt us to revise our mental models. We proposed that feedback falls into two general classes. *Extrinsic feedback* dominates during the early repetitions, since we do not possess the appropriate mental model needed to successfully complete the task. Instead, the requisite mental models reside within the instructor.[4,5,11,20,21] The instructor compares our performance with the desired results and reports the difference as feedback.

From an information gathering standpoint, it can be argued that we learn nothing new from cases in which everything agrees exactly with our expectations.[19] In such cases, no new information is available to refine our mental model. Some may oppose this viewpoint and argue that they have often learned from successful outcomes because those desired results confirmed that their approach to the problem was valid. In such cases, they are admitting that the outcome was in doubt. Such equipoise means that two mental models were being considered, and

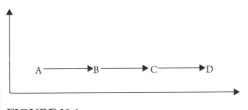

FIGURE 20.4

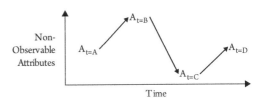

FIGURE 20.6 How nonobservable task attributes can further confound repeated measures of what seems to be an identical task.

the result served to favor one over the other. Stated another way, one mental model was erroneous, and this supports the contention that everything we learn is based on analysis of our mistakes.

As we develop our own mental models, we acquire the ability to provide internal feedback. This self-assessment is driven by an internal comparison of self-generated expectations and actual performance.[1,9] Self-assessment not only frees us from the necessity of being supervised, but allows us to mentally rehearse the procedure.

As shown in Equation 7, the feedback factor (α) can be separated into internal and external components. In this model, the external feedback quality factor can range from –1 to 1 since learning rates on a task could be confounded by deliberately misinforming the trainee about his/her performance. In contrast, the internal feedback quality factor ranges from 0 to 1. Negative values for internal feedback are not permitted because, as illustrated in Example 7, we cannot deliberately misinform ourselves.

$$\alpha = \alpha_I + \alpha_E \qquad \text{(Equation 7)}$$

Example 7: Negative Feedback

A mischievous instructor can easily provide negative feedback by reversing the answer key. Consider practice sessions in which our hypothetical field goal kicker was not able to observe the results. The kicker would depend on an observer to report whether or not the attempt was good. A malicious observer would deliberately misinform the kicker of the results and, since this was the only means the kicker had of updating his mental model, we expect the model would soon reproducibly yield undesirable results.

Next, consider a kicker with poor vision and no coach. The kicker's poor vision leads to scoring errors, in which as a portion of successful kicks are registered as misses and errant kicks are scored as field goals. Although such scoring errors will impede progress, they do not lead to a continual increase in the probability of undesirable results. Some might argue that we consider the case in which the kicker misinterpreted the scoring criteria and mistakenly believed that it was desirable to kick the ball so that it bounced off the goal post. While practicing, the kicker would observe the flight of the ball and use that intrinsic feedback to improve his performance. During practice, this kicker would continually refine his flawed mental model and improve his ball striking and aiming skills. The kicker would clearly be learning, but the results would be confusing to an observer until a coach or other source of extrinsic feedback clarified the scoring criteria.

SKILL LOSS

Unused skills are lost over time. Although some have modeled skill loss as a linear function,[18] we agree

(A)

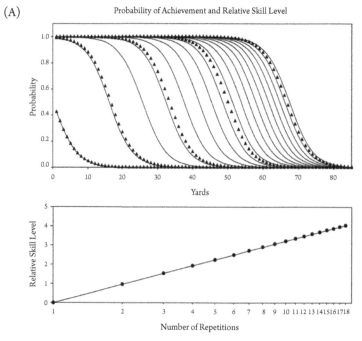

Probability of Achievement and Relative Skill Level

FIGURE 20.7 Rates of improvement vary according to feedback and skill decay. This figure helps visualize skill development for a football kicker. In these simulations, every consecutive line depicts the skill level at the end of 1,000 repetitions. (A) **k** is constant, and there is no decay; the player needs about 15,000 repetitions to reach a skill level of 4. (B) k is lowered by about 30% with no decay; the player needs about 55,000 repetitions to reach the same level. (C) k is restored to its original value but decay is introduced; the kicker needs about 106,000 repetitions to reach the same level. Decay is obvious in the first early trials of (C) but its effect on skill acquisition decreases as the kicker acquires more skill.

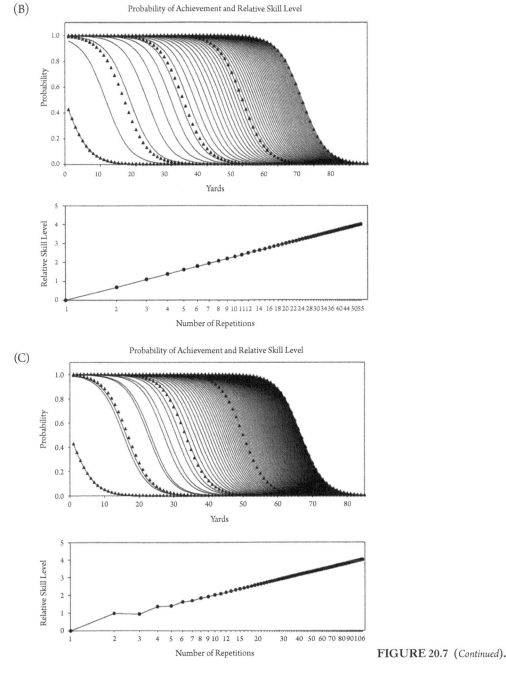

FIGURE 20.7 (*Continued*).

with those who have modeled skill loss as a power function similar to those used to describe radioactive decay. As a result, the amount of skill lost during some time interval (T) depends on the prior level of skill and the time constant of skill decay (τ) as shown in Equation 8. In almost every case, training intervals are small relative to this time constant since, if this were not true, any attempt to acquire skill through training would be futile.

$$S_t = S_{t=0} + \alpha\beta_{P \to A}\ln(n) - S_{t\,at\,n-1}(1-e^{-T/\tau}) \quad (\text{Equation 8})$$

Results of This Model

This model predicts that skill with a particular task will increase with practice. As shown in Figure 20.7, small decreases in feedback or transfer make it substantially harder to attain higher levels of skill. The importance of feedback and well-designed practice activities makes it clear that skill acquisition requires more than just "going through the motions." High skill levels can only be attained through what Ericsson described as *deliberate practice,* which is practice specifically designed to improve performance.[3,4] Skill loss between practice sessions will also make it hard to reach higher skill levels. This model suggests that the major factor limiting skill attainment is the amount of time one devotes to practice.[22] Accurate feedback, whether provided by a coach, teacher, or the task itself, will certainly facilitate skill acquisition, but it cannot substitute for practice. Practice activities that reproduce the important attributes of the assessment task will also promote skill acquisition.

WHAT CONSTITUTES PRACTICE?

Since transfer of training involves multiple dimensions (Example 6), we suggest that any experience should be considered when calculating potential practice repetitions. Experience with unrelated tasks will not significantly contribute to skill since the transfer factor (β) will be near zero. However, we advise caution before completely discounting the importance of experience in a seemingly unrelated task. For example, the mental models regarding how to best display the splenic flexure on a barium study are transferred to mesenteric arteriography since colonic anatomy is a shared feature. It is also possible that shared features will fail to improve performance if the task at hand does not depend on those shared features. For example, extensive experience in detecting and categorizing patterns in adult chest radiographs will not automatically improve performance when interpreting neonatal chest radiographs.

As a result, practice venues are myriad. Although it is common to consider physical repetitions of the task, mental task repetitions should also be considered since they can lead to improved performance.[9,23,24] Once we have developed the capacity for internal feedback, these mental repetitions provide an opportunity to test and refine our mental models. We also use simulation when we attempt to understand another individual's mental models. As we listen to their words, review their notes, or watch their actions, we often attempt to make sense of their instructions by comparing their ideas for solving a particular problem to our internal store of related events.[1] From a biologic perspective, our ability to refine our mental models without physically performing a task provides a tremendous evolutionary advantage.[25] It allows us to improve our future

performance on a dangerous or physically demanding task with minimal risk or effort.

The ability to transfer skills learned in one set of circumstances to another task is imperative. We contend that even familiar tasks differ in the time dimension, and there is no conceivable way of preparing preprogrammed responses to every possible contingency. Rather, we strive to develop an assortment of flexible mental models capable of transforming variable inputs into the desired outputs. These mental models are modular and lead many to suggest that human cognition works in the same general way that computer programs process information.[23,26] They suggest that humans and computers both use a hierarchy of routines and subroutines to transform inputs into actions.

The need to add modular and hierarchical properties to our model suggests expressing skill at any multifaceted task as the sum of skill contained in multiple mental models. The skill available for this tasks (task x) is represented as S_x, and the importance of any particular component skill (S_i) depends on how well practice with the ith task will impact performance during task x. This relationship is shown in Equation 9, where the transfer factor is represented as $B_{i \to x}$. The resulting model suggests that it is reasonable to expect that practice in any activity may influence performance on the task of interest. However, since their transfer factors may be close to zero, and performance is influenced by factors other than skill, the observable impact can easily escape detection. However, practice on a closely related task will have a greater influence on future performance. Thus, our model acknowledges that skill is largely domain-specific.[4] The factor for transfer across domains ($B_{i \to x}$) is distinct from the domain specific transfer factor ($\beta_{P \to A}$). Within a domain, transfer is always positive, and thus $\beta_{P \to A}$ will vary from 0 to 1.0 and usually be greater than 0.5. When crossing domains, we acknowledge that mental models learned and refined in one domain can compete with development of skill in another domain. Thus, the $B_{i \to x}$ factor can vary between -1 to 1 and will frequently be zero.

$$S_x = S_{x,t=0} + \Sigma\, B_{i \to x} S_i \qquad \text{(Equation 9)}$$

Where S_i refers to the ith skill and $B_{i \to x}$ reflects how these skills influence performance on the task at hand.

RESULTING MODEL

By combining equations 1–9, we arrive at our final model (Equation 10). This model predicts performance at time (t) will be best represented by a probability distribution in which the central tendency of the distribution will depend on initial skill, practice, time, feedback, and transfer of training. The model no longer requires a separate factor describing the problem difficulty since any variation in the factors that influence problem difficulty will also influence transfer. However, given the difficulty of accurately measuring the numerous transfer factors, and the relative ease of measuring problem attributes, it will often be easier to predict task performance using a problem difficulty factor. The resulting model is far from complete, but it does provide some insights into why observed performance might deviate from the result predicted by the power law of practice. Prior models suffered because they equated performance with skill. Further, the prior models equated gains in performance with learning. This model acknowledges that skill is only the capacity for performance, and learning can still occur even without any changes in the observed performance. This model explicitly accounts for how subtle factors such as chance, feedback, transfer, and time can subvert the linkage between practice and performance.

$$P_x(t) = F((S_{x,t=0} + \Sigma\, B_{i \to x} S_i)) \qquad \text{(Equation 10)}$$

Example 8: How Multiple Different Skills Are Applied to a Task

Consider how the skills needed to pass a high-stakes assessment like the American Board of Radiology (ABR) certification exam in diagnostic radiology are acquired. Verbal skills clearly play a role in this oral exam (Figure 20.8). Verbal skill development starts in childhood, but our model include a second increase that reflects how one's medical vocabulary increases during the first 2 years of medical school. Knowledge of radiation physics plays a role, and these skills are typically gained in high school, college, and residency. In our model, physics knowledge decreases after each course ends. Verbal debating skills can be problematic during the ABR oral exam, and our model suggests that the propensity to argue with an authority figure, such as an examiner, might reach its peak during the teenage years. Finally, the skills used to interpret radiographs begin increasing in medical school and rapidly expand during one's radiology residency. These skill sets and their ability to transfer to tasks encountered during the ABR oral exam are depicted in panel E. We have used a vari-

ety of transfer factors to estimate the relevant skill needed to pass the ABR exam over the same time period. The resulting skill was then used to predict the probability of passing the ABR oral exam. As expected, this probability remains low until the last year of one's radiology residency.

TRAINING STRATEGIES

To be useful, this model should predict successful strategies for improving future performance on different tasks. Training can be accelerated by predicting exactly what tasks will be important in the future workplace and designing practice repetitions that help trainees acquire or refine the necessary mental models. During the initial stages of training, trainees will lack an appropriate mental model and thus skill acquisition will depend on extrinsic feedback. As skill is gained, extrinsic feedback should be faded, so that the trainee learns to generate and rely on internal feedback. This model acknowledges that we learn nothing new when our predictions are fulfilled. Rather, learning is based on discovering errors in our mental models.

The model predicts that on-the-job training will be useful since it maximizes transfer. However, the model also argues that the utility of on-the-job training can be hampered if the training repetitions are not accompanied by clear and effective feedback. Junior radiology residents depend on instructors to provide extrinsic feedback. Skills can clearly continue increasing after formal training ends, but such continued on-the-job training will depend on feedback. The feedback can include follow-up of difficult cases, analysis of missed cases, or investigation of complications.

Our model also predicts that simulation offers an efficient and effective method of improving performance. Radiology residents devote a large amount of their ABR exam preparation to taking cases in the presence of simulated ABR examiners. During case conferences, residents will often mentally simulate what they might have said if they were presented the case by an ABR examiner. This suggests that simulated image interpretation sessions should be part of every radiology curriculum. These teaching conferences are an excellent example of simulation-based training. Individuals are asked to describe their thought process as they examine a series of images of radiographs with known findings. By thinking aloud, the trainees communicate their mental models, and the instructor bases his or her feedback on whether the trainees are using robust or flawed mental models.

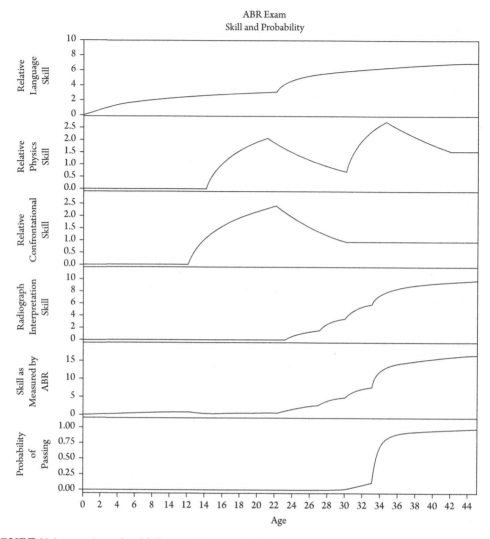

FIGURE 20.8 How a hierarchy of skills is needed to pass a high stakes examination in radiology.

Simulation also allows the instructor to select the training stimuli so as to sequence and segment content.[27] Since the goal is to improve workplace performance, the instructor selects instructive cases from normal workflow and uses them to move the trainee rapidly up the learning curve. Initially, the cases concentrate on normal anatomy and common diseases because the aim is to build strong mental models capable of handling problems commonly encountered in the workplace. This strategy strengthens mental models that prompt one to "think of horses, not zebras when you hear hoof beats." As trainees move further up the learning curve, mental models are revised and refined to accommodate uncommon presentations of common diseases, as well as common presentations of rare entities. Throughout this process, teaching file cases allow the trainee to examine and interpret stimuli that closely resemble what he or she might encounter in the future workplace. This type of training allows trainees to learn from their perceptual and analytical mistakes in a low-risk environment.

The benefits of simulation-based training for image interpretation suggest that mental and hands-on simulation can be used to improve procedural skills. Although we expect a higher transfer factor for hands-on practice with a high-fidelity simulator, we also expect that mental rehearsal of a procedure will prove useful.

CONCLUSION

In summary, we present a model that suggests how future performance can be predicted from analysis of prior activities, including the number of physical and mental task repetitions, feedback, and potential for transfer. The model suggests that simulation is already an integral part of how we learn, and we expect that the rapid advancements in simulation technology and automated feedback can facilitate progress up the learning curve. Although the model is far from complete, it provides a series of testable predictions that can guide our efforts to improve future performance.

REFERENCES

1. Klein GA. *Sources of power: How people make decisions.* Cambridge, MA: MIT Press, 1998.
2. Klein GA. *Streetlights and shadows: Searching for the keys to adaptive decision making.* Boston: MIT Press, 2009.
3. Ericsson K. Deliberate practice and the acquisition and maintenance of expert performance in medicine and related domains. *Acad Med.* 2004;79:S70–S81.
4. Ericsson KA, Charness N, Feltovich PJ, Hoffman RR. *The Cambridge handbook of expertise and expert performance.* Cambridge: Cambridge University Press, 2006: xv.
5. Schmidt R, Lee T. *Motor control and learning: A behavioral emphasis,* 4th ed. Champaign, IL: Human Kinetics, 2005.
6. Senge PM. *The fifth discipline: The art and practice of the learning organization,* rev. and updated. Edition. New York: Doubleday/Currency, 2006.
7. Argote L. *Organizational learning: Creating, retaining and transferring knowledge.* New York: Springer, 2005.
8. Gagne R, Wager W, Golas K, Keller J. *Principles of instructional design,* 5th ed. Belmont, CA: Wadsworth/Thomson Learning, 2005.
9. Williams AM, Hodges NJ. *Skill acquisition in sport: Research, theory and practice.* London/New York: Routledge, 2004: xxii.
10. Singley M, Anderson J. *The transfer of cognitive skill.* Cambridge, MA: Harvard University Press, 1989.
11. Reason JT. *Human error.* New York: Cambridge University Press, 1990.
12. Deming W. *The new economics for industry, government, education,* 2nd ed. Cambridge, MA: MIT Press, 2000.
13. Montgomery D. *Introduction to statistical quality control,* 5th ed. Hoboken, NJ: John Wiley & Sons, 2005.
14. Kubiszyn T, Borich G. *Educational testing and measurement,* 8th ed. Hoboken, NJ: John Wiley & Sons, 2007.
15. Brennan R. *Educational measurement,* 4th ed. Westport, CT: Praeger Publishers, 2006.
16. Embretson SE, Reise SP. *Item response theory for psychologists.* Mahwah, NJ: Lawrence Erlbaum Associates, 2000.
17. Teplitz CJ. *The learning curve deskbook.* New York: Quorum Books, 1991.
18. Argote L. *Organizational learning: Creating, retaining, and transferring.* Norwell: Kluwer Academic Publishers, 1999.
19. Pierce JR. *An introduction to information theory: Symbols, signals & noise,* 2nd rev. ed. New York: Dover Publications, 1980.
20. Speelman CP, Kirsner K. *Beyond the learning curve.* New York: Oxford University Press, 2005.
21. Reason JT. *Managing the risks of organizational accidents.* Brookfield, VT: Ashgate, 1997.
22. Colvin G. *Talent is overrated: What really separates world-class performers from everybody else.* New York: Portfolio, 2008.
23. Minsky M. *Society of the mind.* New York: Simon & Schuster, 1986.
24. Sanders CW, Sadoski M, van Walsum K, Bramson R, Wiprud R, Fossum TW. Learning basic surgical skills with mental imagery: Using the simulation centre in the mind. *Med Educ.* 2008;42:607–12.
25. Medina JJ. *Brain rules: 12 principles for surviving and thriving at work, home, and school.* Seattle, WA: Pear Press, 2008.
26. Polk TA, Seifert CM. *Cognitive modeling.* Cambridge, MA: MIT Press, 2002.
27. Clark R, Nguyen F, Sweller J. *Efficiency in learning: Evidence-based guidelines to manage cognitive load.* San Francisco: Pfeiffer, 2006.

21

Control Charts and Dashboards

JOSEPH R. STEELE, JOHN A. TERRELL, DAVID M. HOVSEPIAN,
AND VICTORIA S. JORDAN

Quality improvement projects often generate too much data with too little information. How does one transform high volumes of project data into the useful information necessary to drive quality improvement within an organization? In essence, how does one find the "signal among the noise"? Control charts and performance dashboards are tools that can help. These two commonly used displays can help visualize data on various metrics and facilitate monitoring and analysis of those data. Control charts and performance dashboards are particularly relevant to radiologists because we are visual learners, for whom images and graphs tend to be more appealing than spreadsheets and columns of numbers.

Control charts summarize how well individual processes are producing the desired outcomes. Performance dashboards, which are often built on the more detailed information provided by control charts (Figure 21.1), provide a "30,000-foot-overview" of the key performance indicators of an organization—metrics that reflect underlying processes thought to be critical to the institution's mission. In health care, key performance indicators could reflect daily operations, publicly reported values, or necessary regulatory information.

Control charts and dashboards are key tools for statistical process control (SPC), an approach that was originally developed for use in manufacturing but that can be tremendously useful for health care applications as well.

STATISTICAL PROCESS CONTROL

When presented with the proposition that medicine is more similar than different from industrial manufacturing, most physicians will bristle and promptly retort something along the lines of, "Patients are not widgets." True—each patient is unique and has unique medical needs. However, health care delivery *is* a process—a very complicated process, but a process nonetheless—and in few areas of medicine is this more apparent than in radiology. In radiology, a predictable sequence of steps is performed, from ordering an examination to its completion and interpretation.

American physicist and engineer Walter Shewhart defined a process as "a series of linked steps, often but not necessarily sequential, designed to cause some set of outcomes to occur, transform inputs to outputs, generate useful information and/or add value".[1] A process leads to the highest-quality product (e.g., imaging studies) at the lowest cost when variation, errors, and waste are decreased through standardization. During his work at the Western Electric Company and later the Bell Telephone Laboratories, Shewhart developed SPC to improve manufacturing by refocusing attention on systems instead of events, processes rather than individuals, and scientifically acquired data above anecdotal experience.

Statistical process control was further developed by W. Edwards Deming, Joseph Juran, and

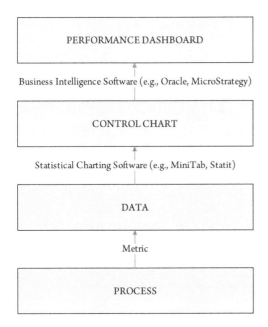

FIGURE 21.1 Control charts help link processes to performance dashboards.

others, and has been the cornerstone of continuous quality improvement programs since.[2] The potential for use of SPC in health care delivery was initially recognized in the 1950s,[3] and renewed attention to the use of SPC in health care was stimulated in the 1980s by Donald Berwick,[3,4] formerly president and CEO of the Institute for Healthcare Improvement and currently director of the Centers for Medicare and Medicaid Services. To date, over 50 articles have been published in the medical literature on SPC, many of them reports on scientifically conducted studies that clearly demonstrate that the use of SPC improves patient care processes.[5]

Critical to understanding SPC is understanding the concept of variation. Although it is accepted and positive that every snowflake is different and every golf game provides new challenges, substantial variation is not acceptable in health care delivery. If outpatient magnetic resonance imaging (MRI) volumes drop for three consecutive months or the number of patient falls within the radiology department rises over two quarters, it is unlikely that these changes will be attributed to just "variation in the system." However, variation is unavoidable in any process or system, and the more complicated the process or system—i.e., the more subprocesses or steps—the greater the potential for cumulative variation. Deming and Shewhart both noted this

phenomenon in manufacturing and coined terms to describe it. Deming termed the inherent variation in a process the "common cause" variation.[6,7] This variation is the result of a system's current design, its regular rhythm, and cannot be traced back to a single root cause. It represents the noise within the system and can be accounted for and predicted when the system is stable and remains "in control." Conversely, Deming used the term "special cause" variation to refer to variation resulting from events rising above the background noise of the process due to events outside and not inherent to the process. These events *do have* a traceable root cause that can be mitigated and, when necessary, eliminated. Occasionally, special cause variation may unearth a previously unappreciated beneficial event that can be formally incorporated to improve the process.

What is most important about special cause variation data points is that they represent improvement opportunities. These points represent unique events outside the normal operation of the process (e.g., a drop in outpatient MRI volumes that should be concerning), and investigation of the underlying causes can reveal unforeseen problems and potential solutions. Focusing efforts on special cause variation can bring a process into control—which is the situation when a process has only common cause variation and is, within some limits, predictable. Differentiating common cause from special cause variation is one of the greatest values of control charts.

CONTROL CHARTS

Process output and its variation can be depicted in one of two basic formats: static or dynamic.[8] Commonly used static representations of process output include tabular values such as mean, median, variance, and standard deviation, which are displayed using histograms, bar charts, or tables. Dynamic displays of process output include run charts and control charts, in which data is plotted over time. The stream of points in a run chart or control chart is similar to the stream of frames in a movie about a process: Each new data point in the control chart reflects the process output at a new point in time.

Both run charts (Figure 21.2) and control charts (Figure 21.3) are two-dimensional, with time plotted on the x-axis and data points generated from the process in question plotted on the y-axis. Run charts are centered on the median, whereas control charts are centered on the mean. Control charts are more powerful than run charts and apply a set of decision rules based on probabilities according to the population

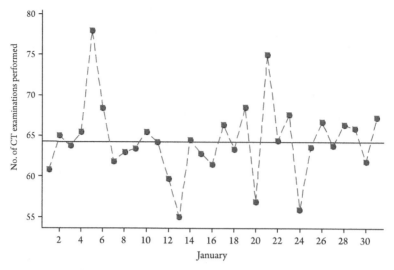

FIGURE 21.2 Run chart demonstrating the number of computed tomography scans performed in January.

from which the data are collected. In addition to the center line, which is set at the mean, control charts include upper and lower control limits, which are a function of the standard deviation (σ).[9,10] The upper and lower control limits are used to distinguish common cause from special cause variation.

According to Shewhart, "a phenomenon will be said to be controlled when, through the use of past experience, we can predict, at least within limits, how the phenomenon may be expected to vary in the future."[11] Statistical control is indicated on a control

chart when the data are evenly distributed around the centerline (without trends, shifts, or oscillations) and are entirely contained within the upper and lower control limits. A process in statistical control has common cause variation but is currently unaffected by special causes. Therefore, the future performance of the system may be considered predictable.

It is important to understand that a process can be in control and still fail to obtain its desired objective. This state is referred to as "out of specification" and indicates the need for process reengineering.

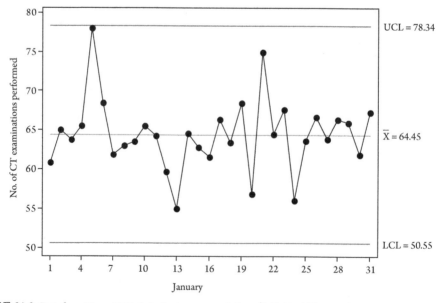

FIGURE 21.3 Data from Figure 21.2 plotted using a control chart (Individual Chart without an accompanying Moving Range chart).

In health care, it is critically important to distinguish processes that are out of specification from processes that are out of control; otherwise, a large amount of effort may be wasted attempting to improve a process that does not have the capability of producing the desired outcome.

INTERPRETING CONTROL CHARTS: TYPE 1 AND TYPE 2 ERRORS

Like most tools, a control chart can be very useful when used properly and potentially dangerous when used incorrectly. To understand the limitations of control charts, one must first understand type 1 and type 2 errors.

Historically, the upper and lower control limits have been set at 3σ above and below the center line, respectively. Control charts are typically designed such that the likelihood of getting a point inside these control limits, if the process remains in control, is 99.75%. If control limits narrower than 3σ are chosen, there is a higher risk that data points that actually do not represent special cause variation will fall outside the control limits and be interpreted as representing special cause variation. (This risk is

also known as α *risk*.) When such findings are acted upon, a type 1 error has been committed; "tampering" with the process has occurred. The type 1 error is similar to the phenomenon of "overcalling" with which we are faced in radiology, which often causes more harm than good.

Alternatively, if control limits wider than 3σ used, there is a higher risk that data points that do represent special cause variation will fall within the control limits and be interpreted as representing common cause variation. (This risk is also known as β *risk*.) When such findings lead to inactivity when activity was desirable, a type 2 error has been committed; opportunities for improvement in the process have been lost. The type 2 error is similar to the phenomenon of "undercalling" in radiology.

Some authors have suggested that, in certain scenarios in which the well-being of patients is at risk, the control limits should be narrowed.[12] It has been postulated that if the β risk (undercalling) far outweighs the α risk (overcalling), the control limits should be set at less than 3σ; however, this practice has not been widely accepted or consistently applied. Others believe that control limits should vary based on the number of plotted points, such that if the number of data points is 10–35, 3σ is most

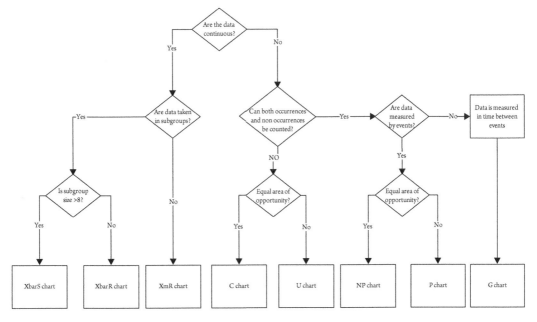

FIGURE 21.4 Decision tree for choosing the appropriate control chart, depending on whether the data are continuous or discontinuous and the size and distribution of the samples. The area of opportunity for attribute charts may be physical (e.g., per surgical case), geographical (e.g., per outpatient clinic), or the time during which the event *could* happen (e.g., per hospital day). The area of opportunity is similar to the sample size; an equal area of opportunity is a constant sample size, whereas an unequal area of opportunity is a changing sample size.

appropriate; if there are fewer data points, the control limits should be narrowed; and if there are more data points, the control limits should be widened. It is important to realize that this is a gross oversimplification. Operating characteristics (OC) curves measure the tradeoff between α and β risk and the relationship to the variance and sample sizes.

CHOOSING THE BEST CONTROL CHART

To maximize the value and ensure the accuracy of any control chart, the correct chart must be used. Control charts fall into two basic categories:

- *Variables charts*, which are used for continuous data that are measured on a scale (e.g., time, weight)

- *Attributes charts*, which are used for discrete data that are counted using integers or categories (e.g., number of events, infected vs. noninfected)

Attribute charts can be divided further into two types: charts for use when both the occurrence and the nonoccurrence are known, and charts for use when the nonoccurrences are unknown. For example, in a chart of intravenous contrast reactions, the number of reactions would be the occurrences, and the number of times contrast was administered without a reaction would be the nonoccurrences. Whether or not the nonoccurrences are known dictates which attribute chart is applicable. The decision tree below (Figure 21.4) is a guide for choosing the most appropriate chart for the data type being analyzed.

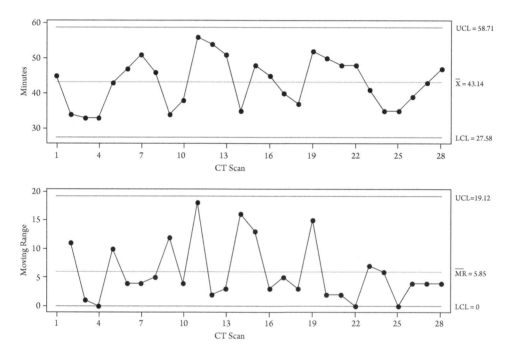

FIGURE 21.5 XmR chart of turnaround times for sequential emergency room computed tomography scans on a single day. Each data point represents the number of minutes between completion of the exam and communication of the report to the emergency physician. When each charted subgroup (data point) represents *more* than one observation, an Xbar chart is used (Figure 21.6). This is most commonly seen when each point on the y-axis reflects the mean of a sample. Frequently, when evaluating trends in health care, we study large groups of data using averages. For example, an individual data point might represent the average blood sugar level of a subpopulation of diabetics. If subgroups are based on eight or fewer observations an Xbar-R chart is used; if subgroups are based on more than eight observations, an Xbar-S chart is used. Similar to the XmR chart, the Xbar-R and Xbar-S charts are paired charts:

1. Xbar chart plots the average value of a subgroup or sample over time.
2. Complementary chart:
    A. Range chart (Xbar-R) displays the range of the subgroup.
    B. Sigma chart (Xbar-S) displays the standard deviation of the subgroup.

This can be further simplified. Are the numerator and the dominator the same unit of measurement (e.g., number of contrast reactions during contrast administration and the total number of contrast administrations) or different (e.g., the number of contrast reactions and a unit of time [day, week, month])?

Variables

A commonly used variable chart is the *individual moving range* or XmR chart (Figure 21.5). It is actually a paired chart, consisting of two charts:

- *Individuals chart.* Plots the individual value of interest over time
- *Moving range chart.* Plots the difference in values *between* measurements

XmR charts are used when each charted subgroup (data point) represents only *one* observation; for example, the time for *one* emergent head computed tomography (CT) scan to be completed, the glucose level for *one* diabetic, or the blood pressure of *one* person with hypertension (Figure 21.6).

Attributes Charts

Attribute charts are used for discrete data that are counted using integers or categories (e.g., number of events, infected vs. noninfected). Often, their statistical power is less than that of charts created using continuous variables. The data reflected in attribute charts are limited and sometimes binomial (e.g., infected/noninfected, on time/delayed); therefore, attribute charts do not communicate the same breadth of information as those created using continuous data. For example, an attribute chart showing the percentage of emergent head CTs performed and interpreted in under 45 minutes does not provide the same amount of information about the underlying process as a variables chart showing the time required for each head CT. On the attribute chart, a head CT that takes 46 minutes and a head CT that takes 1 hour and 46 minutes are treated the same way—they are both categorized in the group of "not completed in under 45 minutes." Therefore, variables charts are more powerful than attribute charts and can detect change in the process more quickly.

Five types of attribute charts can easily be applied to radiology, depending on what, how, and how many is being measured.

When both the events and the nonevents are known, either a P-chart or an NP-chart is used. Whether a P-chart or an NP-chart should be used depends on whether the number of observations

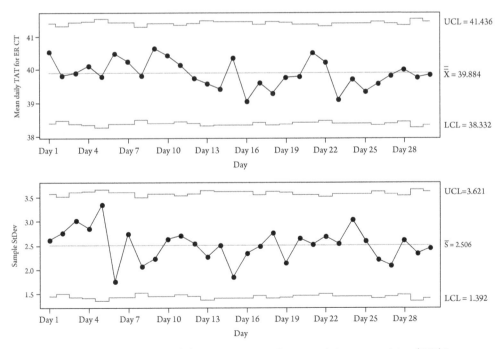

FIGURE 21.6 Xbar-S chart in which each data point represents the average daily turnaround time (TAT) for an emergency room computed tomography scan. Since the subgroups are based on eight or more observations, an Xbar-S chart is used.

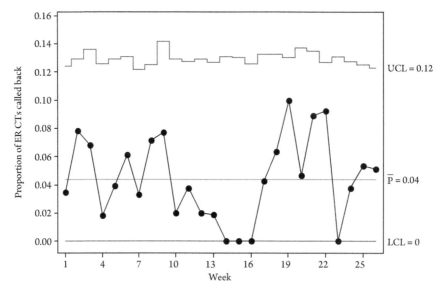

FIGURE 21.7 P-chart demonstrating proportion of emergency room computed tomography (CT) patients each week called back for additional imaging. Since the subgroup size varies weekly, and number of events (CT studies requiring additional images) and nonevents (emergency room CT scans not requiring additional images) are both known, a P-chart is most appropriate.

varies or is constant. P-charts are used when the number of observations per subgroup is variable (e.g., percentage of emergency room patients with the diagnosis of headache receiving a head CT every day), and NP-charts are used when the number of observations per subgroup is constant (e.g., percentage of patients with the diagnosis of headache receiving a head CT from a random sample of 50 emergency room patients each day). Since the sample size in a P-chart varies, control limits in P-charts vary. In contrast, since the sample size in an NP-chart is constant, the control limits in an NP-chart are straight.

An example may help to clarify these concepts. Suppose that, in an effort to increase throughput, a radiology department has implemented standard CT protocols and no longer has the radiologist check the images before the patient is removed from the scanner. To ensure that the initial imaging is adequate, the call-back rate for emergency room CT scans is recorded and plotted using a P-chart (Figure 21.7).

Alternatively, if a random audit method was applied and 50 emergency room CT scans were reviewed weekly, an NP-chart would be used (Figure 21.8). Since the subgroup size is constant, the control limits are straight.

Two additional attribute charts that are commonly used in radiology are C-charts and U-charts. These are somewhat analogous to NP-charts and P-charts but are designed for count data that follow a Poisson distribution, meaning that they track relatively infrequent events. C-charts and U-charts are used when only the number of events is known and the number of nonevents is not. The number of nonevents may be too large or impractical to measure. For example, patient falls are relatively rare, and non-falls are immeasurable.

Whether a C-chart or a U-chart should be used depends on whether the area of opportunity is constant or varies. The area of opportunity represents the potential for the event to occur (e.g., the time period during which a patient could fall). If the area of opportunity is a constant value (e.g., patient falls per day), a C-chart is used. Alternatively, if the area of opportunity varies (e.g., patient falls per patient day, where a patient day is the hospital census at a specific time of day), a U-chart is used. Parallel to the situation with NP-charts and P-charts, in a C-chart, the control limits are straight because the area of opportunity is constant, and in a U-chart, the control limits vary because the area of opportunity varies (Figures 21.9 and 21.10).

In the setting of very rare events, such as wrong-site surgeries or anaphylactic reaction to contrast, a seldom used but very helpful chart is the G-chart.[13] In a G-chart, the data points, rather than representing events themselves, represent *time between events*. The two types of data most commonly plotted are number of nonevents and the time elapsed between events.

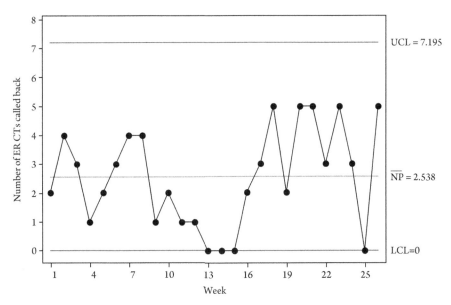

FIGURE 21.8 NP-chart demonstrating the number of emergency room patients who required additional imaging. Data were accumulated from a random weekly sample of 50 emergency room patients who underwent computed tomography imaging.

For wrong-site surgeries, it is preferable to record the number of nonevents (i.e., number of surgeries without mishap), rather than the time elapsed between events. Since the number of surgeries varies from day to day, its measurement provides a better reflection of what is happening in the process. However, it is sometimes impractical or difficult to collect nonevents (correct site surgeries), in which case the time interval between events may be an appropriate alternative. The G-chart follows a geometric distribution. Figure 21.11 is a plot of the number of days between moderate contrast reactions.

The choice of control chart is a function of the question being asked. If the question has already been asked, the methodology used for data collection (e.g., type of data, choice of subgroups, and area

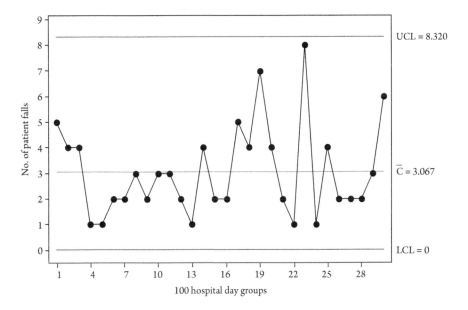

FIGURE 21.9 C-chart of the total number of patient falls within the hospital per 100 hospital days for a 2-year period.

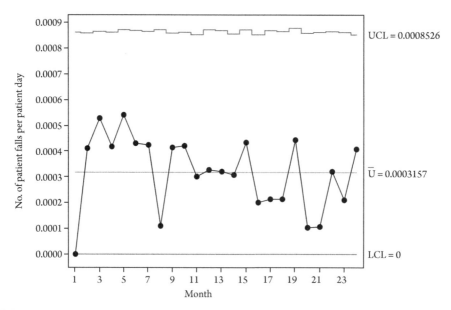

FIGURE 21.10 U-chart of the number of patient falls per patient day in a 500-bed tertiary care hospital. Patient day is defined as the hospital census at 0800.

of opportunity) dictates the choice of control chart. However, if the question has not already been asked, by working backward and using a thorough understanding of control charts, a quality improvement study can be designed with questions that enable utilization of the more powerful and informative charts. The more powerful the chart, the more useful the information obtained. When possible the following are preferred:

- Variables charts using continuous data rather than attribute charts using discrete data
- Large subgroups rather than individual or small subgroups

For example, Table 21.1 shows how the same data can be expressed differently, depending on the question asked.[8]

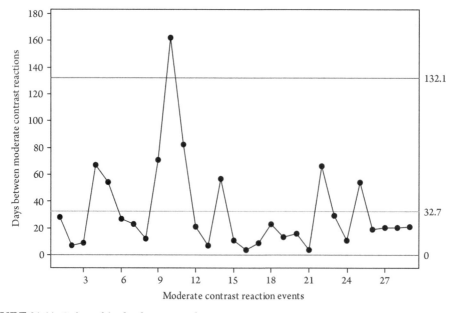

FIGURE 21.11 G-chart of the days between moderate contrast reactions.

TABLE 21.1   HOW THE CHOICE OF CONTROL CHART CHANGES WITH HOW THE QUERY IS STRUCTURED

Analysis of Fluoroscopy Use	Type of Chart
What are the fluoroscopy times for placement of central venous catheters?	XmR chart
For a weekly sample of five central venous catheters, what is the fluoroscopy time?	Xbar-R chart
For a monthly sample of 20 central venous catheters, what is the fluoroscopy time?	Xbar-S chart
For all central venous catheters placed each month, what percentage required over 1 minute of fluoroscopy time?	P-chart
For a sample of 25 central venous catheters placed each month, what percentage required over 1 minute of fluoroscopy time?	NP-chart
For all central venous catheters placed each month, how many required over 1 minute of fluoroscopy time?	U-chart
For a sample of 25 central venous catheters placed each month, how many required over 1 minute of fluoroscopy time?	C-chart

INTERPRETATION OF CONTROL CHARTS

The interpretation of control charts is a delicate science. Charts can be made more powerful by increasing the sample size or decreasing the variation in the process. However, a fine line exists between increasing the power of the control chart to detect special cause variation and increasing the risk of type 1 error. Many different decision rules have been developed to help detect nonrandom, out-of-control

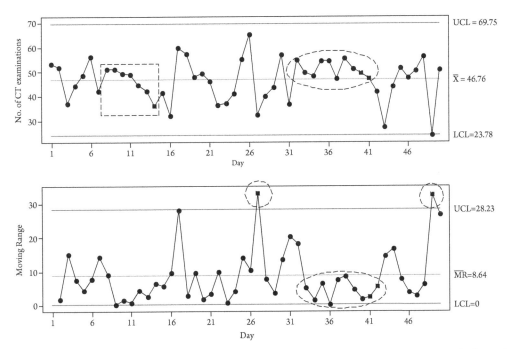

FIGURE 21.12 XmR chart of the computed tomography examinations performed over a 50-day period. These rules provide the tools for a cursory check to identify patterns or trends indicating that nonrandom influences are at work, indicating opportunities for improvement. However, they provide only rough snapshots, not robust statistical analysis. The rules used to interpret control charts are based on probability and introduce a small amount of error; therefore, the more rules applied, the greater the possibility of false alarms. Concurrent use of multiple rules could lead to increased false-positives and tampering with a healthy process (type 1 error). Continually testing the interpretation of control charts against one's knowledge of the process is critical. Charts are only one tool and do not invalidate clinical expertise. As the analysis becomes more complicated, the assistance of a statistician may prove invaluable to ensure accuracy.

conditions. Although a thorough discussion of these rules is beyond the scope of this chapter, their importance warrants a brief overview.

To analyze control charts, most quality improvement professionals use a combination of the Western Electric Rules,[14] first described in 1956, and the Nelson Rules,[15] published in 1984. These rules apply to all types of control charts. Three simple and often used rules are:

1. One point more than 3 standard deviations from the mean is an *outlier.*
2. Nine or more points in a row on the same side of the mean constitute a *shift.*
3. Six or more points in a row that are continually increasing or decreasing constitute a *trend.*

The XmR chart (Figure 21.12) plots the CT examinations performed in a radiology department over a 50-day period. Analysis with the run rules demonstrates an outlier (*circle*), shift (*ellipse*), and a trend (*rectangle*).

SCORECARDS AND DASHBOARDS

Scorecards and dashboards are used to track results within an organization. The terms are often used interchangeably, but actually scorecards and dashboards are different tools. Scorecards are strategic and used to monitor progress toward identified objectives, while dashboards are operational and used to monitor clinical and nonclinical processes.[16] Scorecards and dashboards are closely linked, however, as scorecards can reflect the contents of a dashboard. Both often include gauges, color (e.g., green, yellow, and red), graphs, and charts in their display of business performance data. Results are measured against specific targets or thresholds, which may be historical results, industry standards, or institutional goals. Both scorecards and dashboards may provide "drill-down" ("linkage") capability, which allows users to "peel back" to the next lower level of data (e.g., the department, unit, or provider level), which are often displayed using control charts.

The difference between scorecards and dashboards becomes more evident when they are used. The scorecard approach has been in use since the early part of the 20th century, but it gained much popularity after the introduction of the Balanced Scorecard methodology by Kaplan and Norton in the early 1990s. This approach uses four aspects of the strategic management of an organization: Financial, Internal Business Processes, Learning and Growth, and Customer.[17] Scorecards link the strategic objective formulated by the leadership

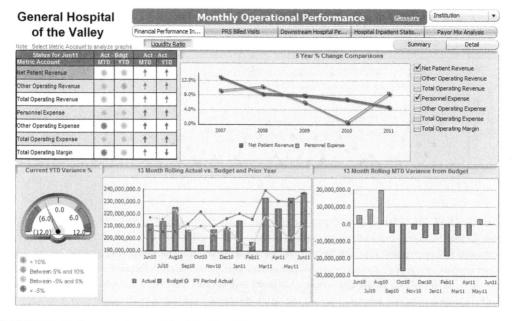

FIGURE 21.13 Scorecard of General Hospital of the Valley.

Profile for Physician 14
Clinical Department: DEPARTMENT X
06/01/09

Status	Indicator	My Score	Peers Score	Target	SPC Alert
	Medical Knowledge				
	BETA OPPE Number of Inpatient Deaths	n/a	2.0	n/a	
	BETA OPPE Percent Mortality	n/a	7.18%	n/a	
—	**BETA** OPPE Readmissions within 48 hrs of discharge	0.00%	2.09%	n/a	
	Patient Care - Activity Data				
▼	**BETA** OPPE Number of Inpatient Admissions	4	12.6	n/a	
	BETA OPPE Number of Inpatient Days	n/a	267.2	n/a	
	BETA OPPE Number of Inpatient Discharges	n/a	24.5	n/a	
	Systems - Bassed Practice				
	BETA OPPE Inpatient ALOS	n/a	10.96	n/a	

Profile Generated 06/09/2010 11:02:22.

FIGURE 21.14 Dashboard of performance indicators for Department X at General Hospital of the Valley (used with permission from MIDAS+ Statit Solutions Group).

with the performance of the institution. In contrast, dashboards are used to display data. Dashboards can be more real time, giving feedback on current and ongoing practices and processes throughout the organization.

Figure 21.13 is a Scorecard of General Hospital of the Valley. It summarizes key performance indicators as defined by the executive team.

General Hospital of the Valley also uses dashboards. To monitor the complete spectrum of

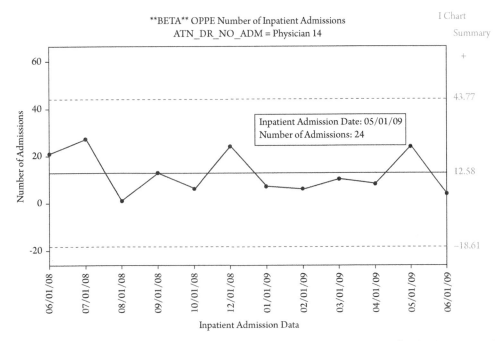

FIGURE 21.15 The first level of "drill-down," showing inpatient admissions for physician 14 (used with permission from MIDAS+ Statit Solutions Group).

BETA OPPE Number of Inpatient Admissions ATN_DR_NO_ADM=Physician 14

5/1/2009

24 Records

	PT BIRTH DATE	PT AGE	PT RACE	PT SEX	ADMISSION DESCRIP-TION	DAYS TO READMIT	ADM DTM	MDC DESC	DRG DESC	ICD DX DESC
Details	15-Sep-54	63	W	M	Emergency		5/5/2009 0:35	DISEASES & DISORDERS OF BLOOD, BLOOD FORMING ORGANS, IMMUNOLOG DISORD	MAJOR HEMATOL/IMMUN DIAG EXC SICKLE CELL CRISIS & COAGUL W MCC	NEUTROPENIA DUE TO INFECTION
Details	5-Jul-46	40	U	W	Emergency	2	5/5/2009 17:14	DISEASES & DISORDERS OF THE HEPATOBILIARY SYSTEM & PANCREAS	DISORDERS OF PANCREAS EXCEPT MALIGNANCY W CC	ACUTE PANCREATITIS
Details	13-Sep-46	55	W	W	Elective		5/5/2009 18:15	DISEASES & DISORDERS OF THE RESPIRATORY SYSTEM	RESPIRATORY SYSTEM DIAGNOSIS W VENTILATOR SUPPORT 96+ HOURS	ACUTE RESPIRATORY FAILURE
Details	12-Aug-23	58	W	M	Elective	19	5/5/2009 18:25	DISEASES & DISORDERS OF THE RESPIRATORY SYSTEM	SIMPLE PNEUMONIA & PLEURISY W CC	PNEUMONIA, ORGANISM UNSPECIFIED

FIGURE 21.16 The second level of "drill-down," showing the patients admitted by physician 14 (used with permission from MIDAS+ Statit Solutions Group).

physician clinical competence, as defined by the six core competencies of the Accreditation Council for Graduate Medical Education, data are collected for each physician. One metric that is closely followed is the number of inpatient admissions. The dashboard shows the number of patient admissions for Department X. Drill-down capability allow the user to further analyze the data, at both the individual physician and patient levels (see Figures 21.14, 21.15, 21.15).

CONCLUSION

Quality and process improvement are becoming a cornerstone of health care delivery. As efforts increase to build evidence-based, consistent, and safe care delivery models, radiologists will have numerous opportunities for involvement. Knowledge of control charts, dashboards, and other process improvement tools will be necessary. These tools have proved effective across various industries and are becoming widely used and accepted in health care. Radiologists are visual learners, which should lead to easy acceptance and understanding of control charts and dashboards in radiology. Initially, these tools may seem cumbersome and confusing, but with practice, use of control charts and dashboards can be an excellent method for identifying opportunities for improvement and monitoring changes that are made.

REFERENCES

1. Shewhart WA. *Economic control of quality of manufactured product*. Milwaukee, WI: American Society for Quality Control, 1980.
2. Deming WE. *Out of the crisis*. Cambridge, MA: MIT Press, 2000.
3. Levey S. The use of control charts in the clinical laboratory. *Am J Clin Path*. 1950;20:1059–66.
4. Berwick DM. Continuous improvement as an ideal in health care. *N Engl J Med*. 1989;320:53–56.
5. Thor J, Lundberg J, Ask J, et al. Application of statistical process control in healthcare improvement: Systematic review. *Qual Saf Health Care*. 2007;16:387–99.
6. Carey RG. *Improving healthcare with control charts: Basic and advanced SPC methods and case studies*. Milwaukee, WI: ASQ Quality Press, 2003.
7. Duncan AJ. *Quality control and industrial statistics*. Homewood, IL: Irwin, 1986.
8. Carey RG, Lloyd RC. *Measuring quality improvement in healthcare: A guide to statistical process control applications*. New York: Quality Resources, 1995.
9. Ziegenfuss JT, Jr., McKenna CK. Ten tools of continuous quality improvement: A review and case example of hospital discharge. *Am J Med Qual*. 1995;10:213–20.
10. Montgomery DC. *Introduction to statistical quality control*. Hoboken, NJ: Wiley, 2009.
11. Shewhart WA. *Economic control of quality of manufactured product*. New York: D. Van Nostrand Company, Inc., 1931.
12. Blumenthal D. Total quality management and physicians' clinical decisions. *JAMA*. 1993;269:2775–8.

13. Benneyan JC. Performance of number-between g-type statistical control charts for monitoring adverse events. *Health Care Manag Sci.* 2001;4:319–36.

14. Western Electric Company. *Statistical quality control handbook.* Indianapolis: Western Electric Co., 1956.

15. Nelson LS. Technical aids. *J Qual Technol.* 1984;16:238–9.

16. Cokins G. How are balanced scorecards and dashboards different? In: Cokins G, ed. *Performance management: Integrating strategy, execution,methodologies, risk and analysis.* Hoboken, NJ: John Wiley & Sons, 2009:91–115.,

17. Kaplan RS, Norton DP. *The balanced scorecard: Translating strategy into action.* Boston, MA: Harvard Business School Press, 1996.

22

Governmental and Outside Agencies' Influence on Radiology Quality

DIPTI NEVREKAR, JAMES P. BORGSTEDE, AND JUDY BURLESON

Rapid advances in medical care have contributed greatly to improved patient outcomes, with significant reductions in morbidity and mortality. An aging and expanding population with ever-increasing, complex medical needs challenges the capacity of the health care system to deliver timely, effective, and safe care, and expanding costs place health care beyond the budget of many patients. Health care reform has evolved as one of the defining issues of the past several decades, and the United States is on the cusp of meaningful change to reduce waste, control costs, increase quality, and ensure access for more people.

FOCUS ON QUALITY

Quality health care can be defined as the ability of a health care system to deliver goods and services to produce positive outcomes. Value in a health care system is seen as achieving the highest quality for the lowest cost. A quantification of quality can be expressed as:

Quality = Value × Price/Time

Recent initiatives in the public and private sector have focused on quantifying health care quality and rewarding providers for measuring and achieving quality metrics. In theory, the selection of meaningful metrics should correlate with improved health care outcomes.

EFFECTORS OF QUALITY

Effectors of quality include governmental, quasi-governmental, private agencies and organizations, and their subordinates. Throughout this chapter, a Venn diagram approach to the relationship of these effectors will be used to clarify what has become a complex morass of interrelated groups all addressing the quality topic. As each group and subgroup is discussed, its relationship to the global topic of quality will be added to the Venn diagram. A qualitative attempt to identify the significance of each effector is indicated by the proportional size of each circle.

The global organizational relationship is defined in Figure 22.1 .

GOVERNMENTAL INFLUENCES ON QUALITY

Federal Government

In the United States, the single largest governmental influence on health care quality comes from the federal government, through either legislation or executive branch rule-making (Figure 22.2). Congressional legislation, although more difficult to alter, is also more difficult to create and easier to defeat. Presidential rule-making, although easier to accomplish, is also more capricious. Often, these two vehicles that affect health care quality are linked because legislation typically does not address the specific details of implementation but instead addresses broad concepts and philosophies, with the understanding that legislated changes will be implemented by executive branch agencies, such as the Centers for Medicare and Medicaid Services (CMS). As well, federal legislation may direct states to undertake quality efforts, with or without commensurate federal funding.

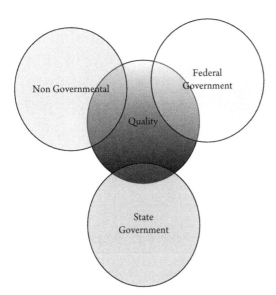

FIGURE 22.1 Global organizational relationship.

Legislative Efforts on Quality

Health Care Legislation

Health care legislation has held center stage in the U.S. political system for over a decade now (Figure 22.3). President Obama and Congress have a strong interests in reducing waste in the current system and in modeling new health care systems based on the quality equation above. Both Congress and the executive branch desire health systems that "offer high-quality care at costs below average" and want to "encourage adoption of these common-sense best practices by doctors and medical professionals throughout the system."[1]

On March 23, 2010, President Obama signed a landmark comprehensive reform bill entitled the Patient Protection and Affordable Care Act

(PPACA) that could permanently alter the landscape of health care delivery in the United States. Major tenets of the bill include extensive health insurance reform that prohibits denial of insurance coverage based on preexisting conditions, prohibits differential pricing for health status, features an individual mandate to purchase insurance, recommends state-based health insurance exchanges for the self- and unemployed, and provides subsidies for families to purchase insurance. New Medicare and "Cadillac Plan" taxes will fund the new coverage for the currently 30 million uninsured Americans.

Details of this 2,000-plus page legislation are beyond the scope of this chapter, and implementation of the bill through rule-making is uncertain; however, the bill has two very important features that address health care quality.

Independent Medicare Advisory Board

The PPACA created the Independent Medicare Advisory Board (IMAB), an independent commission with the authority to make proposals that will save Medicare dollars. The board will review Medicare reimbursement levels, make recommendations and develop proposals to extend Medicare solvency, reduce the rate of per capita Medicare spending, and improve the quality of care in Medicare. The Board will also make annual recommendations on actions to improve quality and constrain the rate of growth of health care costs in the private sector. In the past, pilot reimbursement cuts had to be approved; this new authority will give the CMS more freedom to turn Medicare into a savvier purchaser of health care services, because recommendations from the IMAB do not need Congressional approval for implementation. The IMAB's predecessor, the Medicare Payment Advisory Commission (MEDPAC), was not independent and acted only in an advisory capacity to Congress. The implications of a small, independent board making major health care decisions is stunning, not only for radiology but for all of health care. The potential impact of this board on radiology is unique because the rapid growth of imaging services for Medicare patients in recent years exceeds the growth of virtually all other medical services. [From the Blue Cross/Blue Shield *Medical Cost Reference Guide* 2008, published by the Blue Cross/Blue Shield Association. Available online at http://apps.bcbs.com/.] Therefore, it is likely that the IMAB will target imaging services.

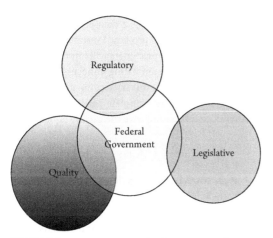

FIGURE 22.2 Governmental influences on quality.

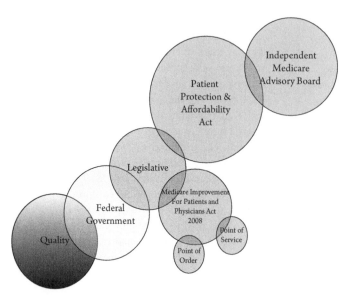

FIGURE 22.3 Legislative effects on quality.

Medicare Improvements for Patients and Providers Act and Medicare Imaging Demonstration

In 2008, Congress passed the Medicare Improvements for Patients and Providers Act (MIPPA) mandating a 2-year demonstration project to evaluate the appropriate use of imaging services, beginning in 2010. Data collection focused on physician compliance with the appropriateness criteria of advanced diagnostic imaging services including magnetic resonance imaging (MRI), computed tomography (CT), nuclear medicine (NM), and positron emission tomography (PET) for Medicare beneficiaries. Physician participants are eligible for reimbursement for reasonable administrative costs, as well as for incentives to encourage participation.[2]

The appropriateness criteria were developed with input from several medical specialty societies, such as the American College of Radiology (ACR), American College of Cardiology (ACC), and American College of Physicians (ACP), to name a few. These criteria must be developed or endorsed by the specialty society involved, and the criteria must adhere to principles developed by a consensus organization, such as the AQA Alliance, a coalition of the American Academy of Family Physicians (AAFP), the ACP, America's Health Insurance Plans (AHIP), and the Agency for Healthcare Research and Quality (AHRQ), originally known as the Ambulatory Care Quality Alliance.

Data collection on physician compliance will be confirmed using one of two models. A point-of-order (POO) model uses a computerized physician order entry (CPOE) system that requires information input at the time of referral. This system can also provide feedback on the appropriateness of the order, with input from embedded decision support systems in the electronic health record (EHR).[3] Alternatively, a point-of-service (POS) model may be used that allows practices with less electronic integration to participate in the demonstration. If the practice providing the imaging service does not have a CPOE system to received imaging orders, then an alternative electronic order submission is required. A POS model may be used by a physician practice that both orders and furnishes the imaging service, such as a cardiology practice, and the practice will receive feedback on the order appropriateness. The CMS is not allowed to use prior authorization, such as a radiology benefit management (RBM) service, as a data collection model for the demonstration project. Presumably, refinement in imaging appropriateness will improve quality by reducing cost and eliminating unnecessary examinations. Reducing unnecessary examinations should also reduce the time to complete patient evaluations and therefore further improve the quality equation.

Regulatory Efforts on Quality

Centers for Medicare & Medicaid Services

As the single largest health care payer in the United States, the CMS provides health benefits for nearly 90 million Americans, including individuals over

65 years of age, low-income individuals and families, and children (Figure 22.4). As an agency of the U.S. Department of Health and Human Services (DHHS), the CMS is a part of the executive branch of government. The CMS administers health benefits through Medicare, Medicaid, and the State Children's Health Insurance Program (SCHIP).

Through recent legislation described above, the CMS began implementing a transition to value-based purchasing (VBP) of Medicare payments for hospital inpatient services, hospital outpatient services, and physician care. The CMS's goal is to become an active purchaser of high-quality, efficient health care. The principle of VBP is to incentivize health care providers to deliver high-quality care at lower costs. Goals for value-based purchasing include[4]:

- *Financial viability.* Protecting the traditional fee-for-service program for beneficiaries and taxpayers
- *Payment incentive.* Linking Medicare payments to value, quality, and efficiency of care provided
- *Joint accountability.* Holding health care providers to clinical and financial accountability in their communities

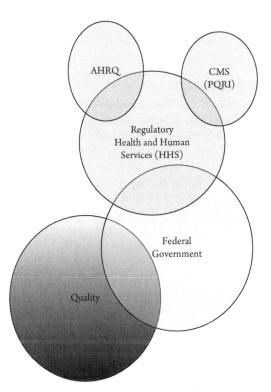

FIGURE 22.4 Regulatory effects on quality.

- *Effectiveness.* Providing evidence-based and outcomes-driven disease management and complication prevention
- *Ensuring access.* Restructuring fee-for-service payment system for equal access to high-quality, affordable care.
- *Safety and transparency.* Providing beneficiaries with information on the quality, cost, and safety of their health care
- *Smooth transitions.* Using payment systems that support well-coordinated care across different providers and settings
- *Electronic health records (EHR).* Using information technology that enables providers to deliver high-quality, efficient, well-coordinated care

The CMS is developing an array of tools to obtain the right type and mix of quality services at a reasonable cost, including:

- *Performance measurement,* using a combination of quality metrics, resource utilization tools, and cost information
- *Payment incentives,* for reporting, performance, attainment, or improvement; penalties for poor performance; no payment for hospital-acquired conditions
- *Alignment of financial incentives,* so that provider and payer share savings
- *Transparency and public reporting,* to enhance patient choice of high-quality providers
- *Conditions of participation* and accreditation requirements, such as those for imaging services under MIPPA
- *EHR and health information technology (IT) adoption*

The Medicare Quality Improvement Community (MedQIC) website is an online forum for sharing quality improvement resources, including interventions, tools, and literature that can influence processes, structures, and behaviors in health care settings.[5]

The primary tool that CMS has initiated to achieve value-based services is public reporting of quality measures in various settings or at various levels of health care (i.e., physician, hospitals, nursing homes, home health agencies, hospitals, and kidney dialysis facilities). The information from these quality measures can assist consumers, patients, and providers in making better health care choices or decisions. Two such quality reporting programs are described below.

Hospital Outpatient Quality Data Reporting Program

The Hospital Outpatient Quality Data Reporting Program (HOPQDRP) is modeled after the CMS hospital inpatient quality reporting program and is administered through the Hospital Outpatient Prospective Payment System (OPPS). In 2011, the program name was changed to the Hospital Outpatient Quality Reporting Program (HOQR). Under this program, hospitals report data on the quality of hospital outpatient care services to receive the full annual update to their OPPS payment rate (2%); the program became effective for payments beginning in calendar year (CY) 2009.

In 2010, to meet HOQR requirements, hospitals must submit data for seven quality measures for three medical conditions. Four imaging efficiency measures are also included in HOQR in 2010, but are calculated from hospital Medicare fee-for-service claims data paid under OPPS. Hospitals need not submit any additional data for these four imaging measures. Four additional imaging efficiency measures have been proposed for CY 2011, and an additional two more for 2012 and 2013.

In 2010, hospital performance rates for the measures included in HOQR were posted for the first time on the CMS Hospital Compare website, thus allowing patients and consumers to compare rates on certain conditions and procedures (see http://www.qualitynet.org/dcs/ContentServer?c=Page&pagename=QnetPublic%2FPage%2FQnetTier2&cid=1191255879384).

Physician Quality and Reporting System

The Tax Relief and Health Care Act of 2006 (TRHCA) established the Physician Quality and Reporting Initiative (PQRS) under the authority of the CMS. In 2011, the CMS changed the program name to the Physician Quality Reporting System (PQRS), in order to denote the permanence of the program. The PQRS is a type of pay-for-performance program administered through the CMS Physician Fee Schedule (PFS) to reduce unnecessary expenses for Medicare beneficiaries. Eligible professionals who voluntarily participate in the program and meet the reporting requirements earned up to 1% bonus on CMS charges in 2007, and 2% in 2009 and 2010; this decreased in 2011 to a 1% bonus, and to a 0.5% bonus in 2012–2014. Starting in 2015, nonparticipation carries a penalty of 1.5%,

increasing to 2% in 2016 and beyond. Achieving the PQRS reporting goals requires a reporting compliance rate of 80% (or 50% if reporting through claims) of a particular measure, calculated as the following:

Metric score = # billable events applicable to the metric/total number of billable events reported under metric

The bonus applies to *all* Medicare charges billed by an individual and not only to the specific PQRS metrics. The bonus payments could lead to a substantial increase in reimbursements for participants meeting PQRS reporting measures, and the penalties could lead to substantial decreases in reimbursement for those not participating.

Radiology PQRS Measures

Although most of the metrics focus on primary care management of common health conditions such as diabetes and coronary artery disease, five imaging-related metrics have been developed[6]:

- *Fluoroscopy. Exposure time reported for procedures using fluoroscopy*: Percentage of final reports for procedures using fluoroscopy that include documentation of radiation exposure or exposure time
- *Mammography. Inappropriate use of "probably benign" assessment category in mammography screening*: Percentage of final reports for screening mammograms that are classified as "probably benign"
- *Nuclear medicine. Correlation with existing imaging studies for all patients undergoing bone scintigraphy*: Percentage of final reports for all patients, regardless of age, undergoing bone scintigraphy that include physician documentation of correlation with existing relevant imaging studies (e.g., x-ray, MRI, CT, etc.) that were performed
- *Neuroradiology. Stroke and stroke rehabilitation: CT or MRI reports*: Percentage of final reports for CT or MRI studies of the brain performed either in the hospital within 24 hours of arrival, or in an outpatient imaging center to confirm initial diagnosis of stroke, transient ischemic attack (TIA), or intracranial hemorrhage, for patients aged 18 years and older with either a diagnosis of ischemic stroke or TIA or intracranial hemorrhage, or at least one documented symptom consistent with ischemic stroke or TIA or intracranial hemorrhage that includes documentation of

the presence or absence of each of the following: hemorrhage, mass lesion, acute infarction

- *Neuroradiology. Stenosis measurement in carotid imaging studies.* Percentage of final reports for all patients, regardless of age, for carotid imaging studies (neck MR angiography [MRA], neck CT angiography [CTA], neck duplex ultrasound, carotid angiogram) performed that include direct or indirect reference to measurements of distal internal carotid diameter as the denominator for stenosis measurement
- *Mammography (anticipated 2011)*.Reminder system for mammograms; percentage of patients aged 40 years and older undergoing a screening mammogram whose information is entered into a reminder system with a target due date for the next mammogram.

These metrics are designed to improve patient care and increase quality. For example, recent headlines regarding therapeutic and diagnostic radiation overexposure resulting in severe mortality in radiation therapy patients reinforce the need for more thorough monitoring and documentation of patient radiation dose. Reporting fluoroscopic exposure time could improve patient care by creating a record of patient dose, and could guide future management to reduce unnecessary imaging studies and possibly reduce future risk of cancer for these patients. As another example, the inappropriate use of the "probably benign" assessment category in mammography screening exams does little to guide clinicians in their patient management; reducing the "probably benign" assessment category will lead to better quality care. As further evidence of how these metrics can improve care, using standardized terminology for stenosis quantification or to describe the potential of stroke in a patient can play a vital role in the initial treatment decisions made for such patients.

In 2008, only 16% of radiologists eligible to participate in PQRS measures took advantage of this opportunity.

Agency for Healthcare Research and Quality

The AHRQ was founded in 1989 as a division of the U.S. DHHS and was charged with health services research. The National Institutes of Health (NIH) is a sister organization within HHS, charged with biomedical research. Other organizations within HHS include the Centers for Disease Control and Prevention (CDC) and the Food and Drug Administration (FDA). Major areas of AHRQ research focus on quality improvement in patient safety, access, outcomes, technology, and health care organization and delivery. The AHRQ fosters health services research at the university level to expand knowledge in evidence-based medicine for translation into practice and policy.

State and Regional Initiatives
Cooperatives

In the last 5–10 years, many private-sector initiatives surfaced with the goal of improving health care quality (Figure 22.5). Public reporting efforts, particularly for hospitals, have accelerated, bringing with them increased interest in comparative quality data for hospitals, health plans, and physicians.

Collaborative partnerships at the state level have been formed, with membership from health plans, physician groups, and hospital systems, along with other stakeholders, including academia and representatives for consumers, purchasers, pharmaceutical companies, and technology providers. One well-known collaboration is the Integrated Healthcare Association (IHA), whose principal projects include programs for pay-for-performance (P4P), medical technology assessment and purchasing, measurement and reward of efficiency in health care, and disease prevention. The IHA's P4P program is the largest physician incentive program in the United States.

Other programs, such as the Institute for Healthcare Improvement (IHI) and Bridges to Excellence (BTE), have launched campaigns targeting reducing unnecessary hospital deaths and have

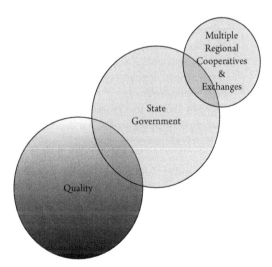

FIGURE 22.5 State and regional governmental impacts.

developed physician incentive programs for use of better systems of care, reengineering physician practice, and use of IT.

More than 70 ongoing regional initiatives are centered around quality measurement and public reporting in the United States, including private, public, regional, and nonregional quality organizations.[7] In 2006, the CMS launched the Better Quality Information to Improve Care for Medicare Beneficiaries or BQI project. Under the guidance of the DHHS Value-Drive Health Care Initiative, project goals included evaluation of Medicare and regional quality data to calculate ambulatory care quality measures, and the benefits of reporting quality measures to physicians, providers, and patients. Six regional collaboratives were selected as participants[8]:

- *California Cooperative Healthcare Reporting Initiative, San Francisco.* Focused on performance data, quality measures, data collection to reduce burden and cost (www.cchri.org/)
- *Indiana Health Information Exchange, Indianapolis.* Expanding information sharing with electronic infrastructure (www.ihie.com)
- *Massachusetts Health Quality Partners, Boston.* Broad-based health care coalition to promote valid, comparable measures to drive quality improvement (www.mhqp.org)
- *Minnesota Community Measurement, Minneapolis.* Focused on improving care and support through quality initiatives, reducing reporting expenses, and communicating findings in a fair, usable, and reliable way (www.mnhealthscores.org/)
- *Arizona State University—Center for Health Information & Research (CHIR), Tempe.* A multidisciplinary team focusing on health care, clinical quality, the health care workforce, occupational illness and injury, medical malpractice, health care economics, and disability (chir.asu.edu/)
- *Wisconsin Collaborative for Healthcare Quality, Madison.* Developing verifiable measures for public reporting. www.wchq.org/

By pooling private data with Medicare claims data, these sites can produce more accurate and comprehensive provider quality measures. Information fed back to physicians can improve quality of care and provide Medicare beneficiaries with performance information to be used when selecting health care providers.[9] With the current emphasis

on imaging appropriateness, many of these collaboratives are likely to begin, or have begun focusing efforts to address this issue. For example, the Minnesota Community Measurement is developing a new performance measure aimed at high-technology diagnostic imaging (HTDI) procedures for its *HealthScores* product.

Regional Health Information Organizations

Health care data collection and information exchange is vital for meaningful measurement and reporting. As a result, several Regional Health Information Organizations (RHIOs) have been developed to form the building blocks of the proposed National Health Information Network (NHIN) initiative of the Office of the National Coordinator for Health Information Technology (ONCHIT). The RHIOs are funded by grants from the Health Resources and Services Administration (HRSA) and the AHRQ. Alternatively, they can be independently funded by private insurers, nonprofit philanthropic organizations, health care systems, and health information management system vendors. More than 150 RHIO-type organizations have been formed all over the country, chartered with cross-jurisdictional health care data-sharing and facilitating standards for data exchange over electronic networks. Sharing specific patient data can reduce medical errors, such as adverse drug reactions; enable better decision-making; and improve health care delivery.[10]

PRIVATE-SECTOR QUALITY EFFORTS

American Board of Medical Specialties Maintenance of Certification

By the end of the 19th century, medical practice in the United States mirrored the lawless Wild West (Figure 22.6). There was no centralized credentialing organization for physicians, and no way to verify the qualifications of a practicing physician. Medical education was unregulated, with no minimum achievement standard required. In response, specialty boards were first proposed in the early 1900s as a vehicle for credentialing, specialty qualification, and examination, and were required for practice in a given specialty. In 1933, the American Board of Medical Specialties (ABMS) originated from a small cadre of physicians determined to build a national system of standards for recognizing specialists and providing information to the public.

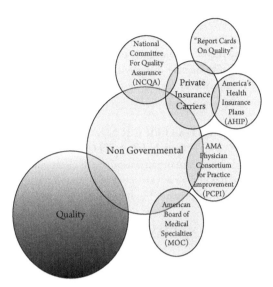

FIGURE 22.6 The impact of nongovernmental organizations (NGOs).

communication skills, professionalism, practice-based learning and improvement, and systems-based practice. These competencies are evaluated with the components listed above. The professional standing component is met by maintaining a current medical license. Lifelong learning and self-assessment is achieved through regular participation in continuing medical education (CME) and self-assessment modules (SAMs). Documentation of cognitive expertise is attained by passing a high-stakes examination. The goal of PQI competency is to improve quality of care delivery, reduce errors, and improve safety. A radiologist meets the PQI goal by completing three projects in one or more of five categories: patient safety, accuracy of interpretation, report timeliness, practice guidelines and technical standards, and referring physician surveys over the 10-year MOC cycle.[12]

The ABMS created the infrastructure for standards of excellence in the medical specialties, which physicians pursue and on which the public relies. This internal self-regulation helped assure the public of physician qualification, competency, and the ability to deliver high-quality care.

Today, maintenance of certification (MOC) is required by every ABMS member board. The American Board of Radiology (ABR) is one of these member boards. The MOC requirements include the components of professionalism, lifelong learning and periodic self-assessment, cognitive expertise, and practice performance. Practice performance is documented by completing regular practice quality improvement (PQI) projects. The goal of MOC is to ensure physician commitment to lifelong education and core competency in a chosen specialty. The MOC certification can be used as a metric by patients, employers, and health plans to choose physicians who adhere to high-quality standards. A provision in the Patient Protection and Affordable Care Act of 2010 (PPACA) includes an additional pathway and incentive payments for physicians to fulfill the CMS PQRS requirement by participating in an ABMS-approved MOC PQI project.[11] Currently, the ABR is collaborating with the AMA PCPI, ACR, and ABMS to develop performance measures that can be used for PQI projects, and potentially in the CMS PQRS MOC option. The measures focus on patient radiation dose optimization in CT procedures.

The MOC focuses on six core areas: medical knowledge, patient care, interpersonal and

Private Health Care Plans

Private health organizations are continually evolving to reflect the public's demand for quality, cost efficiency, and accountability in health care service and delivery. Private insurance plans are instituting their own internal quality programs to reward those providers and health care centers that meet certain metrics. Several private insurers have initiated report card concepts to evaluate physicians by using predefined metrics. These report cards focus on preventative and chronic care metrics, such as immunization, diabetic care, and patient reminders for upcoming screening exams. Member satisfaction can be evaluated by surveying patients on key areas of care and service.

Some insurers recognize those physicians who meet certain cost efficiency and quality standards by awarding them a certain number of stars. Recognition of specialty centers in areas such as cardiac care, neonatology, and joint replacements can be achieved through a comparison of quality of care and cost efficiency standards. Patients/customers may then choose physicians or care centers based on this quality designation.[13] Medical facilities that deliver quality care based on evidence-based selection criteria can also be recognized. These efforts encourage providers to implement quality improvement practices for better patient outcomes, and they provide consumers with information to make informed decisions regarding their providers.[14]

Other insurers or health plans have implemented cost containment or utilization control tools, such as prior notification when ordering HTDI procedures, such as CT, MRI, NM, and PET. Prior notification entails contacting a radiology business management (RBM) firm under contract with the insurer. Using this system, some health plans have seen a decrease in the number of exams ordered, although it is unclear if the ordered tests were more appropriate. Additionally, the RBM process may delay tests, thus potentially affecting the speed of diagnosis and resulting care.

Alternatively, appropriateness criteria guidelines have been used. For example, in Minnesota, a pilot program was developed through the Institute for Clinical Systems Improvement (ICSI) with six medical groups, five insurance companies, and the Minnesota Department of Human Services to use a point-of-service decision support tool to assess imaging procedure appropriateness.

Physician Consortium for Performance Improvement

The American Medical Association (AMA) originated the Physician Consortium for Performance Improvement (PCPI)[15] to develop evidence-based performance measures to improve health care quality and patient safety. This ongoing effort includes over 170 national and state medical societies, the ABMS, health care professional organizations, federal agencies, and others. Many of the PCPI measures are employed by the CMS for the PQRS. The ACR continues to develop radiology-specific measures through the PCPI, and these are included in the PQRS listed above.[16] Other metrics include communication of suspicious findings from a diagnostic mammogram to the ongoing care management physician and CT radiation dose reduction. Additionally, radiation oncology has several metrics for the management of prostate cancer and general metrics for oncology care.

America's Health Insurance Plans

America's Health Insurance Plans is a national group representing private health insurers that provide coverage to the majority of Americans. These companies provide medical, dental, long-term care, disability, and other health-related insurance products to individual consumers, and to private and public employers. The AHIP's goals are to expand coverage to all Americans through increased affordability and quality. The AHIP's purpose, however, is to represent the interests of insurance carriers

in legislative and regulatory issues at the state and federal level.[17] To this end, the AHIP either may be synergistic with quality efforts by the radiology community or may differ with the opinions of the ACR and others regarding the appropriateness of imaging.

QUASI-GOVERNMENTAL ORGANIZATIONS

Included here are organizations with close governmental ties and/or government contracts, but which are ostensibly private (Figure 22.7).

National Quality Forum

In 1998, the President's Advisory Commission on Consumer Protection and Quality in the Health Care Industry published a report entitled *Quality First: Better Health Care for All Americans*, which brought the issues of health care errors front and center. The report concluded that the top priority for the health care industry should be error reduction. From this report, the National Quality Forum (NQF) was born. Since its inception, the NQF has produced an array of products that focus on measuring, evaluating, reporting, and preventing patient safety events.

The NQF is a nonprofit organization with a mission to improve the health care of Americans by setting goals for performance improvement, endorsing quality standards, and supporting education and outreach. The organization comprises

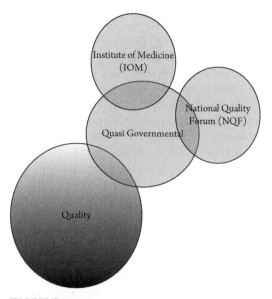

FIGURE 22.7 Quasi-govermental organizations.

over 375 stakeholders, including consumer organizations, public and private purchasers, physicians, nurses, hospitals, accrediting and certifying bodies, supporting industries, and health care research and quality improvement organizations. Its goal is to improve quality through measurement and evidence-based quality reporting. Organizations such as the CMS rely on NQF endorsement to set meaningful standards and improve health care performance. Over 500 measures have been developed to date, including radiology-specific measures, such as guidelines for imaging for low back pain, timing of brain imaging for inpatients with a stroke diagnosis, and correlating old studies for bone scintigraphy.[18]

The NQF is currently conducting a second imaging efficiency project, which should close in October 2010. Many of the imaging efficiency measures that the CMS has included or plans to include in the HOQR were evaluated through this and the preceding imaging efficiency project, such as the low back pain study (already mentioned), mammography recall rate, use of combined with/without contrast CT exams, simultaneous use of CT brain and sinus scans, and several other appropriateness measures.

One of the NQF's priority topics is safety, with numerous ongoing projects in that area, such as the Serious Reportable Events and the Safe Practices project. Safe pediatric imaging, based on the *Image Gently* concept, has been included as Safe Practice 34.

In 2008, a provision of MIPPA directed the Secretary of Health and Human Services to contract with an agency such as the NQF to help establish quality and efficiency metrics to help the federal government evaluate how health care spending is achieving results for patients and taxpayers. The $10 million awarded to the NQF in fiscal year 2009, with yearly renewal options through 2010, is administered by the CMS. The General Accounting Office report is available at http://www.gao.gov/new.items/d10737.pdf.

National Committee for Quality Assurance

The National Committee for Quality Assurance (NCQA) is a nonprofit organization that develops programs to improve health care quality and patient safety. Through measurement and transparency, the group develops specific disease-related performance measures and methods to evaluate physicians on chronic disease-management issues, as for diabetes, heart disease, and back pain. The NCQA

has created the Healthcare Effectiveness Data and Information Set (HEDIS) as a tool for health plan quality measurement, to evaluate how well plans follow standards of medical care. Using measures such as effectiveness, access, quality, cost, and utilization, HEDIS sets performance measures for health plans by focusing on public health and chronic diseases, such as smoking, heart disease, asthma, and cancer. Founded in 1990, the NCQA has helped build consensus around health care quality issues by collaborating with various stakeholders such as physicians, patients, health plans, large employers, and policy-makers. The NCQA guides decisions on metric selection, measurement, and improvement, and is also involved with accreditation, certification, recognition, and evaluation. Achieving accreditation requires reporting performance on more than 60 standards to earn the NCQA's seal of approval. Health plans in every state, the District of Columbia, and Puerto Rico are NCQA accredited, and almost 75% of all Americans are enrolled in NCQA-accredited health plans.[19] Regarding imaging, the Back Pain Recognition Project is an NCQA-sponsored initiative to guide clinicians in the evidence-based management of uncomplicated back pain, with criteria to minimize overuse of imaging.

Institute of Medicine

The Institute of Medicine (IOM) is a nonprofit, nongovernmental organization that functions as the health care arm of the National Academy of Sciences. The purpose of the IOM is to help health care leaders make informed, evidence-guided decisions on many areas of health policy. Studies undertaken by the IOM are often under congressional mandate. The IOM also facilitates open forums to promote discovery and forward thinking.

In 1999, the IOM published a groundbreaking publication entitled *To Err Is Human*, describing strategies to reduce medical errors. It focused on medical errors and patient safety by reporting that as many as 98,000 people die each year from medical errors, and the report ignited a professional and public dialogue on the topic. These medical errors increase cost, length of hospital stay, pain, and suffering. The report laid out a multitiered approach to error reduction, with specific recommendations focusing on leadership, research, mandatory error reporting, raising quality standards, and creation of safe practices and systems within health care organizations.

Another IOM consensus report, *Crossing the Quality Chasm*, expanded on the concept of health care quality and proposed the essential elements of a quality health care system. The landmark report documented the fundamental need for a new approach in the American health care system by providing six "aims for improvement": safety, timeliness, effectiveness, efficiency, equity, and patient-centeredness (STEEP).[20]

Research

Because of the efforts described throughout this chapter, a new focus has been placed on quality in health care. Some of the major current research projects that support this focus are briefly discussed here. Each of these research efforts includes topics related to imaging and spotlights issues regarding imaging quality and utilization.

A 2002 Rand study, "The Quality of Health Care Delivered to Adults in the United States," cited that a little more than half of the American population gets basic recommended preventive care. A 2003 IOM report, "Unequal Treatment, Confronting Racial and Ethnic Disparities in Health care," found that minorities "tend to receive a lower quality of health care than whites do, even when access-related factors such as insurance status and income are controlled." In 2007, the Kaiser Family foundation published a report showing that health care spending per capita in the United States grew at an average annual rate of 4.4% from 1980–2003, the highest rate among countries in the Organization for Economic Cooperation and Development, but without a significant difference in key health care quality metrics such as life expectancy and infant mortality.

Nonprofit research groups such as the Robert Wood Johnson Foundation (RWJF), the Brookings Institute, and The Commonwealth Fund conduct or fund research projects, pilots, and demonstrations to support health care quality measurement and improvement. A recent initiative funded by RWJF and directed by Brookings is the High Value Health Care Project (HVHC). The goal of HVHC is to develop consistent and useful information about the quality and cost of health care, and to make this information available to patients, medical professionals, hospitals, insurers, and others. The Commonwealth Fund has described a high drug error rate in hospital radiology departments that perform complex procedures with high-risk drugs and that feature several

opportunities for communication breakdown between staff and requesting physicians and nurses.

INTERNATIONAL HEALTH CARE QUALITY

Quality improvement in health care is a global effort. In the past 20 years, interest in accountability and health care effectiveness has grown considerably as the governments of developed countries around the world seek an accounting of health care financial expenditure and value. Information sharing among new and established programs for health care accreditation from a variety of countries is in high demand.[21]

In the mid-1990s, quality evaluation in health care, business, and government burgeoned. The International Organization for Standards (ISO) emerged as a globally recognized process for quality monitoring across public and private business enterprises, and some governments looked to the ISO as a health care monitoring process. Health care systems in countries such as Canada, Australia, New Zealand, the United Kingdom, and the United States already had accreditation programs in place, such as the U.S. Joint Commission on Accreditation of Health care Organizations (JCAHO). Leaders from these organizations created an external peer review process to assess accreditation bodies. The ISO published health care sector guidelines in 2005.

The International Society for Quality in Health Care (ISQua)'s mission is to promote access to safe, quality health care.[22] A working group of the ISQua, the Agenda for Leadership in Programs for Healthcare Accreditation (ALPHA), is focused on international accreditation, with the goal of promoting facilitation and collaboration in the evaluation of worldwide health care organizations. The ALPHA has created specific guidelines on how health care standards could be developed, applied, and evaluated across a variety of systems.[23]

Many international health organizations already focus on a variety of quality standards to improve health and sustain quality of life at the population level. For example, the World Health Organization (WHO) has created standards for hospital-based heath promotion using measurable quality goals, including development of a written policy, assessment of patient needs, distribution of patient-specific information for health conditions, development of the hospital as a healthy workplace, and a planned approach to collaboration with other health service organizations.[24]

Other groups set standards for patient and provider safety. The International Atomic Energy Agency (IAEA) sets standards for occupational protection from ionizing radiation and guidelines for the disposal and transport of radioactive materials. Creation of evidence-based referral guidelines will help to limit the use of ionizing radiation to only those cases in which the benefits outweighs patient risk. However, vigilance must be maintained by the radiology physician community to ensure appropriateness in guideline development.

Collaboration with international agencies is key to the current U.S. political climate. Many of these international agencies, such as those sponsored by the United Nations, work exclusively with other international agencies. Therefore, it is imperative that U.S. radiologists integrate their efforts in the quality arena through membership and participation in these international agencies and international projects.

CONCLUSION

An analysis of the governmental and outside agencies that affect health care quality can be considered either a morass of confused standards or a monumental advance in the quality of radiology services; however, if we return to the quality equation (Quality = Value × Price/Time), several important concepts become evident:

1. Many organizations are interested in quality. Some of these groups work synergistically and in concert, whereas others work in opposition to each other. This results in challenges for the practicing radiologist, who must evaluate each of these groups and his or her relationship with them.
2. Radiologists must act as leaders in quality and integrate themselves in these organizations if they are to remain relevant in health care.
3. Radiologists must establish both the value of their services and cost containment to validate quality to the governmental and private sector if they are to survive and thrive as a specialty.
4. Radiologists must be transparent to public and private agencies, payers, and patients in their quality efforts.
5. Above all, radiologists must support patient primacy in quality health care because linked

directly to every scanner, PACS, accession number, and film is a patient who is worried, afraid, and relying on his radiologist to provide the very best effort possible. Radiologists must keep that patient first and never abrogate that responsibility.

REFERENCES

1. President Obama's address on healthcare to the Joint Session of Congress, September 9, 2009.
2. Centers for Medicare and Medicaid Services. The Medicare imaging demonstration (slide presentation) Accessed April 20, 2010, at:https://www.cms.gov/DemoProjectsEvalRpts/downloads/AUI_Oct_ODF.pdf
3. Khorasani R. Health care reform through meaningful use of health care IT: Implications for radiologists. *J Am Coll Radiol.* 2010;7(2):152–3.
4. Centers for Medicare and Medicaid Services. Roadmap for implementing value driven health care in the traditional Medicare fee-for-service program. Accessed April 20, 2010, at: http://www.cms.gov/QualityInitiativesGenInfo/downloads/VBPRoadmap_OEA_1-16_508.pdf
5. Medicare Quality Improvement Community (MedQIC). Accessed at: http://www.qualitynet.org
6. U.S. Department of Health & Human Services, Centers for Medicare and Medicare Services. Physicians Quality Reporting Initiative. Accessed at: http://www.cms.gov/PQRI/Downloads/2010_PQRI_Measureslist_111309.pdf
7. Health Quality Alliance. Accessed at: http://www.healthqualityalliance.org/initiatives
8. Department of Health and Human Services. Accessed at: http://archive.hhs.gov/valuedriven/pilot/index.html
9. CMS. Better Quality Information to Improve Care for Medicare Beneficiaries (BQI) Project. Accessed at: http://www.cms.gov/BQI/Downloads/BQIFinalReport.zip
10. E-HIM Work Group on Patient Identification in RHIOs. Surveying the RHIO landscape: A description of current RHIO models, with a focus on patient identification. *J AHIMA.* 2006; 77(1):64A–D. Accessed April 19, 2010, at: http://library.ahima.org/xpedio/groups/public/documents/ahima/bok1_028980.hcsp?dDocName=bok1_028980
11. American Board of Medical Specialties. Accessed at: http://www.abms.org/News_and_Events/Media_Newsroom/Releases/release_ABMSMOCInHlthcareBill_03232010.aspx
12. American College of Radiology. Accessed at http://theabr.org/moc/moc_dr_landing.html
13. United Healthcare. Accessed at http://www.uhc.com/individuals_families/health_care_quality.htm

14. BlueCross BlueShield. Blue Distinction. Accessed at: http://www.bcbs.com/innovations/bluedistinction/

15. American Medical Association Physician Consortium for Practice Improvement. Accessed at: http://www.amaassn.org/ama/pub/physician-resources/clinical-practice-improvement/clinical-quality/physician-consortiumperformance-improvement.shtml

16. American Medical Association. Accessed at: http://www.ama-assn.org/ama1/pub/upload/mm/370/radiology-ms.pdf

17. American's Health Insurance Plans. Accessed at: http://www.ahip.org/

18. National Quality Forum. Accessed at: http://www.qualityforum.org/

19. National Committee for Quality Assurance. Accessed at: http://www.ncqa.org/

20. Institute of Medicine. Accessed at: http://www.iom.edu

21. Heidemann E. Moving to global standards for accreditation processes. *Int J Qual Health Care.* 2000;12:227–30.

22. Shaw CD. Accreditation and ISO: International convergence on health care standards. ISQua position paper—October 1996. *Int J Qual Health Care.* 1997 Feb;9(1):11–13.

23. Heidemann EG. Editorial: The ALPHA program. *Int J Qual Health Care.* 1999;11:275–7.

24. World Health Organization. Standards for Health Promotion in Hospitals, WHO European Office for Integrated Health Care Services, 2004. WHO Regional Office for Europe. Accessed at: http://www.euro.who.int/document/e82490.pdf

Pay-for-Performance and Quality in Radiology

DAVID A. ROSMAN AND SANJAY SAINI

In November 1999, the Institute of Medicine (IOM) published its hallmark report, *To Err Is Human*.[1] In it, claims were made of 98,000 deaths a year caused by medical error. Headlines flooded the nation's newspapers. Congressional hearings were convened, and a full-throated cry for a renewed quality movement was heard throughout the medical community.

Health care organizations and particularly individual practitioners were put on the defensive, and many initiatives were launched in the name of quality. Shortly thereafter, the IOM followed with another seminal work: *Crossing the Quality Chasm*.[2] In this, it suggested that our health care system needed fundamental change in order to provide the care that the American people deserved. The authors of both reports urged many changes. Central to the success of a quality transformation was a system of payment incentives. They urged that "payment policies be aligned to encourage and support quality improvement."[2] Thus was born the pay-for-performance (also known as P4P) movement in health care in the United States.

At the same time that the quality movement was urging radical transformation, another force was brewing: escalating cost. As insurance companies, and more importantly businesses, watched health cost spiral higher, they claimed the pay-for-performance movement as their own. A report assembled for the Leapfrog group, an association of many large corporations that are purchasers of health care, noted that "the momentum behind pay-for-performance comes from a response to rising medical cost trends, the growth in chronic care conditions, health care utilization, consumer-directed health care and demands by purchasers for improvements in quality care."[3] Although quality was mentioned here, a clear driver was undoubtedly a desire to control costs.

It is the coexistence of these two drivers—increasing safety and quality and decreasing costs—that defines the pay-for-performance movement. These two drivers give the movement purpose and power. However, the concern also exists that the drive to improve safety and quality will give way to the drive to decrease costs.

In this chapter, we first define pay-for-performance, then explore more fully the drivers of pay-for-performance programs in health care. We will look at various models that have been implemented within health care, and at specific examples. In addition to its broad applications, we will look at the limited experience of pay-for-performance as specifically applied to radiology. As pay-for-performance has often been bathed in controversy, we will address the skepticism regarding its use. Finally, we will look to the future of pay-for-performance as it may relate to radiology and examine how it can function as a transformational force in health care delivery.

WHAT IS PAY-FOR-PERFORMANCE?

Broadly, pay-for-performance is a simple and intuitive concept: Pay people more when they do their job well, and pay them less when their performance lags. We see it in bonus structures in athletic contracts and in incentive plans for everyone from business executives to hotel employees. It exists in many industries and has for decades—sometimes with great effect and sometimes less so. In health care, "pay-for-performance" is a title given to a variety of incentive programs and payment schema that differentiate payments to providers based on their performance on quality and efficiency measures. In theory, instituting payment incentives or penalties based on how well a physician conforms to certain standards should, in the long run, increase conformity and improve outcomes.

DRIVERS

Quality and Safety
The two seminal works of the IOM mentioned above made two remarkable assertions. In *To Err Is Human*, the IOM claimed that nearly 100,000 preventable deaths were occurring every year. In *Crossing the Quality Chasm*, the assertion was that a radical transformation of the health delivery system was needed, and that aligning payment with outcomes was a critical pathway to achieving that end goal. The combination of these two assertions leads to the conclusion that aligning payment with quality would help reduce medical errors and deaths.

As an aside, it is important to note that *To Err Is Human* emphasized changing systems rather than individuals to eliminate errors: "The focus must shift from blaming individuals for past errors to a focus on preventing future errors by designing safety into the system. This does not mean that individuals can be careless. People must still be vigilant and held responsible for their actions. But when an error occurs, blaming an individual does little to make the system safer and prevent someone else from committing the same error."[1] This approach has been advocated by Donald Berwick and the Institution on Healthcare Improvement, the Joint Commission, the Agency for Healthcare Research and Quality, and many others, with significant impact on the institutions of U.S. health care delivery.

However, shifting attention back to individuals, the pay-for-performance movement received another boost from the IOM in *Crossing the Quality Chasm*. This report put the problem in stark terms: "As medical science and technology have advanced at a rapid pace [over the last decade] the health care delivery system has floundered in its ability to provide consistently high-quality care to all Americans. Research on the quality of care reveals a health care system that frequently falls short in its ability to translate knowledge into practice, and to apply new technology safely and appropriately" (p. 181).[2] They argued further that, although clinicians often know how to translate the new research into practice, doing so is costly to practices that are already stretched thin financially. They concluded that purchasers of care must "align financial incentives with the implementation of care processes based on best practices and the achievement of better patient outcomes. Substantial improvements in quality are most likely to be obtained when providers are highly motivated and rewarded for carefully designing and fine-tuning care processes to achieve increasingly higher levels of safety, effectiveness, patient-centeredness, timeliness, efficiency, and equity" (p. 18).[2]

Costs
In a presentation at the Press Ganey National Conference, Leah Binder, the CEO of the Leapfrog group, declared the 9%–20% annual escalation in health care "untenable."[4] In the same conference, she noted $100 billion of avoidable health expenses due to errors, and $690 billion of health expenditures attributable to regional variations in care. She decried that "companies [are] unable to absorb growing medical cost through product price increases." Although the Leapfrog group is a leader that looks to and tries to drive quality, costs are undoubtedly a huge driver and motivator in the business community's demands for pay-for-performance.

It is this combination of reducing costs and improving quality that makes pay-for-performance so attractive to purchasers of care. The Leapfrog group noted that, "numerous attempts at containing costs and improving quality have been previously attempted, but with little success. Initiatives based on quality alone have not worked to contain the growth of healthcare expenditures. Likewise, purely utilization-driven programs, such as generalized preauthorization have proven burdensome and financially ineffective. Pay-for-performance programs, in contrast, hold promise for effectively addressing these dual concerns."[5]

MODELS OF PAY-FOR-PERFORMANCE
Pay-for-performance incentives take many forms. As the name implies, most are financial, although there are also indirect incentives within the rubric

of pay-for-performance which, although not directly resulting in payments or financial penalties to the physician, can still have a profound effect on income. There are also variations, with incentives going to groups rather than individuals.

Direct Incentives

The most common type of financial incentive is a simple bonus. These are often set up to correlate with meeting target requirements for clinical measures such as hemoglobin A1c or appropriate medications on discharge after myocardial infarction. This type of plan is often easy to create and implement. These incentives are popular because they do not require renegotiated contracts, and companies rarely get pushback regarding increases in pay.

A related financial incentive is a *withhold* or *at-risk financial model*. Withholds usually aren't additional funds but rather a percentage of a physician's base pay, which is withheld unless the doctor meets the target requirements. For obvious reasons, individual physicians are loathe to enter into these sorts of agreements.

Tiering has become increasingly popular and can have many meanings within the pay-for-performance context. As a direct financial incentive, insurance companies are empowered through their payment contracts to set their payment rates to individual (or groups of) physicians. One mechanism of accomplishing this is via an adjustable fee schedule, in which the fee schedule can be retroactively increased or decreased based on the doctor's conformance to particular measures during the period in question.

Indirect Incentives

Authorization for referrals can be a bane for many physicians. The insurance companies are aware that the complexity of the authorization process can be a disincentive for primary care physicians to make referrals or for patients to follow through on them. As a result, one particularly appealing incentive is to eliminate the authorization step and automatically preapprove a particular specialist who has a high level of conformity to their standards—so-called "high performers."

As opposed to tiering the physician fee schedule, an action invisible to the patient, another form of tiering is to give the price decision to the patient. Much like tiering of copayments for medications, this system is set up to disincentivize the "more expensive choice." If a doctor conforms to the mandated measures, the copay to see them will be lower. If they do not conform, their copay will be higher. This choice is particularly appealing to insurance companies as it can be done in a budget-neutral or even positive fashion and requires no acquiescence from the physicians involved.

Not all pay-for-performance programs are directed at individual doctors or groups. Hospitals too can be targeted as conformers or nonconformers to the standards set by the payers. Public report cards, rankings, and honor rolls are believed by some to have a community impact and to direct more or fewer patients to individual hospitals.

MEASURES USED IN PAY-FOR-PERFORMANCE

The most common measure is the Healthcare Effectiveness Data and Information Set (HEDIS) created by the National Committee for Quality Assurance (NCQA). Over 90% of health plans use the HEDIS data, which consists of 71 measures across many domains of care. Included are things such as childhood immunization status, persistence of β blockade after myocardial infarction, and items relevant to radiology such as breast cancer screening and colon cancer screening.[6]

The Physician Consortium for Performance Improvement (PCPI), convened by the American Medical Association (AMA), chooses clinical topics, and for each given clinical topic, develops a comprehensive set of measures that can be used for quality improvement and accountability. The PCPI now has 266 measures across 42 topics. Within these lists are included radiology-specific measures such as chest radiography for suspected pneumonia and barium swallow for gastroesophageal reflux disease.

In an era of customer-driven health care, customer satisfaction is increasingly important. The Consumer Assessment of Healthcare Providers and Systems (CAHPS), developed by the Agency for Healthcare Research and Quality (AHRQ), is a popular tool to capture patient satisfaction and in turn drive tiering and compensation.

Many other groups, including medical specialty society groups, as well as insurance plans and even state-based groups such as the Massachusetts Health Quality Partner (MHQP), form their own measures.

SKEPTICISM REGARDING PAY-FOR-PERFORMANCE

There are many skeptics regarding pay-for-performance, and the skepticism comes in many forms. Some simply question the means, while others question whether payers, conflicted by financial interest, can be sincere about the ends. Unintended consequences are another fear regarding pay-for-performance.

Donald Berwick, Director of the Centers for Medicare and Medicaid Services (CMS), who until recently was the chairman of the Institute for Healthcare Improvement (IHI) and one of the champions of eliminating the errors brought to light in *To Err Is Human,* recently said, "I'm a skeptic. I have some pretty serious doubts about whether pay-for-performance helps... quality to get better."[7] No one can doubt Dr. Berwick's intentions or claim that he is a defender of the status quo. As evidenced by the phenomenal and transformational work that the IHI has done, Dr. Berwick is extremely dissatisfied by the status quo and determined to make change. However, supported by the research of Alfie Kohn in his book *Punished by Rewards,* he claims that paying to change performance can have the paradoxical effect of reducing performance. Kohn and Berwick argue that incentives can have this effect by degrading and demoralizing people who would otherwise already intend to do a good job. He admits that pay-for-performance sometimes works, but that the end goals of a particular measure, for example compliance with β blockade or improved hemoglobin A1c, haven't always correlated with improved outcomes.

A related criticism of pay-for-performance is that, by the nature of the measures, they are narrow. Narrow measures inevitably intensify focus, and given the incontrovertible limits of time, focus on a particular issue will almost assuredly mean paying less attention to other, equally valid concerns. To be specific, if a program incentivizes ensuring that a physician has a current hemoglobin A1c on all of her patients, it may be that while attending to a patient's bloodwork that she ignores the counseling required to improve that patient's glucose control. Alternatively, if the measure is to lower the A1c, while concentrating on the patient's diabetes, the physician may pay less attention to breast and/or colon screening or cardiac care. Adding more measures can exacerbate this problem, thus interfering with the physician's ability to embrace a holistic approach.

Although some fear that pay-for-performance can have unintended consequences on the individual level, there is a similar concern on the macro level. In particular, physicians and advocacy groups worry that pay-for-performance will increase inequities in care—particularly with regards to racial and ethnic disparities in care.[8] Casalino et al. suggested several ways that pay-for-performance can exacerbate disparities. First, pay-for-performance could result in income reductions for physicians in poor minority communities. This can happen because, in these communities, a higher percentage of uninsured and Medicaid patients results in lower average payments and thus less available capital for a practice to invest in the information technology that may be needed to achieve better scores. Further, substantial research has shown that, for a variety of reasons, the patients in these communities may be less likely to adhere to treatment recommendations,[9] which will ultimately lower the conformance score and thus income for those communities' physicians. Although data on the topic are scarce, the British experience has corroborated this fear.[10]

Although these issues have a deleterious effect on the physicians, the logical next step is *adverse selection*: Doctors, in order to keep their practices solvent, may avoid patients who are likely to lower their conformance scores.[11,12] Similarly, as certain measures will demand lower utilization and/or improved outcomes, doctors may also avoid sicker patients whose illnesses may lower their scores on these counts.

Both patient and physician groups are also skeptical regarding pay-for-performance, albeit for different reasons. Their fear is that an insurance company, with its need to show profits to shareholders or other interested parties, may be inclined to use pay-for-performance not to improve performance, but rather to lower pay. It is for this reason that the American Medical Association, along with the state and specialty medical societies that make up its policy-making body, created their principles and guidelines for pay-for-performance, which begin with ensuring quality of care and include such principles as fostering the patient–physician relationship, voluntary participation, accuracy of data, and fair and equitable program incentives.[13]

EXAMPLES OF PAY-FOR-PERFORMANCE AND THEIR OUTCOMES

California Integrated Healthcare and PacifiCare Health Systems

In an unplanned, fortuitous natural experiment, PacifiCare Health Systems, a large network HMO, instituted a pay-for-performance program called the quality incentive program (QIP) in 2002. A year later, a coalition of health plans, physician groups, and purchasers called the California Integrated Healthcare Association (IHA) instituted a separate but related pay-for-performance effort. In a remarkable article, Mullen et al. compared the performance of the groups affected by one or both of these programs with each other, as well as with nearby Northwest groups not affected by either program.[14] This was a massive and expensive experiment in which the combined payout of pay-for-performance bonuses was $122.7 million in 2004 and $139.5 million in 2005. Mullen noted that "of the six measures initially rewarded by the IHA, only cervical cancer screening showed consistently positive returns.... On the other hand, appropriate asthma medication rates actually decreased even though it was...linked to significant potential monetary payouts." Additionally, both preferred (rewarded by QIP) as well as appropriate (rewarded by both) antibiotic usage rates also declined. Of further concern, and supporting the fear of that such incentives could result in the provision of less care in unrewarded areas of care, a decrease of *Chlamydia* screening was seen in the test group when compared to the rest of the Pacific Northwest. This trend reversed when *Chlamydia* screening was added to the rewarded measure set. Mullen noted that the "results highlight the fact that pay-for-performance may not necessarily have the dramatic and or even predictable effects touted by its enthusiasts.... In the end, we fail to find evidence that a large P4P initiative either resulted in major improvement in quality or notable disruption to care.... This result casts doubt on the promise of P4P as a transformative mechanism for improving the general quality of the healthcare system."

United Kingdom Incentives for Family Practices

In 2004, the U.K. government introduced a pay-for-performance program for the nation's family practitioners; 99.6% of the physicians participate, and the payments are substantial, making up approximately 25% of the average physician's income. Campbell et al. conducted an extensive review of the effect of the program.[15] Because of the high penetration, the only comparison group was the same physicians prior to the implementation of the program. The program focused on asthma, diabetes, and heart disease. Intriguingly, this experiment was conducted against the background of a trend of improvement in care in all of these clinical scenarios. Against this background, Campbell

et al.'s results demonstrated short-term accelerated improvements in quality for asthma and diabetes, but not for cardiac care. Further, the result was not sustained and, once the targets were reached, the rate of improvement fell below baseline (perhaps confirming Berwick and Kohn's posit). The group also "found significant differences between aspects of care that were linked to incentives and...[those] not linked.... Mean quality scores for aspects of care that were not linked to incentives dropped between 2005 and 2007." Discouragingly, "for all aspects of care—whether associated with incentives or not...rates of quality improvement slowed considerably after 2005."

Massachusetts Group Insurance Commission and the Clinical Performance Improvement Initiative

The Group Insurance Commission (GIC) was established in Massachusetts in 1955, to provide and administer health insurance and other benefits to the employees and retirees of the Commonwealth.[16] In 2003, the GIC launched the Clinical Performance Improvement Initiative (CPII) to improve quality and decrease costs. In its first stage, the CPII collected data from the GIC health plans. In July 2006, group tiering of physicians began. Shortly thereafter, the CPII began tiering individual physicians and, as time passed, moved increasingly from group tiering to individual tiering. The tiering affects both physician and hospital copayments. In its annual report, the GIC claims that the tiering is working and that costs are rising at a slower rate than the national average.

Physician groups, particularly the Massachusetts Medical Society (MMS), feared that tiering would be done based on inadequate or inaccurate data. In an analysis using aggregated claims data, Adams et al. concluded that 59% of physicians had cost-profile scores with reliabilities of less than 0.70 and that approximately a quarter of physicians would be misclassified in a two-tier system (CPII uses three tiers, likely increasing the probability of mistiering).[17] The MMS has an ongoing lawsuit against GIC claiming harm caused by mistiering and tiering from inadequate and misapplied information. One plaintiff "found that 68 percent of the patients attributed to him were not his."[18]

The challenges with implementation of the CPII aren't a condemnation of all tiering programs, although they highlight the challenge of moving from theory to practice.

PAY-FOR-PERFORMANCE AND RADIOLOGY

Physician Quality Reporting Initiative

The 2006 Tax Relief and Health Care Act established a physician quality reporting system that would incentivize physicians who satisfactorily report data on quality measures. Administered by the CMS, the program was called the Physician Quality Reporting Initiative (PQRI). Very little information is yet available as it is a reporting initiative and, unlike the programs above, there is no incentive to change practice patterns, only to report according to the measures established. There are 179 quality measures, including several pertaining to radiology:

Measure 10. Stroke and Stroke Rehabilitation
Computed Tomography (CT) or Magnetic Resonance Imaging (MRI) Reports

Percentage of final reports for CT or MRI studies of the brain performed either: In the hospital with 24 hours of arrival OR In an outpatient imaging center to confirm initial diagnosis of the stroke, transient ischemic attack (TIA) or intracranial hemorrhage. For Patients aged 18 years and older with either a diagnosis of ischemic stroke or TIA of intracranial hemorrhage OR at least one documented symptom consistent with ischemic stroke or TIA or intracranial hemorrhage that includes documentation of the presence or absence of each of the following: hemorrhage and mass lesion and acute infarction

Measure 145. Radiology: Exposure Time Reported for Procedures Using Fluoroscopy

Percentage of final reports for procedures using fluoroscopy that include documentation of radiation exposure or exposure time.

Measure 146. Radiology: Inappropriate use of "Probably Benign" Assessment Category in Mammography Screening

Percentage of final reports for screening mammograms that are classified as "probably benign"

Measure 147. Nuclear Medicine: Correlation with Existing Imaging Studies for All Patients Undergoing Bone Scintigraphy

Percentage of final reports for all patients regardless of age, undergoing bone scintigraphy that include physician documentation of correlation with existing relevant imaging studies (e.g., x-ray, MRI, CT, etc.) that were performed.

Measure 195. Stenosis Measurement in Carotid Imaging Studies

Percentage of final reports for all patients, regardless of age, for carotid imaging studies (neck MR angiography [MRA], neck CT angiography [CTA], neck duplex ultrasound, carotid angiogram) performed that include direct or indirect reference to measurements of distal internal carotid diameter as the denominator for stenosis measurement.[19]

PQRI is still nascent and what will become of the data and whether it will be used by CMS as part of a pay-for-performance program is yet unknown.

WHAT'S NEXT FOR RADIOLOGY AND PAY-FOR-PERFORMANCE?

As can be seen from the discussion above, much of the history and origin of pay-for-performance has had little interaction with radiology. Its primary emphasis has been disease prevention and management in a few areas such as cardiac disease, asthma, and diabetes.

However, it is easy to imagine three additional types of standards that could be applied to radiology in the future:

- Measures that discourage inappropriate imaging utilization from referring physicians
- Measures that encourage appropriate imaging recommendations from interpreting radiologists
- Measures that aim to minimize radiation exposure to patients

The American College of Radiology has created an extensive set of appropriateness criteria, which, as the name implies, give evidenced-based arguments and guidelines for the appropriate use of imaging across nearly all clinical scenarios. One can imagine that conformity to the appropriateness criteria could be a measure to which payers link payment incentives. Aside from the creation of the appropriateness criteria however, this is a metric that has secondary rather than primary effects on radiologists.

Radiologists can have a much more direct effect on utilization by recommending further imaging. Measures could be created demanding conformity to standards of recommendations, such as the Fleischner Society guidelines for pulmonary nodules.

Last, as both medical and lay concerns regarding radiation dosage continue to escalate, it is easy to imagine radiation protection measures, which take a step beyond the ALARA principle or perhaps move to systematizing ALARA, such that all reports must include both instant and cumulative radiation dose. Measures regarding radiation dose in fluoroscopy already exist, and others regarding CT could easily follow.

Hearing of such proposed measures likely creates a visceral response in physicians who can foresee examples in which particular dose demands would worsen the care provided to a patient or, conversely, could set a bar too low and discourage further dose reduction after a certain goal is met. The exceptions are easy to imagine (which is likewise true when treating a diabetic or asthmatic), and this explains why so many physicians have an inherent unease with pay-for-performance. It is not the resistance to improving care, controlling costs, or adhering to evidence-based principles, but rather the understanding that, along with the science of medicine, there remains an art that may somehow become lost in a series of measurements.

CONCLUSION

Despite the somewhat disappointing results of the pay-for-performance experiments that have occurred to date, it is unlikely that the era of pay-for-performance is over. There are powerful forces that, working together, have the synergy to drive pay-for-performance forward. The most important is the need for an improved health system. *To Err Is Human* raised compelling and disturbing arguments about our health system, and our conscience demands that they be addressed. The second force is economic. The continual increases in health costs have been declared untenable by individuals, businesses, and politicians. The Medicare trust fund's solvency is debated, but by the latest report of its own trustees, the fund will be exhausted by 2017.[20] Many will argue that, given the results to this point, pay-for-performance is the answer for neither the quality nor the cost deficiencies in our health care system. Many decision makers, however, seem to believe there is too great a need to improve outcomes and decrease costs to give up on pay-for-performance at this time. In times that demand "all hands on deck," it seems even ineffective hands must be put to work.

Despite the criticism inherent in the analyses, one could argue that many pay-for-performance schema have worked. They might not have resulted in the end goal that administrators wanted—better health outcomes—but they often resulted in the end goals that were paid for: more β blockade or improved usage of asthma medications. Pay-for-performance often works by getting people to do more of what they are paid to do. Pay-for-performance fails when it works on faulty information or incentivizes intermediate steps (more asthma medication) rather than end goals (better health outcomes for asthmatics).

Donald Berwick declared, "I think what you'll see change, is not the investment in pay-for-performance but rather the definition of performance itself."[7] The performance we truly want to incentivize is improvement in patients' health, function, and comfort. Pay-for-performance is not the only methodology of accomplishing this. Berwick's work at IHI strives to eliminate errors and inappropriate utilization but uses substantially different methods from pay-for-performance. Reading the IHI annual report gives hope that the system can be fundamentally changed. Individual hospitals innovate in an effort to eliminate system error. For example, the Massachusetts General Hospital employed smart pumps to eliminate infused medication errors and has shared that technology. Other innovators are doing the same and are making strides in safety unmatched by pay-for-performance.

Perhaps pay-for-performance should be scrapped altogether. However, if that is not to be its future, the next phase in pay-for-performance could involve a shift of focus from measures such as hemoglobin A1c, which are easy and convenient to track, to measures such as health, function, and comfort, which are far more elusive.[21] It may be harder, but it is the honest end goal. Implemented correctly, paying for performance might work. In its next iteration, it is critical to ensure that it is implemented correctly and works for the good of patients.

REFERENCES

1. Kohn LT, Corrigan JM, Donaldson MS, eds. *To err is human: Building a safer health system*. Washington, DC: National Academy Press, Institute of Medicine, 1999.
2. Committee on Quality of Health Care in America, Institute of Medicine. *Crossing the quality chasm: A new health system for the 21st century*. Washington, DC: National Academy Press, 2001.
3. Baker G, Jaughton J, Mongroo P. *Executive briefing. Pay for performance incentive programs in healthcare: Market dynamics and business process*. San Francisco, CA: Med-Vantage. Retrieved April 19, 2008, from http://www.leapfroggroup.org/media/file/Leapfrog-Pay_for_Performance_Briefing.pdf.

4. Pay-for-performance: The National Landscape; Press Ganey National Client Conference. Leah Binder, CEO Leapfrog Group

5. Pay-for-performance Incentive Programs in Healthcare: Market Dynamics and Business Process, Executive Briefing, 2003. Geoffrey Baker, MBA.

6. Accessed at: http://www.ncqa.org/tabid/187/Default.aspx

7. Berwick D. On call: Does pay-for-performance work?" IHI open school, June 24, 2009.

8. Casalino LP, Elster A, et al. Will pay-for-performance and quality reporting affect health care disparities? *Health Affairs*. 2007;26(3):w405–14.

9. Holt K, et al. Mammography self-report and mammography claims: Racial, ethnic, and socioeconomic disparities among elderly women. *Med Care*. 2006;44(6):513–8.

10. Doran T, et al. Pay-for-performance programs in family practices in the United Kingdom. *N Engl J Med*. 2006;355(4): 75–84.

11. Omoigui NA, et al. Outmigration for coronary bypass surgery in an era of public dissemination of clinical outcomes. *Circulation*. 1996;93(1): 27–33.

12. Werner RM, Asch DA, Polsky D. Racial profiling: The unintended consequences of coronary artery bypass graft report cards. *Circulation*. 2005;111(10):1257–63.

13. Snyder L, Neubauer RL; the American College of Physicians Ethics, Professionalism and Human Rights Committee. Pay for performance principles that promote patient-centered care: An ethics manifesto. *Ann Int Med*. 2007;147(11):752–94.

14. Mullen KJ, Frank RG, Rosenthal MB. Can you get what you pay for? Pay-for-performance and the quality of healthcare providers. *Rand J Econom*. 2010;41(1): 64–91.

15. Campbell SM, et al. Effects of pay-for-performance on the quality of primary care in England. *N Engl J Med*. 2009;361:4.

16. Accessed at: http://www.mass.gov/

17. Adams JL, et al. Physician cost profiling: Reliability and risk of misclassification. *N Engl J Med*. 2010;362:11.

18. Accessed at: http://www.massmed.org/AM/Template.cfm?Section=Home6&TEMPLATE=/CM/ContentDisplay.cfm&CONTENTID=33038

19. 2010 PQRI Measures List. Accessed at: http://www.cms.hhs.gov/PQRI/15_MeasuresCodes.asp#TopOfPage

20. Accessed at: http://www.ssa.gov/OACT/TRSUM/index.html

21. Berwick DM. Measuring physician's quality and performance: Adrift on Lake Wobegon. *JAMA*. 2009;302(22):2485–6.

24

ACR Appropriateness Criteria

MICHAEL A. BETTMANN

Imaging is increasingly complex, as well as increasingly central to modern medical care. It is also an increasingly important component of the cost of medical care, with the growth in the cost of medical imaging outpacing the growth of the rest of health care over the last decade. Further, it is essentially universally accepted that a considerable percentage of all imaging performed is not appropriate to the clinical situation. This chapter focuses on the reasons why clinical imaging guidelines are important, reasons for inappropriate imaging and associated barriers to the use of clinical imaging guidelines, and finally, on the American College of Radiology (ACR) Appropriateness Criteria° as clinical imaging guidelines, with a discussion of their methodology and their utilization.

WHY ARE CLINICAL IMAGING GUIDELINES NECESSARY?

All decisions in health care require a consideration, either implicitly or explicitly, of the risk–benefit ratio of that approach, whether it be a laboratory test, an imaging study, or the use of a drug or a procedure. The benefits of imaging are clearly related to the information that confirms, excludes, or helps to delineate pathology. Although it is hard to overstate the worldwide importance of imaging in modern medical care, as with all aspects of medical care, there are concerns associated with its use. First, imaging is not always accurate; false positives and false negatives both occur. Additionally, unexpected incidental findings are increasingly

common as the sensitivity of imaging has increased. Some may lead to complex and expensive further work-up, without real gain. The likelihood of significant incidental findings, and of their positive or negative implications, cannot be defined before the study is performed. There are implications for patient health and longevity, anxiety, risk from further investigations or interventions, and cost. It has also become common to rely on imaging to the exclusion of other means of evaluation, including physical diagnosis. Further, costs clearly are associated with imaging. Although it is often difficult to define costs precisely, the equipment used in imaging, particularly high-technology imaging such as computed tomography (CT), magnetic resonance (MR), and positron emission tomography (PET), is substantial. Although equipment costs are widely recognized, there is an understandable and probably universal interest in having the best quality equipment available whenever possible. When equipment is available, there is clearly impetus to use it, even in situations in which there may be marginal likelihood of direct benefit. For all these reasons, there has been a disparate growth in the expenditures on imaging over the last two decades, as a function of total health care dollars.

Finally, there are concerns regarding the direct risks of imaging itself. These include reactions to contrast agents and, more significantly, radiation exposure. Although contrast agents are among the safest of all medications, reactions are associated with them. Most are not clinically significant, but rare severe reactions and even fatalities do occur, and such adverse events must figure into any risk–benefit balance.[1] Similarly, risks are associated with MRI. Again, these are small and include the direct risks in certain patients, such as those with pacemakers or aneurysm clips, as well as risks of accidents associated with the magnet itself. Overall, a far greater concern is radiation exposure.[2,3] On the one hand, the direct association between radiation and adverse effects is not at all clear. It is incontrovertible that, at very high doses, radiation has significant ill effects. These include alopecia and skin burns at high focal doses, as occurs, albeit infrequently, with certain interventional procedures. Of greater concern, and more difficult to quantitate, is the risk of carcinogenesis. Direct evidence for this derives primarily from studies of survivors of atom bomb exposure during World War II. The direct effects of diagnostic-level radiation, either in single doses in the unusual high-dose studies, or cumulatively with multiple diagnostic studies, is unknown. It is reasonable to assume that there is no direct benefit to diagnostic radiation, and that risk increases in some relationship with increasing dose. The specific relationship between diagnostic-level doses and long-term adverse sequelae, however, remains unknown in the face of so many relevant variables. What is clear is that there is widespread concern, within the medical profession as well as among the public, about the possible ill effects of radiation.[4] This concern must be taken into account whenever the use of ionizing radiation is considered. It has been made more immediate by unintended overexposure over the last few years, specifically in CT brain perfusion studies. This must be put in the perspective of the dramatic increase in the use of high-technology imaging, primarily CT and nuclear medicine studies, over the last several decades. According to the National Council on Radiation Protection and Measurements (NCRP), in the 1980s, medical radiation accounted for 15% of the radiation exposure to the general public, with most of the remainder coming from background sources. By 2006, although the amount of background exposure had stayed constant, medical exposure now accounted for 48% of overall exposure (Figure 24.1). Largely because of this, the average dose per individual had risen from 3.6 to 6.2 mSv per year.[5]

WHAT ARE OBSTACLES TO THE APPROPRIATE USE OF IMAGING AND OF CLINICAL IMAGING GUIDELINES?

As helpful as diagnostic imaging is, it is also important, for cost and public health reasons, that it be used appropriately. That is, imaging should be used only when a clear potential benefit outweighs any personal or societal risks. It is interesting that it is widely accepted that imaging is overused, and that this is thought to occur 20%–50% of the time. This observation applies not only to the United States,

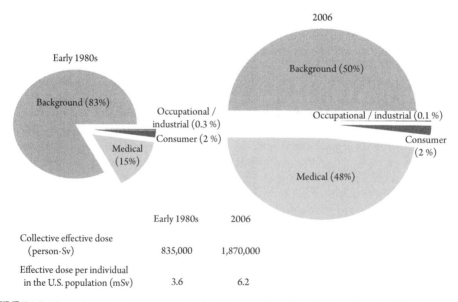

FIGURE 24.1 Change in population exposure to ionizing radiation from the 1980s to 2006. From NCRP Report No. 160, Ionizing Radiation Exposure of the Population of the United States. Reprinted with permission of the National Council on Radiation Protection and Measurements, http://NCRPpublications.org.

but has been accepted worldwide. It is reasonable, then, to suggest that the use of imaging should be based on clinical decision support tools that will help to decrease (although they can almost certainly not eliminate) the inappropriate use of imaging— whether overuse, underuse, or an inappropriate choice of an exam to a specific clinical situation. Although it is easy to accept that evidence-based guidelines for the use of imaging are a good idea, as is evidence-based medicine in general, several significant barriers exist to guideline implementation (Table 24.1). Perhaps most importantly, medicine in general is increasingly complex, and the evidence base for the use of imaging is incomplete. There are many clinical situations in which it is simply not known whether any imaging study is likely to be helpful, or whether one particular type is preferable to another (e.g., plain x-ray vs. ultrasound vs. CT). Further, with the increasing complexity of modern health care, individual knowledge and experience are both limited and essential. Individual preference, on the part of either the radiologist or the referring health care provider, may play a large role in the choice of an imaging study. As all health care providers are aware, it is very tempting to practice based on the last case or the last similar experience, whether good or bad. Although this does not mean that, in a given situation that has been dealt with before, a specific imaging study is not appropriate, it similarly does not necessarily guarantee that it is. The use of guidelines, particularly in relatively unusual situations, is likely to provide significant benefit, but this does not eliminate some reluctance to rely on them as opposed to individual experience or preference.

Another major motivator for inappropriate imaging, and a roadblock for the use of clinical imaging guidelines, is patient preference. Many patients believe that an imaging study will provide "the truth" in any given situation, and are disappointed if one is not obtained. This is analogous to a patient wanting an antibiotics prescription for a cold. It is often easier for the busy health care provider to prescribe antibiotics than to explain at length (and often without acceptance) why they are not indicated. Similarly with imaging, although patient preference or desire does not necessarily mean that a specific study will not be helpful, it is relatively unusual when patient desire is the prime motivator that such a study will actually provide important and relevant information. Realistically, it is often easier for a health care provider to recommend an imaging study than to try to argue a patient out of one. Patients are often disconnected from actual costs and even from true utility. Also, in the West, it is common to see young athletes referred for complex imaging exams, creating the impression that such exams are or should be readily available to all at short notice. For example, if a 20-year-old college football player can be taken for an immediate CT scan during a game on a Saturday afternoon, why can't everyone? Another major barrier to appropriate use of imaging is that for reasons of efficiency and ease, particularly in emergency rooms, it may be easier to establish fairly broad screening criteria so that a patient who comes in can first have a CT scan, x-ray, or ultrasound, and then be clinically evaluated.

Fear of litigation is another major reason for inappropriate use of imaging. The reality is that most physicians are sued rarely, if ever, over the course of their careers, and the overwhelming majority of suits that come to trial are settled in favor of defendant physician. This reality, however, does not eliminate the fairly common fear of litigation. This is particularly true in the United States, but also seems to be increasingly true in other developed nations. A study from the Massachusetts Medical Society[6] indicated that concern about litigation affected the decision-making of a majority of the doctors surveyed. Overall, 83% indicated that they practiced defensive medicine, and 28% indicated that fear of litigation affected their treatment of patients "a lot." These physicians not only ordered imaging exams that they did not think were medically necessary, but also ordered laboratory tests, hospital admission, prolongation of admission, and consultation with specialists simply because of fear that they might be sued. This fear, then, is clearly a major consideration in the inappropriate use of imaging. Although malpractice premiums nationwide were thought to cost $26,000,000,000 in 2007,[6] this is only one obvious

---

TABLE 24.1 REASONS FOR INAPPROPRIATE IMAGING

- Patient expectations and demands for imaging
- Concerns of liability exposure if diagnosis is delayed
- Conflict of interest presented by physician ownership of imaging equipment (self-referral)
- Lack of specific guidance from radiologists
- Lack of knowledge by ordering physicians and other providers (increasing number of exams ordered by non-physicians; e.g., "customary practice")

part of the total bill. Total expenditures on defensive medicine have been estimated to add as much as $56,000,000,000 per year, roughly 3%, to the U.S. health care budget.[7] Actual jury awards, settlements, and related expenses are thought to amount to about $10,000,000,000. Litigation reform is likely to help to address this specific cause of over- and inappropriate utilization, but the use of clinical decision support systems, such as imaging guidelines, will also likely be helpful, because reliance on high-quality, widely accepted clinical imaging practice guidelines is a ready defense against accusations of inappropriate care.

Finally, it is important to recognize that financial considerations play a role in the inappropriate use of imaging.[8] It is very difficult to quantitate the extent to which this is true. It is apparent, however, that ownership of an imaging facility, as is common in the United States, or payment that is linked directly to use, can stimulate the use of imaging when it may not be medically necessary. It is obvious that it is not always true that overutilization of imaging is linked to financial gain, but it is impossible to avoid the conclusion that it is a significant factor.

DEVELOPING AND USING CLINICAL IMAGING GUIDELINES

The development and utilization of clinical imaging guidelines can play a major role in optimizing imaging and significantly limiting inappropriate use. Many imaging guidelines have been developed, including ones that are components of focused clinical guidelines as produced by organizations as diverse as the American College of Physicians, the American Academy of Neurology, and the American Heart Association. The American College of Radiology Appropriateness Criteria are currently the most robust, widely used, and widely accepted specific clinical imaging guidelines. Although the principles of guideline writing have been widely debated, there are certain widely accepted methodologic requirements for any clinical decision support guidelines. For the most part, they are based on the methodology developed by the Rand Corporation more than a decade ago and widely discussed and improved since then.[9–12] The first principle is that such clinical guidelines must be based to as great an extent as possible on high-quality, peer-reviewed evidence.

Further, the methodology used to develop guidelines must be clearly stated, rigorously followed, and transparent. That is, it must be clear how the evidence to be evaluated (in the form of published peer-reviewed articles) is identified, what the criteria for inclusion or exclusion of articles are, how the articles are rated, how the evidence is synthesized, and then how the synthesized information is utilized to develop recommendations. The review, selection, and evaluation of available evidence is generally the most difficult and time-consuming part of the construction of guidelines. It is a reality, however, that data are essentially never sufficiently complete to allow robust guidelines to be based solely on evidence. A need always exists for the evidence to be supplemented by expert opinion. The extent to which expert opinion is used should first be minimized and then should be explicitly and transparently defined. To some extent, this can be accomplished by using a standardized format for rating the strength of evidence on which conclusions and recommendations are based.[12,13]

Next, the topic must be very clearly defined. This is not a simple task, as it requires an understanding of what questions need to be answered and why. Among the important considerations are prevalence of a disease, impact on morbidity and mortality of target populations, treatment and diagnostic options, potential for improved care, and economic impact of the condition. For imaging guidelines, it is also important to determine whether imaging is actually relevant in a particular setting. This is not to say that imaging must be used in order to develop guidelines, but rather that it must be clear that it is relevant to ask whether or not to use imaging, and/ or whether one imaging modality or study is better.

There has been much discussion about the constitution of groups that write guidelines.[10–13] It is generally accepted that the group must be both diverse and knowledgeable. To this end, it is often suggested that specific experts, nonexpert health care practitioners, methodologists, and even patients should be included. The actual constitution of the group must take into account not only this theoretical ideal, but also practical concerns such as interest of prospective panelists, their willingness to commit time and energy to the process, and sufficient knowledge base and expertise to allow them to be able to judge proposed guidelines. Another major consideration is the need for clarity and rigor in decision-making. The modified Delphi formula is usually followed. Using this formula, the group involved in constructing a guideline is asked to vote on specific questions. The vote is followed by discussion and then revoting is held as necessary to achieve consensus. The definition of what constitutes consensus must also be clear and consistent. Usually, agreement of 80% of the group within three voting rounds is accepted. It is unrealistic to expect or require unanimity.

It is also important that guidelines be as current as possible. Particularly in imaging, with the very rapid technological advances that occur, guidelines that are more than 2 or 3 years old may well not reflect current knowledge, and their validity and utility are, therefore, limited. Finally, clear definition of any conflicts of interest and collaborations with industry that exist among the authors must be not only indicated but available to all who review the guidelines. It is not sufficient to say that no conflict exists. The parameters for determining when a conflict exists, in terms of monetary relationships and other involvement, must be stated clearly, and the criteria that would disqualify individuals from participation in construction of a guideline must be both publically available and rigorously followed.

Although no guidelines are perfect, the ACR Appropriateness Criteria (available at www.acr. org/ac) are robust, well-established clinical imaging guidelines. There are currently approximately 180 topics with a total of over 800 variants included in the Appropriateness Criteria, constructed by 20 specific panels. Eleven of these are diagnostic, including panels such as pediatrics, musculoskeletal, and cardiac. A separate panel on interventional radiology exists. There are also eight panels, with a slightly different focus but common methodology, that deal with radiation oncology. Each panel consists of 10–18 members, and each has a chair and vice chair, with a 2-year term of service with the option of renewal for a second term. The chair and vice chair are recognized experts in the field. Each panel is diverse; each includes members in private practice, as well as in academics, with expertise in specific imaging modalities and with geographic diversity. Further, each panel includes two or more members who are not imagers. For example, orthopedic surgeons sit on the musculoskeletal panel, neurosurgeons on neurologic panels, and cardiologists and vascular surgeons on the vascular panel. Each panel begins by choosing a topic. The topic is chosen, as suggested above, by addressing factors such as incidence, frequency of consideration of imaging, socioeconomic importance, medical impact, and the availability of high-quality information. If no studies are available on a particular topic, the topic is not suitable for development as an appropriateness criterion. After the topic is defined by the panel, a methodologist conducts a literature review focusing on citations in major databases (e.g., PubMed). A panelist is chosen as first author, and this panelist then reviews the selected literature for inclusiveness and relevance. The author determines which citations should be included. Each potential citation is then rated on a defined scale as to type of article (e.g., case report, review, single-center experience, case-controlled study, prospective randomized trial) and strength of conclusions. A brief summary of the conclusions is prepared. All of this information forms an Evidence Table that then becomes

TABLE 24.2   CATEGORY NAME AND DEFINITION

Diagnostic Procedures		
Rating	Category Name	Category Definition
7, 8, or 9	Usually appropriate	The study or procedure is indicated in certain clinical settings at a favorable risk–benefit ratio for patients, as supported by published peer-reviewed scientific studies, supplemented by expert opinion
4, 5, or 6	May be appropriate	The study or procedure may be indicated in certain clinical settings, or the risk–benefit ratio for patients may be equivocal as shown in published peer-reviewed, scientific studies supplemented by expert opinion
1, 2, or 3	Usually not appropriate	Under most circumstances, the study or procedure is unlikely to be indicated in these specific clinical settings, or the risk–benefit ratio for patients is likely to be unfavorable, as shown in published peer-reviewed, scientific studies supplemented by expert opinion
Unrated	No Consensus	Either high-quality, relevant clinical studies are not available or are inconclusive, or expert consensus could not be reached regarding the use of this study/procedure for this clinical scenario

December 26, 2010.

TABLE 24.3   APPROPRIATENESS CRITERIA: LOW BACK PAIN

Variant 1: Uncomplicated. No red flags. (Red flags defined in text.)

Variant 2: Low-velocity trauma, osteoporosis, and/or age >70

Variant 3: Suspicion of cancer, infection, or immunosuppression

Variant 4: Radiculopathy

Variant 5: Prior lumbar surgery

Variant 6: Cauda equina syndrome

the basis of both a narrative and of the panel review and decision-making. The unfortunate reality is that true prospective randomized controlled trials of imaging are relatively infrequent in medical literature, so there is a need to rely on additional studies and, as noted, expert opinion.

The author constructs a narrative, describing the clinical scenario and then evaluating each of the relevant imaging modalities based on the available, cited literature. Then, the author creates a draft table containing each relevant imaging modality, with an Appropriateness Criteria table for each relevant variant. For example, in the specific clinical topic of low back pain, there are six variants, ranging from uncomplicated back pain with no risk factors, to back pain after surgery in patient with known metastatic process (Table 24.2). The evidence table, narrative, and draft appropriateness criterion table(s) are then circulated to the panel chair, vice chair, and panel members for review and comment. After revision by the author, they are then distributed for voting. There are three voting rounds. Each panelist is required to vote on a scale of 1–9, with 1 being the least appropriate and 9 the most appropriate, for each imaging modality and each variant table

(Table 24.3). Consensus is defined as 80% agreement among panelists within one or two numbers. If agreement is not reached on the first round, a second round is held, with circulation of comments from the panel members. If necessary to achieve consensus, a conference call is then held followed by a third voting round. After the third round, the topic is considered finalized. Panelists are reminded that each vote should be on the basis of published, high-quality evidence to as great an extent as possible. A sample Appropriateness Criteria table is shown in Table 24.4. It includes the clinical topic, in this case "headache," the specific variant ("suspected complication of sinusitis or mastoiditis"), the relevant imaging modalities, and then the consensus rating, with comments as needed. Also included is a relative radiation level (RRL), compiled by a committee of physicists and clinical radiologists. As with the Appropriateness Criteria overall, the RRL are based on available literature, and indicate the relative radiation exposure of each exam.

On occasion, it may not be possible to reach consensus, for one of two reasons. First, it may become apparent that insufficient evidence exists to allow a clear conclusion. Alternatively, there may be disagreement among panelists in the interpretation of the evidence, with the result that consensus cannot be reached. In either case, lack of consensus is noted in the appropriateness criterion table. By definition, to aid in clinical utility, a rating of 1, 2, or 3 is considered "not usually appropriate." A rating of 4, 5, or 6 is considered "may be appropriate." A rating of 7, 8, or 9 is defined as "usually appropriate" (Table 24.2). The graduated scale and the phraseology are necessary, given the available information and the large number of variables that may exist, including considerations such as availability of expertise or of

TABLE 24.4   SAMPLE VARIANT TABLE

Clinical condition: Headache

Variant 5: Headache, suspected intracranial complication of sinusitis and/or mastoiditis (see the ACR Appropriateness Criteria® on "Sinonasal Disease")

Radiologic Procedure	Rating	Comments	RRL*
MRI head without contrast	8	See statement regarding contrast in text under "Anticipated Exceptions"	O
CT head without contrast	7	Sinus imaging may also be indicated	☢☢☢
MRI head without contrast	7		None
CT head without and with contrast	6	Sinus imaging may also be indicated	O

Rating Scale: 1, 2, 3 usually not appropriate; 7, 8, 9 usually appropriate.

* Relative Radiation Level.

particular technologies. For example, if MR is considered "usually appropriate" for a specific clinical setting, but an MR unit is not available, then an alternative exam, such as CT may in that particular setting be more appropriate. Finally, each topic is reviewed and revised as necessary every 2 years. It is important to point out that the ACR Appropriateness Criteria are in fact clinical imaging guidelines. The ACR has a separate series of guidelines and standards that are intended to guide how an imaging study is actually done, rather than as a guide to which study is appropriate in a given clinical setting. For example, the ACR Guidelines for mammography indicate how a mammogram should be performed, as well as the format for the readings and requirements for correlations and review. The ACR Breast Imaging Appropriateness Criteria address, instead, which specific study should be utilized for further evaluation of a palpable mass, a known tumor, or a specific calcification pattern (Table 24.5). Basically, the entry question for the ACR Appropriateness Criteria is "I'm considering an imaging study in this clinical setting. Which, if any, imaging study should I order?"

CONCLUSION

The ACR Appropriateness Criteria have been used for two main purposes. First, they are useful for educational purposes, for medical students, radiology residents, and others.[14,15] Second, they have been used as decision support tools, both formally and informally.[16,17] They are available to anyone at no cost on the ACR website (www.acr.org/ac). They are searchable by panel (that is by organ system), by topic, and by imaging modality. The format, with the appropriateness criterion table, allows easy use in any common clinical situations. A database version is also available for smart phones and related devices, in a database format, for a nominal fee. The appropriateness criteria have also been used as the basis for clinical decision support systems by several different institutions and vendors.[16,17] To ensure appropriate use of imaging in the future, it is important that the ACR Appropriateness Criteria, or other robust clinical imaging guidelines, be disseminated and used, optimally as part of a clinical decision support system, in a computerized physician order entry system. Currently, no others are as methodologically strong or as broad. When this broad use occurs, it will facilitate more effective utilization of imaging, in this era of increased attention to both evidence-based medicine and fiscal responsibility.

REFERENCES

1. Bettmann MA, Heeren T, Greenfield A, Goudy C. Adverse events with radiographic contrast agents: Results of the SCVIR registry. Radiology. 1997;203:611–20.
2. Shuryak I, Sachs RK, Brenner DJ. Cancer risks after radiation exposure in middle age. *J Natl Cancer Inst.* 2010 Nov 3;102(21):1628–36.
3. Accessed at: http://www.nlm.nih.gov/medlineplus/radiationexposure.html
4. Fazel R, Krumholz HM, Wang Y, Ross JS, Chen J, Ting HH, et al. Exposure to low-dose ionizing radiation from medical imaging procedures. *N Engl J Med.* 2009;361:849–57.
5. Schauer DA, Linton OW. NCRP Report No. 160, Ionizing Radiation Exposure of the Population of the United States, medical exposure—are we doing less with more, and is there a role for health physicists? *Health Phys.* 2009;97(1):1–5. doi: 10.1097/01.HP.0000356672.44380.b7
6. MMS. First-of-its-kind survey of physicians shows extent and cost of the practice of defensive medicine and its multiple effects of health care on the state. Accessed at: http://www.massmed.org/AM/Template.cfm?Section=Advocacy_and_Policy&TEMPLATE=/CM/ContentDisplay.cfm&CONTENTID=23559.
7. Mello MM, Chandra A, Gawande AA, Studdert D. National costs of the medical liability system. *Health Affairs.* September 2010;29(9):1569–77.
8. Casalino LP. Physician self-referral and physician-owned specialty facilities. Research Synthesis Report No. 15. Princeton, NJ: Robert Wood Johnson Foundation, June 2008.
9. Mitchell JM. The prevalence of physician self-referral arrangements after Stark II: Evidence from advanced diagnostic imaging. *Health Affairs.* May/June 2007;26(3): w415–24. Published online only: doi: 10.1377/hlthaff.26.3.w415.
10. Brook RH. The RAND/UCLA appropriateness method. In: McCormick KA, Moore SR, Siegel RA, eds. *Methodology perspectives.* AHCPR Pub. NO. 95-0009. Rockville, MD: Public Health Service, U.S. Department of Health and Human Services,1994:59–70.

11. Hussain T, Michel G, Shiffman RN. The Yale Guideline Recommendation Corpus: A representative sample of the knowledge content of guidelines. *Int J Med Inform.* 2009;78(5):354–63.

12. Rosenfeld RM, Shiffman RN. Clinical practice guideline development manual: A quality-driven approach for translating evidence into action. *Otolaryngol Head Neck Surg.* 2009;140(6 Suppl):S1–S43.

13. Smith FG, Tong JL, Smith JE. Evidence-based medicine. *Contin Educ Anaesth, Crit Care Pain.* 2006;6(4):148–51.

14. Dillon JE, Slanetz PJ. Teaching evidence-based imaging in the radiology clerkship using the ACR Appropriateness Criteria. *Acad Radiol.* 2010;17:912–6.

15. Levy G, Blachar A, Goldstein L, Pas I, Sharon Olsh S, Atar E, et al. Nonradiologist utilization of American College of Radiology Appropriateness Criteria in a preauthorization center for MRI requests: Applicability and effects *AJR.* 2006;187:855–8.

16. Sistrom CL, Dang PA, Weilburg JB, Dreyer KJ, Rosenthal DI, Thrall JH. Effect of computerized order entry with integrated decision support on the growth of outpatient procedure volumes: Seven-year time series analysis. *Radiology.* 2009;251(1):147–55.

17. Vartanians VM, Sistrom CL, Weilburg JB, Rosenthal DI, Thrall JH. Increasing the appropriateness of outpatient imaging: Effects of a barrier to ordering low-yield examinations. *Radiology.* 2010;255(3):842–9.

III

Educational and Special Concepts in Radiology Quality & Safety

25

Teaching Quality and Safety to Radiology Residents and Fellows

MICHAEL A. BRUNO AND DONALD J. FLEMMING

One of the characteristic features that defines a field of endeavor as a "profession," as opposed to a population of skilled workers, is an imperative that members transmit an essential core body of knowledge, priorities, and skills to those who wish to enter the profession. This knowledge transfer has several functions for a profession: it is needed to enable the trainees to ultimately function as members of the profession, it helps to bind the entering members to the group, and it is essential to maintain the continued existence of the profession itself. By this criterion, radiology may be deemed a distinct "profession" within the larger medical profession, as can any working group that maintains its own teaching academies or programs, including such things as law, music, nursing, teaching, and engineering.

Like all medical specialties, the sole vehicle of entry into the profession of diagnostic radiology is through a residency program, which involves experienced radiologists imparting, through mentorship, didactics, and supervised work experience, a sufficient amount of radiologic knowledge and skill to the trainees over a 4-year period, so that they may ultimately practice radiology independently at a basic level of competence. In a majority of cases, the basic residency training and experience is supplemented by an additional dedicated year or two of subspecialty training fellowship.

As faculty members in an academic medical center, we have become very comfortable teaching radiology residents how to interpret radiographic findings, synthesize the findings into a reasonable differential diagnosis, and consult with clinicians in directing the care of patients. This makes sense as the primary goals of residency education. Many faculty members are significantly less comfortable, however, in teaching residents and fellows nonclinical skills, especially those that fall under the Accreditation Council on Graduate Medical Education (ACGME) category of "systems-based practice." This is one of the six "core competencies" that residency programs are required to teach our trainees. Those of us involved in resident education are also charged to objectively assess competence in these core areas, in order to determine that a resident is ready to be released from training and can enter the certification process.

Much of what is involved under the general category of systems-based practice involves the basic topics of quality assessment and process improvement as applied to radiology. Central to these is the concept that many important sources of clinical error that can harm patients are actually caused by (or are, at the very least, latent within) the systems in which we work. In fact, it is a national expectation that graduate medical education in radiology, as in other fields, will include teaching residents these concepts and helping them to develop the skills they will need to perform the essential tasks of ongoing practice quality improvement (or PQI) in their future professional lives.

Most radiologists-in-training are by now familiar with the term "PQI" because of the requirements imposed by the ACGME and the American Board of Radiology, both physician-driven organizations that govern their training and certification, allowing them to formally enter the profession and both establish and maintain their standing as members of the profession. In fact, the radiology RRC places such importance on this topic that all radiology residents are now required to satisfactorily complete a systems-based practice (SBP) project in order to graduate. This requirement has only been in effect since 2008, but has already caused great anxiety for residents and faculty alike, since most do not feel that they are well-prepared to address this requirement. The new requirements for SBP experience during residency foreshadow the PQI requirements that radiologists will face after each 10 years of practice under the American Board of Radiology's maintenance of certification (MOC) process. Taken together, these external pressures (new RRC requirements and the Board's MOC process) are accelerating a realignment of the training priorities for residents and fellows in radiology to emphasize quality and safety (Q&S) concepts and PQI methods. This, of course, is causing significant anxiety among both groups—the trainers as much as their trainees.

Medical school is a highly standardized basic experience, and does a very good job at providing new physicians with the basic knowledge of disease and health, medical thinking and jargon, and an orientation to the systems that provide the structure of medical practice. Some medical schools even do a passable job at teaching basic quantitative analysis, rudimentary statistical reasoning, and the like. None truly attempts to tackle the topic of PQI, which is left for the graduate medical education process, arguably where it belongs, since the issues of practice quality are relatively specific to each specialty. But, for those of us who teach residents and fellows, this means that we must typically start "from scratch," often being the first to broach the subjects, topics, and concepts underlying PQI with our trainees. In doing so, we must first overcome the barrier of the trainees' having a not inconsiderable amount of skepticism and even cynicism—in essence "if-this-is-so-important-then-why-haven't-I-heard-of-it-before?"

Many senior faculty members express similar feelings. To successfully teach Q&S concepts and skills, we as a faculty must suspend any disbelief and skepticism of our own, and find for ourselves the value of this relatively young area of professional effort in radiology.

THE PENN STATE HERSHEY MEDICAL CENTER EXPERIENCE

In our respective roles as Director of Quality and Safety (MAB) and Vice Chair for Education/Residency Program Director (DJF), the teaching of Q&S topics to our residents has become a high priority for both of us, and is perhaps the most significant way in which our departmental roles overlap. When we first began thinking about how to approach this task together, and began planning our educational strategy back in the early months of 2006, we quickly realized we were navigating uncharted waters. Needless to say, not everything we thought of or tried since that time has worked out well, and it is also a fair assessment to say that we both had underestimated the difficulty of preparing and delivering such an unaccustomed curriculum to our residents. Our "target audience" proved at once receptive toward, and also skeptical of, our message. We had to first somehow convince them to suspend their disbelief and approach this novel topic with open minds. We are quite convinced that this was only possible because we had previously established a learner–teacher "alliance," a sense of trust, rapport, and a level of mentorship in the daily education and work environment. An outside "guest" speaker or nonclinical quality consultant would not likely have the same impact. Our first conclusion from this exercise is that the faculty who teach Q&S must have "street credibility" with the audience as teachers and practitioners of radiology for the message to be accepted. The second lesson that we learned in the beginning of this process was that the preacher must also be a "true believer" in the basic doctrines; for example, the idea that quantitative analysis and measurable indices of performance can truly lead to better outcomes in practice.

One of the most difficult concepts to convey to residents is the central, essential and inescapable imperative of cultural change. In the Q&S field, many recognized "Quality Gurus" are fond of saying "culture eats [you name it] for lunch," a group mantra that serves to refocus priorities, akin to the real-estate industry's familiar incantation of "location location *location*." The creation of a passable "culture of safety" at our own institution was years in the making, and our residents and fellows were among the earliest adopters of the sort of mindfulness of safety and quality that is needed. A cynical person might conclude that this was because they had fewer ingrained bad habits to unlearn; however, we feel that it is more likely that residents as a group are unusually motivated to seek solutions to problems. They are the "first responders" at the scene of most problems as they occur, and frequently have dealt with issues definitively before faculty are even aware of them.

In our estimation, the single most important factor for success in developing and delivering an effective quality curriculum to residents and fellows is having committed departmental leadership. We were blessed with a department chairperson who embraced the imperative of quality and safety long before it was fashionable to do so, and it was our chairperson who championed the cause in our department, including early involvement of our trainees at every level in the process. Her sincerity and enthusiasm made our success at developing a comprehensive educational program in Q&S almost inevitable. Conversely, without the strong support of the departmental chair and institutional leadership, the required cultural changes for a successful Q&S program would most likely be impossible to achieve—and without the underlying cultural paradigm in place, trying to teach this material to residents would almost certainly be a futile exercise.

In developing our quality curriculum, we have relied less on the traditional didactic education model (i.e., in which the faculty are in the role of the "sage-on-the-stage") and more on a project-based "hands-on" approach (i.e., in which the faculty serve as the "guide-on-the-side"), which seems to bring about more lasting learning for our adult-learner population, as well as a deeper appreciation of the procedures involved in PQI. One of us (MAB) nonetheless provides lectures on the basics of Q&S each year to the residents for about 2 hours, and we include at least one visiting professor per year on these topics. There are some assigned readings and, occasionally, current articles from radiology journals (especially the *JACR*) are circulated for the residents and fellows to read. The visiting professors are chosen to reinforce key aspects of the didactic core, such as radiation safety and utilization control, practice quality assessment, and so forth. The bulk of our Q&S teaching lies in the process of residents developing their own PQI projects and initiatives, largely of their own design, and under one-on-one faculty supervision and guidance.

A majority of faculty members have made themselves available to serve as mentors to our residents in this endeavor, although the two of us are tapped more frequently for this than are most other faculty members. Considering all of the demands on our faculty member's time and effort, it came as somewhat of a pleasant surprise to us that an overwhelming majority of our faculty members are quite enthusiastic about participating in this work. It is a testimony to the professionalism of our faculty that Q&S efforts are viewed as being highly meaningful activities that add significant value to our practice. Faculty participation is encouraged by small cash incentives—paid to faculty members who are the primary supervisors of resident-completed PQI projects. Furthermore, faculty members who are enrolled in the ABR MOC process can meet their own PQI requirements through mentoring a resident through a substantive project.

In these ways, we find that we have been able to develop an approach to teaching Q&S concepts that mimics very closely the method we use to teach clinical radiology, with a split of approximately 10% didactics and prescribed readings and 90% supervised "practice" of the subject matter. We feel that this leverages the synergistic learning boost that can only be obtained from the firsthand experience of trial and error, and in that order!

A RESIDENT PQI PROJECT "CLEARING HOUSE"

Early in this process, we realized that better organization and proactive planning on our part was going be needed to deal with the burgeoning demand for resident PQI projects, both to streamline the residents' and faculty members' experience and also to assure that the projects chosen were helpful to the department's and the overall institution's Q&S goals. Two years ago, our department's Quality & Safety Committee, a 28-member body composed of faculty physicians and senior (lead) technologists, nursing leaders, operations managers, and administrative personnel—as well as two radiology residents—spawned a subcommittee for education that was charged initially with developing a "menu" of preapproved PQI projects to help guide residents in their own project development. Our PQI project menu currently includes more than a dozen items, mostly preidentified quality problems or issues taken from across our entire organization, which our sub-committee members feel would be of value for resident projects to address. The menu offerings are developed with varying degrees of specificity and guidance for the residents, and are focused within every subspecialty in the department. They are designed to appeal to the full range of potential resident interest. Some are extremely ambitious and relatively labor-intensive, and these are designated as being "group projects," ideal for a small group of three or four residents to tackle together. Others are completed more easily by one person over a period of just a few weeks. We also encourage residents to develop their own individualized projects, with faculty guidance, but these must be approved before work is started. The two of us also evaluate each project at its completion, to verify that the work has been done properly and the lesson(s) of the data are indeed learned and shared appropriately with those in the department who can make use of the results to improve patient care. When appropriate, we also strongly encourage our residents to submit abstracts of their work to local and national meetings. Many of our residents have presented PQI abstracts in various venues such as the Hershey Medical Center Resident Research Day, the Pennsylvania Radiological Society Annual Meeting, the Association of University Radiologists (AUR), the Radiological Association of North America (RSNA), and the American Roentgen Ray Society (ARRS) Annual Meetings. When the project has sufficient merit, we also strongly encourage our residents to pursue publication of their projects in peer-reviewed radiology journals.

CONCLUSION

Some Final Thoughts and Future Directions

In summary, with approximately 6 years' experience in teaching Q&S to residents "under our belts," we are only just beginning to believe that we are close to having the sort of Q&S educational program that we had hoped to achieve here at the Penn State Hershey Medical Center—one in which graduating residents understand the concepts and have developed the skills needed to competently conduct PQI efforts in the future. More importantly, we seek to develop residency graduates who have come to believe in and embrace the core cultural beliefs and ingrained patterns of behavior that will make them effective at PQI throughout their radiological careers. We like to think that our residents find their PQI experiences to be enriching rather than drudgery, and not as merely another "unfunded mandate," needlessly consuming precious time and energy that would be better spent on their clinical studies.

Again, we believe the sort of "cultural learning" that we want our residents to achieve is best imparted through direct mentorship and faculty leadership. We believe leadership by example is the single most important aspect of our Q&S teaching program. We feel gratified that such cultural learning is evident in the types of (relatively ambitious) projects that our residents choose and in seeing how they throw themselves into this work with care and enthusiasm. The results they achieve from their PQI projects are equally gratifying for the trainee and mentor, and are absolutely essential for the growth and development of the residency and radiology department. Based on this, we feel that we have achieved a measure of success in our Q&S teaching program so far. But our work in this area must still be considered a work in progress, and perhaps always will be. Our next challenge will be to develop better tools to assess the resident's grasp of the material and also, importantly, for us to provide a deeper level of feedback to our trainees in Q&S, as we do for all other aspects of our residency training program. Also, and importantly, most of our Q&S training efforts have been directed toward residents in radiology, and these need to be expanded to include our subspecialty fellows as well.

There is still very clearly a need for us to provide more and better instruction to the faculty, so that they can perform better in their role as faculty mentors for resident PQI efforts. We have presented lecture-type material at faculty meetings and also at faculty workshops, but there may be some advantage to be gained by more intensively developing a small cadre of "faculty subject matter experts," to extend our efforts and ultimately serve as mentors to faculty members, especially our junior faculty, in the development of their own skill set and knowledge base in this arena.

To date, none of our recent graduates have had to run the gauntlet of the new MOC process of the ABR, which has a significant PQI component. If we achieve our training goals, our residency/fellowship graduates will think of the PQI process and its underlying conceptual basis in radiology Q&S to be second nature for them—they won't have to struggle to create a PQI project to merely to satisfy the MOC requirement, but rather, hopefully, they'll already be engaged in continuous improvement efforts as part of their overall professional life as radiologists, immersed in a quality culture within their own practices not unlike the proverbial fish swimming in a bowl of water that never pauses to realize that it is wet.

26

Simulation

SHARJEEL H. SABIR AND JEFFREY B. COOPER

uality and safety have come to the fore of national attention since the publication of the Institute of Medicine (IOM) report, *To Err Is Human: Building a Safer Health System*, revealed the heavy price patients have had to pay for major shortcomings in the health care system.[1] Fortunately, the health care industry, beginning with anesthesia, took its lead from other complex, high-risk endeavors like aviation in addressing these shortcomings. Thus, rather than reacting with recrimination and punishment, health care organizations have worked to improve safety by emphasizing human factors and attending to the faulty workflow, organizational, and training systems that lead to errors and adverse events.[2–4] Many of the ways for improving quality and safety are addressed in other chapters in this book. Yet, several critical elements for creating a safe system of care can be addressed by a technological and educational approach that is generally referred to as "simulation." Simulation has long been used in other industries for training and education outside of the production environment for the development of teamwork; the assessment of competencies; the evaluation of new procedures, processes, and technologies; and other uses. In this chapter, we review how simulation is being applied in radiology and how it can be further employed to achieve the fundamental goal of patient safety: so that radiologists can be sure that no patient is harmed during their care.

EDUCATION AND TRAINING IN HEALTH CARE

The traditional method of medical training is an apprenticeship, in which a more experienced practitioner demonstrates the practices of the trade to the trainee. The trainee is then expected to learn these practices by applying them over a traditionally set period of time, with periodic critiques from the experienced practitioner to bring the trainee into line with the experienced practitioner's methods. The success of this process is assessed by testing intermittently during training and also near the completion of training, usually via paper, computer, or oral examination. Although this apprenticeship model has been employed since the time of the ancient Egyptians, the current version of this model was promulgated by Abraham Flexner and William Stuart Halsted in the early 20th century.[5] An integral part of the current approach to clinical training is the use of patients as the primary teaching materials, with trainees given increasing autonomy with concomitantly increasing responsibility over the training period.

Unfortunately, the sole use of this approach is in direct conflict with the central medical ethical principle of *nonmaleficence*. The principle of nonmaleficence is more than the classic dictum, "Primum non nocere" ("First, do no harm"). Health care professionals also have an obligation to *beneficence*, namely providing safe and effective care.[6] They can only do that if they are adequately trained. Yet, health care trainees cannot learn the complexity of caring for patients without actually providing care during their training. Thus, the need to protect patients from harm must be tempered with the need to train competent health care professionals who will be able to provide safe and effective care for their future patients. This conflict between the principles of nonmaleficence and beneficence requires us to find ways to limit the harm to patients while training health care professionals to perform competently. One of the ways to deal with this conflict is to use alternate training methods during the early phase of training, methods that limit the potential harm an unskilled trainee may do to a patient.

Even after this initial phase of training, sole reliance on the apprenticeship model may not be enough to produce truly competent health care workers. Ericsson, who has done extensive work on the nature of expertise and how it is obtained, has stated that, "superior performance does not automatically develop from extensive experience, general education, and domain related knowledge."[7] When applied to medicine, this statement can be interpreted to mean that the traditional apprenticeship model of health care training may not be enough when relied upon exclusively to produce the level of expertise expected from competent health care workers. Rather, "superior performance requires the acquisition of complex integrated systems of representations for the execution, monitoring, planning, and analyses of performance."[7] These "complex integrated systems of representations" that form the basis for superior performance are the fruits of deliberate practice, which will be discussed further in the next section.

These shortcomings of the traditional apprenticeship model necessitate that supplements to the traditional model of training must be found that avoid conflict with the principle of nonmaleficence and also adhere to the guidelines of deliberate practice. Other potentially hazardous and complex industries, such as aviation, nuclear power, and the military, have addressed this issue with the use of simulation during training.[8] Medicine has begun to embrace this philosophy.

SIMULATION AS MEDICAL PRACTICE

Simulation has been defined as "a technique, not a technology, to replace or amplify real experiences with guided experiences, often immersive in nature, that evoke or replicate substantial aspects of the real world in a fully interactive fashion."[9] But this technique must be used in accordance with the guidelines of deliberate practice, so that the trainee can develop those complex integrated systems of representations that form the basis for superior performance.

Ericsson describes four aspects of deliberate practice (Table 26.1). First, a training task must have clearly delineated goals. Second, the trainee must have a motivation to improve his or her performance. Third, the trainee must be provided with a critique of his or her performance. Finally, the trainee must be given the chance to repeat the training task and gradually refine his or her performance.[7] The importance of these four elements in promoting learning was also emphasized by Issenberg and colleagues in their review of the available evidence on aspects of simulation that lead to effective learning.[10]

With simulation, the trainee can make errors and learn from those errors without harmful consequences to any patients. Therefore, instead of the typical trainee response to medical errors of denial, mitigating responsibility, and/or distancing from the consequences,[11] the simulated environment allows errors to occur and be openly analyzed to enable behavior modification. Learning from errors is an essential part of enhancing expertise and helps redirect behavior in the future.[12–13]

The second aspect of deliberate practice—a trainee's motivation to improve his or her performance—cannot be affected directly by simulation. But, simulation may provide a palpable reminder of the potential consequences of medical errors, thereby motivating the trainee to acquire the skills and knowledge required to avoid such errors. Since most people involved in the health care field are motivated by a desire to improve the lives of others, having a simulated patient be harmed or even die because of their actions would be a strong motivator to alter the errors in practice and fill in the lacunae in knowledge that led to that harm. However, this motivation would be fruitless without the implementation of the third aspect of deliberate practice: namely, an assessment and critique of the trainee's performance to point out errors in practice and gaps in knowledge.

Thus, the capacity of simulation-based training to allow more thorough assessment of competence

---

TABLE 26.1   FOUR ELEMENTS OF DELIBERATE PRACTICE

Clearly delineated goals
Motivation to improve performance
Critique of performance
Opportunity to repeat training task and gradually refine performance

From Ericsson KA. Deliberate practice and acquisition of expert performance: A general overview. *Acad Emer Med.* 2008;15:988–94.

with associated critiques of any deficits is a great asset to a medical training program. Oral, paper, or computer-based tests are the traditional means of assessment and criticism. These types of tests focus on assessing cognitive abilities and neglect the broader range of abilities integral to medical practice such as procedural, communication, and teamwork skills. As a result, these essential skills are not given appropriate attention during training. But this neglect must be overcome since shortcomings in these abilities have been shown to be causal factors in poor outcomes.[14–15]

Simulation-based assessment can be used to test much of the range of abilities required for the safe and effective delivery of health care. This is already being done in various specialties, including radiology.[16–21] Further adoption of simulation as an assessment tool will be seen as professional boards begin to include simulation in their certification and recertification procedures.[22–23] By enabling assessment of the whole range of abilities integral to the practice of medicine, rather than to just the cognitive abilities that have traditionally been emphasized, simulation will ensure that these abilities are attended to during training. Simulation will thus become a new tool for reducing errors and making care safer.

Fundamental changes in the way medicine is practiced today compared to how it was practiced during the time of Flexner and Halsted have made it difficult to fulfill the fourth aspect of deliberate practice—the chance to repeat the training task and gradually refine performance. Outpatient care has become emphasized, and the patients who are admitted to the hospital tend to be more ill. Hospital stays have decreased in length. Minimally invasive therapies have become preferred over more invasive options, and the procedures that are performed tend to be more complicated. In addition, significant work hour restrictions for residents have been put into place by the federal government.[24] All of these factors limit the variety of training, as well as the time available for training.[25–27] It is interesting to note that, in certain European countries, it is not uncommon for surgical residents to undertake operative fellowships after residency to acquire adequate experience. Simulation-based training may obviate the need for such drastic measures by providing the trainee experience with a wide variety of clinical and procedural situations, thus ensuring they are prepared for unusual presentations, rare diseases, and crises. In addition, simulation allows trainees to learn and practice at a self-directed pace rather than the often hectic pace dictated by the schedule of daily clinical practice.[28–29]

THE MODES OF SIMULATION

There are numerous methods by which the technique of simulation may be deployed. Some of these methods rely on no technology, while others rely on a simulator of varying levels of sophistication. A simulator (as distinct from "simulation") can be defined as "a *device* that presents a simulated patient (or part of a patient) and interacts appropriately with the actions taken by the simulation participant."[9] Gaba enumerates 11 different "domains" of simulation, describing each as a spectrum of elements that can make up a given simulation event. These include the types of applications (e.g., basic skills training to research in pedagogy), the unit of participation (individuals to entire organizations), and the technologies through which simulation is delivered. He also offered a taxonomy of types of technologies used for health care simulation[9] (Table 26.2). Note that the use of animals for training was not included in this list but may be considered by some as a type of simulator.

The first two methods of simulation need little explanation. Part-task trainers include a wide spectrum of devices for learning specific skills, replicating only a portion of the entire patient care environment. They can be as simple as a piece of cloth used to simulate skin while suturing or more complex devices used for learning laparoscopic surgery skills.[30] Virtual reality (VR) technologies can range from replicating parts of tasks to more immersive techniques to simulate a full experience. Virtual reality is generally interpreted as recreating some aspects of the patient and environment within a computer, without physical representation

---

TABLE 26.2 TYPES OF SIMULATION TECHNOLOGIES

Verbal (e.g., role playing)
Standardized patient actor
Part-task trainer
Virtual reality (ranging from screen-based to immersive with haptics)
Mannequins (alone or in full clinical environment)

From Gaba DM. The future vision of simulation in health care. *Qual Saf Health Care.* 2004;13(Suppl 1):i2–i10.

of a body, as would be done with a mannequin simulator. Virtual reality simulators can range from a screen-based, multimedia program playing various heart sounds to train a novice auscultator to a fully immersive recreation of complex surgical procedures as accessed via goggles displaying a three-dimensional representation of a patient and haptic interface equipment, such as gloves, that provide tactile sensation to the trainee.[30] Finally, the mannequin method of simulation refers to using simulators that physically replicate the whole patient to varying degrees of complexity and representativeness of clinical situations.[30-31]

The usefulness of these various methods of simulation can be validated in several ways[24] (Table 26.3). *Face validity* indicates the level of similarity between the appearance of the simulator and real-life objects, such as parts of the patient or medical implements, being simulated. *Content validity* refers to the extent to which the knowledge that the simulation is attempting to teach or assess is actually taught or assessed. *Concurrent validity* and *discriminant validity* refer to the correlation or distinction, respectively, of the results of simulation compared with other validated measures of assessment or training. Finally, *predictive validity* describes how well the manner in which a trainee performs on the simulator correlates with the way in which the trainee performs in a real clinical scenario.

Simulation has been used in medicine since at least the 16th, century when mannequins were employed in obstetrics training to lessen maternal and infant mortality.[32] Although animal models have been used for training in the past, they are becoming less acceptable because of ethical concerns. Verbal and standardized patient actor methods have not been widely described in the radiology literature. In contrast, the last three methods outlined above hold special interest for training and assessment in radiology. A more complete list of possible uses

of simulation is given in Table 26.4, adapted from Dawson.[24]

For nearly 20 years, non–animal based simulation has come into use in many medical specialties. The technologies and the ways in which they are applied have become increasingly sophisticated. There is now extensive use of simulation for training in clinical/technical skills in essentially every medical procedural specialty, at least for basic skills training.[33] As the technology advances, we can expect to see the uses in training increase throughout the professional life of all clinicians, both for obtaining new skills and for maintaining them, especially those skills that are not used frequently. Simulation is also being more widely applied to teach what are termed "behavioral" skills; that is, to teach professionals to interact better with their colleagues, to act optimally in teams, and also to develop cognitive and decision-making skills more deliberately and effectively.

One of the most common and obvious uses for simulation is for the practice of critical and/or rare events in any health care domain. A large literature describes the uses of various types of simulation, from the lowest to highest fidelity, for teaching and practice of crisis management skills. Gaba and colleagues coined the term *crises resource management* (CRM), based on crew resource management developed in aviation, and applied it first in anesthesia.[34-36] Crises resource management is now widely applied with and without simulation, and has been shown to improve the performance of individuals and teams, although improvement in clinical outcomes has been more challenging to demonstrate.

SIMULATION IN RADIOLOGY

Several forms of simulation are used in radiology for various purposes. Although it may not be thought as being simulation, the case conference educational

TABLE 26.3   WAYS TO ANALYZE THE VALIDITY OF A SIMULATOR

Face validity	Similarity between simulator and real life objects
Construct validity	Ability of simulator to differentiate operators of different levels of expertise
Content validity	Ability of simulator to teach or assess desired knowledge
Concurrent validity	Correlation of results of simulation with other measure of assessment
Discriminant validity	Distinction of results of simulation from other measures of assessment
Predictive validity	Correlation between performance on simulator with performance in real clinical scenarios

From Dawson S. Procedural simulation: A primer. *JVIR.* 2006;17:205–13 and Ahmed K, et al. Role of virtual reality simulation in teaching and assessing technical skills in endovascular intervention. *J Vasc Interv Radiol.* 2010;21:55–66.

TABLE 26.4   POTENTIAL APPLICATIONS
FOR SIMULATION

Testing aptitude
Developing basic skills before patient contact
Developing advanced skills before performing complex
    procedures on patients
Maintaining skills
Training for teamwork
Training for management of critical and/or rare events
Rehearsing procedure before performing it on a patient
Credentialing and certification
Developing new or advanced skills among experienced
    practitioners
Inventing new procedures
Evaluating new technologies or procedures
Conducting research in human performance, pedagogical
    methods, etc.

From Dawson S. Procedural simulation: A primer. *JVIR.*
2006;17:205–13.

format is an amalgam of both a screen-based VR
simulation and verbal simulation. An attending physician presents an image or a series of images from
an actual case, usually one interpreted previously by
the attending. The images are displayed most often
via an electronic projector but occasionally via traditional view boxes. A resident physician is called upon
to discuss the images. After discussing the findings,
the resident physician concludes with either a final
diagnosis or a differential diagnosis for the findings, as well as recommendations for further management. If appropriate, the attending may display
further images from the case, usually demonstrating
the findings via other modalities, which the resident
is expected to discuss in the same manner and use
in narrowing the differential diagnosis. Finally, the
attending critiques the discussion. The process of
analyzing radiologic images, discussing the findings,
and drawing a conclusion about potential diagnoses
nearly exactly replicates the daily work of a diagnostic radiologist. It is thus a form of fairly high-fidelity
simulation and is fairly well representative of actual
clinical work, yet conducted with simple technology. What makes it a simulation is that, although the
images presented are from an actual case, the task of
primary interpretation has already been completed
and the resident's interpretation does not influence
patient management. Thus, this process meets the
definition of simulation, namely, "a technique, not
a technology, to replace or amplify real experiences
with guided experiences, often immersive in nature,
that evoke or replicate substantial aspects of the real

world in a fully interactive fashion."[9] This process
also complies with all four of the requirements for
deliberate practice.

The oral board examination is also a form of
simulation, used for assessment rather than training, although practice for the exam with mock exam
sessions also serves an educational function. (The
oral board examination will soon be replaced by a
computer-based examination.)

In addition to these traditional uses of simulation in radiology, there have been reports of innovative uses of simulation methods in radiology for the
purposes of training and assessment.

Towbin and colleagues[37] created a picture
archiving and communication system (PACS) simulator that allowed the display of the complete set of
images from a case, allowing a trainee to give a list of
findings and differentials with immediate feedback
provided. This feedback consisted of the findings and
differential generated by an expert radiologist for
that case. This article provides an excellent example
of a pure screen-based VR simulator. Unfortunately,
this article merely described the simulator and did
not assess its effectiveness.

Ganguli and colleagues[17-19] used a pure screen-
based VR application for assessment. They created
a month-long emergency radiology curriculum that
they taught via a didactic presentation to all of the
residents in their residency program during a 5-year
period. The material was based on the American
Society of Emergency Radiology (ASER) curriculum, which consists of multiple 45-minute lectures on various topics. The assessment employed a
screen-based VR application to simulate the PACS
system in use at their institution. The exam included
20 cases demonstrating pathologies deemed
essential for a competent radiologist to know. The
residents were presented with these cases via the
simulator and were asked to formulate their findings and impression within a limited time. Each case
included only a limited clinical history, in order to
simulate what the authors considered to be the typical situation encountered in the clinical setting of
emergency radiology. The residents' answers were
scored by a subspecialty radiologist. The study gives
a powerful example of the maturity of simulation as
a means of thorough assessment, since simulation
was the sole means of assessment used to determine
the effectiveness of the didactic curriculum in preparing the residents for overnight calls.

Several mannequin-based and VR systems have
been described that simulate more complex tasks

in radiology, such as the management of a contrast reaction or performance of endovascular diagnosis and therapy.

One of the earliest descriptions of a mannequin-based simulator application for radiology was by Sica and colleagues.[38] One of the early models of mannequin simulators was deployed with a CT-scanner to simulate a clinical emergency in that setting. The mannequin was capable of exhibiting various physiological responses such as pulses, papillary and lid reflexes, temperature probe variations, and heart and breath sounds, as well as voice via a remote actor communicating via a microphone. The mannequin had provisions for simulation of intravenous medication administration. Using resident subjects, several scenarios were conducted involving various contrast reactions and similar emergent situations that can occur during diagnostic CT procedures. The residents were randomized to a control group that performed the scenarios without prior instruction and a test groups that performed the scenarios after watching a video lecture. The scenarios were taped and reviewed by expert physicians. This article provides an excellent example of the use of mannequin based-simulation for assessment of essential skills. Several subsequent papers have used other mannequin-based patient simulators to assess radiology resident preparedness for dealing with contrast reactions in both adults and children.[39-40] These are examples of the common use of simulations for training in a spectrum of clinical emergencies in essentially every health care domain in which such situations are encountered. Simulation is useful in practicing for such relatively rare events and especially in training teamwork.

Although simulation is used in many areas of radiology, it is most likely that new developments in simulation technologies will have the biggest impact in interventional radiology. Several endovascular simulators are available that allow training in catheter and guidewire manipulation, contrast injection, and fluoroscopy[41] (Table 26.5). These simulators tend to use a combination of a complete or partial mannequin form and a screen-based VR application. The technology developed for training for a new percutaneous carotid stent is a good example. The U.S. Food and Drug Administration (FDA) required that the manufacturer devise a safe training method for the procedure. The Center for Medicare and Medicaid Services required that physicians seeking payment for services in placing the device undergo training on the simulator. These actions established a new threshold for training with high-risk new medical technologies, recognizing that patients should not be put at risk during the inevitable learning curve. This has given a strong motivation for the development and use of simulators in interventional radiology.[42] Several studies describing the use of simulation in interventional radiology both for training and assessment are discussed in a review article by Ahmed and colleagues.[43]

One of the earliest descriptions of an endovascular simulator was presented in the cardiology literature. This device, created by Dawson and colleagues, was called the Interventional Cardiology Training System (ICTS), and allowed simulation of right- and left-heart catheterization. Even though this was an early effort, this simulator already included the essential elements of an endovascular simulator. It allowed trainees to manipulate actual catheters and guidewires. These movements, including insertion, withdrawal, and torquing, were sensed by electromechanical sensors located within a haptics device through which the catheters and guidewires were inserted. The system was then able to provide simulated visual feedback similar to what interventionalists see on a fluoroscopy monitor. The system included sophisticated geometric and physical monitoring of the involved anatomy and physiology, as well as advanced modeling of the physics of catheter manipulation. In addition to sophisticated modeling, the simulator included an educational core of standardized patients. Also, the simulator provided several features to augment reality, such as pause and undo, that allowed trainees to both learn from their mistakes and redo the procedure until they did it correctly, essential elements of deliberate practice.[44]

In addition to descriptive articles showing how endovascular simulation may be performed, multiple publications have demonstrated the effectiveness of endovascular simulation as a training method both in the radiology and nonradiology literature.[45-46] Two studies are of special interest because they focused on the benefits of endovascular simulation in novices and in experienced practitioners.

TABLE 26.5   COMMONLY AVAILABLE COMMERCIAL ENDOVASCULAR SIMULATORS

Simulator	Manufacturer
Procedicus VIST	Mentice
Angio Mentor	Simbionix USA Corporation
Simsuite	Medical Simulation Corporation

Coates and colleagues studied both the ability of the simulator to discriminate a novice from an experienced practitioner (construct validity) and the educational effectiveness of the Procedicus Vist simulator, as shown in Figure 26.1. The assessment compared the performance of the study subjects on three basic interventional radiology tasks: flush arteriography, selective renal angiography, and ipsilateral iliac artery angioplasty. The objective outcomes measures used to compare the novice versus the experienced groups were total time to perform the task, fluoroscopy time used for the task, and volume of contrast medium injected during the procedure. The more experienced group performed better than the novice group, with statistically significant differences found for total time of procedure and nearly statistically significant differences found in the other two outcome measures.[47]

Next, Coates and colleagues assessed the content validity of the simulator; namely, the ability of the simulator to teach the desired task. The study was performed with 14 first-year radiology residents without prior interventional radiology experience. After receiving a brief introduction to the simulator, the study subjects performed the three basic interventional radiology tasks used to assess construct validity, which were assessed by the same objective outcome measures. The investigators also measured more subjective outcome variables for this group including the number of major errors made and a subjective overall evaluation of the operator's performance on the three tasks. In addition, the study

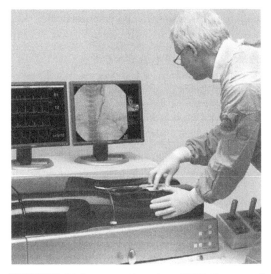

FIGURE 26.1 Mentice Procedicus VIST. Courtesy of Mentice, Inc. Copyright 2010. Reprinted with permission.

subjects also evaluated their feelings about their performance, as well as their confidence about future performance of the procedure. After this preintervention performance, the study subjects underwent 2 hours of structured training on the simulator followed by 1 hour of guided practice on the device. Following this training period, the study subjects repeated the three basic interventional radiology tasks, and the previously described subjective and objective measures were recorded. Statistically significant improvements were demonstrated in terms of mean fluoroscopy time, mean task time, and mean number of major errors. In addition, the performer's self-assessment, as well as the supervisor's overall assessment, all significantly improved.[47] Although this study has its limitations, it adds weight to the evidence for using endovascular simulators as an effective training tool, specifically to train novices in the techniques required to perform basic interventional radiology procedures.

Van Herzeele and colleagues performed an experiment to show that simulator-based training could also be helpful for experienced interventionalists. Their study sample consisted of 11 experienced attendings. The simulator used in the study was the Angiomentor, as shown in Figure 26.2. Although the device can be used to simulate endovascular interventions in carotid, coronary, renal, iliac, and femoral vessels, this study focused on the carotid module. Participants were introduced to the simulator, then they were asked to perform a carotid artery stenting procedure on the simulator. The subjects then underwent a 2-day course with both cognitive and technical skills training. The technical skills training was carried out using various carotid modules available on the simulator. At the end of the course, the participants performed the same assessment module that they had performed before the course. The performance of the participants was assessed on numerous objective and subjective criteria. In addition, the satisfaction of the participants was also evaluated. The participants found the face validity of the simulator to be good and were extremely satisfied with the 2-day course. After they completed the 2-day course, the study subjects performed the procedure significantly more rapidly, exposed the virtual patient to significantly less fluoroscopy time, and after selecting the embolic protection device, they retrieved it much more expeditiously. An additional parameter that improved significantly was the advancement of the guiding catheter or sheath without a leading wire,

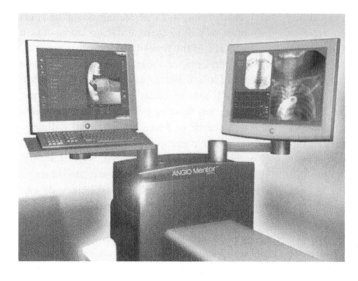

FIGURE   26.2 Simbionix ANGIO Mentor™. ANGIO Mentor™ by Simbionix USA Corp. Reprinted with permission.

which occurred far less frequently after the course. The occurrence of carotid artery spasm was significantly reduced after the course. The median number of errors observed by the study proctors decreased significantly following the course.[48] This study, although limited, further supports the position that endovascular simulators can be an effective training tool even for experienced interventionalists who may need to learn a new procedure.

CONCLUSION

Although the apprenticeship model of medical education has been in use for centuries, the changing practice of medicine demands that novel means of training be developed and put into use. The fundamental principle of nonmaleficence requires that medical training be performed in a way that prevents harm to any patients involved in the training process. However, given the complexity of medical practice, trainees do eventually need to learn to work with real patients in order to provide effective care. Thus, the use of alternative methods during the early phases of training is essential. The changes in the practice model of medical practice, with shorter hospital stays and duty hour restrictions, also demands alternative training methods. Furthermore, there is rightfully an increasing demand for objective measures of procedural, teamwork, and other skills that are not well assessed via traditional means. Simulation, which is widely used for all of these purposes in other high-risk industries, is an enabling solution to all of these challenges. Making simulation-based training an integral part of medical training from the earliest phases of the process will ensure that

patients are protected from the learning curve that all novices traverse. It can allow those novices to learn from their mistakes in a safe environment and in accordance with the principles of deliberate practice. In addition, experienced practitioners can add new skills to their repertoire safely and effectively. Finally, simulation can allow a more thorough and realistic assessment of the full set of skills required by a trainee to perform at a high level.

Although many studies have been performed using simulators as both training and assessment tools, not enough studies have been done to show how trainees perform in real-life situations after simulation training. By adding these types of studies to the weight of evidence for using simulation, we may be able to change this transformative method of training and assessment into a practical reality.

REFERENCES

1. Kohn LT, Corrigan JM, Donaldson MS. *To err is human: Building a safer health system.* Washington, DC: National Academy Press, 1999.
2. Berwick DM, Leape LL. Reducing errors in medicine: It's time to take this more seriously. *BMJ.* 1999;319:136–7.
3. Frankel A, Gandhi TK, Bates DW. Improving patient safety across a large integrated health care delivery system. *Int J for Qual in Health Care.* 2003;15(supplement I):i31–i40.
4. Hanscom R. Medical simulation from an insurance perspective. *Acad Emer Med.* 2008;15:984–7.
5. Long DM. Competency-based residency training: The next advance in graduate medical education. *Acad Med.* 2000;75:1178–83.
6. Raanan G. "Primum non nocere" and the principle of non-maleficence. *BMJ.* 1985;291:130–1.

7. Ericsson KA. Deliberate practice and acquisition of expert performance: A general overview. *Acad Emer Med.* 2008;15:988–94.

8. Gaba D. Structural and organization issues in patient safety: A comparison of health care to other high-hazard industries. *California Management Rev.* 2001;43:83–102.

9. Gaba DM. The future vision of simulation in health care. *Qual Saf Health Care.* 2004;13(Suppl 1):i2–i10.

10. Issenberg SB, et al. Features and uses of high-fidelity medical simulations that lead to effective learning: A BEME systematic review. *Med Teacher.* 2005;27:10–28.

11. Mizrahi T. Managing medical mistakes: Ideology, insularity and accountability among internists-in-training. *Soc Sci Med.* 1984;19:135–46.

12. Blumenthal D. Making medical errors into medical treasures. *JAMA.* 1994;272:1867–8.

13. Rasmussen J. The role of error in organizing behavior. *Ergonomics.* 1990;33:1185–99.

14. Levinson W, Roter DL, Mulooly JP, et al. Physician-patient communication. *JAMA.* 1997;277:553–9.

15. Risser DT, Rice MM, Salisbury M, et al. The MedTeams Research Consortium. The potential for improved teamwork to reduce medical errors in the emergency department. *Ann Emerg Med.* 1999;34:373–84.

16. Issenberg SB, McGaghie WC, Hart IR, et al. Simulation technology for health care professional skills training and assessment. *JAMA.* 1999;282:861–6.

17. Ganguli S, Pedrosa I, Yam CS, Appignani B, et al. Part I: Preparing first-year radiology residents and assessing their readiness for on-call responsibilities. *Acad Radiol.* 2006;13(6):764–9.

18. Yam CS, Kruskal J, Pedrosa I, Kressel H. Part II: Preparing and assessing first-year radiology resident on-call readiness technical implementation. *Acad Radiol.* 2006;13(6):770–3.

19. Ganguli S, Camacho M, Yam CS, Pedrosa I. Preparing first-year radiology residents and assessing their readiness for on-call responsibilities: Results over 5 years. *Am J Roentgenol.* 2009;192(2):539–44.

20. Gaca AM, Frush DP, Hohenhaus SM, et al. Enhancing pediatric safety: Using simulation to assess radiology resident preparedness for anaphylaxis from intravenous contrast media. *Radiology.* 2007;245(1):236–44.

21. Tubbs RJ, Murphy B, Mainiero MB, et al. High fidelity medical simulation as an assessment tool for radiology residents' acute contrast reaction management skills. *J Am Coll Radiol.* 2009;6:582–7.

22. Murray D. Clinical simulation: Technical novelty or innovation in education. *Anesthesiology.* 1998;89:1–2.

23. Gould D, Patel A, Becker G, et al. SIR/RSNA/CIRSE joint medical simulation task force strategic plan executive summary. *J Vasc Interv Radiol.* 2009;20:S284–S286.

24. Dawson S. Procedural simulation: A primer. *JVIR.* 2006;17:205–13.

25. MacDonald R. How protective is the working time directive? *BMJ.* 2004;329:301–2.

26. Fletcher KE, Saint S, Mangrulkar RS. Balancing continuity of care with residents' limited work hours: Defining the implications. *Acad Med.* 2005;80(1):39–43.

27. Romanchuk K. The effect of limiting residents' work hours on their surgical training: A Canadian perspective. *Acad Med.* 2004;79(5):384–5.

28. Ziv A, Wolpe PR, Small SD, Glick S. Simulation-based medical education: An ethical imperative. *Simul Healthcare.* 2006;1:252–6.

29. Gordon JA. High-fidelity patient simulation: A revolution in medical education. In: Dunn WF, ed. *Simulators in critical care and beyond.* Des Plaines, IL: Society of Critical Care Medicine 2004;3–6.

30. Bradley P. The history of simulation in medical education and possible future directions. *Med Educ.* 2006;40:254–62.

31. Cooper JB, Taqueti VR. A brief history of the development of mannequin simulators for clinical education and training. *Qual Saf Health Care.* 2004;13(Suppl 1):i11–i18.

32. Buck GH. Development of simulators in medical education. *Gesnerus.* 1991;48 Pt 1:7–28.

33. McGaghie WC, Issenberg SB, Petrusa ER, Scalese RJ. A critical review of simulation-based medical education research: 2003–2009. *Med Educ.* Jan 2010;44:50–63.

34. Gaba D, Fish K, Howard S. *Crisis management in anesthesiology.* Philadelphia: Churchill Livingstone, 1994.

35. Gaba DM, Howard SK, Fish K, Smith B, Sowb Y. Simulation-based training in anesthesia crisis resource management (ACRM): A decade of experience. *Simulation & Gaming.* 2001;32(2):175–93.

36. Howard SK, Gaba DM, Fish KJ, Yang G, Sarnquist FH. Anesthesia crisis resource management training: Teaching anesthesiologists to handle critical incidents. *Aviat Space Environ Med.* 1992;63(9):763–70.

37. Towbin AJ, Paterson BA, Chang PJ. Computer-based simulator for radiology: An educational tool. *Radiographics.* 2008;28:309–16.

38. Sica GT, et al. Computerized realistic simulation: A teaching module for crisis management in radiology. *AJR.* 1999;172:301–304.

39. Tubbs RJ, et al. High-fidelity medical simulation as an assessment tool for Radiology residents' acute contrast reaction management skills. *J Am Coll Radiol.* 2009;6:582–7.

40. Gaca AM, et al. Enhancing pediatric safety: Using simulation to assess radiology resident preparedness for anaphylaxis from intravenous contrast media. *Radiology.* 2007;245: 236–44.

41. Desser TS. Simulation-based training: The next revolution in radiology education? *J Am Coll Radiol.* 2007;4:816–24.

42. Gallagher AG, Cates CU. Approval of virtual reality training for carotid stenting: What this means for procedure-based medicine. *JAMA*. 2004;292:3024–6.
43. Ahmed K, et al. Role of virtual reality simulation in teaching and assessing technical skills in endovascular intervention. *J Vasc Interv Radiol*. 2010;21:55–66.
44. Dawson SL, et al. Designing a computer-based simulator for interventional cardiology training. *Cathet Cardiovasc Intervent*. 2000;51:522–7.
45. Berry M, et al. Porcine transfer study: Virtual reality simulator training compared with porcine training in endovascular novices. *Cardiovasc Intervent Radiol*. 2007;30:455–61.
46. Chaer RA, et al. Simulation improves resident performance in catheter-based intervention: Results of a randomized, controlled study. *Ann Surg*. 2006;244: 344–52.
47. Coates JB, Zealley IA, Chatraverty S. Endovascular simulator is of benefit in the acquisition of basic skills by novice operators. *J Vasc Interv Radiol*. 2010;21:130–4.
48. Van Herzeele I, et al. Experienced endovascular interventionalists objectively improve their skills by attending carotid artery stent training courses. *Eur J Vasc Endovasc Surg*. 2007;35:541–50.

27

Evidence-based Radiology and Its Relationship with Quality

FRANCESCO SARDANELLI

The principle of *evidence-based medicine* (EBM) is to define clinical practice on the basis of the critical evaluation of results, the proofs (the evidence) supplied by the best medical research. This discipline is increasingly expanding into health care, bringing with it a striking change not only in clinical practice but also in teaching and learning, as well as in decision-making by administrators and policymakers. Evidence-based medicine has entered radiology after a relative delay, but with a substantial impact, as emphasized by the increasingly prevalent role of web-based search tools that allow real-time access to medical journals and other sources of information on medical research solely available through the Internet.

The aim of this chapter is to provide an outline of the EBM's historical origins and an overview of this discipline in relation to radiology (*evidence-based radiology*, EBR). We will describe EBM's impact on clinical radiology in terms of more appropriate and safer use of imaging and higher intrinsic and perceived quality of radiologic procedures.

A LONG HISTORY

Evidence-based Medicine Definition and Conceptual Framework

About 10 years ago, EBM (often referred to as *evidence-based health care* or *evidence-based practice*[1]) was defined as "the systematic application of the best evidence to evaluate the available options and decision making in clinical management and policy settings,"[2] or "integrating clinical expertise with the best available external clinical evidence from research."[2]

Evidence-based medicine has its roots in clinical epidemiology. Here, we explore the historical process that produced this benchmark for all specialties of contemporary medicine, including diagnostic and interventional radiology.

In the last two centuries, medicine was practiced (and is still practiced today) by balancing the tension between a theoretical, causative, dogmatic, and deterministic approach and a practical, clinical, probabilistic approach. Evidence-based medicine is probably the best result of the latter approach. However, many doctors—and radiologists among them—reject statistics and see EBM as a complex and theoretical approach, difficult to use as a problem-solving method in clinical practice. For these, EBM is believed to be an impractical, dogmatic tool. This view of EMB is something of a paradox. In fact, the historical origins of EBM are in the observational medicine of the 19th century, which was a strong reaction against then-current theories (from bloodletting as a method to cure inflammation to the position of the stars interplaying with Galenic humors).[3] Today, EBM is a reaction against the power of modern basic medical science: EBM should be regarded as an advanced scientific clinical viewpoint that affirms the role of clinical practice over any physiopathological theory or laboratory-, cell-, or animal-based model demonstration.

In this framework, radiology should refuse to play a laboratory-only role (with the obvious exception of basic radiological research) and instead gain power as a clinical specialty. This transformation implies the use of probabilistic thinking and the rapid adoption of EBR principles because clinical medicine—especially when a diagnosis is under consideration—is always relatively uncertain and therefore intrinsically probabilistic.

Birth of Clinical Epidemiology During the Early 19th Century

Traces of ideas not too distant from modern controlled clinical trials can be seen during the 12th century, when Frederick II (1194–1250) studied the effect of exercise on digestion. He gave identical meals to a couple of knights, one sent out hunting, the other ordered to bed, and then observed the contents of their stomach and bowels.[4] Later, during the 17th century, Jan B. Van Helmont (1579–1644) proposed to randomize a large sample of patients to bloodletting or not bloodletting and then to count the number of funerals.[4]

During the fourth decade of the 19th century, Pierre C.A. Luis (1787–1872) initiated in postrevolutionary Paris a new way of medical thinking—which he called *médecine d'observation*—that rejected the approaches of traditional medical authorities.[3] According to this new view, physicians would not base their decision-making only on personal experience or theoretical speculations on the possible causes of symptoms and diseases; instead, they would consider the objective numbers of results of large, systematic series of experimental cases concerning the effect of a medical treatment.[3] Louis' motto was *"Ars medica tota in observationibus"* ("Medical art entirely consists of observations").[5,6] He developed a numerical method of standardized data collection and analysis that he used to define new clinical entities, such as typhoid fever. In those times, bloodletting (by surgical bleeding or using leeches) was advocated as a universal treatment for inflammation and other diseases. Louis analyzed the clinical records of 77 patients with pneumonia, 41 of whom underwent early bloodletting (first bleeding on day 1–4 from clinical onset) and 36 of whom underwent late bloodletting (first bleeding on day 5–9 from clinical onset). The age of the two groups was comparable, and the mean number of bleedings was 2.8 in the early bloodletting group and 2.3 in the late bloodletting group. Average disease duration was 17.8 days and 20.8 days, but mortality was 44%

and 25%, respectively. Considering only patients who survived, disease duration was 17.7 versus 20.3 days; considering only those who died, 51 versus 43 days, respectively.[5]

A modern calculation performed by Alfred Morabia on Louis' data[5] resulted in a relative risk of death for the early bloodletting group of 1.8 (95% confidence interval, 0.9–3.5), using the mortality rate of the late bloodletting group as a reference (1.0). Louis concluded that the effect of bloodletting was "much less than has been commonly believed," that it was useful but potentially dangerous, and that its validity should be restricted to severe inflammations of important organs. Moreover, he was in favor of abundant bleeding and thought that "the use of the lancet should be preferred to that of leeches."[5] Morabia commented: "These conclusion were balanced but still provocative in 1830 medicine."[5] Apart from the discussion on the absence of formal statistical significance and on mistakes in computing means in the original French version of Louis' work,[5] these data showed that early bloodletting reduced pneumonitis duration but also increased short-term mortality.

Louis' study initiated a change, not only in considering the value of bloodletting as a universal medical treatment, but in how medical practitioners thought. What was new?: Standardized data collection, quantitative analysis, grouping patients into two groups differently exposed to a cause, and evaluating the effect of the cause in each of the two groups, looking for a difference. From a modern viewpoint, Louis' study has the great limitation of using nonrandomized assignment to the two groups, so that a selection bias could have influenced the results. Louis discussed the necessity of a balance for all factors other than treatment, but he thought that using large samples would be enough to obtain similar conditions and error compensation, which we know is not true, especially for misclassification bias.[5] Nonetheless, Louis' work laid the foundation of a new scientific discipline that we today know as *clinical epidemiology*, based on probability and population thinking. And, as noted earlier, EBM can be considered an offshoot of this discipline.[3]

However, Louis' way of thinking was not embraced by clinical medicine during the 19th century, because the current trend for Positivism was not a good philosophical environment for probabilistic medical thinking. Claude Bernard (1813–1878), a famous French physiologist who advocated the experimental method for medical science, wrote that "if based on statistics, medicine can never be anything but a conjectural science."[7] The success of deterministic instead of a probabilistic thinking was also favored by the success of bacteriology, which greatly influenced medicine in the second half of the 19th century.[3]

The 20th Century and EBM Foundations: A Late Louis' Victory

The application of probabilistic thinking to clinical medicine flourished into clinical epidemiology and then into EBM only during the 20th century, especially after World War II.

An essential contribution to this process came from British geneticist and statistician Ronald A. Fisher (1890–1962), who first described the relevance of random sampling in the experimental design, whose principles were defined in his book entitled *The Design of Experiments*, published in 1935. He introduced the concepts of null hypothesis (H_0) and experimental hypothesis (H_1), thus building the theoretical framework of statistical significance which all of us use in scientific research. When we get a *p* lower than 0.05, we think to demonstrate H_1 while we are only rejecting H_0. However, the *acceptance* of H_1 as a result of the rejection of H_0 is still matter of debate.[8] After World War II, British epidemiologists Austin Bradford Hill (1897–1991) and Richard Doll (1912–2005) demonstrated the association between cigarette smoking and lung cancer. The former defined the so-called Bradford-Hill criteria for determining a causal association. Another pioneer was the Scottish epidemiologist Archie Cochrane (1909–1988), who promoted the use of randomized controlled trials (RCTs). From this initial experience was derived the development of the Cochrane Library Database of Systematic Reviews, the establishment of the U.K. Cochrane Centre in Oxford, and the international Cochrane Collaboration.[4]

However, it was not until the last decades of the 20th century that the Canadian School, led by Gordon Guyatt and Dave L. Sackett at McMaster University (Hamilton, Ontario, Canada), promoted the idea of guiding clinical practice using the best results—the proofs, the *evidence*—produced by scientific research.[2,4] This approach was officially presented in the medical literature in 1992, in an article published in the *Journal of the American Medical Association*[9] and further refined by the Centre for Evidence-based Medicine (CEBM) at the Oxford University, England.[1,10]

In the historical 1992 article, the EBM working group (Gordon Guyatt being the first author)[9] wrote:

Evidence-based medicine de-emphasizes intuition, unsystematic clinical experience, and pathophysiologic rationale as sufficient grounds for clinical decision making and stresses the examination of evidence from clinical research. Evidence-based medicine requires new skills of the physician, including efficient literature searching and the application of formal rules of evidence evaluating the clinical literature.

In 1996, Dave L. Sackett[11] said that:

Evidence based medicine is the conscientious, explicit, and judicious use of current best evidence in making decision about the care of individual patients. The practice of evidence-based medicine means integrating individual clinical expertise with the best available external evidence from systematic research.

A highly attractive, but more technical EBM definition, which explicitly includes diagnosis and investigation, has been proposed by Anna Donald and Trisha Greenhalgh:[12]

Evidence-based medicine is the use of mathematical estimates of the risk of benefit and harm, derived from high-quality research on population samples, to inform clinical decision making in the diagnosis, investigation or management of individual patients.

Evidence-based medicine has deeply penetrated the world of academic and clinical medicine, such that one of the most important challenges facing medical specialties is keeping up with the rapid adoption of EBM principles. Unfortunately, as we will see, not all clinical practice can be evidence-based, and this is particularly true for radiology. However, the future of medical professionalism is certainly connected with increasing EBM penetration and acceptance. Thus, at the borders between competing specialties (as happens today with many imaging techniques), those physicians who can quickly demonstrate the evidence of their contributions to patient outcome and use EBM as a clinical problem-solving approach will prevail over those who are slower to use it. Thus, 160 years later, Pierre C.A. Louis won.

THE ETERNAL TENSION BETWEEN THEORY AND PRACTICE IN MEDICINE: RADIOLOGY'S STANCE

As mentioned above, Louis' late triumph can be found in the restless "tension between the theoretical and the empirical side of medicine."[3]

This tension can be traced to ancient Greek philosophy and medicine, which favored medical theory and process, rather than patient outcome. On the side of theoretical medicine we find Galen of Pergamon (129–199 or 217 CE), the prominent Roman physician and philosopher of Greek origin who was strongly influenced by Hippocrates' humoral theory. In his view, "one could reason about the human body in a perfect syllogistic way."[3] On the empirical side, we find Alexander of Aphrodisias (late 2nd–early 3rd century CE), peripatetic philosopher and commentator on the writings of Aristotle. He thought that medicine should be entirely empirical, because "it is impossible to infer from theory what will happen to a patient when a drug is administered" and "anyway the result is going to be highly variable over patients because there is so much that we do not know."[3] Thus, whereas Galen's idea of medicine was deterministic, that of Alexander was stochastic. On one side, the syllogism (if A is equal to B and B is equal to C, then A is equal to C); on the other, uncertainty and probability (A is the event in most cases, B is relatively rare, but C cannot be completely excluded).

In the 2,000 years that separate modern medicine from the ancient Greeks, an extraordinary amount of correct medical theory has been produced. However, medical thinking remains (and will remain) probabilistic. The reason is not a lack of knowledge; the reason lies in the intrinsic variability of biological processes. To be accepted as a medical rule, theory must be proved in clinical practice by means of high-quality studies. This forms the EBM (and EBR) point of view.

As Louis reacted to dogmatic theories about bloodletting, clinical epidemiology and EBM react to the "success of the theoretical, explanatory, and technical parts of medicine,"[3] including the extraordinary success of molecular biology, genomics, metabolomics, and other advances of the last few decades. Most of the future of medical science will come from these exciting research fields. Where, then, should we position radiology?

In 1996, Dutch epidemiologist Jan P. Vandenbroucke[3] positioned radiology solely on the side of explanatory, technical medicine, drawing some worrisome conclusions. He wrote:

I do not need to pause here about the success of molecular techniques, for example in diagnostic pathologist, nor about the wonderful images from [computed tomography] CT-scans or Magnetic Resonance. Again, physicians have tended to react by arguing that there is more to medicine than applied molecular pathology or radiology. One cannot leave a patient to a committee of radiologists and pathologists, at least as long as the patient is alive. And no committee of molecular biologists will ever be able to monitor a patient on artificial respiration in an intensive care unit, even each of the chemical reactions that goes on inside the patient can be explained by one of them. The complexity of the whole cannot be reduced to individual chemical reactions, and mastering the whole organ or the whole patient as in an intensive care unit is a science in itself.

It would be too easy to comment on the outcomes of leaving a living patient with a relevant diagnostic clinical problem to a committee of epidemiologists. Notably, that same year (1996), Sackett's famous article was published in the BMJ,[11] in which he placed radiology squarely in the EBM field of action. Vaunderbroucke not only totally overlooked interventional radiology, but also considered diagnostic radiology as a pure laboratory tool, an image-centered and not patient-centered specialty, unable to understand "the complexity of the whole."[3] This judgment entirely negates the clinical role of diagnostic radiology, in which signs on images are interpreted and reported in the light of a patient's history and of the clinical question asked by the referring physician, in which conclusions are mandatory and, if necessary, further diagnostic steps or specific clinical actions are requested at the end of the report.

Here, radiologists must acknowledge some blame, at least in the past decades. We have not always been enthusiastic members of a fully patient-centered clinical specialty. A prime example of a purely technical, rather than patient-centered, behavior is the performance of an imaging-guided needle biopsy done without closing the diagnostic pathway by comparing the pathological (or cytological) report with the radiologic appearance of the sampled lesion. This final comparison is of paramount importance to avoid false-negative cases due to sampling error or to pathologic misclassification. As an example, in breast imaging (and this can be extended to many other fields of radiology), if the lesion seems to be a cancer (e.g., a BI-RADS 4 or 5 finding) and the fine needle aspiration cytology and/or the core or vacuum-assisted biopsy has turned out to be negative, with a puzzling discordance in respect to imaging features, the radiologist should acknowledge this discordance in the final report and strongly suggest repeating the needle biopsy or going directly to surgical biopsy.[13]

Another example of deficient patient-centeredness in radiology is the frequent lack of a direct connection with the patient during the crucial phase of report communication. The use of the Internet allows the radiologist to send reports and make images available to the referring physician (if the patient agrees to this). This is correct modern management in our relation with the referring colleague, but it is not a patient-centered clinical behavior. Especially when breaking bad news, we should have a *direct clinical conversation with the patient* (and/or with his or her relatives, when indicated). I am aware of the time constraints we live under, but if we want to be clinicians, this is a must.[14]

These are only two small examples of ways of being *clinical* radiologists. The expanding role of imaging, notwithstanding Vandenbroucke's opinion,[3] frequently puts the patient entirely in our hands. His or her life (or quality of life) mainly depends on our evaluation and decision. It is not as immediate a responsibility as managing a patient in an intensive care unit, but the outcome's impact can be exactly the same.

Thus, EBM should be regarded as the clinical, practical side of medicine, and EBR as the clinical, practical side of radiology. This clinical view is not limited to personal experience and anecdotal episodes, but is elevated to the science of probabilistic thinking based on the best external evidence available in the literature. As we will see below, technical expertise also is crucial for radiology but is not enough to produce high-quality radiologic professionalism. To be clinicians, we also need to apply EBM to radiology.

WHAT IS EBM? INTEGRATING THEORY AND PRACTICE IN MEDICAL THINKING

The Hidden Side of EBM: The Patient's Values and Choice

Evidence-based medicine is not only the combination of current best available external evidence coupled with individual clinical expertise. "It cannot result in slavish, cookbook approaches to individual patient care."[11] A third factor must be included: The patient's values and choice. Thus, EBM should be considered as the integration of evidence from research, clinical expertise, and the patient's values and preferences.[1,11,15]

Clinical expertise "decides whether the external evidence applies to the individual patient," evaluating "how it matches the patient's clinical state, predicament, and preferences."[11] A synopsis of this process is given in Figure 27.1.

The integration of patient values and choice is commonly not sufficiently considered in the structure of EBM, especially when EBM principles are advocated by administrators and policy-makers with the aim of cutting health care expenditures. We should strongly stress that no EBM applications can be done without careful consideration of the patient's viewpoint. As for a diagnostic pathway, the clinical radiologist is the integrator of the patient's viewpoint with the best external evidence. Further, the radiologist must use his or her technical and clinical expertise in combination with a fourth dimension, the *as low as reasonably achievable* (ALARA) principle, aimed at the maximal reduction of radiation exposure.

Two-way EBM and Critically Appraised Topics

We can apply EBM according to two different approaches,[16-18] as shown in Figure 27.2.

Top-down EBM is at work when researchers provide high-quality primary studies (original researches), secondary studies (such as systematic

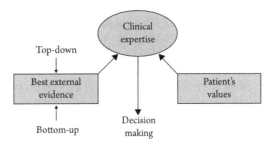

FIGURE 27.1 Evidence-based medicine. See Figure 27.2 for the top-down and bottom-up approaches to the best external evidence.

Reprinted from Sardanelli F, Di Leo G. *Biostatistics for radiologists*. Milan: Springer-Verlag, 2009:3, with permission of the publisher, Springer Science+Business Media.

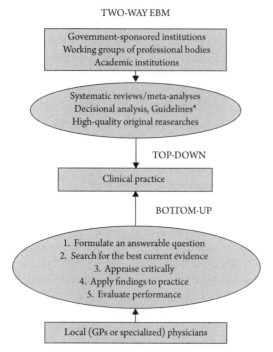

TWO-WAY EBM

Government-sponsored institutions
Working groups of professional bodies
Academic institutions

Systematic reviews/meta-analyses
Decisional analysis, Guidelines*
High-quality original reasearches

TOP-DOWN

Clinical practice

BOTTOM-UP

1. Formulate an answerable question
2. Search for the best current evidence
3. Appraise critically
4. Apply findings to practice
5. Evaluate performance

Local (GPs or specialized) physicians

FIGURE 27.2 Top-down and bottom-up evidence-based medicine (EBM). Appropriateness criteria are not included in top-down EBM due to their common production on the basis of expert opinion, even though formalized procedures (such as the modified Delphi protocol) are frequently used and experts commonly base their opinion on systematic reviews and meta-analyses. Note that the recently (2010) revised versions of the American College of Radiology (ACR) appropriateness criteria have references embedded, thus linking them with the evidence on which these criteria are based.[155] GPs = general practitioners.

reviews and meta-analyses), or applications of decision analysis, or when panels of experts on behalf of medical bodies, such as the American College of Radiology (ACR),[19] or specialized organizations, such as the Cochrane Collaboration,[20] issue evidence-based guidelines and make efforts to integrate them into practice.

Bottom-up EBM is at work when general practitioners or other physicians working in a day-to-day practice are able to ask a question, search and appraise the literature, and then apply best current evidence to the local setting.

A particular aspect of EBM is the so-called *critically appraisal topics* (CATs).[21] When published as articles in medical journals, these should be considered as a kind of top-down EBM. However, a CAT is usually designed to solve a particular clinical problem in an individual patient. A clinical question is

generated, and a search is prompted for published studies to answer the question. With reference to radiology, relevant articles are selected and summarized in order to produce measures of diagnostic performance, therapeutic efficacy, risk, or patient outcome. Differing from a formal meta-analysis, a CAT does not require complex statistical methodology and can be performed in a relatively short time. Thus, it mimics what a single physician (radiologist) could do in practice to apply bottom-up EBM (EBR) to answer a pressing or recurring clinical question.

Both EBM methods can open a so-called *audit cycle*, in which one physician takes a standard and measures his or her own practice against it. However, the top-down approach involves a small number of people considered as experts and does not involve physicians acting at the local level. There is a difference between the production of systematic reviews and meta-analyses (that are welcome as an important source of information by local physicians who want to practice the bottom-up model) and the production of guidelines, which could be considered as an external "cookbook" approach, especially (when confused as a mandatory standard of practice) by physicians who feel themselves removed from the decision-making process.[18]

Notably, the bottom-up approach to EBM preceded the top-down approach.[22] However, bottom-up EBM implies a higher level of knowledge of medical research methodology and EBM techniques by local physicians than that demanded by the top-down approach. In either case, a qualitative improvement in patient care is expected, and clinical expertise plays a pivotal role in integrating external evidence with patient's values and choice. When decision analyses, meta-analyses, and guidelines provide only part of the external evidence found by the practicing physician, then the two models act together.

A particular aim of the top-down approach is the identification of knowledge gaps to be filled in by future research. In this way, EBM becomes a method to redirect medical research toward an improved medical practice.[22] At the end of this chapter, we will discuss the role of EBM-driven research and of the relevance of freedom of scientific research in radiology.

EBM limitations, Criticisms of EBM, and Integration of EBM with Causative Medical Thinking

Evidence-based medicine is not free of limitations. It has been judged as unproved, very time-consuming (and therefore expensive), narrowing the research agenda and patients' options, facilitating cost cutting, and threatening professional autonomy and clinical freedom.[11,17,23] In an objective evaluation, these criticisms seem to be substantially weak. In fact, EBM gives a pivotal role to "individual clinical expertise" with the general aim "to maximize the quality and quantity of life for individual patient," which "may raise rather than lower the cost of their care" as pointed out by Sackett in 1996.[11]

Of course, we should not be surprised that administrators, managers of insurance companies, and policy-makers try to use EBM to cut health care costs. It is appropriate to their role. Despite a large range of differences between the health care systems of the United States and the European Union, and between advanced and developing countries, control of health care expenditure is a worldwide priority, especially as an aging population is becoming more and more relevant. But EBM applications cannot be left only in the hands of administrators. Evidence-based medicine can be used not only to spend less; it can be used to more effectively spend the same amount of money or to even spend more money when there are good reasons for doing so. Thinking about the increasing role of imaging in health care, we should advocate the correct use of EBR to justify diagnostic and interventional radiological procedures. To do this, we should have a deep knowledge of EBM and EBR and of the methods these approaches use, including statistics.

Other limitations attributed to EBM seem to be more relevant, particularly for imaging and radiology. On the one hand, large clinical areas have not been sufficiently explored by high-quality studies, according to EBM criteria. On the other hand, real patients can be totally different from those described in the literature, especially due to the presence of comorbidities, thus making the conclusions of studies not directly applicable to clinical practice. This situation is day-to-day reality in geriatric medicine. The aging populations of Western countries has created a difficult benchmark for EBM.

These limitations of EBM could be related to a more general criticism, which considers that, using the EBM perspective, the central feature is the patient population and not the individual patient.[24,25] This a key point: "Medicine is about individual patients, not about groups" is a very old criticism of EBM[3] and one that should be carefully taken into account.

In his 1996 article,[3] Jan P. Vandenbroucke commented on a criticism of EBM published in 1993

by a philosopher, Sandra J. Tanenbaum, writing in the *New England Journal of Medicine*.[26] The author's question was: Is statistical analysis (and EBM) superior to other forms of medical knowledge, in particular to clinical experience or basic science? Moreover, she highlighted that "reasoning about an individual is not probabilistic" but "framed in causal terms." Vandenbroucke's view is that this causative reasoning is what really happens in decision-making at the bedside. In other words, a cardiologist uses thrombolytic treatment for myocardial infarction "because it dissolves the clot," not "because of GISSI-1, 2, 3 or whatever megatrial."[3] This causative, not probabilistic, thinking helps in applying this treatment to individual patients. The logical chain should be completed by adding that doctors know that the clot-dissolving capability of thrombolytic treatment was shown to have a positive impact on patient outcomes by means of those trials. Thus, we memorize the results of RCTs and other studies in terms of causative, nonprobabilistic, deterministic thinking and use these in clinical decision-making.

A radiological example on the difference between the population *epidemiologic* viewpoint and the individual subject *clinical* viewpoint can be supplied by considering mammographic screening for breast cancer. This example is relevant because it remains entirely in the EBM field but concerns the kind of data should we use in a given setting.

Randomized controlled trials showed that screening mammography allows for a breast cancer mortality rate reduction of between 15% and 31%,[27–30] thanks to a sensitivity estimated to be 80% in women between 49 and 69 years of age.[31,32] The real advantage of periodical mammography in this age interval is certainly higher for the individual woman who gets a mammogram every 12–24 months. In fact, the rate of specific mortality reduction in the screened arm of RCTs is calculated on all women invited to the screening (i.e., both those who accepted the invitation and those who refused). This is correct from the viewpoint of public health programs and of administrators and policy-makers because it measures the effectiveness of doing mammographic screening in a population. However, when we tell a 49-year-old woman that an annual or biannual mammogram reduces her risk of dying from breast cancer, we should consider that, if she accepts, she will have a greater reduction of specific mortality than that reported in RCTs for the women invited to attend the screening program. *Case–control studies are more suitable for this calculation.* Comparing the specific mortality of women with breast cancer who got screening mammograms with that of women with breast cancer who did not, mortality reduction has been recently estimated equal to 45%–48%.[33,34] This is the mortality reduction we should present to an individual woman who is deciding whether to undergo a screening mammogram.

Randomized controlled trials are not always the best source of data. On the other hand, data for well-conducted retrospective studies (typically using case–control design) can be very useful in giving a patient reliable estimates of his or her own risk reduction. Here, probabilistic thinking is applied to an individual subject and translated into causative, quasi-deterministic thought: If you get a periodic mammogram, an earlier detection of a potentially killer cancer will be possible and you will reduce your related death probability by 50%.

Coming back to the Vandenbroucke's article,[3] we agree with his general statement:

> Completely empirical knowledge cannot exist, because it would not be knowledge. It would be only a collection of facts, like a pile of grains of sand, without any structure. One cannot do anything with a collection of facts without the cement of theory that gives meaning and especially purpose to the facts.

To summarize, we need facts (analyzed with EBM) to show that theories work for patients. At the end of the day, this refers to the eternal cycle of hypothesis and observations in (basic) science.[8] "Theory guides. Experiment decides."[35] The British astrophysicist Arthur S. Eddington (1882–1944) wrote:[36]

> Observation and theory get on best when they are mixed together, both helping one another in the pursuit of truth. It is a good rule not to put overmuch confidence in a theory until it has been confirmed by observation. I hope I shall not shock the experimental physicists too much if I add that it is also a good rule not to put overmuch confidence in the observational results that are put forward until they have been confirmed by theory.

Evidence-based medicine is not medical theory, if that is defined as nothing more than clinical observations (and sophisticated techniques for their analysis). Basically, the value of EBM should be borne in mind, as EBM aims to provide the best choice for the individual patient with the use of probabilistic reasoning, even though we use this tool within a knowledge framework given by medical theory and basic science.

Finally, not all that appears in the medical literature as an EBM product is really to be considered a high-quality tool. In particular, we should avoid an unbridled enthusiasm for some clinical guidelines (which theoretically should be one of the best uses of top-down EBM), even when issued by important medical bodies, especially if they there is a lack of clarity explaining how they were reached or if questionable methods were used.[37] We will come back on this point later in this chapter.

DELAYED DIFFUSION OF EBM IN RADIOLOGY: FOUR-DIMENSION EBR

Radiology is not outside of EBM, as stated by Sackett in 1996: "EBM is not restricted to randomised trials and meta-analyses.... To find out about the accuracy of a diagnostic test, we need to find proper cross-sectional studies of patients clinically suspected of harbouring the relevant disorder, not a randomised trial."[11] Evidence-based radiology, also called *evidence-based imaging*, first appeared in the literature only recently. The term "evidence-based radiology" will be used here, not to restrict the field of interest but to highlight that radiologists play a main role in this field. Radiologists are the interpreters of the images and are required to understand the implications of their findings and reports in the context of the available evidence from the literature.

The diffusion of EBM into radiology was delayed. Until 2000, few papers on EBR were published in nonradiological journals,[38,39] mainly regarding ultrasound imaging in pregnancy,[40–42] and in one journal specializing in dentomaxillofacial radiology.[43] From 2001 to 2005, several papers introduced the EBM approach in radiology.[2,44–59] In 2006, the first edition of the book *Evidence-based Imaging*, by L. Santiago Medina and C. Craig Blackmore, was published.[60] These authors contended that radiology was "behind other specialties" in embracing EBM.[60] According to Medina and Blackmore "only around 30% of what constitutes 'imaging knowledge' is substantiated by reliable scientific inquiry."[61] Other authors estimate that less than 10% of standard imaging procedures are supported by sufficient RCTs, meta-analyses, or systematic reviews.[38,48,62]

We could summarize these evaluations by concluding that less than one-third of our day-to-day use of diagnostic imaging has an EBR reference. However, the gap between the EBM approach and clinical practice cannot be entirely avoided, no matter what medical discipline is considered. Not all of practice medicine can be supported in terms of EBM. Dr. Fergus Macbeth, Consultant Oncologist and Director of the Centre for Clinical Practice at the U.K. National Institute for Clinical Excellence (NICE), recently affirmed that about 30% of the content of guidelines issued by the NICE are necessarily based on expert panel opinion due to the lack of evidence in the literature [communication during the Royal College of Radiologist Breast Group Meeting, Belfast, November 1–3, 2009].[63] If we compare this gap with that of radiology, we have a measure of our delay in applying EBM to our discipline: the ratio between EBM-unsupported and EBM-supported practice is about 1:2 for the whole of medicine, while it is about 2:1 for radiology.

Several particular traits of our discipline explain this EBR delay. The comparison between two diagnostic imaging modalities differs greatly from the well-known comparison between two treatments (typically between a new drug and a placebo or the standard care). Thus, the classical design of RCTs is not the standard for radiological studies. We normally do not measure patient outcome to evaluate the quality of a diagnostic test, even though we should do this more and more in the future. So, what peculiar features of radiology should be considered?

First, the evaluation of the diagnostic performance of imaging modalities must be based on a deep knowledge of the technology used for image generation and postprocessing. As a consequence, *technical expertise* has to be combined with clinical expertise in judging when and how the best available external evidence can be applied to a clinical case. In radiology, this aspect is as important as *clinical expertise* (i.e., knowledge of indications for an imaging procedure, imaging interpretation and reporting, etc.). Dodd et al.[55] showed the consequences of ignoring a technical detail, such as the slice thickness, in evaluating the diagnostic performance of magnetic resonance (MR) cholangiopancreatography. Using a 5 mm instead of a 3 mm thickness, the diagnostic performance for the detection of choledocholithiasis changed from 0.57 sensitivity and 1.0 specificity to 0.92 sensitivity and 0.97 specificity.[55] If the results of technically inadequate imaging protocols are included in a meta-analysis, the consequence will be underestimation of diagnostic performance. Thus, technical expertise is crucial for EBR.

At times, progress in clinical imaging is essentially driven by the development of new technology, as was the case for MR imaging at the beginning of the 1980s. However, more frequently, an important gain in spatial or temporal resolution, in signal-to-noise or contrast-to-noise ratio is attained through hardware and/or software innovations in preexisting technology. This new step broadens the clinical applicability of the technology, as was the case for CT, which evolved from helical single-slice to multidetector row scanners, thus opening the way to cardiac CT and CT angiography of the coronary arteries. To stay up-to-date with technological developments is a hard task for radiologists, and a relevant part of their time not spent with imaging interpretation should be dedicated to the study of new imaging techniques or modalities. In radiological research, each new technology appearing on the market is tested with studies of its technical performance.

Second, the increasing availability of multiple options in diagnostic imaging should be taken into consideration, along with their continuous and sometimes unexpected technological development and sophistication. Thus, the high speed of technological evolution creates not only the need to study theory and the practical applications of new tools, but also to repeatedly consider studies on technical performance, reproducibility, and diagnostic performance. The faster the advances in technical development, the more difficult it is to do the job in time. This development is often much more rapid than the time required for performing clinical studies for the basic evaluation of diagnostic performance. From this viewpoint, *we are often too late with our assessment studies*. In particular, the evaluation of intraobserver, interobserver, and interstudy reproducibility of imaging modalities is an emergent research area that requires dedicated study designs and statistical methods that depend on the type of variables under consideration (e.g., Bland-Altman analysis for continuous variables, Cohen's κ statistics for categorical variables).[64] In fact, if a test shows poor reproducibility, it will never provide good diagnostic performance. Good reproducibility is a necessary (but insufficient) condition for a test to be useful.

The consequence of the combination of the need for technical expertise and continuous technological evolution is that radiologists are very busy with the technical aspects of their profession, both for research academic purposes and for high-quality clinical practice. This is not the case for other specialties. A cardiologist or an oncologist can use a new drug or be an active participant in an RCT without knowing the technical aspects of the drug's production, the details of basic research that allowed the new molecule to be synthesized, or the outcomes of studies of the drug in cell or animal models. Conversely, if a new MR sequence (e.g., diffusion weighted imaging) or a new CT acquisition technique (e.g., dual source/dual energy CT) emerges, radiologists have to study carefully the technical details of the hardware and software of these new approaches. A period of training with the use of the new technique is needed, or no clinical or research purpose is affordable. This creates an objective delay for the evaluation of these new tools according to EBR principles.

Last, we should specifically integrate into EBR one final aspect: the need to avoid unnecessary ionizing radiation exposure, according to the ALARA principle[65-67] and to government regulations.[68-70] The ALARA principle might be considered as embedded in radiological technical and clinical expertise. However, in our opinion, it should be regarded as *a fourth dimension of EBR*, due to the increasing relevance of radio-protection issues in radiological thinking. The best external evidence (first dimension) has to be integrated with patient's values (second dimension) by the radiologist's technical and clinical expertise (third dimension), while taking in the highest consideration the ALARA principle (fourth dimension). A graphical representation of the EBR process, including the ALARA principle, is provided in Figure 27.3.

EVIDENCE BASED MEDICINE

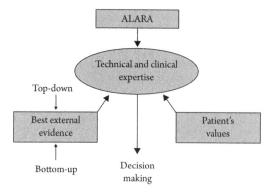

FIGURE 27.3 Evidence-based radiology. ALARA, as low as reasonably achievable, referred to ionizing radiation exposure.

Reprinted from Sardanelli F, Di Leo G. *Biostatistics for radiologists.* Milan: Springer-Verlag, 2009:7, with permission of the publisher, Springer Science+Business Media.

REAL BENEFIT VERSUS DIAGNOSTIC BENEFIT: OVERDIAGNOSIS AND OVERTREATMENT

The most important problem to be considered with any new diagnostic technology is that "a balance must be struck between apparent (e.g., diagnostic) benefit and real benefit to the patient."[38] In fact, a qualitative leap in radiologic research is now expected: from demonstrating the increasing ability to see more and better, to demonstrating a significant change in treatment planning or, at best, a significant gain in patient health and/or quality of life— the patient outcome.

This is a not simple issue because multiple aspects are at work. We must first distinguish between diagnostic and interventional radiology, putting all imaging-guided biopsy procedures in the field of diagnostic radiology and considering only those procedures aimed at treating diseases as interventional radiology.

Interventional radiology is a pure *clinical* specialty. As a consequence, it must be studied on the basis of a classical application of EBM to clinical medicine. Randomized controlled trials should be the rule, especially when we want to demonstrate the superiority or noninferiority of an imaging-guided treatment in comparison to a standard surgical treatment. This implies the use of all the tools of clinical epidemiology, from complex forms of randomization to *intention-to-treat* analysis, from disease-free or overall survival analysis to the calculation of number needed to treat (NNT) (i.e., the number of patients we should treat to typically avoid an unwanted event),[71] and more. Percentages of immediate success of the procedure are only technical evaluations of the procedure itself. We cannot hope to be high-quality treating physicians unless we have expert knowledge of these methodological tools, as well as a simple understanding of the literature on the procedures we perform day-by-day.

Diagnostic radiology is quite different. A diagnostic procedure is performed to benefit the patient, as is for an interventional procedure. However, while the value of an interventional procedure should be finally evaluated with outcome analysis (and percentages of technical success remain only a necessary but preliminary evaluation), a diagnostic procedure is commonly evaluated using measures of diagnostic performance (sensitivity, specificity, accuracy, etc.), which can be considered a kind of measure of *immediate success*. Currently, outcome analysis is not common in diagnostic radiology; the reason lies with the historical process of clinical medicine.

For thousands of years, medicine was practiced by men and women who tried to cure patients, to care for human beings suffering from some symptom or disease. It was only with the dawn of the 20th century that a patient had more probability of advantage than disadvantage if he looked to a doctor to cure his symptoms.[72] At that time, a good diagnosis began to be associated with a good probability of benefit to the patient. If a diagnostic test revealed the truth about a symptom, the physician could then try to use his or her knowledge to obtain a better patient outcome. In this old framework, a good diagnosis almost always implied a potentially better outcome.

In the last 50 years, and especially in the last two or three decades, this scenario dramatically changed. First, modern medicine developed a long series of different diagnostic tests, including those using imaging techniques, each competing with the other for accuracy, associated risks, invasiveness, cost, etc. The choice of the right test and of the right sequence of tests (i.e., the diagnostic pathway) has become challenging due to the fact that the number of possible test combinations grows exponentially with every new discovery. Second, physicians began using diagnostic tests on healthy populations in an attempt to screen for the early diagnoses of diseases such as breast, uterine, lung, or prostate cancer, to reduce mortality from these diseases. Third, the advent of tomographic imaging techniques such as B-mode ultrasonography, CT, single-photon emission tomography (SPECT), positron emission tomography (PET), and MRI, and their combinations performed through hybrid units, opened a new era in medical imaging: *you may be looking for something, but you find something else.* As a matter of fact, nowadays, more than 50% of renal tumors are incidentally diagnosed at ultrasonography, CT, or MRI, and increasing rates of incidental diagnosis are reported.[73] As an example, the number of patients with relevant additional findings has been recently estimated at 15% in a cohort of subjects undergoing a CT angiography of the abdominal aorta and the lower extremities.[74] We have similar percentage in consecutive series of contrast-enhanced CT examination of both inpatients and outpatients (unpublished data). Notably, a rate of 10% of findings of potential clinical relevance (e.g., arteriovenous malformations, cavernomas, pituitary abnormalities) requiring further diagnostic investigations has been reported in a cohort of *healthy* subjects who underwent a cranial MRI for research purposes.[75]

Thus, on a day-to-day basis, we perform unordered screenings for a number of diseases. Not insignificantly, the need to control health care expenditures makes it important to justify imaging procedures on the basis of cost-effectiveness analysis.

To understand this new era, we should examine some typically relevant problems of screening theory. The diagnosis of an asymptomatic disease is a challenge, not only because of the need of sensitivity (e.g., interpreting less prominent imaging signs as relevant), but also because of two phenomena well-known by the epidemiological science: *lead time bias* and *length bias.*

These are two particular types of disease progression bias we encounter in screening programs when a randomized control group is not available.[76] In lead time bias, the earlier diagnosis creates a false effect of prolonged survival for the group of subjects who were screened (Figure 27.4). In length bias, a differing disease progression makes the diagnosis of less aggressive tumors more probable in the group of subjects who were screened (Figure 27.5).

Moreover, when an asymptomatic disease is diagnosed (either by a screening program or as an additional finding in clinical imaging), we have the possibility of *overdiagnosis.* It is an extreme case of length bias: The disease, typically a tumor, is so indolent (slowly growing) or stable that it would not have been clinically relevant during the subject's life—taking into account the concurrent action of other causes of death—without the medical act of preclinical detection. The difference between diagnosis and overdiagnosis is clearly represented in Figure 27.6. The impact of an unknown overdiagnosis on the evaluation of the effect of a screening program is illustrated in Figure 27.7.

Overdiagnosis cannot be avoided in any screening program: Due to biological variability, we will invariably find some fraction of indolent diseases (e.g., tumors). We must accept a tradeoff between reduction of disease mortality and overdiagnosis. The problem is that quantification of overdiagnosis is not an easy task. It requires a complex statistical analysis considering a cohort of screened subjects for many years during and after the screening. A hot debate is now brewing on the amount of overdiagnosis due to mammographic screening programs. The size of overdiagnosis has been recently estimated to be as much as 25% of mammographically detected

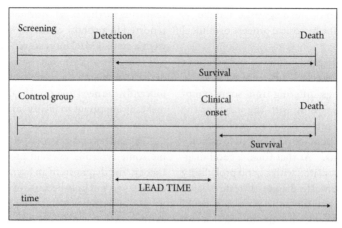

FIGURE 27.4 Lead time bias. Comparison between a group of screened subjects and a control group. The survival in the screened subjects appears double that of the controls. However, if the control group has been formed as a result of correct randomization (with the same probability of disease of the same mean severity as the screened group), the increase in survival is revealed as only apparent, solely due to earlier diagnosis. The difference between apparent and real survival in the screened group is the lead time.

Reprinted from Sardanelli F, Di Leo G. *Biostatistics for radiologists.* Milan: Springer-Verlag, 2009:177, with permission of the publisher, Springer Science+Business Media.

breast cancers, 50% of chest x-ray and/or sputum-detected lung cancers, and 60% of prostate-specific antigen-detected prostate cancers.[77]

As mentioned, we cannot achieve earlier and earlier diagnoses without a percentage of overdiagnosis. Up to now, no method, including advanced molecular gene profiling of tumor cells, is available to stratify malignant lesions (including breast grade 1 ductal carcinoma in situ) into those to be treated and those not to treat. This possibility is not achievable just around the corner and probably is beyond the current strategic horizon. Moreover, RCTs on this topic reveal relevant ethical problems that are highly difficult to resolve. Thus, when we find a small cancer, we are compelled to treat it. As a logical consequence, overdiagnosis causes *overtreatment*. In those

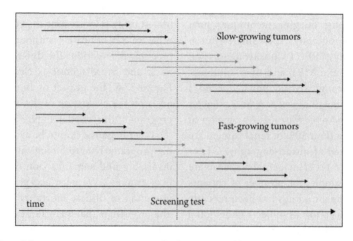

FIGURE 27.5 Length bias. A screening event, given a fixed time interval between one event and the next, more probably reveals slow-growing tumors than fast-growing tumors. The extent of the arrows represents the time between subclinical detectability and clinical onset. Black arrows represent tumors not detected at the screening test (interval cancers), whereas gray arrows represent screen-detected tumors.

Reprinted from Sardanelli F, Di Leo G. *Biostatistics for radiologists.* Milan: Springer-Verlag, 2009:177, with permission of the publisher, Springer Science+Business Media.

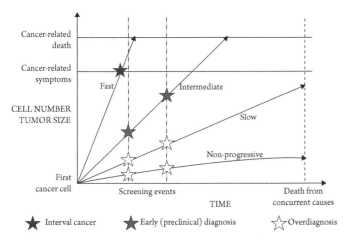

FIGURE 27.6 Overdiagnosis. The graph shows the influence of the growth speed on the screening diagnosis. Fast-growing tumors can present as interval cancer, tumors with intermediate growth speed are typically screen-detected, slow and nonprogressive tumors are overdiagnosed.

overdiagnosed cases, any treatment is overtreatment. The challenge is to minimize the treatment.

From that perspective, interventional radiology can do the job of minimizing biological and economic costs. If we find smaller and smaller tumors thanks to screening programs and the diagnostic performance of ultrasonography, CT, and MRI, then to treat these lesions using old surgical protocols well known to be effective for large, symptomatic lesions makes no sense. A spectrum of tools (radiofrequency ablation, focused ultrasound, lasertherapy, cryotherapy) under the guidance of various imaging techniques (US, CT, MRI) is now in the hands of interventional radiologists.

We should be aware that overdiagnosis is a not negligible problem and that it can be reduced by eliminating inappropriate imaging. However, we should be able to compensate for the unavoidable overdiagnosis by means of reducing the aggressiveness of treatment by means of interventional radiology. This perspective is open for debate, but needs to be backed by high-quality research, in particular RCTs comparing imaging-guided interventional procedures with standard surgical interventions for asymptomatic small tumors. In this way, we will able to guarantee the quality and safety of diagnostic and therapeutic procedures within the radiologic environment.

HOW TO MEASURE THE QUALITY OF DIAGNOSIS: RADIOLOGIST'S SKILL AND VALUE OF REPORTS

The application of EBM presents a fundamental difficulty. Producing scientific evidence, as well as reading and correctly understanding the primary

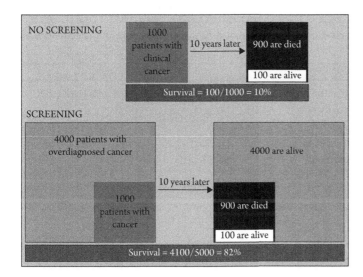

FIGURE 27.7 Effect of overdiagnosis. This comparison shows how an unknown overdiagnosis affects the estimated gain in survival rate of a screening program. In this theoretical case, we imagine a cancer disease composed of two different population of tumors, one fast-growing killer cancer with a clinical course not influenced by early diagnosis and one slowly growing cancer, overdiagnosed. The survival rate seems to change from 10% to 82%. However, this gain is only apparent.

evidence (original articles) and, in particular, the secondary evidence (basically, systematic reviews and meta-analyses), requires a knowledge of and confidence in the principles and techniques of descriptive and inferential statistics as applied to medical research. In fact, this is the only way to quantify the uncertainty associated with biological variability and the changes brought about by the patient's disease. It also allows one to manage treatment, using the indices and parameters involved in these studies, and it is the only means by which to judge their quality level. This methodological background is emerging as a very important expertise for any physician practicing in the new millennium.

As already stated, the methods for evaluating therapeutic interventional radiology are very similar to those for any surgical therapy, with RCTs being the principal tools for demonstrating the value of imaging-guided approaches. At first glance, diagnostic radiology may appear to be simpler, because it is limited to the analysis of diagnostic performance (i.e., a simple problem of sensitivity and specificity). We will show that this is not the case and that to analyze diagnostic performance is a complex matter having relevant theoretical and practical implications. Considering that making diagnoses is part of the radiologist's day-to-day job, he or she should be expert in handling the analysis of diagnostic performance.

This has great impact on quality because, in the radiologist's diagnostic performance, we should distinguish two issues:

- *Intrinsic quality*, which is basically related to the radiologist's skill and to the quality of the diagnostic process, including the quality of machines and the skill of the entire radiologic team. This intrinsic quality is measured

by means of indices such as sensitivity and specificity.
- *Value*, which is the reliability of radiological reports for the patient and the referring physician. This also depends on sensitivity and specificity, but is measured by means of indexes, such as positive and negative predictive values.

The main message here is that, depending on disease prevalence, we can have very high sensitivity or specificity, but also very low positive or negative predictive values (and vice versa, although less important). Notably, we are judged by patients and referring physicians on the basis of predictive values.

We need some simple definitions and formulas, starting with a two-by-two contingency table that considers the comparison between the results of a test and the standard of reference (Table 27.1). We do not comment here on the differences among the per-lesion, per-segment, per-organ, and per-patient analysis of diagnostic performance. Remember that in an early phase of test evaluation (when the test is initially introduced in clinical research), the per-lesion analysis is highly useful, whereas from a clinical viewpoint (when we want to test the value of the test for clinical practice), the per-patient approach is generally preferred.[78]

The numbers of true positives (TP), false positives (FP), true negatives (TN), and false negatives (FN) are used to calculate a series of indices that measure diagnostic performance, as shown in Table 27.2.

To describe each of these ten indices is beyond the scope of this chapter. However, I want to draw your attention to a particular aspect concerning the quality of diagnosis. Sensitivity and specificity are

TABLE 27.1 TWO-BY-TWO CONTINGENCY TABLE FOR A COMPARISON BETWEEN THE RESULTS OF A DIAGNOSTIC TEST AND THOSE OF A REFERENCE STANDARD IN A SERIES OF SUBJECTS

		Reference Standard		
		Affected	Unaffected	Total
Diagnostic test	Positive	True positives (TP)	False positives (FP)	All positives (TP + FP)
	Negative	False negatives (FN)	True negatives (TN)	All negatives (FN + TN)
Total		All affected (TP + FN)	All unaffected (FP +TN)	Grand total (TP + FN + FP + TN)

TABLE 27.2   INDICES MEASURING THE DIAGNOSTIC PERFORMANCE

Index	Definition	Formula	Interval	Dependence on Disease Prevalence
1. Sensitivity	Ability to identify the presence of disease	TP/(TP+FN)	0.0–1.0 (0%–100%)	No
2. Specificity	Ability to identify the presence of disease	VN/(VN+FP)	0.0–1.0 (0%–100%)	No
3. Positive predictive value	Reliability of the positive result	TP/(TP+FP)	0.0–1.0 (0%–100%)	Yes
4. Negative predictive value	Reliability of the negative result	TN/(TN+FN)	0.0–1.0 (0%–100%)	Yes
5. FN rate	Proportion between FN and all affected	FN/(FN+TP) = (1–Sensitivity)	0.0–1.0 (0%–100%)	No
6. FP rate	Proportion between FP and all unaffected	FP/(FP+TN) = (1–Specificity)	0.0–1.0 (0%–100%)	No
7. Accuracy	Global reliability	(TP+TN)/ (TP+TN+FP+FN)	0.0–1.0 (0%–100%)	Yes
8. Positive likelihood ratio (LR+)	Increase in disease probability when the result is positive	Sensitivity/ (1–Specificity)	1.0–∞	No
9. Negative likelihood ratio (LR–)	Decrease in disease probability when the result is negative	(1–Sensitivity)/ Specificity	0.0–1.0	No
10. Diagnostic odds ratio	Discriminating power	(TP×TN)/(FP×FN) = LR+/LR–	0.0–∞	No

commonly accepted by radiologists as the measures of their own quality and of the quality of the entire radiological process, including that of the radiological team (technicians, nurses, etc.), imaging machines, software, and so on. Sensitivity answers the fundamental question: How many of the affected patients am I able to diagnose as affected? Specificity answer another fundamental question (although commonly perceived as a less important than the former): How many of the unaffected patients am I able to diagnose as unaffected? Most believe that if these two indices are high, all is well. This is not true.

Quality for patients and referring physician is not measured by sensitivity and specificity. Radiologists look at the reliability of test results. How many times was I right when I reported the test as positive (positive predictive value)? How many times was I right when I reported the test as negative (negative predictive value)? How many times was I right when I reported the test as positive or negative (accuracy)? These indices are totally different from measures of sensitivity and specificity. The problem is that sensitivity and specificity concern affected or unaffected subjects, separately. As a consequence, the proportion between affected and unaffected subjects, or between affected subjects and the total number of

subjects (i.e., the disease prevalence) does not influence the measure. This is not the case with other indices: They address a mixture of affected and unaffected subjects (predictive values) or the total sample (accuracy). All of these three indices are influenced by disease prevalence. For mathematical reasons, this influence is relatively light for accuracy (which ranges between the value of sensitivity and the value of specificity) but dramatically heavy for both predictive values, as shown in Figure 27.8.

As you can see in Figure 27.8, with relatively high levels of sensitivity and specificity, depending on disease prevalence, accuracy ranges within the interval between them, but predictive values stay within this range only for a relatively narrow interval of disease prevalence, approximately from 45% to 75%. Outside of these values, predictive values are forced to go up to 1.00 (100%) or down to 0.00 (0%). This tremendous effect can be intuitively understood by considering that, if we do not have unaffected subjects in the sample, the diagnosis (prediction) of absence of disease will be always wrong; whereas, if we do not have affected subjects in the samples, the diagnosis (prediction) of disease will be always wrong.

Thus, we must understand that, given our *intrinsic quality* (sensitivity and specificity), the *perceived*

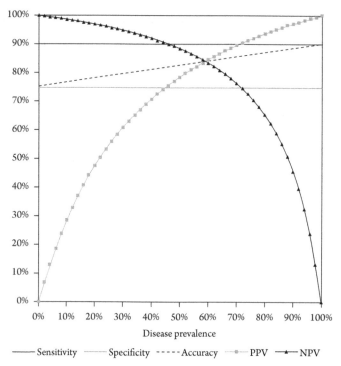

FIGURE 27.8 Distribution of positive predictive value (PPV), negative predictive value (NPV), and diagnostic accuracy as a function of disease prevalence (sensitivity and specificity being constant, equal to 90% and 75%, respectively). Note that disease prevalence changes the predictive values from 0% to 100% according two different curves, while accuracy increase linearly from 75% (the value of specificity) to 90% (the value of sensitivity). At a disease prevalence of about 60% accuracy, PPV and NPV tend to be equal (about 85%). The likelihood ratios (LRs), here not represented, depending on sensitivity and specificity, are constant too, equal to 3.60 (positive LR) and 0.13 (negative LR).

quality of our work (predictive values) depends on disease prevalence. Notably, accuracy—which has a reduced range of variation—is a quite unusable index in clinical practice. What patients and clinicians want to know is the reliability of a single positive or negative result, not a mean of correctness over the entire sample of patients. Thus, the value of our reports depends on disease prevalence. Disease prevalence is basically the result of patient selection.

What factors influence patient selection? We will consider three different scenarios, in logic order, from lower to higher disease prevalence, even though the practical experience is inverted (one usually first undertakes clinical practice, then screening).

The first scenario is classic organized screening. The archetype is the biannual mammographic screening, with the invitation of asymptomatic women from 49 to 69 years of age, performed in many European countries. Here, after the first round, the prevalence is about 0.3%–0.5% (technically, this is an incidence, calculated as number of new cases per year). This is due to the fact that, if the lifetime risk of being diagnosed with a breast cancer is about 9%-14% across European countries,[79] a large fraction of tumors is diagnosed between 45 and 75 years of age. For instance, suppose that lifetime risk is 10% and that 60% of cancers appear from 49 and 69 years of age. The probability of facing a cancer in this age interval (20 years) with a screening event every 2 years will be $0.10 \times 0.60 \times 0.10 = 0.006 = 0.6\%$. The annual incidence will be 0.3%. Thus, for every 100 women we screen, we will find less than one cancer. Numbers can change due to different general lifetime risks, screening intervals, and other factors, but what counts here is the scale of the phenomenon. Suppose that we have 0.6 women with cancer out of every 100 screened biannually. Importantly, even with good sensitivity (say, 75%), if we recall 10% of the screened women for further imaging, our positive predictive value will be $(0.6 \times 0.75/10) = 0.045 = 4.5\%$.

The second scenario is screening in a high-risk asymptomatic population. Consider the case of

MRI annual screening of BRCA1 or BRCA2 mutation carriers and women with a strong family history of breast and/or ovarian cancer. Here, the lifetime risk is about 70%, and first cancers appear earlier.[80] From 30 to 50 years of age, you see probably 90% of the first breast cancers. The annual incidence will be $0.7 \times 0.9 \times 0.05 = 0.0315 = 3.2\%$, more than 10 times that seen in the first scenario. After screening every year in these women with a high sensitivity technique such as contrast-enhanced MR imaging (with, say, a 90% sensitivity), if you recall 10% of patients for further imaging, the positive predictive value will be $(3.2 \times 0.9/10) = 0.288 = 28.8\%$. As you see, the merit of this sixfold performance in terms of positive predictive value in comparison with screening mammography is not mainly due to the higher sensitivity of MR imaging but to the higher disease prevalence (we are using incidence data because we are reasoning on a yearly basis). You can verify what happens using mammography in this setting by positing that sensitivity is only about 50%: if other conditions remain unchanged, then the predictive value will be about 16%.

Importantly, in both these scenarios concerning asymptomatic women, the so-called pretest disease probability is equal to the disease prevalence in the population under consideration. In other words, we did not make any further patient selections.

The third scenario is clinical mammography, when this imaging technique is applied to symptomatic women from 40 to 70 years of age. Suppose we are considering women with a new palpable breast nodule and that this symptoms implies a cancer probability of about 40%. With the same sensitivity supposed for screening mammography (75%), and also with a recall for further imaging equal to 70%, the positive predictive value will be $(40 \times 0.75/70) = 0.428 = 43\%$. The consequence is a strongly increased reliability (in terms of positive predictive value) for the radiologist's report, even though sensitivity remains unchanged in comparison to that of the first scenario. The perceived quality of the radiologic examination went up solely due to the increased disease prevalence. Here, the woman (with self-palpation) or the referring physician (with clinical breast examination) made the patient selection.

However, in this setting, sensitivity will probably be higher. Using a sensitivity level (90%) that takes into account that the potential cancer is larger (palpable) and that the radiologist knows where the cancer is, the positive predictive value will be $(40 \times$ $0.9/70) = 0.514 = 51\%$. From this viewpoint, when patient selection impacts on disease severity, sensitivity and specificity can be strongly influenced. In other words, sensitivity and specificity are independent from disease prevalence but not from disease severity. Patient selection frequently changes not only prevalence but also disease severity. Four different settings showing this mixed influence are presented in Figure 27.9.

The message here is that *patient selection is crucial for quality of radiology*. This is true also for screening. To extend the screening program to women from 39 to 49 years of age is a change of subject selection and may change the global disease prevalence and, as a consequence, aspects of the diagnostic performance. We should therefore educate clinicians to perform correct patient selection, giving them updated information about the indications and limitations of imaging methods in different clinical and screening settings. One way to do this is to discuss with clinicians their questionable requests for imaging examinations, so that the radiologist's expertise plays a strong role in the final decision.

THE DIAGNOSTIC PATHWAY: GRAPHS OF CONDITIONAL PROBABILITY

In clinical practice, a diagnostic pathway frequently includes a planned sequence of multiple examinations, each determining a new disease probability. If one examination is useful, it lowers or increases the disease probability to a relevant extent. The relevance of this decrease or increase can be defined only from a clinical perspective, weighting the impact of residual risk of false-negative and false-positive results in a particular setting. In other words, here you see how a statistically significant increase or decrease of disease probability may be clinically irrelevant. Would you stop the diagnostic pathway if your test (e.g., a negative chest x-ray examination) tells you that the probability of lung cancer for your patient (a symptomatic strong smoker) is decreased from 60% to 30%? I think not, even though the probability has been halved. All of us would still request a chest CT.

The theoretical framework of this approach is the Bayes' theorem, proposed by the Thomas Bayes (1702–1761) and published posthumously in 1763. If we know the pretest disease probability and the sensitivity and specificity of the test, the theorem allows us to calculate the disease probability after

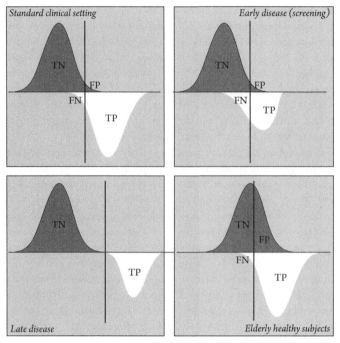

FIGURE 27.9 Effect of changes of spectrum of disease and of healthy condition on diagnostic performance. The area under the curve of the distribution of healthy subjects is white; the area under the curve of the distribution of the patients affected with the disease is gray. *Upper left* (clinical setting for outpatients): Only about 50% of the symptomatic subjects is really affected with the disease; only a few subjects resulted in false-negative (high sensitivity) or false-positive (high specificity) results. *Upper right* (screening setting): The patients affected with the disease are reduced in number, but they also have a disease with a lower mean level of gravity. As a consequence, the gray area under the curve is reduced in size and shifted toward left, with a larger superimposition on the white area of the healthy subjects: We have more false negatives as well as lower sensitivity and negative predictive value. *Lower left* (late disease, e.g., clinical setting for inpatients): The mean level of disease gravity is higher; the gray area is reduced (some patients are dead) and shifted toward right; shifting the cutoff toward the right, we can distinguish perfectly between patients with the disease and healthy subjects (no false negative or false positive). *Lower right* (elderly healthy subjects): A more aged healthy population shifts the white area to the right, giving more false positives, as well as reduced specificity and positive predictive value.

having obtained a positive or negative result (i.e., *the post-test probability*). This approach is exploited by Fagan's Bayesian nomogram,[81] which transforms a pretest disease probability into a post-test disease probability using the likelihood ratio as geometrical projection, without any need for calculation (Figure 27.10). It uses the graphic solution of an equation with multiple variables. The slope of the straight line on the nomogram allows us to see graphically the power of the examination.

How do we define the right sequence of examinations for a particular clinical problem? When can we decide to stop the sequence, concluding in favor of the presence or absence of the disease? This problem can be solved using graphs of conditional probability. These graphs supply a visual representation of the change in disease probability obtained using

a diagnostic examination in a given clinical setting. The diagnostic performance can be appreciated on the graphs in terms of modification of disease probability for positive and negative results at all points within the range of pretest disease probability, and the contribution of different techniques can be evaluated to design efficient diagnostic algorithms. An example is shown for a diagnostic algorithm including a D-dimer test, CT pulmonary angiography, and indirect CT venography in diagnosing pulmonary embolism (Figure 27.11).[17]

Importantly, data to be entered in these graphical calculations—both Fagan's nomogram and graphs of conditional probability—should be extracted from the *best external evidence* available in the literature. These are the initial pretest probability and the positive and negative likelihood ratio of

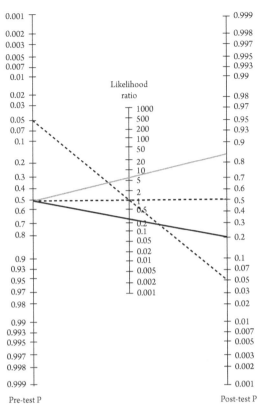

FIGURE 27.10 Fagan's Bayesian nomogram. On the central vertical axis, the positive and negative likelihood ratio (LR) values; on the vertical axis on the left side, the pretest disease probability (pre-test P); on the vertical axis on the right side, the post-test disease probability (post-test P). The oblique gray line shows how a positive LR equal to +5 changes a pretest disease probability of 0.5 (i.e., an absolute uncertainty) into a post-test disease probability of about 0.83 (i.e., a relatively high disease probability). The two dotted lines show how an examination with a LR equal to 1 left the disease probability unchanged. The oblique black line shows how a negative LR equal to 0.35 changes a pretest disease probability of 0.5 into a post-test disease probability of 0.2. In this way, LRs act as angular coefficients of the straight lines designed on the Bayesian nomogram.

Reprinted from Sardanelli F, Di Leo G. Biostatistics for radiologists. Milan: Springer-Verlag, 2009: 35, with permission of the publisher, Springer Science+Business Media.

the diagnostic tests. To best use this approach, we should examine the sensitivity and specificity (and, as a consequence, the likelihood ratios) of the test performed at the particular center or hospital under consideration, which may be lower (or higher) than those reported in the literature. Theoretically, we could calibrate our calculations on the real diagnostic performances we offer to our patients. This strategic target for quality in diagnostic radiology is very difficult, but all of us should be aware that clinical medicine is evolving in that direction. We should take into account this perspective.

HEALTH TECHNOLOGY ASSESSMENT IN RADIOLOGY

The Six-level Scale

In the framework described earlier, EBM and EBR are based on the possibility of getting the best external evidence for a specific clinical question. Now the problem is: How is this evidence produced? In other words, which methods should be used to demonstrate the value of a diagnostic imaging technology? This field is known as *health technology assessment* (HTA), and particular features of HTA are important in radiology.

Performance can be measured using three different terms. While *efficacy* reflects the performance of medical technology under ideal conditions, *effectiveness* evaluates the same performance under ordinary conditions, and *efficiency* measures the cost-effectiveness.[82] In this way, the development of a procedure in specialized or academic centers (efficacy) is distinguished from its application to routine clinical practice (effectiveness) and from the inevitable role played by the economic costs associated with implementation of the procedure (cost-effectiveness).

To evaluate the impact of the results of studies (i.e., the level at which the HTA was performed), we need a hierarchy of values. Such a hierarchy has been generically proposed for diagnostic tests and is also accepted for diagnostic imaging investigations. During the 1970s, the first classification proposed five levels for the analysis of the diagnostic and therapeutic impact of cranial CT.[83] By the 1990s,[84] this classification had evolved into a six-level scale, thanks to the addition of a top level called *societal impact*.[85–87] A description of this scale was recently presented in the radiologic literature.[2,88,89] This six-level scale is currently widely accepted as a foundation for the HTA of diagnostic tools.

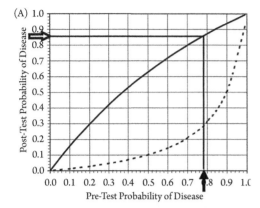

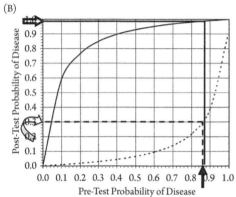

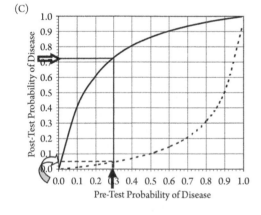

FIGURE 27.11 Graphs of conditional probability. Diagnostic performance of D-dimer (A), CT pulmonary angiography (B), and indirect CT venography (C) for pulmonary embolism and deep venous thrombosis. Positive result of the examination, solid curve line; negative result of the examination, dashed curve line. For a pretest probability (on the x-axis), the post-test probability of a positive or negative test is derived by drawing a perpendicular line up to the solid line or dashed line, respectively, and then across to the y-axis. For a patient with a high pretest probability of pulmonary embolism, the prevalence is 78% (*solid arrow* in A). Post-test probability for a positive D-dimer result is 85% (*open arrow* in A), which warrants further investigation. This post-test probability is then applied as pretest probability to the graph for CT pulmonary angiography (*solid arrow* in B). If the result is positive, post-test probability is 99% (*open arrow* in B) and the diagnosis is confirmed. If the result is negative, post-test probability is 30% (*curved arrow* in B), which does not allow the disease to be ruled out: further investigation is warranted. This post-test probability is finally applied as pretest probability to the graph for indirect CT venography (*solid arrow* in C). If the result is positive, post-test probability of deep vein thrombosis is greater than 72% (*open arrow* in C) and diagnosis is confirmed. If the result is negative, post-test probability of deep venous thrombosis is less than 5% (*curved arrow* in C) and the diagnosis is excluded.

From Dodd JD. Evidence-based practice in radiology: Steps 3 and 4—appraise and apply diagnostic radiology literature. *Radiology.* 2007;242:342–54, with permission of the author and of copyright owner, RSNA.

This hierarchy is presented here (Table 27.3) with the introduction reproducibility studies, usually not considered, at the level 2, because of the increasing importance of these studies for quality assessment in radiology. From a strictly logical viewpoint, reproducibility is a complex issue that combines different aspects dealing with factors related to technical performance and factors related to the observer's reliability. It may be proposed as intermediate level between levels 1 and 2. However, we should take into account that (intra- and interobserver) reproducibility mainly depends on observers'

performance and that results on reproducibility are frequently reported within studies evaluating classic measures of diagnostic performance (sensitivity, specificity, etc.). Thus, they can be introduced as an aspect of level 2 of the HTA hierarchy. Moreover, the introduction of safety issues at level 1, as proposed recently,[89] seems to be a smart approach that links quality to safety at the first (i.e., preliminary) level of evaluation. This method takes advantage of the common practice of evaluating safety and technical performance together when a new technology is introduced. An alternative may be to introduce

TABLE 27.3   HIERARCHY OF STUDIES ON DIAGNOSTIC TESTS

Level	Parameters Under Investigation
6. Societal impact	Benefit–cost and cost effectiveness analysis from a social perspective
5. Patient outcomes	Fraction of patients improved with the test compared with that of those improved without the test; difference in morbidity between the patients with the test and those without the test; gain in quality-adjusted life years (QALYs) obtained by the patients with the test compared with those without the test
4. Therapeutic impact	Fraction of patients for whom the test is judged useful for treatment planning or for whom the treatment planning is modified on the basis of the information supplied by the test
3. Diagnostic impact	Fraction of patients for whom the test is judged useful for rendering the diagnosis or for whom the diagnosis is substantially modified after the test; positive and negative likelihood ratios
2. Diagnostic performance	Sensitivity, specificity, accuracy, positive predictive value, negative predictive value, and receiver operator characteristic (ROC) analysis; intraobserver, interobserver, and interstudy reproducibility
1. Safety and technical performance	Mechanical and electric safety; radiation dose (if relevant); gray scale range; modulation transfer function change; sharpness; spatial resolution, in-plane (line pairs per mm, pixel size) and through-the-plane (slice thickness), integrated in voxel size; signal-to-noise ratio; contrast resolution (contrast-to-noise ratio); time resolution (images/sec) etc;

a new level, namely *level 0*, which considers solely safety issues.

This scale offers an opportunity to assess a diagnostic technology from differing viewpoints. Studies on safety and technical performance (level 1) are of key importance as initial gatekeepers for further research, whereas those concerning diagnostic performance and reproducibility (level 2) are the basis for adopting a new technique. However, radiologists and clinicians are also interested in how an imaging technique impacts patient management for diagnosis (level 3), therapy (level 4), and patient outcomes (level 5). Health care providers wish to ascertain the costs and benefits of reimbursing a new technique from a societal perspective (level 6). Governments are mainly concerned about the societal impact of new technology in comparison to that of other initiatives they may be considering.

A crucial point here is the apparently small jump from level 2 to level 3. A technique can offer optimal diagnostic performance without making any impact on diagnosis (when symptoms are already highly suggestive for disease). Or, a technique can offer an optimal diagnostic performance (level 2) and have high diagnostic impact (level 3) without having any impact on therapy (when a disease is diagnosed but cannot be cured). In the latter case, an early asymptomatic diagnosis only achieves a dramatic worsening in the quality of life of the preclinical-phase patient.

This hierarchical order is *a one-way logical chain*. A positive effect at any level generally implies a positive effect at all preceding levels, but not vice versa.[22] In fact, although a new diagnostic technology with a positive impact on patient outcome commonly has better technical performance and higher diagnostic accuracy compared with the standard technology, there is no certainty that a radiologic test with a higher diagnostic performance results in better patient outcomes. If we demonstrate high diagnostic performance for a new test (level 2), the impact on a higher level depends on the clinical setting and frequently on conditions external to radiology. Thus, diagnostic performance must be demonstrated with specifically designed studies. The HTA should examine the link between each level in the chain of this hierarchy to establish the clinical value of a radiological test.

Cost effectiveness can be included in HTA at any level of the hierarchic scale, as cost per examination (level 1), per correct diagnosis (level 2), per invasive test avoided (level 3), per changed therapeutic plan (level 4), and per gained quality-adjusted life expectancy or per saved life (levels 5–6).[22] Recommendations for the performance of cost effectiveness analyses, however, advocate calculating incremental costs per quality-adjusted life year gained and doing this from the health care or societal perspective. Only then are the results comparable and meaningful when setting priorities.

New equipment or a new imaging procedure should undergo HTA assessment before it is adopted by day-to-day practice. Indeed, the radiological literature is mainly composed of level 1 (safety and technical performance) and level 2 (diagnostic performance) studies. This is almost inevitable since the evaluation of the technical and diagnostic performance of medical imaging is a typical function of radiologic research. However, radiologists less frequently study the diagnostic impact (level 3) or therapeutic impact (level 4) of medical imaging, and outcome (level 5) and societal impact (level 6) analysis is rare in radiologic research. In 2001, a "shortage of coherent and consistent scientific evidence in the radiology literature" to be used for a wide application of EBR was claimed.[2] Ten years later, much work remains to be done.

This urgent problem has been recently highlighted by Kuhl et al. for the clinical value of 3.0-T MR imaging. These authors state that, "Although for most neurologic and angiographic applications 3.0 T yields technical advantages compared to 1.5 T, the evidence regarding the added clinical value of high-field strength MR is very limited. There is no paucity of articles that focus on the technical evaluation of neurologic and angiographic applications at 3.0 T. This technology-driven science absorbs a lot of time and energy—energy that is not available for research on the actual clinical utility of high-field MR imaging."[90]

There are genuine reasons why radiological research rarely attains the highest impact levels of efficacy. On the one hand, increasingly rapid technologic development forces an endless return to low impact levels (radiology was judged as the most rapidly evolving specialty in medicine).[38] On the other hand, level 5 and 6 studies entail long performance times, huge economic costs, and a high degree of organization and management for longitudinal data gathering on patient outcomes, and these studies often require a randomized design. The average time for 59 studies in radiation oncology was reported to be about 11 years.[91] In this setting, there are two essential needs: full cooperation with clinicians who manage the patient before and after a diagnostic examination, and methodological/statistical expertise regarding RCTs. Radiologists should not shun this type of research because it is not unfamiliar territory: More than three decades ago, mammographic screening created a scenario in which early diagnosis by imaging contributed to a worldwide reduction in mortality from breast cancer, producing high societal impact.

A simple way to appraise the intrinsic difficulty in HTA of radiological procedures is to compare radiological with pharmacological research. After chemical discovery of an active molecule, development, cell and animal testing, and phase I and II studies are carried out by the industry and a very few cooperating clinicians (for phase I and II studies). In this long phase (commonly about 10 years), the majority of academic institutions and large hospitals are not involved. When clinicians are involved in phase III studies (i.e., large randomized trials for registration), the aims are already at level 5 (outcome impact). *Radiologists have to climb four levels of impact before reaching the outcome level.* We can imagine a world in which new radiologic procedures also are tested for cost effectiveness or patient outcome endpoints before entering routine clinical practice, but the real world is different, and we have much more technology-driven research from radiologists than radiologist-driven research on technology.

Several countries have well-developed strategies for HTA. Radiologists in the United States have formed the ACR Imaging Network (www.ACRIN.org). In Europe, the European Institute for Biomedical Imaging Research, promoted by the European Society of Radiology, has formed the European Network for Assessment of Imaging in Medicine (http://www.eibir.org/cms/website.php?id=/en/joint_initiatives/euroaim.htm). In the United Kingdom, the government funds a HTA program in which topics are prioritized and work is commissioned in relevant areas. In Italy, the Section of Economics in Radiology of the Italian Society of Medical Radiology has connections with the Italian Society of HTA for dedicated research projects. Since 2005, the Royal Australian and New Zealand College of Radiologists have developed a program focusing on implementing evidence into practice in radiology: the Quality Use of Diagnostic Imaging (QUDI) program (http://www.ranzcr.edu.au/qualityprograms/qudi/index.cfm). The program is fully funded by the Australian government and managed by the College.

It is important that new technologies are appropriately assessed before being adopted into practice. However, with new technology, the problem of deciding when to undertake a formal HTA is difficult. Often, the technology is still being developed and refined. An early assessment, which can take several years, might not be relevant if the technology is still undergoing continual improvement. However, if we wait until a technology is mature, then it may already have been widely adopted into practice, and most clinicians and radiologists are very reluctant to randomize patients into a study that might deprive them of the newest imaging test.

With increasingly expensive technology, new funding mechanisms may be required to create partnerships among industry, the research community, and the health care system that will allow the timely, planned introduction of these techniques into practice so the benefit to patients and society can be fully explored before widespread adoption takes place.

Alternative to Randomized Controlled Trials: Pragmatic (or Quasi-experimental) Studies and Decision Analysis

The conduction of classic RCTs in radiology is not the standard for clinical research. In fact, this study design was born in a context characterized by a slower technological evolution and is frequently not feasible in the clinical radiological setting. New possibilities now exist, however. These are the so-called *pragmatic* or *quasi-experimental studies* and *decision analysis*.

A pragmatic study examines the concurrent development, assessment, and implementation of new diagnostic technologies.[92] An empirically based study, preferably using controlled randomization, integrates research aims with clinical practice, using outcome measures reflecting the clinical decision-making process and acceptance of the new test. Outcome measures include additional imaging studies requested, costs of diagnostic workup and treatments, confidence in therapeutic decision-making, recruitment rate, and patient's outcome measures. Importantly, *time is used as fundamental dimension*, as an explanatory variable in data analysis to model the learning curve, technical developments, and interpretation skill. Limitations of this approach can be the need for dedicated and specifically trained personnel and the related economic costs to be covered (presumably by governmental agencies).[93] However, this type of study has the potential to answer the double demand of increasingly rapid technological evolution in radiology and the need to attain higher quality in radiological studies, thus providing a unique approach to obtaining data on diagnostic confidence, effect on therapy planning, patient outcome measures, and cost-effectiveness analysis. Currently, very few pragmatic radiological studies have been published.[94–99]

Decision analysis integrates the best available evidence and patient values in a mathematical model of possible strategies, their consequences, and the associated outcomes. By analyzing the sensitivity of model results to varying assumptions, it can explore the effects of the limited external validity associated with clinical trials.[15,100] It is a particularly useful tool for evaluating diagnostic tests by combining intermediate outcome measures, such as sensitivity and specificity obtained from published studies and meta-analyses, with long-term consequences of TP, FP, TN, and PN outcomes. Different diagnostic or therapeutic alternatives are visually represented by means of a decision tree, and dedicated statistical methods are used (e.g., Markov model, Monte Carlo simulation).[15,101] This method is typically used for cost effectiveness analysis.

This approach has been evaluated in 111 radiology-related articles over a 20-year period, starting in 1985, when the first article concerning cost effectiveness analysis in medical imaging was published.[102] The average number of studies increased from 1.6 per year (1985–1995) to 9.4 per year (1996–2005). Eighty-six studies were performed to evaluate diagnostic imaging technologies, and 25 were performed to evaluate interventional imaging technologies. Ultrasonography (35%), angiography (32%), MR imaging (23%), and CT (20%) were evaluated most frequently. Using a seven-point scale, from 1 = low to 7 = high, the mean quality score was 4.23 ± 1.12 (mean ± standard deviation), without significant improvement over time. Note that quality was measured according to U.S. recommendations for cost effectiveness analyses, which are not identical to European standards, and the power to demonstrate an improvement was limited.[103] The authors concluded that "improvement in the quality of analyses is needed."[102]

Levels of Evidence and Degrees of Recommendation

The need to evaluate the relevance of the various studies in relation to reported levels of evidence generated a hierarchy of the levels of evidence based on study type and design.

According to the Centre for Evidence-based Medicine (Oxford, U.K.),[10] studies on diagnostic performance can be ranked on a scale, from 1 to 5 (Table 27.4). Based on similar scales, four degrees of recommendations, from A to D, can be distinguished (Table 27.5).

Many different classification levels exist by which to rank evidence and recommendations, and because the same degree of recommendation can be represented differently in different systems (by letter grade, numerical rank, etc.) confusion and errors are possible clinical practice.

TABLE 27.4   LEVELS OF EVIDENCE OF STUDIES ON DIAGNOSTIC PERFORMANCE

Level of Evidence	Study Type
1a	Systematic reviews with homogeneous meta-analyses of level-1 studies
	Multicenter studies, in consecutive patients with a reliable and systematically applied reference standard, of diagnostic criteria previously established by explorative studies
1b	Single-center studies, in consecutive patients with a reliable and systematically applied reference standard, of diagnostic criteria previously established by explorative studies
1c	Studies of diagnostic examinations with very high sensitivity (absolute *snout*) and of diagnostic examinations with very high specificity (absolute *spin*)*
2a	Systematic reviews with homogeneous meta-analyses of level 2 or higher studies
2b	Explorative studies of diagnostic criteria in cohorts of patients with a reliable and systematically applied reference standard; definition of diagnostic criteria on parts of cohorts or on databases
3a	Systematic reviews with homogeneous meta-analyses of level 3 or higher studies
3b	Studies of nonconsecutive patients and/or without systematic application of the reference standard
4	Case–control studies
	Studies with inadequate or nonindependent reference standard
5	Experts' opinions without critical evaluation of the literature

From Centre for Evidence-Based Medicine, Oxford University, England. Accessed July 9, 2010, at: http://cebm.net; and Dodd JD, MacEneaney PM, Malone DE. Evidence-based radiology: How to quickly assess the validity and strength of publications in the diagnostic radiology literature. *Eur Radiol.* 2004;14(5):915–22, with modifications.
* An examination is *snout* when its negative result excludes the possibility of the presence of the disease (when a test has a very high sensitivity, a negative result rules *out* the diagnosis); it is instead *spin* when its positive result definitely confirms the presence of the disease (when a test has a very high specificity, a positive result rules *in* the diagnosis).

A new approach to evidence classification has been recently proposed by the GRADE working group,[104] with special attention paid to the definition of standardized criteria for releasing and applying clinical guidelines. The GRADE system states the need of an explicit declaration of the methodological core of a guideline, with particular regard to quality of evidence, relative importance, risk–benefit balance, and the value of the incremental benefit for each outcome. This complex method finally provides four simple levels of evidence: *high,* when further research is thought unlikely to modify the level of confidence of the estimated effect; *moderate,* when further research is thought likely to modify the level of confidence of the estimated effect and the estimate itself of the effect; *low,* when further research is thought very likely to modify the level of confidence of the estimated effect and the estimate itself of the effect; and *very low,* when the estimate of the effect is highly uncertain. Similarly, the risk–benefit ratio is classified as follows: *net benefit,* when the treatment clearly provides more benefits than risks; *moderate,* when, even though the treatment provides important benefits, a tradeoff occurs in terms of risks; *uncertain,* when we do not know whether the treatment provides more benefits than risks; *lack of net benefit,* when the treatment clearly provides more risks than benefits. The procedure gives four possible recommendation levels: *do it* or *don't do it,* when we think that the large majority of well-informed people would make this decision; *probably do*

TABLE 27.5   DEGREES OF RECOMMENDATION

Degree of Recommendation	Study Type
A	Level 1 studies
B	Consistent level 2 or 3 studies or extrapolations* from level 1 studies
C	Consistent level 4 studies or extrapolations* from level 2 or 3 studies
D	Level 5 studies or low-quality or inconclusive studies of any level

From Centre for Evidence-based Medicine, Oxford University, England. Accessed February 24, 2008, at: http://www.cebm.net/index.aspx?o=1025; with modifications.
* *Extrapolation* is the translation of a study to clinical situations different from those of the original study.

it or *probably don't do it*, when we think that the majority of well-informed people would make this decision, but a substantial minority would have an opposite opinion. The GRADE system finally differentiates between *strong recommendations* and *weak recommendations*, making guideline application to clinical practice easier. Methods for applying the GRADE system to diagnostic tests were issued.[105]

QUALITY OF RESEARCH ON DIAGNOSTIC RADIOLOGY

Sources of Bias in Studies on Diagnostic Performance

The quality of HTA studies is determined by the quality of the information provided by the original primary studies on which they are based. Thus, the quality of the original studies is the key point for implementing EBR.

What are the most important sources of bias for the studies on diagnostic performance? We must distinguish between biases influencing the *external validity* of a study—that is, the applicability of its results to clinical practice—and biases influencing the *internal validity* of a study—that is, its inherent coherence. Bias influencing external validity are mainly due to selection of subjects and choice of techniques leading to lack of generalizability. Bias influencing the internal validity are due to errors in the methods used in the study (Figure 27.12). External and internal validity are related concepts: Internal validity is a necessary but not sufficient condition to ensure that a study has external validity.[106]

Thus, all kinds of bias influence the external validity of a study. Although lack of generalizability has a negative effect on external validity, the study can retain its internal validity; errors in performing the study have a negative effect primarily on internal validity and only secondarily on external validity. The lack of internal validity makes the results themselves unreliable. In this case, the question of external validity (i.e., the application of the results to clinical practice) is pointless. As a consequence, only the results of a study not flawed by errors in planning and performance can be applied to clinical practice.[107]

Several items are present in both planning and performing a study. Consider the reference standard: an error in planning occurs when the researcher chooses an inadequate reference standard (imperfect reference standard bias); an error in performing the study occurs when there is an incorrect use of the planned reference standard. We can go wrong either in choosing incorrect rules or by applying right rules incorrectly (but also adding errors in the application of already incorrect rules). There is probably only one right way to do a study, but infinite ways to introduce errors that make a study useless.

Bias in performing the study can be due to:

- Defects in protocol application
- Unforeseen events or events due to insufficient protocol specification
- Methods defined in the study protocol that imply errors in performing the study

For the last two items, the defects in performing the study depend in some way on error in planning.

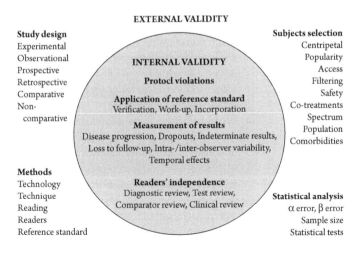

EXTERNAL VALIDITY		
Study design		**Subjects selection**
Experimental		Centripetal
Observational	**INTERNAL VALIDITY**	Popularity
Prospective		Access
Retrospective	**Protocl violations**	Filtering
Comparative		Safety
Non-	**Application of reference standard**	Co-treatments
comparative	Verification, Work-up, Incorporation	Spectrum
	Measurement of results	Population
	Disease progression, Dropouts, Indeterminate results,	Comorbidities
	Loss to follow-up, Intra-/inter-observer variability,	
	Temporal effects	
Methods		
Technology	**Readers' independence**	
Technique	Diagnostic review, Test review,	**Statistical analysis**
Reading	Comparator review, Clinical review	α error, β error
Readers		Sample size
Reference standard		Statistical tests

FIGURE 27.12 Synopsis of the sources of bias in the studies on diagnostic performance. To apply the results of a study to clinical practice, it must have internal validity (i.e., absence of substantial errors in the methods used in the study) and external validity (i.e., generalizability to other settings). For more details on each of the sources of bias, see references 106–108.

Reprinted from Sardanelli F, Di Leo G. *Biostatistics for radiologists.* Milan: Springer-Verlag, 2008:166, with permission of the publisher, Springer Science+Business Media.

This does not seem to be the case for the first item. However, if a study has many protocol violations, then the study protocol was probably theoretically correct but only partially applicable. In other words, biases in performing the study frequently have their ultimate origin in planning errors.

More details on each source of bias can be found in articles by Kelly et al.[107] and Sica et al.[108]

The STARD Initiative

The need for an improved quality of studies on diagnostic performance has been present for many years. In 1995, Reid et al.[109] published the results of their analysis on 112 articles regarding diagnostic tests published from 1978 to1993 in four important medical journals. Overall, over 80% of the studies had relevant biases flawing their estimates of diagnostic performance. In particular, only 27% of the studies reported the disease spectrum of the patients; only 46% of the studies had no workup bias; only 38% had no review bias; only 11% reported the confidence intervals associated with the point estimates of sensitivity, specificity, predictive values, etc.; only 22% reported the frequency of indeterminate results and how they were managed; and only 23% of the studies reported a reproducibility of the results.

In this context, a detailed presentation of rules for a quality original article on diagnostic performance was outlined in an important paper,[110] "Towards Complete and Accurate Reporting of Studies of Diagnostic Accuracy: The STARD Initiative," published in 2003 in many renowned radiological journals. The work provides a practical short manual to check the quality of a manuscript or published paper. An extremely useful checklist is provided so that authors can avoid omitting important information. STARD is an acronym for Standards for Reporting of Diagnostic Accuracy. The authors evaluated 33 papers that proposed a checklist for studies on diagnostic performance. From a list of 75 recommendations, 25 were judged important. The gap to be filled in was outlined by Smidt et al. in a study published in 2005.[111] These researchers evaluated 124 articles on diagnostic performance published in 12 journals with an impact factor of 4 or higher using the 25-item STARD checklist. Only 41% of articles covered more than 50% of STARD items, while no articles covered more than 80%. A flowchart of the study was presented in only two articles. The mean number of reported STARD items was 11.9. These authors concluded that "Quality of reporting

in diagnostic accuracy articles published in 2000 is less than optimal, even in journals with high impact factor."[111]

The relatively low quality of studies on diagnostic performance is a relevant threat to the successful implementation of EBR. Hopefully, the adoption of the STARD requisites will improve the quality of radiological studies, but the process seems to be very slow,[22] as demonstrated by the recent work by Wilczynski.[112]

Other rule lists are available for articles reporting the results of randomized controlled trials (the CONSORT statement,[113] recently extended to trials assessing nonpharmacological treatments),[114] and meta-analyses (the QUOROM statement).[115]

In particular, systematic reviews and meta-analyses in radiology should evaluate study validity for specific issues[55]: detailed imaging methods, level of excellence of both imaging and reference standard, adequacy of technology generation, level of ionizing radiation exposure, and viewing (hard vs. soft copy).

EVIDENCE-BASED RADIOLOGY AND SAFETY

The Impact of Evidence-based Radiology on Patient Safety

An evidence-based approach has relevant impact on patient safety. This occurs at different levels by means of the use of diagnostic tests in optimized diagnostic pathways. An EBR approach may imply:

- Better diagnoses in terms of expert use of predictive values in defined clinical settings (e.g., using graphs of conditional probability)
- Reduction in time needed for diagnosis
- Reduction in number of tests used for diagnosis
- Reduction in invasiveness of tests used for diagnosis, including a smart choice of diagnostic techniques not necessitating the administration of contrast material and/or ionizing radiation exposure
- When contrast material administration is necessary, higher patient protection against unwanted effects from diagnostic imaging, such as contrast-induced nephropathy (CIN) and nephrogenic systemic fibrosis (NSF), including reduced doses of contrast material and management of contrast material-induced reactions

- When exposure to ionizing radiation is necessary, reduction in dose according to the ALARA principle

The excessive exposure of patients to ionizing radiation is one of most important issues for safety in radiology. The overuse of CT is under consideration for its paramount contribution to an unsafe approach to medical imaging: the number of CT scans performed in the U.S. has increased from 3,000,000 in 1980 to 62,000,000 in 2006, with about 4%-11% of them performed in pediatric patients (4,000,000–7,000,000 scans).[116] This trend has not been changed. According to the same author, the estimated number of CT scans in the U.S. will be over 70,000,000 in 2010, and guidelines are commonly not adopted in clinical practice.[117] A large number (1.9%) of emergency department patients undergoing CT of the neck, chest, abdomen, or pelvis have had a high number (median 10, mean 13, maximum 70) of previous multiple scans during the prior 7.7 years, with a cumulative average CT dose of 122 mSv.[118] Using a risk model of one cancer per 1,000 patients receiving a 10-mSv dose, the average risk for these patients is 1:82.[118] Another alarming report[119] showed that a sample of over 32,000 patients who underwent CT in 2007 had undergone over 190,000 CT scans during the prior 22 years. On this basis, the authors estimate that CT produces 0.7% of total expected baseline cancer incidence and 1% of total cancer mortality. Moreover, 7% of patients had an estimated lifetime attributable risk greater than 1%, of which 40% (2.8% of the total) had either no malignancy history or had a cancer history of successful treatment without evidence of residual disease.[119] Useless ionizing radiation exposure should be avoided also for low-dose x-ray examination, as recently shown by a meta-analysis that favored abandoning daily routine chest radiography in the intensive care unit.[120] Worldwide, the average annual per-capita effective dose from medical imaging has approximately doubled in the past 10–15 years.[121] Data from a report of the National Council on Radiation and Measurements confirmed this trend in the United States.[122,123] The recent concern about the alarming use of brain-perfusion CT scans in the emergency setting—which uses three times the daily dose of radiation treatment for brain cancer[124]—refueled the debate on "the uncritical use of high-tech medical imaging" in the *New England Journal of Medicine*.[125] More on this matter can be found in the Chapter 9 of this book, which is entirely dedicated to radiation dose reduction in medical imaging.

Notably, all these safety topics are being continuously updated on the basis of the best external evidence; thus, a review of primary literature is useful, as well as a reading of systematic reviews and meta-analyses. Advanced secondary sources—such as evidence-based websites and guidelines, etc.—is also helpful.

Lessons from the Nephrogenic Systemic Fibrosis Perfect Storm

For the last 4 years, NSF has been a hot topic for safety in radiology. Gadolinium (Gd)-based contrast agents (GBCAs) have been routinely used for over 20 years, based on their strong evidence of diagnostic value in clinical practice.[126] More than 200 million patients have been intravenously administered a GBCA, with rare adverse events of any kind. Moderate or severe allergic reactions to GBCAs were reported to have a frequency of 1:10,000,[127] and no fatal event had been reported. In 2001, the safety of GBCAs for hemodialysis patients was reported.[128] In this context, high doses (up to 0.4 mmol/kg) of GBCA were used also in CT or in x-ray examinations, typically in digital subtraction angiography, which exploited the high molecular weight of Gd; in cases of significant renal impairment; in prior severe generalized adverse reaction to iodinated contrast media; and in imminent thyroid treatment with radioactive iodine, even though GBCAs were not approved for this use.[129,130] In 2003, I contributed to the opinion on GBCAs safety by reporting[131] about the use of a long-term monthly triple dose (0.3 mmol/kg) of gadodiamide in 10 patients affected with secondary progressive multiple sclerosis. These patients were studied before and after autologous hematopoietic stem cell transplantation, and received a total of 170 triple-dose GBCA injections (17 injections per patient). The dose per patients was over 5 mmol/kg. No side effects were reported.[131]

This scenario dramatically changed in the first months of 2006, when Grobner et al. first reported on an association between GBCA intravenous administration and the development of NSF.[132] The disease originally had been seen in 1977 and reported in 2000 as a scleromyxedema-like disease in renal dialysis patients, which warranted its designation as a new clinico-pathological entity.[133] Nephrogenic systemic fibrosis emerged as a systemic fibrosing disorder, clinically characterized by pain, dermopathy, and joint contractures, affecting the skin, skeletal muscle, esophagus, lungs, heart, and kidneys.[126] In June 2006, the U.S. Food and Drug Administration (FDA) issued a public health advisory.[134] In January 2007, the European Agency for Evaluation of Medicinal Products (European Medicines Agency, EMEA) reported an association between GBCAs administration and NSF.[135] On May 2007, FDA called for a black box warning for GBCAs.[136,137] A deluge of publications appeared on the Internet. By August 14, 2010, 546 papers on NSF were available on PubMed (160 of them being reviews), more than one paper per NSF case reported.

What we learned from this story can be summarized as follows:[126,138–142]

- The relation between GBCAs administration and NSF is probably true, as demonstrated by the precipitous drop of biopsy-confirmed NSF cases after 2007 and by the lack of convincing proof of NSF without GBCA administration.
- Nephrogenic systemic fibrosis is a rare disease: considering the 325 biopsy-confirmed cases or 500 cases reported in peer-reviewed journals, there is an incidence of 1:616,000 to 1:400,000 per GBCA administered dose. Hypothesizing one unreported case for every one reported case, the ratio is 1:200,000. Moreover, most high-risk patients do not develop NSF after GBCA administration.
- Nephrogenic systemic fibrosis occurs almost only in patients with acute kidney disease (AKD) or severe chronic kidney disease (CKD) (i.e., estimated glomerular filtration rate [eGFR] <30 mL/min × 1.73 m^2), the vast majority of the latter being on dialysis at the time of exposure.
- The risk of NSF is higher with GBCAs with low kinetic stability, and there are relevant differences in NSF incidence according to the type of GBCA used.
- High cumulative doses of low-kinetic-stability GBCAs confer a higher risk for NSF.
- Risk should be evaluated as relative and not as absolute (the risk of NSF with GBCA-enhanced MRI may be small if compared to the risk of contrast-induced nephropathy with iodinated contrast-enhanced CT).
- Patients scheduled for any type of GBCA should undergo a screening procedure aimed at excluding severe renal disease (e.g., questionnaires, serum creatinine levels, and eGFR).

- In hemodialysis patients, if GBCA administration is necessary, a hemodialysis session immediately after the MRI examination confers efficient protection against the risk of NSF.

Notably positive consequences of the warning issued by FDA, EMEA, and other state agencies were:

- To stop (or drastically reduce) the use if GBCA in high-risk patients.
- To stop (or drastically reduce) the use of GBCA doses higher than 0.1 mmol/kg, in particular, double and triple doses, especially for MR angiography.
- To extend the use of GBCA doses measured as mmol/kg of body weight instead of fixed doses such as 15 or 20 mL, which means different doses in patients of differing body weight.
- To initiate the habit of exactly reporting type and dose of contrast agent for each contrast-enhanced MRI examination (here, a safe practice is testified to by a high-quality of technical report).

However, important questions were not able to be answered. Why do only some high-risk patients develop NSF after GBCA exposure while others (the vast majority) do not? It is speculated that one or more concomitant factors may play a role in the development of NSF, and a long list of candidate cofactors has been proposed,[143] although for none of these factors are convincing proofs shown. Can certain classes, types, or molecules of GBCA be considered positively NSF-risk free? At what level of renal function does the risk for NSF outweigh the risk for CIN?

Thus, a fundamental scientific and ethical question remains about the use of GBCAs. Leiner and Kucharczyk[126] asked "would we not expect some adverse effects eventually to surface? We were injecting a heavy metal (albeit as a chelate), in ever larger doses, often multiple times, and often in patients with severely compromised renal excretion, knowing that these agents were primarily excreted by the kidneys."[126] Discussing the use of GBCAs for MR angiography, including high-dose applications, Weinreb and Abu-Alfa[139] highlighted that, in the United States, no prohibition exists for the off-label use of an FDA-approved drug[144]: "Off-label use is a common medical practice and is permitted if it is based on firm scientific rationale and sound medical evidence, and the agent is used for indications that are widely recognized by a medical specialty."[144] In other words, the *best external evidence* was in favor of the use of (high doses of) GBCA for MR angiography, even in patients with renal failure.

The "perfect storm" swirling about NSF[145] raises many complex questions. There is the apparent mystery of the double nine-year interval: from 1988 to 1997 (9 years of use of GBCA without any reported cases of NSF) and from 1997 to 2006 (9 years before beginning to suspect an association between GBCA exposure and NSF).[139] The explanation is probably related to the introduction of MRA with high-doses GBCA only after 1997, as well as to the absence of careful registration of GBCA use by radiologists and to the difficulties in creating an epidemiological registry of the disease, perhaps enhanced by the introduction of regulations for the use and disclosure of Protected Health Information, under the Health Insurance Portability and Accountability Act (HIPAA) privacy rule.[139]

The lesson derived from the NSF issue is this: exercise caution when using evidence-based practice. Not all problems can be solved by searching for the *best external evidence*. When a medical error is hidden in a successful procedure presented in the literature, evidence-based practice can spread the error throughout the medical community. And, this also can happen as a consequence of publication bias. We should be aware that there is a much higher probability of patients receiving better care if we follow an evidence-based approach. However, science is not faith, and a probabilistic reasoning works also for EBM (and EBR).

EVIDENCE-BASED RADIOLOGICAL GUIDELINES

Clinical guidelines are defined by the Institute of Medicine as "systematically developed statements to assist practitioners and patient decisions about appropriate health care for specific clinical circumstances."[37,146,147]

Sistrom recently reviewed the concept of appropriateness for diagnostic imaging,[89] and showed that "the appropriateness of diagnostic imaging can only be meaningfully discussed for specifically defined imaging procedures performed in the setting of clearly articulated clinical scenarios." He quoted the formal definition of appropriateness from the Rand/UCLA health care utilization studies:[89]

The indication to perform a medical procedure is appropriate when the expected health

benefit (i.e., increased life expectancy, relief of pain, reduction in anxiety, improved functional capacity) exceeds the expected negative consequences (i.e., mortality, morbidity, anxiety of anticipating the procedure, pain produced by the procedure) by a sufficiently wide margin that the procedure is worth doing.

In a guideline, the aim of supporting appropriateness is reached by seeking "to make the strengths, weaknesses, and relevance of research findings transparent to clinicians."[148] Guidelines also must be evaluated on a benefit–harm continuum,[37] from both a humanitarian and legal viewpoint,[148] and only rigorously developed evidence-based guidelines minimize potential harms.[37,48] But rigorously developed evidence-based guidelines are not purely objective products; they imply a decision-making process in which opinion is gathered and used, at least because "conclusive evidence exists for relatively few health care procedures" and "deriving recommendations only in areas of strong evidence would lead to a guideline of limited scope and applicability."[149] Thus, a guideline is a sum of evidence and expert opinion, taking into account "resource implications and feasibility of interventions."[149] As a matter of fact, "strong evidence does not always produce a strong recommendation."[149]

The application of a clinical guideline involves interpretation, as embodied in the EBM principle of combining the best external evidence from research with clinical expertise for each specific case and patient. As stated also by the World Health Organization: "Guidelines should provide extensive, critical, and well-balanced information on benefits and limitations of the various diagnostic and therapeutic interventions so that the physician may exert the most careful judgment in individual cases."[150]

A number of bodies have produced guidelines for imaging; examples include the ACR,[151] the Canadian Association of Radiologists,[152] the European Society of Radiology and the European subspecialty societies,[153] as well as the radiological societies of individual European countries.

The U.K. Royal College of Radiologists has produced guidance on making the best use of the radiology (MBUR) department for over 10 years and most recently has published MBUR6.[154] In 2001, a fundamental shift occurred in the way the U.K. guidelines were developed through the adoption of a more formal approach to the process of gathering and synthesizing evidence. A template was provided to individual radiologists tasked with providing an imaging recommendation, thus providing transparency on how literature was collected and distilled before a guideline was produced. The more formal process of gathering evidence highlighted the deficiencies of the imaging literature—there were relatively few outcome studies on the impact on patient management or health outcome, a number of studies in which the reference standard had been suboptimal, and many others in which the study methodology had been inadequately described.

Although some of these guidelines are based on strong evidence resulting from systematic reviews and meta-analyses, others were formulated only on the basis of consensus of expert opinion. Where consensus is used, guidance can be conflicting, even when this has been developed in the same country. Although there may be cogent reasons why a particular guideline varies from one country to another, it is somewhat surprising that so much variation is present when these guidelines are supposedly based on evidence. To clarify the leakage to evidence, the ACR's tables of appropriateness criteria, revised in 2010 have references embedded.[155]

We should remember that, as highlighted by Kainberger et al.,[48] guidelines may be issued, but they are commonly accepted by very few clinicians[156] or radiologists.[157] In fact, in a paper by Tigges et al.,[157] U.S. musculoskeletal radiologists, including those of the Society of Skeletal Radiology, were surveyed in 1998 regarding their use of the musculoskeletal appropriateness criteria issued by the ACR. The response rate was 298/465 (64%), and only 30% of respondents reported using the appropriateness criteria, with no difference among organizations or for private practice compared with academic radiologists.[157]

Guidelines should deliver according to EBM (and EBR) principles. Examples of these rules can be found at the website of the AGREE Collaboration.[158] From this perspective, a guideline should include:

- Selection and description of the objectives
- Methods for literature searching
- Methods for classification of the evidence extracted by the literature
- Summary of the evidence extracted by the literature
- Practical recommendations, each of them validated by one or more citations and tagged with the level of evidence upon which it is based

- Instructions for application in clinical practice

Importantly, *guidelines should identify clearly which contents are evidence-based and which contents are based on expert panel opinion.*[159] Before the final release of a guideline, external reviewer should ensure its validity (experts in clinical content), clarity (expert in systematic reviews or guidelines development), and applicability (potential users).[149] Moreover, a date for updating the systematic review that underpins the guideline should be specified.[149]

Thus, the usual method, consisting of experts' opinions combined with a nonsystematic (narrative) review, should be discarded.

CONCLUSION

The evidence-based approach is changing clinical practice. This approach is already impacting the day-to-day practice of radiology, although the greatest changes are expected in the upcoming years. This process will be mainly pushed by the desire for higher quality and safety. Patients and their advocacy associations will ask for an evidence-based practice of radiology.

We must be prepared for this. The application of EBM and EBR can no longer be limited to the bottom-down approach used when academic radiologists or radiologists working at large medical centers are involved in producing guidelines, refereeing manuscripts, publishing papers, or undertaking research. Cognizance of EBR principles should be increased at all levels of our profession because quality and safety are requirements for all radiologists and all patients. Evidence-based radiology should be considered as part of the core curriculum of a radiology residency. Efforts in this direction have been made in the United States by the Radiology Residency Review Committee, the American Board of Radiology, and the Association of Program Directors in Radiology, as well as by the Education Committee of the European Society of Radiology.

Moreover, we should be aware that another challenge is on its way: from morphologic, qualitative, and descriptive radiology to *quantitative radiology*. Numbers will substitute for words in important sections of radiological reports of the next generation. Important examples of this trend are perfusion CT or MRI studies, cardiac MRI, diffusion-weighted MRI, MR spectroscopy, bone densitometry, and all examinations in which quantification is based on the measurement of continuous variables. In this era, a high degree of reproducibility will be a must, not an option. We must find a way to ride the wave of this trend.

In 1996,[160] while commenting on "two centuries of conflict-collaboration between medicine and mathematics" (i.e., on the change of medicine from art to science), Alvan R. Feinstein focused on the "quality of data" as "a major scientific problem" and on an "unrecognized and unrepaired observer variability in radiologists." Quality of data is still the challenge. The evidence-based approach can provide the pathway to meeting this challenge.

Finally, imagine a scenario in which clinical practice will be more and more determined by an evidence-based approach, synthesized through recommendations, guidelines, and appropriateness and cost-effectiveness rules. Some may believe this undermines our freedom as professionals. To prevent this, a strictly evidence-based approach to research should be avoided. Secondary studies, such as systematic reviews and meta-analyses or gap-analyses, may certainly redirect primary research toward objectives that arise from the critical evaluation of evidence.[22] However, while using correct scientific methods and fulfilling ethical requirements, we must also give basic and clinical research as much freedom as possible to follow unexplored pathways, new hypotheses, and dreams. Basically, all of us are the sons and daughters of one discovery: x-rays, which characterized the crisis of physics more than one century ago and changed medicine dramatically. However, let us not forget that this discovery happened by chance. The historical merit of Wilhelm C. Roentgen was to be able to see the practical application behind the novelty.

REFERENCES

1. Malone DE. Evidence-based practice in radiology: An introduction to the series. *Radiology.* 2007;242(1):12–14.
2. Evidence-Based Radiology Working Group. Evidence-based radiology: A new approach to the practice of radiology. *Radiology.* 2001;220(3):566–75.
3. Vandenbroucke JP. Evidence-based medicine and "médecine d'observation." *J Clin Epidemiol.* 1996;49(12):1335–8.
4. Weatherall DJ. Foreword to first edition by Professor Sir David Weatherall. In: Greenhalgh T., ed. *How to read a paper. The basics of evidence-based medicine,* 3rd ed. Oxford, England: Blackwell, 2006: ix–x.
5. Morabia A PCA. Louis and the birth of clinical epidemiology. *J Clin Epidemiol.* 1996;49(12):1327–33.
6. Massey RU. Reflections on medicine. Pierre Louis and his numerical method. *Conn Med.* 1989;53(10):613.
7. Bernard C. *An introduction to the study of experimental medicine.* New York: Dover, 1957: 139.
8. Sardanelli F, Di Leo G. *Biostatistics for radiologists.* Milan: Springer-Verlag, 2008:67–69.
9. Evidence-Based Medicine Working Group. Evidence-based medicine. A new approach to teaching the practice of medicine. *JAMA.* 1992;268(17):2420–5.
10. Centre for Evidence-Based Medicine, Oxford University, England. Accessed July 9, 2010, at: http://cebm.net
11. Sackett DL, Rosenberg WM, Gray JA, Haynes RB, Richardson WS. Evidence based medicine: What it is and what it isn't. *BMJ.* 1996;312(7023):71–72.
12. Greenhalgh T. *How to read a paper. The basics of evidence-based medicine,* 3rd ed. Oxford, England: Blackwell, 2006: 1–3.
13. Crystal P, Koretz M, Shcharynsky S, Makarov V, Strano S. Accuracy of sonographically guided 14-gauge core-needle biopsy: Results of 715 consecutive breast biopsies with at least two-year follow-up of benign lesions. *J Clin Ultrasound.* 2005;33(2):47–52.
14. Berlin L. Communicating results of all outpatient radiologic examinations directly to patients: The time has come. *AJR Am J Roentgenol.* 2009;192(3):571–3.
15. Hunink MGM, Glasziou PP, Siegel JE, et al. *Decision making in health and medicine: Integrating evidence and values.* Cambridge, UK: Cambridge University Press, 2001.
16. Malone DE, Staunton M. Evidence-based practice in radiology: Step 5 (evaluate)–Caveats and common questions. *Radiology.* 2007;243(2):319–28.
17. Dodd JD. Evidence-based practice in radiology: Steps 3 and 4–Appraise and apply diagnostic radiology literature. *Radiology.* 2007;242(2):342–54.
18. van Beek EJ, Malone DE. Evidence-based practice in radiology education: Why and how should we teach it? *Radiology.* 2007;243(3):633–40.
19. American College of *Radiology.* Accessed July 14, 2010, at: http://www.acr.org/SecondaryMainMenuCategories/quality_safety/guidelines.aspx
20. Cochrane collaboration. Accessed July 12, 2010, at: http://www.cochrane.org/cochrane-reviews
21. Shannon S. Critically appraised topics (CATs). *Can Assoc Radiol J.* 2001;52(5):286–7.
22. Hollingworth W, Jarvik JG. Technology assessment in radiology: Putting the evidence in evidence-based radiology. *Radiology.* 2007;244(1):31–38.
23. Trinder L. A critical appraisal of evidence-based practice. In: Trinder L, Reynolds S, eds. *Evidence-based practice: A critical appraisal.* Oxford, England: Blackwell Science, 2000:212–4.
24. Tonelli MR. The philosophical limits of evidence-based medicine. *Acad Med.* 1998;73(12):1234–40.
25. Raymond J, Trop I. The practice of ethics in the era of evidence-based radiology. *Radiology.* 2007;244(3):643–9.
26. Tanenbaum SJ. What physicians know. *N Engl J Med.* 1993;329(17):1268–71.

27. Humphrey LL, Helfand M, Chan BK, Woolf SH. Breast cancer screening: A summary of the evidence for the U.S. Preventive Services Task Force. *Ann Intern Med.* 2002;137 (5 Part 1):347–60.

28. de Koning HJ. Mammographic screening: Evidence from randomised controlled trials. *Ann Oncol.* 2003 Aug;14(8):1185–9.

29. Harris R. Effectiveness: The next question for breast cancer screening. *J Natl Cancer Inst.* 2005;97(14):1021–3

30. Gøtzsche PC, Nielsen M Screening for breast cancer with mammography. *Cochrane Database Syst Rev.* 2006;(4):CD001877.

31. Feig SA. Screening mammography controversies: Resolved, partly resolved, and unresolved. *Breast J.* 2005;11(Suppl 1):S3–6.

32. Dent R, Warner E. Screening for hereditary breast cancer. *Semin Oncol.* 2007;34(5):392–400.

33. Puliti D, Miccinesi G, Collina N, et al., IMPACT Working Group. Effectiveness of service screening: A case-control study to assess breast cancer mortality reduction. *Br J Cancer.* 2008;99(3):423–7.

34. Allgood PC, Warwick J, Warren RM, Day NE, Duffy SW. A case-control study of the impact of the East Anglian breast screening programme on breast cancer mortality. *Br J Cancer.* 2008;98(1):206–9.

35. Science quote. Accessed July 12, 2010, at: http://www.lhup.edu/~dsimanek/sciquote.htm.

36. Eddington AS. *New pathways in science.* Ann Arbor: The University of Michigan Press, 1959:211.

37. Woolf SH, Grol R, Hutchinson A, Eccles M, Grimshaw J. Clinical guidelines: Potential benefits, limitations, and harms of clinical guidelines. *BMJ.* 1999;318(7182):527–30.

38. Dixon AK. Evidence-based diagnostic radiology. *Lancet.* 1997;350(9076):509–12.

39. Mukerjee A. Towards evidence based emergency medicine: Best BETs from the Manchester Royal Infirmary. Magnetic resonance imaging in acute knee haemarthrosis. *J Accid Emerg Med.* 1999;16(3):216–7.

40. Acheson L, Mitchell L. The routine antenatal diagnostic imaging with ultrasound study. The challenge to practice evidence-based obstetrics. *Arch Fam Med.* 1993;2(12):1229–31.

41. Anonymous. Routine ultrasound imaging in pregnancy: How evidence-based are the guidelines? *Int J Technol Assess Health Care.* 1997;13(3):475–7.

42. Anonymous. Reports from the British Columbia Office of Health Technology Assessment (BCOHTA). Routine ultrasound imaging in pregnancy: How evidence-based are the guidelines? *Int J Technol Assess Health Care.* 1997;13(4): 633–7.

43. Liedberg J, Panmekiate S, Petersson A, Rohlin M. Evidence-based evaluation of three imaging methods for the temporomandibular disc. *Dentomaxillofac Radiol.* 1996;25(5):234–41.

44. Taïeb S, Vennin P. Evidence-based medicine: Towards evidence-based radiology. *J Radiol.* 2001;82(8):887–90.

45. Arrivé L, Tubiana JM. "Evidence-based" radiology. *J Radiol.* 2002;83(5):661.

46. Bui AA, Taira RK, Dionisio JD, Aberle DR, El-Saden S, Kangarloo H. Evidence-based radiology: Requirements for electronic access. *Acad Radiol.* 2002;9(6):662–9.

47. Guillerman RP, Brody AS, Kraus SJ. Evidence-based guidelines for pediatric imaging: The example of the child with possible appendicitis. *Pediatr Ann.* 2002;31(10):629–40.

48. Kainberger F, Czembirek H, Frühwald F, Pokieser P, Imhof H. Guidelines and algorithms: Strategies for standardization of referral criteria in diagnostic radiology. *Eur Radiol.* 2002;12(3):673–9.

49. Bennett JD. Evidence-based radiology problems. Covered stent treatment of an axillary artery pseudo-aneurysm: June 2003–June 2004. *Can Assoc Radiol J.* 2003;54(3):140–3.

50. Blackmore CC. Evidence-based imaging evaluation of the cervical spine in trauma. *Neuroimaging Clin N Am.* 2003;13(2):283–91.

51. Cohen WA, Giauque AP, Hallam DK, Linnau KF, Mann FA. Evidence-based approach to use of MR imaging in acute spinal trauma. *Eur J Radiol.* 2003;48(1):49–60.

52. Goergen SK, Fong C, Dalziel K, Fennessy G. Development of an evidence-based guideline for imaging in cervical spine trauma. *Australas Radiol.* 2003;47(3):240–6.

53. Medina LS, Aguirre E, Zurakowski D. Introduction to evidence-based imaging. *Neuroimaging Clin N Am.* 2003;13(2):157–65.

54. Blackmore CC. Critically assessing the radiology literature. *Acad Radiol.* 2004;11(2):134–40.

55. Dodd JD, MacEneaney PM, Malone DE. Evidence-based radiology: How to quickly assess the validity and strength of publications in the diagnostic radiology literature. *Eur Radiol.* 2004;14(5):915–22.

56. Erden A. Evidence based radiology. *Tani Girisim Radyol.* 2004;10(2):89–91.

57. Gilbert FJ, Grant AM, Gillan MG, et al., Scottish Back Trial Group. Low back pain: Influence of early MR imaging or CT on treatment and outcome—multicenter randomized trial. *Radiology.* 2004;231(2):343–51.

58. Matowe L, Gilbert FJ. How to synthesize evidence for imaging guidelines. *Clin Radiol.* 2004;59(1):63–68.

59. Giovagnoni A, Ottaviani L, Mensà A, Durastanti M, Floriani I, Cascinu S. Evidence Based Medicine (EBM) and Evidence Based Radiology (EBR) in the follow-up of the patients after surgery for lung and colon-rectal carcinoma. *Radiol Med.* 2005;109(4):345–57.

60. Medina LS, Blackmore CC. *Evidence-based imaging,* 1st ed. New York: Springer, 2006.

61. Medina LS, Blackmore CC. Evidence-based radiology: Review and dissemination. *Radiology.* 2007;244(2):331–6.

62. Royal College of Radiologists Working Party. *Making the best use of a department of clinical radiology: Guidelines for doctors,* 4th ed. London: The Royal College of Radiologists, 1998.

63. RCR Breast Group 2009 Annual Scientific Meeting. Accessed July 15, 2010, at: http://www.rcrbreastgroup.com/meetings/ASM/ASMarchive/ASM2009prog.pdf

64. Sardanelli F, Di Leo G. *Biostatistics for radiologists.* Milan: Springer-Verlag, 2008:125–40.

65. Anonymous. Proceedings of the Second ALARA Conference. February 28, 2004. Houston, Texas, USA. *Pediatr Radiol.* 2004;34 (Suppl 3):S162–246.

66. Prasad KN, Cole WC, Haase GM. Radiation protection in humans: Extending the concept of as low as reasonably achievable (ALARA) from dose to biological damage. *Br J Radiol.* 2004;77(914):97–99.

67. Semelka RC, Armao DM, Elias J Jr, Huda W. Imaging strategies to reduce the risk of radiation in CT studies, including selective substitution with MRI. *J Magn Reson Imaging.* 2007;25(5):900–909.

68. Council of the European Union. Council Directive 97/43/Euratom of 30 June 1997 on health protection of individuals against the dangers of ionizing radiation in relation with medical exposure, and repealing Directive 84/466/Euratom. *Official J European Communities L.* 1997;180:22–27. Accessed July 9, 2010, at: http://ec.europa.eu/energy/nuclear/radioprotection/doc/legislation/9743_en.pdf

69. Barr HJ, Ohlhaber T, Finder C. Focusing in on dose reduction: The FDA perspective. *AJR Am J Roentgenol.* 2006;186(6):1716–7.

70. FDA Radiological Health Program. Accessed July 9, 2010, at: http://www.fda.gov/Radiation-EmittingProducts/FDARadiologicalHealthProgram/default.htm

71. Altman DG, Andersen PK. Calculating the number needed to treat for trials where the outcome is time to an event. *BMJ.* 1999;319(7223):1492–5.

72. Attali J. *Cannibalism and civilization: Life and death in the history of medicine.* Italian Edition. Milan: Feltrinelli, 1980.

73. Chow WH, Dong LM, Devesa SS. Epidemiology and risk factors for kidney cancer. *Nat Rev Urol.* 2010;7(5):245–57.

74. Naidu SG, Hara AK, Brandis AR, Stone WM. Incidence of highly important extravascular findings detected on CT angiography of the abdominal aorta and the lower extremities. *AJR Am J Roentgenol.* 2010 Jun;194(6):1630–4.

75. Hartwigsen G, Siebner HR, Deuschl G, Jansen O, Ulmer S. Incidental findings are frequent in young healthy individuals undergoing magnetic resonance imaging in brain research imaging studies: A prospective single-center study. *J Comput Assist Tomogr.* 2010;34(4):596–600.

76. Sardanelli F, Di Leo G. *Biostatistics for radiologists.* Milan: Springer-Verlag, 2008:176–7.

77. Welch HG, Black WC. Overdiagnosis in cancer. *J Natl Cancer Inst.* 2010 May 5;102(9):605–13. Epub 2010 Apr 22.

78. Sardanelli F, Di Leo G. *Biostatistics for Radiologists.* Milan: Springer-Verlag, 2008:20–21.

79. Sardanelli F, Boetes C, Borisch B, et al. Magnetic resonance imaging of the breast: Recommendations from the EUSOMA working group. *Eur J Cancer.* 2010;46(8):1296–1316.

80. Sardanelli F, Podo F. Breast MR imaging in women at high-risk of breast cancer. Is something changing in early breast cancer detection? *Eur Radiol.* 2007;17(4):873–87.

81. Fagan TJ. Letter: Nomogram for Bayes theorem. *N Engl J Med.* 1975;293(5):257.

82. Hillman BJ, Gatsonis CA. When is the right time to conduct a clinical trial of a diagnostic imaging technology? *Radiology.* 2008;248(1):12–15.

83. Fineberg HV, Bauman R, Sosman M. Computerized cranial tomography. Effect on diagnostic and therapeutic plans. *JAMA.* 1977;238(3):224–7.

84. Fryback DG, Thornbury JR. The efficacy of diagnostic imaging. *Med Decis Making.* 1991;11(2):88–94.

85. Thornbury JR. Eugene W. Caldwell Lecture. Clinical efficacy of diagnostic imaging: Love it or leave it. *AJR Am J Roentgenol.* 1994;162(1):1–8.

86. Mackenzie R, Dixon AK. Measuring the effects of imaging: An evaluative framework. *Clin Radiol.* 1995;50(8):513–8.

87. Thornbury JR. Intermediate outcomes: Diagnostic and therapeutic impact. *Acad Radiol.* 1999;6(Suppl 1):S58–S65.

88. Sunshine JH, Applegate KE. Technology assessment for Radiologists. *Radiology.* 2004;230(2):309–14.

89. Sistrom CL. The appropriateness of imaging: A comprehensive conceptual framework. *Radiology.* 2009;251(3):637–49.

90. Kuhl CK, Träber F, Schild HH. Whole-body high-field-strength (3.0-T) MR Imaging in Clinical Practice. Part I. Technical considerations and clinical applications. *Radiology.* 2008;246(3):675–96.

91. Soares HP, Kumar A, Daniels S, et al. Evaluation of new treatments in radiation oncology: Are they better than standard treatments? *JAMA.* 2005;293(8):970–8.

92. Hunink MG, Krestin GP. Study design for concurrent development, assessment, and implementation of new diagnostic imaging technology. *Radiology.* 2002;222(3):604–14.

93. Jarvik JG. Study design for the new millennium: Changing how we perform research and practice medicine. *Radiology.* 2002:222(3):593–4.

94. Eccles M, Steen N, Grimshaw J, et al. Effect of audit and feedback, and reminder messages on

primary-care radiology referrals: A randomised trial. *Lancet*. 2001 May 5;357(9266):1406–9.

95. Gilbert FJ, Grant AM, Gillan MG, et al. Does early imaging influence management and improve outcome in patients with low back pain? A pragmatic randomised controlled trial. *Health Technol Assess*. 2004 May;8(17):iii, 1–131.

96. af Geijerstam JL, Oredsson S, Britton M; OCTOPUS Study Investigators. Medical outcome after immediate computed tomography or admission for observation in patients with mild head injury: Randomised controlled trial. *BMJ*. 2006 Sep 2;333(7566):465.

97. Norlund A, Marké LA, af Geijerstam JL, Oredsson S, Britton M; OCTOPUS Study. Immediate computed tomography or admission for observation after mild head injury: Cost comparison in randomised controlled trial. *BMJ*. 2006 Sep 2;333(7566):469.

98. Brealey SD; DAMASK (Direct Access to Magnetic Resonance Imaging: Assessment for Suspect Knees) Trial Team. Influence of magnetic resonance of the knee on GPs' decisions: A randomised trial. *Br J Gen Pract*. 2007 Aug;57(541):622–9.

99. Rahman NM, Singanayagam A, Davies HE, et al. Diagnostic accuracy, safety and utilisation of respiratory physician-delivered thoracic ultrasound. *Thorax*. 2010 May;65(5):449–53.

100. Launois R. Economic assessment, a field between clinical research and observational studies. *Bull Cancer*. 2003;90(1):97–104.

101. Plevritis SK. Decision analysis and simulation modeling for evaluating diagnostic tests on the basis of patient outcomes. *AJR Am J Roentgenol*. 2005;185(3):581–90.

102. Otero HJ, Rybicki FJ, Greenberg D, Neumann PJ. Twenty years of cost-effectiveness analysis in medical imaging: Are we improving? *Radiology*. 2008;249(3):917–25.

103. Hunink MG. Cost-effectiveness analysis: Some clarifications. *Radiology*. 2008;249(3):753–5.

104. Atkins D, Best D, Briss PA et al.; GRADE working group. Grading quality of evidence and strength of recommendations. *BMJ*. 2004;328(7454):1490. Accessed July 9, 2010, at: http://www.bmj.com/cgi/content/full/328/7454/1490

105. Schünemann HJ, Oxman AD, Brozek J et al.; GRADE Working Group. Grading quality of evidence and strength of recommendations for diagnostic tests and strategies. *BMJ*. 2008;336(7653):1106–10.

106. Sardanelli F, Di Leo G. *Biostatistics for radiologists*. Milan: Springer-Verlag, 2008:165–79.

107. Kelly S, Berry E, Roderick P, et al. The identification of bias in studies of the diagnostic performance of imaging modalities. *Br J Radiol*. 1997;70(838):1028–35.

108. Sica GT. Bias in research studies. *Radiology*. 2006;238(3):780–9.

109. Reid MC, Lachs MS, Feinstein AR. Use of methodological standards in diagnostic test research. Getting better but still not good. *JAMA*. 1995;274(8):645–51.

110. Bossuyt PM, Reitsma JB, Bruns DE, et al. Towards complete and accurate reporting of studies of diagnostic accuracy: The STARD Initiative. *Radiology*. 2003;226(1):24–28.

111. Smidt N, Rutjes AW, van der Windt DA, et al. Quality of reporting of diagnostic accuracy studies. *Radiology*. 2005;235(2):347–53.

112. Wilczynski NL. Quality of reporting of diagnostic accuracy studies: No change since STARD statement publication—before-and-after study. *Radiology*. 2008;248(3):817–23.

113. Moher D, Schulz KF, Altman DG. The CONSORT statement: Revised recommendations for improving the quality of reports of parallel-group randomised trials. *Lancet*. 2001;357(9263):1191–4.

114. Boutron I, Moher D, Altman DG, Schulz KF, Ravaud P; CONSORT Group. Methods and processes of the CONSORT Group: Example of an extension for trials assessing nonpharmacologic treatments. *Ann Intern Med*. 2008;148(4):W60–66.

115. Moher D, Cook DJ, Eastwood S, Olkin I, Rennie D, Stroup DF. Improving the quality of reports of meta-analyses of randomised controlled trials: The QUOROM statement. Quality of Reporting of Meta-analyses. *Lancet*. 1999;354(9193):1896–1900.

116. Brenner DJ. Medical imaging in the 21st century—getting the best bang for the rad. *N Engl J Med*. 2010 11;362(10):943–5.

117. Brenner DJ, Hall EJ. Computed tomography—an increasing source of radiation exposure. *N Engl J Med*. 2007 29;357(22):2277–84.

118. Griffey RT, Sodickson A. Cumulative radiation exposure and cancer risk estimates in emergency department patients undergoing repeat or multiple CT. *AJR Am J Roentgenol*. 2009;192(4):887–92.

119. Sodickson A, Baeyens PF, Andriole KP, et al. Recurrent CT, cumulative radiation exposure, and associated radiation-induced cancer risks from CT of adults. *Radiology*. 2009;251(1):175–84.

120. Oba Y, Zaza T. Abandoning daily routine chest radiography in the intensive care unit: Meta-analysis. *Radiology*. 2010;255(2):386–95.

121. Mettler FA Jr, Bhargavan M, Faulkner K, et al. Radiologic and nuclear medicine studies in the United States and worldwide: Frequency, radiation dose, and comparison with other radiation sources—1950–2007. *Radiology*. 2009;253(2):520–31.

122. National Council on Radiation Protection and Measurements. Ionizing radiation exposure of the population of the United States. National Council on Radiation Protection report no. 160. Bethesda, MD: National Council on Radiation Protection and Measurements, 2009.

123. Schauer DA, Linton OW. National Council on Radiation Protection and Measurements report

shows substantial medical exposure increase. *Radiology.* 2009;253(2):293–6.

124. Smith-Bindman R. Is computed tomography safe? *N Engl J Med.* 2010;363(1):1–4.

125. Hillman BJ, Goldsmith JC. The uncritical use of high-tech medical imaging. *N Engl J Med.* 2010 Jul 1;363(1):4–6.

126. Leiner T, Kucharczyk W. Special issue: Nephrogenic systemic fibrosis. *J Magn Reson Imaging.* 2009;30(6):1233–5.

127. De Ridder F, De Maeseneer M, Stadnik T, Luypaert R, Osteaux M. Severe adverse reactions with contrast agents for magnetic resonance: Clinical experience in 30,000 MR examinations. *JBR-BTR.* 2001;84(4):150–2.

128. Okada S, Katagiri K, Kumazaki T, Yokoyama H. Safety of gadolinium contrast agent in hemodialysis patients. *Acta Radiol.* 2001;42(3):339–41.

129. Albrecht T, Dawson P. Gadolinium-DTPA as X-ray contrast medium in clinical studies. *Br J Radiol.* 2000;73:878–82.

130. Thomsen HS, Almèn T, Morcos SK. Gadolinium-containing contrast media for radiographic examination: A position paper. *Eur Radiol.* 2002;12:2600–5.

131. Sardanelli F, Mancardi G, Filippi M. Safety of the long-time monthly triple dose of a Gd-based contrast agent. *Eur Radiol.* 2003 Dec;13 Suppl 4:L243–4.

132. Grobner T. Gadolinium—a specific trigger for the development of nephrogenic fibrosing dermopathy and nephrogenic systemic fibrosis? *Nephrol Dial Transplant.* 2006;21(4):1104–8. Erratum in: *Nephrol Dial Transplant.* 2006;21(6):1745.

133. Cowper SE, Robin HS, Steinberg SM, Su LD, Gupta S, LeBoit PE. Scleromyxedema-like cutaneous diseases in renal-dialysis patients. *Lancet.* 2000;356(9234):1000–1.

134. United States Food and Drug Administration. Public health advisory update on magnetic resonance imaging (MRI) contrast agents containing gadolinium and nephrogenic fibrosing dermopathy, 2006. Accessed September 28, 2009, at: http://www.fda.gov/Drugs/DrugSafety/PublicHealthAdvisories/ucrn124344.htm

135. Committee for Medicinal Products for Human Use CHMP. Committee of the European Medicines Agency (EMEA). Accessed July 1, 2008, at: http://www.emea.europa.eu

136. United States Food and Drug Administration. FDA requests boxed warning for contrast agents used to improve MRI images. Accessed September 21, 2009, at: http://www.fda.gov/NewsEvents/Newsroom/PressAnnouncements/2007/ucm108919.htm

137. United States Food and Drug Administration. Information for healthcare professionals gadolinium-based contrast agents for magnetic resonance imaging (marketed as Magnevist, MultiHance, Omniscan, OptiMARK, ProHance). Accessed January 24, 2008, at: http://www.fda.gov/cder/drug/InfoSheets/HCP/gcca_200705.htm

138. Prince MR, Zhang H, Morris M, et al. Incidence of nephrogenic systemic fibrosis at two large medical centers. *Radiology.* 2008;248(3):807–16.

139. Weinreb JC, Abu-Alfa AK. Gadolinium-based contrast agents and nephrogenic systemic fibrosis: Why did it happen and what have we learned? *J Magn Reson Imaging.* 2009;30(6):1236–9.

140. Altun E, Martin DR, Wertman R, Lugo-Somolinos A, Fuller ER 3rd, Semelka RC. Nephrogenic systemic fibrosis: Change in incidence following a switch in gadolinium agents and adoption of a gadolinium policy—report from two U.S. universities. *Radiology.* 2009;253(3):689–96.

141. Martin DR, Semelka RC, Chapman A, et al. Nephrogenic systemic fibrosis versus contrast-induced nephropathy: Risks and benefits of contrast-enhanced MR and CT in renally impaired patients. *J Magn Reson Imaging.* 2009;30:1350–6.

142. Agarwal R, Brunelli SM, Williams K, Mitchell MD, Feldman HI, Umscheid CA. Gadolinium-based contrast agents and nephrogenic systemic fibrosis: A systematic review and meta-analysis. *Nephrol Dial Transplant.* 2009;24(3):856–63.

143. Peak AS, Sheller A. Risk factors for developing gadolinium-induced nephrogenic systemic fibrosis. *Ann Pharmacother.* 2007;41(9):1481–5.

144. Nightingale SL. Unlabeled uses of approved drugs. *Drug Info* (II.I). 1991;26:141–7.

145. Colletti PM. Nephrogenic systemic fibrosis and gadolinium: A perfect storm. *AJR Am J Roentgenol.* 2008;191(4):1150–3.

146. Field MJ, Lohr KN, eds. *Guidelines for clinical practice: From development to use.* Washington DC: National Academy Press, 1992.

147. Lohr KN. Reasonable expectations: From the Institute of Medicine. Interview by Paul M. Schyve. *QRB Qual Rev Bull.* 1992;18(12):393–6.

148. Hurwitz B. Legal and political considerations of clinical practice guidelines. *BJM.* 1999;318(7184):661–4.

149. Shekelle PG, Woolf SH, Eccles M, Grimshaw J. Clinical guidelines: Developing guidelines. *BJM.* 1999;318(7183):593–6.

150. Schmidt HG, van der Arend A, Moust JH, Kokx I, Boon L. Influence of tutors' subject-matter expertise on student effort and achievement in problem-based learning. *Acad Med.* 1993;68(10):784–91.

151. American College of Radiologists. Guidelines. Accessed July 9, 2010, at: http://www.acr.org/SecondaryMainMenuCategories/quality_safety/guidelines.aspx

152. Canadian Association of Radiologists. Guidelines. Accessed July 9, 2010, at: http://www.car.ca/content.aspx?pg=Guidelines&spg=home&lang=E&lID=

153. European Society of Radiology. Document on revision of Referral Guidelines for Imaging. Accessed July 9, 2010, at: http://www.myesr.org/cms/website.php?id=/en/eu_affairs/newfilename.htm

154. Royal College of Radiologists. Making the best use of clinical radiology services (MBUR), 6th ed., 2007. Accessed July 9, 2010, at: http://www.rcr.ac.uk/content.aspx?PageID=995

155. American College of Radiology. Appropriateness criteria. Accessed August 15, 2010, at: http://www.acr.org/secondarymainmenucategories/quality_safety/app_criteria.aspx

156. Cabana MD, Rand CS, Powe NR, et al. Why don't physicians follow clinical practice guidelines? A framework for improvement. *JAMA*. 1999; 282(15):1458–65.

157. Tigges S, Sutherland D, Manaster BJ. Do radiologists use the American College of radiology musculoskeletal appropriateness criteria? *AJR Am J Roentgenol*. 2000;175(2):545–7.

158. Appraisal of Guidelines Research and Evaluation (AGREE). Accessed July 9, 2010, at: http://www.agreecollaboration.org/instrument/

159. Brink JA. The art and science of medical guidelines: What we know and what we believe. *Radiology*. 2010;254(1):20–21.

160. Feinstein AR. Two centuries of conflict: Collaboration between medicine and mathematics. *J Clin Epidemiol*. 1996;49(12):1339–43.

28

Quality in Pediatric Imaging

SJIRK J. WESTRA

To describe the concept of "quality" in pediatric radiology is a difficult proposition, since it is a very subjective term—similar to beauty, which, as we are frequently reminded, is in the eye of the beholder.[1] For our patients and their parents, a high-quality pediatric radiology service may mean convenience of scheduling and access, pleasant bedside manners, and a child-friendly environment; for our referring physicians, it may include fast service when needed, well-structured and accurate reports, rapid and effective communications of unexpected and emergency findings, and consultations that are helpful in clinical management; and for our pediatric radiology colleagues and coworkers, quality may be defined by considering which facility would we pick if our own child needs imaging, or which colleague would we trust most for performing a difficult procedure or rendering a definitive opinion on a difficult case.

Most approaches to quality assessment in health care use the "structure, process, outcome" algorithm that was first proposed by Donabedian in 1988.[2] For example, in pediatric radiology, "structure" may refer to having a fluoroscope with pulsed tube output in use for children, so as to reduce radiation.[3-5] "Process" may refer to the monitored introduction of computed tomography (CT) dose reduction following the institution of age-, weight-, and indication-based protocols,[6] and educational efforts aimed at referring physicians to decrease unnecessary referral for CT imaging.[7] Other publications have described "best practices" to standardize across institutions the performance of common pediatric radiological procedures, such as the voiding cystourethrogram.[8] "Outcome" is always more difficult to address in radiology, because of the many links external to our specialty that exist between providing a radiology report and a change in clinical management, but may refer to better prognostication and possibly better outcomes by the evidence-based application of neuroimaging techniques in neonates[9] or screening for developmental dysplasia of the hip.[10]

DEFINITION

Most references to quality in medicine quote two pivotal publications regarding medical errors and their prevention, *To Err Is Human: Building a Safer Healthcare System*[11] and *Crossing the Quality Chasm: A New Health Care System for the 21st Century*.[12] Accordingly, the definition of quality, as it pertains to medical imaging, echoes the Institute of Medicine definition:

> Quality of care is the degree to which health services for individuals and populations increase the likelihood of desired health outcomes and are consistent with current professional knowledge. Specifically with regard to diagnostic imaging and image-guided treatment, quality is the extent to which the right procedure is done in the right way, at the right time, and the correct interpretation is accurately and quickly communicated to the patient and referring physician. The goals are to maximize the likelihood of desired health outcomes and to satisfy the patient.[13]

This definition contains elements of infrastructure, professional competence (process), and outcome, and includes the perspective of our consumers (referring physicians and patients). Notably absent in this definition is any reference to the concept of cost-effectiveness of medical care.

Interestingly, a "Guide to Health Care Quality" for patients, issued by the Agency for Healthcare Research and Quality from the U.S. Department of Health and Human Services,[14] carries the subtitle "How to Know It When You See It," borrowed from the famous quotation of Supreme Court Justice Potter Steward.[1,15] Many people believe that quality in medicine seems to have some gestalt-like "know-it-when-I-see-it" aspects that cannot be defined or measured, but are presumed to be self-evident to the "consumer," be it the patient, parents, or referring physician. In my opinion, however, it would be highly unrealistic to assume that a layperson, in the dependent role of a patient or parent, has the ability to clearly identify quality "when he or she sees it."[16] Therefore, society has put in place a number of measures that are supposed to ensure that "quality" is always being delivered by health care practitioners. Organized radiology has taken the issue of quality improvement seriously, and several excellent review articles have been published on this topic,[13,17–20] and these are discussed in more detail elsewhere in this book. Practice leaders in organized radiology have convened at a number of meetings and symposia under the auspices of the American College of Radiology (ACR) in order to develop benchmarks and methodologies to measure quality and safety in imaging, and to formulate recommendations to improve the same in the future.

INITIAL QUALIFICATION OF PEDIATRIC RADIOLOGY PRACTITIONERS

The medical imaging profession has attempted to operationally define the quality of its members by means of the certification process (American Board of Radiology [ABR] certification, Certificate of Added Qualification [CAQ], Maintenance of Certification [MOC]).[21,22] Impending changes to the radiology board certification process, with more emphasis on testing knowledge in chosen subspecialty areas rather than administering a uniform exam that all radiologists must pass, have led some[23] to question the validity of such a process to ensure that all certified radiologists answer to basic quality criteria, thus promoting the commodification of radiology and exposing the graduates to future legal challenges. Proponents of these certification process changes maintain that increased subspecialization in radiology is inevitable to answer societal demands for quality in our specialty.[24] Thus, even the basic requirements that radiologists have to answer to in order to be admitted to the profession are currently under intense discussion.

Whereas the ABR certification process defines minimum requirements to be admitted to the profession, it is by no means a comprehensive assessment of the fitness for independent practice of its diplomates. This point is illustrated by a study of graduating anesthesia residents[25]: when polled, program directors would not trust a substantial number of their own board-certified graduates to perform complex anesthesia procedures on themselves. All experienced radiology educators know of instances when candidates were able to pass through the whole training and certification process, but whom they would not consider to be competent radiologists.

MAINTENANCE OF CERTIFICATION AND (RE-)CREDENTIALING

Life-long practice performance evaluation is an essential part of the MOC process as implemented by the ABR,[22] which constitutes the minimum requirements to remain certified to practice in the (sub)specialty. The ABR has developed a 10-year cycle of recertification for pediatric radiologists, which includes the monitored completion of at least one practice quality improvement (PQI) project per cycle. Established web-based PQI modules are available through the websites of the Society for Pediatric Radiology (SPR), in the area of radiation safety for pediatric CT and the performance of voiding cystourethrogram (VCUG) examinations. At the institutional and practice levels, performance evaluation is delegated to hospital (re)credentialing committees; this evaluation is implemented in a nonuniform manner across radiology practices and does not have quality improvement as its primary goal.

Donnelly et al. have developed objective guidelines for performance-based assessment of radiology faculty in a large children's hospital through a formal peer-review process that also satisfies the requirements for re-credentialing mandated by the Joint Commission.[26,27] This formal peer-review process includes evaluation of the following elements:

professionalism, interpersonal and communications skills, medical knowledge, clinical judgment, clinical and technical skills, and system-based practice improvement. Of these, professionalism and effective communication are probably the most difficult to define and evaluate.[28]

QUALITY IN PEDIATRIC RADIOLOGY: THE PRODUCTION MODEL AND ITS LIMITATIONS

Another approach is to examine the quality of the product of our services, rather than the qualifications of its practitioners. Such an approach has often invoked the application of a market model, and comparisons are made between radiology and other "industries" where quality and outcome metrics are more clearly defined.[13] This approach attempts to look at the concept of "value" in radiology, defining the outcome of radiology services in strictly monetary terms: What is society willing to pay for it? In their 2009 article entitled "Value in Radiology,"[16] Gunderman and Boland pointed out the moral limitations of such an approach, but nonetheless this approach has found increasing application, with the recent emphasis on *pay-for-performance* (P4P) measures.[29–31] Pay-for-performance metrics are difficult to develop for radiology, since the measured clinical outcomes cannot often be related to radiologists' performance in a simple and straightforward manner (except when radiologists assume primary responsibility for patients' outcomes, such as in interventional radiology and perhaps mammography). I am not aware of any meaningful pay-for-performance measure having been instituted that are applicable to the practice of pediatric radiology, but it seems likely that political pressures may change this in the near future, especially in light of impending financial reform of the health care system.

QUALITY IN PEDIATRIC RADIOLOGY: THE PROFESSIONAL MODEL

In a seminal publication on quality in radiology,[20] Blackmore distinguishes the professional versus the production model to define quality in radiology. As mentioned earlier, the production model pertains to the process through which images are produced and interpreted, and results are communicated. The radiology report is the final product of this process, and the measurable elements of the quality of this product and its production process are discussed. The professional model goes beyond the mere production of a report to include such elements as appropriateness of imaging and effects on patient outcome. There is limited literature on the completeness of radiology requests,[32,33] suggesting that existing processes (including computerized order entry) may impede rather than enhance communication between referring physicians and radiologists. Introduction of the ACR appropriateness criteria, and in particular linking these with computerized radiology order entry, has reduced the number of duplicate and otherwise inappropriate requests,[34,35] but there is little evidence that this approach has worked well in pediatric radiology. In addition, there is also a dearth of high-level-of-evidence outcomes studies in pediatric radiology, such as randomized controlled clinical trials and meta-analysis studies,[36] that prove the value of the subspecialty for disease prevention, diagnosis, and cure in children. Nevertheless, pediatric radiologists, embedded as they are in the larger framework of pediatric care, are not satisfied with simply applying the descriptors of the production model for assessment of quality and safety, and would generally prefer to be evaluated according the professional model.

QUALITY METRICS IN PEDIATRIC RADIOLOGY

As opposed to subjective aspects of quality in health care, the more objective aspects can be operationally defined and therefore measured. The assumption is that what can be measured or otherwise quantified has relevance to quality, and any attempt at quality improvement should start with a measurement of the status quo, followed by tailored interventions and then reassessment.[37] Although this statement in general is true, the reverse ("what cannot be measured is unimportant") clearly is not. Nonetheless, fueled by the current political and economic climate to hold health care facilities accountable for the quality they provide, the managers of large radiology departments have embarked on instituting a host of quality metric initiatives, which are often tabulated and reviewed by administrators in the form of a performance review "dashboard."[38] This approach favors measures that can be collected with relative ease, such as report turnaround times,[39] average time of notification of important findings, patient and referring physician satisfaction scores, wait times, examination volumes (professional and technical radiology value unit [RVUs]), and so forth.[38] All of these activities operate within the production model in radiology and, as such, have limited value and do not address the more important aspects of quality as outlined in the professional model. For instance, most departments collect data of report turnaround from the moment the patient arrives at the imaging facility to the final signoff of the report. Whereas timeliness of communication of radiological findings to referring physicians has some relevance to quality, this preoccupation with report turnaround times ignores the fact that frequently findings have already been communicated before signoff, at the time when clinical decisions are made. For instance, a radiology resident or fellow may have made a preliminary interpretation, or the case may have been discussed at morning x-ray rounds, through a telephone communication of an important or unexpected finding, or during an informal "curb-side" consult before final report signoff. In addition, many experienced referring physicians make the critical decisions that affect patient management before and often without (completely) reading the radiology reports, based on their own review of the images.[40] The challenge of the quality assurance process then becomes to ensure that unexpected and subtle findings are brought to the attention of the referring physician, and that the information in the final report does not in any way contradict any initial communications that took place. If a discrepancy with a preliminary interpretation is felt to be necessary by the final signer taking responsibility for the radiology report, it is of utmost importance that he or she resolves these discrepancies with thorough documentation of the information exchange.

Only when done in a clinically relevant manner may the ability of information technology to collect reproducible quality metrics be of some help to differentiate successful pediatric radiology practices from others, thereby counteracting recent trends to regard and treat our subspecialty as a mere commodity.[41]

THE PEDIATRIC RADIOLOGY REPORT: STRUCTURE

The radiology report being the most important and most tangible product of our work, it is not surprising that many quality assurance processes in radiology have attempted to measure the quality of this product in some manner.[42–44] Since the provocative publication by Hall on language that should be avoided in radiology reports,[45] most publications focus on the lexicon and the structure of the report,[40,42–44,46–51] aspects that can relatively easily be evaluated and that bear some relevance to the information exchange between radiologist and referring physicians. Proponents of the use of structured reporting state that it is preferred by referring physicians, and that its uniform implementation should ensure that radiologists are less likely to "forget" to address essential elements in their reports. However, one could argue that a well-structured free-style report can equally well comply with the basic quality requirements of a radiology report that were formulated by Armas in his 1998 letter to the *American Journal of Roentgenology* (AJR)[52]: clarity, correctness, confidence, concision, completeness, and consistency (the 6 C's). The limitations of the traditional prose style of reporting that has dominated radiology for the past 110 years have also been summarized in a review article by Reiner et al.[46] These authors have advocated the increased use of information technology to eventually produce radiology reports that are devoid of text but are purely based on images, with appropriate pictorial annotations.[46] This approach was elegantly criticized by Berlin,[53] who maintained that descriptive text will always be a needed part of radiology reports. Opinion articles on optimization of radiology reporting in the future[48,51] predict that structured reporting with the use of macro templates will become more prevalent, not just in mammography, but in other disciplines of radiology as well, using a standardized radiology lexicon developed under the auspices of the Radiological Society of North American (RSNA; RadLex®). The assumption that use of standardized terminology will reduce confusion and improve communication of imaging findings, and may lead to better deductive reasoning to arrive at the correct radiological diagnosis seems well founded,[50] although this paper concludes: "Of paramount importance is the approach, not the lexicon." In addition, the preference for use of standardized terminology does not necessarily imply that standardization of the *structure* of the radiology report will also accomplish these goals independently. Very few empirical studies have been published on the accuracy of structured versus traditional free-style text reports. A perhaps unexpected outcome of Johnson's study, comparing a structured reporting template (that allowed only mouse-clicks of predefined diagnostic categories and no free text) with conventional dictation, was that this kind of structured reporting actually lowered accuracy and completeness to report cranial magnetic resonance imaging (MRI) studies.[43]

A study of the perspective of referring physicians in a children's hospital on the value of radiology reports[40] emphasized the fact that the reports need to specifically address the clinical question posed in the referral, and must be tailored to the level of expertise of the person receiving the report—generalist versus specialist—conditions that are difficult to meet when rigid standardized report templates are adapted. This is echoed in Hall's opinion article,[48] which makes an argument for more "patient-centered care" in radiology and states that, in the future, not only referring physicians, but also patients will manage their own radiology reports. This applies in particular to the practice of pediatric radiology, which is characterized by more direct patient and family interaction than most other disciplines in radiology. Compared to adult subspecialists, pediatric radiologists have more frequent direct interaction with referring physicians as well, even in the current era of electronic medical records and availability of medical images on personal computers throughout the medical enterprise. Pediatric radiologists have often emphasized the continued importance of face-to-face consultations between radiologists and referring physicians to ensure optimal care for children.[54] They have been creative in overcoming some obstacles brought forth by the digital information age to ensure that critical clinical information continues to be available at the time of image interpretation.[55]

In my opinion, it is unlikely that a rigid reporting structure will be able to satisfy a correct description and interpretation of imaging findings for all possible patient encounters that occur in pediatric radiology practice over the entire age spectrum of 0–18 years. I believe that more efforts should be devoted to teaching trainees (and perhaps even today's generation of younger radiologists!) the analytical skills needed to convey radiographic findings in a clear and unambiguous manner to referring physicians, rather than abandoning free-style text altogether in reports.

THE PEDIATRIC RADIOLOGY REPORT: CONTENT

A more fundamental aspect of radiology report quality is the accuracy of the report content, which is the topic of fewer publications,[32,56,57] since this is much more difficult to assess than report structure.[57] This process requires radiologists to agree on what imaging findings are present and their relevance to the clinical question at hand. This is usually done through the process of trainee[56] and peer review,[58] which is subject to observer variability, unless an independent and accepted gold standard is available to compare the elements of the report content against. In pediatric radiology, studies have focused on errors made in plain film interpretations by trainees, mainly in the diagnosis of subtle buckle fractures and Salter injuries that are specific to the pediatric age group, and in the overdiagnosis of normal variants as pathology.[56] This study has emphasized the need for better trainee education to prevent them from making these pediatric-specific errors when they are in general practice.

ORGANIZATIONAL CULTURE AND QUALITY OF HEALTH CARE

Recent publications have looked at the culture of large health care organizations and how fostering a culture of quality and safety within such organizations may effect change.[59] Within pediatric radiology, the largest body of work in this area has been described in the publications of Frush et al., from Duke Medical Center, and Donnelly et al., from the Cincinnati Children's Hospital.[60-64] The latter group has implemented an integrated patient safety and quality improvement program that is actively supported by the leadership of the department, and constitutes the following elements:

- Structural vertical and horizontal interventions,[60] which refer, respectively, to a systematic response to incident reports, in order to enhance error prevention practices related to a particular process that has led to (potential) errors,[60,65] and the fostering of a general culture of safety among all employees of the department
- Institution of regularly scheduled operational rounds in all areas of the department,[63] in which all employees are encouraged to freely voice quality and safety concerns that are actively addressed by the department leadership to ensure adequate follow-up until resolution of the issues
- A safety coach program,[64] in which specific interested employees are trained and empowered to act as safety coaches

- A "Lessons Learned and Communication Program,"[60-62] which actively tracks the incidence of serious safety breaches in a transparent manner, visible at all times on the department intranet web page.

EXAMPLES OF QUALITY ASSURANCE IN PEDIATRIC RADIOLOGY: CT RADIATION DOSE MONITORING

Many recent studies have dealt with the systematic collection of data on radiation exposure for pediatric radiology procedures,[66-69] in particular for CT and positron emission tomography (PET) imaging. Approximately 62 million CT scans are performed annually in the United States, with at least 4 million of those scans performed in children.[70] Despite this widespread use, the typical radiation doses associated with these procedures are not well known.[71] Extrapolation from survivors of the Japanese atomic bombings during World War II, as well as other instances of high radiation exposure, demonstrate increased incidence of cancer after exposure, particularly in children.[70] Pediatric patients are at particular risk as their growing cells and longer life expectancy may increase their lifetime risk of cancer. Although there is no certainty that the type of radiation and dose ranges used in medical imaging cause cancer, the pediatric radiology community has set out to monitor the use of CT and PET technology, and to use as low a radiation dose as possible to yield the required information (optimization).[6]

The risks of cumulative radiation exposure from repeated CT scans have been estimated in the adult population by a recent study,[72] which showed that many patients accumulated radiation above levels that are thought to be associated with an increased risk of cancer. The professional radiology and pediatric organizations, as well as the U.S. Food and Drug Administration (FDA) and other public agencies have issued public warnings about these potential radiation risks, and CT radiation protection, particularly in children, has become an important quality improvement issue throughout the radiological community.[73] We have performed a CT dose survey in our institution, following systematic efforts at dose reduction in children based on size, clinical indication, and number of prior CT scans performed.[6] We also have measured radiation exposure directly in children undergoing CT

angiography of the chest (Figure 28.1), in order to balance dose with image quality. We, as well as others,[71] have surveyed the variability of pediatric CT doses across regional hospital networks, for the purpose of reducing among hospitals dose outliers and undesirable variability that is not explained by patient factors.

Currently, no national benchmarks guide radiologists on what technical parameters or target CT dose index should be used to optimize radiation exposure of children in the United States. This deficiency will be addressed in the near future by the first national pediatric CT dose registry,[74] established by Dr. Marilyn Goske, the chair and founder of the Alliance for Radiation Safety in Pediatric Imaging, which in 2008 launched the now international Image Gently campaign,[75] aimed at raising awareness of the opportunities to lower radiation dose in the imaging of children. In recent years, pediatric radiologists have been on the forefront of patient advocacy,[76] supported by these and other SPR initiatives. Many of the recent publications in our (sub) specialty journals actively address the recent CT and PET radiation "crisis" through developing techniques to lower doses and advocating nonirradiating alternatives, such as ultrasound for appendicitis and MRI for follow-up of tumors and inflammatory bowel disease.

EVOLUTION OF IMAGING IN DIAGNOSING ACUTE APPENDICITIS: AN OUTCOME-BASED QUALITY IMPROVEMENT INITIATIVE

The application of the professional model of quality is illustrated by the ongoing controversy about the optimal imaging strategy of a common pediatric disorder: acute appendicitis. Until the 1980s, imaging played a very small role in this diagnosis, which changed after Puylaert's publications describing sonographic diagnosis.[77] The use of CT was popularized by the publications of Rao et al.[78] The advantages of CT over ultrasound include higher sensitivity and specificity, less operator dependency, and a greater ability of CT to demonstrate the normal appendix. The past two decades are characterized by increased CT utilization for this diagnosis in children, and due to its initial success, the threshold for performing abdominal CT in a child has nearly disappeared, and its use has diffused to broader indications, such as the evaluation for nonspecific abdominal pain, the search for inflammatory bowel disease, and

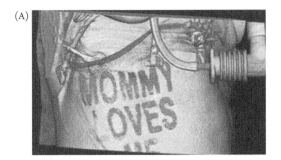

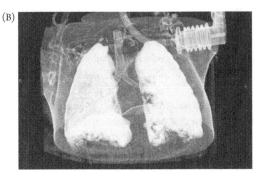

FIGURE 28.1. Example of a radiation safety quality improvement project: Intra-procedural measurement of surface absorbed radiation (SAD, which was equaled to breast dose) to monitor balance between radiation exposure and image quality in a cardiac computed tomography (CT) angiogram of a 3-month-old 10 kg male infant under general anesthesia. The study was done at 80 kV, 35 mAs, CTDI = 1.4 mGy, SAD = 1.2 mGy (= less than one mammogram), DLP = 7 mGy.cm, effective dose = 0.71 mSv. Shaded surface rendition of CTA demonstrates the placement of the Unfors™ Patient Skin Dosimeter solid-state dose detectors on the chest. The radiopaque text on the shirt of this infant is a reminder that parents entrust us with the care of their most valuable assets, their children, and it is our professional obligation to always try to optimize the balance between diagnostic value and potential harm. Coronal images of the chest were evaluated for image quality, which was rated as excellent to address the clinical question, despite a radiation exposure that was an order of magnitude lower than published reference values for this type of exam.

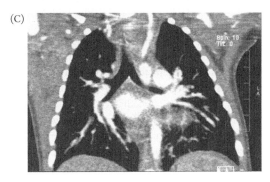

the primary evaluation of small bowel obstruction. After the initial promotion of CT, skepticism set in among pediatric radiologists,[79] after it was realized that the initial papers overestimated the value of CT in the pediatric population.

Papers have appeared in the pediatric surgical literature questioning the value of imaging altogether[80] and proposing to revert to a diagnostic algorithm that focuses on physical examination as the primary triage technique.[81] For reasons of radiation protection and cost-effectiveness,[80] the pendulum is currently swinging back to no imaging at all for typical cases of acute appendicitis,[82] and to defining a role for ultrasound first to screen children with equivocal clinical findings, followed by CT only if ultrasound is inconclusive[83] or if there are complications (perforation, abscess) that might impact on surgical management.

It is of paramount importance to have an adequate clinical triage process in place to raise the disease prevalence, and therefore increase the pretest probability, before children are referred for any imaging test. An important meta-analysis predicted that for every 10,000 young children scanned with ultrasound first rather than CT, 13 could be prevented from developing a future cancer.[36] However, with this strategy, assuming an appendicitis prevalence of 31%, 280 (2.8%) would have a missed diagnosis. The clinical consequences of this can be ameliorated, however, by performing CT in all cases in which ultrasound is equivocal (i.e., ultrasound does not demonstrate the normal appendix, or shows only the secondary signs of acute appendicitis), and by having a thorough clinical follow-up protocol in place that generally would require hospital admission for observation.

In this diagnostic strategy, the role of the pediatric radiologists has evolved to become one that fosters a cost-effective utilization of imaging resources that minimizes exposure of children to ionizing radiation. This excellently illustrates the efforts that the pediatric radiology community can make to accomplish an outcome-based quality improvement initiative. It requires pediatric radiologists to work with their pediatric emergency and surgical colleagues to help develop diagnostic algorithms that can be implemented effectively, taking local resources into consideration. One aspect may be that some pediatric radiologists will need to enhance their own ultrasound scanning skills and to make their expertise available through direct hands-on instruction to ultrasound technologists and radiology trainees, so as to ensure a reliable and consistent diagnostic service, not only during regular office hours but also on evenings and weekends.

Similar arguments can be used to develop evidence-based clinical algorithms for the evaluation of trauma of the cervical spine,[84] chest,[85] and abdomen,[86–88] cognizant of the lack of direct treatment implications that many CT findings have in children subjected to blunt injuries. Following these guidelines should serve to lower the exposure of children to radiation and improve the cost-effectiveness of imaging.

CONCLUSION

The subspecialty of pediatric radiology has a long and rich tradition of addressing the issues of quality and patient safety that are encountered by the profession as a whole.[7,26–28,40,54,60–63,65,74] Traditionally, because pediatric radiologists are working with children who are frequently uncooperative, pediatric radiologists have a higher tolerance for technical imperfections and suboptimal imaging results than their adult counterparts. Through their training, pediatric radiologists are traditionally confident in plain film interpretation and competent in hands-on ultrasound and fluoroscopy as problem-solving tools, rather than having to resort to the more expensive cross-sectional imaging tools of CT and MRI. The contributions to child health for which the subspecialty is most credited, such as the initial description of child abuse and neglect by John Caffey in 1946, the original description of bronchopulmonary dysplasia in premature infants by William Northway in 1967, and the systematic description and categorization of congenital syndromes and skeletal dysplasias by Hooshang Taybi in 1975, to mention a few, are all in the realm of plain film diagnosis. Since, in general, there is a lower pretest probability for malignant disease in pediatrics, well-trained, experienced, and confident pediatric radiologists do not experience the burdens of medicolegal pressure to the same degree as adult radiologists, and consequently operate less with the prevailing "rule-out" mindset that has spurred the extraordinary increase in utilization of advanced and expensive medical imaging that we have seen in recent years. Financial constrains resulting from the impending financial overhaul of the U.S. health care system will hopefully stimulate pediatric radiologists to practice medicine that is even more evidence-based and cost-effective in the future.

I firmly believe that the unique role and qualities required from a pediatric radiologist cannot be fully characterized and measured using the simplistic quality metrics that are derived from the production model for quality assessment and the proposed pay-for-performance measures. I hope that the subspecialty may continue to move forward in a more

TABLE 28.1 MOST IMPORTANT QUALITY IMPROVEMENT INITIATIVES SPECIFIC FOR PEDIATRIC RADIOLOGY

- Optimization of radiation exposure of children, through:
    Using pulsed fluoroscopy, and limiting fluoroscopy time and field
    Child-sizing radiation exposure in pediatric computed tomography (CT) and positron emission tomography (PET) following the recommendations of the Image Gently campaign
    Instituting a local CT radiation safety monitoring program and/or participating with a national CT dose registry
    Further exploring the potential for using alternatives to CT and PET, such as conventional radiography, ultrasound, and magnetic resonance imaging (MRI)
    Consider the use of shielding during CT (thyroid, breasts, gonads)
- Improving the cost-effectiveness of pediatric imaging through:
    Collaboration with referring physicians in outcomes research
    Developing evidence-based diagnostic algorithms for common pediatric conditions (acute appendicitis, inflammatory bowel disease, other chronic conditions, trauma)

holistic approach to quality and safety, and, supported by rigorous outcomes and cost-effectiveness research, may enhance its recognition as being a valuable resource for the welfare of pediatric patients (see Table 28.1).

REFERENCES

1. Guaspari J. I know it when I see it: A modern fable about quality. AMACOM, 1985.
2. Donabedian A. The quality of care. How can it be assessed? *JAMA*. 1988;260:1743–8.
3. Brown PH, Silberberg PJ, Thomas RD, Strife JL, Towbin RB. A multihospital survey of radiation exposure and image quality in pediatric fluoroscopy. *Pediatr Radiol*. 2000;30:236–42.
4. Brown PH, Thomas RD, Silberberg PJ, Johnson LM. Optimization of a fluoroscope to reduce radiation exposure in pediatric imaging. *Pediatr Radiol*. 2000;30:229–35.
5. Ward VL. Patient dose reduction during voiding cystourethrography. *Pediatr Radiol*. 2006;36(Suppl 2):168–72.
6. Singh S, Kalra MK, Moore MA, Shailam R, Liu B, Toth TL, et al. Dose reduction and compliance with pediatric CT protocols adapted to patient size, clinical indication, and number of prior studies. *Radiology*. 2009;252:200–208.
7. Donnelly LF. Reducing radiation dose associated with pediatric CT by decreasing unnecessary examinations. *AJR*. 2005;184:655–7.
8. Agrawalla S, Pearce R, Goodman TR. How to perform the perfect voiding cystourethrogram. *Pediatr Radiol*. 2004;34:114–9.
9. Ment LR, Bada HS, Barnes P, et al. Practice parameter: Neuroimaging of the neonate: report of the Quality Standards Subcommittee of the American Academy of Neurology and the Practice Committee of the Child Neurology Society. *Neurology*. 2002;58:1726–38.
10. Shipman SA, Helfand M, Moyer VA, Yawn BP. Screening for developmental dysplasia of the hip: a systematic literature review for the US Preventive Services Task Force. *Pediatrics*. 2006;117:e557–76.
11. Kohn L CJ, Donaldson M, editors. *To err is human: Building a safer healthcare system*. Washington, DC: National Academy Press, 1999.
12. Multiple authors. *Crossing the quality chasm: a new health care system for the 21st century*. Washington DC: National Academy Press, 2001.
13. Hillman BJ, Amis ES, Jr., Neiman HL. The future quality and safety of medical imaging: proceedings of the third annual ACR FORUM. *J Am Coll Radiol*. 2004;1:33–39.
14. Agency for Healthcare Research and Quality (AHRQ). Guide to health care quality: How to know it when you see it. US Department of Health and Human Services, ed. Publication No. 05-0088. Rockville MD: AHRQ, 2005. Accessed at: http://www.ahrq/consumer/guidetoq/
15. Silver J. Movie day at the Supreme Court or "I Know It When I See It": A history of the definition of obscenity. Findlaw® On-line reference publication for legal professionals, 2003. Accessed December 8, 2011 at: http://library.findlaw.com/2003/May/15/132747.html.
16. Gunderman RB, Boland GW. Value in radiology. *Radiology*. 2009;253:597–9.
17. Thrall JH. Quality and safety revolution in health care. *Radiology*. 2004;233:3–6.
18. Borgstede JP, Zinninger MD. Radiology and patient safety. *Acad Radiol*. 2004;11:322–32.
19. Johnson CD, Swensen SJ, Applegate KE, et al. Quality improvement in radiology: White paper report of the Sun Valley Group meeting. *J Am Coll Radiol*. 2006;3:544–9.
20. Blackmore CC. Defining quality in radiology. *J Am Coll Radiol*. 2007;4:217–23.
21. Friedenberg RM. An endangered art: Teaching. *Radiology*. 2000;214:317–9.
22. Strife JL, Gary LE, Becker J, Dunnick NR, Bosma J, Hattery RR. The American Board of Radiology perspective on maintenance of certification: Part IV—Practice quality improvement in diagnostic radiology. *AJR*. 2007;188:1183–6.
23. Christian BA. The great internal threat to our specialty: The lack of a standardized board-certifying examination in radiology. *J Am Coll Radiol*. 2008;5:1029–31.
24. Dunnick NR, Becker GJ. Commentary on "The great internal threat to our specialty: The lack of a standardized board-certifying examination in radiology." *J Am Coll Radiol*. 2008;5:1032–33.
25. Slogoff S, Hughes FP, Hug CC, Jr., Longnecker DE, Saidman LJ. A demonstration of validity for certification by the American Board of Anesthesiology. *Acad Med*. 1994;69:740–6.
26. Donnelly LF. Performance-based assessment of radiology practitioners: Promoting improvement in accordance with the 2007 joint commission standards. *J Am Coll Radiol*. 2007;4:699–703.
27. Donnelly LF, Strife JL. Performance-based assessment of radiology faculty: A practical plan to promote improvement and meet JCAHO standards. *AJR*. 2005;184:1398–1401.
28. Donnelly LF, Strife JL. Establishing a program to promote professionalism and effective communication in radiology. *Radiology*. 2006;238:773–9.
29. Hillman BJ. Who gets paid with "pay-for-performance"? *J Am Coll Radiol*. 2004;1:891–2.
30. Moser JW, Wilcox PA, Bjork SS, et al. Pay for performance in radiology: ACR white paper. *J Am Coll Radiol*. 2006;3:650–64.
31. Seidel RL, Nash DB. Paying for performance in diagnostic imaging: Current challenges and future prospects. *J Am Coll Radiol*. 2004;1:952–6.
32. Stavem K, Foss T, Botnmark O, Andersen OK, Erikssen J. Inter-observer agreement in audit of

quality of radiology requests and reports. *Clin Radiol.* 2004;59:1018–24.

33. Cohen MD, Curtin S, Lee R. Evaluation of the quality of radiology requisitions for intensive care unit patients. *Acad Radiol.* 2006;13:236–40.

34. Sistrom CL, Dang PA, Weilburg JB, Dreyer KJ, Rosenthal DI, Thrall JH. Effect of computerized order entry with integrated decision support on the growth of outpatient procedure volumes: Seven-year time series analysis. *Radiology.* 2009;251:147–55.

35. Sistrom CL, Dreyer KJ, Dang PP, et al. Recommendations for additional imaging in radiology reports: Multifactorial analysis of 5.9 million examinations. *Radiology.* 2009;253:453–61.

36. Doria AS, Moineddin R, Kellenberger CJ, et al. US or CT for diagnosis of appendicitis in children and adults? A meta-analysis. *Radiology.* 2006;241:83–94.

37. Langley GJ, Moen RD, Nolan KM, Nolan TW, Norman CL, Provost LP. *The improvement guide: A practical approach to enhancing organizational performance,* 2nd ed. San Francisco, CA: Jossey-Bass, 2009.

38. Seltzer SE, Kelly P, Deibel GM, Ros P. Radiology quality and performance metrics on the Web: A management information and communications tool. *Acad Radiol.* 2000;7:981–5.

39. Seltzer SE, Kelly P, Adams DF, et al. Expediting the turnaround of radiology reports: Use of total quality management to facilitate radiologists' report signing. *AJR.* 1994;162:775–81.

40. Gunderman R, Ambrosius WT, Cohen M. Radiology reporting in an academic children's hospital: What referring physicians think. *Pediatr Radiol.* 2000;30:307–14.

41. Reiner BI, Siegel EL. Decommoditizing radiology. *J Am Coll Radiol.* 2009;6:167–70.

42. Johnson AJ. Radiology report quality: A cohort study of point-and-click structured reporting versus conventional dictation. *Acad Radiol.* 2002;9:1056–61.

43. Johnson AJ, Chen MY, Swan JS, Applegate KE, Littenberg B. Cohort study of structured reporting compared with conventional dictation. *Radiology.* 2009;253:74–80.

44. Johnson AJ, Ying J, Swan JS, Williams LS, Applegate KE, Littenberg B. Improving the quality of radiology reporting: A physician survey to define the target. *J Am Coll Radiol.* 2004;1:497–505.

45. Hall FM. Language of the radiology report: Primer for residents and wayward radiologists. *AJR.* 2000;175:1239–42.

46. Reiner BI, Knight N, Siegel EL. Radiology reporting, past, present, and future: The radiologist's perspective. *J Am Coll Radiol.* 2007;4:313–9.

47. Lee R, Cohen MD, Jennings GS. A new method of evaluating the quality of radiology reports. *Acad Radiol.* 2006;13:241–8.

48. Hall FM. The radiology report of the future. *Radiology.* 2009;251:313–6.

49. Weiss DL, Langlotz CP. Structured reporting: Patient care enhancement or productivity nightmare? *Radiology.* 2008;249:739–47.

50. Brenner RJ. On the logistics of interpretive radiology reporting: Moving beyond Procrustes. *J Am Coll Radiol.* 2009;6:544–6.

51. Dunnick NR, Langlotz CP. The radiology report of the future: A summary of the 2007 Intersociety Conference. *J Am Coll Radiol.* 2008;5:626–9.

52. Armas RR. Qualities of a good radiology report. *AJR.* 1998;170:1110.

53. Berlin L. Replacing traditional text radiology reports with image-centric reports: A shift from epiphany to enigma? *AJR.* 2006;187:1156–9.

54. Slovis TL, Frush D. Getting back to basics. *Pediatr Radiol.* 2005;35:839–40.

55. Cohen MD, Alam K. Radiology clinical synopsis: A simple solution for obtaining an adequate clinical history for the accurate reporting of imaging studies on patients in intensive care units. *Pediatr Radiol.* 2005;35:918–22.

56. Halsted MJ, Kumar H, Paquin JJ, et al. Diagnostic errors by radiology residents in interpreting pediatric radiographs in an emergency setting. *Pediatr Radiol.* 2004;34:331–6.

57. Lee JK. Quality—a radiology imperative: Interpretation accuracy and pertinence. *J Am Coll Radiol.* 2007;4:162–5.

58. Borgstede JP, Lewis RS, Bhargavan M, Sunshine JH. RADPEER quality assurance program: A multifacility study of interpretive disagreement rates. *J Am Coll Radiol.* 2004;1:59–65.

59. Davies HT, Nutley SM, Mannion R. Organisational culture and quality of health care. *Qual Health Care.* 2000;9:111–9.

60. Donnelly LF, Dickerson JM, Goodfriend MA, Muething SE. Improving patient safety in radiology. *AJR.* 2010;194:1183–7.

61. Donnelly LF, Dickerson JM, Goodfriend MA, Muething SE. Improving patient safety in radiology: Concepts for a comprehensive patient safety program. Seminars in ultrasound, CT, and MR. 2010;31:67–70.

62. Donnelly LF, Dickerson JM, Goodfriend MA, Muething SE. Improving patient safety: Effects of a safety program on performance and culture in a department of radiology. *AJR.* 2009;193:165–71.

63. Donnelly LF, Dickerson JM, Lehkamp TW, Gessner KE, Moskovitz J, Hutchinson S. IRQN award paper: Operational rounds: A practical administrative process to improve safety and clinical services in radiology. *J Am Coll Radiol.* 2008;5:1142–9.

64. Dickerson JM, Koch BL, Adams JM, Goodfriend MA, Donnelly LF. Safety coaches in radiology: Decreasing human error and minimizing patient harm. *Pediatr Radiol.* 2010;40:1545–51.

65. Frush KS, Alton M, Frush DP. Development and implementation of a hospital-based patient safety program. *Pediatr Radiol.* 2006;36:291–8.

66. Reiner BI. Quantifying radiation safety and quality in medical imaging, part 3: The quality assurance scorecard. *J Am Coll Radiol.* 2009;6:694–700.

67. Reiner BI. Quantifying radiation safety and quality in medical imaging, part 2: The radiation scorecard. *J Am Coll Radiol.* 2009;6:615–9.

68. Reiner BI. Quantifying radiation safety and quality in medical imaging, part 1: Creating the infrastructure. *J Am Coll Radiol.* 2009;6:558–61.

69. Reiner BI. Automating quality assurance for digital radiography. *J Am Coll Radiol.* 2009;6:486–90.

70. Brenner DJ, Hall EJ. Computed tomography—an increasing source of radiation exposure. *N Engl J Med.* 2007;357:2277–84.

71. Smith-Bindman R, Lipson J, Marcus R, et al. Radiation dose associated with common computed tomography examinations and the associated lifetime attributable risk of cancer. *Arch Intern Med.* 2009;169:2078–86.

72. Sodickson A, Baeyens PF, Andriole KP, et al. Recurrent CT, cumulative radiation exposure, and associated radiation-induced cancer risks from CT of adults. *Radiology.* 2009;251:175–84.

73. Amis ES, Jr., Butler PF, Applegate KE, et al. American College of Radiology white paper on radiation dose in medicine. *J Am Coll Radiol.* 2007;4:272–84.

74. Goske M. First national children's dose registry to ensure necessary, safe imaging. In: *RSNA News.* Oak Brook, IL: RSNA, 2010. Accessed at: http://www.rsna.org/Publications/RSNAnews/August2010/dose_registry_feature.cfm

75. Goske MJ, Applegate KE, Boylan J, et al. The Image Gently campaign: Working together to change practice. *AJR.* 2008;190:273–4.

76. Larson DB, Rader SB, Forman HP, Fenton LZ. Informing parents about CT radiation exposure in children: It's OK to tell them. *AJR.* 2007;189:271–5.

77. Puylaert JB. Acute appendicitis: US evaluation using graded compression. *Radiology.* 1986;158:355–60.

78. Rao PM, Rhea JT, Novelline RA, et al. Helical CT technique for the diagnosis of appendicitis: Prospective evaluation of a focused appendix CT examination. *Radiology.* 1997;202:139–44.

79. Strouse PJ. Pediatric appendicitis: An argument for US. *Radiology.* 2010;255:8–13.

80. York D, Smith A, Phillips JD, von Allmen D. The influence of advanced radiographic imaging on the treatment of pediatric appendicitis. *J Pediatr Surg.* 2005;40:1908–11.

81. Kosloske AM, Love CL, Rohrer JE, Goldthorn JF, Lacey SR. The diagnosis of appendicitis in children: Outcomes of a strategy based on pediatric surgical evaluation. *Pediatrics.* 2004;113:29–34.

82. Shorvon PJ. Imaging of appendicitis: A cautionary note. *Br J Radiol.* 2002;75:717–20.

83. Wan MJ, Krahn M, Ungar WJ, et al. Acute appendicitis in young children: Cost-effectiveness of US versus CT in diagnosis—a Markov decision analytic model. *Radiology.* 2009;250:378–86.

84. Jimenez RR, Deguzman MA, Shiran S, Karrellas A, Lorenzo RL. CT versus plain radiographs for evaluation of c-spine injury in young children: do benefits outweigh risks? *Pediatr Radiol.* 2008;38:635–44.

85. Moore MA, Wallace EC, Westra SJ. The imaging of paediatric thoracic trauma. *Pediatr Radiol.* 2009;39:485–96.

86. Retzlaff T, Hirsch W, Till H, Rolle U. Is sonography reliable for the diagnosis of pediatric blunt abdominal trauma? *J Pediatr Surg.* 2010;45:912–5.

87. Deunk J, Brink M, Dekker HM, et al. Predictors for the selection of patients for abdominal CT after blunt trauma: A proposal for a diagnostic algorithm. *Ann Surg.* 2010;251:512–20.

88. Sola JE, Cheung MC, Yang R, et al. Pediatric FAST and elevated liver transaminases: An effective screening tool in blunt abdominal trauma. *J Surg Res.* 2009;157:103–7.

29

Quality in Interventional Radiology

GLORIA M. SALAZAR AND HANI H. ABUDUJUHEH

The incorporation of initiatives to promote safety and maintain quality in the care of patients is paramount to delivering accurate, timely, and efficacious clinical services in interventional radiology (IR). Assuring proper patient management requires the use of a focused and inclusive clinical protocol that should be reproducible in different clinical scenarios. In this setting, establishing a program that includes a continuous assessment of clinical outcomes that allow the identification of problems within our field and areas to be improved is desirable to minimize risks and maintain a low incidence of patient complications. In fact, these initiatives are required by the Joint Commission for hospital accreditation. To ensure quality of care in vascular and interventional radiology, the Society of Interventional Radiology (SIR) has been actively involved, through the Standards Division, in developing evidence-based standards and clinical practice guidelines. In spite of the variation and heterogeneity of procedures performed in IR, several safety prac-tices can significantly reduce errors and complications and provide the best quality of care to patients. This chapter presents an overview of the process of quality and assurance in IR at different stages of patient care (preprocedural verification, procedural indications, complications thresholds, and clinical outcomes), and for various levels of health care providers (physicians, nurses, technologists, physician assistants, and radiology trainees).

LEVELS OF INTERVENTION FOR PATIENT SAFETY

The process of ensuring quality patient care begins at the organizational level, with proper planning and allocation of those resources needed to accomplish the desired outcome: a high level of clinical success with a low incidence of complications and adverse events. Main quality initiatives in radiology include safety, process improvement, and data collection, and the recommendations for implementation suggest that partnership with registered nurses and personnel with specialized training in process improvement can be very efficacious.[1] Therefore, given the complexity and variety of procedures performed in IR, it is imperative that a multidisciplinary team works together in determining clinical protocols tailored for specific patient and disease processes.

With this goal in mind, safety initiatives in IR can be stratified into the following groups: organizational, clinical and procedural care, materials and resources, radiologic reporting, health care providers, and training standards. At an organizational level, an IR section should provide effective services for scheduling clinical consults and procedures, reporting critical findings, determining staff hours and availability of services, coordinating patient workflow, and assigning individuals of different capacities for monitoring safety issues. For clinical issues, the American College of Radiology (ACR), in collaboration with the Standards Committee of the

SIR and the Society of Neurointerventional Surgery (SNIS), has developed the IR practice guideline defining the infrastructural requirements needed in this setting.[2] Procedural care parameters can be utilized depending on the nature of procedures, but in general, continuous monitoring of the incidence of infections, complications, and adverse events should be performed. Specific procedural threshold recommendations are described in several SIR quality improvement guidelines. In addition, the application of the Joint Commission's guidelines for labeling medications[3] and preventing "wrong site, wrong procedure, and wrong person surgery" to the preoperative verification process[4] is indicated for all procedures. Determination of appropriate resources and materials is also a very important aspect of IR practice, and specific requirements are described by the ACR guidelines.[2] Moreover, ongoing evaluation of the performance of medical devices utilized for procedures is paramount to safe patient care, as is establishing a regular program of equipment maintenance. Radiologic report safety and process metrics are similar to those used in other imaging subspecialties, and include critical test reporting, standardized protocol use rate, and finalization time of reports.[1] Finally, all health care providers should follow clinical protocols and Joint Commission guidelines, work together to maintain the standard quality of care, and be systematically evaluated for appropriateness in their competency to deliver such clinical services.

Likewise, in the academic setting, proper supervision and education of trainees is performed according to Accreditation Council for Graduate Medical Education (ACGME), the ACR, and SIR training standards.

In summary, a wide range of safety initiatives can be represented in a quality assurance (QA) program in IR, and this program should include continuous standardized monitoring of outcomes and parameters representing all levels of patient care.

OVERVIEW OF QUALITY ASSURANCE PROGRAMS IN INTERVENTIONAL RADIOLOGY

A QA evaluation should be performed systematically to allow for proper identification of problems and prompt response to an issue when further action is required. Both a departmental committee and a responsible physician within the IR section should be present to collect data and employ clinically recommended thresholds to evaluate a potential risk or complication. Particularly in the academic environment, quarterly or monthly morbidity and mortality sessions should be presented to trainees, in order to demonstrate how to manage or avoid a specific complication. The process of determining appropriate action for a specific situation is not intended to penalize involved health care providers, but to identify causes and to improve departmental clinical guidelines. Moreover, such a process allows an opportunity to review the guidelines and to change clinical practices based on discussion with different hospital staff members.

The guidelines established by the SIR Standards of Practice Committee recommend 10 steps to design a QA program.[5] These are: assigning responsibility for the monitoring and evaluation (M&E) program; delineating the scope of the care provided; identifying important aspects of care; identifying indicators related to the important aspects of care; establishing the thresholds for evaluation related to the indicators; collecting and organizing data; evaluating care when thresholds are reached; taking action to resolve identified problems; determining whether care or service has improved and documenting improvement; and communicating relevant information to the facility-wide QA program.

These guidelines also establish that the chief of vascular and interventional radiology should be responsible for monitoring and evaluating the M&E program, although each staff physician is responsible for ensuring proper documentation of his or her procedures, as well as for recording procedural complications. Identified complications are classified according to SIR standards by outcome (Table 29.1).[6] Determination of the scope of care is based on the volume and related risks of a specific procedure. Important aspects of procedural care include appropriateness, efficacy, and safety, and evaluation with indicator thresholds for a specific procedure. When indications or success rates fall below a minimum threshold, or when complication rates exceed a maximum threshold, a review should be performed to determine causes and to implement changes, if necessary.[6] Data collection should consist of studying the logs of vascular and interventional radiology procedures performed in the radiology department, and includes documenting the patient's name, medical

TABLE 29.1   SOCIETY OF INTERVENTIONAL RADIOLOGY (SIR) CLASSIFICATION
SYSTEM FOR COMPLICATIONS BY OUTCOME

Minor Complications

A. No therapy, no consequence

B. Nominal therapy, no consequence; includes overnight admission for observation only

Major Complications

C. Require therapy, minor hospitalization(<48 hours)

D. Require major therapy, unplanned increase in level of care, prolonged hospitalization (>48 hours)

E. Permanent adverse sequelae

F. Death

Reprinted from Sacks D, McClenny TE, Cardella JF, Lewis CA. Society of Interventional Radiology clinical practice guidelines. *J Vasc Interv Radiol.* 2003;14:S199–S202, with permission from Elsevier.

record number, operating physician, date, indication, and the specific procedure done. Records of complications should be maintained in a separate log, with a brief summary of the reported event. All this information will be monitored as part of the department's confidential peer review file.

Discussion of the complications at monthly QA meetings should include the responsible staff physician presenting the circumstances of the event, with classification of the complication as avoidable or unavoidable by the staff. A discussion regarding the prevention of avoidable complications will take place in the monthly meeting, and agreement should be reached. Cumulative data should also be presented in departmental meetings every 6 months. Complications rates will be discussed with the individual staff and with the department, and a review will be performed if thresholds of appropriateness, efficacy, and safety are reached. When individual or departmental appropriateness thresholds are exceeded, the specific cases will be discussed. As a result of the review, the procedure indications may need to be broadened, or reemphasis of the consensus for procedural indications will occur. When efficacy or safety thresholds are exceeded, the review will focus on specific cases, expertise, patient population, and equipment-related issues. The formulation of a specific plan of action may include changing thresholds secondary to patient population characteristics, recommending continuing medical education courses for some practitioners, and instituting voluntary limitations of privileges. This plan should be implemented by the chief of interventional radiology, who will monitor the outcomes of the action taken.

If the problem recurs, or an individual fails to meet the standards outlined by the department, and no sufficient improvement occurs after the recommended actions, involuntary limitations of privileges may be considered, following the hospital's medical staff bylaws and procedures.

The results of departmental meetings should be reported to the hospital's QA committee, including the specific actions recommended and taken, and the outcome data. Any recommendation to alter hospital privileges for any medical staff will be also presented.

THE ROLE OF MORTALITY AND MORBIDITY (M&M) REVIEWS

A departmental discussion of complications is the most important initiative to educate staff and maintain a safer patient environment, and therefore these reviews should be a systematic part of any QA program. Mortality and morbidity (M&M) reviews not only allow practitioners to learn from errors, but also promotes education for all levels of providers by discussing issues and adverse events, reviewing clinical protocols, and raising awareness about specific patient characteristics. The academic importance of M&M sessions resides in providing trainees with an opportunity to develop competency in the core areas required by the ACGME, including system-based practice, practice-based learning, professionalism, and communication (although the value of the educational impact for modeling error recognition is still questionable in other areas of medicine, with the emphasis placed mostly on complication-related deaths).[7] Moreover, systematic review of complications not only stimulates standardization and modification of practices, but also improves communication and teamwork, resulting in a more efficient delivery of patient care.

In the IR literature, a paucity of studies evaluates the importance of such sessions, but recently Tuong et al. described their experience in conducting multidisciplinary M&M reviews in a pediatric IR service over a 10-year period.[8] As a result of a retrospective analysis of the database, the authors found that 80% of the recommendations made at M&M sessions were implemented in their practice. This publication highlights the importance of M&M as a method for improving QA in an IR service by using predefined methodology in the sessions. As an example, the authors classified the complications or issues in 10 categories (device-related, ethics-related, management-/education-/compliance-related, medication-related, near-miss/catch, other, patient-related, procedure-related, process-related, and sedation-/anesthesia-related) and the recommendations in six categories (discussion, educational, manufacturer, process, technical, other). With these tools, the M&M reviews yielded a precise assessment of different areas, thus promoting a more focused implementation of changes and improvements tailored to their patient's population characteristics. This experience functions as a model for other IR services to implement or enhance M&M reviews.

CLINICAL INDICATORS FOR CONTINUOUS MONITORING OF PATIENT SAFETY IN INTERVENTIONAL RADIOLOGY

Appropriate development and selection of clinical indicators are needed for systematic evaluation of patient care. In general, most of the data assessing safety issues in medicine relies on reporting systems and the analysis of events (such as root cause analysis) to prompt for modification and improvement.[9] Ideally, clinical indicators should be determined by research-based outcomes; however, if the evidence in the literature is conflicting or weak, indicators are derived from professional expert panels using a consensus process. Indicators can be expressed as numbers, rates, or averages, and may include

measures of structure, process, and outcome for general or specific disease-processes.[10] In general, safety parameters that are considered important for radiology include radiology-generated infections, medication errors rates, patient falls, contrast material-induced nephropathy, critical test reporting, specimen labeling errors, Universal Protocol, hand hygiene, medication reconciliation, and correct image labeling.[1]

Due to the variety of procedures performed in IR, different parameters are used to continuously monitor patient safety for vascular and nonvascular procedures, as recommended by the SIR Clinical Practice Guidelines documents. These include documents on quality improvement, consensus, reporting standards, emerging technologies, position statements, and health and safety guidelines.[11] The purposes of SIR documents are to optimize the quality of care of patients, assure consistency and comparability in the publication of clinical and basic science research, establish QA programs with action thresholds, and provide knowledge about new topics for IR.[11] Accordingly, indicators for outcomes utilized by these documents are indications, effectiveness (success), and complications rates.[12] The methodology employed to create these documents is described in the literature[12] and has been recently updated with the addition of collaborative work with other relevant societies and revision of documents every 5 years.[11] For example, quality improvement guidelines are systematically developed, evidence-based, consensus documents including definitions, indications, efficacy, success, and complications thresholds that assist medical decision-making for a given procedure/technique in IR.[12] As previously discussed, IR services are encouraged to use these indicators to evaluate their outcomes on a regular basis and at QA meetings. By defining the most suitable level of patient care, these guidelines are helpful resources for IR staff and are intended to be reproducible in different clinical environments, thus reducing clinical variation.

The Safety and Health Committee of the SIR has also published several documents regarding patient and provider safety. The most relevant documents adapted from Joint Commission guidelines are summarized in the following sections. The steps presented by the quality improvement documents of SIR provide an organized and comprehensive review of Joint Commission guidelines as applied to IR.

SOCIETY OF INTERVENTIONAL RADIOLOGY GUIDELINES FOR PREVENTING WRONG SITE, WRONG PROCEDURE, AND WRONG PERSON ERRORS: APPLICATION OF THE UNIVERSAL PROTOCOL IN INTERVENTIONAL RADIOLOGY

The SIR has published guidelines for application of the Joint Commission process for preprocedure verification (Universal Protocol for preventing wrong site, wrong procedure and wrong person surgery[13]) to IR practice, which is indicated for all procedures. A detailed description of the document has been published elsewhere; the most important points include a time-out process, preprocedural side/site marking, and postprocedure briefings.

The IR time-out should occur after the patient is placed on the procedure table, regardless of the location, and before the invasive procedure has started. All personnel involved in the procedure should be present and participate in the process.

The correct side/site must be marked on the skin and be visible during the procedure, whenever the side/site or individual structure to be intervened upon is known. However, this is not always possible for certain IR procedures, given that site marking may not be visible—for example, in a right renal artery angioplasty procedure. In such instances, the SIR recommends the use of appropriate intraprocedural imaging to confirm the side/site and level of intervention. Other situations excluded from the skin marking requirement include performing vascular access as a route for a procedure or for central venous access, unless otherwise specified by the referring physician or contraindicated.

In summary, although preprocedural marking is rarely required in IR, identification of the correct structure/side/site to be treated with prior imaging is necessary and should be performed by the interventional radiologist or designee before the procedure. Ideally, the site and side of the procedure should be indicated at the time of scheduling, and all pertinent imaging studies should be available before the procedure's date. After completion of the procedure, correct labeling of images identifying the site/structure of intervention should be done before archiving.

SOCIETY OF INTERVENTIONAL RADIOLOGY GUIDELINES FOR LABELING MEDICATIONS

Specific recommendations for labeling medications are guided by the Joint Commission 2007 National Patient Safety Goals (NPSGs),[14] and were summarized by the SIR guidelines in 2009 (15). The most important points include the following:

- All solution containers and syringes must be labeled at the time of preparation, including contrast material loaded into power injectors.[14] The label must include drug name, strength, amount, expiration date when not used within 24 hours, expiration time if less than 24 hours, date prepared, and the diluent for all compounded admixtures.
- Label syringes and containers of medications on the procedure table using sterile labels and a sterile marking pen or preprinted labels.
- Remove skin preparation substances (e.g., povidone iodine, alcohol, chlorhexidine) from the table as soon as the patient is prepared and draped, or use a second table for patient preparation materials.
- Encourage the use of single-use vials.
- Do not use unlabeled medications: discard them immediately.

Other pertinent recommendations encourage the teamwork environment, in which physicians, nurses, and technologists review the patient's allergies list and communicate verification of the physician's verbal orders.

PREVENTABLE ADVERSE EVENTS

Reporting adverse events in IR is important to prevent the future occurrence of such complications. The goal is to evaluate the causes that led to the event and to establish clinical protocols to prevent recurrence of such events. A list of possible causes of preventable adverse events was published in 2007 by Miller,[16] and it was adapted by the SIR Task Force on Medical Errors (Table 29.2). Knowing the potential causes of preventable complications may prompt specific actions to develop standardized protocol checklists that can be used by all the health care providers in IR.

TABLE 29.2 POSSIBLE CAUSES OF PREVENTABLE ADVERSE EVENTS

Before Procedure

1. Necessary equipment not available for a case
2. Incomplete necessary history or examination
3. Predisposition for hemorrhage is not know due to insufficient documentation or inadequate history
4. Patient ate before a procedure requiring an empty stomach
5. Wrong patient sent from ward
6. Patients allergies not checked
7. Vitals signs and/or patient assessment not done before sedation or procedure
8. No consent before the procedure

During Procedure

1. Procedure performed in the wrong patient, side or organ
2. Wrong patient is indicated on monitor and/or fluoroscopy equipment
3. Handed the wrong equipment during a case
4. Handed equipment incorrectly during a case
5. Asked for wrong equipment
6. Incorrect medication or dose of medication given (by operator or nurse)
7. Medication on procedure table incorrectly labeled or not labeled
8. Administration of medication to patient with a known allergy to the drug
9. Fluid overload due to high intravenous fluid administration rate
10. Stopcock blows off during power injection
11. Contrast medium injected but no images are obtained
12. Images are obtained but contrast medium injector did not inject
13. Patient falls off stretcher or table during transfer or procedure
14. Break in sterile technique
15. Power failure
16. Access lost catheter or guide wire inadvertently removed from the patient
17. Misinterpretation of arterial anatomy or miss of relevant findings
18. Patient radiation greater than optimum

Procedure-specific

1. Performance of pulmonary arteriography in a patient with known left bundle branch block
2. Placement of inferior vena cava filter in gonadal vein or hepatic vein

3. Embolization of bronchial artery without recognition of the artery of Adamkiewicz; risk of cord ischemia
4. Ureteral stent deployed with tip in the renal parenchyma or coiled in the ureter
5. Excessive oversizing of balloon or stent in artery, with risk of rupture
6. Perforation of renal capsule with a guide wire during renal intervention
7. Radiofrequency ablation in a patient with a pacemaker
8. Intraarterial placement of a venous access device
9. Placement of nitinol stent or filter in a patient with nickel allergy
10. Injecting CO_2 in a patient with a right-to-left shunt

Postprocedure

1. Attempt an arterial line placement in a patient undergoing thrombolytic therapy
2. Inadequate postprocedural monitoring or instructions leading to delayed therapy of a substantial postprocedural complication (e.g., infection after uterine artery embolization, pneumothorax after lung biopsy, neurologic complication of lytic therapy)
3. Images incorrectly labeled
4. Official report with correct dictation in incorrect patient
5. Official report with incorrect dictation in correct patient
6. Patient and/or family is not advised of a high radiation dose to skin and appropriate follow-up

Reprinted from Miller DL. Safety in interventional radiology. *J Vasc Interv Radiol.* 2007;18:1–3, with permission from Elsevier.

INDICATOR THRESHOLDS FOR SPECIFIC PROCEDURES

Important aspects of care involving specific procedures were established by SIR committees through quality improvement publications. Given the wide range of procedures in IR, universal indicator thresholds are very difficult to determine as they may be influenced by patient referral and characteristics; therefore, each department is encouraged to review its data from systematic safety monitoring and customize thresholds based on its own clinical outcomes. The following indicator thresholds are recommended by the SIR for some of the high-volume procedures performed in IR.

Diagnostic Angiography

Indications for diagnostic arteriography have been described by SIR committees for pulmonary, spinal, bronchial, aorta, abdominal visceral, renal, pelvic, and extremity arteriography.[17] The threshold for these indications is 95%. When fewer than 95% of the procedures are for these indications, the department will review the process of patient selection. Complications may be divided into three groups: puncture site, systemic, and catheter-induced.

Puncture site-related complications thresholds are hematoma (0.5%), occlusion (0.2%), and pseudoaneurysm/arteriovenous fistula formation (0.2%).

The catheter-induced complications threshold is 0.5% and includes distal emboli, arterial dissection/subintimal passage, and subintimal injection of contrast.

The major contrast reactions threshold is 0.5%, whereas contrast media-associated nephrotoxicity is 0.2%. The overall procedure threshold for major complications is 1.0%.[17]

Central Venous Access

Threshold rates for success in placement of central venous access, for both peripherally inserted central catheters and peripherally implanted ports in the adult population, are 95% for internal jugular approach and 90% for subclavian vein and translumbar approaches.[18]

Specific major complication thresholds for venous access via subclavian and jugular approaches are pneumothorax (3%), hemothorax (2%), hematoma (2%), perforation (2%), air embolism (2%), wound dehiscence (2%), procedure-induced sepsis (2%), and thrombosis (8%).

Specific major complication thresholds for peripheral PICC and ports are pneumothorax/hemothorax (0%), hematoma (2%), wound dehiscence (2%), phlebitis (8%), arterial injury (1%), thrombosis (6%), and procedure-induced sepsis (2%).

The overall procedure threshold for major complications related to image-guided central venous access (subclavian, jugular, and peripheral approaches) is 3%.

Inferior Vena Cava Filters

Absolute and relative indications for inferior vena cava (IVC) filter placement have been described by SIR guidelines.[19] Technical success for placement is expected to be 97%; therefore, the threshold for review of technical failures is 3%. Complication thresholds are recurrent pulmonary embolism (5%), IVC occlusion (10%), filter embolization (2%), access site thrombosis (1%), and death (<1%).

Percutaneous Transcatheter Embolization

For percutaneous transcatheter embolization, specific indications were already determined by the SIR guidelines,[20] and overall technical and clinical success thresholds are 95% and 85%, respectively; these include bronchial, pulmonary, renal, hypogastric, pancreatic, and splenic arteries, as well as gastrointestinal embolization for bleeding and varicocele. The overall complication threshold is 6%, and specific complication thresholds are sepsis (1%), abscess (1%), target ischemia (4%), nontarget embolization (2.5%), hemorrhage (<1%), spinal infarction (<1%), and procedure-related death (1%). The splenic embolization-related overall major complication threshold is 15%, and specific thresholds are abscess/sepsis (5%), pneumonia (8%), pleural effusion (4%), and death (2%).

INTERVENTIONAL TECHNOLOGIES AND DEVICE SAFETY

Interventional radiology is highly dependent on the use of technologies and devices. Although evolving technologies and devices provide a broad spectrum of treatment options for different patient populations, variable clinical efficacy is associated with their use. From the process of clearance and approval for usage from the U.S. Food and Drug Administration (FDA), to the demonstration of clinical efficacy recognized in well-designed randomized trials, several factors might result in safety issues and/or undesired clinical outcomes for patients.

Medical devices sold in the United States are regulated by the FDA's Center for Devices and Radiological Health (CDRH) and are classified into class I, II, and III (21) devices, according to their corresponding risk. Regulatory control increases from class I to class III. Current standards for determining the safety and effectiveness of new devices are based on the Code of Federal Regulations, which requires premarket approval (PMA) for class III devices. PMA is the most stringent type of device marketing application and is based on a determination by the FDA that the PMA contains sufficiently valid scientific evidence to provide reasonable assurance that the device is safe and effective for its intended use or uses.[22] These include evidence from well-controlled investigations, partially controlled studies, studies and objective trials without matched controls, well-documented case histories conducted by qualified experts, and reports of significant human experience with a marketed device, from which it can fairly and responsibly be concluded by qualified experts that there is reasonable assurance of the safety and effectiveness of a device under its conditions of use.[23]

Evolving technology used to manufacture new materials approved by the FDA can offer great benefits to our patient population, even in "off-label" circumstances, thus prompting physicians to use devices for unapproved indications. However, there are concerns regarding the meanings of FDA approval criteria, which do not specifically include studies with sufficient scientific strength, such as comparative effectiveness research data with known current standard treatments.[24,25]

Moreover, the lack of an adequate demonstration of comparative effectiveness in well-designed studies can lead to serious risks and adverse events for patients in the long-term. One particular example in IR refers to the use of embolic agents in the treatment of uterine leiomyomas (fibroids). The efficacy and safety of uterine artery embolization (UAE) for treatment of symptomatic fibroids is well established in the literature, with the publication of high-level scientific evidence.[26,27] Likewise, polyvinyl alcohol (PVA) particles and trisacryl gelatin microspheres (Embospheres; Biosphere Medical, Rockland, Massachusetts) became the standard embolic agents for UAE, with effective fibroid infarction.[28] Subsequently, new agents, such as spherical PVA particles (sPVA; Contour SE; Boston Scientific, Natick, Massachusetts) were introduced to the market after approval from FDA. Although, sPVA particles were initially proved to yield symptom improvement and fibroid reduction as compared to myomectomy,[29] no contrast-enhanced magnetic resonance (MR) imaging was available for postprocedural patient evaluation at that time, which is now considered the standard to evaluate fibroid infarction and therefore treatment success.[30] It was assumed that sPVA was as effective as the standard particles for fibroid infarction, and therefore, several interventionalists employed sPVA for UAE in their practice, resulting in a high incidence of treatment failures. The clinical indication that sPVA was actually not as effective as the standard particles prompted the initiation of a clinical trial that was halted after demonstrating a very high rate of uninfarcted leiomyomas on follow-up.[31] Later, similar findings of less fibroid shrinkage and less clinical improvement with the use of sPVA as compared to PVA were demonstrated in a prospective study.[32] It became evident that clinical success with the UAE technique is highly dependent of the type of particle. Thus, careful evaluation, through developing well-designed randomized comparative trials assessing the use of standard versus novel agents, should be done before a new agent is introduced into IR practice.

Such examples highlight the importance of maintaining high-quality care in IR by demanding scientific evidence through an ongoing evaluation of new techniques by experts in the field, in conjunction with the SIR and beyond the FDA approval process. It also demonstrates the need to incorporate changes into the current process of FDA approval by addressing the clinical superiority of new treatments over known and well-established therapies, and therefore providing real benefit to the targeted patient population.

Although the use of devices is an essential part of IR practice, ongoing manufacturer monitoring of device-related problems (e.g., malfunction, adverse events, and deaths) is not required after FDA approval. Most of the adverse events data involving medical devices are recorded by the Manufacturer and User Facility Device Experience (MAUDE), the FDA's voluntary reporting system. Moreover, unlike drugs, which can be discontinued after evidence serious adverse events, many devices are implanted within patients, thus making safety issues of great concern. Even when devices can be removed after their intended use (such as retrievable IVC filters), long-term effects should be evaluated carefully, and under intense medical scrutiny, to avoid serious complications to patients.

As an example, in the case of retrievable IVC filters, three devices were approved for use in 2005, including the Recovery filter (CR Bard, Tempe, Arizona). At that time, there were concerns regarding fatal filter migration, thus demonstrating the need for further studies to evaluate safety issues.[33] Although IVC filter fracture/migration is a known complication, and the recommended SIR threshold for this occurrence is not to exceed 3%,[19] the Recovery filter had been reported to have a 21% filter arm fracture and migration rate[34] and a 27.4% vena cava penetration rate[35] in subsequent studies. As a result, the manufacturer withdrew the product from the market in 2005, and replaced it with the G2 filter, a second-generation device designed for increased resistance to migration and fracture. Although, the G2 filter was reported to be associated with less filter fracture and tilt, and greater technical success of placement as compared to the Recovery, more caudal filter migration occurs with the G2 filter.[36] To date, the G2 filter has been reported to have a 12% caudal migration rate and 1.2% rate of filter fracture,[37] and at the time of publication, seven major complications were reported in the MAUDE database associated with the G2 filter.[38]

Safety issues with approved devices can be associated with serious complications in clinical practice, even when PMA is applied, thus raising concerns about the strength of evidence required for this process.[25] Moreover, such events raise concerns about the follow-up surveillance of FDA-approved devices.

In this setting, the SIR plays an important role in providing support to interventionalists by proposing guidelines for the scientific evaluation of new technology[11] through its emerging technologies committee and by the release of position statement documents. The purpose of these initiatives is to provide information about future methods and techniques that may impact IR practice and to write statements that clarify or emphasize SIR positions regarding new procedures.

In summary, before instituting a new treatment into clinical practice, careful consideration of clinical evidence is required, together with postsurveillance evaluation of performance, outcomes, and adverse events, to ensure high-quality care for our patient population.

SAFETY INITIATIVES IN TRAINING PROGRAMS

Safe practices in the academic environment are highly dependent on the direct supervision of trainees. In IR, supervised teaching of procedures is based on the master–apprentice model, in which a staged learning curve allows the trainee to master the procedural technique over a certain period of time. As with surgical skills, catheter-based techniques are acquired in a "hands-on" fashion, although recently, using new technologies, it is possible to employ simulation models for this purpose. Although few publications evaluate the impact of trainees in patient procedural care, a 2007 study demonstrated no statistical difference in procedural-related complications for central venous access placement when

comparing radiology practitioner assistants, IR faculty members, and IR fellows and residents.[39] Patient safety during the training of more complex procedures, which usually require more time, radiation, and costs, is more difficult to determine in our specialty. Therefore, the use of simulators in IR training programs is an alternative to enhance patient safety while increasing opportunities for trainees to improve skills and refine techniques.[40,41]

The integration of virtual reality (VR) simulation models in IR has been developed by academic groups[42] and commercial manufacturers,[43,44] with significant benefits to procedural training, particularly in carotid interventions.[45] Moreover, computer-based haptic simulators have been used to train catheter-based techniques to improve residents' performance[46] and to objectively evaluate proficiency and efficiency in the training of fellows.[47]

To increase the use of simulation in the proper training of IR fellows, the executive councils of the SIR and the Cardiovascular and Interventional Radiological Society of Europe (CIRSE), together with the Board of Directors of the Radiological Society of North America (RSNA), have charged the Joint Simulation Task Force (JSTF) with recommending a plan to integrate the analysis, development, assessment, application, and dissemination of medical simulation in IR.[48]

TOOLS FOR PREVENTING COMPLICATIONS AND ADVERSE EVENTS

As previously discussed, the use and evaluation of clinical indicators are necessary for quality improvement projects. This process can be performed most efficiently when incorporated into routine patient care, as part of the required information on patient characteristics and care delivery included in clinician and administrative documentation.[10] Therefore, in order to achieve this goal, checklists, reporting systems, standardized clinical protocols, and guidelines should be used as tools for quality and safety improvements. In IR, most of the areas for safety projects were discussed earlier in this chapter. Specifically, the use of checklists can be incorporated at all levels of procedural care: scheduling, patients' clinical workup, Universal Protocol, medication reconciliation, and postprocedural care. The checklists are helpful resources to maintain systematic and adequate control of clinical issues that may result in preventable adverse events, while including pertinent information readily available for other staff members.

Another strategy, proved to enhance personnel communication in the operating room, is the utilization of preprocedural briefings to avoid wrong-site surgery.[49] This tool should also be used in IR, in addition to the time-out, in order to discuss and communicate with the team potential hazards issues for patients, the anticipated treatment of complications, and procedural planning, and to review critical information.

Most importantly, to ensure the application of these tools in clinical practice, IR services should promote continuous educational activities, evaluation of clinical outcomes, and observation of adherence to standardized protocols by assigning leadership roles among staff members.

CONCLUSION

Quality and safety initiatives involve a wide range of clinical and administrative procedures that can be effectively integrated within an IR program. These initiatives should include continuous monitoring and evaluation of parameters from several aspects of patient care, with the goal of identifying areas for improvement. As a result, these projects may enhance patient care, service efficacy, and collaboration among staff members. Establishing a QA program and delivering a clinical service in accordance with regulatory accreditation bodies and to the recommendations of SIR guidelines are paramount to maintain a standardized level of patient care in IR.

REFERENCES

1. Johnson CD, Krecke KN, Miranda R, Roberts CC, Denham C. Quality initiatives: Developing a radiology quality and safety program: A primer. *Radiographics.* 2009; 29:951–959.
2. American College of Radiology, Society of interventional Radiology, and Society of Neurointerventional Surgery. Practice guideline for interventional clinical practice. Accessed March 22, 2010, at: http://www.acr.org/SecondaryMainMenuCategories/quality_safety/guidelines/iv/interventional_clinical_practice.aspx
3. Statler JD, Towbin RB, Ronsivalle JA, Oteham, A., Miller, DL, Grassi, CJ, et al. Recommendations for the implementation of Joint Commission Guidelines for labeling medications. *J Vasc Interv Radiol.* 2008;19:(11):1531–5.
4. Angle JF, Nemcek AA, Cohen AM, et al. Quality Improvement Guidelines for preventing wrong site, wrong procedure, and wrong person errors: Application of the Joint Commission "Universal protocol for preventing wrong site, wrong procedure, wrong person surgery" to the practice of Interventional Radiology. *J Vasc Interv Radiol.* 2009;20:S256–S262.
5. Society of Interventional Radiology Standards of Practice Committee. Vascular guidelines for establishing a quality assurance program in vascular and interventional radiology. *J Vasc Interv Radiol.* 2003;14:S203–S207.
6. Sacks D, McClenny TE, Cardella JF, Lewis CA. Society of Interventional Radiology clinical practice guidelines. *JVIR.* 2003;14:S199–S202.
7. Pierluissi EP, Fischer MA, Campbell AR, Landefeld CS. Discussion of medical errors in Morbidity and Mortality conferences. *JAMA.* 2003;290:2838–42.
8. Tuong B, Shnitzer Z, Pehora C, et al. The experience of conducting Mortality and Morbidity reviews in a pediatric Interventional Radiology service: A retrospective study. *J Vasc Interv Radiol.* 2009; 20:77–86.
9. Stecker MS. Root cause analysis. *J Vasc Interv Radiol.* 2007;18:5–8
10. Mainz J. Defining and classifying clinical indicators for quality improvement. *Int J Qual Health Care.* 2003;15:523–30.
11. Cardella JF, Kundu S, Miller DL, Millward SF, Sacks D. Society of Interventional Radiology clinical practice guidelines. *J Vasc Interv Radiol.* 2009;20:S189–S191.
12. Sacks D, McClenny TE, Cardella JF, Lewis CA. Society of Interventional Radiology clinical practice guidelines. *J Vasc Interv Radiol.* 2003;14:S199–S202.
13. Angle JF, Nemcek AA, Cohen AM, et al. Quality Improvement Guidelines for preventing wrong site, wrong procedure, and wrong person errors: Application of the Joint Commission "Universal protocol for preventing wrong site, wrong procedure, wrong person surgery" to the practice of Interventional Radiology. *J Vasc Interv Radiol.* 2009; 20:S256–S262
14. Joint Commission. 2007 National Patient Safety Goals Hospital Version Manual Chapter, including Implementation Expectations. Accessed March 25, 2010, at: http://www.jointcommission.org/PatientSafety/NationalPatientSafetyGoals/07_hap_cah_npsgs.htm
15. Statler JD, Towbin RB, Ronsivalle JA, et al. Recommendations for the implementation of Joint Commission Guidelines for labeling medications. *J Vasc Interv Radiol.* 2009;20:S251–S255.
16. Miller DL. Safety in interventional radiology. *J Vasc Interv Radiol.* 2007;18:1–3.
17. Singh H, Cardella JF, Cole PE, Grassi CJ, McCowan TC, Swan TL, et al.; for the Society of Interventional

Radiology Standards of Practice Committee. Quality Improvement Guidelines for diagnostic arteriography. *J Vasc Interv Radiol.* 2003;14:S283–S288.

18. Lewis CA, Allen TE, Burke DR, et al.; for the Society of Interventional Radiology Standards of Practice Committee. Quality Improvement Guidelines for central venous access. *J Vasc Interv Radiol.* 2003; 14:S231–S235.

19. Grassi CJ, Swan TL, Cardella JF, et al.; for the Society of Interventional Radiology Standards of Practice Committee. Quality Improvement Guidelines for percutaneous permanent inferior vena cava filter placement for the prevention of pulmonary embolism. *J Vasc Interv Radiol.* 2003;14:S271–S275.

20. Drooz AT, Lewis CA, Allen TE, et al.; for the Society of Interventional Radiology Standards of Practice Committee. Quality Improvement Guidelines for percutaneous transcatheter embolization. *J Vasc Interv Radiol.* 2003;14:S237–S242.

21. Overview of device regulation. US Food and Drug Administration. Accessed March 15, 2010, at: http://www.fda.gov/MedicalDevices/Device RegulationandGuidance/Overview/default.htm

22. Device Approvals and Clearances. US Food and Drug Administration. Accessed March 15, 2010, at: http://www.fda.gov/MedicalDevices/Products andMedicalProcedures/DeviceApprovalsand Clearances/default.htm

23. Code of Federal Regulations. Tittle 21, part 860 – Medical Device Classification procedures: subpart A – general. Section 860.7 – Determination of safety and effectiveness. Accessed March 15, 2010, at: http://www.accessdata.fda.gov/scripts/cdrh/cfd ocs/cfcfr/CFRSearch.cfm?fr=860.7

24. O'Connor AB. Building comparative efficacy and tolerability into the FDA approval process. *JAMA.* 2010;303:979–80.

25. Dhruva SS, Bero LA, Redberg RF. Strength of study evidence examined by the FDA in premarket approval of cardiovascular devices. *JAMA.* 2009;302:2679–85.

26. Edwards RD, Moss JG, Lumsden MA, et al. Uterine-artery embolization versus surgery for symptomatic uterine fibroids. *N Engl J Med.* 2007;356:360–70.

27. Hehenkamp WJ, Volkers NA, Birnie E, Reekers JA, Ankum WM. Symptomatic uterine fibroids: Treatment with uterine artery embolization or hysterectomy- results from the randomized clinical embolisation versus hysterectomy (EMMY) trial. *Radiology.* 2008;246:823–32.

28. Spies J, Allison S, Sterbis K, et al. Polyvinyl alcohol particles and tris acryl gelatin microspheres for uterine artery embolization for leiomyomas: Results of a randomized comparative study. *J Vasc Radiol.* 2004;15:793–800.

29. Goodwin SC, Bradley LD, Lipman JC, et al. Uterine artery embolization versus myomectomy: A multicenter comparative study. *Fertil Steril.* 2006;85:14–21.

30. Spies JB. What evidence should we demand before accepting a new embolic material for uterine artery embolization? *J Vasc Interv Radiol.* 2009;20:567–70.

31. Spies JB, Allison S, Flick P, et al. Spherical polyvinyl alcohol versus tris acryl gelatin microspheres for uterine artery embolization for leiomyomas: Results of a limited randomized comparative study. *J Vasc Interv Radiol.* 2005;16:1431–7.

32. Rasuli P, Hammond I, Al-Mutairi B, et al. Spherical versus conventional polyvinyl alcohol particles for uterine artery embolization. *J Vasc Interv Radiol.* 2008;19:42–46.

33. Millward SF. Vena cava filters: Continuing the search for an ideal device. *J Vasc Interv Radiol.* 2005;423–5.

34. Hull JE, Robertson SW. Bard Recovery Filter: Evaluation and management of vena cava limb perforation, fracture, and migration. *J Vasc Interv Radiol.* 2009;20:52–60.

35. Kalva SP, Athanasoulis CA, Fan C M, et al. Recovery vena cava filter: Experience in 96 patients. *Cardiovasc Intervent Radiol.* 2006;29:559–64.

36. Cantwell CP, Pennypacker J, Singh H, et al. Comparison of the Recovery and G2 filter as retrievable inferior vena cava filters. *J Vasc Interv Radiol.* 2009;20:1193–9.

37. Binkert CA, Drooz AT, Caridi JG, et al. Technical success and safety of retrieval of the G2 filter in a prospective, multicenter study. *J Vasc Interv Radiol.* 2009;20:1449–53.

38. MAUDE – Manufacturer and User Facility Device Experience. Accessed March 15, 2010, at: http://www.accessdata.fda.gov/scripts/cdrh/cfdocs/cfMAUDE/search.CFM.

39. Benham JR, Culp WC, Wright LB, et al. Complication rate of venous access procedures performed by a radiology practitioner assistant compared with interventional radiology physicians and supervised trainees. *J Vasc Interv Radiol.* 2007;18:1001–4.

40. Dawson S. Procedural simulation: A primer. *J Vasc Interv Radiol.* 2006;17:205–13.

41. Gould DA. Interventional radiology simulation: Prepare for a virtual revolution in training. *J Vasc Interv Radiol.* 2007;18:483–90.

42. CIMIT endovascular simulator. EVE: Real-time endovascular simulator. Accessed June 7, 2009, at: http://www.medicalsim.org/endovasc.htm

43. ANGIO Mentor˚. Accessed June 7, 2009, at: http://www.simbionix.com/ANGIO_Mentor.html

44. Mentice VIST˚. Accessed June 7, 2009, at: http://www.mentice.com/default.asp

45. Herzeele IV, Aggarwal R, Neequaye S, et al. Experienced endovascular interventionalists objectively improve their skills by attending carotid artery stent training courses. *Eur J Vasc Endovasc Surg.* 2008;35:541–50.

46. Chaer RA, DeRubertis BG, Lin SC, et al. Simulation improves resident performance in catheter-based

intervention: results of a randomized, controlled study. *Ann Surg.* 2006;244:343–52.

47. Glaiberman CB, Jacobs B, Street M, et al. Simulation in-training: One-year experience using an efficiency index to assess interventional radiology fellow training status. *J Vasc Radiol.* 2008;19: 1366–71.

48. Gould D, Patel A, Becker G, et al. SIR/RSNA/CIRSE Joint Medical Simulation Task Force Strategic Plan Executive Summary. *J Vasc Interv Radiol.* 2007;18:953–5.

49. Makary MA, Mukherjee A, Sexton JB, et al. Operating room briefings and wrong-site surgery. *J Am Coll Surg.* 2007;204:236–43.

30

Pregnancy in Radiology

MANNUDEEP K. KALRA, MICHAEL F. GREENE, AND ROBERT L. BRENT

Diagnostic imaging examinations performed during pregnancy are not uncommon and are often clinically necessary for the management of a pregnant patient, as determined by an experienced physician who has evaluated the benefits of various procedures. From the well-being of the mother derives the well-being of the fetus, and therefore, radiologists, radiation physicists, and physicians must evaluate the possible effects of each imaging modality on the fetus, along with the necessity of the examination for the mother, in order to expedite indicated imaging studies and avoid nonessential exams. Knowledge of the benefits and potential risks of radiological studies used for assessing illnesses in pregnancy can help in selecting an appropriate imaging study for the evaluation of a pregnant woman. This is of particular importance as recent studies have reported that physicians who care for pregnant women and do not perform an evaluation of potential risks may recommend an abortion on the basis of an overestimated teratogenic risk from radiological studies.[1,2] Misconceptions regarding the use of imaging in pregnancy can also delay necessary and urgent radiological studies in pregnant women and increase anxiety in pregnant patients seeking counseling.[3,4] Therefore, experienced and well-trained physicians, health physicists, and geneticists who are familiar with the fields of developmental biology, teratology, epidemiology, and genetics must counsel pregnant women or the parents of a child with congenital malformations to avoid excessive emphasis on epidemiological data that may be meager or insufficient for a rational conclusion.[5] When facing the dilemma of imaging studies in pregnancy, a "Combination of uncertainty and radiation is the formula for actuating anxiety and fear."[6] And, "Education is usually the answer to fear of the unknown, but it is not an easy task when the subject is radiation."[6]

The potential risks of radiological exposure include reproductive effects such as birth defects, miscarriage, growth retardation, premature birth, and stillbirths.

QUANTITATIVE MEASURES OF EXPOSURE IN DIAGNOSTIC IMAGING

Conventional Radiography, Fluoroscopy, and Computed Tomography Scanning

X-rays and γ rays ionize atoms and molecules in human tissues by the deposition of energy, a phenomenon that has the potential for increasing risks of teratogenesis and mutagenesis. Contrary to popular misconception, x-rays from radiographic and computed tomography (CT) examinations are not more harmful than γ rays or neutron radiation.[7]

Typically, ionizing chamber dosimeters are used for measuring exposure associated with ionizing radiation. When an ionizing chamber is exposed to ionizing radiation, air molecules are ionized and the resultant ionic charges are detected and measured as coulomb per kilogram of air or as units of Roentgen.

The *entrance skin exposure* is frequently used to compare radiation delivered from different conventional radiography and fluoroscopy procedures.[8] The quantity exposure (measured in Roentgen) has been replaced with the quantity *air kerma* (kinetic energy released per unit mass), which quantifies the energy transferred to charged particles from ionizing radiation per unit mass in the medium of interest. The SI unit of *kerma* is the Gray, which is defined as the transfer of 1.0 joule of energy to charged particles per kilogram of tissue (Gray replaces the previously used unit rad; 1 Gray = 100 rad; 1 milliGray = 0.1 rad). *Absorbed dose* refers to the quantity of energy deposited locally in an absorbing medium by ionizing radiation. Some unit measurements have been introduced to take into account the different extent of tissue damage caused by different types of ionizing radiation. These include *equivalent dose* and *effective dose*. Equivalent dose is the product of the averaged absorbed dose in a tissue or organ and its associated radiation-weighting factor. The SI unit of equivalent dose is the Sievert (Sv replaces previously used rem, 1 Sv = 100 rem). As the quality factor for all diagnostic radiations is 1, numerically, an absorbed dose of 1 Gy is the same as an equivalent dose of 1 Sv for low linear energy transfer (LET) radiation.

As sensitivities of tissues differ for ionizing radiation, additional weighting factors have been introduced to estimate the associated risks of specific tissues for adverse effects. These tissue-weighting factors relate to the risk of cancer in different organs and the hereditary risks for future offspring. Effective dose, a measure introduced by the International Commission on Radiological Protection (ICRP) to estimate the risk resulting from a radiation exposure, represents the sum of the products of equivalent doses for irradiated tissues or organs and the appropriate tissue-weighting factor. The organ dose refers to the absorbed dose delivered to the organs of a patient during a radiologic examination.[9]

The same type of radiation is used in CT examinations and conventional radiography. Therefore, like conventional radiography, radiation dose associated with CT scanning is based on the x-ray beam energy (which is determined by the applied tube potential or peak kilovoltage, kVp) and photon fluence (which depends on the tube current-time product or milliAmpere seconds, mAs) intensity.[10] However, as CT radiation dose is distributed more homogeneously in the scan plane because the patient is equally irradiated from all directions, a comparison of radiation dose with CT scanning and radiography in terms of skin dose or skin entrance exposure is not appropriate.

The CT dose index (CTDI), measured in mGy, and the dose length product (DLP), measured in mGy.cm, are the most commonly used CT radiation dose indices and provide an estimate of radiation dose associated with CT scanning.[10] Although these indices do not represent the actual radiation dose, they can be used to calculate the effective dose. The CTDI represents the average radiation dose delivered within and beyond the scan volume. For contiguous acquisitions, the weighted CTDI (CTDIw) averages variations in the absorbed dose from the periphery to the center of the object in the region of scan volume. The CTDI volume or CTDI vol is used to describe the radiation dose if there are gaps or overlap between sequential scans. The CTDI vol represents the average dose within a scan series. The term *dose length product* (DLP) is used to represent the integrated dose and is equal to the average dose within the scan volume (CTDI vol) times the total scan length (in centimeters). This parameter is also displayed on some CT systems. The CTDI and DLP values can be used to calculate the effective dose associated with CT scanning.

Nuclear Medicine

The effects of external irradiation with x-rays on the embryo differ from those of radiopharmaceutical agents. In nuclear medicine studies, the radiation exposure to the fetus depends on several factors, such as whether the isotope crosses the placenta; the distribution or tissue affinity of the isotope, the nature of the radiation emitted (α, β, or γ), and the amount of radioactivity (rate at which nuclei in a radiopharmaceutical agent undergo spontaneous emission of radiation, which is also called *disintegration rate* or *decay rate*) administered to the patient.[12] The decay rate is directly proportional to the number of radionuclei present in the sample. The SI unit of radioactivity is the Becquerel (Bq, which has replaced Curie [Ci]). Each radiopharmaceutical agent has its own correlation with the absorbed dose, which is dependent on the amount of radiopharmaceutical agent administered, its half-life, radioactive emission, and metabolism.[12]

Placental transfer and fetal dose estimates have been published for women in early pregnancy and at the end of each trimester for a large number of radiopharmaceuticals based on available information in the literature.[13-15] A recent publication has also reported quantitative values for maternal and fetal uptake of fluorodeoxyglucose (18F-FDG) in primates, along with estimated values of uptake in fetal brain and heart.[16] In addition, the Medical Internal Radiation Dose (MIRD) Committee has also published new values for 18F-FDG kinetics and fetal dose.[17] Estimated mean fetal dose from intravenous administration of 18F-FDG ranges from 0.017 to 0.022 mGy/MBq (the usual administered activity for a FDG-PET study is 370MBq).

Ultrasonography

The American Institute of Ultrasound in Medicine (AIUM) and the National Electrical Manufacturers Association (NEMA) have developed unitless indices to estimate the bioeffects of ultrasound waves.[18] The thermal indices, soft tissue thermal index, and thermal index for bone located at the focal level describe tissue heating with ultrasound waves. In addition to the hyperthermic effect of ultrasound, other nonthermal effects of ultrasound are described by mechanical index (MI), which cause hypothetical stable or transient cavitation from torque, pressure forces, and streaming, and depend on peak rarefaction pressure and the frequency of the ultrasound beam.[18-21]

The soft tissue thermal index (TIS) is a conservative approximation of the possible temperature rise in soft tissues for conditions encountered in medical imaging.[18] As a rise in temperature is more likely to occur in bones than in the soft tissues, due to greater beam reflection and attenuation in bones, the thermal index for bone (TIB) located at focus provides an estimate of the possible rise in temperature of the bone located at the beam focus.[18]

As exposure to ultrasound can elevate the temperature of an embryo, use of ultrasonography must take into account the hyperthermic potential, as well as the hypothetical additional risk of performing sonography in pregnant patients who are febrile. However, there is no measurable risk of embryonic or fetal adverse effects if the embryonic temperature never exceeds 39°C.[19] The Bioeffects Committee of the AIUM has recommended that diagnostic ultrasound exposures should not result in a temperature rise of 1°C above normal physiological levels.[22] In general, currently used diagnostic pulse echo ultrasonography equipment is unlikely to cause a substantial increase in the temperature of exposed tissue.[19,20,23]

Magnetic Resonance Imaging

Magnetic field strength, magnetic field gradients and switching rates, and specific absorption rate are the most important factors in the estimation of bioeffects of magnetic resonance (MR) imaging. The SI units for magnetic field strength, magnetic field gradient, and switching rate are the Tesla, milli-Tesla/meter, and Tesla/second, respectively. Generally, the magnetic fields currently used in diagnostic imaging range between 0.5 and 3 Tesla. Magnetic field gradients refer to changes in magnetic field strength related to position. The *specific absorption rate* (SAR) refers to the amount of radiofrequency energy absorbed by human tissue, which corresponds to the dose rate from ionizing radiation, albeit with a thermal (not ionizing) mechanism.[24] To date, there are no epidemiology reproductive studies or anecdotal reports documenting ill effects of MR imaging in pregnancy.[25-27]

EFFECTS OF DIAGNOSTIC IMAGING ON PREGNANCY AND CONCEPTUS

Ionizing Radiation

Ionizing radiation can occur from either direct or scattered external beams. Direct exposure occurs in the region being examined with ionizing radiation-based imaging techniques such as radiography, fluoroscopy, and CT scanning. For instance, abdominal or pelvic radiography, fluoroscopy, and CT scanning lead to direct exposure of abdominal and pelvic regions. Scattered exposure, which may occur outside the body or during passage of the beam within the body, is generally less than direct exposure. In pregnancy, such exposure to a fetus occurs from radiography, fluoroscopy, or CT scanning of regions outside the abdomen and pelvis. In most cases, any direct or indirect interaction leading to an adverse event, such as cell damage, is repaired so that the event is inconsequential to the cell. In some instances, if the repair process is unsuccessful, the affected cell may die or become dysfunctional.

Ionizing radiation-induced effects are usually classified as stochastic or deterministic.[28] *Deterministic effects* are predictable events that occur when doses above a minimum threshold radiation dose are received.[29] These effects infer that the effects have a threshold for a particular effect or a *no observed adverse effect level* (NOAEL).[30] The probability and severity of these effects depends on the number of affected cells and the amount of radiation delivered. Epidemiological studies and animal studies

TABLE 30.1 DETERMINISTIC RISK
EFFECTS OF IONIZING RADIATION
RELATED TO PREGNANCY

Lethality (resorption)
Gross congenital malformations
Growth retardation (at term)
Growth retardation (as adult)
Sterility
Cataracts
Mental retardation
Lower intelligence quotient
Small head size

indicate a NOAEL of 200 mGy for deterministic effects (Table 30.1),[30] whereas radiation doses from diagnostic examinations are usually much lower than 200 mGy. It is important to remember that reproductive issues including sterility, infertility, abortion (miscarriage), stillbirth, congenital malformations (due to environmental or hereditary etiologies), fetal growth retardation, and prematurity, are relatively common in the general population and therefore, it is not easy to corroborate association of these issues with environmental or diagnostic radiation exposure.[30] Therefore, patients exposed to diagnostic radiation must be informed about the background reproductive risks.

In contradistinction, *stochastic effects* are chance events that have a linear relationship with radiation dose and have a theoretical risk to zero exposure. These effects can result from changes in a single cell (the usual site of damage is the DNA), and thus the probability of the event relates to the number of cells altered and to the dose delivered. At low radiation exposure, spontaneous reproductive effects dwarf the theoretical effects at exposures in the 200–300 mGy range. Embryonic and fetal stochastic risk effects include mutagenesis and carcinogenesis.[30] Preconception exposure to ionizing radiation can result in point mutations and chromosomal abnormalities that can be transmitted or result in germ cell death. Abnormalities of the DNA at the molecular level of the nucleotides that provide genetic messages to the cell, such as deletions and duplications, are an important contribution to the dominant lethal effect of preconception ionizing radiation.[26] It has been difficult to demonstrate a definite increased occurrence of genetic disease in populations that have received low preconception exposures to ionizing

radiation.[30] As the incidence of mutagenesis and carcinogenesis is low in the absence of any obvious environmental insult, the increase in incidence of these problems is also relatively small from a modest exposure from diagnostic radiations, and a statistically meaningful statement would require a large numbers of observations. This may be explained on the basis of *biological filtration*, which has been used to describe the ameliorating effects of fetal development in decreasing the manifestation of genetic effects, because of the propensity for the genetically damaged cells to be "lost" during gonadogenesis, fertilization, and organogenesis.[30]

Follow-up studies in 50 pregnant women exposed to diagnostic levels of ionizing radiation over a period of 10 years have shown that the threshold doses suggested by the National Radiological Protection Board[31] are well above the mean fetal doses for diagnostic radiological exams included in these studies.[32] The risk of death or gross congenital malformation in the patients was comparable to the estimated background risk in the natural course of clinically recognized pregnancy, which is 15% for spontaneous abortion, 3% for children with major malformations at term, and 6%–8% when all malformation and genetic diseases are considered.[32,33] The U.S. National Council on Radiation Protection (NCRP) states that the risk of induced miscarriages, malignancies, or major congenital malformations in an embryo or fetus exposed to doses of 50 mGy or less is not measurably increased compared with the spontaneous risk in an unexposed pregnant woman.[34]

Most information about the effects of human exposure to radiation, including teratogenic effects, abnormal development of the brain and nervous system, and intrauterine growth retardation, is derived from the exposure to high levels of radiation by the large populations surviving the Hiroshima and Nagasaki atomic explosions.[35-38] As a result of these explosions, more than 2,800 pregnant women were exposed, and 500 conceptuses received more than 100 mGy of radiation.[35] The results of follow-up studies in these pregnant women are often controversial, as the contributions of neutron radiation and environmental conditions remain uncertain.[35,41,90]

Most recently, data from animal studies[41,42] and human exposures to diagnostic and therapeutic radiation[43,44] have been used to study and classify the potential effects from radiation exposure into three categories: mutagenesis, teratogenesis, and carcinogenesis (Table 30.2).

TABLE 30.2   RADIATION EXPOSURE AND RISK AT DIFFERENT GESTATION PHASES

Gestation weeks	Effects
First week:	Minimum human lethal dose (from animal studies) In first week = 100 mGy Most sensitive period for prenatal death. Before implantation, likely effect of radiation is failure to implant or death of conceptus

2–8 weeks:	Minimum lethal dose (from animal studies)
	    At 18 days = 250 mGy
	    After 50 days >500 mGy
	Embryo is predisposed to teratogenesis and growth retardation.
	Minimum dose for growth retardation
	    At 18–36 days = 200–500 mGy
	    At 36–110 days = 250–500 mGy

2–15 weeks:	Minimum dose for fetal malformations of central nervous system At 2–15 weeks >100 to 1,500 mGy Most sensitive period for small head size and growth retardation. Small head size is most frequent effect and appears alone at low doses. At higher doses, small head size occurs with severe mental retardation

8–15 weeks	Minimum lethal dose threshold (from animal studies)
	    At 8–15 weeks >1,000 mGy
	No severe teratogenesis except genitourinary and organ hypoplasia (brain and testis)
	Most sensitive period for severe mental retardation
	Intelligence quotient decreases by 30 points per Gy.
	Minimum dose for severe mental retardation
	    At 8–15 weeks = 570 mGy

15 weeks– term	No documented risk for teratogenesis
	Minimum lethal dose threshold (from animal studies)
	    At 15 weeks to term >1,500 mGy
	Minimum dose for severe mental retardation
	    At 15 weeks to term >1,500 mGy

There is no evidence that radiation exposure in the diagnostic ranges (<200 mGy) is associated with a measurably increased incidence of congenital malformation, still birth, miscarriage, growth retardation, and mental retardation.

Mutagenesis

Radiation-induced mutagenesis includes germ-line alterations and mutations, which can potentially affect future generations. Although the exact frequency of mutagenetic risks from fetal radiation exposure is not known, the risk is extremely small and of little concern from diagnostic radiation exposures. With a dose of 10 mGy, risk of radiation-induced genetic disease in future generations has been estimated to lie between 0.012% and 0.099%.[45] According to the NRPB, during the most sensitive period (8–15 weeks postconception), the risk coefficient for hereditary effects in all future generations can be assumed to be about 2.4×10^{-2} per Gy.[46] The natural frequency of genetic disease manifesting at birth in the unexposed general population has been estimated to be 1 $\times 10^{-2}$ to 3×10^{-2} (up to about 5×10^{-2} to 6×10^{-2} if

congenital abnormalities are included).[46] The Biological Effects of Ionizing Radiation (BEIR 5) report states that mutagenesis in the offspring of radiated patients has not been demonstrated in humans, although these effects have been demonstrated in plants and animals at high radiation doses.[33]

Teratogenesis

Radiation-induced teratogenesis is a deterministic effect that results in fetal malformations from injury to multiple cells and occurs at a radiation dose of greater than 200 mGy.[30] Fetal irradiation from diagnostic radiation exposures of less than 50 mGy (<5 rad) has not been demonstrated to cause congenital malformation or growth retardation.[30] As the expression of deterministic effects depends on the proportion of differentiating cells injured, the occurrence of these effects also depends on the age of the conceptus (Table 30.2)[47,48]

Carcinogenesis

Although initial case–control studies suggested a possible increase in the incidence of cancer following prenatal radiation exposure,[49–52] subsequent cohort studies have failed to document any substantial correlation between prenatal exposure and cancer.[53–57] An initial 14-year follow-up study conducted by the Oxford Survey of Childhood Cancer reported a 1.92 relative risk for leukemia in children of mothers exposed to prenatal abdominal radiation, and 1.19 relative risk for nonabdominal exposure.[58] However, later publication of extended series of this study showed that there is no excess risk of solid cancer related to prenatal exposure.[59] The authors concluded that uncertainties in risk estimates make it difficult to define what the risk at these low doses might be, beyond the inference that the risk was not zero.[60] Other studies have also been unable to document an association between prenatal exposure to diagnostic radiation and malignancy.[61–64] Although an association between risk for cancer and prenatal radiation exposure is not questioned, the etiologic significance of radiation remains controversial.[65]

Iodinated Contrast Agents in Radiography and Computed Tomography Scanning

Both ionic and nonionic iodinated contrasts have been used in pregnancy for various radiological studies, including angiography and amniography.[66] No mutagenic or teratogenic effects of ionic or nonionic agents have been shown in either in vitro or in vivo animal studies.[67,68] Prior studies have shown no substantial change in fetal T_3 and T_4 levels following administration of iodinated contrast agent in amniotic fluid.[69] A recent publication from the Contrast Media Safety Committee of the European Society of Urogenital Radiology has recommended that when a radiographic examination or CT scanning is necessary in pregnancy, iodinated contrast agent may be administered.[66] The committee recommended evaluation of thyroid functions in the neonate during the first week following administration of iodinated agents to the mother during pregnancy.

According to the American College of Radiology (ACR)'s Committee on Drug and Contrast Media, there is neither a proof that iodinated contrast agents pose risk to fetus nor sufficient evidence to label contrast agents as safe for use in pregnancy (accessed at http://www.acr.org/contrast-manual, on January 26, 2010). Thus, the committee recommends three steps for radiologists prior to administration of iodinated contrast agents to pregnant patients. First, check with the ordering physician about the absolute need of iodinated contrast agent for information that cannot be obtained without contrast administration. Second, ensure that the information obtained following contrast administration will affect the care of patient and fetus during the pregnancy. And finally, seek the opinion of the physician that it is not wise to postpone the procedure until after the pregnancy. The ACR also recommends that radiologists obtain informed consent from such patients after informing them about the risk versus benefit aspects and making them aware of the alternative options if available.

Nuclear Medicine

Radiopharmaceutical agents may be occasionally administered to a pregnant patient when the maternal or fetal benefits of the study make any radiation risk subservient, or when the mother is not aware of her pregnancy and the prenatal irradiation is accidental. To eliminate the possibility of accidental exposure in pregnancy, the Society of Nuclear Medicine recommends pregnancy testing before any procedure that will expose the fetus to greater than 50 mGy.[70–72] As the fetal dose from most diagnostic nuclear medicine studies is below 10 mGy, the risk of detrimental deterministic effects on the embryo or fetus due to radiation from most diagnostic nuclear medicine procedures is not increased.[11]

In nuclear medicine studies, fetal exposure depends on the physical and biochemical properties of the radioisotope. Radioactive iodine readily crosses the placenta and can adversely affect the fetal thyroid, especially after 10–12 weeks of postconception age, when it can lead to diminished thyroid function or thyroid aplasia in the fetus.[60] However, most radiopharmaceutical agents for lung, bladder, kidney, bone, and bleeding scans are labeled with ^{99}Tc and deliver fetal doses as low as 5 mGy.[70–72] The route of administration also affects fetal dose, such as xenon (127 or 133) administered in ventilation scans for suspected pulmonary embolism.[71–72]

Radiation dose from radiopharmaceutical agents is normally protracted and therefore is less effective than a similar acute dose.[34] Accordingly, threshold dose levels for fetal effects, estimated from human and animal studies involving acute radiation exposure, may actually be higher for some or all radiopharmaceutical agents.[34]

Ultrasonography

Several retrospective and prospective studies have shown no evidence of risk for abnormalities of organogenesis and growth retardation following prenatal ultrasound.[19-21,73-81] Based on thorough reviews of reports on biological effects from the use of diagnostic ultrasound, the AIUM has reported that there was no consistent evidence of risks for the conceptus.[83] The AIUM Official Statement on Clinical Safety, revised and approved in March 1988 stated that "no confirmed biological effects on patients or instruments' operators caused by exposures to intensities typical of present diagnostic ultrasound instruments have ever been reported."[83] Likewise, the American College of Obstetricians and Gynecologists (ACOG) has reported that there are no contraindications to ultrasound procedures during pregnancy at energy exposures from ultrasonography arbitrarily limited to 94 mW/cm^2 by the U.S. Food and Drug Administration (FDA).[82] Likewise, the Routine Antenatal Diagnostic Imaging with Ultrasound (RADIUS) study found no increase in fetal abnormalities following antenatal ultrasonography in 15,530 pregnant patients.[84]

Interestingly, a study performed in 6,858 men born between 1973 and 1978 with an in utero ultrasound and 172,537 men born in the same period without exposure to ultrasound demonstrated that ultrasound exposure in utero increases the risk of left-handedness in men by 3 per 100.[85] Increased risk of left-handedness in individuals exposed to a first-trimester ultrasound study was similar to that in the second trimester.[86] Subsequent case–control studies have shown no significant statistical difference between the rate of delayed speech development, delayed motor development, reduced hearing, reduced vision, and behavioral disorders in groups with and without in utero exposure to ultrasound.[87] Biological effects are unlikely to appear in diagnostic ultrasound due to the frequency of the diagnostic beam and the relatively short time required for ultrasound examinations.[74] Indeed, animal studies suggest that diagnostic levels of ultrasound are safe and do not elevate the fetal temperature into the region at which deleterious reproductive effects occur.[20] Similarly, analysis of human epidemiologic studies does not indicate that diagnostic ultrasound presents a measurable risk to the developing embryo or fetus.[19]

Magnetic Resonance Imaging

Brent et al. have reported that there does not appear to be a measurable risk of birth defects from electromagnetic field exposure in humans.[26] Indeed, current MR imaging protocols within standard safety recommendations have not revealed any harmful effect on the fetus, especially in late pregnancy.[24,88] No increase in the risk of teratogenesis, intrauterine growth restriction, delayed central nervous system development, or childhood malignancy has been demonstrated with current MRI protocols.[88]

Static magnetic fields, changing magnetic fields, and pulsed radiofrequency (RF) have been assessed for possible harmful effects from MR imaging in vivo.[89] Fluctuating magnetic field and pulsed radiofrequencies can cause tissue heating. Pulsed radiofrequencies have been shown to produce nonthermal effects leading to altered cellular membrane calcium flux and degraded lymphocytic function at frequencies considerably higher than those employed for diagnostic imaging (several GHz versus the diagnostic range of 4–60 MHz).[90] Animal studies have also shown that prolonged exposure (8 hours) to a high field MR (4.7 T) in the period of gonad differentiation causes reduction in the daily sperm production.[91] However, studies in human fetuses with routine MR protocols within standard safety recommendations performed during the late postconception period have not revealed any harmful effect on the fetus.[92-94] In addition, no harmful effects of prenatal MR exposure in the third trimester of pregnancy have been detected at the SAR limits proposed in the MR safety guidelines of the U.S. FDA.[24]

The ACOG has issued the following statement about the exposure of a conceptus to electromagnetic fields: "although there have been no documented adverse fetal effects reported, the National Radiological Protection Board arbitrarily advises against its use in the first trimester."[82] Although MR imaging should be performed if medically indicated, the International Non-Ionizing Radiation Committee of the International Radiation Protection Association states that "there is no firm evidence that mammalian embryos are sensitive to the magnetic fields encountered in magnetic resonance systems. However, it is recommended that elective examination of pregnant women should be postponed until after the first trimester."[48]

Gadolinium-based MR contrast agents have been used in pregnancy without adverse effect.[66] Gadolinium readily crosses the placenta and is excreted by the fetus. Thus, it is retained in the amniotic fluid, where its components dissociate and may reassociate to form other compounds. The Contrast Media Safety Committee of the European Society of Urogenital Radiology has recommended that when MR examination is necessary, gadolinium media may be given to the pregnant mother.[66] Furthermore, the committee does not recommend any neonatal tests following administration of gadolinium-based contrast agents to the mother during pregnancy.

In the United States, MR contrast agents with current FDA approval are considered pregnancy class C agents, which imply that risk to the developing fetus cannot be excluded. Consequently, the ACR recommends a similar approach to the MR contrast agents as described for the iodinated contrast agents in the preceding section of this chapter. Additionally, the ACR also recommends obtaining informed consent from pregnant patients receiving gadolinium-based contrast agents.

STRATEGIES FOR DIAGNOSTIC IMAGING IN PREGNANCY

Conventional Radiography

The use of radiography for clinically appropriate indications during pregnancy is acceptable medical practice. Several factors affect radiation dose associated with conventional radiography, including fluoroscopic or exposure time, number of radiographic views, milliamperage, tube potential, focal spot to patient distance, and shielding devices.[9] Other factors that affect the radiation exposure to embryo/fetus also include the output intensity (measured in mGy) of the x-ray equipment for radiographic exposures, the entrance exposure (measured in mGy/seconds) for fluoroscopic exposures, and the protraction and fractionation of fetal radiation exposure.[8] In addition, prior animal studies have shown that protraction (exposure over several hours or days) and fractionation (exposure in two or more fractions) of the radiation dose to the embryo decrease incidence of fetal death, congenital malformations, and growth retardation.[95,96]

Information necessary to calculate the fetal dose includes the fetal age at the time of the exposure, the mother's size or thickness, and the depth of the fetus.[9,97] The reported mean fetal exposures for the most commonly performed examinations are summarized in Table 30.3.[47,97–101] Although absorbed doses for the same diagnostic procedure can vary considerably for different patients depending on the types of equipment and technique, along with variations of patient anatomy, fetal doses from extraabdominal, as well as from abdominal, pelvic, and lumbar radiographic studies, are much lower than the threshold dose for deterministic effects (200 mGy).[47] In fact, doses from these examinations are usually lower than the dose received over 9 months from environmental radiation (the average natural background exposure at sea level is estimated at about 3 mGy/year). Conversely, abdominal, pelvic, and lumbar examinations deliver higher doses to the embryo or fetus.

General strategies adopted to achieve as low as reasonably achievable (ALARA principle) radiation dose for all radiologic examinations must be used in pregnant patients. These include:

- Limit the number of exposures and projections. For example, for a maternal chest x-ray, the incidental fetal dose can be reduced by using a 72 inch distance between the focal spot and film to reduce scatter and by excluding the lateral view.
- Minimize repeat radiography by reducing technical errors (such as miscentering) and patient factors (such as motion).
- Limit the amount of fluoroscopic time.
- Know that although grids improve image quality by reducing scattered radiation, they cause an increase in radiation dose by a factor of two or more.[9]
- Use an optimum kVp and tube current. Reduce beam milliamperage in digital imaging (phosphor screen storage technology allows reduction of mAs).
- Be aware that the convenience and immediacy of a bedside chest radiograph are, unfortunately, associated with increased fetal dose and decreased spatial resolution. The portable generator is incapable of achieving the same tube current as those in the radiology department, and it is less efficient in delivering the peak kV of the beam.
- Collimate the x-ray beam to the size of the anatomical area of interest as the fetal radiation dose depends on the primary x-ray field.
- Use shielding such as lead aprons, lead blockers, and anatomically cut lead blockers that may be used as shields of the abdomen and pelvis for examinations of neighboring structures.[9] Shielding is of limited value when

TABLE 30.3   APPROXIMATE MEAN FETAL DOSE (IN MGY) ASSOCIATED WITH THE MOST COMMON DIAGNOSTIC EXAMINATIONS[2,3]

Radiological Procedure	Mean Fetal Dose in mGy
Dental	<0.01 (maximum dose <0.01)
Head/cervical Spine	<0.01 (maximum dose <0.01)
Chest (AP)	<0.01 (maximum dose <0.01–0.01)
Chest (PA)	<0.01 (maximum dose <0.01)
Thoracic spine (AP)	<0.01 (maximum dose <0.01)

Radiological Procedure	Mean Fetal Dose in mGy
Thoracic spine (LAT)	<0.01 (maximum dose <0.01)
Abdomen (AP)	2.9 (range = 0.26–15.0)
Abdomen (PA)	1.3 (range = 0.64–3.0)
Lumbar spine (AP)	7.5 (range = 0.31–40.0)
Lumbar spine (LAT)	0.91 (range = 0.09–3.5)
Lumbar spine (Oblique)	1.3 (range = 0.61–2.0)
Lumbosacral joint (LAT)	1.1 (range = 0.10–2.0)
Pelvis	3.4 (range = 1.4–15.0)
Hip joint (AP)	0.9 (range = 0.11–2.1)
Distal femur	<0.01 (maximum dose <0.01)
Upper G.I. series	1.1 (<0.01–12.3)
Cholecystography/Cholangiogram	1.5 (range = 0.01–16)
Barium enema	6.1 (range = 0.3–10.4)
Intravenous urography	7.0 (range = 0.5–40)
Retrograde pyelogram	8.0 (range = 0.85–40)
Urinary bladder (AP)	3.9 (range = 0.56–11.0)
Urethrocystography	15.0 (range = 2.0–30.0)
Barium meal	1.5 (range = 0.1–2.3)
ERCP	4.0 (range = 0.1–18.0)
Mammogram	<0.01 (maximum dose <0.20)
Dual X-ray absorptiometry (lumbar spine)	< 0.01 (maximum dose <0.01)
Cerebral angiography	N/A (maximum dose <0.1)
Pulmonary angiography (femoral route)	N/A (maximum dose <3.74)
Pulmonary angiography (brachial route)	N/A (maximum dose <0.5)
CT head	<0.01 (maximum dose <0.01)
CT chest	0.06 (maximum dose = 0.96)
CT abdomen	8.0 (maximum dose = 49)
CT pelvis	**25.0 (maximum dose = 79.0)**
CT lumbar spine	2.4 (maximum dose = 8.6)

Computed tomography (CT) scanning of pelvis may be associated with a fetal radiation dose greater than 50 mGy. N/A, not available.

the fetus is positioned outside the field of view as the bulk of the fetal exposure will come from indirect scattered radiation from maternal tissues. However, in these cases, collimation of the radiation beam should be adapted to the size of the anatomical area of interest.

• Properly position the patient to reduce radiation dose: For radiographic examinations of the abdomen, pelvis, and lumber spine, where shields cannot cover the area being assessed, the prone position should be used to shield the fetus from the softer x-rays and thus reduce the fetal dose.

Angiography and Interventional Radiology

Like most radiological examinations, angiography and IR procedures are not contraindicated for appropriate maternal indications. General rules for radiation dose reduction with conventional radiography also apply to these invasive procedures. When radiographic examination or CT scanning is necessary in pregnancy, iodinated contrast agent may be administered.[66] The committee recommended evaluation of thyroid functions in the neonate during the first week following administration of iodinated agents to the mother during pregnancy. Strategies that can be adopted to reduce dose from interventional procedures include:

- Limiting fluoroscopy to short episodes.
- Recording the fluoroscopy time, kVp, and mAs for dose estimation (dose-area product meters on new fluoroscopy systems provide dose estimates).
- Avoiding use of the magnification mode to reduce the field of view as it increases the associated dose. Poor-quality TV tubes and electronic gain control can also affect the dose.[102]
- Holding the last image on the fluoroscopy screen.
- Use of electronic collimation features to restrict the area of exposure.[103]
- Fluoroscopy, a modest source of fetal dose compared to the dose from filming during the injection of angiographic contrast medium, can be readily reduced or eliminated during angiography. For example, fluoroscopy can be eliminated or performed with little fluoroscopic time (30 seconds) for IVC venography in pregnant patients.
- Choosing an alternative access route distant from the uterus can reduce fetal dose. For example, calculated fetal dose with pulmonary angiography via the femoral route can be reduced with use of the brachial route.

Computed Tomography Scanning

When performing a CT examination in a pregnant patient, radiation dose should be kept as low as reasonably achievable (the ALARA principle). Several scanning parameters that affect radiation dose to the conceptus from CT include tube current and potential, scanning modes, scan length, beam collimation, table speed and pitch, gantry rotation time, and shielding. The technologist monitoring the scan has control over most scanning parameters and can modulate them to obtain the desired image quality and dose reduction. Strategies to reduce dose include:

- Increasing beam collimation and pitch, and decreasing mAs, kV, and scan volume. Tube current adjustment is the most commonly used method of reducing radiation. Increasing the tube voltage from 110 to 140 kV increases the dose by about 60% (at constant mA).[104]
- Strict x-ray beam collimation in modern CT scanners allows very little scattered radiation dose. Thus, the radiation dose to the conceptus from CT of regions other than the pelvis and abdomen is not substantial.
- For abdominal-pelvic CT, scanning parameters must be selected to reduce the fetal dose. For example, for CT in a pregnant patient with suspected appendicitis, the scan volume must be restricted to the necessary anatomy, and dual-pass (with and without contrast) studies should be avoided.[104, 105]
- A "step-and-scan protocol" may help in terminating the study when the appendix is scanned.[104] Likewise, in CT for renal calculi in pregnancy, fetal dose must be reduced with use of low mAs, high pitch, and a limited scan volume, without substantially compromising the study quality.[106]
- Computed tomography angiography of chest for evaluation of pulmonary embolism in pregnant patients can be performed with no technical modifications other than pelvic shielding. Radiation dose should be reduced using lower mAs or appropriate settings of automatic exposure control techniques for smaller patients. Another important but simple step toward radiation dose reduction to fetus from chest CT is to administer up to 30% barium sulphate, which acts a 1 mm lead shield between the chest and the fetus. Ultrasound examination of the lower extremities should be performed, and CT angiography of pelvis and lower extremities should be excluded to

minimize radiation dose to the fetus. Fetal radiation dose from these studies is lower than the dose associated with a ventilation–perfusion scan during all trimesters.[106]

Nuclear Medicine

Most commonly used radiopharmaceutical agents, including ^{99}Tc, can be used during pregnancy since the fetal exposures are less than 5 mGy (Table 30.4). Furthermore, in pregnant patients, the common practice of halving the dose and collecting the data in a doubled time to maintain the information density and the accuracy of diagnosis helps in reducing dose.[107,108] It is prudent to avoid radioactive iodine during pregnancy, unless it is essential for medical care of the mother and there is no substitute.[107,109] However, if a diagnostic scan is necessary, ^{123}I or ^{99}Tc can be used in place of [131]I.[101] The total dose to the embryo must be estimated even if it is administered during first 5–6 weeks of pregnancy, when the fetal thyroid is not yet developed. As the fetal thyroid gland does not concentrate iodine until the 8th to 11th weeks, administration of [123]Iodine (3.7–14.8 MBq) before 8 weeks of postconception age is associated with a whole fetal dose of 148 μGy and negligible thyroid dose.[109]

Likewise, bone scan agents do not concentrate in fetal bones until after the 18th week, and the largest portion of the absorbed dose comes from the maternal bladder.[107] Fetal radiation exposure can be reduced by asking the patient to drink copious fluids and to void frequently.[110]

Ultrasound

As no relationship between dose and effect has been confirmed, ultrasound is unlikely to have

TABLE 30.4   FETAL DOSE ESTIMATES FROM VARIOUS NUCLEAR MEDICINE PROCEDURES (MATERNAL AND FETAL DOSE CONTRIBUTIONS)

Radioisotope	Activity Administered (MBq)	Range of Exposure (mGy)
[67]Ga Citrate	190	18.0–38.0
[131]I NaI (diagnostic thyroid uptake)	0.55	0.037–0.15
[131]I NaI (therapeutic thyroid uptake)	**350**	**23.0–95.0**
[99m]Tc DTPA (Kidney imaging, glomerular filtration)	750	3.1–9.0
[99m]Tc DTPA (aerosol)	40	0.092–0.23
[99m]Tc HDP	750	1.9–4.1
[99m]Tc MAA (Lung imaging)	200	0.56–1.0
[99m]Tc MDP	750	1.8–4.6
[99m]Tc Pertechnetate		
Thyroid	400	3.7–8.8
Blood pool imaging	1100	1.0–2.4
Cardiovascular shunt detection	550	5.1–12.0
[99m]Tc Blood pool imaging	700	2.0–4.6
[99m]Tc sulfur colloid (Liver–spleen imaging)	300	0.54–1.1
[18]F FDG (maternal contribution only)	370	1.0–6.3
[111]In white blood cell (maternal contribution only)	20	1.9–2.6
[99m]Tc MAG 3 (maternal contribution only)	750	4.1–14.0
[99m]Tc MIBI (maternal contribution only)		
Rest	1100	5.9–17.0
Stress	1100	4.8–13.0

Reprinted with permission from Russell JR, Stabin MG, Sparks RB, Watson E. Radiation absorbed dose to the embryo/fetus from radiopharmaceuticals. *Health Phys.* 1997;73:756–69.

Most radioisotopes, with exception of [131]I NaI for therapeutic thyroid uptake, are associated with less than 50 mGy radiation exposure.

deleterious effect on the fetus. The ACOG recommends that ultrasound be limited by minimizing the extent and duration of the examination, by training those acquiring the images, and by quality control performed at the ultrasound facility.[111]

Although there are no confirmed biological effects on patients caused by exposures from present diagnostic ultrasound instruments, the possibility that such biological effects may be identified in the future is possible. Consequently, the nonmedical use of ultrasound for psychosocial or entertainment purposes is strongly discouraged. The use of either two-dimensional (2D) or three-dimensional (3D) ultrasound to only view the fetus, to obtain a picture of the fetus, or to determine the fetal gender without a medical indication is regarded as inappropriate and contrary to responsible medical practice. Thus, ultrasound should be used in a prudent manner to provide medical benefit to the patient.

Magnetic Resonance Imaging

According to the safety committee of the Society for Magnetic Resonance Imaging (SMR), MR imaging is indicated for use in pregnant women when the result of nonionizing diagnostic imaging is inadequate for diagnosis or when MRI is expected to provide information for proper treatment of the fetus or mother.[24,112-114] Some investigators urge extra caution during the first trimester of pregnancy (organogenesis), when the fetus might be more vulnerable to any unknown bioeffects of MR imaging.[82] Use of gadolinium-enhanced MR imaging is relatively contraindicated in pregnancy, as the risk to the fetus has not been excluded. When contrast-enhanced MR examination is essential, gadolinium contrast media may be given to the pregnant mother.

RECOMMENDATIONS FOR IMAGING A PREGNANT PATIENT

Each radiology department must develop recommendations for imaging in pregnancy. As lack of knowledge can lead to anxiety and probably unnecessary termination of pregnancies, these recommendations must be specifically designed to expedite imaging studies when pregnant patients are involved, while limiting fetal radiation dose (Figure 30.1).[115-117] These recommendations must define safe imaging practice in pregnant patients for radiologists, physicists, residents, fellows, and technologists, as well as for referring physicians. The guidelines must help to protect both the mother and the fetus and encompass all imaging scenarios and indications. We propose the adoption of a sensible radiology practice for imaging in pregnancy, which should include the following.

Standard Protocols for Radiological Examinations in Pregnancy

A standard practice protocol must dictate that most radiological examinations can be performed in pregnant patients for appropriate indications. Radiologists and physicians must discuss the indication for imaging, keeping in mind that radiologic procedures should only be performed during pregnancy when medically indicated for the care of the patient and when the necessary information cannot be obtained by other means.

In life-threatening conditions, indicated radiological examinations should be performed without delay. Although an attempt should be made to keep the fetal dose at 50 mGy or less, the dose can be allowed to exceed 50 mGy (which itself allows a large safety margin, as the actual threshold level for fetal effects is 200 mGy in the most sensitive period of gestation) if the procedure is vital for the health of the mother and fetus.[115] Once the patient is stabilized, the result of a pregnancy test must be transmitted to radiology personnel and physicist to determine fetal radiation exposure.

For non–life-threatening conditions, women with childbearing capacity undergoing radiological examinations must be asked about the date of their last menstrual period and whether they think they might be pregnant. A sign must be posted in all radiology waiting areas requesting patients who suspect they may be pregnant to notify the technologist. As most radiological examinations, including those of abdomen, pelvis, and lumbar spine, are associated with radiation exposures of less than 200 mGy, pregnancy testing may be performed for a number of reasons, including the possibility of pregnancy in the differential diagnosis, so that a small percentage of studies may no longer be considered necessary; to determine pregnancy status, so that it is much less likely that patients who have undergone or will be undergoing radiological examination will be upset if they prove to be pregnant; and, to prevent possible allegations of malpractice from surprise and provocation of anxiety.[34,115] However,

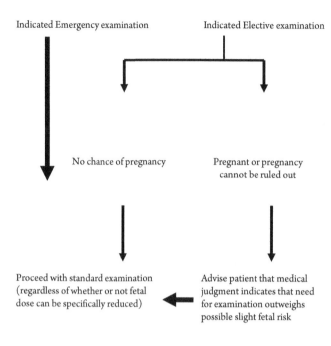

Indicated Emergency examination   Indicated Elective examination

No chance of pregnancy   Pregnant or pregnancy
                                cannot be ruled out

Proceed with standard examination   Advise patient that medical
(regardless of whether or not fetal   judgment indicates that need
dose can be specifically reduced)   for examination outweighs
                                           possible slight fetal risk

FIGURE 30.1 Proposed decision tree that might be used in women with childbearing capacity. An elective procedure may be described as those examinations that are not of immediate importance to the patient's health. Modification of a standard examination to specifically reduce fetal dose is warranted only if the tailored examination can be performed without substantial jeopardy to the medical care of the patient and/or her unborn child.

Adapted from National Council on Radiation Protection (NCRP) reports. Medical radiation exposure of the pregnant and potentially pregnant women. Report no. 54. Washington, DC: National Council on Radiation Protection and Measurements, July 15, 1977.

when a radiographic exam does not directly expose the uterus or its vicinity, pregnancy testing is not mandatory and patient shielding is recommended when appropriate. In these instances, examination techniques must reduce radiation exposure to the uterus (embryo or fetus) only if the diagnostic information obtained from the examination is not compromised.[34] Radiological examinations must not be performed in a woman for elective preemployment screening or follow-up, unless pregnancy has been excluded.

Assurance and Counseling of Pregnant Patients

Regardless of the indications of the study, all pregnant patients must be informed about the benefit of (reason for) the imaging study and informed that the proposed diagnostic imaging exams do not reach exposure levels sufficient to cause fetal adverse effects. Pregnant patients must be informed that it is extremely rare that diagnostic radiological studies will exceed the 200mGy threshold for radiation exposure. If higher radiation levels are related to an imaging study, the radiologist, referring physician, and patient should make an informed decision to protect the health of the mother and fetus.

For pregnant patients who are undergoing or have undergone radiological examination, and for parents of children born with congenital malformation following radiological examination in pregnancy,

the ultimate message should be that diagnostic radiation doses are associated with an extremely small risk of potential cancer, but no evidence has been found of any measurable increase in miscarriage, prematurity, stillbirth, mental retardation, congenital malformations, or microcephaly.[112, 115] For radiation doses of less than 100 mGy, a conservative estimate of the lifetime risk of radiation-induced childhood cancer or leukemia is about 1 in 170 (or 0.006%), which is extremely small compared to the natural background risk of 1 in 3 (or 33.33%), without radiation exposure.[112]

Since ignorance is responsible for anxiety and probably unnecessary termination of pregnancies, indicated imaging studies must be expedited in pregnancy, while limiting fetal radiation dose. Health personnel with comprehensive knowledge about the effects of imaging in pregnancy should advise pregnant patients. Information pertaining to radiation exposure must also be conveyed to the referring physician, so that he or she can counsel the pregnant patient and help her to make an informed decision regarding the potential impact of the radiation exposure on the offspring.

Facts Pertaining to Risk of Imaging

Radiation dose and risks should be evaluated and discussed with the patient, comparing them with other risks of pregnancy and with the exposure to background radiation. Evaluation and discussion of risks of radiological investigations are important when imaging has been performed in patients unaware of pregnancy or when imaging is being performed in patients with known pregnancy, as well as after pregnancy, when a reproductive problem has occurred. In either case, patients must also be informed that every healthy mother begins a pregnancy with 15% risk for miscarriage, 4% risk of prematurity, 4% risk of growth retardation, 3% risk for birth defects, and 1% risk of mental retardation or neurologic developmental problems, which are population background risks for reproductive effects.[115]

The ACOG Committee guidelines published in 1995 proposed counseling women that exposures of less than 50 mGy have not been associated with an increase in fetal anomalies or pregnancy loss.[82] At the same time, other imaging modalities not associated with ionizing radiation, such as ultrasonography and MRI, should be considered when appropriate. Thus, MR imaging can be performed, when indicated for medical reasons in pregnancy, although extra caution might be needed in the first trimester of pregnancy (organogenesis).[118] When contrast-enhanced MR is indicated in pregnancy, gadolinium-based contrast agents can be administered.

In the past, physicians have frequently relied on the Danish rule as a guideline for recommending therapeutic abortion following irradiation.[116] This rule advised therapeutic abortion for fetal exposures of greater than 100 mGy, but did not give consideration to other biomedical or personal factors.[97] According to the ICRP guidelines, fetal doses of less than 100 mGy must not be a reason for terminating the pregnancy.[112] For most of pregnancy, the fetal effect threshold is greater than 200 mGy (which is the threshold in the most sensitive stage), so medical termination of pregnancy for exposures of less than 200 mGy is incorrect.[115] Furthermore, higher fetal doses of 100–200 mGy with diagnostic imaging usually occur from multiple examinations (fractionation) or from radionuclide imaging with long half-lives (protraction), both of which leads to lower risk than does acute exposure.[115,119] Radioactive iodine is contraindicated for therapeutic use in pregnancy.[111]

CONCLUSION

In conclusion, it is clear that imaging in pregnancy is an important medical dilemma with a significant emotional impact for both patients and their physicians. Knowledge of the known risks of fetal radiation exposure during medical imaging can allay unnecessary anxiety and optimize expedited patient care. The adoption of the appropriate radiology practice for imaging in pregnancy can help us better serve our pregnant patients and their as yet unborn children.

APPENDIX

Definition of the following terms will be helpful in understanding the concepts described in the article:

Gestational age (or *menstrual age*) is the time elapsed between the first day of the last normal menstrual period and the day of delivery.

Conceptional age is the time elapsed between the day of conception and the day of delivery. The convention for calculating gestational age when the date of conception is known is to add 2 weeks to the conceptional age.

REFERENCES

1. Einarson A, Park A, Koren G. How physicians perceive and utilize information from a teratogen information service: The Motherisk Program. *BMC Med Educ.* 2004;4:6
2. Joerg NE. A personal story about pregnancy radiation risk counseling. *Teratology.* 1999;59:314–5.
3. Ratnapalan S, Bona N, Chandra K, Koren G. Physicians' perceptions of teratogenic risk associated with radiography and CT during early pregnancy. *AJR.* 2004;182:1107–9.
4. Lowe SA. Diagnostic radiography in pregnancy: Risks and reality. *Aust N Z J Obstet Gynaecol.* 2004;44:191–6.
5. Graham JM Jr, Jones KL, Brent RL. Contribution of clinical teratologists and geneticists to the evaluation of the etiology of congenital malformations alleged to be caused by environmental agents: Ionizing radiation, electromagnetic fields, microwaves, radionuclides, and ultrasound. *Teratology.* 1999;59:307–13.
6. Brent RL. Introduction. *Teratology.* 1999;59:299–300.
7. Solomon HM, Beckman DA, Buck SJ, Gorson RO, Mills RE, Brent RL. Comparative effects of neutron irradiation and X irradiation on the embryonic development of the rat. *Radiat Res.* 1994;137:226–30.
8. Brateman L. Radiation Safety considerations for diagnostic radiology personnel. *Radiographics.* 1999;19:1037–55.
9. Parry RA, Glaze SA, Archer BR. Typical patient radiation doses in diagnostic radiology. *Radiographics.* 1999;19:1289–1302.
10. Kalra MK, Maher MM, Toth TL, et al. Strategies for CT radiation dose optimization. *Radiology.* 2004;230:619–28.
11. Brent RL. Drug and chemical action in pregnancy. In Fabro S, Scialli AR, et al., eds., *Pharmacologic and*

toxicologic principles, 1st ed., Chapter 17. New York: Marcel Dekker1986:427–38.

12. Wyckoff HO, Allisy A, Liden K. The new special names of SI units in the field of ionizing radiations. *Radiology*. 1976;118:233–4.

13. Russell JR, Stabin MG, Sparks RB. Placental transfer of radiopharmaceuticals and dosimetry in pregnancy. *Health Phys*. 1997;73:747–55.

14. Russell JR, Stabin MG, Sparks RB, Watson E. Radiation absorbed dose to the embryo/fetus from radiopharmaceuticals. *Health Phys*. 1997;73:756–69.

15. Stabin MG. Proposed addendum to previously published fetal dose estimate tables for 18F-FDG. *J Nucl Med*. 2004;45:634–5.

16. Benveniste H, Fowler JS, Rooney WD, et al. Maternal-fetal in vivo imaging: a combined PET and MRI study. *J Nucl Med*. 2003;44:1522–30.

17. Stabin MG. Proposed addendum to previously published fetal dose estimate tables for 18F-FDG. *J Nucl Med*. 2004;45:634–5.

18. AIUM-NEMA. Standard for Real-Time display of thermal and mechanical acoustic output indices on diagnostic ultrasound equipment. Rockville, MD: AIUM, 1992.

19. Brent RL, Jensh RP, Beckman DA. Medical sonography: Reproductive effects and risks. *Teratology*. 1991;44:123–46.

20. Jensh RP, Brent RL. Intrauterine effects of ultrasound: Animal studies. *Teratology*. 1999;59:240–51.

21. Jensh RP, Lewin PA, Poczobutt MT, Goldberg BB, Oler J, Brent RL. The effects of prenatal ultrasound exposure on postnatal growth and acquisition of reflexes. *Radiat Res*. 1994;140:284–93.

22. American Institute of Ultrasound in Medicine Bioeffects Committee. Bioeffects Considerations for the Safety of Diagnostic Ultrasound. *J Ultrasound Med*. 1988;7(Suppl 9):S1–38.

23. Nyborg WL. Mechanisms. In: Nyborg WL, Ziskin MC, eds. *Biological effects of ultrasound*, Chapter 1. New York: Churchill Livingstone, 1985:24.

24. Kok RD, de Vries MM, Heerschap A, van den Berg PP. Absence of harmful effects of magnetic resonance exposure at 1.5 T in utero during the third trimester of pregnancy: A follow-up study. *Magn Reson Imaging*. 2004;22:851–4.

25. Brent RL. Reproductive and teratologic effects of low-frequency electromagnetic fields: A review of in vivo and in vitro studies using animal models. *Teratology*. 1999;59:261–86.

26. Brent RL, Gordon WE, Bennett WR, Beckman DA. Reproductive and teratologic effects of electromagnetic fields. *Reprod Toxicol*. 1993;7:535–80.

27. Brent RL, Beckman DA, Landel CP. Clinical teratology. *Curr Opin Pediatr*. 1993;5:201–11.

28. Little MP. Risks associated with ionizing radiation. *Br Med Bull*. 2003;68:259–75.

29. Edwards AA, Lloyd DC. Risk from deterministic effects of ionizing radiation. *Docs NRPB*. 1996;7:1–31.

30. Brent RL. Utilization of developmental basic science principles in the evaluation of reproductive risks from pre- and post conception environmental radiation exposures. *Teratology*. 1999;59:182–204.

31. Cox, R ad KMac Gibbon, B.H. Documents of the National Radiation Protection Board (NRPB). Estimates of late radiation risks to the UK population: Chapter 6 – Irradiation in utero. Doc. NRPB, 4, No. 4. 1993: 105–25. Available for purchase at the UK National Radiological Protection Board at http://www.hpa.org.uk. ISBN: 0–85951-365–3.

32. Brent RL. Radiation teratogenesis. *Teratology*. 1980;21:281–98.

33. National Academy of Sciences/National Research Council (NAS/NRC). Health effects of exposure to low levels of ionizing radiation. Committee on the Biological Effects of Ionizing Radiation. BEIR V. Washington, DC: National Academy Press, 1990.

34. National Council on Radiation Protection (NCRP) reports. Medical radiation exposure of the pregnant and potentially pregnant women. Report no. 54. Washington, DC: NCRP, July 15, 1977.

35. Blot WJ, Miller RW. Mental retardation following in utero exposure to the atomic bombs of Hiroshima and Nagasaki. *Radiology*. 1973;106:617–9.

36. Yonehara S, Brenner AV, Kishikawa M, Inskip, PD, Preston, DL, Ron, E, Mabuchi, K, Tokuoka, S. Clinical and epidemiologic characteristics of first primary tumors of the central nervous system and related organs among atomic bomb survivors in Hiroshima and Nagasaki, 1958–1995. *Cancer*. 2004;101:1644–54.

37. Yamada M, Sasaki H, Kasagi F, et al. Study of cognitive function among the Adult Health Study (AHS) population in Hiroshima and Nagasaki. *Radiat Res*. 2002;158:236–40.

38. Kodama Y, Pawel D, Nakamura N, et al. Stable chromosome aberrations in atomic bomb survivors: Results from 25 years of investigation. *Radiat Res*. 2001;156:337–46.

39. Otake M , Schull WJ. Radiation-related brain damage and growth retardation among the prenatally exposed atomic bomb survivors. *Int J Radiat Biol*.1998;74:159–71.

40. Schull WJ, Orake M, Yoshimaru H. Effect on intelligence test score of prenatal exposure to ionizing radiation in Hiroshima and Nagasaki: A comparison of T65DR and D586 Dosimetry system. Radiation Effects Research Foundation Technical Report. Radiation Effects Research Foundation, 1988:3–88. Available online at http://www.rerf.or.jp/library/scidata/trs_e/80–89/tr8803.htm.

41. Edwards FM. Risk of medical imaging. In: Putnam CE, Ravin CE, eds. *Fundamentals of diagnostic*

imaging, 2nd ed. Philadelphia: W. B. Saunders, 1994:83–97.

42. Brent RL. The effects of embryonic and fetal exposure to x-rays, microwaves and ultrasound. *Clin Obstet Gynecol.* 1983;26:484–510.

43. International Commission on Radiological Protection. Pregnancy and medical radiation. *Ann ICRP.* 2000;30:iii-viii, 1–43.

44. Streffer C, Shore R, Konermann G, et al. Biological effects after prenatal irradiation (embryo and fetus). A report of the International Commission on Radiological Protection. *Ann ICRP.* 2003;33(1–2):5–206.

45. Steenvoorde P, Pauwels EK, Harding LK, Bourguignon M, Mariere B, Broerse JJ. Diagnostic nuclear medicine and risk for the fetus. *Eur J Nucl Med.* 1998;25:193–9.

46. National Radiological Protection Board. Diagnostic medical exposures: Exposure to ionizing radiation of pregnant women-biological basis of the board's statement. *Doc NRPB.* 1993;4:7–14.

47. Osei EK, Faulkner K. Fetal doses from radiological examinations. *Br J Radiol.* 1999;72:773–80.

48. Wagner LK, Lester RG, Saldana LR. *Exposure of the pregnant patient to diagnostic radiations: A guide to medical management*, 2nd ed. Madison, WI: Medical Physics Publishing, 1997.

49. Inskip PD, Harvey EB, Boice JD Jr, et al. Incidence of childhood cancer in twins. *Cancer Causes Control.* 1991;2:315–24.

50. Rodvall Y, Pershagen G, Hrubec Z, Ahlbom A, Pedersen NL, Boice JD. Prenatal X-ray exposure and childhood cancer in Swedish twins. *Int J Cancer.* 1990;46:362–5.

51. United Nations Scientific Committee on the effects of Atomic Radiation (UNSCEAR). *Sources and effects of ionizing radiation*. No. E.94.IX.11. New York: United Nations, 1994.

52. National Academy of Scences. *The effects on populations of exposure to low levels of ionizing radiation*. Washington, DC: National Academy Press, 1980.

53. Jablon S, Kato H. Childhood cancer in relation to prenatal exposure to atomic-bomb radiation. *Lancet.* 1970;14:1000–1003.

54. Yoshimoto Y, Kato H, Schull WJ. Risk of cancer among children exposed in utero to A-bomb radiations, 1950–84. *Lancet.* 1988;2:665–9.

55. Court Brown WM, Doll R, Hill RB. Incidence of leukaemia after exposure to diagnostic radiation in utero. *Br Med J.* 1960;5212:1539–45.

56. Diamond EL, Schmerler H, Lilienfeld AM. The relationship of intra-uterine radiation to subsequent mortality and development of leukemia in children. A prospective study. *Am J Epidemiol.* 1973;97:283–313.

57. Giles D, Hewitt D, Stewart A, Webb J. Malignant disease in childhood and diagnostic irradiation in utero. *Lancet.* 1956;271:447.

58. Dekaban AS. Abnormalities in children exposed to x-radiation during various stages of gestation: Tentative timetable of radiation injury to the human fetus. *J Nucl Med.* 1968; 9:471–7.

59. Monson RR, McMahon B. Prenatal X-ray exposure and cancer in children. In: Boice JD Jr, Fraumeni JF Jr, eds., *Radiation carcinogenesis: Epidemiology and biological significance*. New York: Raven Press, 1984:97–104.

60. Wakeford R, Little MP. Risk coefficients for childhood cancer after intrauterine irradiation: A review. *Int J Radiat Biol.* 2003;79:293–309.

61. Brent RL. The effect of embryonic and fetal exposure to x-ray, microwaves, and ultrasound: Counseling the pregnant and non-pregnant patient about these risks. *Semin Oncol.* 1989;16:347–68.

62. Court Brown WM, Doll R, Hill RB. Incidence of leukaemia after exposure to diagnostic radiation in utero. *Br Med J.* 1960;5212:1539–45.

63. MacMahon B. Prenatal x-ray exposure and childhood cancer. *J Natl Cancer Inst.* 1962;28:1173–91.

64. Mole RH. Childhood cancer after prenatal exposure to diagnostic X-ray examinations in Britain. *Br J Cancer.* 1990;62:152–68.

65. Boice JD Jr, Miller RW. Childhood and adult cancer after intrauterine exposure to ionizing radiation. *Teratology.* 1999;59:227–33.

66. Webb JA, Thomsen HS, Morcos SK; Members of Contrast Media Safety Committee of European Society of Urogenital Radiology (ESUR). The use of iodinated and gadolinium contrast media during pregnancy and lactation. *Eur Radiol.* 2003;13:181–4.

67. Felder E. Iopamidol toxicology. *Invest Radiol.* 1984;19(Suppl):S168–S170.

68. Shaw DD, Potts DG. Toxicology of iohexol. *Invest Radiol.* 1985;20(Suppl 1):S10–S13.

69. Morrison JC, Boyd M, Friedman BI, et al. The effects of Renografin-60 on the fetal thyroid. *Obstet Gynecol.* 1973;42:99–103.

70. Parker JA, Yester MV, Daube-Witherspoon E, Todd-Pokropek AE, Royal HJ. Procedure guideline for general imaging: 1.0. Society of Nuclear Medicine. *J Nucl Med.* 1996;37:2087–92.

71. Russell JR, Stabin MG, Sparks RB. Placental transfer of radiopharmaceuticals and dosimetry in pregnancy. *Health Phys.* 1997;73:747–55.

72. Russell JR, Stabin MG, Sparks RB, Watson E. Radiation absorbed dose to the embryo/fetus from radiopharmaceuticals. *Health Phys.* 1997;73:756–69.

73. Barnett SB, Ter Haar GR, Ziskin MC, Rott HD, Duck FA, Maeda K. International recommendations and guidelines for the safe use of diagnostic ultrasound in medicine. *Ultrasound Med Biol.* 2000; 26:355–66.

74. Ziskin MC. Intrauterine effects of ultrasound: Human epidemiology. *Teratology.* 1999;59:252–60.

75. Heyner S, Abraham V, Wikarczuk ML, Ziskin MC. Effects of ultrasound on DNA and RNA synthesis in preimplantation mouse embryos. *Mol Reprod Dev.* 1990;25:209–14.

76. Margulies N, Abraham V, Way JS, Ziskin MC. Effect of ultrasound on the neonatal rat brain. *Ultrasound Med Biol.* 1992;18:459–64.

77. Takabayashi T, Sato S, Sato A, et al. Influence of pulse-wave ultrasonic irradiation on the prenatal development of mouse. *Tohoku J Exp Med.* 1985;147:403–10.

78. Child SZ, Carstensen EL, Gates AH, Hall WJ. Testing for the teratogenicity of pulsed ultrasound in mice. *Ultrasound Med Biol.*1988;14:493–8.

79. Carnes KI, Hess RA, Dunn F. The effect of ultrasound exposure in utero on the development of the fetal mouse testis: Adult consequences. *Ultrasound Med Biol.*1995;21:1247–57.

80. Child SZ, Hoffman D, Norton S, Carstensen EL, Cox C, Gates AH. Pulsed ultrasound and the hyperbarically exposed mouse fetus. *Ultrasound Med Biol.* 1991;17:367–71.

81. Newnham JP, Evans SF, Michael CA, Stanley FJ, Landau LI. Effects of frequent ultrasound during pregnancy: A randomized controlled trial. *Lancet.* 1993;342:887–91.

82. American College of Obstetricians and Gynecologists, Committee on Obstetric Practice. Guidelines for diagnostic Imaging during pregnancy. ACOG Committee opinion no.158. *Int J Gynaecol Obstet.* 1995; 51:288–91.

83. AIUM. Report. *J Ultrasound Med.* 1988;7:S1–S38.

84. LeFevre ML, Bain RP, Ewigman BG, Frigoletto FD, Crane JP, McNellis D. A randomized trial of prenatal ultrasonographic screening: Impact on maternal management and outcome. RADIUS (Routine Antenatal Diagnostic Imaging with Ultrasound) Study Group. *Am J Obstet Gynecol.* 1993; 169:483–9.

85. Kieler H, Cnattingius S, Haglund B, Palmgren J, Axelsson O. Sinistrality—a side-effect of prenatal sonography: A comparative study of young men. *Epidemiology.* 2001;12:618–23.

86. Kieler H, Cnattingius S, Palmgren J, Haglund B, Axelsson O. First trimester ultrasound scans and left-handedness. Epidemiology. 2002;13:370.

87. Kieler H, Ahlsten G, Haglund B, Salvesen K, Axelsson O. Routine ultrasound screening in pregnancy and the children's subsequent neurologic development. *Obstet Gynecol.*1998;91:750–6.

88. Glover P, Hykin J, Gowland P, Wright J, Johnson I, Mansfield P. An assessment of the intrauterine sound intensity level during obstetric echo-planar magnetic resonance imaging. *Br J Radiol.* 1995; 68:1090–4.

89. Budinger TF. Nuclear magnetic resonance (NMR) in vivo studies: Known thresholds for health effects. *J Comput Assist Tomogr.* 1981;5:800–11.

90. Edwards FM. Risk of medical imaging. In: Putnam CE, Ravin CE, eds., *Fundamentals of diagnostic imaging,* 2nd ed. Philadelphia: W. B. Saunders, 1994:83–97.

91. Carnes KI, Magin RL. Effects of in utero exposure to 4.7 T MR imaging conditions on fetal growth and testicular development in the mouse. *Magn Reson Imaging.* 1996;14:263–74.

92. Baker PN, Johnson IR, Harvey PR, Gowland PA, Mansfield P. A three-year follow-up of children imaged in utero with echo-planar magnetic resonance. *Am J Obstet Gynecol.*1994; 170:32–33.

93. Myers C, Duncan KR, Gowland PA, Johnson IR, Baker PN. Failure to detect intrauterine growth restriction following in utero exposure to MRI. *Br J Radiol.* 1998: 71:549–51.

94. Clements H, Duncan KR, Fielding PA, Gowland PA, Johnson IR, Baker PN. Infants exposed to MRI in utero have a normal paediatric assessment at 9 months of age. *Br J Radiol.* 2000;73:190–4.

95. Jacobs LA, Brizzee KR. Effects of total-body x-irradiation in single and fractionated doses on developing cerebral cortex in rat foetus. *Nature.* 1966;210:31–3.

96. Brent RL. The response of the 9 and one-half-day-old-rat embryo to variations in exposure rate of 150 R x-irradiation. *Radiat Res.* 1971;45:127–36.

97. Mossman KL, Hill LT. Radiation risks in pregnancy. *Obstet Gynecol.* 1982;60:237–42.

98. Cunningham FG, MacDonald PC, Gant NF, Leveno KJ, Gilstrap LC, eds. *Williams obstetrics,* 20th ed. Stamford, CT: Appleton & Lange, 1997:1045–57.

99. Winer-Muram HT, Boone JM, Brown HL, Jennings SG, Mabie WC, Lombardo GT. Pulmonary embolism in pregnant patients: Fetal radiation dose with helical CT. *Radiology.* 2002;224:487–92.

100. Brent RL, Gorson RO. Radiation exposure in pregnancy. In: *Current problems in radiology technique of pneumoencephalography.* Chicago: Year Book Medical, 1972:1–47.

101. Ginsberg JS, Hirsh J, Rainbow AJ, Coates G. Risks to the fetus of radiologic procedures used in the diagnosis of maternal venous thromboembolic disease. *Thromb Haemost.* 1989;61:189–96.

102. Marshall NW. Optimisation of dose per image in digital imaging. *Radiat Prot Dosimetry.* 2001;94:83–87.

103. El-Khoury GY, Madsen MT, Blake ME, Yankowitz J. A new pregnancy policy for a new era. *AJR.* 2003; 181:335–40.

104. Wagner LK, Huda W. When a pregnant woman with suspected appendicitis is referred for a CT scan, what should a radiologist do to minimize potential radiation risks? *Pediatr Radiol.* 2004;34:589–90.

105. Ames Castro M, Shipp TD, Castro EE, Ouzounian J, Rao P. The use of helical computed tomography in pregnancy for the diagnosis of acute appendicitis. *Am J Obstet Gynecol.* 2001;184:954–7.

106. Forsted DH, Kalbhen CL. CT of pregnant women for urinary tract calculi, pulmonary thromboembolism, and acute appendicitis. *AJR*. 2002;178:1285.

107. Adelstein SJ. Administered radionuclides in pregnancy. *Teratology*. 1999;59:236–9.

108. Marcus CS, Mason GR, Kuperus JH, Mena I. Pulmonary imaging in pregnancy. Maternal risk and fetal dosimetry. *Clin Nucl Med*. 1985;10:1–4.

109. Watson EE. Radiation absorbed dose to the human fetal thyroid. In: Watson EE, Schlafke-Stelson AT, eds. Fifth International Radiopharmaceutical Dosimetry Symposium. Oak Ridge, TN: Oak Ridge Associated Universities, 1991:179–87.

110. Baker J, Ali A, Groch MW, Fordham E, Economou SG. Bone scanning in pregnant patients with breast carcinoma. *Clin Nucl Med*. 1987;12:519–24.

111. ACOG Committee on Ethics. ACOG Committee Opinion. Number 297, August 2004. Nonmedical use of obstetric ultrasonography. *Obstet Gynecol*. 2004;104:423–4.

112. Anonymous. Protection of the patient undergoing a magnetic resonance examination. International Non-Ionizing Radiation Committee of the International Radiation Protection Association. *Health Phys*. 1991;61:923–98.

113. American Academy of Pediatrics/American College of Obstetricians and Gynecologists (AAP/ACOG). *Guidelines for perinatal care*, 3rd ed. Elk Grove Village, IL: American Academy of Pediatrics and American College of Obstetricians and Gynecologists, 1992:210–3.

114. Kanal E, Shellock FG. Policies, guidelines, and recommendations for MR imaging safety and patient management. SMRI Safety Committee. *J Magn Reson Imaging*. 1992;2:247–8.

115. Brent RL, Mettler FA. Pregnancy policy. *AJR*. 2004;182:819–22; author reply 822.

116. Hammer-Jacobsen E. Therapeutic abortion on account of x-ray examination during pregnancy. *Dan Med Bull*. 1959;6:113–22.

117. National Council on Radiation Protection and Measurements (NCRP). Limitation of exposure to ionizing radiation NCRP report no. 116. Bethesda, MD: NCRP, 1993.

118. Garden AS, Weindling AM, Griffiths RD, Martin PA. Fast-scan magnetic resonance imaging of fetal anomalies. *Br J Obstet Gynaecol*. 1991;98:1217–22.

119. Beckman DA, Solomon HM, Buck SJ, Gorson RO, Mills RE, Brent RL. Effects of dose and dose protraction on embryotoxicity of 14.1 MeV neutron irradiation in rats. *Radiat Res*. 1994;138:337–42.

31

Afterword: Quality and Ethics

RICHARD GUNDERMAN AND JORDAN SWENSSON

And what is good, Phaedrus, and what is not good—need we ask anyone to tell us these things?

—PLATO, PHAEDRUS

One of the most famous inquiries into the subject of quality over the last half century was Robert Pirsig's *Zen and the Art of Motorcycle Maintenance.*[1] Published in 1974, the book was originally rejected by 121 publishers, more than any other best-selling book, although it went on to sell more than 4 million copies and has been translated into no fewer than 27 languages. The book represents an inquiry into quality, and in particular, a "metaphysics of quality," an idea that the author deems impossible to define. To say that quality is indefinable, however, does not imply that it is not worth thinking about, and in fact the failure to think deeply and well about quality is one of the most important problems and opportunities before the field of radiology today.

What makes for a great motorcycle? To what degree does a great motorcycle require a great motorcyclist, and to what extent do great motorcyclists understand and care for their machines? Is motorcycle maintenance the epitome of drudgery or an engaging art, and what difference does this make? What makes for great radiology? To what degree does great radiology require a great radiologist, and to what extent do great radiologists understand and care first and foremost for the machinery of radiology? Is the care and feeding of radiologists the epitome of drudgery or an engaging art, and what difference does this make in the career trajectories we craft for ourselves as individual radiologists and members of the field of radiology?

Can we reliably and accurately differentiate between good radiologists and bad radiologists, and between merely good radiologists and great radiologists? What makes it valid to speak of great radiology and great radiologists? If there is such a thing as a great radiologist, and perhaps even great radiology, what does it look like? What would we need to know about a radiologist or a radiology practice to determine whether or not it is great? Would the volume of studies tell the tale? How about the number of RVUs or the amount of revenue generated? What about error rates, or the clinical relevance of observations and recommendations? How about patient or referring physician satisfaction scores? Would we need to know something about health outcomes? Could we identify great radiologists from electronic reports, or would you need to observe them in action to discern greatness?

Although quality is devilishly difficult to define, there are constituents of quality that must be mentioned in any even quasi-comprehensive account of it. Among these constituents are precision, accuracy, safety, efficiency, and efficacy. In this chapter, we briefly examine these five elements, attempting to define their individual roles in the larger economy of quality, and noting, where relevant, their inherent ambiguities and tensions as well as their strengths. Thereafter, we return to the concept of quality writ large, attempting to understand the relationship between quality and another complex concept, that of appropriateness. We conclude with an examination of the enduring importance of discernment, a resource for which no quality algorithm can ever substitute.

FIVE FEATURES OF QUALITY

Precision

Precision describes how tightly results are clustered together, the reproducibility of findings. Common examples in radiology include interobserver and intraobserver variability. Do different radiologists looking at the same chest radiograph or mammogram reach the same conclusions regarding whether or not it is normal, the number and nature of positive findings, the differential diagnostic possibilities, or the implications for further diagnostic evaluation or treatment? The same questions can be posed concerning a single radiologist who interprets the same imaging study on multiple occasions. To an important degree, wide variation in these parameters constitutes de facto evidence that quality could be improved.

Suppose, for example, that a motorcyclist takes his machine to a several repair shops for routine maintenance. At one shop, he is told that the fuel injectors are becoming clogged and need to be replaced. At another shop, he is told that he needs new spark plugs. At a third shop, he is told that his motorcycle is in perfect condition and receives commendation for the terrific job he is doing maintaining it. What is our motorcyclist to think of these conflicting diagnostic and therapeutic recommendations? This general problem is one of the reasons behind efforts to standardize the reporting of radiology studies, such as the BI-RADS system in breast imaging. However, merely reducing the radiologist's discretion in the wording of reports does not necessarily induce a greater degree of diagnostic agreement.

Moreover, precision alone is not sufficient to guarantee high-quality radiology. Although the reliability of a diagnostic impression probably increases to some extent in proportion to the number of radiologists who agree on it, there are still situations in which even large numbers of observers may be wrong. This is especially likely in situations where independence of assessment is low or the imperative for consensus is high. For example, if one senior radiologist asks a room full of junior colleagues whether they agree with her impression, the probability of uniformity may be higher than if each radiologist comes to an independent assessment. Likewise, people who feel compelled to agree may be more likely to do so than those under no pressure to reach consensus.[2]

Accuracy

In contrast to precision, which refers to variability, accuracy concerns the degree to which impressions correctly represent reality. If a radiologist says that a lung or breast lesion represents cancer and a biopsy is performed, does the pathologist interpret the histologic morphology of the lesion as malignant? Other types of diagnostic studies, such as laboratory testing of blood and urine samples, may play an equally important confirmatory role. A joint effusion and synovial enhancement that appear to the radiologist to represent either an infectious or inflammatory arthritis may be easily distinguished by laboratory analysis of aspirated joint fluid. Even the pathologist needs guidance regarding which fluid or tissue was sampled, and in this sense no medical specialty sees everything.

Pathology has often been regarded as the final arbiter of truth when it comes to radiological performance, but this is not always justified. For one thing, pathologists are fallible, and sometimes make mistakes. Moreover, the material the pathologist is working with may be flawed in some way. For example, the tissue sample may be from the wrong patient, or the biopsy may have failed to obtain tissue from the lesion seen on imaging. In some cases, pathology itself may be unreliable. For example, a biopsy sample obtained from a healing fracture may appear indistinguishable from an osteogenic osteosarcoma, and the only way for a pathologist to tell the difference may be to rely on a radiograph of the lesion.

Aside from the difficulty of establishing gold standards against which to assay radiologic interpretations is another important limitation on the assessment of radiologic accuracy.[3] In many cases, radiologic impressions are not subjected to rigorous verification. For example, when the computed tomography (CT) pulmonary arteriogram shows a filling defect in a pulmonary artery branch, the patient is simply treated for acute pulmonary thromboembolism, with no further diagnostic evaluation. When the chest radiograph shows an airspace opacity in a patient with a fever, the patient is treated for pneumonia. The point is not that radiology is inherently unreliable, but simply that many radiologic diagnoses, even some skeletal fractures and pneumothoraces, are hypotheses, and should be treated as such.

Safety

Safety has been receiving more and more attention of late, fueled in part by reports in the popular media of excessive doses of radiation delivered to patients during diagnostic and therapeutic radiologic procedures. Since the era of Hippocrates, one of the first principles of medicine has been "Do no harm."[4] This idea is represented in the ethical principle of non-maleficence, which many ethicists regard as more fundamental than the principle of beneficence.[5] The former states that health professionals should protect patients from harm, while the later states that they should promote patient's welfare. This means that physicians and other health professionals need to anticipate possible harms before they occur and take steps to prevent them.

Of course, safety is not quite so simple. For one thing, there is the issue of whose safety the physician is called upon to look out for. Does the umbrella of professional responsibility extend only to patients under the physician's direct care, or to other patients, family members, health professionals, and other employees of the health care organization, and the community at large? In one sense, the responsibility seems greatest for patients under the physician's direct care, but it can and often does extend beyond this, as when a nuclear medicine physician counsels patients to avoid direct contact with family members after radiotherapy. Moreover, radiologists often need to enlist the aid of others, including friends and family members, to protect patients, for example by ensuring that someone is available to drive a patient home after completing a procedure under sedation or general anesthesia.

Safety is an important goal, but it is not the only goal, and in some cases, it may be appropriate to compromise safety in pursuit of other worthy objectives. Safety measures tend to be tied to the status quo, aimed at managing risks inherent in current practices. In some cases, safety may be compromised for the sake of innovation. Investigational protocols involve an increased level of risk, because the element of the unknown is inevitably increased. Where levels of anxiety and fear of the unknown are high, innovation may be unduly stifled. For example, the first nuclear medicine hepatobiliary imaging agents were inadvertently discovered during a search for effective cardiac radiopharmaceuticals.[6] Preventing investigators and patients from taking risks to which reasonable people might reasonably agree for the sake of advancing knowledge and improving on current standards of diagnosis and therapy would be a mistake.[7]

Efficiency

Efficiency may be defined as the ratio of results achieved to resources expended. Efficiency can be increased either by improving results while keeping resources expenditures constant, or by achieving the same results with fewer resources. Such resources may include time, effort, and money. In an era when commerce plays an increasing role in health care, there is a strong tendency to focus where possible on fungible resources, those that can be valued in dollars and cents. This tendency is abetted by a legal system that seeks to assign monetary values to civil damages, such as the loss of a body part, the loss of functional capacity, and the loss of years of life. Even health care-specific metrics such as quality-adjusted life years (QALYs) beg an important question: How much is a life, or a year of life, worth?

As Pirsig implies in *Zen and the Art of Motorcycle Maintenance*, we cannot always tell how good something is, or even what it is worth, in monetary terms. As most radiologists appear to have recognized by the positions they have opted to accept, the job most worth having is not necessarily the one that pays the most. The highest paying position may need to pay well for a reason, such as an extreme workload, a high level of stress, unpleasant working conditions, undesirable location, and in general, a relative dearth of intrinsic rewards, such as professional fulfillment, that must be balanced by the extrinsic incentive of extra compensation. Likewise, the steps that would be necessary to maximize the economic efficiency of a radiology practice might entail the neglect of other goals that make radiologists' work meaningful and rewarding.

Suppose, for example, that a group decides to forego adding additional radiologists to its workforce, despite a growing workload. For a time, increases in productivity, such as those made possible by picture archiving and communication system (PACS) and other electronic work systems, may make such strategies successful. At some point, however, further increases in productivity may require substantial reductions in quality of work life, with increased rates of burnout, errors, and defections, and associated losses in morale and fulfillment. This serves as an example of how a relentless focus on efficiency, and in particular, on one aspect of efficiency, can ultimately undermine the performance of radiologists and produce more harm than benefit.

Efficacy

Efficacy focuses on the relative effectiveness of different alternative courses of action, omitting to consider the risks and costs associated with each. Efficacy is highly desirable, but needs to be tempered by other considerations, including efficiency.

For example, we could dramatically decrease the incidence of cancer in various organs such as the thyroid gland, the breast, and the gonads, by surgically removing them. The efficacy of this practice, measured in terms of the reduction in risk of cancer, would be very high. Yet the simple fact that an intervention has a high level of efficacy does not reliably establish it as the appropriate alternative. The cost of surgically removing such organs is very high, and the price paid per cancer-free year of life might be astronomical. Such practices might make more sense in patients at high risk, such as those harboring a *BRCA* mutation, but even in these cases the issues are complex.

In other words, efficacy is not an absolute but a relative concept. For one thing, it is important to clarify the ends we are attempting to achieve. As Fryback and Thornbury have shown,[8] the efficacy of diagnostic testing can be assessed at many levels, including technical efficacy (How well can I see it?), diagnostic accuracy (How well does it reveal the pathology?), diagnostic thinking (Does it change my diagnosis?), therapeutic effect (Does it change therapy?), patient outcomes (Does the patient do better?), and societal outcomes (Is it cost effective?). Increasing technical efficacy may compromise patient outcomes (increasing radiation doses to make images as attractive as possible), and increasing patient outcomes may militate against societal efficacy (ignoring cumulative imaging costs to ensure that each patient gets the best possible diagnostic evaluation).

Appropriateness

In principle, products, services, and performances of higher quality are to be preferred over those of lower quality. As a consumer, no one wants to spend money on poorly constructed and executed goods that manifest shoddy workmanship or inattention to functionality and aesthetics. Likewise, no producer wants to be responsible for shabby work. Each of us wants to do work that we can be proud of. Hence, a reasonably high level of quality is a reasonable expectation. Yet the pursuit of quality has its limits, and these limits are not purely the product of a lack of commitment to quality. In some situations, a product, service, or performance of lower quality is not only acceptable but actually preferable to one of high quality. For example, most of us would prefer to hear "Happy Birthday" sung by our own friends and loved ones than by a world-famous vocalist. In musical terms, the quality may be lower, but it means more to us.

This introduces the crucial theme of value. When some connoisseurs buy a motorcar, they want nothing but the best, and will invest large sums of money to acquire a product of unsurpassed quality. Most of us, however, are content with a less-than-optimal product. We want an automobile that is attractive, reliable, and performs well, but we do not insist on having the most exotic, luxurious, and high-performance model available. It is not just that we cannot afford such a vehicle, although for many of us this is a factor. Instead, we do not care so much for motorcars and simply want one that will reliably get us about town. Even if we possessed a vast fortune and could purchase any model we chose, we would still spend our time and energy on concerns other than automobiles.

Something similar applies in radiology. We could focus a great deal of time and energy on acquiring the very best equipment, maintaining it consummately, upgrading at every opportunity, and producing the very best images possible. To some extent, the field needs people who operate this way, to keep raising the bar. Yet many radiologists may judge that they can get by with less. That is, they do not need the absolute latest and best equipment to acquit themselves admirably as radiologists. They can make the diagnoses they need to make with equipment that is several years old, that does not have the latest upgrades, and whose images are not always appropriate for publication in the best journals. They recognize that, in most cases, the goal of the radiologist is not to produce the most aesthetically pleasing images, but to contribute to health care decision-making.[9]

Consider the implications of quality for imaging strategy. If the goal of imaging were to be as confident as possible that the patient harbors no radiologically detectable pathology, then every patient with a headache might need a brain MRI, every patient with a cough might need a chest CT, and many patients with a history of malignancy might need a PET/CT scan. In fact, even asymptomatic patients might need whole-body cross-sectional screening examinations, depending on the level of intolerance to letting lesions go undetected. However, the goal of imaging is not to enhance sensitivity to the highest possible level or to decrease diagnostic uncertainty to as low as level as possible. The goal of radiology at its best is to make valuable contributions to the medical care and health outcomes of patients. In many cases, when the pretest probability of disease is very low and the management implications are minimal, this may mean foregoing imaging entirely.

What is value, as opposed to quality? Value concerns the ratio of quality over price or cost.[10] In most circumstances in life, it makes sense to settle for less than the very best, because achieving the absolute highest level of quality is so costly that it quickly displaces other goods that are equally important. Even if it were within the realm of possibility, to become the world's greatest tennis player or pianist might require so many other sacrifices, including giving up the practice of medicine, that it is not a sacrifice radiologists would be prepared to make. If the clinical situation involves an acute, life-threatening diagnosis that mandates immediate and effective treatment—for example, a patient with suspected aortic dissection—and if imaging can confirm or rule out this diagnosis with a high degree of probability, then few compromises are warranted.

In other situations, however, less costly alternatives may be more appropriate. For example, in most cases of suspected skeletal fracture, two-view, orthogonal radiographs are adequate for radiological evaluation. If such radiographs are negative and clinical suspicion for fracture is high, additional views may be warranted. In high-stakes situations, such as suspected cervical spine injury or Lisfranc fracture, it may be appropriate to employ an additional modality, such as CT. However, in the vast majority of cases, the first-line imaging modality in suspected fracture should not be CT. It is ironic but true that the best is not in fact the best—that is, the highest-technology, most sensitive, and most costly examination is not the most appropriate choice for most patients. The issue is not just one of value, but one of appropriateness.

This principle is familiar to any experienced consumer. There are situations in which the highest-value purchase is not the most appropriate purchase. For example, it might be possible to maximize the ratio of quality over cost by purchasing a large quantity of a particular item. Suppose, for example, that we could procure the very best stockings for the lowest per-unit cost by purchasing a lot of 1,000 pairs. In absolute terms, purchasing 1,000 pairs would provide the best value. Yet value is not synonymous with appropriateness, and due to inconvenience, storage costs, and the improbability of using 1,000 pairs of socks in a lifetime, it would probably make sense to accept a somewhat higher unit cost and take home a lower number of items. Appropriateness, then, as distinct from value, is always defined in relation to the means and objectives of the people involved.

Discernment

Appropriateness is thus situational. It depends of the who, what, when, where, how, and why of the situation at hand. To determine an appropriate course of action requires knowledge of the specific circumstances. Is the patient a world-class athlete or a nursing home resident? Is the suspected lesion a disc herniation or a metastasis? Did the symptoms arise in the past few days or have they been present off and on for years? Are we practicing medicine in Miami, Florida, or rural Haiti? Are we seeing the case in the course of routine clinical practice or consulting on a medico-legal dispute? Is the patient seeking consultation to prove fitness for work or competition or in hopes of receiving compensation for injuries suffered on the job? Depending on the answers to such questions, the appropriate imaging recommendations may differ substantially.

In other words, discernment and judgment will remain an irreplaceable and irreducible aspect of high-quality radiology practice. Irreplaceable because, when it comes to applying general principles to particular situations, there is no substitute for a thorough understanding of the particulars. Irreducible because no level of detail and sophistication in clinical pathways, algorithms, and heuristics can ever equal the perspective of an expert who knows the distinctive features of the situation well. We want quality, but not at the expense of value. And we want value, but not at the expense of appropriateness. Ultimately, educating great radiologists means not only transferring knowledge and skills, but cultivating the faculty of discernment, which manifests itself nowhere more so than in an educator's level of respect and trust in their former pupils.

CONCLUSION

One implication is clear—health care cannot simply import the quality and safety methodologies of other businesses and industries. There is much to be learned from nonmedical sources, but medicine is a distinct field, marked by distinctive quality and safety considerations.[11] What works in manufacture, where the goal may be merely to reduce deviations from a standard, may not work in health care, where patients and providers differ from one another in important respects. Merely appointing quality and safety officers will not solve the problem either, although such individuals can make important contributions. For example, decreasing repeat rates and improving compliance with hand hygiene protocols represent important goals, but the practice of medicine cannot be entirely reduced to such parameters. Such quality specialists should not focus all of their time on developing rules and protocols, and should instead be available to consult with health professionals seeking to enhance quality. Such consultations would result in short-term quality improvements and, by fostering reflection and conversation about quality, provide important longer-term educational benefits.

Every physician has a professional responsibility to pursue improvements in quality, and doing so can be one of the most fulfilling aspects of a career, inasmuch as it can enrich the care of many patients and help colleagues practice better medicine. In pursuing quality, however, we must look beyond the low-hanging fruit of simplistic quality models. Thomas Pinchon once said, "If they can get you asking the wrong questions, they don't have to worry about the answers."[12] Physicians above all need to act as vigilant, creative, and energetic advocates for quality in the health care system. And doing so requires a rich understanding of the relationship between quality, value, and appropriateness, so that we focus quality improvement efforts on the most important questions. Doing so requires no less artistry than scientific rigor, and above all, the Zen-like quality of discernment.

REFERENCES

1. Pirsig R. *Zen and the art of motorcycle maintenance.* New York, NY: William Morrow, 1974.
2. Scott EA, Black N. When does consensus exist in expert panels? *J Pub Health Med.* 1991;13(1):35–39.
3. Lee JKT. Quality—A radiology imperative: Interpretation accuracy and pertinence. *J Am Coll Radiol.* 2007;3(4):162–65.
4. Lloyd G, ed., Chadwick, J, trans. *Hippocratic writings.* New York: Penguin Classics, 1978.
5. Beauchamp T, Childress J. *Principles of biomedical ethics,* 5th ed. New York: Oxford University Press, 2001.
6. Loberg M, Harvey E. Development of new radiopharmaceuticals based on N-substituation of iminodiacetic acid. *J Nucl Med.* 1976;17:633–8.
7. Ghaemi SN, Goodwin FK. The ethics of clinical innovation in psychopharmacology: Challenging traditional bioethics. *Philosophy Ethic, Humanities Med.* 2007;2:26.
8. Fryback DG, Thornbury JR. The efficacy of diagnostic imaging. *Med Decision Making.* 1991;11(2):88–94.
9. Poletti P, Platon A, Rutschmann, OT, Schmidlin, FR, Iselin, CE, Becker, CD. Low-dose versus standard-dose CT protocol in patients with clinically suspected renal colic. *AJR.* 2007;188:927–33.
10. Gunderman R, Boland G. Value in radiology. *Radiology.* 2009;253(3):597–9.
11. Erturk SM, Ondategui-Parra, S, Ros PR. Quality management in radiology: Historical aspects and basic definitions. *J Am Coll Radiol.* 2005;2(12):985–91.
12. Pynchon T. *Gravity's rainbow.* New York: The Viking Press, 1973.

INDEX

AAFP. *See* American Academy of Family Physicians
ABMS. *See* American Board of Medical Specialties
ABR. *See* American Board of Radiology
Abu-Alfa, Ali K., 282
ACC. *See* American College of Cardiology
Accreditation Council for Graduate Medical Education
    (ACGME), 12
  Outcome Project, 22
  peer review for, 118
accreditation requirements, for diagnostic radiology,
    81, 82
  ACR, 10
ACGME. *See* Accreditation Council for Graduate Medical
    Education
ACP. *See* American College of Physicians
ACR. *See* American College of Radiology
active failures, in diagnostic radiology, 100–101
  of execution, 100
  latent failures compared to, 99
  mistakes of intention, 101
Adams, John L., 227
adaptive section collimation, in CT, 135
adverse events, 93
  in interventional radiology, prevention of, 306, 310–311
    causes of, 307
  reporting systems for, 13
    in interventional radiology, 306
AEC techniques, with CT, 135–136
Agency for Healthcare Quality and Research (AHRQ), 4,
    212, 215
  just culture and, 52
  MGH pilot program and, survey for, 70, 72–73
AHIP. *See* America's Health Insurance Plan
ALARA principle. *See* "as low as reasonably achievable"
    principle
Alexander of Aphrodisias, 258
American Academy of Family Physicians (AAFP), 212
American Academy of Orthopaedic Surgeons, 112
American Board of Medical Specialties (ABMS), 118
  MOC by, 177, 216–217
    core areas for, 217
    pediatric radiology certification and, 292–293
    under PPACA, 217

American Board of Radiology (ABR), 12, 147
American College of Cardiology (ACC), 212
American College of Physicians (ACP), 212
American College of Radiology (ACR), 10, 12, 212
  accreditation programs of, 10
  appropriateness criteria, 231–232, 237
    for breast imaging, 237
    categorization of, 235
    conflict awareness in, 235
    as current, 235
    development of, 234–237
    group sources for, 234–235
    inappropriate imaging and, 233
    litigation fears and, 233–234
    for low back pain, 236
    obstacles to utilization of, 232–234
    patient preferences in, 233
    variant tables, 236
  communication standards, 60–61
    practice guidelines in, 61
    revisions for, 61
    technical, 61
  RADPEER program, 18, 122–123
American Recover and Reinvestment Act, 65
America's Health Insurance Plan (AHIP), 212, 218
angiography. *See* diagnostic angiography
apology, act of
  benefits of, 110
  definition of, 104, 105
    contemporary, 105
  disclosure and, 106–110
  elements of, 105–106
  after errors, 104
  in health care system, 104–105
  patient perspectives on, 107
  by physicians, as protective act, 107, 107–108
    "I am sorry I harmed you" laws, 108–109, 109, 108
    legislation and, 108–109
    malpractice claims, 108
  psychology of, 106
  utility of, 106
appointment setting, in radiology quality map, 8
apprenticeship, for clinical training, 245, 246

"as low as reasonably achievable" (ALARA) principle, 264
 for radiology dosage, during pregnancy, 321–323
Associates in Process Improvement, 24
asynchronous communication, in radiology, 65
ATNA Integration Profile. *See* Audit Trail and Node
        Authentication Integration Profile
at-risk behaviors, 56–57, 58
 incentives for, 56, 56–57, 57
 punishment responses to, 57
attributes charts, 201–204
audits
 in EBM, 260
 of performance improvement programs, 14–15
  for critical results communication, 64–65
Audit Trail and Node Authentication (ATNA) Integration
        Profile, 65, 66

balloon angioplasty, 180
Bayes, Thomas, 271
Bayes theorem, 271–272
Bernard, Claude, 256
Berwick, Donald, 197, 224, 226, 229
bias
 in EBR research, 279–280
 in peer review process, 121–122
Blackmore, Craig, 262, 293
"blame-free" culture, 52
bottom-up EBM, 260
Bradford-Hill criteria, 257
breasts, imaging for, 237
briefings, in CRM, 69
"bubble up" concept, in KPIs, 21

Caffey, John, 298
CAHPS. *See* Consumer Assessment of Healthcare Providers
        and Systems
California Integrated Health Care (IHC), 226–227
Campbell, Stephen, 227
Canadian Orthopaedic Association, 112
cancer, diagnostic radiology and, 127
 with CT, 127
 during pregnancy, 319
caregivers, on RCA teams, 40
Cascade, Philip, 124
CATs. *See* critically appraisal topics
C-chart, 202
Center for Medicare and Medicaid Services (CMS), 80, 81, 81,
        212–214
 IMAB, 211
 under MEDPAC, 211
 under MIPPA, 81, 212
 payment development strategies, 213
 radiology performance guidelines, 147
 VBP by, 213
cervical spine trauma, CT for, 132
chest, CT for, 132–133
clinical training. *See also* simulation, as medical practice
 for diagnostic radiology
  culture change and, 242–243
  future applications for, 244
  in MGH pilot program, 70–71

 at Penn State Hershey Medical Center, 242–243
  PQI projects for, 243–244
  purpose of, 241–242
  for quality and safety, 241–244
  systems-based, 241–242
  for systems performance predictions, transfer of training
        and, 188–189
  teamwork and, 76
 in health care, 245–246
  through apprenticeship, 245, 246
  principle of non-maleficence, 245–246
  through simulation, 246–252
 for interventional radiology, safety initiatives in, 310
  with simulation models, 310
closed loop information, in CRM, 69
CMS. *See* Center for Medicare and Medicaid Services
Cochrane, Archie, 257
color-coding
 in CQI, 32
 in dose reduction strategies, for CT, 130, 131
communication, in diagnostic radiology
 ACR standards, 60–61
  practice guidelines in, 61
  revisions for, 61
  technical, 61
 aspects of, 59
 asynchronous, 65
 for critical results, 62–65
  audits for, 64–65
  compliance guidelines for, 64–65
  with ED physicians, 65
  elements of, 64
  implementation of, 62
  methods of, 62–63
  NPSG for, 62–65
  policy development for, 63–64, 63
  requirements of, 62
 with CRMT, 66–67
  commercial availability for, 66
  early issues with, 66
  functional applications of, 66
  under HIPPA, 66
  IHE, 66
  PHI in, 66
  selection of, 67
  Veriphy, 66
 errors in, 97–99, 99
  in communication loop, 99–100
 function of, 59
 with information systems, 65–66
  ATNA Integration Profile, 65, 66
  EHRs, 65
  EMRs, 65
 legal issues for, 59–60
  liability in, 60
  for radiologists, 60
 of mammography reports, 61–62
  under MSQA, 61
 PCP reviews in, 60
 in peer review process, 121
 synchronous, 65

Communication Results Management Tool (CRMT), 66–67
  commercial availability for, 66
  early issues with, 66
  functional applications of, 66
  under HIPPA, 66
  IHE, 66
  PHI in, 66
  selection of, 67
    escalation algorithm for, 67
  Veriphy, 66
computed tomography (CT)
  appropriateness of, 127–128
  cancer risks with, 127
  for cervical spine trauma, 132
  for chest diseases, 132–133
  for craniosynostosis, 132
  CTDI for, 315
  deterministic risks with, 126–127
  DLP for, 315
  dose reduction strategies
    with adaptive section collimation, 135
    with AEC techniques, 135–136
    clinical indications from, 130–134
    color-coded protocol systems, 130, 131
    with FBP, 138
    for follow-up exams, 134–135
    gantry location adjustments, 137
    gantry rotation time and, 129
    historical background for, 126, 127
    magnitude of use for, 126
    with noise reduction filters, 137–138
    pitch in, 129
    protection agents in, 129–130
    risks and, 126–127
    scanning parameters for, 128–130, 128
    size based, 130
    with technology, 135–140
    with tube modulation, 136–137
    tube volume and, 129
  with fluoroscopy, 133
  for gastrointestinal abnormalities, 133
  for hydrocephalus, 132
  for orthopedic trauma, 134
  for paranasal sinus abnormalities, 132
  for perfusion, 132
  during pregnancy, 315
    dosing strategies for, 323–324
  stochastic risks with, 127
  for urinary tract abnormalities, 133–134
Computerized Physician Order Entry (CPOE) system, 212
  EHR in, 212
Consumer Assessment of Healthcare Providers and Systems (CAHPS), 225
continuous quality improvement (CQI)
  applications for, 8
  components of, 163
  functions of, 8, 29
  goals of, 27
  in health care, 163
  interventions in, 35–36

as iterative process, 36
process of, 29–30, 33
for quality and safety in care, 7–8
for radiologists
  color-coding, 32
  continuous philosophy, 32
  dashboards, 32
  data communication, 32, 36
  impact awareness, 32–33
  through leadership, 32
  plain film quality, as case study, 36–38, 36
  project selection by, 33
  pulmonary embolism, as case study, 33–34, 34, 34
  requisition history, as case study, 34–36, 35
  reward awareness, 32–33
roadblocks to, 30–31, 31–32
  distractions as, 30–31
  insufficient resources as, 31
  lack of training as, 30
  resource allocation in, 31
  work culture as, 31
control charts, 196, 197–206. See also Shewhart charts
  attributes, 201–204
  interpretation of, 199–200
    for type 1 errors, 199
    for type 2 errors, 199
  "out of specification" state in, 198–199
  run charts, 197–198
  selection criteria for, 200–204
    attributes charts, 201–204
    by query structure, 205
    variable charts, 201
  in SPC, 196
  variable, 201
cooperatives, quality of health care and, 215–216
  by region, 216
counseling, during pregnancy, 326
CPOE system. See Computerized Physician Order Entry system
CQI. See continuous quality improvement
craniosynostosis, CT for, 132
crew resource management (CRM), 69, 69–70
  briefings in, 69
  closed loop communication in, 69
  debriefing in, 69–70
  measurement of success with, 78
  SAQ in, 69
  SBAR communication in, 69
critically appraisal topics (CATs), 260
critical results, communication for, 64, 62–65
  audits for, 64–65
  compliance guidelines for, 64–65
  with ED physicians, 65
  elements of, 64
  implementation of, 62
  methods of, 62–63
  NPSG for, 62–65
  policy development for, 63–64, 63
  requirements of, 62
CRM. See crew resource management
CRMT. See Communication Results Management Tool

Crossing the Quality Chasm (IOM), 3, 223, 224
CT. *See* computed tomography
CT Dose Index (CTDI), 315
culture, of work environment
    for CQI, 31
    just culture, 13
    quality of care and, 295–296
    for safety, in diagnostic radiology, 27
customer surveys, in performance improvement programs, 20

dashboards. *See* performance dashboards
data communication, for CQI, 32, 36
debriefing, in CRM, 69–70
decision support (DS) tools, 168
delayed diffusion, in EBR, 262–264
deliberate practice, 246
    simulation in, 246–247
Deming, W. Edward, 3, 3, 9, 196
deterministic risks
    with CT, 126–127
    during pregnancy, from radiology, 317
diagnostic angiography, during pregnancy, 308, 323
diagnostic radiology. *See also* American College of Radiology;
        clinical training, for diagnostic radiology; computed
        tomography; dose reduction strategies; interventional
        radiology; pediatric radiology; radiologists; radiology
        quality map
    ABR performance guidelines, 147
    for breasts, 237
    cancer risks from, 127
    classification of errors in, 93, 95, 95–101
        active, 100–101
        in communication, 97–99, 99–100
        with documentation, 99
        with external causes, 101
        latent failures, 95, 97
        patient-based, 101
        Swiss Cheese model for, 95
        systems development for, 95
    clinical training for
        culture change and, 242–243
        future applications for, 244
        in MGH pilot program, 70–71
        at Penn State Hershey Medical Center, 242–243
        PQI projects for, 243–244
        purpose of, 241–242
        for quality and safety, 241–244
        systems-based, 241–242
        for systems performance, 185, 188–189, 193, 193–194
        teamwork and, 76
    CMS performance guidelines, 147
    communication in
        ACR standards, 60–61
        aspects of, 59
        asynchronous, 65
        for critical results, 62–65
        with CRMT, 66–67
        errors in, 97–99, 99–100
        function of, 59
        with information systems, 65–66
        legal issues for, 59–60

    of mammography reports, 61–62
    PCP reviews in, 60
    synchronous, 65
culture of safety in, 27
deterministic risks with, 126–127
development of, ix, 47
EBR, 264–265
    ALARA principle in, 264
    definition of, 262–264
    delayed diffusion in, 262–264
    evolution of, 263–264
    guidelines for, 283–284
    integration of, 264
    practice use for, 262–263
    research on, quality of, 279–280
    safety and, 280–283
errors in
    adverse events and, 93
    classification of, 93, 95–101
    consequences of, 101–102
    global considerations from, 102
    management of, 102
    morbidity rates from, 93
    near miss events and, 93–94
    patient impact from, 101
    as process-related, 94–95
    rates of, 94
    staff impact from, 101–102
    as system-related, 94–95
exposure limit recommendations, for adults, 296
JC and, 80–86
    accreditation requirements under, 81, 82
    future challenges for, 92
    for mammography reports, 81
    at MGH, 86–92
    NPSGs for, 82–86, 84–85
    nuclear medicine licensing guidelines, 81–82
    performance criteria for, 82–86, 147
    regulatory readiness for, 86
    for sentinel events, 82, 87
    standards for, 82–86
KPIs for, 27, 153–154, 151
    for financial management, 156
    for operations management, 154, 155
    for patient safety, 156
    PQRI guidelines, 153–154
    for stakeholder management, 157, 158
for low back pain, 236
medicinal theory *vs.* practice and, 258–259
patient perspectives on, analysis of, 48–51
    anxiety stressors, for patients, 49
    examination conclusion, 50
    for expectation setting, 49–50
    for follow-up procedures, 50–51
    for greetings, 49
    for imaging event, 50
    pre-arrival assessment in, 48–49
    site assessment in, 49
    technologist assessment, 49–50
pay for performance and, 228–229
    future applications for, 228–229

under PQRI, 228
peer review process in, 18, 118–123, 171
  bias minimization in, 121–122, 122
  case assignment in, 120
  case identification in, 120
  case/rating scoring in, 122, 123
  committee review, 120–121
  communication of decision in, 121
  decision-making in, 121
  development of, 119
  eRADPEER program, 122–123
  from external sources, 123
  method adaptation in, 121
  proactive method in, 119
  RADPEER program, 18, 122–123
  reactive method in, 119
  target input, 121
PIs for, 153–154, 159
  ABR guidelines, 147
  CMS guidelines, 147
  under JC, 82–86, 147
  KPIs, 27, 153–154
under PQRI, 214–215
  pay for performance and, 228
QC guidelines for, 6
quantitative, 284–285
RFMEA, 45, 44
simulation for, 248–252
  with ICTS, 250
  for interventional radiology, 250
  mannequin method, 250
  with Procedus Vist simulator, 251–252
  with VR, 249
stakeholders and, increased expectations with, 166
stochastic risks with, 127
training for
  in MGH pilot program, 70–71
  systems-based, 241–242
  teamwork and, 76
diagrams. See graphical tools, for quality and safety; Ishikawa
      diagram
direct financial incentives, in pay for performance models,
      225
disclosure, apology and, 106–110
DLP. See dose-length product
documentation errors, in diagnostic radiology, 99
  through inaccurate or incomplete information, 99
Doll, Richard, 257
Donald, Anna, 257
dose-length product (DLP), 315
dose reduction strategies, for CT
  with adaptive section collimation, 135
  with AEC techniques, 135–136
  clinical indications from, 130–134
  color-coded protocol systems, 130, 131
  with FBP, 138
  for follow-up exams, 134–135
  gantry location adjustments, 137
  gantry rotation time and, 129
  historical background for, 126, 127
  magnitude of use for, 126

  with noise reduction filters, 137–138
  pitch in, 129
  protection agents in, 129–130
  risks and, 126–127
  scanning parameters for, 128–130, 128
  size based, 130
  with technology, 135–140
  with tube modulation, 136–137
  tube volume and, 129
drifting, 54, 54
"drill down" concept, in KPIs, 21
  in RCA, 41
DS tools. See decision support tools

EBM. See evidence-based medicine
EBR. See evidence-based radiology
ED. See emergency department physicians
Eddington, Arthur, 262
electronic health record (EHR), 65
  in CPOE, 212
electronic medical record (EMR), 65
  imaging in, 171
emergency department (ED) physicians, 65
EMR. See electronic medical record
eRADPEER program, 122–123
errors
  apology after, 104
  causes of, 94
  classification of, in radiology, 93, 95, 95–101
    active, 100–101
    in communication, 97–99, 99–100
    with documentation, 99
    with external causes, 101
    latent failures, 95, 97
    patient-based, 101
    Swiss Cheese model for, 95
    systems development for, 95
  common myths about, 94, 94–95
  definition of, 93
  in diagnostic radiology
    adverse events and, 93
    classification of, 93, 95–101
    consequences of, 101–102
    global considerations from, 102
    management of, 102
    morbidity rates from, 93
    near miss events and, 93–94
    patient impact from, 101
    as process-related, 94–95
    rates of, 94
    staff impact from, 101–102
    as system-related, 94–95
  lapses, 100
  in medical practices, 94
  mistakes of intention, 101
  slips, 100
  type 1, in control charts, 199
  type 2, in control charts, 199
escalation algorithm, for CRMT, 67
ethics, quality and, 332–336
Evidence-based Imaging (Medina/Blackmore), 262

evidence-based medicine (EBM)
  during 19th century, 256–257
  during 20th century, 257
  audit cycles in, 260
  bottom-up, 260
  CATs in, 260
  as clinical, 259
  clinical epidemiology and, 256–257
    bloodletting study as, 256
  contingency table for, 268
  criticisms of, 261
  definitions of, 255, 257
  diagnostic pathways in, 271–273
    with Bayes theorem, 271–272
  diagnostic tests
    evidence levels in studies, 278
    hierarchy of studies, 273
    indices, 269
  EBR, 264–265
    ALARA principle in, 264
    definition of, 262–264
    delayed diffusion, 262–264
    evolution of, 263–264
    guidelines for, 283–284
    integration of, 264
    practice use for, 262–263
    research on, quality of, 279–280
    safety and, 280–283
  HTA in, 273–279
    with decisional analysis, 277
    degrees of recommendations in, 277–279, 278
    evidence levels in, 277–279
    international applications for, 276
    with pragmatic studies, 277
    with six-level scale, 273–277
  interventional radiology and, 264
  lead time bias in, 265
  length bias in, 265
  limitations of, 260–261
  overdiagnosis and, 265–267
  overtreatment and, 264–265
  patient perspectives and, 259
  philosophy of, 255
  principles of, 255
  quality measures for, 268–271, 267–268
    with asymptomatic population, 270–271
    with general organized screening, 270
    with symptomatic population, 271
  random sampling in, 257
  RCTs in, 261–262
  top-down, 259–260
evidence-based radiology (EBR), 264–265
  ALARA principle in, 264
  definition of, 262–264
  delayed diffusion in, 262–264
  evolution of, 263–264
  guidelines for, 283–284
    organizations for, 283–284
  integration of, 264
  practice use for, 262–263

research on, quality of, 279–280
  bias in, 279–280
  in STARD initiative, 280
safety and, 280–283
  NSF and, 281–283
  for patients, 280–281

failure modes, in Healthcare FMEA, 43
  hazard analysis for, 44
  scoring matrix for, 44, 44
FBP. See filtered back projection
FDA. See Food and Drug Administration
filtered back projection (FBP), 138
"first do no harm." See principle of non-maleficence, in health
    care
Fisher, Ronald A., 257
Five Rules of Causation, 41, 42
Fleming, Alexander, 94
Flexner, Abraham, 245
flow charts
  for quality and safety, 4–6, 4–6
    function of, 6
    Pareto chart, 6
    Shewhart charts, 4–5
  in RCA, 41
fluoroscopy, with CT, 133, 180–181
FMEA. See Healthcare Failure Mode and Effect Analysis
focused professional practice evaluation (FPPE), 117
Food and Drug Administration (FDA), 61, 81
FPPE. See focused professional practice evaluation
Funstein, Alvan, 285

gadolinium-based contrast agents (GBCAs), 281–283
Galen of Pergamon, 258
gastrointestinal abnormalities, CT for, 133
Gauss, Carl, 162
GBCAs. See gadolinium-based contrast agents
G-chart, 202–203
GIC. See Group Performance Commission
Goffman, Erving, 105
Google, Inc., ix
Goske, Marilyn, 296
governments, quality of care through, 210–211
  through CMS, 80, 81, 81, 212–214
    IMAB, 211
    under MEDPAC, 211
    under MIPPA, 81, 212
    payment development strategies, 213
    radiology performance guidelines, 147
    VBP by, 213
  at federal level, 210
  at legislative level, 211
    appropriateness criteria development, 212
    MIPPA, 81, 212
    physician compliance under, tools for, 212
    PPACA, 211
  through regulatory agencies, 212–215
    AHRQ, 4, 212, 215
    CMS, 80, 81, 81, 212–214
    HOPQDRP, 214

PQRI, 153–154, 214–215
  at state and regional level, 215–216
    with cooperatives, 215–216
    with RHIOs, 216
grand rounds, in QA, 22–24
graphical tools, for quality and safety, 4–6. *See also* flow
    charts, for quality and safety
  histograms, 5–6
  Ishikawa diagram, 4
  radiology quality map, 8–9
  scatter plots, 6
Greenhalgh, Trisha, 257
Group Performance Commission (GIC), 227
Guyatt, Gordon, 257, 257

Halsted, William Stuart, 245
Hawthorne Effect, 179
hazard analysis, for Healthcare FMEA, 44
  failure modes in, 44
  scoring matrix for, 44, 44
HCUP. *See* health care utilization project
health care. *See also* patient perspectives, on health care;
    quality of care
  apology in, impact of, 104–105
  clinical training for, 245–246
    through apprenticeship, 245, 246
    principle of non-maleficence in, 245–246
    through simulation, 246–252
  consumer revolution in, 47–48
    for customer service, 47
    in technical knowledge, of patients, 47–48
  CQI in, 163
  lean management methodology for, 162–164
  Lean Six Sigma management strategy in, 163–164
  PIs for, 148–153
    for care providers, 150
    development of, 149–152
    implementation of, 152–153
    outcome as, 148–149
    for patients, 150
    pitfalls in, 157–159
    process as, 149
    structure as, 149
    for third-party payers, 150
    variations in interpretation for, 154–157
  under PPACA, 211
  professionalism in, foundations of, x
  quality assessment of, 147–148
  Six Sigma management strategy for, 162–164
    implementation costs for, 163
  SPC in, 197
  TQM in, 3, 163
Healthcare Effectiveness Data and Information Set (HEDIS),
  225
Healthcare Failure Mode and Effect Analysis (FMEA), 43–45
  failure modes in, 43
    in hazard analysis, 44
    scoring matrix for, 44, 44
  functional goals of, 43
  hazard analysis for, 44

    failure modes in, 44
    scoring matrix for, 44, 44
  outcome measures in, 44–45
  process description in, 44
  RFMEA, 45
    five steps of, 44
  team assembly in, 44
  topic definition in, 43–44
  US Veteran's Administration use of, 43
health care utilization project (HCUP), 4
Health Insurance Portability and Accountability Act
  (HIPPA), 66
health technology assessment (HTA), 273–279
  with decisional analysis, 277
  degrees of recommendations in, 277–279, 278
  evidence levels in, 277–279
  international applications for, 276
  with pragmatic studies, 277
  with six-level scale, 273–277
    cost-effectiveness in, 275
HEDIS. *See* Healthcare Effectiveness Data and Information
  Set
"highly punitive" culture, 52
High Value Health Care (HVHC) project, 220
Hill, Austin Bradford, 257
HIPPA. *See* Health Insurance Portability and Accountability
  Act
histograms, for quality and safety, 5–6
Hospital Outpatient Quality Data Reporting Program
  (HOPQDRP), 214
human behavior, in just culture, 53
  at-risk behaviors, 56–57, 58
  human error, 55–56, 58
  job performance reliability, 55
  punishment responses to, 57–58
  reckless behaviors, 57, 58
  risk management for, 55–58
  stress as influence on, 55–56
human error, 55–56, 58. *See also* active failures, in
  diagnostic radiology; errors, in diagnostic radiology
HVHC project. *See* High Value Health Care project
hydrocephalus, CT for, 132

IAC. *See* Intersocial Accreditation Commission
IAEA. *See* International Atomic Energy Agency
"I am sorry I harmed you" laws, 108–109, 109, 108
  radiologists under, 109
ICTS. *See* Interventional Cardiology Training System
IHC. *See* California Integrated Health Care
IHE. *See* Integrating Healthcare Enterprise
IMAB. *See* Independent Medicare Advisory Board
imaging. *See* diagnostic radiology
Independent Medicare Advisory Board (IMAB), 211
indirect financial incentives, in pay for performance models,
  225
inferior vena cava (IVC) filters, 308
information systems, for radiology communication, 65–66
  ATNA Integration Profile, 65, 66
  EHRs, 65
  EMRs, 65

Institute for Safe Medication Practices (ISMP), 44
Institute of Medicine (IOM), 219–220
    Crossing the Quality Chasm, 3, 223, 224
    To Err is Human: Building a Safer Health System, ix, 3, 28,
        219, 223
        system reform in, 224
    manifesto of, 107, 219
institutional leadership
    in performance improvement programs, 12–13
        through just culture, 13
        staff engagement under, 13
        with team formation, 13
    for radiologists, with CQI, 32
Integrating Healthcare Enterprise (IHE), 66
intentional risk behavior. *See* drifting
International Atomic Energy Agency (IAEA), 221
International Organization for Standards (ISO), 220
International Society for Quality in Health Care (ISQua), 220
Intersocial Accreditation Commission (IAC), 81
Intersociety Conference, 4
Interventional Cardiology Training System (ICTS), 250
interventional radiology, 250
    adverse events in, prevention of, 306, 310–311
        causes of, 307
    device safety with, 309–310
    EBM and, 264
    evolution of technology for, 308–309
    with ICTS, 250
    indicator thresholds in, 307–308
        for central venous access, 308
        for diagnostic angiography, 308
        for IVC filters, 308
        for percutaneous catheter embolization, 308
    M&M reviews for, 304–305
    practice guidelines for, 302–303
    QA programs for, 303–304
    quality in, 302
        at organizational level, 302–303
    safety in, 302
        clinical indicators for, 305
        of devices, 309–310
        practice guidelines for, 305
        with simulation models, 310
        in training programs, 310
    SIR guidelines for, 306, 304
        for medication labeling, 306
        UP applications under, 306
intrinsic values, professionalism from, x
IOM. *See* Institute of Medicine
ionizing radiation, during pregnancy, 316–317
IRT. *See* Item Response Theory
Ishikawa diagram, 4
ISMP. *See* Institute for Safe Medication Practices
ISO. *See* International Organization for Standards
ISQua. *See* International Society for Quality in Health Care
Item Response Theory (IRT), 182–183

IVC filters. *See* inferior vena cava filters
JC. *See* Joint Commission
JCAHO. *See* Joint Commission on Accreditation of
    Healthcare Organizations

job performance reliability, 55
Joint Commission (JC)
    CMS and, 80, 81, 81
    diagnostic radiology and, 80–86
        accreditation requirements for, 81, 82
        future challenges for, 92
        mammography report guidelines, 81
        at MGH, 86–92
        NPSGs for, 82–86, 84–85
        nuclear medicine licensing guidelines for, 81–82
        performance criteria for, 82–86, 147
        regulatory readiness for, 86
        sentinel event response, 82, 87
        standards for, 82–86
    establishment of, 80
    functions of, 80–81
    at MGH, 86–92
        priority setting at, 89–91
        regulatory readiness maintenance for, 91–92
        safety reporting at, 92
    peer review process under, 117
    RCA use by, 39–40
    UP and, 111
Joint Commission on Accreditation of Healthcare
        Organizations (JCAHO), 52
Juran, Joseph, 196
just culture, 13
    accountability in, 52–53, 54–55
    AHRQ and, 52
    beliefs in, 53–55
        accountability, 52–53, 54–55
        drifting as realistic event, 54
        error as realistic event, 54
        management support of value system, 54
        progress measures, 55
        risk events, likelihood of, 54
    commitment to, 58
    function of, 52–53
    human behavior in, 53
        at-risk behaviors, 56–57, 58
        human error, 55–56, 58
        job performance reliability, 55
        punishment responses to, 57–58
        reckless behaviors, 57, 58
        risk management for, 55–58
        stress as influence on, 55–56
    JCAHO and, 52
    learning systems for, 52
    as model, philosophy of, 58
    system design for, 53

KAP. *See* kerma area product
Kaplan, Robert, 24
kerma area product (KAP), 181–182
key performance indicators (KPIs), 152
    for diagnostic radiology, 27, 153–154, 151
        for financial management, 156
        for operations management, 154, 155
        for patient safety, 156
        PQRI guidelines, 153–154
        for stakeholder management, 157, 158

implementation of, 152–153
in performance improvement programs, 20–22
    "bubble up" concept in, 21
    development of, 21
    "drill down" concept in, 21
    goals of, 21, 22
    management of, 21
    mission statement for, 21
    objectives for, 21
    optimization of, 21
    strategic planning for, 21
for physician peer review, 20
for radiologists, 172
knowledge-based mistakes, 101
Kohn, Alfie, 226
KPIs. *See* key performance indicators
Krafcik, John, 161
Kucharczyk, Walter, 282

lapses, in errors, 100
latent failures, in diagnostic radiology, 95, 97
active compared to, 99
system, 97
technical, 97
laws. *See also* governments, quality of care through
communication in radiology and, 59–60
    court assessment of, for radiologists, 60
    liability in, 60
"I am sorry I harmed you" laws, 108–109, 109, 108
for quality of health care, 211
    appropriateness criteria development, 212
    MIPPA, 81, 212
    under MIPPA, 212
    physician compliance under, tools for, 212
    PPACA, 211
leadership, 75. *See also* institutional leadership
lead time bias, in EBM, 265
lean management methodology, 8, 10, 161–162
development of, 10
goals of, 161
for health care, 162–164
mistake proofing in, 10
principles of, 10, 161, 161
production leveling in, 10
value stream mapping in, 10
waste and, types of, 161
Lean Six Sigma management strategy, in health care, 163–164
learning systems, for just culture, 52
Leiner, Tim, 282
length bias, in EBM, 265
Louis, Pierre C.A., 256, 258
low back pain, imaging for, 236

magnetic resonance imaging (MRI), 316, 320–321
dosing strategies for, 324–325
Maimonides, 106
Maintenance of Certification (MOC), 177, 216–217
core areas for, 217
for pediatric radiology, 292–293
under PPACA, 217
malpractice claims, apologies by physicians and, 108

"I am sorry I harmed you" laws, 108–109, 109, 108
    legislation for, 108–109
Mammography Quality Standard Act (MQSA), 61, 81
mammography reports, 61–62
    JC guidelines for, 81
    under MSQA, 61
mannequin method, of simulation, 248, 250
Marx, David, 13, 13
Massachusetts Coalition for the Prevention of Medical Errors (MCPME), 63
Massachusetts Health Quality Partner (MHQP), 225
Massachusetts Medical Society (MMS), 227
MCPME. *See* Massachusetts Coalition for the Prevention of Medical Errors
Medicaid. *See* Center for Medicare and Medicaid Services
medical errors, 94
Medicare. *See* Center for Medicare and Medicaid Services
Medicare Improvements for Patients and Providers Act (MIPPA), 81, 212
Medicare Payment Advisory Commission (MEDPAC), 211
medicine. *See also* evidence-based medicine
theory *vs.* practice in, 258–259
    diagnostic radiology and, 258–259
Medina, L. Santiago, 262
MEDPAC. *See* Medicare Payment Advisory Commission
metrics, for quality and safety, 4
AHRQ guidelines for, 4
assessment guidelines for, 4
HCUP, 4
in pediatric radiology, 293–294
MGH pilot program
under JC guidelines, for diagnostic radiology applications, 86–92
    priority setting in, 89–91
    regulatory readiness maintenance for, 91–92
    safety reporting in, 92
teamwork process in, 70–72
    AHRQ survey of, 70, 72–73
    framing in, 70
    observational scores for, 73–75
    SAQs in, 70
    sustainment measures in, 71–72
    training in, 70–71
MHQP. *See* Massachusetts Health Quality Partner
Miller, Donald, 306
MIPPA. *See* Medicare Improvements for Patients and Providers Act
mistake proofing, in lean management, 10
mistakes, of intention, 101
    knowledge-based, 101
    motivation-based, 101
    substitution test for, 101
M&M reviews. *See* mortality and morbidity reviews
MMS. *See* Massachusetts Medical Society
MOC. *See* Maintenance of Certification
Morabia, Alfred, 256
mortality and morbidity (M&M) reviews, 304–305
motivation-based mistakes, 101
MQSA. *See* Mammography Quality Standard Act
MRI. *See* magnetic resonance imaging
Mullen, Kathleen, 227

mutagenesis, from radiation during pregnancy, 318
mystery shoppers, in performance improvement programs, 20

National Committee for Quality Assurance (NCQA), 219
National Council on Radiation Protection (NCRP), 126
National Patient Safety Goals (NPSG), 13–14
    for critical results communication of, 62–65
    under JC, 82–86, 84–85
    performance improvement program compliance under, 15–16
    requirements of, 62
National Quality Forum (NQF), 82, 83, 218–219
NCQA. See National Committee for Quality Assurance
NCRP. See National Council on Radiation Protection
near miss events, 93–94
nephrogenic systemic fibrosis (NSF), 281–283
    from GBCAs, 281–283
noise reduction filters, in CT, 137–138
Northway, William, 298
Norton, David, 24
NP-chart, 201–202
NPSG. See National Patient Safety Goals
NQF. See National Quality Forum
NRC. See Nuclear Regulatory Commission
NSF. See nephrogenic systemic fibrosis
nuclear medicine
    licensing guidelines for, 81–82
    during pregnancy, 315–316, 319–320
        dosing strategies for, 324, 324
Nuclear Regulatory Commission (NRC), 81–82

Obama, Barack, 211
ongoing professional practice evaluation (OPPE), 117
    for performance assessment, 182–183
        IRT in, 182–183
        simulation-based, 177
on-the-job training, in systems performance predictions, 193
OPPE. See ongoing professional practice evaluation
orthopedic trauma, CT for, 134
Outcome Project, ACGME, 22
"out of specification" state, in control charts, 198–199

PacifiCare Health Systems, 226–227
PACS. See picture archiving and communication systems
PACS system, ix
paranasal sinus abnormalities, for CT, 132
Pareto chart, 6
patient perspectives, on health care
    for apologies from medical personnel, 107
    consumer revolution and, 47–48
        for customer service, 47
        in technical knowledge, of patients, 47–48
    diagnostic radiology errors and, 101–102
    for EBM, 259
    patient needs and, 48
    pay for performance, criticism of, 226
    PIs in, 150
    radiologists and, 169–170
    radiology appropriateness and, 233
    for radiology services, analysis of, 48–51
        anxiety stressors, for patients, 49

examination conclusion, 50
for expectation setting, 49–50
for follow-up procedures, 50–51
for greetings, 49
for imaging event, 50
pre-arrival assessment in, 48–49
site assessment in, 49
technologist assessment, 49–50
Patient Protection and Affordable Care Act (PPACA), 211
    ABMS MOC under, 217
    IMAB under, 211
patient safety, guiding principles for, 26–27
pay for performance
    in California IHC, 226–227
    criticism of, 225–226
        by patient advocacy groups, 226
        by physicians, 226
    definition of, 223–224
    drivers in, 224
        costs as, 224
        quality and safety as, 224
    future applications for, 229
        with radiology, 228–229
    in GIC, 227
    measures in, 225
        CAHPS, 225
        depth of, 226
        HEDIS, 225
        MHQP, 225
        PCPI, 225
    models of, 224–225
        direct incentives, 225
        indirect incentives, 225
    in PacifiCare Health Systems, 226–227
    "quality and safety" movement and, 223
    radiology and, 228–229
        future applications for, 228–229
        under PQRI, 228
    in UK health care systems, 227
"pay for performance" plans, 27–28
P-chart, 201–202
PCPI. See Physician Consortium for Performance Improvement
PCP reviews. See primary care physician reviews
PDSA cycle. See Plan-Do-Study-Act cycle
pediatric radiology
    under ABR MOC guidelines, 292–293
    for acute appendicitis, as case study, 296–298
    definition of, 291–292
    evolution of, 296–298
    exposure limit recommendations for, 296
    initial qualifications for, 292
    organizational culture and, 295–296
    quality in, 291
        improvement initiatives for, 298
        metrics for, 293–294
        production model for, 293
        professional model for, 293
        QA for, 296
    reports, 294–295

content of, 295
structure of, 294–295
peer review process, 17–18, 117–118
    for ACGME, 118
    definition of, 118
    in diagnostic radiology, 18, 118–123, 171
        bias minimization in, 121–122, 122
        case assignment in, 120
        case identification in, 120
        case/rating scoring in, 122, 123
        committee review, 120–121
        communication of decision in, 121
        decision-making in, 121
        development of, 119
        eRADPEER program, 122–123
        from external sources, 123
        method adaptation in, 121
        proactive method in, 119
        RADPEER program, 18, 122–123
        reactive method in, 119
        target input, 121
    under JC, 117
    limitations of, 124
    measurement tools for, 118
    morbidity in, 22
    mortality in, 22
    for physicians, 18, 20
    quality assurance elective programs in, 22
Penn State Hershey Medical Center, 242–243
performance assessment. See also health technology
        assessment
    OPPE for, 182–183
        IRT in, 182–183
        in simulation-based assessment, 177
    for physicians, 175–176
        Hawthorne Effect in, 179
        observed event conversion in, 179
        score conversion in, 179
        simulation-based, 177–178
        test stimuli in, 177
        validity of, 176
        in workplace, 178–179
    for radiologists
        during fluoroscopic procedures, 180–181
        KAP and, 181–182
        of radiation use from daily work, 181–182
        with RIS, 181
        in workplace, 180
performance dashboards, 196, 206–208
    in CQI, 32
    functions of, 207
    scorecards compared to, 206
    in SPC, 196
performance improvement programs, 12
    Associates in Process Improvement, 24
    customer surveys for, 20
    educational components of, 22–24
        ACGME Outcome Project, 22
    institutional leadership in, 12–13
        through just culture, 13

staff engagement under, 13
with team formation, 13
KPIs in, 20–22
    "bubble up" concept in, 21
    development of, 21
    "drill down" concept in, 21
    goals of, 21, 22
    management of, 21
    mission statement for, 21
    objectives for, 21
    optimization of, 21
    for physician peer review, 20
    strategic planning for, 21
monitoring of, 12
mystery shoppers in, 20
peer review process in, 17–18
    morbidity in, 22
    mortality in, 22
    for physicians, 18
    for radiologists, 18
quality assurance elective programs, 22
    grand rounds, 22–24
safety issues in, 13–16
    adverse event reporting systems in, 13
    audits of, 14–15
    NPSG compliance, 15–16
    result communication systems for, 13–14
    risk reporting mechanisms for, 15
    walkabouts for, 15
performance indicators (PIs). See also key performance
        indicators
    development of, 149–152, 148
        aspect of care selection in, 150–151
        assessment team organization in, 150
        clinical area choice in, 150
        indicator specifications in, 151
        preliminary testing in, 151–152
        scoring in, 152
        stakeholder definition in, 149–150
    for diagnostic radiology, 153–154, 159
        ABR guidelines, 147
        CMS guidelines, 147
        under JC, 82–86, 147
        KPIs, 153–154, 151
        PQRI guidelines, 153–154
    for health care, 148–153
        for care providers, 150
        development of, 149–152
        implementation of, 152–153
        outcome as, 148–149
        for patients, 150
        pitfalls in, 157–159
        process as, 149
        structure as, 149
        for third-party payers, 150
        variations in interpretation for, 154–157
perfusion, CT for, 132
PHI. See protected health information
Physician Consortium for Performance Improvement
        (PCPI), 218
    in pay for performance, 225

Physician Insurers Association of America (PIAA), 60
Physician Quality Reporting Initiative (PQRI), 153–154,
        214–215
    for radiology, 214–215
        pay for performance, 228
    TRHCA and, 214
physicians. *See also* teamwork
    apology by, as protection, 107, 107–108
        "I am sorry I harmed you" laws, 108–109, 109, 108
        legislation for, 108–109
        malpractice claims and, 108
    ED, critical results communication with, 65
    intrinsic values of, professionalism as, x
    legal compliance of, for health care legislation, 212
        with CPOE, 212
    pay for performance for, criticism of, 226
    peer review process for, 18, 20, 117–118
        under ACGME, 118
        definition of, 118
        under JC, 117
        KPIs in, 20
        limitations of, 124
        measurement tools for, 118
        morbidity in, 22
        mortality in, 22
    performance assessment for, 175–176
        Hawthorne Effect in, 179
        observed event conversion in, 179
        score conversion in, 179
        simulation-based, 177–178
        test stimuli in, 177
        validity of, 176
        in workplace, 178–179
    on RCA teams, 40
PIAA. *See* Physician Insurers Association of America
picture archiving and communication systems (PACS),
        170–171
Pirsig, Robert, 332
PIs. *See* performance indicators
pitch, in CT, 129
plain film quality, with CQI, 36–38, 36
Plan-Do-Study-Act (PDSA) cycle, 3, 9
    in QI, 8
    for RCA, 42
PPACA. *See* Patient Protection and Affordable Care Act
PQI projects, for radiology training, 243–244
PQRI. *See* Physician Quality Reporting Initiative
pregnancy, radiology use during
    clinical uses of, 314
    dosing strategies for, 321–325, 322
        ALARA principle in, 321–323
        for angiography, 323
        for CT, 323–324
        nuclear medicine, 324, 324
        ultrasonography, 324–325
    effects of, 316–321
        carcinogenesis, 319
        from contrast agents, 319
        deterministic risks, 317
        by gestation phase, 318
        from ionizing radiation, 316–317

        mutagenesis, 318
        teratogenesis, 318–319
    quantitative exposure measures, 314–316
        for conventional radiology, 314–315
        with CT, 315
        with MRI, 316, 320–321
        with nuclear medicine, 315–316, 319–320
        with ultrasonography, 316, 320
    recommendation guidelines for, 325–327
        for patient counseling, 326
        for risk information, 326–327
        with standard practice protocols, 325–326
primary care physician (PCP) reviews, 60
principle of non-maleficence, in health care, 245–246
private sector, quality health care efforts and, 216–218
    ABMS MOC, 177, 216–217
        core areas for, 217
        under PPACA, 217
    AHIP, 212, 218
    PCPI, 218
    private health care plans, 217–218
Procedus Vist simulator, 251–252
production leveling, in lean management, 10
professionalism
    as intrinsic value, x
    in "quality and safety" movement, x
    for radiologists, x
protected health information (PHI), 66
pulmonary embolism, CQI for, 33–34, 34, 34
punishment responses, in risk management, 57–58
    for at-risk behaviors, 57, 58
    to reckless behaviors, 57–58, 58
Pynchon, Thomas, 337

QA. *See* quality assurance
QC. *See* quality control
QI. *See* quality improvement
"quality and safety" movement, ix, ix
    core concepts in, ix
    foundations for, x
    patient safety issues, 26–27
    pay for performance and, 223
    professionalism in, x
    program development in, ix
quality assurance (QA)
    elective programs, 22
    grand rounds, 22–24
    for interventional radiology, 303–304
    NCQA, 219
    for pediatric radiology, 296
    for quality and safety in care, 6–7
quality control (QC)
    for diagnostic radiology, 6
    for quality and safety in care, 6
quality improvement (QI). *See also* performance improvement
            programs; radiologists
    CQI
        applications for, 8
        functions of, 8, 29
        goals of, 27
        interventions in, 35–36

as iterative process, 36
process of, 29–30
for quality and safety in care, 7–8
roadblocks to, 30–31, 31–32
functional applications for, 8
with lean management, 8, 10
methodologies for, 8
with PDSA, 3, 9
for quality and safety in care, 7–8
RCA in, 10
with Six Sigma, 9–10
quality of care, 10
accuracy in, 333
ACR guidelines for, 10
appropriateness in, 335–336
CQI of, 7–8
definition of, 3, 210
discernment in, 336
effectors of, 210
efficacy in, 334–335
efficiency in, 334
flow charts in, 4–6
governmental influences on, 210–211
through CMS, 80, 81, 81, 212–214
at federal level, 210
IMAB as, 211
at legislative level, 211
through regulatory agencies, 212–215
at state and regional level, 215–216
graphical tools for, 4–6
in international contexts, 220–221
through IAEA, 221
under ISO, 220
ISQua, 220
by WHO, 220–221
in interventional radiology, 302
at organizational level, 302–303
laws for, 211
appropriateness criteria development, 212
MIPPA, 81, 212
physician compliance under, tools for, 212
PPACA, 211
metrics for, 4
organizational culture and, 295–296
pay for performance and, 224
in pediatric radiology, 291
improvement initiatives for, 298
metrics for, 293–294
production model for, 293
professional model for, 293
QA for, 296
precision in, 333
in private sector, 216–218
through ABMS MOC, 177, 216–217
through AHIP, 212, 218
through PCPI, 218
through private health care plans, 217–218
QA for, 6–7
QC for, 6
QI in, 7–8
with quasi-governmental organizations, 218–220

IOM, ix, 3, 3, 28, 219, 219–220
NCQA, 219
NQF, 82, 83, 218–219
research by, 220
safety as aspect of, 333–334
"structure, process, outcome" algorithm for, 291
systems failures in, 3–4
TQM for, 3
training for, in diagnostic radiology, 241–242
culture change and, 242–243
future applications for, 244
at Penn State Hershey Medical Center, 242–243
PQI projects for, 243–244
quantitative radiology, 284–285
"quick fix" design implementation, in RCA, 41

radiologists. See also American College of Radiology;
teamwork
communication in radiology, legal liability of, 60
CQI for
color-coding in, 32
continuous philosophy in, 32
dashboards in, 32
data communication in, 32, 36
impact awareness in, 32–33
through leadership, 32
for plain film quality, as case study, 36–38, 36
project selection in, 33
for pulmonary embolism, as case study, 33–34, 34, 34
requisition history for, as case study, 34–36, 35
reward awareness in, 32–33
under "I am sorry I harmed you" laws, 109
imaging and
dosing and, 168–169
with DS tools, 168
EMRs and, 171
interpretation issues, 170–171
modality safety and, 170
with PACS, 170–171
patient access and, 169–170
procedural safety and, 170, 172
protocols for, 168
report formatting and delivery, 172, 171–172
utilization management by, 167–168
KPIs for, 172
patient safety and, 28
peer review process for, 18, 118–123, 171
bias minimization in, 121–122, 122
case assignment in, 120
case identification in, 120
case/rating scoring in, 122, 123
committee review, 120–121
communication of decision in, 121
decision-making in, 121
development of, 119
eRADPEER program, 122–123
from external sources, 123
method adaptation in, 121
proactive method in, 119
RADPEER program, 18, 122–123
reactive method in, 119

radiologists (*Cont.*)
    target input, 121
    performance assessment for
        during fluoroscopic procedures, 180–181
        KAP and, 181–182
        of radiation use from daily work, 181–182
        with RIS, 181
        in workplace, 180
    professionalism for, x
    quality and safety factors for, 167
        KPIs in, 172
        for patients, 28
radiology. *See* diagnostic radiology; interventional radiology;
        pediatric radiology; quantitative radiology
radiology benefit management (RBM), 212
radiology Failure Mode and Effect Analysis (RFMEA), 44
Radiology Information System (RIS), 181
radiology quality map, 8–9
    appointment setting in, 8
    communication in, 9
    examination protocol in, 9
    examination selection in, 8
    imaging performance in, 9
    interpretation of examination in, 9
    office encounter in, 8–9
    report finalization in, 9
RADPEER program, 18, 122–123
randomized clinical trials (RCTs), 261–262
RBM. *See* radiology benefit management
RCA. *See* root cause analysis
RCTs. *See* randomized clinical trials
Reason, James, 94, 95
reckless behaviors, 57, 58
    punishment responses to, 57–58
regional health information organizations (RHIOs),
        216
reports, by radiologists, 171–172
    with voice recognition, 172
requisition history, in CQI, 34–36, 35
result communication systems, in performance improvement
        programs, 13–14
RFMEA. *See* radiology Failure Mode and Effect Analysis
RHIOs. *See* regional health information organizations
RIS. *See* Radiology Information System
risk management, human behaviors for, 55–58
    at-risk behaviors, 56–57, 58
    human error, 55–56, 58
    job performance reliability, 55
    punishment responses to, 57–58
    reckless behaviors, 57, 58
    stress as influence on, 55–56
risk-reduction strategies, from RCA, 41–42
    Six Thinking Hats process, 41
risk reporting mechanisms, in performance improvement
        programs, 15
Roentgen, Wilhelm, 285
root cause analysis (RCA), 10, 39–43, 40
    communication of results for, 43
    definitions of, 39
    event definition in, 40
    event-related processes in, identification of, 41

    flow charts for, 41
    functional goals of, 39–40
    improvement action plan, 42–43
        evaluation of, 42
        PDSA cycle for, 42
    JC use of, 39–40
    limitations of, 43
    proximate cause identification in, 41
    "quick fix" design implementation in, 41
    results evaluation for, 43
    risk-reduction strategies from, 41–42
        Six Thinking Hats process, 41
    root cause identification, 41
        contributing causes, 41
        "drill down" concept for, 41
        Five Rules of Causation in, 41, 42
        presumptive causes, 41
    sentinel events in, 40
    as structured process, 39
    for systems-related issues, 41
    team organization for, 40
        with caregivers, 40
        with physicians, 40
run charts, 197–198

Sackett, Dave L., 257, 257
safety, in care, 10. *See also* patient safety, guiding principles for
    CQI of, 7–8
    definition of, 3
    EBR and, 280–283
        NSF and, 281–283
        for patients, 280–281
    flow charts in, 4–6
    graphical tools for, 4–6
    in interventional radiology, 302
        clinical indicators for, 305
        practice guidelines for, 305
        with simulation models, 310
        in training programs, 310
    KPIs for, in diagnostic radiology, 156
    metrics for, 4
    for patients
        "pay for performance" plans and, 27–28
        in "quality and safety" movement, 26–27
    pay for performance and, 224
    performance improvement programs for, 13–16
        adverse event reporting systems in, 13
        audits of, 14–15
        NPSG compliance, 15–16
        result communication systems in, 13–14
        risk reporting mechanisms in, 15
        walkabouts as part of, 15
    QA for, 6–7
    QC for, 6
    QI in, 7–8
    as quality, 333–334
    for radiologists, 170, 172
        for patients, 28
    systems failures in, 3–4
    TQM for, 3
    training for, in diagnostic radiology, 241–242

culture change and, 242–243
future applications for, 244
at Penn State Hershey Medical Center, 242–243
PQI projects for, 243–244
safety attitudinal questionnaires (SAQs), 69, 70
SBAR communication, in CRM, 69
scatter plots, 6
scorecards, 206–207, 206–208
dashboards compared to, 206
sentinel events, 40
JCAHO guidelines for, 52
JC standards for, 82, 87
serious reportable events (SREs), 82, 83. *See also* sentinel
events
Seward, Potter, 292
Shewhart, Walter, 162, 196
Shewhart charts, 4–5
simulation, as medical practice, 246, 246–252
in deliberate practice, 246–247
modes of, 247–248, 247
animal models in, 248
mannequin method, 248
non-animal models in, 248
part-task trainers, 247
with rare events, 248
with VR, 247–248
potential applications for, 249, 250
in radiology, 248–252
with ICTS, 250
for interventional radiology, 250
mannequin method for, 250
with Procedus Vist simulator, 251–252
with VR, 249
validity analysis for, 248
simulation-based assessment, for physicians, 177–178
design for, 177
domain modeling for, 177
with MOC, 177
with OPPE, 177, 182–183
task model selection in, 177–178
SIR. *See* Society of Interventional Radiology
Sistrom, Christopher, 283
Six Sigma management strategy, 9–10, 162
development of, 9, 162
disadvantages of, 10
for health care, 162–164
implementation costs for, 163
phases of, 9–10, 162
as process improvement, 162
in QI, 8
Six Thinking Hats process, 41
slips, in errors, 100
Smith, Bill, 162
SNIS. *See* Society of Neurointerventional Surgery
Society of Interventional Radiology (SIR), 113
interventional radiology guidelines, 306, 304
for medication labeling, 306
UP applications under, 306
Society of Neurointerventional Surgery (SNIS), 303
Society of Skeletal Radiology, 284
Soft Tissue Thermal Index, 316

SPC. *See* statistical process control
SREs. *See* serious reportable events
staffing
errors and, impact on, 101–102
institutional leadership and, 13
stakeholders
diagnostic radiology and, increased expectations with, 166
KPIs for, 157, 158
PIs for, definition of, 149–150
Standards for Reporting of Diagnostic Accuracy (STARD)
initiative, 280
statistical process control (SPC), 196–197
in control charts, 196
in dashboards, 196
development of, 196–197
in health care systems, 197
Shewhart and, 196
variation in, 197
stochastic risks, with CT, 127
stress, risk management and, 55–56
strokes. *See* perfusion, CT for
"structure, process, outcome" algorithm, 291
substitution test, mistake assessment, 101
Swiss Cheese model, for errors, 95
person approach in, 95
system approach in, 95
synchronous communication, in radiology, 65
system performance, predictions for
feedback factors in, 189–190
measurement metrics for, 185–186
mental models in
results of, 191–192, 192–193
revision of, 184–185
transfer of training in, 185, 188–189
practice in, 192
property additions in, 192
venues for, 192
from prior experience, 184–185
skills and
acquisition of, 188
changes over time for, 188
loss of, 190–191
by task difficulty, 186–188
test theory in, 186
training strategies in, 193–194
on-the-job, 193
with simulations, 193–194
transfer of training and, 185, 188–189
limitations of, 185
time factors in, 189
systems failures, in quality and safety, 3–4, 4
RCA for, 41

Tannenbaum, Sandra, 261
Tavuchis, N., 105
Tax Relief and Health Care Act (TRHCA), 214
Taybi, Hooshang, 298
teamwork
continuous learning and, 76–77, 75–77
with CRM, 69–70
briefings in, 69

teamwork (*Cont.*)
    closed loop communication in, 69
    debriefing in, 69–70
    functions of, 69
    measurement of success with, 78
    SAQ in, 69
    SBAR communication in, 69
    for Healthcare FMEA, 44
    implementation of, 75
    leadership and, 75
    measurement of, 77–79
        with CRM, 78
    in MGH pilot program, 70–72
        AHRQ survey of, 70, 72–73
        framing in, 70
        observational scores for, 73–75
        SAQs in, 70
        sustainment measures in, 71–72
        training in, 70–71
    in performance improvement programs, 13
    performance results from, 68
    for RCA, 40
        with caregivers, 40
        with physicians, 40
    reinforcement of, 75–77
    site-based observation for, 76
    training and, 76
teratogenesis, from radiation during pregnancy, 318–319
test theory, in systems performance, 186
To Err is Human: Building a Safer Health System (IOM), ix, 3, 28, 219, 223
    system reform in, 224
top-down EBM, 259–260
total quality management (TQM), 3
    components of, 163
    in health care, 163
    origins of, 3
    PDSA cycle in, 3
    processes in, success of, 3
training. *See* clinical training
TRHCA. *See* Tax Relief and Health Care Act
type 1 errors, in control charts, 199
type 2 errors, in control charts, 199

U-chart, 202
ultrasonography, during pregnancy, 316, 320

dosing strategies for, 324–325
    Soft Tissue Thermal Index for, 316
United Kingdom (UK), pay for performance in, 227
United Kingdom National Patient Safety Agency, 53
Universal Protocol (UP), 113
    application factors for, 112–113
    components of, 113–115, 113
        pre-procedural verification, 114
        procedure site marking, 114
        time-outs, 114–115
    establishment of, 111
    JC and, 111
    outcomes for, 115
    parameters for, 112
    wrong-site surgery/procedures under, 111–112
        causes for, 111–112
        incidence rates for, 111
        prevention efforts, 112
        WHO guidelines, 112
urinary tract abnormalities, CT for, 133–134

validity, in performance assessment, 176, 176
value based purchasing (VBP), 213
value stream mapping, in lean management, 10
Vanderbroucke, Jan P., 258, 261
Van Helmont, Jan B., 256
variable charts, 201
VBP. *See* value based purchasing
Veriphy, 66
Veteran's Administration, US., Healthcare FMEA use by, 43
virtual reality (VR) simulation, 247–248, 249
voice recognition, 172
VR simulation. *See* virtual reality simulation

walkabouts, in performance improvement programs, 15
Weinreb, Jeffrey, 282
World Health Organization (WHO)
    quality health care strategies, 220–221
    wrong-site surgery/procedures guidelines, 112
wrong-site surgery/procedures, under UP, 111–112
    causes for, 111–112
    incidence rates for, 111
    prevention efforts, 112
    WHO guidelines, 112

Zen and the Art of Motorcycle Maintenance (Pirsig), 332

CPSIA information can be obtained at www.ICGtesting.com
Printed in the USA
BVOW11s1428161014

371052BV00004B/7/P

9 780199 735754